RAISED FROM
THE DEAD

*"Why should it be thought a thing incredible,
that God should raise the dead?"*

—Acts 26:8

OTHER BOOKS BY THE AUTHOR

Mary, Our Blessed Lady (poems)
A Christ-Filled World (poems)
Priestly Celibacy—Lasting Value and Recurrent Battle
Mary, Our Blessed Mother (poems)
The Tears of Mary and Fatima—Why?
Mary, Why Do You Cry?
A Prayerbook of Favorite Litanies
Prophecies! The Chastisement and Purification!
Mary and Her Hidden Life

RAISED FROM THE DEAD

True Stories of
400 Resurrection Miracles

by

Father Albert J. Hebert, S.M.

"Heal the sick, raise the dead, cleanse the lepers, cast out devils: freely have you received, freely give."
—Words of Jesus Christ
to His Apostles (*Matt.* 10:8)

TAN BOOKS AND PUBLISHERS, INC.
Rockford, Illinois 61105

Nihil Obstat:	Fortune Frenoy, S.M. Censor Deputatus
Imprimi Potest:	Donald A. Romito Provincialis
Nihil Obstat:	Cage Gordon, V.G. Censor Librorum
Imprimatur:	✠ Joseph V. Sullivan, S.T.D. Bishop of Baton Rouge, Louisiana

The *Nihil Obstat* and *Imprimatur* are official declarations that a book is free of doctrinal or moral error. No implication is contained therein that those who have granted the *Nihil Obstat* and *Imprimatur* agree with the contents, opinions, or statements expressed.

In no case do the *Nihil Obstat* and *Imprimatur* constitute an approval of any private revelations, prophecies, or possible new devotions or cults connected therewith if these have not been officially approved by the Church. Where such are treated as historical accounts or are reported as news of the day, the Catholic reader may form his own opinion or judgment according to the facts presented. However, he must be ready to submit to the judgment of the Church if and when it is made; and at the place of source, the instructions of the local Ordinary should be obeyed.

With regard to declarations on miracles, holiness of individuals, or other supernatural matters, the author in no way presumes to anticipate the judgment of Holy Mother Church. In conformity with the decree of Pope Urban VIII, the author declares his intention to attach purely human credibility to such events narrated in this book.

TAN BOOKS AND PUBLISHERS, INC.
P.O. Box 424
Rockford, Illinois 61105

1986

"Believe you not that I am in the Father, and the Father in me? Otherwise believe for the very works' sake. Amen, amen I say to you, he that believeth in me, the works that I do, he also shall do; and greater than these shall he do."

—*Words of Our Lord*
(*John* 14:11-12)

CONTENTS

THE BLESSED VIRGIN MARY

— PART THREE —
OTHER WONDERS:
FURTHER SIGNS OF IMMORTALITY

— PART FOUR —
CONCLUSIONS

FOREWORD

What is more important to any man or woman than to know, to be sure, that he or she will rise from the dead someday?

Nothing is better established as fact in the history of the Old and New Testaments and in the Catholic Christian centuries than the raising of dead persons to life—some of these in fairly recent times. Although these privileged persons all had to die again, their "temporary" resurrections confirm the Christian's faith in the great resurrection of the body which will come at the end of the world. The entire Christian era—20 centuries—is the fruit of that great belief, that great hope.

True, there are people today, as there always have been, who will attack the teaching of the resurrection of the body. The Sadducees of Jesus' day challenged Him on the doctrine of a bodily resurrection. But before the Master's words they retired in confusion.

Miracles of the dead being returned to life need not be accepted on faith; they are a matter of historical record. The accounts presented here, at least taken as a whole, will show the impossibility of denying these miracles. There are just too many great saints involved—St. Benedict, St. Martin of Tours, St. Bernard of Clairvaux, St. Dominic, St. Vincent Ferrer, and St. Francis Xavier, to name but a few. To deny the works of such men of history is to affront the faculty of reason.

It is hoped that this book's account of so many wonders—both resurrection miracles and other miracles—will show the utter foolishness and poor scholarship of those so-called exegetes, theologians, and other writers, even within the Church, who deny the fact of miracles. The poorest of scholars and researchers can attest to the many historical reports of persons raised from the dead by any number of Catholic saints.

In commissioning His twelve Apostles, Our Lord gave them the power of working miracles to witness to the divine Source of their teachings. He said to them, "And going, preach, saying: The kingdom of heaven is at hand. Heal the sick, raise the dead, cleanse the lepers, cast out devils: freely have you received, freely give." (*Matt.* 10:8).

Our Lord stated that His great miracles were meant to lead men to faith, and He prophesied even greater wonders to come: "Believe you not that I am in the Father, and the Father in me? Otherwise believe for the very works' sake. Amen, Amen I say to you, he that believeth in me, the works that I do, he also shall do; and greater than these shall he do." (*John* 14:11-12).

Following in the footsteps of the Apostles, the Catholic saints have brought the teachings and the Baptism of Our Lord Jesus Christ to vast numbers of people. God has often seen fit to back up the teachings of His later "Apostles," also, with miracles—healings, the casting out of devils, and the raising of the dead. It is particularly to His great *missionary* saints, those who received the vocation and the stupendous responsibility of converting *thousands,* that God has given the power to raise the dead.

The great number of resurrection miracles worked by the saints of God constitute divine approval of the Catholic Church—of her claim to be founded by Jesus Christ Himself, and of her claim to be the ark of eternal salvation. These saints were instruments of God, and their miracles were primarily *His* action, not theirs. These great miracles are God's testimony to the truth of the Catholic Faith. He has not so testified to the truth of any other religion.

As Vatican Council I (1870) proclaimed,

> "In order that the obedience of our faith might be
> in harmony with reason, God willed that to the in-
> terior help of the Holy Spirit there should be

joined exterior proofs of His revelation, to wit, divine facts, and especially miracles and prophecies, which, as they manifestly display the omnipotence and infinite knowledge of God, are most certain proofs of His divine revelation adapted to the intelligence of all men. Wherefore, both Moses and the Prophets, and most especially Christ Our Lord Himself, showed forth many and most evident miracles and prophecies, and of the Apostles we read: 'But they, going forth, preached everywhere, the Lord working withal, and confirming the word with signs that followed.'"

These resurrection miracles also make it easier for one to accept the miracles reported of Our Lord Himself in the Gospels—including His raising of three persons from the dead. If the servants of God can perform such great works, why not the Master Himself? He is truly the Lord of the living and the dead: "I am the resurrection and the life: he that believeth in me, although he be dead, shall live." (*John* 11:25). Further, the miracles recounted in this book indicate how easy it was for Our Lord Jesus Christ, the Source of the saints' power, to rise from the dead. The Resurrection of Christ the Son of God by His own power transcends every other wonder. It is the Miracle of miracles! It is the basis for all our hopes of our own resurrection on Judgment Day.

The Resurrection of Our Lord Jesus Christ, as well as the resurrection miracles performed by the saints, provide a guarantee of Christ's promise to every faithful Catholic: "I will raise him up in the last day." (*John* 6:44).

INTRODUCTION
Have the Dead Really Been Raised to Life?

Have you ever wondered whether, outside of the Scriptural accounts, dead persons have ever *really* been raised to life again?

This book is full of such cases. No, they did not revive and live forever on this earth; though they were raised from death once, eventually each one had to pay the penalty of all human beings and die again. The permanent Resurrection will be only on Judgment Day. But its credibility increases as one learns of the many persons who were not only raised from the dead, but often also healed when diseased or mangled in body.

This book is not intended to be an encyclopedia of every instance of resurrection from the dead; nor is it an exhaustive scientific work with many documentary notes and critical comments. But neither is it intended to be a book of sensationalism. Rather, it is meant to be a reliable, popularly-written book.

In most of this book I have endeavored to recount miracles of proven or accepted authenticity. But I must make a distinction regarding miracles: between biblical miracles (those found in the Sacred Scriptures) and ecclesiastical miracles (those occuring within the later history of the Church, and not recorded in the Bible).

The biblical miracles, as Cardinal Newman (long before he became a Catholic) points out in his essays on miracles, are in a superior class. They have a certain majesty, clarity, objectivity, decisiveness and powerful action. Even if I were not a Catholic I would accept, along with all reasonable historians, that the accounts of the dead raised by the prophets and Apostles, and particularly by Jesus Christ, are matters of historical record: they are *facts.*

I must make another distinction regarding the biblical wonders. In holding to our main theme, the raising of the dead, I accept as a matter of well-attested historical record the fact that Christ rose from the dead. But I *believe* that it was a *divine* Person who rose from the dead that first Easter Sunday. I *believe,* because seeing the divine nature of Christ is not possible to my senses and judgment, nor to the discernment of others witnessing for me. But the historical fact of Christ's Resurrection, along with His wise and holy teachings, shows that He came from God, and that the power of God was with Him. God worked this stupendous miracle to witness to the truth of Christ's teaching—and Christ taught that He was God.

Similarly, I *believe* in Mary's bodily Assumption into Heaven as a revealed truth, for it is hard to show any factual evidence or historical witnesses to it. Although the Assumption is not mentioned in the sacred Scriptures, I believe it on the authority of the Church, which draws on its memory of Tradition (in the strict ecclesiastical sense). The Church is a living teacher, not just an inanimate (though wonderful) book.

The Church as a living teacher holds that Book, the Bible, in her hands while she also recalls all the treasures of divine Tradition received from Christ—the great truths which she faithfully hands down over the centuries. Only the Church has a memory and understanding assisted by the divine guidance which was promised to her by Christ. The Church is guided by the Holy Ghost, and she passes this guidance on to the faithful through the teachings of the Holy Father, who is the Vicar of Christ, and the teachings of the Magisterium in union with him.

On the other hand, Catholics are not obligated to believe in ecclesiastical miracles, those performed since Biblical days (that is, they are not obligated to believe in any individual miracle—but they must believe that God is still able to perform miracles). Of course, such miracles must be subjected to the canons of reason; to the ecclesiastical tribunals—as in canonization processes of candidates for saint-hood; to the testimonies of medical experts—as at the shrine of Our Lady of Lourdes in France; and to the general norms for judging historical reports. But when a miracle passes these tests, no man of integrity—Christian or pagan—is free to deny it, to abrogate the testimony of sound senses and reason. One has a duty to truth and to the God-given faculties of examination and judgment.

A juror, for instance, cannot reject factual (not circum-stantial) evidence and endanger society by permitting a criminal to venture abroad as if he were innocent. Con-versely, where the evidence of innocence is conclusive, no juror or judge can outrage intellect and justice by sending a guiltless party to the electric chair. Still, recalling bitter ex-periences of some deceits, mankind must be astute. Though they remain innocent as doves in genuine sincerity and simplicity of approach, persons should be wise as serpents in reasonable prudence and precautions.

However, some persons, perhaps because of limited back-ground and education, *a priori* disregard all miracles as im-possible from the start. That is a blind, blocked, unscientific and unreasonable approach which we hope and pray may be corrected. But if it is insisted upon, it leaves such persons outside the pale of evidence and rational judgment. It diminishes men who are gifted with intellect—and a certain responsibility to its Creator for its proper use.

It must be remembered that in many cases the accounts of saints and their miracles have been unjustly pre-judged. Too many writers too freely label the miracles of the saints as "legendary." However, the reasonable approach, sane scrutiny, and scientifically objective judgment of the judicial processes of the canonical commissions of the twentieth-cen-tury Church, in her acceptance or rejection of candidates for canonization, is readily apparent to any observer. These modern records are scarcely in the class of the "legendary," with their assemblage of competent witnesses, corps of medical consultants, and other collaborating scientists who attend and testify.

But does that mean that the lives of saints and the accounts of miraculous nappenings of past centuries are not valid because they did not have today's so-called "scientific" and "historical" criteria by which to establish them? Nonsense! Men of every age had sense and intelligence. If that requirement were applied to other areas of study, we would have to forget major parts of what we consider history. Indeed, those who have given testimony for the Church over the centuries are far wiser and more truthful than some of those writers devoted to portraying many secular episodes of history.

Admittedly, there have been both true and false prophets, true and false private revelations, as well as actual demons and merely apparent demons in certain psychiatric disorders or sicknesses. And, yes, there have been true and false mystics, and true and false miracles.

But that which is true seems to have more staying power. One can recall a number of true prophets in the Old and New Testaments and down the centuries. But how many false prophets can one name? How many false miracle-workers can one recall! Only Simon the Magician might be remembered, simply because he was so popularized. But who is he beside Peter, Paul, John, Stephen and a host of early great saints?

In recent times, after the apparitions of the Blessed Virgin Mary to Bernadette at Lourdes and to the three children at Fatima, there were also false seers claiming this and that. Bernadette is well-known (even through the movie, *The Song of Bernadette*), as are Lucy, Jacinta and Francisco. But where now are the false seers so prevalent after the above little seers became known?

Miraculous happenings that come down to us in the lives of the saints are often unjustly called "mere legends" (as though legends cannot be true), or "myths used to express certain Christian concepts." However, for the most part the miracle workers were good and holy persons. Even their enemies will admit this. Surely "good" and "holy" saints cannot practice deceit and lies about their activities. The saints have been people of true insight; how can one even accuse them of naivete and stupidity?

From that which is good must come down to us good, and from the holy ones of God comes the supernatural. Unless fraud is actually proven, one should accept as true the traditional beliefs about the saints, the reverences of the people, and the stories of their lively hope for miracles from the saints. These represent something real in history. The false saints, false miracle-workers, false mystics, are seldom revered and remembered. But when a true and saintly miracle-worker appears on earth, the memory of man is longer than printed records, and the total human experience much larger and fuller than books and documents.

So, out of a mass of evidence and common sense, the material in this book shall be confined to those events which are reasonably accepted as miracles of the dead being raised to life. Also noted in an appendix are many cases where the dead were reported as raised, but which lack more conclusive or well-known evidence; it would be unfair not to report them at all. Their relegation to an appendix does not mean I regard them as merely "legendary"; it simply means that I would like more information and certainty about them.

I would never deny God one atom of glory; all miracles give glory to Him. Nor would I detract from the God-given glory of the saints. At the same time I am open to any additional information, pro or con, on individual saints or the miracles attributed to any one of them. But let objectors prove their objections with facts and not with vague insinuations, sophisticated scorn, or condescending smiles. In the meantime let people judge for themselves whether, "O Agrippa, it is deemed incredible with you if God does raise the dead!"

Finally, for anyone desiring to do fuller and more exhaustive research, the references in this book will give a very good start. Who knows, more manuscripts may be turned up to afford more evidence and even more favorable judgments.

Christ gave orders to His Apostles to raise the dead. Why should we be surprised that the saints have followed those instructions?

—PART ONE—

RESURRECTION MIRACLES IN BIBLICAL DAYS

"And I look for the resurrection of the dead,
and the life of the world to come. Amen."
—*The Niceno-Constantinopolitan Creed*
381 *A.D.*

THE OLD TESTAMENT
Elias and Eliseus Raise the Dead

> *" . . . and behold the child lay dead on*
> *his bed. . . . And going in he [Eliseus]*
> *. . . prayed to the Lord. . . . and the child's*
> *flesh grew warm. . . . and the child gaped*
> *seven times, and opened his eyes."*
> —4 Kings 4:32-35

There may have been others, but the first *recorded* instances of the dead being brought back to life occur in the third and fourth books of Kings. It was the pleadings of their mothers that brought about the miraculous resurrections of these two boys.

Elias the Thesbite, who rated later on to stand beside Jesus along with Moses on the Mount of the Transfiguration, lived in the ninth century B.C. In the time of Achab, that evil king of Israel, Achab, whose pagan wife was the wicked Jezabel of Tyre, Elias predicted a three-year drought: God had, for a time, put the control of rain into the prophet's hands.

Elias first lived by the torrent Carith, but when it dried up the Lord sent him to a widow of Sarephta of Sidon with the promise that the widow would look after his needs. The widow, in the midst of famine, had only enough oil and bread to prepare a last meal for her son and herself, "that we may eat it, and die." (*3 Kings* 17:12). But Elias tried her faith by ordering her first to cook for himself. When she obeyed she found that fresh oil and flour kept appearing, and she and her son—and Elias—were able to eat from it for a year. "The pot of meal wasted not, and the cruse of oil was

3

not diminished, according to the word of the Lord, which he spoke in the hand of Elias." (*3 Kgs.* 17:16).

That in itself, most would agree, was an impressive miracle—one that was granted in response to trust and obedience. There are some, of course, who will accept certain miracles but balk at what they deem "super-actions," as if God were limited by human conceptions and abilities. But it costs God no more effort to provide life to the dead than it did to provide life in the form of oil and bread for the living. And that is just what God did, through Elias, for the widow's son. Later, after the miracle during the famine, the widow's son fell sick, his illness grew more severe, and finally he stopped breathing.

"What have I to do with thee, thou man of God?" she cried.

"Give me thy son," Elias said, and he took him from her lap, carried him to his own upper room and laid him on the bed, praying, "O Lord, my God, hast thou afflicted also the widow with whom I am after a sort maintained, so as to kill her son?" Elias stretched himself out three times on the child and pleaded with the Lord: "O Lord, my God, let the soul of this child, I beseech thee, return into his body." The Lord heard his prayer; He returned the soul to the child's body. The prophet brought him downstairs and gave him to his mother with the words, "Behold, thy son liveth."

That was the first bringing back from the dead. Read more details in Chapter 17 of the third book of *Kings*.

Eliseus was a great prophet, too, and like Elias, another wonder-worker. One can find various miracles of both in the books of Kings. It was upon Eliseus' shoulders that Elias' mantle fell as Elias went up to Heaven in the fiery chariot.

Eliseus raised a boy from the dead in a case somewhat similar to that of Elias. By his prayers, Eliseus obtained the son for the woman in the first place, a son that he later brought back to life. It came about this way.

Eliseus once came to Sunam, where a good woman of position and influence urged him to dine with her. As

Eliseus had a habit of passing by that way, he also got into the habit of dining there. The woman suggested to her husband that they should do something for this holy man of God who visited them so often.

"Let us therefore make him a little chamber, and put a little bed in it for him and a table and a stool, and a candlestick, that when he cometh to us he may abide there." (*4 Kgs.* 4:10).

The husband agreed, so Eliseus had a comfortable stopover place. On one overnight visit Eliseus said to his servant Giezi, "Call this Sunamitess." Eliseus expressed his thanks to her: "Behold, thou hast diligently served us in all things; what wilt thou have me to do for thee? Hast thou any business, and wilt thou that I speak to the king, or to the general of the army?"

"I dwell in the midst of my own people," she replied, which seems to indicate that she was sufficiently taken care of.

Later Eliseus asked his servant, "What will she then that I do for her?"

Giezi answered, "Do not ask, for she has no son, and her husband is old." Eliseus bade the servant call the woman. When she stood at the door, Eliseus promised, "At this time [next year] and this same hour, if life accompany, thou shalt have a son in thy womb."

"Do not, I beseech thee, my lord, thou man of God, do not lie to thy handmaiden," she pleaded. But Eliseus did not take back his words. The same time the following year, the woman had a son.

Thus there came to pass another impressive miracle—a woman who had never conceived brought forth a child, and the sex was correctly forecast. This came about because of the prophet's prayer to Yahweh in gratitude to the couple for their kindness, services and hospitality, as well as for their respect and reverence.

But "the Lord giveth and the Lord taketh away." The day came when the son of the Sunamitess was old enough to go out with his father among the reapers. While with them one day he complained to his father that his head hurt.

"Carry him to his mother," the father said to a servant, who did so, and then stayed with the anxious mother. At noon the boy died in her lap. The brokenhearted mother took him upstairs and laid the body on the bed of the prophet. She closed the door and then acted with that single-mindedness that has for centuries marked the manner of mothers in similar circumstances. Her actions expressed an utter confidence in the intercessory powers of those special souls of God such as the prophets or the saints. The Sunamitess called out to her husband, "Send with me, I beseech thee, one of thy servants, and an ass that I may run to the man of God, and I come again."

"Why dost thou go to him?" he asked, "today is neither new moon nor sabbath."

But his wife bade him goodbye, and when the donkey was saddled she ordered the servant, "Drive, and make haste, make no stay in going."

From his place on Mount Carmel, Eliseus spied her coming: "Behold, that Sunamitess. Go therefore to meet her . . ."

She greeted Giezi, but hurried on to the man of God on the mountain, where she clasped his feet. Giezi came near to push her away, but Eliseus told him:

"Let her alone for her soul is in anguish, and the Lord hath hid it from me and hath not told me."

"Did I ask a son of my lord?" she cried out. "Did I not say to thee: Do not deceive me?"

"Gird up thy loins," Eliseus said to Giezi. He then told him to take his (the prophet's) staff, to return with the Sunamitess, not to pause on the way, and to lay the staff upon the boy's face.

"As the Lord liveth," the mother cried out, "and as thy soul liveth, I will not leave thee." So Eliseus started back with her.

In the meantime Giezi had gone ahead and had laid the staff on the boy with no results—no sound, no sign of life.

When Eliseus reached the house he found the boy lying dead. Eliseus prayed and stretched himself upon the boy as Elias had done, and the body began to grow warm. He repeated his action, and the boy gaped seven times and opened his eyes.

"Call the Sunamitess," Eliseus told his servant. "Take up thy son," he said to the mother, who fell in gratitude at his feet, and then took her son.

It is important to note here that it is only to the Lord that these great servants of God attribute their miracles. Elias and Eliseus prayed, God answered. And there was also the persevering, even vehement, faith of the mothers.

That the power of raising the dead is only from God is easily seen in the third restoration account in the Old Testament.

Eliseus came to the end of his days, died, and was buried. It happened in those days that bands of wandering Moabites used to raid the land each year. One day a local funeral procession was passing by the tomb of Eliseus when suddenly a band of marauders came into view. Fearing more danger to themselves than to the dead man, the frightened bier-bearers cast the corpse of the dead man into the grave of Eliseus and fled. "And when it had touched the bones of Eliseus, the man came to life, and stood upon his feet."(*4 Kgs.* 13:21). (It is not stated whether it was then the marauders' turn to flee!)

Centuries later, in a similar manner, the woman with the issue of blood would be cured merely by touching Our Lord's garment. And after Pentecost, the sick would wait by the roadside for even the shadow of St. Peter to fall upon them; many would thus be cured. Similarly, in the centuries after the Apostles, innumerable people would be cured or even restored to life merely by touching the relics of the saints.

2

THE GOSPELS
Jesus Raises the Widow's Son, The Daughter of Jairus, and Lazarus

"And presently he that had been dead came forth, bound feet and hands with winding bands... Jesus said to them: Loose him, and let him go."
—John 11:44

Like the first miracle of the dead being raised to life in the Old Testament, the first instance in the New Testament concerns a widow's son. But this time it was a grown man, apparently the only support of his mother.

After Our Lord had cured the Roman centurion's servant and praised the faith of that military captain, He went away from Capharnaum, over the high hills of His native Nazareth, to a town called Naim. There He met a funeral procession coming from the gate of the town. On the litter was the body of a man; as St. Luke sympathetically notes, "He was the only son of a mother, and she was a widow." The case must have touched the hearts of many, for Luke observes that a goodly number of townsfolk accompanied the sorrowing mother.

Did Our Lord then picture a mournful procession in Jerusalem wending its way toward Calvary not long hence? And a shorter one carrying His own Body from the cross to His borrowed tomb? Did He see His own Mother standing there—*Stabat Mater!*—the chief mourner?

St. Luke tells us that "being moved with mercy toward her, he said to her, 'Weep not.'" Then Jesus stepped forward and touched the stretcher; at this the bearers stood still.

Jesus said, "Young man, I say to thee, arise." "And he that was dead, sat up, and began to speak. And he gave him to his mother." (*Luke* 7:11-15).

One can imagine the happiness of that widowed mother, and the surprise and joy of her son! Picture the astonishment of the crowd at seeing this unexpected reunion, this return from the grave! But they were also full of fear, for the Gospel says, "and there came a fear on them all." But it was a healthy fear, for they began to praise and glorify God. And they understood, saying, "A great prophet is risen up among us, and God hath visited his people." That was a good description of the reality of miracles; the same thought would often be expressed years later concerning the saints. Through miracles God *does* visit His people, so that His people will listen to His word.

St. Luke, the physician evangelist, is the only Gospel writer to record the miracle of the widow's son. Sympathy for women is consistent throughout his Gospel, as is the inclusion of other incidents regarding women in the life of Our Lord. But Matthew and Mark also relate the next raising of the dead.

The daughter of Jairus was a young girl 12 years of age. She is the first *known* female to be brought back to life—but she is not necessarily the first female to be raised, because some time before this incident Jesus had told disciples of John the Baptist to report to John that "the dead rise," along with many other miracles. One could infer that other dead besides the widow's son had already been raised.

Be that as it may, to return to the young girl, her father, Jairus, was a man of prominence in Capharnaum. He is called a ruler of the synagogue, an official. After Jesus had called the tax collector Levi to become the Apostle Matthew, when Jesus was near Capharnaum, Jairus came up to Him and did Him reverence, saying, "My daughter is at the point of death; come, lay thy hand upon her, that she may be safe, and may live." (*Mark* 5:23).

Jesus and Jairus went off together, a large crowd following and pushing about Jesus. Undoubtedly there were many whose sympathy was aroused as they accompanied this pleading father who expressed such confidence in the Master. And the father was apparently a good man.

On the way, a woman troubled with a hemorrhage for a dozen years, having exhausted her doctors and her money, was convinced that she would be cured if she could but touch Jesus' cloak. In the pressing crowd she came from behind and touched a tassel on His cloak. She was instantly healed. Jesus had scarcely finished praising her faith when a messenger from Jairus' house arrived with news of the daughter's death. "Thy daughter is dead: why dost thou trouble the master any further?" But Jesus said to Jairus, "Fear not, only believe."

Jesus went on to Jairus' house, taking only Peter, James and John. They found the flute players and the crowd making a din, and the people wailing and lamenting. Jesus ordered the crowd to depart: "Give place, for the girl is not dead, but sleepeth." At this they "laughed him to scorn." But Jesus had said this to reassure them as He went in.

He entered with the child's parents and Peter, James and John. Inside the room where the little girl lay, Jesus took her hand and said, "Talitha, cumi," which means, "Damsel (I say to thee) arise!" "Talitha" immediately got up and began to walk around. Jesus, being very practical-minded, told her parents to give their child something to eat. It was as if He said, "Do not stand there in astonishment. What you have witnessed was real. Now make the girl feel at home." That, perhaps, was why He excluded the crowd. Two or three witnesses were sufficient to testify to what had happened. And the poor child, on coming back to life, might have been frightened to find a crowd pressing about her.

Reflecting on these two episodes, one sees that the people involved believed that Jesus could both cure illness and prevent death. But since the householders of the synagogue leader gave up when the girl died, it seems they did not believe Jesus could actually *raise* someone from the dead.

To men, the one restoration—from death—seems a much more difficult accomplishment than restoration from sickness. But to God's power there is no difference. And if the touch of the hem of Christ's garment could cure, what then could the touch of His hand do? And what of His will? The simple truth is that it costs God no more "effort" to raise Lazarus from the tomb than it does for Him to heal a toothache or restore a withered arm. It is no more difficult for God to raise one Lazarus from the tomb than to raise a few billion or a hundred billion on Judgment Day. To think that God will have to work awfully hard on Judgment Day is an utter misconception. It is all effortless to the Almighty.

Our Lord may have worked an appreciable number of miracles around Jerusalem, but not as many have been recorded for that area as for around Galilee and other territories. One probable reason is that Jesus did not want to attract too much attention too often in the domain of His enemies.

Thus, Jesus reserved one of His greatest miracles for the latter days of His public ministry. He knew beforehand that it would be yet another occasion for His enemies to quicken their plots to destroy Him—another "death warrant" for the Author of Life. How foolish and blind men can be!

Jesus performed His greatest resurrection miracle—raising Lazarus from the dead—almost at the gates of Jerusalem in nearby Bethania. And not far off is the Valley of Josaphat, which is associated with the general Resurrection at the end of the world.

St. John is the only evangelist to record the miracle of the raising of Lazarus. Some scholars postulate that if the earlier Gospels had run such an account it might have reminded Jews hostile to the new way that Lazarus yet alive posed a threat to them. They had once plotted to kill Lazarus along with Jesus because the raising of Lazarus was a "super-miracle" right in their own front yard, that is, in

Bethania, near Jerusalem, and it had greatly enhanced Our Lord's prestige among the people.

This miracle was one more sign to prepare the people for Christ's own pre-announced Resurrection. If Jesus could raise a man who had lain wrapped in a tomb for four days (along with all the other marvelous instances of His control over man and nature, life and death), certainly His own Resurrection would cause no difficulty. He is *above* nature; the one who could give life must be Life Itself—"I am the way, and the truth, and the life." (*John* 14:6).

Lazarus, it would seem, was a fairly young man. At any rate he was a good Jew and well-respected in the Jerusalem area. Lazarus was well-off, or at least sufficiently comfortable to be able to put up Jesus and His Apostles regularly (along with a number of others who traveled with Jesus). Another sign of some affluence was the fact that the family tomb was a large one, provided with a big closing stone. The prosperous Joseph of Arimathea would provide a similar one for Jesus' burial, but that would be several days hence and several miles away.

Lazarus' house was also a popular gathering place because of his two sisters—and future saints—Martha and Mary. Contemplative Mary had, sometime before, sat at the feet of Jesus, drinking of the waters of life, while Martha had busied herself as hostess. "Now Jesus loved Martha, and her sister Mary, and Lazarus." (*John* 11:5). These words of John state beautifully the relationship of Jesus with these dear friends. So when the sisters sent messengers to Jesus, bearing their plea: ""Lord, behold, he whom thou lovest is sick," the Apostles were amazed that Jesus did not stir. Rather, Jesus said, "This sickness is not unto death, but for the glory of God: that the Son of God may be glorified by it." Jesus did not mean that Lazarus was not going to die; He meant that Lazarus' death was not going to *end* in death. And Jesus stayed on where He was for two days.

Imagine how Martha and Mary felt as the anxious days passed and Jesus did not arrive; then their brother died. And the Apostles also, must have been distressed, for they too were friends of Lazarus and his sisters. How typical this is of the way human beings wonder or complain at the way God handles things, or seems not to answer their prayers— and all the while the Lord is preparing something better.

Finally Jesus said to the Apostles, "Let us go into Judea again." (This would indicate that they were some distance from Jerusalem. And one can also surmise that Martha and Mary delayed Lazarus' burial as long as possible, hoping for Jesus' arrival.) "Rabbi," protested the Apostles, "the Jews but now sought to stone thee; and thou goest thither again?" The Apostles recognized that Jesus was again facing death for a friend. But Our Lord said, "Lazarus our friend sleepeth; but I go that I may awake him out of sleep." At this the Apostles answered, "Lord, if he sleeps, he shall do well."

It is important to note here what St. John then observes, because it adds to the facts that prove Lazarus was really raised from the dead. St. John says, "But Jesus spoke of his death, and they thought that he spoke of the repose of sleep. Then therefore Jesus said to them plainly: 'Lazarus is dead. And I am glad, for your sakes, that I was not there, that you may believe: but let us go to him.'"

What Jesus was saying was that it was propitious that He had not been there when Lazarus was sick and still alive, because everyone would have expected Jesus to cure him. Note that Jesus told the Apostles that He was happy not to have been at Lazarus' side, because now He could give them a much greater sign, a resurrection that would almost demand belief in Him and in His own coming Resurrection.

When Jesus and His band arrived at Bethania they found that Lazarus had already been in the tomb for four days. At Lazarus' house the sisters learned that Jesus was on the way, and Martha went out to meet Him some distance from the house. Mary stayed home with her many guests, Jewish people who had come to console the two sisters.

When Martha met Jesus she exclaimed, "Lord, if thou

hadst been here my brother had not died. But now also I know that whatsoever thou wilt ask of God, God will give it thee."

"Thy brother shall rise again," Jesus assured her. Martha answered, "I know that he will rise again, in the resurrection, at the last day."

One must note here the Jewish belief in the resurrection of the body. But Our Lord meant the words "rise again" to apply right then and there; the truth of the resurrection of the Last Day would be demonstrated immediately. Note Our Lord's next words very carefully: He then said, "I am the resurrection and the life: he that believeth in me, although he be dead, shall live; and every one that liveth, and believeth in me, shall not die forever. Believest thou this?"

Our Lord was telling Martha, and all of us, that the same power of resurrection as that of the Last Day would appear right before her. Our Lord was—Our Lord *is*—the Resurrection and the Life! Jesus was about to give a sort of preview of Judgment Day.

When they finally got to the house, Mary, Martha and the crowd of mourners all went to the tomb with Jesus. "Where have you laid him?" He asked.

"Lord, come and see."

"And Jesus wept." The Jews therefore said, "Behold how he loved him." Jesus was proving His human nature, His deep sorrow over a lost friend, but also over death itself and the sorrow of others at death—and the evil of sin that had brought death into the world in the first place.

Some of the Jews said, "Could not he that opened the eyes of the man born blind, have caused that this man should not die?" But the faith of such questioners does not go far enough. They were blind as to just what Jesus was permitting and just what He was about to do. Jesus' weeping showed that Lazarus was really dead. His purpose in not keeping Lazarus from dying was to manifest His power to defeat death. "Jesus therefore again groaning in himself, cometh to the sepulchre."

The tomb (representing death) was a cave with a big stone across it. Jesus ordered, "Take away the stone" (and also the stone of unbelief)! Martha, the practical one, cried out realistically, "Lord, by this time he stinketh, for he is now of four days."

Four days! That was just why Jesus had delayed. Jesus wanted all to know, and all history to know, that Lazarus was "plenty" dead. He couldn't be much "deader," having died and lain four days in a tomb, bound hand and foot with linen strips, his face wrapped in a cloth.

Our Lord said, "Did I not say to thee that if thou believe thou shalt see the glory of God?" So at Jesus' words they took away the stone. Jesus lifted up His eyes, prayed, and then cried out in a loud voice: "LAZARUS, COME FORTH!"

Those words of absolute authority were not just for Lazarus; they were for all the people there. Those words were for all of us, who on Judgment Day will rise from the great terrestrial tomb of earth. (The Valley of Josaphat, traditionally regarded as the site of the Last Judgment, was only a few miles away).

At Christ's words the dead man came out from his grave. Jesus said, "Loose him and let him go."

Unbind him! Untie him! Let Lazarus go free! Let all the dead be untied from death! Let the whole world be freed from death! The Resurrection, the Life of the world, was standing there before that crowd which represented the whole world.

Jesus had said earlier, "As the living Father hath sent me, and I live by the Father, so he that eateth me, the same also shall live by me." (*John* 6:58). He was speaking of the Holy Eucharist, which He would soon institute—that great Sacrament by which we receive the very life of God, and a pledge of eternal life in Heaven.

The great miracle of the raising of Lazarus from the dead led many Jews who had witnessed it to believe in Jesus. Others, however, reported the miracle to the Pharisees, and the Sanhedrin held a hurried session and definitely determined to put Jesus to death. At that meeting Caiphas the High Priest argued: "You know nothing. Neither do you consider that it is expedient for you that one man should die for the people, and that the whole nation perish not." (*John* 11:50). Caiphas did not realize that this was exactly what Jesus would do: die, one God-Man for all, so that the people would be able to receive redemption, salvation and eternal life.

Not many days later, when Jesus came back to Bethania, Lazarus and his sisters gave Jesus a banquet, and Mary used a costly perfume to anoint Jesus' feet. Perhaps Mary had an intuition (or maybe she had simply absorbed Jesus' repeated prophecies of His death) that her Lord would soon be in a tomb instead of the brother He had given back to her. When Judas complained about the "waste" of the precious nard, Jesus said, "Let her alone, that she may keep it against the day of my burial." (*John* 12:7).

Lazarus, having been raised from the dead, was of great interest to everyone in the area. Many Jews even came out from Jerusalem to see Jesus and Lazarus, so the chief priests planned to kill Lazarus too. What foolishness! As if anyone could keep someone dead if the Son of God wanted him kept alive! As if they could really destroy Life Itself! How inane poor mortals can be.

While there are more details to the story of Jesus and Lazarus in St. John's Gospel, this account is sufficient to show the tremendous importance of that historical event. Yet despite the tremendous impression it must have made, it was only a short time later at the time of Jesus' death and burial, that the Apostles had apparently forgotten His frequent prediction of His own Resurrection within three days. It would seem that the presence of Lazarus might have helped sustain their hope.

The Apostles must also have temporarily forgotten, in their grief, those other momentous words of Jesus: "Heal the sick, raise the dead, cleanse the lepers, cast out devils:

freely have you received, freely give." (*Matt.* 10:8). The Apostles knew the powers He had given them—including raising the dead—so why should they have worried about the Lord taking care of Himself? Why did they act as if He were not the Resurrection and Life Himself—the *Alpha* and the *Omega!*

3

THE ACTS OF THE APOSTLES
Peter Raises Dorcas, Paul Raises Eutychus

*"Peter kneeling down prayed, and turn-
ing to the body, he said: Tabitha, arise.
And she opened her eyes; and seeing
Peter, she sat up."*

—Acts 9:40

If the "apostles" of the Old Testament, that is, the
prophets Elias and Eliseus, raised the dead to life, surely the
Apostles of the New Testament would perform even greater
works.

When the Lord sent the Apostles out to minister while He
was yet alive and active in the Holy Land, He gave them
many powers, including that of raising the dead. "Heal the
sick, raise the dead, cleanse the lepers, cast out devils."
(*Matt.* 10:8). It is most probable that all of the 12 Apostles,
along with St. Paul, raised the dead at some point in their
missionary lives. Otherwise there was no point in Jesus giving them this power, adding, "Freely you have received,
freely give."

Just as only a sampling of Jesus' miracles was given in the
Gospels, the inspired writers often noting that "many other
miracles Jesus did," so too is there only a small sampling in
the Acts of what the Apostles actually did. Remember, there
were 13 apostolic lives involved, and for the most part little
is known of the accomplishments of most of the Apostles.

The Apostle Peter, among his many journeys, once went
to see God's people at Lydda on the Palestinian coast. There
he cured a paralytic who had been bedridden for eight years.
In fact, St. Peter cured so many people on his preaching

tours that the people laid the sick by the side of the road, hoping St. Peter's mere shadow would cure them.

At Joppe, not far away on the same coast, there was a woman convert, Tabitha, whose name in Greek was Dorcas, meaning "gazelle." Dorcas died after a life of constant good deeds and acts of charity. Her body was washed and laid in an upstairs room. The Christians there heard that St. Peter was at Lydda and sent two men with an urgent request for him to come to Joppe.

When Peter arrived at the house of Dorcas, the weeping widows of the area showed him the various garments Dorcas had made for them. At her bedside Peter made the others leave; he knelt down and prayed, and then, "turning to the body, he said: 'Tabitha, arise.' And she opened her eyes; and seeing Peter, she sat up." (*Acts* 9:40).

Then Peter gave Dorcas his hand, and helped her to her feet. He called in the mourners, and all the widows rejoiced to see Dorcas alive again. This miracle led many in Joppe to believe.

Note those words, "led many to believe," for that spiritual wonder, conversion, often follows upon the working of miracles—particularly after *great* miracles. The charism of miracles among the saints and missionaries was one of the chief means of converting pagans to the Faith and of bringing about repentance and renewal among believers.

St. Paul, on one of his many missionary journeys, set sail from Philippi and joined other disciples in Troas five days later. On the first day of the week they had gathered for the "breaking of the bread," and Paul, because he planned to leave the next day, spoke until midnight. St. Luke observes that there were many lamps in the upstairs room of the assembly. As Paul talked on, a young man, Eutychus, fell asleep, perhaps partly because of the smoke and warm air from the lamps escaping through the window over the sill on which he was sitting. (It may cheer many a preacher to know that even St. Paul once put a listener to sleep.) Sound asleep, Eutychus fell out the window, plunging all the way from the third story to the ground.

Eutychus was picked up dead. When St. Paul heard this he hurried down, threw himself upon him, embraced him and, for the sake of the bystanders, said, "Be not troubled, for his soul is in him." (At times saints say such things, apparently to hide the greatness of their miracles and to avoid the attention and honors they get because of them.) After restoring Eutychus to life, St. Paul went upstairs again, broke bread, and talked until dawn. Apparently the lad kept awake this time, for the account ends with the words, "And they brought the youth alive, and were not a little comforted." (*Acts* 20:12).

St. Paul was such a tremendous missionary, the accepted greatest of all time, that he must have raised the dead many times, although the above case is the only one recorded. And what St. Peter and St. Paul did has also been done by numerous later saints down through the Christian centuries.

4

THE ASSUMPTION
OF THE BLESSED VIRGIN MARY

"Arise, make haste, my love, my dove,
my beautiful one, and come."
—Canticle of Canticles 2:10

Tota pulchra es, Maria! "You are all-beautiful, O Mary!"
And there is in you no stain of original sin. Nor, by the
special assistance and grace of God, did you ever commit the
least actual sin.

What then of the disposition at death of that immaculate
body of Mary, Mother of the Saviour, Mother of God,
Virgin of Virgins, Queen of angels and men? *Mater
Purissima, Mater Castissima, Mater Inviolata!* (Mother Most
Pure, Mother Most Chaste, Mother Inviolate!)

The first woman, Eve, would not have been subject to
death had she not sinned. Adam and Eve, in their state of
original innocence in the Garden, over and above the
possession of their wonderful pristine natural powers, were
elevated by supernatural grace. They also had preternatural
gifts such as original integrity and freedom from sickness.

If our original parents had not fallen from grace, they
would have passed through some form of deathless transition to the Beatific Vision and the joys of Heaven, after they
had proven themselves faithful and obedient for a while on
earth. But with their fall, sin came into the world, and with
sin, death—and with sin and death, the destiny of Hell, like
that of the fallen angels.

Jesus and Mary were the new and perfect Adam and Eve.
Jesus, of course, was also divine; Mary, although only a
human being, was the greatest, purest, and most wonderful

23

of all God's creations, both in nature and in grace. One would have to be another Mary to be able to contemplate all the wonders in Mary—*Tota pulchra es!*

With Christ and Mary came the New Creation, the reality of redemption, salvation and perfection. Although Mary was Christ's Mother according to the flesh, Christ and Mary, in a real sense, were the new spiritual "parents" of the race. In them that original purity was restored. Though the effects of the Redemption usually take place in the baptized soul only gradually, the Christian should grow continually in sanctifying grace, approaching closer and closer to the innocence of Jesus and Mary. He should become able to say with St. Paul, "No longer I, but Christ lives in me." (*Gal.* 2:20).

And as Jesus came to us through Mary, we go to Jesus through Mary. As Mary mothered His physical body, she also mothers all the members of His Mystical Body. Both Mary and the Church are the spiritual mother of Christian souls, enabling them to grow in holiness, making them ever more pleasing to God.

Little by little Mary forms us, little by little she brings us more to Jesus so that we become more and more like her elder Son, our Brother. Mary's love is continually directed toward the glory of Christ and the Father through the fulfillment of God's will in perfected souls.

What then would Jesus do at the death of His Mother, whose virginal body had been a living temple for Him for nine months? This is the very best, the holiest Mother, the new Eve, the spiritual Mother of the children of God.

"Thou shalt not suffer thy holy one to see corruption" (*Acts* 13:35), says the Bible regarding Our Lord Jesus Christ. These beautiful words also express God's will regarding His holy Mother.

Mystics and scholars might argue about the site and place of Mary's death and burial. Ephesus or Jerusalem—it matters little. There is a shrine, visited by Pope John Paul II, near Ephesus. It is the ancient house where Mary, according to early traditions, lived with St. John the Evangelist, to whose care she had been committed by her Son from the cross. But in Jerusalem one also can visit the Church of the Dormition (the "Falling Asleep," which is the Byzantine name for the Assumption), and near this church is the shrine where she is reputed to have been buried briefly before her Assumption. Fittingly, Mary's Jerusalem "burial site" shrine, like that of her ascended Son, is not far from the resurrection valley of Josaphat.

But the teaching of the Church should suffice. The solemn definitive declaration of the divinely revealed dogma of the Assumption of Mary proclaims: "The Immaculate Mother of God, Mary ever Virgin, after her life on earth, was assumed, body and soul, to the glory of Heaven." Thus reads the bull, *Munificentissimus Deus,* of Pope Pius XII, November 1, 1950.

Many a saint's body has remained incorrupt for centuries. Joan Carroll Cruz's book, *The Incorruptibles*, deals with over a hundred cases of incorruption to greater or lesser degree and shorter or longer time among God's holy ones. Yet these were bodies that once housed some sin and evil, despite whatever great virtues and holiness these saints were able to achieve by God's redeeming grace.

What, then, might one expect for the incredibly holy Mother of God, who, from her own pure body, gave Jesus His perfect one by the intervention of the Holy Spirit Himself? In her was utter purity, utter holiness, fullness of grace, and many other glories as well. So it would seem that the only fitting action on the part of her divine Son would be to take her body and soul into Heaven after her death, without her body undergoing the least corruption.

The legend is that St. Thomas was away (doubting and missing Thomas!) when the Apostles buried Mary. Arriving later, Thomas asked for the tomb to be reopened so he could have one last gaze upon that dear Mother who had encouraged them all, the Mother of their Master, the Queen of the Apostles and the fairest of all women. They found her tomb empty.

In any case we believe, in accord with the infallible teaching of the Church, that Mary lives in Heaven in her glorified body, with her Son who likewise reigns there in His glorious body. Their presence in their glorified bodies is a promise to all those blessed souls in Heaven who are at present without their bodies: at Judgment Day, the latter, too, will rejoice in restored, spiritualized and glorified bodies.

Although they are not a part of Catholic doctrine, and although the dogma of the Assumption in no way depends upon them, Mary's innumerable apparitions over the Christian centuries give the Christian a certain reassurance about the presence of Mary, body and soul, in Heaven. These are not part of the deposit of Faith which must be accepted by all Catholics. Yet the Church also teaches that individuals cannot lightly reject the verified experiences of the supernatural. When the Church, or an individual ordinary of a diocese, rules that certain apparitions are worthy of a Catholic's belief, when popes and saints have endorsed the shrines of such apparitions by their words or presence, when there are numerous well-established miracles and all sorts of spiritual favors, then one is very temerarious to reject such claims.

One must distinguish between apparitions and appearances. Jesus *appeared* to His Apostles and the others after His Resurrection. He told them to touch and feel His hands and side, to see that He was not a ghost (or apparition), to give Him something to eat. Normally what we call "apparitions" do not eat, drink, etc.

It will be argued among "experts" whether all apparitions of Mary or even of Christ are actual appearances in their real bodies. In many cases, they look strikingly alive, just like they did on earth, but with superior beauty, light and radiance, which leads the privileged seers to consider their heavenly (or purgatorial) visitors for all practical purposes as completely present—that is, with their bodies also. There are also certain mysteries that are simply incomprehensible. For instance, some saints while yet on earth, by a supernatural help or charism, could bilocate. They were seen active in a distant place, as real to observers there as where they actually were back at their permanent location or "home base." So perhaps a soul (and in Thomistic philosophy the soul is said to *inform* the body) is able to project a realistic image of the body of the person in an apparition.

Mary has appeared at times, especially in her most famous "Marian apparitions," as if she were there with her real body. For example, when St. Catherine Labouré was called by the angel to the chapel of the Sisters of Charity at their rue du Bac convent in Paris, she heard a rustling as of a silk dress when Mary took her seat there. Further, Catherine fell on her knees and clasped her hands upon the knees of the Blessed Virgin and listened as she spoke to her for a long time. At a subsequent apparition, Our Lady was to show Catherine the design for the Miraculous Medal.

At Fatima, those who did not see Mary could note her arrival or departure by the motion of the little holm oak on which she stood. It remains a fact that many seers—whether they witnessed great apparitions like that of the Blessed Virgin Mary to the three children at Fatima or that of Our Lord to St. Margaret Mary, or just had visions of the saints—are convinced that they saw real persons.

There have been many apparitions of Mary over the centuries—particularly in recent history. There are shelves of volumes recounting these apparitions: Miraculous Medal, La Salette, Lourdes, Pontmain, Pellevoisin, Knock, Fatima, Beauraing, Banneux, to mention the most famous. (All of these mentioned have been approved by the Church.)

These celestial happenings on earth are a very good private argument, and a substantial one, for the actuality of Mary dwelling with her glorified body in Heaven, having been raised from the earth by her Son long ago. Mary gave her Son flesh-and-blood life. It is not surprising that in her own flesh and blood, in her spiritualized, risen, glorified body, she visits the children of earth again and again.

Ave Maria! Hail Mary! Mother of God, Virgin Most

Powerful, Queen assumed into Heaven, Gate of Heaven, *Ora pro nobis!*

—PART TWO—

RESURRECTION MIRACLES IN THE CHRISTIAN ERA

"At His [Christ's] coming, all men are to arise with their own bodies; and they are to give an account of their lives. Those who have done good deeds will go into eternal life; those who have done evil will go into everlasting fire.

"This is the Catholic faith. Everyone must believe it, firmly and steadfastly; otherwise, he cannot be saved."

*—The Athanasian Creed
(Fifth Century)*

THE EARLY CENTURIES

5

MIRACLES IN THE EARLY CHURCH

Testimony of St. Irenaeus and Others;
Resurrection Miracles Performed by St. Hilary
of Poitiers, St. Ambrose, and Others

> *"God, whom he believed, who quickeneth
> the dead . . ."*
> —Romans 4:17

There was a time during the past century when some non-Catholic Christians tried to deny "Catholic" miracles and to limit miracles to the times of the very first Christians. The truth is that there were many miracles not only in the first days of the Church, but also in the early centuries, and ever since—miracles which include the raising of the dead.

The last miracle of the dead raised by an Apostle (outside the scriptural accounts) is that of St. John the Evangelist. Appolonius, a Greek Father, claims that St. John raised a dead man to life at Ephesus.

St. John the Evangelist had a famous disciple, St. Polycarp, Bishop of Smyrna (died in 156). St. Polycarp, in turn, had a celebrated disciple, the great St. Irenaeus (c. 130-220) who became Bishop of Lyons. Irenaeus knew the early Church very well, east and west; as a famous apologist for the Church, he wrote five influential volumes entitled *Against the Heresies*.

In that work Irenaeus says, "Some persons that were dead have been raised again and have continued among us many years." He affirms this in an almost casual manner; in a word, Irenaeus assumes that Christians took this sort of happening for granted, recognizing it as unchallengeable. He continues: "Nor can we sum up the miraculous works which the Church, by the gift of God, performs every day over the whole world in the Name of Jesus Christ."

Writing about the inability of Simon Magus (the Magician) and his disciples to work real miracles, Irenaeus states, "So far are they from raising the dead, as Our Lord raised them, and as the Apostles did by prayer, *and as in the brotherhood oftentimes is done,* when the whole church of the place hath begged it with much fasting and prayer, and the spirit of the dead man hath returned and the man hath been given back to the prayers of the saints." (Emphasis added).

St. Justin Martyr (c. 100-165) also speaks of miracles in general worked in his time, as do others. But the testimony of Irenaeus is particularly important. Irenaeus, praised by many of the early learned saints for his exhaustive research into pagan philosophies and myths, was well qualified to refute the heresies connected with them. One can rely on his declaration that there were many miracles of the dead being raised in his time, even though there may not have survived any records of detailed accounts of them. St. Irenaeus' work was unchallengeable even by pagans.

John Henry Cardinal Newman, eminent and saintly scholar of the past century, quotes the writer Douglas concerning "the testimonies of Papias and Irenaeus, who speak of raising the dead." Of course, other ancient writers who lived after St. Justin Martyr—Origen, Tertullian and St. Cyprian, for instance—refer to miracles, cures, the driving out of demons, etc. Newman also quotes Middleton and on the whole affirms his reference to "the power of raising the dead" and other wonders worked in the primitive Church. But that power did not end with the second or third-century Christians.

St. Gregory of Nazianzus (329-390) was one of the three great "Cappadocian" Fathers and Doctors of the Eastern Church in Cappadocia in the fourth century (the other two being Basil and Gregory of Nyssa). About 379 he was made Bishop of Constantinople. This church had been spiritually ravaged for 40 years because it was controlled by the

Arians, who denied the divinity of Christ.

St. Gregory, on his entry to his see city, then a great metropolis and the seat of the Emperor of the Roman Empire in the East, could not retake possession of even one of the churches that had been usurped by the Arians. So he gathered the faithful Catholics in a palace belonging to some of his relatives, and converted it into a small church. It was there that he gave some of his famous theological discourses.

Gregory named the place "Anastasis" (Anastasia), meaning "Resurrection"; he meant it to be a symbol of the true Catholic Faith resurrected, as it were, from the grave of heresy. A miracle occurred there which seemed to confirm the site's name. It also recalls the words of St. Irenaeus about the wonders obtained through the prayers of the "saints," that is, members of the congregation.

Sozomen (d. 447-8), a reliable Church historian not long after Gregory's time, related the miraculous revival of a woman who was killed when she fell from a gallery in the converted palace. The woman was also with child. This miracle was not credited to St. Gregory, the pastor and bishop, but to the faith of the congregation, by whose prayers she was returned to life.

St. Gregory of Nyssa, friend of St. Gregory of Nazianzus and younger brother of St. Basil, also had some apt comments regarding miracles. Gregory of Nyssa was the philosopher of the three (and not as bold as Basil). When his sister, St. Macrina, died, Gregory wrote about her saintly life, mentioning miracles such as the cure of a blind girl, daughter of the military commander of a district of Pontus, and other cures.

Gregory also recorded other wonders connected with his sister: the grain that did not give out in famine, devils cast out, prophecies of future events. All these, he wrote, were well known to her associates. But St. Macrina's wise and saintly brother apparently hesitated to mention Macrina's greater miracles, for he wrote, "I do not think it wise to add to my story all the other details we heard from those who lived with her and knew her life accurately, for most men judge the credibility of what they hear according to the measure of their own experience, and what is beyond the power of the hearer they insult with the suspicion of falsehood, as outside of the truth."

These early Fathers and Doctors, of course, lived not in peaceful times but in times of hard debate and often bitter opposition. There were doubters back then even as there are doubters now. St. Gregory's statement still gives a superb and classic description of the mind-set of skeptics, even "Christian" skeptics; it shows how they exclude themselves from certain facts by close-mindedly clinging to the notion that miracles are impossible.

As Cardinal Newman points out, the Fathers and early writers of the Church took for granted that their fellow Christians knew of the wonders that had been worked among them. Thus these leaders might refer to them, but they felt no need to try to prove them. They spoke to their own people; and since "everybody" knew of demons cast out, of miraculous cures, and even of the dead being raised, any burden of disproof was on the objectors.

It was in these early centuries that the resurrection miracle of Macarius the Egyptian, a monk who lived in the desert and died at the age of 90, was performed. Macarius had special powers of interpreting the Scriptures, a power over demons, and the gift of prophecy. He once foretold to a disciple named John, who had an avaricious bent, that if he did not change he would someday suffer the punishment of Giezi, the servant of the prophet Eliseus. And indeed, John later died of leprosy.

Palladius, who wrote in about the year 420, and had traveled extensively among the desert monks in many areas and interviewed a great number of them, relates the following of Macarius the Egyptian. There was a certain heathen who did not believe in the Resurrection. To convince him, Macarius brought back to life a man who had died. This miracle was spoken of throughout the desert.

The above information comes from the writings of Palladius entitled *The Lausiac History*; another version of this work is known as *The Paradise of Palladius*. Sir Ernest A. Wallis Budge, Kt., Litt. D., a well-respected North Africa and Near East scholar translated the *Stories of the Holy Fathers,* which included *The Paradise of Palladius,* from an old manuscript he discovered in ancient Nineveh, that is, from the Syrian of Anan Isho, a seventh-century monk of the monastery of Beth Abhe. Budge judged Palladius and his work to be genuine and true, as did Dom Cuthbert Butler, who wrote the authoritative *Palladius: The Lausiac History.* (*The Lausiac History* was named after the wealthy prefect, Lausus, who requested the writing of Palladius' original manuscript.)

Fitting well into this company is St. Hilary of Poitiers (315?-368), Bishop and Doctor of the Church. He fought the Arians and wrote deeply and brilliantly on the Blessed Trinity, especially about the Second Person. For his orthodoxy and his refusal to attend a synod at which the bishops present were required to sign a condemnation of St. Athanasius, St. Hilary was exiled from Gaul by the Emperor, and sent to Phrygia far away in the East. There he wrote a great deal, raised a dead man to life, and worked other miracles. When the Arians of the East became upset by Hilary's blasting of their heretical views, the Emperor Constantius sent him back to France, where the people of Poitiers welcomed him with joy. There Hilary brought back to life an infant who had died unbaptized. This same St. Hilary was the inspiration and spiritual guide of the great St. Martin of Tours, *Trium mortuorum suscitator*—the "Raiser of Three Dead"; St. Martin's miracles are recounted in a subsequent chapter of this book.

It is easily seen that there was a continuity and "interlacing" among the early great saints, especially bishops, wherein the matter of raising the dead was taken for granted as an accepted fact and almost normal happening. The knowledge and experience of these facts augmented and encouraged the faith of succeeding saints.

However, at this point in time came a different sort of saint and circumstance, in the Holy Land. It was the Empress St. Helena (c. 250-c. 330), mother of Constantine, searching for the True Cross. Constantine had won an inspired victory over Maxentius at the Milvian Bridge after he saw a cross of light in the sky with the words: *In hoc signo vinces!* "In this sign thou shalt conquer!" The victorious emperor then issued his famous Edict of Milan which gave Christians the freedom to practice their religion.

Some time after her conversion to Christianity, Helena set off for Jerusalem to find the True Cross. From the tradition handed down over the years (with some variations), it is known how this most precious Christian relic was found and authenticated.

In Helena's diggings at the traditional site, three crosses were uncovered. This put the emperor's mother and those with her—and an impressive party they were—into a quandary. That Helena prayed is beyond doubt. One account says that all with her, at least the Christians, also prayed. At any event, Helena had an inspiration. To determine which of the three crosses buried on Calvary was the true one, she touched the corpse of a dead man to each. When the dead man returned to life after touching one of the three crosses, it was considered a sign from Heaven: Here was the True Cross on which the Saviour had died. And it was not far from that very spot—where He had been crucified, and where St. Helena had dug so diligently—that Christ had gloriously defeated death some 300 years earlier.

Sts. Cyril of Jerusalem, Paulinus of Nola and Ambrose of Milan all record St. Helena's search for and discovery of the True Cross. It is not hard to believe that St. Helena received this special divine assistance to help her to find such an important and glorious relic; one might even be surprised if she had not received some special help from God.

St. Ambrose (c. 340-397), by the way, was the one who baptized St. Augustine. He once said to St. Monica, who was weeping over her wayward son, Augustine, that the child of so many prayers and tears would not be lost. St. Ambrose had held a high office in the Roman Empire, and when he was elected Bishop of Milan, a seat of the empire (by acclamation, through the inspired cry of a boy), he dealt gently but firmly with the supreme political rulers, the Roman emperors. Once he denied the great Emperor Theodosius entrance to the cathedral at Milan until he had performed public penance for having ordered the slaughter of a number of people.

It is due to St. Ambrose that one of the best attested miracles in history came about—the cure of the blind butcher Severus. Ambrose had found the tombs of Sts. Gervase and Protase, early martyrs, and Severus was cured by touching the relics on the bier with his handkerchief and then applying the cloth to his sightless eyes. This happened before a great crowd; it was also testified to by St. Augustine (then in Milan) and by Paulinus, secretary to St. Ambrose. Many of the sick and possessed were healed at this shrine; even a Protestant, Dr. Cave, admitted the truth of these miracles.

St. Ambrose once stayed at the home of Decentius, an illustrious Christian of Florence. The son of Decentius, Pansopius, who had been troubled by an unclean spirit, was healed by frequent prayers and the laying on of the holy bishop's hands. Some days later the lad was seized by a sudden attack of illness and died. But what seemed an apparent defeat was only ordered, as often happens, for the greater glory of God and for the bestowal of a smile of approval upon His saint.

Ambrose had been out of the house at the time the boy died. In the absence of the saint, the devout mother took the corpse of her son from the upper part of the house to the lower and placed him on the bishop's couch. When Ambrose returned, he restored Pansopius to life. He also wrote a book of wise and helpful instructions specifically for this privileged boy.

St. Ambrose had gone to Florence not to perform miracles

but to consecrate the "Ambrosian" basilica. But Decentius was an important citizen there, and it seems that this miracle was an expression of a beautiful friendship on the part of St. Ambrose. It is said that Ambrose laid himself out over the lifeless child, rather like Eliseus had done, and restored Pansopius by his prayers. There are a number of cases in which—especially among the early great saints—these holy revivers of the dead followed the example of Eliseus in stretching themselves out over the lifeless body as they prayed.

This account of St. Ambrose and Pansopius is from the life of Ambrose written by Paulinus, the saint's companion and secretary. St. Ambrose is also renowned for many other great accomplishments.

6

RESURRECTION MIRACLES PUBLICIZED BY ST. AUGUSTINE

*"Accounting that God is able to raise up
even from the dead."*
—Hebrews 11:19

Anyone who reads the writings of St. Augustine can see that the great miracles of the primitive Church continued. Given Augustine's lifespan, 354-430, it becomes evident that miracles were still being performed in the fifth century.

St. Augustine was one of the greatest men of all time. If we cannot accept his testimony, both reason and history are meaningless. After spending his youth and early manhood in wayward living and in philosophical studies, searching for truth, St. Augustine was converted (through the prayers of his mother, St. Monica, and the preaching of St. Ambrose), gave up his concubine, and became perhaps the greatest and most brilliant theologian in the history of the Church—as well as a great saint.

Bishop of Hippo (not far from ancient Carthage, in northern Africa) for 35 years, Augustine was also an orator, rhetorician, teacher, philosopher, apologist, spiritual leader, psychologist of the soul, guide, and writer of over a hundred books. He led the fight against three major heresies: Manichaeism, Donatism, and Pelagianism, and he is one of the four great founders of religious orders. St. Augustine's influence over the currents of history has lasted well beyond his own time, and his integrity and his ability are beyond question.

In what is perhaps Augustine's greatest work, *De Civitate Dei, (The City of God)*, amid other displays of his vast knowledge and competence, Augustine speaks of miracles. He considers the complaint that has been voiced in every age: How is it that *today* we do not have the miracles that were seen in the *early* days of the Church? (There is nothing new under the sun!) Augustine replies:

> "The truth is that even today miracles are being wrought in the Name of Christ, sometimes through His Sacraments and sometimes through the intercession of the relics of His saints. Only, such miracles do not strike the imagination with the same flashing brilliance as the earlier miracles, and so they do not get the same flashing publicity as the others did."

Augustine points out how the miracle accounts of the canon of the Gospels (the genuine Scripture Gospels) were heard regularly by all, and that they carried the full authority of the Church. But there were many other miracles scarcely known about except by a few, even in the big cities; these were seldom backed by ecclesiastical authority.

Similarly, it is very likely that there are many miracles occurring today, as they have throughout Christian history, which receive little attention from ecclesiastical authority, that is, from the bishops and priests in positions of leadership.

True, these miracles, in and of themselves, are not objects of divine faith, and one has no specific duty to promulgate individual miracles as if they were. But Bishop and writer Augustine knew that one function of miracles was to strengthen the faith of the people by endorsing the authenticity of the Catholic Faith, echoing those well-known wonders of Our Lord and His Apostles.

Moreover, Augustine saw a subtler, deeper, hidden attack in the words of those who attempted to deny the miracles taking place in his own time: "It is sometimes objected that the miracles which Christians claim, no longer happen . . .

However the malice of the objection is in the insinuation that not even the earlier miracles ought to be believed."

If only Augustine were alive today to confront some of the so-called Catholic Scripture scholars and exegetes who insinuate or declare that even biblical miracles should not be treated as objective occurrences! St. Augustine would be a master trial lawyer today, questioning such "scholars" and confounding them with his irrefutable logic. Such were the gifts of reasoning and rhetoric that helped him to overcome so many heretical opponents.

Augustine was right: There *have* been miracles in every age (in addition to those of the Old Testament period), from the water Christ turned into wine and the daughter of Jairus brought back to life, to the latest twentieth-century saints such as Pope St. Pius X healing the sick, Padre Pio restoring sight to the blind, or the miracle of the sun at Fatima. St. Augustine himself relates, among a number of other miracles, four accounts of the dead being raised. (Cardinal Newman credits him with accounts of five.)

In Chapter 8 of Book XXII of *The City of God,* Augustine speaks of a relic of the martyr St. Stephen. A Spanish priest, Eucharius, who was stationed in Calama, was cured of "stone" when Bishop Possidius applied to him the relic of St. Stephen. Later the same priest was near death from another sickness—he was so far gone that they had already bound his hands. They took the priest's tunic to the shrine and touched it to the relic of St. Stephen. When they returned to the apparently dead body of Eucharius, they placed the garment on him, and he was restored to life.

Near Audurus, at an estate called Villa Caspaliana, a consecrated virgin became sick and was on the brink of death. Her parents took her habit and set out for the shrine of St. Stephen in Audurus to touch it to his relic. In the meantime, the nun died. When the parents returned, they clothed the corpse with the habit; the moment they did this, their daughter came back to life.

There was a Syrian named Bassus who lived in Hippo (the

see city of St. Augustine). He had a daughter in danger of death, and he took her robe to touch the relic of St. Stephen. He was still praying there at the shrine when his servants came to tell him that his daughter was dead (reminiscent of the daughter of Jairus). However, the friends who were with Bassus saw the servants first, and forbade them to tell their master the bad news lest he break down in public. When they got back home, Bassus found the house loud with the wailing of mourners. He threw the girl's robe on the corpse. Her life was restored.

Also in Hippo, the son of a certain tax collector named Irenaeus died; he was one of St. Augustine's neighbors. The corpse had been laid out and the funeral arranged. A friend attending the funeral suggested that the boy's body be anointed with oil from the shrine of St. Stephen. The family followed his suggestion, and the boy came back to life.

After relating a good number of miracles of various sorts, Augustine goes on to say: "How can I tell all the miracles I know . . . I know that many of my fellow Catholics will complain that I have left out any number of miracles which they happen to know as well as I do." So, limiting himself as to the narration of such miracles for lack of time and space, Augustine observes: "I should have to fill several volumes [of miracles] . . . officially recorded and attested for *public reading* in our churches." (Emphasis added). And Augustine was limiting himself to those miracles at St. Stephen's shrine, and at Calama and his own Hippo.

Note here several important facts. In one see city and two nearby places alone, a great scholar and discerning saint, Bishop and Father of the Church, relates a number of miracles as "official" and tells of many others that are simply known to all. Nor does he, apparently, claim credit for working any of them, or admit directly to any of his own. He assumes that everyone is aware of these miracles, almost as common occurrences—even the raising of the dead.

Yet there were many bishops in Africa at that time. And there were many other great sees—Rome, Constantinople,

Antioch, Ephesus, Jerusalem, Edessa, Florence, Milan, Lyons, Tours, and on and on. Then there were the great desert areas and wildernesses of the hermits and monks. One needs little imagination to guess at the great number of miracles worked not only in those days, but also in later days, including the raising of the dead. These miracles were not "legends," "myths," or mere poetical expressions of certain truths or beliefs.

After the example of other prelates, St. Augustine began to record the miracles at Hippo. He states that within just two years he recorded nearly 70 miracles and that he knew for certain of many others not officially recorded at the time of his writings. Moreover, he said that at Calama, where recording had begun earlier and miracles were more frequent, the number of attested cases there was "incomparably greater."

Augustine did what other bishops might do well to imitate today. He publicized in his own church the miracles of which he was aware. And, when possible, he had the beneficiaries present as proof. The twentieth-century faithful, too, are entitled to hear of such examined and attested miracles. And there *are* still miracles today, although perhaps not in the same great numbers as in "the ages of faith." When people do not hear of miracles—whether of the past or the present— they are not encouraged to pray for them. Those priests who "hide," dodge or scoff at such miracles may have much to answer for.

In answer to those who doubt the miracles attested to by Ambrose or Augustine, or other truly great men, Cardinal Newman stated well, decades before he became a Catholic, that there "will appear no reason, except to vexed and heated minds, for accusing the holy Ambrose of imposture, or the keen, practiced, and experienced intellect of Augustine of abject credulity."

7

ST. MARTIN OF TOURS, THE "RAISER OF THREE DEAD"

"That I may know him and the power of his resurrection."
—Philippians 3:10

Martin of Tours (316-397) has always been one of the most attractive of saints. As I type this in the home of a priest friend, on the wall nearby is a colorful bas-relief of Martin astride his militarily caparisoned horse. It portrays the young Roman officer in the legion of the Emperor Julian in his armor, with his sword raised to divide his military cloak. Except for his armor, the cloak is his only clothing.

At the Gate of Amiens, sitting on the ground on a cold winter day, a beggar, piteously naked, looks up to Martin. It is to this impoverished man that Martin gives half his cloak. Some of his fellow soldiers were amused to see Martin return to camp with only half his cloak—scarcely army propriety. But that night Christ appeared to Martin with a throng of accompanying angels; He said to them, "Martin, still a catechumen, has covered Me with his cloak."

The accepted life of Martin is that written by Sulpicius Severus, a Roman nobleman, in his *Dialogues*. Sulpicius was not only a friend of Martin, but he also kept up with Martin's disciples after the saint's death. In 396, about a year before Martin's death, Sulpicius wrote the biography that became so famous and which stirred up so much emulation of the lives of early holy monks. It ultimately became a model for other biographies of saints. Church historians such as Poulet-Raemers and Father Hippolyte Delehaye, S.J., critical Bollandist scholar, have accepted this work as authentic. (Those who wish to learn more of Martin than space permits here would do well to refer to the popular life written by Henri Gheon and translated by Frank Sheed, *St. Martin of Tours*—a book based largely on the *Dialogues* of Sulpicius.)

Sulpicius, born about 360, knew St. Paulinus of Nola, with whom he corresponded. He was also a contemporary of Sts. Ambrose, Augustine and Jerome. Sulpicius compared Martin with the Apostles. He might very well do so, and even be excused for any excess enthusiasm, for Martin, a holy soldier who courageously stood up to Emperor Julian (the Apostate), became a hermit, monk, founder, bishop, pastor and worker of great miracles and wonders in his missionary labors.

In fourth-century Gaul, Christianity had followers only in large cities like Lyons. The countryside was still predominantly pagan. It was Martin who would begin to change that condition. By his works he would set an example for parish organization, for a bishop's visitations, and for pastoral solicitude.

St. Martin's beginnings were in far-off Sabaria, a town of Pannonia (area of modern Hungary). But he was reared in Ticinun Ita (Pavia) where his father was a soldier, and later a military tribune. Martin became a catechumen in 325 and remained in the catechumenate until his Baptism in 337. In the meantime he was conscripted into the military in 330, and began active service with the Roman legions in 334 under Emperors Constantius and Julian. Following his penchant for solitude and contemplation, he left the legions when he was about 25 years old.

Martin knew St. Hilary, Bishop of Poitiers, and eventually put himself under the holy prelate's spiritual direction. But first he tried a hermit's life in a forest by the Rhine. Then he made a trip to his aging parents' home at Sabaria. On his return he established a community at Milan, but was expelled by the Arian bishop, Auxentius.

Hearing that St. Hilary had been released from his exile in

distant Phrygia, Martin (who was at a hermitage at Liguria) tried to meet the saint at Rome. However, he only caught up with Hilary at Poitiers, where he agreed to support him by prayer and penance in Hilary's fight against Arianism. (Earlier, Hilary had inveigled Martin into being ordained an exorcist.)

In a wild and lonely spot about five miles from Poitiers, St. Martin founded the first Gallic monastery at Ligugé (Logoteiacus). He remained at Ligugé from about 361 until about 370, when he was made Bishop of Tours after St. Lidorius died. (When Hilary had died in 368, Martin had managed to avoid being made bishop there.) Fittingly, Tours was the old Roman fortress town of Caesarodunum.

St. Martin of Tours worked many wonders in his life, even before he raised three people from the dead. In the Alps once, he was nearly killed by brigands—but he converted one of them to a blameless life. At Lerroux he kissed and healed a leper. Another time, at Martin's order, a deacon cast a small net to catch an enormous pike when they desperately needed food. And at Paris (Lutetia Parisiorum), as he was coming in from Treves by way of the North Gate, he found a beggar so far gone with leprosy that the crowd following St. Martin withdrew in horror. At the sight of this miserable creature, Martin was filled with compassion; he stopped, and embraced and blessed the leper. The hideous disease vanished instantly.

The Parisians, who were then considered proud, voluptuous and pleasure-mad sybarites, were converted. This took place at the old St. Martin's Gate (*Porte St. Martin*) opposite the *Pont au Change*.

At Chartres, already the seat of the see of Bishop Valentinus, St. Martin met Victricius, Archbishop of Rouen. At that time a father brought before them his 12-year-old daughter who had been mute from birth. Martin asked the other two bishops to cure the child, but they refused. So Martin sent the crowd away, except for the two prelates. He prayed, blessed oil, and poured a few drops into the girl's mouth, holding her tongue in his fingers. Then Martin asked the girl her father's name. She immediately uttered it. Her father sobbed, cried aloud with joy, and embraced Martin's knees. A stream of conversions followed.

St. Martin of Tours fought idolatry and the false gods worshiped by the countryside pagans. At Amboise on the Loire there was a tremendous tower of shaped and polished stones. It rose to a great height and culminated in a cone. Apparently it was the sanctuary of some warrior god. When some of St. Martin's monks, assigned to destroy it, did not have the courage to do so, Martin prayed and a terrific storm arose. It brought the tower down to its very foundations. The people got the message, forsook their god, and Martin built a church and parish there.

At Leprosum, after an initial repulse, he was encouraged by angels. He returned with his band, and while the pagans looked on, seemingly paralyzed, the monks reduced their idolatrous temple to rubble. Martin performed many other wonders, like "freezing" the progress of a pagan procession he thought was carrying an idol.

In considering St. Martin of Tours' three miracles of reviving the dead, keep in mind that Sulpicius gathered these accounts either from the accounts of witnesses or from his own personal observation. It will also help in understanding Martin's gifts during his lifetime to note that after Martin's death, Bishop Gregory of Tours filled four volumes with accounts of his *posthumous* miracles. And Gregory added that hundreds more had been omitted because many persons had left without informing him of their miracles. A register of these miracles was kept in the basilica at Tours.

Before St. Martin became bishop, while he was still at the monastery at Ligugé, a catechumen, one of his first companions there, was seized with faintness and a violent fever while Martin was away. When Martin returned after three days absence, he found the monk dead and the sorrowing brothers preparing his body for burial. St. Martin came weeping to the corpse of this early companion and friend.

Inspired by the Holy Ghost, he ordered the rest of his disciples out of the cell, barred the door and, like the prophet Eliseus, prayed over the corpse. Time passed. St. Martin lifted himself up and gazed on the face of the dead man with confidence in the mercy of God. Hardly two hours of persistent prayer had passed when, little by little, the limbs of the man's body began to stir. His eyes half opened, and he began blinking at the light.

Then St. Martin filled the cell with a loud shout of rejoicing and thanksgiving. The monks outside rushed in to see their confrere, whom they had been mourning as dead, alive once again. This man remained alive for years. He was the first to furnish tangible proof of St. Martin's miracles, and he used to relate what had happened to him when he was "stripped" of his body.

Here is the monk's account: When dead, he had been led to the tribunal of a judge; there he was sentenced to go with a vulgar crowd to a region of darkness. Then word was brought to the judge, by two angels, that this was the man for whom Martin was praying. The angels were then ordered to lead the man back, to restore him to Martin, and to re-establish him in his former life.

The second raising by St. Martin happened a little later. Martin was walking across the property of a certain high-ranking personage named Lupicinus. The saint heard grief-stricken cries; he noted a house nearby, and a sorrowful throng about it. Upon inquiring, he found out that a young slave had hanged himself.

St. Martin set about praying and acting as he had in the previous case. Life reanimated the slave's features, and he opened his eyes to look into the face of Martin. Then, grasping Martin's hand, the man slowly rose to his feet. With all looking on in awe, the young slave walked with Martin to the vestibule of the house.

Gheon, after recounting these two miracles, writes, "I have set down without comment the two spectacular miracles, for they belong to the written record and there is no reason to doubt them unless our eyes are sealed to the evidence when it concerns facts of the supernatural order."

The third miracle of the dead was even more spectacular. It occurred after St. Martin had been made a bishop. On a journey to the Beauce, to a large town (perhaps Vendôme), he found a vast throng of pagans approaching him; they covered the whole plain. (These sort of Gospel scenes were apparently common occurrences in the lives of the great missionary saints.) This multitude had heard of the saint's miracles and wonders. As one writer put it, Martin *sensit operandum*—he saw that it was the moment to act! At times a certain "vibrancy" sprang up within him, which he knew was from the Holy Ghost. As one moved with deep emotion, "in a voice beyond the human," the saint cried out loudly: "How can so great a crowd of souls not know the Lord our Saviour?"

Just then a woman thrust her way through the crowd; in her arms was the lifeless body of a child. She held the corpse out to Martin, crying: "You are God's friend, we know. Give me back my son! He is my only son!" No theologian could have expressed better the relationship between faith, God, His saint, and divine power!

The crowd heard. They saw the reasonableness of the woman's challenge. Martin knew that for the salvation of all these poor people God would not refuse him. He took the child into his arms, knelt down, and prayed. The multitude was silent, expectant. There was an electric feeling of great suspense. Martin finished his prayer, and then arose with a living child in his arms! He handed the child over to the mother.

The Lord had performed a miracle, through His chosen instrument, for the conversion of these precious pagan souls! The whole multitude proclaimed Christ as God! They came in groups and threw themselves at St. Martin's feet, demanding to be made Christians. Martin lost no time. Right there in the field, he laid his hands upon them and made them catechumens.

In the old liturgical books St. Martin of Tours had the designation, *Trium mortuorum Suscitator,* that is, "Raiser of Three Dead." He once observed wryly that he had raised two from the dead before becoming a bishop, but only one afterward.

Along with St. Hilary of Poitiers and St. Geneviève of Paris, both credited with raising the dead, St. Martin of Tours is one of the great patrons of France; he has also traditionally been beloved of Christian soldiers.

8

RESURRECTION MIRACLES OF
ST. BENEDICT AND OTHERS
Testimony of Pope St. Gregory The Great

*"For I know that my Redeemer liveth,
and in the last day I shall rise out of the
earth. And I shall be clothed again with
my skin, and in my flesh I shall see my
God."*

—Job 19:25-26

One day the great abbot St. Benedict (c. 480-c. 547),
returning to the monastery from working in the fields, was
met by a farmer in great distress. "Give me back my son!
Give me back my son!" he cried. Benedict came to a halt.
"But I have not taken your son from you, have I?"
"He is dead. Come! Bring him back to life!"
Some of Benedict's companions started forward eagerly,
as if intending to go along with the distracted father. But
Benedict was stricken over the suggestion implied in the
father's words and cried out: "Stand back, brethren! Stand
back! Such a miracle is beyond our power. The holy Apostles are the only ones who can raise the dead. Why are you
so eager to accept what is impossible for us?" He spoke in
humility.
But the man pleaded on. He even swore an oath that he
would not leave Benedict until the saint restored his son's
life. Benedict may have been troubled by the oath; he asked
the man where the body was. The father told him he had left
the body at the monastery gate and gone to search for
Benedict after being informed of his absence.
When the band arrived at the monastery gate the saint

55

knelt down beside the lifeless body and bent over it. Then he stood and lifted his hands to pray. "O Lord, do not consider my sins but the faith of this man who is asking to see his son alive again, and restore to this body the soul Thou hast taken from it." Benedict's prayer was scarcely over when the body became animate and throbbed with life. All who were present attributed the miracle to heavenly intervention. Once again a saint had restored a child alive and happy to the arms of a jubilant father.

As Pope St. Gregory observes in his narration of this miracle, it was not Benedict who possessed such power in himself; rather, he begged for the miracle from God. This is always the manner of the saints. It was only Jesus who, with the majesty of the Son of God Himself, worked miracles in His own Name. Far from reaching for glory, the saints often tried to obscure their own identification with miracles by various ingenious methods and diversionary tactics. (Recall St. Anthony Mary Claret's myriad cures through "herbal remedies" in the nineteenth century.)

The above account, along with other accounts of Benedict's miracles and of the dead being raised, is from the *Dialogues* of Pope St. Gregory the Great (c. 540-604). Before the age of 30, Pope Gregory was Prefect of the city of Rome under Emperor Justinian II. Gregory became a monk, spent his fortune in founding seven monasteries on his Sicilian estates, and was an apocrisiarius or papal nuncio to the Emperor at Constantinople. He returned to Italy to become an abbot and, finally, by unanimous choice of clergy and laity, was persuaded to accept the office of Pope.

Gregory was considered the saviour of Italy; he was the builder of the Papal States free from the Empire's control, as well as a Doctor of the Church. It is Pope Gregory who is responsible for the conversion of England, as he sent St. Augustine of Canterbury and 40 monks as missionaries to England in the year 596. According to a tradition, Gregory received his first glimpse of Englishmen when he saw some handsome blond Anglo-Saxon youths for sale in a slave market in Rome. When he asked who they were, he was told that they were "Angles." He replied, "Not Angles, but angels!" and resolved to send missionaries to England to win the English people to Christ.

During his life Gregory dealt with emperors, kings, princes and ruthless barbarian invaders. Yet despite his vast accomplishments, Pope Gregory took as his title, "Servant of the Servants of God." It was this great man who wrote the life of St. Benedict.

St. Benedict, born of a distinguished family of Nursia, Italy, and the Father of Western Monasticism, is another of the greatest men of history. The development of medieval and modern Europe hinged upon the monasteries established by Benedict in the decaying Roman Empire. His Rule and works did much to establish order and stability. The great Abbey of Monte Cassino, restored after its destruction during World War II, is a lasting symbol of his life and contributions. This monastery was the birthplace of Western Monasticism, and St. Benedict's influence upon monastic life and upon the whole Church lasted for centuries—and are still felt in our own day.

St. Gregory the Great relates a story of how St. Benedict once had Totila, the cruel King of the Goths, trembling in fear. Benedict said to him, "You are the cause of many evils. You have caused many in the past. Put an end now to your wickedness. You will enter Rome and cross the sea. You have nine more years to rule, and in the tenth year you will die."

King Totila was less cruel after that. Then the prophecies came true, and in the tenth year he lost both his kingdom and his life. Gregory, too, even more so than Benedict, dealt courageously with invaders—for example, Agiluff, the King of the Lombards who was bent on destroying Rome.

It seems incredible that when faced with the talents, leadership, holiness, actions and greatness of such men as Benedict and Gregory, many so-called "historians," while accepting many other "ordinary" facts about these men, will treat their attitude toward miracles as naive. But reason tells us that one can safely trust the discernment of Gregory, whose business it was to discern.

The great 17th-century saint and Doctor of the Church, St. Francis de Sales, has defended the writings of St. Gregory the Great. In one of his Sermons on Our Lady (July 2, 1621), St. Francis de Sales says: "There are some who are ready to banter and jest over the writings of this glorious saint, and indeed wrongfully, for St. Gregory was one of the greatest Popes that ever sat in the chair of Peter; a few years after his elevation to the papacy he withdrew into solitude and wrote the book of his *Dialogues*."

Another raising of the dead by St. Benedict came about as a result of the devil's malice. The monks were at work adding to one of the monastery's walls. While Benedict was in his room praying, the devil appeared to him and remarked sarcastically that he was on his way to visit the monks at work. Benedict sent word at once to the monks to be on guard because the devil was on his way to disturb them. But the devil moved fast and overturned the wall as Benedict's message arrived. Under its ruins lay a very young monk, his body crushed. St. Gregory adds that he was the son of a tax collector.

Aghast, the monks hurried to report the tragedy to the abbot. The young monk had not only died, he had died without the Last Rites, an additional cause for their sorrow. Benedict told them to bring the body of the youth to his room. It was so mangled that both arms and legs were broken and all the bones were crushed. They had to carry the remains in a blanket.

In St. Benedict's room there was a reed-matting, where he was accustomed to pray. Benedict told all to leave, closed the door, and knelt down to pray.

Within that very hour Benedict sent the young man back to work as hale, whole and healthy as he had been before the accident. There were no broken bones, no wounds, not even a bruise. Surrounded by his amazed brethren, the youth helped them to finish the wall. It was a wall built by holy men, a wall of faith.

Many other wonders occurred in St. Benedict's life. When his sister Scholastica died, he saw her soul leave her body and fly to Heaven under the form of a white dove. He also saw the soul of Germanus, the Bishop of Capua, carried up to Heaven by angels in a ball of fire. With the Lord, one wonderful event is as simply arranged as any other.

Gregory recorded other miracles besides those of St. Benedict. There was a monk of Illyria who had been in the monastery at Rome with Gregory. This monk told Gregory the story of a Spanish monk named Peter, who had been with him as a hermit of Illyria in the vast solitude of Erasa.

Before living in the desert, Peter had become sick and had died. On being returned from death to life, Peter declared he had seen Hell, its torments, its pools of fire, and some of the world's outstanding men tossed amidst its flames. When Peter's turn came to be tossed into the flames, an angel in shining white robes suddenly appeared and preserved him from the burning fires. "Leave this place," the angel instructed him, "and consider well how you are to live henceforth."

With those words Peter came back to earth and felt the warmth of life being restored to his cold limbs. He described it all in detail. But even if he had never said a word, his changed life, his penances, and his night watches would have borne sufficient witness to his visit to another world and his subsequent fear of Hell.

A high-ranking man named Stephen, who was known to Gregory personally, told Gregory how he had sickened and died on a business trip to Constantinople. Since no doctor or mortician could be found that day to embalm his body, it was kept until the following night. In the meantime, Stephen found himself on trial before the Judge of the Infernal Court. However, the Judge dismissed him, saying, "I ordered Stephen the *blacksmith* to be brought here—not this man." So the Stephen who stood before the Judge was sent back to earth.

At the same time, the neighbor, who was a blacksmith also named Stephen, died, and so proved that what the first Stephen had heard at the Infernal Court was true. St. Gregory knew of Stephen the blacksmith and wrote that he had indeed died three years earlier of the plague.

Gregory goes on to relate that a soldier at Rome also died and came back to relate what had happened to him. The soldier had found himself on a high bridge over deep, dark, vaporous and smelly waters. There were beautiful meadows and delightful light beyond it, fragrant flowers, white-robed people and lovely dwellings. The soldier saw an overseer of the Church, a man named Peter who had died four years earlier. Peter was sunk in some foul mire below, bound in chains. This was his penalty for the just but cruel punishments he had given out when in authority (and Gregory remarks that everyone knew of these acts).

The soldier also saw the first Stephen, the acquaintance of Pope Gregory, half-hanging over the edge of the bridge. There were princely spirits in white trying to draw Stephen up, while evil spirits from below were trying to pull him down. At that point the soldier was called back to life. This scene showed, as Gregory explained later in the *Dialogues,* that Stephen (whose ways since coming back to life Gregory knew well) had not fully converted his life. So at death Stephen would face a severe struggle between the forces of good and evil over the settlement of his final fate.

In his *Dialogues I,* St. Gregory tells of Abbot Honoratus, whose humble sandals once led to a great miracle. This abbot had built a monastery which housed 200 monks. Abbot Honoratus was very holy. He once stopped a huge rock rolling down the mountain that towered over the monastery; had it continued on its path, it would have destroyed the monastery buildings as well as the monks inside them. Honoratus raised his right hand, made the Sign of the Cross, prayed to Christ, and the rock stopped. St. Gregory said that in his day the rock could still be seen in a position on the verge of falling—seemingly with nothing to hold it back.

When Libertinus became Abbot of Fondi he always carried one of Abbot Honoratus' sandals with him on a journey. He had been a disciple of Honoratus and had been trained by him; he venerated him greatly. Once, on his way to Ravenna, Abbot Libertinus met a woman carrying a dead child in her arms. When the woman recognized who it was, she seized the bridle of the abbot's horse, called on the Name of God, and cried out to him: "You shall not pass until you have brought my son back to life!"

Libertinus was frightened because she had used an oath in her petition. He was also confused because, try as he might, he could not turn out of her way. He struggled between fear and compassion. The mother finally won out, and in doing so showed forth the abbot's true virtue. He dismounted, got on his knees, prayed, and raised his hands to Heaven. Then he took the sandal of the holy Honoratus from the folds of his garment and laid it upon the breast of the dead child. As he continued praying, the child came to life. He took it by the hand and gave it to its weeping, thankful mother, then continued his journey to Ravenna.

Pope St. Gregory also knew of a good man named Marcellus, who lived in Todi (Tuscany) with his two sisters. When Marcellus died his remains had to be carried a good distance. So his funeral was delayed and his two sisters went to inform Bishop Fortunatus of Todi, a mutual friend, of their loss. They said, "We know that you follow in the footsteps of the Apostles, and that you cleanse lepers and give sight to the blind. Come with us and bring our brother back to life."

Fortunatus, while in tears over his friend's death, said to them, "Go home again, and do not insist on this request of yours, for your brother's death occurred by God's decree, which no man can oppose."

The two women left, but before dawn on Easter Sunday, Fortunatus and his two deacons went to Marcellus' home. There Fortunatus went straight to the bier of Marcellus and softly called his friend by name: "Marcellus, Brother Marcellus!"

Marcellus came to life, and seemingly rather puzzledly, asked, "What are you doing?"

"What am I doing?" Fortunatus echoed.

"Yes, two messengers in white came for me. Then another came and said, 'Bishop Fortunatus wants you!'"

Fortunatus told Marcellus that his sisters and friends wanted him to stay a while with them. Pope Gregory observes that since Marcellus seemed destined for Heaven, the Lord knew he would live a good life—as he did for many years afterward—and so would not risk losing Heaven.

The key words in many raisings of the dead, as Marcellus' two sisters demonstrated, are: "We know that you follow in the footsteps of the Apostles." Where there have been "great apostles" there has also been great faith in their power (that is, power ultimately from God) to raise the dead to life.

We note here that St. Gregory the Great wrote to St. Augustine of Canterbury (d. 604), telling him not to be elated by the miracles God had worked through him for the conversion of the people of Britain. St. Augustine of Canterbury (d. 604) had been sent to England to establish the Catholic Church in that land; on Christmas Day of 597 he baptized 10,000 Saxons. St. Augustine of Canterbury is known as the Apostle of the English. He apparently heeded well the admonition of St. Gregory the Great.

St. Benedict and Pope St. Gregory the Great: two great men of history whose greatness, intelligence and supernatural discretionary powers, in addition to their natural talents, should always be remembered whenever they perform or testify to supernatural happenings.

MEDIEVAL WONDER-WORKERS

9

RESURRECTION MIRACLES PERFORMED BY ST. BERNARD OF CLAIRVAUX AND HIS FRIEND ST. MALACHY

> *"Now that the dead rise again, Moses also shewed, at the bush, when he called the Lord The God of Abraham, and the God of Isaac, and the God of Jacob; for he is not the God of the dead, but of the living."*
> —Luke 20:37-38

Regarding St. Bernard of Clairvaux (1090-1153), St. Robert Bellarmine wrote: "Bernard has more miracles to his credit than any other saint whose life has been written." And Ailbe J. Luddy, O. Cist., author of *The Life and Teachings of St. Bernard,* has added: "And the miracles are so well substantiated that to doubt them would mean to discredit all history."

St. Bernard is one of the greatest figures in all history. He completely dominated his era, and is known as "The Oracle of the Twelfth Century." He was a Doctor of the Church, founder of monasteries, reformer of religious life, advisor of popes, preacher, healer of schisms, peacemaker among the mighty, defender of the Church, lover of Mary, mystic, master of the spiritual life, scholar of the Scriptures, great theologian, author of mystical writings, and one of the greatest wonder-workers in the entire history of the Church.

As Luddy quotes the critical historian Luden: "It is absolutely impossible to doubt the authenticity of St. Bernard's miracles, for we cannot suppose any fraud either on the part of those who reported them or on the part of him who wrought them."

Bernard worked many miracles on well-known personages, often before great multitudes, and especially while he was preaching a crusade. These miracles were never challenged by his enemies or their followers. His band of secretaries or chroniclers recorded great numbers of miracles at different places.

At Doningen near Rheifeld, in one day Bernard cured nine blind, ten deaf mutes, and 18 of the lame or paralytic. On the following Wednesday at Schafhausen he performed an even greater number of miracles. And at Constance alone, 53 miracles were recorded in the journal—and that was not the total number that took place there! Because of his vast number of miracles of other kinds, it seems likely that Bernard raised more dead than the case or two that have come down to us.

While St. Bernard was on a preaching tour somewhere near Constance, a young knight named Henry, who spoke both German and French, became an interpreter for him. The young knight had been converted from evil ways by Bernard. But one of the knight's former squires did not like this change in Henry's life. One day when Henry was riding alongside St. Bernard, this squire suddenly appeared and attacked Henry with jeers and insults which also maligned Bernard. "He blasphemed the servant of God, and cried out with all his might, 'Go follow the devil; and may the devil take you!'"

The travelers ignored him. Then there came some people who laid a crippled woman at St. Bernard's feet, entreating his blessing. This made the squire still more furious. But when he saw the woman suddenly cured by St. Bernard, the squire fell back as if struck by an unseen hand. He lay stretched out on the earth, motionless, lifeless.

At this sudden and awful death, Henry, the squire's former master, was horrified. He fell at St. Bernard's feet, begging pity on the squire's soul: "It is on your account, it is because he blasphemed against you, that this terrible judgment has befallen him!"

"God forbid that anyone should die on my account!" Bernard cried, and turned back toward the lifeless body. He leaned over the corpse of the squire and slowly recited the Our Father, his voice trembling with emotion. "Hold him by the head!" Bernard said to the numerous bystanders. Then he anointed him with his spittle (which he frequently used as if it were a medical remedy). Then he commanded the dead squire: "In the Name of the Lord, arise!" Bernard repeated: "In the Name of the Father, and of the Son, and of the Holy Ghost, may God restore thee to life!"

These words fell solemnly amid the silence of the spectators. Then, as they watched, the dead man arose; he looked up to Heaven.

Loud acclamations and expressions of admiration rose from the people. Then Bernard addressed the restored squire: "Now, what are thy dispositions? What art thou about to do?"

The squire answered, "My Father, I will do all you command." True to his word, he changed completely, becoming a crusader.

Had the squire really been dead? He himself stated: "I was dead and I heard the sentence of my condemnation; for if the holy abbot had not interposed, I should now be in Hell."

The squire's former knight, Henry, became a monk at Clairvaux, and often told the above story.

On another famous occasion, St. Bernard beseeched God to back up his preaching by miraculous signs: "What dost Thou expect from me, my Lord and my God? These people seek for miracles, and we shall derive small profit from our words if Thou dost not confirm them by the tokens of Thy power." Bernard said these words as he was leaving the House of the Canons Regular of Toulouse.

At that moment, an ecclesiastic also named Bernard, dying from palsy, sprang from his bed to run after Bernard and thank him for his sudden and perfect recovery. The canons fled with loud cries because they believed that his soul had already left his body, and that this was therefore a phantom. The crowds that gathered after this miracle forced St. Bernard to hide in his cell and guard it. The raised man became a monk of Clairvaux and later abbot of a monastery at Valdeau.

Bernard was a friend of another great wonder-worker of those days, St. Malachy the Irishman, Archbishop of Armagh (1095-1148). St. Bernard, in whose arms Malachy (Malachi) died at Clairvaux, wrote the life of his friend. Malachy was so able that he was ordained five years early by his bishop in order to be his vicar; he was an abbot, and became a bishop by the age of 30. Malachy reformed Christian life in a good part of Ireland. When he died on November 2, 1148, St. Bernard preached at his funeral, and he also preached a year later on the anniversary of his death. Bernard also wrote the life of St. Malachy, and in it he relates a great number of miracles and wonders, of which he says these are only a few.

St. Malachy cured all sorts of people—from a lunatic lad in Ireland to whom he gave a job as porter, to Henry, son of King David of Scotland. The latter two were his friends ever after. Malachy also raised a storm to rout some would-be killers, and he drove out many demons.

St. Bernard tells of a nobleman in the neighborhood of the famous monastery at Bangor, Ireland, who had a wife sick to the point of death. St. Malachy, who occasionally stayed at Bangor, was asked to come and anoint her. At the sight of the saint she revived a bit, so they agreed to wait until morning to anoint her. Malachy left the room with his friends.

Not much later, a great cry of grief echoed throughout the house, and Malachy came running with his disciples. The woman had died! Bitterly St. Malachy reproached himself for having delayed the anointing. He prayed, "I beseech Thee, O Lord, I have acted foolishly. It is I who have sinned, I who have deferred. It was not she; she desired it!" St. Malachy cried aloud that he would take no rest and receive no comfort unless he was allowed to restore the lack of grace he felt he was responsible for. St. Bernard says that instead of the holy oil, St. Malachy dropped tears over the body all night. He told his disciples, "Watch and pray!" So they kept up an all-night vigil with Psalms.

In the morning, the woman opened her eyes and rubbed her forehead and temples with her hands, as people do who rise from a deep sleep. She got up from her couch. She recognized St. Malachy, bowed reverently to him, and devoutly greeted him. Joy was everywhere, and Malachy was full of great thanksgiving. He anointed the woman, and then went on his way.

The woman had been completely cured. She continued in good health, and when she felt better she did the penance Malachy had enjoined. Later on she "fell asleep" again "in a good confession, and went to the Lord."

As mentioned earlier, although St. Bernard recounts a good number of miracles of St. Malachy, he also states that these are only a few of the wonders he performed. For example, he cured a mute girl at Cruggleton village, a madwoman at the village "Church of St. Michael," and a woman whose limbs were completely useless and who was brought to him on a cart; she walked home on her own two feet.

The well-attested miracles of St. Bernard and St. Malachy make it reasonable to assume that there were similar wonders in the lives of other missionary saints who moved among the people—miracles either not recorded, or obscured among the legends of history.

10

RESURRECTION MIRACLES PERFORMED BY ST. ANTHONY OF PADUA

"It is sown a natural body, it shall rise a spiritual body."
—1 Corinthians 15:44

St. Anthony of Padua (1195-1231), born of a noble family in Lisbon, has always been a popular and beloved saint—but not always for the very best reasons. Often he is implored to find various lost objects—and he is exceptionally good at this. Or he is loved for his exceedingly beautiful countenance expressed in paintings and statues showing him during the famous apparition of the Christ Child.

But this Franciscan friar was more than just the "Wonder Worker of Padua." Pope Gregory IX called him "the Ark of both Testaments and the Storehouse of the Sacred Scriptures." Pope Pius XII declared him a Doctor of the Church. Anthony was also known as "The Hammer of Heretics," so many had he converted. Besides working innumerable miracles, he was a great preacher and was often able to reconcile rebellious cities. As the pope's designation indicates, St. Anthony knew the Bible by heart.

St. Anthony had unusual spiritual gifts like reading hearts, speaking to people at a distance by name, remarkable transportation of himself, and bilocation. He was singled out by St. Francis of Assisi, who sensed the humble Anthony's tremendous hidden merits. Anthony also became a provincial in the Franciscan Order, but he declined being elevated to the purple by the Pope. He accomplished all this—or rather, God accomplished it through him—before he died at only 36 years of age.

The Bollandists, in nearly 30 large folio pages, record St. Anthony's "pure miracles" (as Stoddard styled them). And Azevedo wrote a book of four chapters about the miracles of the saint which were selected by the Bollandists as the most authentic. Azevedo categorized the miracles under various headings; for example, there was the category entitled "Error," under which he recorded numerous miracles of conversion—a Calvinist, a Lutheran, an Indian prince, a Turkish lady—through the saint's intercession. There were other headings for miracles involving deliverance from calamities, cures, imprisoned persons freed, condemned persons saved from death, and more. Under the heading of "Death" Azevedo names a dozen cases of the dead being restored to life.

After Anthony's death—which took place with an enrapturing vision during which the saint exclaimed: "I behold my God!"—a flood of miracles broke out around his remains enshrined at the Church of Santa Maria at Padua. The blind, the lame, the sick, the deaf were cured, not only inside the church, but also outside among those unable to make their way through the crowds.

So great were the miracles at his tomb (as well as others through his intercession) that within six months after his death on June 18, 1231, his cause for sainthood was launched. By May 30, 1232, with exceptional rapidity, he was canonized by Gregory IX, who was at Spoleto. Included in the solemn decree of canonization are these words:

> "Having ourselves witnessed the wonderful and holy life of Blessed Anthony, the great wonder-worker of the universal Church, and unwilling to withhold the honor due on earth from one whom Heaven itself has surrounded with glory, we, in virtue of the plenitude of our apostolic authority, after having duly consulted our brethren the cardinals, deem it expedient to inscribe him in the calendar of saints."

The sparse details that have come down to us, though only inadequately depicting the greatness of St. Anthony, reinforce our realization of the magnitude of such saints, making their most amazing miracles of all—the raising of the dead—more credible.

St. Anthony of Padua was actually born Anthony Fernando de Bouillon; he came into the world on August 15, 1195. He was a descendant of the famous Godfrey de Bouillon, leader of the First Crusade and first Frankish King of Jerusalem. His grandfather, Vincenzo, had been made Governor of Lisbon, and Anthony was heir to the office. Anthony was born in a lordly palace near the Cathedral of Lisbon to Don Martino and Doña Teresa, prominent citizens who were in high favor with the King of Portugal.

Years later, when Anthony was a monk in Padua, there occurred what is perhaps the most astonishing miracle of his entire life. It so happened that Anthony's father, Don Martino, was unfairly implicated in a murder, and was imprisoned. Assassins had murdered a young nobleman coming from the cathedral. Don Martino's home was a palace near the cathedral, and the murderers—whether by design or panic—threw the body of their victim into the garden of the palace of Don Martino.

Although Anthony was far away in Padua, Italy, by miraculous knowledge he immediately knew of the plight of his father. He was Provincial of his Franciscan province at the time and had no need to ask, but out of humility he requested permission of the Father Guardian of the convent at Arcella to be absent for a while. He then began the long, weary journey on foot from Padua to Lisbon, wondering if he would arrive in time to help his father.

Steadied by hope, St. Anthony found himself suddenly transported to Lisbon. He immediately entered the courts where the trial had begun and approached the judges, who were amazed to see him there. When Anthony declared his father's innocence, they asked for proof; Anthony replied, "The murdered man shall bear witness as to the truth of my testimony." It would certainly take great faith and trust to venture such a statement, but Anthony confidently led the way to the victim's grave. The judges and an expectant crowd followed.

At the burial site Anthony commanded the grave to be opened and the body uncovered. He then commanded the dead man, in the Name of God, to declare whether or not Martino de Bouillon was his murderer. All gaped as the dead man, in his grave clothes, rose to a sitting position, and rested himself upon one hand. With the other hand raised to Heaven and to God (as one swearing at court), the resuscitated man declared in a loud voice that Martino de Bouillon was innocent.

Then the revived man turned to Anthony and asked absolution from an excommunication he was under. Anthony obliged, and the man sank back in his coffin, a corpse once more.

The judges, caught in an astonishing situation, asked Anthony who, then, *was* the guilty party or parties. Anthony replied, as more than one saint has done in a similar case, "I come to clear the innocent, not to denounce the guilty."

When Anthony arrived back in Padua, he had been absent only two nights and a single day.

On another occasion, when Anthony's father had neglected to get a receipt for a large sum of money belonging to the royal exchequer, the recipients, in a plot to ruin him, denied having received it. Anthony suddenly appeared at his father's side. He described every detail of the transaction, even to the type of coins involved. He demanded and was given a full receipt for his father. Then he disappeared, terminating the bilocation.

There is a time-honored custom—"St. Anthony's Bread"—of giving alms for the poor, which originated when the great basilica was being built in honor of St. Anthony in the thirteenth century. A child of Padua fell into a barrel of water and was drowned. The mother prayed to St. Anthony and promised to give the child's weight in grain to the poor if she were restored to life. The child arose as if from sleep. Thus developed the practice of giving alms for the poor in petition or thanksgiving to St. Anthony.

Such were the miraculous powers which God gave to St. Anthony, and such was his filial devotion. He is not only a pin-finder, but also a great saint, preacher, wonder-worker and Doctor of the Church.

11

RESURRECTION MIRACLES PERFORMED BY BLESSED MARGARET OF CASTELLO
The Blind and Crippled Wonder-Worker

"It is sown in weakness, it shall rise in power."
—1 Corinthians 15:43

Margaret of Castello (also called Margaret of Metola, after her birthplace) was born in 1287, in the castle of the nobleman Parisio and his wife Emilia at Metola. But her father was not really "noble." When his wife was with child, Parisio simply assumed that he would have a healthy son and heir. But the festivities planned to celebrate this joyful event were suddenly called off when the child born was a dreadfully deformed girl.

She was unusually small, hunchbacked, facially deformed, her right leg was shorter than the left, and she was blind. Margaret's parents treated her very badly. They kept the child hidden from relatives and friends, and worse, from themselves. When she was six years old her father walled her up in a cell next to a chapel hidden in a forest. Fourteen years later, her parents took her to a shrine at Città-di-Castello to pray for a cure. When she was not cured, Margarets' parents returned home without a word to their blind, crippled daughter, cruelly abandoning her.

Left to roam the streets, Margaret became a beggar among beggars. She had always been a bright, good child, and had profited from lessons of the castle's chaplain. Left on her own at age 20, she became a holy young woman—blind, but limping around to help others.

On the day she became a Mantellata, a member of the

Third Order of Penance of St. Dominic, the blind Margaret knew about a dozen Psalms by heart. The next morning, she knew all 150 Psalms by heart. She said the knowledge simply came to her.

Despite her deformities, Margaret had always been kind and cheerful. She once made a profound impression on a group of prisoners when she was elevated some 20 inches off the ground in ecstatic prayer and her poor face was transformed in beauty. She made true predictions about what would happen to various individuals. She cured a little girl who was dying, and ended a roaring fire in the home where she lived by throwing her cloak down the stairs upon the flames.

Margaret is also credited with having restored to life a man and two children. A little boy fell into a river and was drowned. When his body was recovered, the heart-broken mother prayed to Margaret, and the child came back to life.

A woodsman was killed by bears. Hours later, his friends found his body, horribly mangled. They carried it to his home. His wife and children gathered around the corpse and implored Margaret to plead with God for the restoration of their husband and father. The man returned to life.

A child fell from a high balcony to the street below and was killed. Through Margaret's intercession he was brought back to life uninjured.

And these are ony a few among the astoundingly long list of miracles attributed to Margaret: the dead brought back to life, healing of the blind, mute, deaf, lame, paralyzed, cancerous, and of people with every kind of sickness and infirmity.

When Margaret died at age 33, on April 13, 1320, the people at her funeral cried out that she was a saint and should have the privilege of being buried inside the church. The local prior saw this devotion as premature and unauthorized as yet. But the crowd was insistent.

A girl, crippled, mute, and with a curvature of the spine, who had never been able to walk, was brought by her parents to the church, Chiesa della Carità. The parents with their helpless child pushed through the disputing crowd to Margaret's bier. There, they pleaded with the cripple who was a friend of God to have pity on a fellow cripple.

Suddenly there was an awed silence as the crowd stared at the left arm of Margaret; it was rising from her side! The arm reached over and touched the young crippled girl beside the bier.

A moment later the girl who had never walked rose to her feet unaided. The girl who had been mute looked around as if in a dream and then screamed: "I have been cured! I have been cured through Margaret!" The one-time mute cripple threw herself into the arms of her father and mother, laughing and crying. Pandemonium broke out in the church. The prior needed nothing further; Margaret's body was buried in a vault in the church.

The Council of Città di Castello assembled at the town house, the Palazzo del Podestà, and made an official inquiry. They found that the girl, mute and crippled from birth, had indeed been cured of both afflictions at the funeral of Margaret. And the fact of the miracle was sworn to by many prominent citizens who had witnessed it.

As Margaret's body lay in the Dominican Church chapel numerous other miracles occurred, were sworn to by notaries, and are recorded in medieval documents. One source claims there were more than 200 miracles worked after her death. One can read of some striking cases in Father William Bonniwell's book, *The Story of Margaret of Metola* (1952 and 1955 editions), including the names of the witnesses and the notaries public.

The first important biography of Margaret was by an unknown canon of the Cathedral of Città di Castello. As a boy he had probably seen Margaret many times. As he grew older he heard so many wonders told about her that he set out to "expose" these gross "exaggerations" or "lies," as he supposed.

But in his research he found many documents and much

evidence to the contrary, showing that these stories were true. He felt he owed Margaret an apology, so he wrote his authoritative life of Margaret; but unfortunately, he wrote in poor Latin. Some years later, in 1397, a Dominican put this work into classical Latin, but he suppressed a number of facts. Later another Dominican translated the work into Italian, but he, too, suppressed facts.

In the meantime both Latin versions were lost and subsequent writers had to rely on the incomplete Italian version. So there was a distorted picture of Margaret for centuries. Finally, in the twentieth century, the early 1360 and 1397 Latin versions were found in the Dominican monastery at Bologna. And so, for the first time in 500 years, the true and complete story of Margaret is now available, along with other old information dug up by Father Bonniwell.

This sequence of translations and discoveries illustrates how the early manuscripts or records concerning saints and their miracles can be lost—even irretrievably. Yet those events are no less real and historical just because the written documentations are gone. It also shows that even if written records are lost, oral traditions handed down and later absorbed by other writers should be respected. One cannot simply dismiss as mere "legend" or ignore as unreliable the many accounts of wonders that are well-known but which lack scientifically established historical documents.

Some time after Margaret's death, her body was exhumed and the heart was examined. It was perfectly preserved, but it was found to contain some foreign objects. When an incision was made in the heart, there rolled out three little pearl-like pellets; one bore an image of a Baby in a manger surrounded by animals, one showed a woman wearing a crown, and the third had two pictures—an old man before whom knelt a girl in the Dominican habit, and a dove. This discovery recalled the great devotion Margaret had had for the Incarnation and Birth of Our Lord, how she loved to speak of these events, and how she used to exclaim: "Oh, if you only knew what I carry in my heart, you would marvel!" Thus had Margaret borne, in her very flesh, miraculous images of the loves of her soul.

Today the body of the blind deformed dwarf saint can be seen, essentially well preserved over 650 years later, in a glass sarcophagus at the School for the Blind in Margaret's adopted hometown, Città di Castello, Italy.

12

MORE RESURRECTION MIRACLES PERFORMED BY WOMEN

St. Elizabeth of Hungary, St. Catherine of Sweden, St. Colette of Corbie, St. Zita, St. Frances of Rome, St. Joan of Arc, and Others

> *"Thy dead men shall live, my slain shall rise; awake and give praise..."*
> —Isaiah 26:19

Princesses, abbesses and "simple" saints—women too have raised the dead!

One of these saints, both lovely and greatly loved, was Princess Elizabeth of Hungary—so young, so attractive and so holy, and she lived so short a time (1207-1231). She is popularly remembered as one of those women saints with a surprise for her husband: Roses appeared miraculously in her apron assuring her noble spouse of her saintly purposes as she went about bringing food to the poor.

Dead and a saint at only 24, Elizabeth was no mere romantic figure. Daily she fed 900 persons at the gates of her castle—and many more poor in other places. When her princely husband, Louis the Landgrave, died on a crusade, the sorrowing widow had the additional trial of being driven out of her castle with her several young children by a powerful and unscrupulous uncle.

Elizabeth had the sympathy of the people, but they feared the powerful lord. She suffered humiliations and hardships. But when the leaders of the nobility and the knights returned from the crusade bearing the body of her saintly husband (to whom miracles have also been attributed), in great indignation they reinstated Elizabeth in her castle. She was most generous with the ignoble uncle.

When Elizabeth died a few years later, she was known far and wide for her sanctity. Her confessor and spiritual director, Father Conrad, told of her wonderful raptures of love, and how her countenance would seem to give forth rays of light after her secret prayers. Many of the sick were cured at her tomb. These miracles were authenticated by Siffrid, Archbishop of Mentz, through juridical examinations. In two sessions (1233 and 1235), commissions taking depositions submitted 130 cases of miracles to Rome.

Not long after her death Elizabeth was canonized by Pope Gregory IX. At the translation of her relics in 1236, the crowd was estimated at 200,000. Emperor Frederick II placed a crown of gold on the grave. The Emperor is reputed to have said something like this: "What you would not have from me as Empress, I place on your grave as saint."

One of the most remarkable miracles worked at her tomb through her intercession involved a boy named Dietrich, age five, born blind with no sign of any eyes on his face. The sockets were completely covered over with skin. His mother prayed and wept at the tomb of Elizabeth, and dust from the tomb was applied to the places where the eyes should have been. The covering skin burst, and normal eyes appeared. Several witnesses testified to the miracle under oath, and Father Conrad affirmed that he himself had seen the healed eyes.

When such a prominent person as Elizabeth is so quickly canonized a saint, and in view of her connections among the highest royal, political and spiritual circles, it is only reasonable to accept the reported facts of her many miracles. Among these wonders were several resurrections of the dead.

The first case was that of a three-year-old boy who had been dead, stiff and cold, for a whole night. His pious grandmother made a vow to give an alms to St. Elizabeth's hospital and to dedicate the boy to the service of God if his life was restored. He returned to life. This miracle in all its circumstances, was attested to by depositions of the mother, father, grandmother and uncle of the child, and by others whose testimony was recorded by Father Conrad.

Another boy of about the same age, Wezelin, who had been ill for five days, was found dead by his mother, Lutrude of Roddenau of the Mainz diocese. The body had been inanimate and rigid for the time (as the old account goes) "it takes to go about four German miles." The mother's bewailing of her dead child summoned the neighbors, who began to prepare burial clothes.

Then Lutrude caught up the body of her child and cried out in a mother's prayer to St. Elizabeth: "Why have I lost my child? Come to my help!" The mother promised various types of gifts equalling the weight of the child's body for St. Elizabeth's tomb if her prayer were heard. Shortly afterward, pulse and life slowly returned to her son.

Wigard of Mederbach of the then Cologne diocese testified that he found Gottfried, a four-year-old child, submerged in a well. He called the villagers. Everyone could see that the child was dead. His mouth was open, his skin was black, his belly swollen, all his limbs rigid. As the child's father was ill and his mother in childbirth, they did not tell her. But they all prayed and made vows to St. Elizabeth. Color and pulse returned, and the child came back to life.

A fourth restoration to life was that of a drowned youth. A fifth was that of a child stillborn and brought to life through the intercession of Elizabeth. As Margaret of Castello, a cripple herself, had healed cripples, so did Elizabeth, young widowed mother of little children, seem especially to favor the little ones. The bereft parents could cry: "You, too, Elizabeth, were a mother!"

The details given above about Elizabeth's life augment the credibility of her miracles. Similarly, where there is a great number of all sorts of miracles by a certain saint, those of the dead being raised often seem more credible. But it is impossible in a single volume to do justice to all the miracles of the saints.

St. Catherine of Sweden (1331-1381) was another princess, daughter of St. Bridget of Sweden (also called St. Birgitta). It is said that St. Bridget herself raised two or three people who had been pronounced dead. Catherine (also called Karin) was married about age fourteen, but she persuaded her husband to join her in taking a vow of perpetual chastity. Catherine became a widow a few years later.

On one occasion a man in St. Catherine's employ was riding atop a coach, according to the custom of those days. He fell from the coach-box and was run over by the wheels; it was found that he was dead. When Catherine heard of it she came immediately. She merely touched the dead man's hand as she prayed, and he was restored to life.

On another occasion a workman fell from the roof of a house to a paved area below. His body was so mutilated that it could not be moved. St. Catherine went to him, simply touched his body, and he came back to life completely and perfectly restored. He was able to return to his work that very same day.

The complete restoration of a mangled body in such miracles illustrates the great power of God, for whom such works are effortless. Compare such an account with those sometimes seen on television shows featuring "incredible" recoveries from bad accidents. The cases are considered unique and the persons heroic by virtue of their long struggle back to normal or semi-normal life. But such cases required all sorts of hospitalization technology and therapy over extended periods of time. They are praiseworthy, but nothing like the instant, unaided (except by God) restoral that the saints effected not only on still-living broken bodies, but also on *dead* broken bodies.

Princess Catherine, like St. Catherine of Siena (whose miracles are described in chapter 14 of this book), was a beautiful woman. Once, when some unchaste youths tried to seduce her, a miraculous hind appeared to defend her. The account of her life was written by a monk of the Brigittine

Order (founded by St. Bridget of Sweden) only 30 days after her death. Catherine organized and gained papal approval for the congregation her mother had founded. She died as superior of the convent her mother had founded at Vadstena, Sweden.

It is a long way from a convent in Scandinavia to a Poor Clare abbey in Corbie, France. St. Colette of Corbie was born Nicolette Boylet at Calcye near Corbie on January 13, 1381. As a practical person—for the saints are the most practical persons in the world, despite some notions to the contrary—Colette reformed many Poor Clare monasteries and established 20 new ones (Colettine Poor Clares). Besides these accomplishments, Colette also performed many miracles.

St. Colette was a friend of St. Juan Capistrano and St. Vincent Ferrer. From her convent at Besançon, she once appeared to Vincent, while he was at prayer in Saragossa, pressing him to end the schism then dividing the Church. She had many friends among the nobility, such as the Duchess of Burgundy; many daughters of princes were sent to her Poor Clare convents of strict reform. She made many prophecies and had many visions.

Once when riding on a mule not far from Besançon, St. Colette fell into an ecstasy and her face became so radiant that a stream of light flowed upon the two friars walking by her side. Along the road people left the fields, coming to touch her mantle, and then her hands and feet as she went on. They were too much in awe to stop her, and Colette was oblivious to their reverent attentions.

As an abbess, Colette once went to Verey to make her eighth monastery foundation. She was welcomed warmly by the Dominican nuns (the spiritual sons and daughters of Dominic, Francis and Clare have always maintained a special friendship). St. Colette embraced and kissed each Dominican nun as they all came forward. But at the end of the greetings Colette noticed a young nun who stood at a distance and made no move to approach. St. Colette said to the Dominican chaplain standing nearby, "Shall I not also kiss her?"

"She is a leper, Reverend Mother," the priest replied in embarrassment. "She cannot live in the community; over there is her house"; he pointed to a small building nearby. "We are sorry to distress you. It would have been better for her to stay away, but she wanted so much to come."

Without a word, Colette quickly walked straight over to the young nun. She put both arms around the pathetic figure and gave her the warmest embrace of all. The other nuns fell back in alarm, and the young nun, not having been embraced for years, also recoiled in horror as she realized she had "contaminated" the famed and holy abbess. The priest moved forward to draw the abbess back.

But Colette quietly announced that everything was all right. And indeed it was—the young nun had been cured of leprosy!

Colette is also credited with raising many to life again, including a nun of Poligny already in her coffin, who had died without absolution, a child who had been buried, four grandees who lived for years afterward, and a goodly number of stillborn children.

One stillborn baby was born to the wife of a man named Prucet, at Besançon. The husband did not want to believe the baby was dead. He seized the lifeless body and ran with it to the church, where he insisted that it be baptized. But the priest had to tell him that it was undoubtedly dead. The father returned home sadly with his tiny, silent burden.

Perhaps to distract his mind, or to give him some hope in his grief, friends and neighbors encouraged him to take the dead infant to the Poor Clare Monastery and ask for the prayers of the Abbess Colette. The father grasped at this hope and went to the monastery, where Colette, when informed of the story, came to the enclosure grate by the parlor.

Prucet fell on his knees and held out the dead infant in mute appeal. The abbess also fell on her knees and began to pray. The friends who had followed Prucet also crowded into the parlor. At the sight of both the father and the abbess on their knees, and of the dead infant, they all fell silent. Then they too sank to their knees and the men doffed their caps in reverence. After a while Colette arose, stepped back from the grate, took off her veil and had it passed out to the father. She said to him, "Wrap the child up in it, and take it back to the church to be baptized."

Prucet obeyed with the simplicity of a child. When he and his friends arrived at the church, Prucet again asked the priest to baptize the baby. The poor priest thought Prucet had lost his senses in his grief. But he was shaken when the familiar cry of an infant came out from under the black veil of the abbess. Prucet told the priest what had happened. The priest, fearing that life might be only temporary, decided not to delay the child's Baptism for even a moment. "What name?" he asked.

"Colette!"

Colette Prucet grew into sturdy girlhood, entered the convent at Besançon, and later made her solemn vows. She became abbess of a Poor Clare monastery at Pont-a-Mousson in Lorraine. Sister Perrine, the faithful biographer of St. Colette, wrote that "Colette Prucet herself told me all this."

St. Colette is credited with many such miracles of raising the dead, four of which were involved in her beatification. Great devotion grew up about St. Colette because of her intercessory powers for childless couples, expectant mothers, and mortally ill infants. After the miracle of baby Colette, many came to her to be cured of sicknesses and other troubles. When Colette herself died in 1447, the marks of her own sickness and suffering disappeared. Her body became incomparably and marvelously beautiful, with skin white as snow, supple limbs, and giving off a lovely fragrance.

Another Mother Superior of a convent, St. Colomba of Rieti (Perugia), was an ecstatic who also healed many of the plague by her touch. Her confessor said that when he first met her he found it hard to believe she had resuscitated a child from death. But he soon became familiar with the wonders she worked. She died in 1501 at the early age of 34.

Truly, the Church has had a marvelous variety of saints. Zita was a single girl who, at the tender age of 12, entered the service of a family other than her own, that of the Fatinellis. There, for some time, she suffered much abuse from both her employers and the other servants. But by heroic patience, meekness and trying to see God in everything, she finally won them over and actually became head of the domestic household. She is a model of faithfulness to domestic duties.

Very generous to the poor, Zita once used her cloak to cover bread she was taking to the poor. To save her from a rebuke, the Lord worked a miracle similar to what He had done for St. Elizabeth of Hungary. When Zita was confronted by her employer, her opened cloak revealed only flowers; after she was safely away, the flowers were replaced again by bread. When a poor man at the well expressed a longing for wine, the water was changed to wine. At another time, Zita was transported suddenly to a distant point, arriving on foot before a horseman who had passed her.

St. Zita died on April 27, 1271. Only eleven years later, Bishop Paganello of Lucca accorded her public honors. The earliest biography of St. Zita was a manuscript belonging to the Fatinelli family. After her death, all kinds of miracles were worked at her tomb in the church of St. Fredian (Frediano) in Lucca. Two of these miracles demonstrate how, in those far-off days, facts could be well attested.

Marie de Sens, daughter of William of Gricu, nobleman of Burgundy, had been lame and blind for ten years. With an attendant she came to Lucca and for ten successive days prayed at the tomb of St. Zita. She had a perfect recovery, enabling her to use both her eyes and her limbs. This miracle was attested on May 6, 1300 by Fatinelli de Migliore, Jacob Senami and Mateo Virani, all three of them notaries public.

Every time there was a miracle through St. Zita's intercession a bell was rung at the church. This annoyed one Maudriano Torsello, a boatman and a scoffer. At the sound of the bell he would explode in coarse expressions. Once he saw a sick man being carried towards St. Zita's tomb: "What now! Place that man on the ground before me—he will be sooner cured!" Immediately the scoffer found himself struck dumb, able to mouth only inarticulate sounds.

The next day, Saturday, the scoffer, much shaken and changed, went to St. Fredian's, wept before the prior in repentance, and was forgiven. Maudriano also wept long before St. Zita's shrine. Then, barefoot and with a cord around his neck, he visited the principal churches of Lucca, humbling himself and praying, and imploring Zita's forgiveness for his irreverence.

Then he went back to St. Fredian's for more long and ardent prayers. There his power of speech returned to him. He subsequently lived a good life and was especially reverent toward God and the saints. This miracle occurred on April 30, 1300, in the presence of numerous witnesses, and was notarized by the aforementioned notary Migliore.

St. Zita is credited with a miracle of raising the dead: The author of a manuscript preserved by the Camaldolese monks affirms that he personally knew of a child of parents devoted to St. Zita who had died and was raised to life through her intercession. The parents swore to the truth of this miracle upon the Holy Gospels.

St. Frances of Rome (1384-1440) was one of those rare persons who have been privileged to visit Hell and Purgatory. Married at age 13 to Lorenzo P. Ponziano, of a wealthy and illustrious family, she pleased him by wearing fine clothes and jewels, but underneath them she wore a hairshirt next to her skin. During the last 23 years of her life she was guided by an archangel whom she could see. She had three children, became a widow after 40 years of marriage, and founded the Olivetan Benedictine Oblates. Her body was perfectly preserved and fragrant for several months after her death.

Frances and her sister-in-law Vannoza, with whom she went about doing good deeds, were walking one day in the old Rioue dei Monti district of Rome. Hearing sobs and cries from a mean-looking dwelling nearby, they entered it. They found a mother weeping over the dead body of her child. The child had died a few hours earlier, without having been baptized. Frances reproved the mother for delaying the child's Baptism. Then she took the corpse of the baby in her arms, prayed, and gave it back to its mother alive.

On another occasion Frances was sitting in a chair reading; she left her devotional book five times in a row to obey successive requests of her husband. When she returned the last time the words of the antiphon in the book had been miraculously changed into letters of gold.

St. Catherine of Bologna (1413-1463) was a woman of the nobility, author of *The Seven Spiritual Weapons,* a painter (also of miniatures) and a patroness of artists; she became abbess of a Franciscan convent in her native Bologna. About 19 days after her death, miracles began to occur at her grave, so her body was exhumed and found undecayed, white and fragrant. Her face appeared joyful.

A special sort of chest-chair was set up in the choir of the convent on which the dead abbess was seated in her nun's robes. This "throne" could be rolled to a window for the public to see her. Once, after her death, Catherine opened her eyes and made a sign for the young Leonora Poggi, then about eleven years old, to approach her: "Leonora, come here! You will be a sister in this convent, where all will love you. And you shall be the guardian of my body."

Eight years later Leonora refused a wealthy suitor and entered the Bologna convent. At the end of the year 1500 the saint appeared to Sister Leonora and requested a special chapel where her body would be kept in a sitting position. Leonora fulfilled this commission, and the faithful then had easy access to the saint's relics. In 1688 an even larger chapel was made for St. Catherine; one can see her incorrupt body enthroned there even today. The body has become

"He is risen, as he said." (*Matt.* 28:6). The Resurrection of Jesus Christ, the historical event which completed His victory over sin and death which had been won on the Cross of Calvary. The Passion, death and Resurrection of Christ constitute the turning point in human history and are the basis of the Christian religion.

Hofmann

Above: "Young man, I say to thee, arise!" The first instance in the New Testament of a person being raised from the dead is Our Lord's raising of the son of the widow of Naim. Our Lord touched the bier and said, "Young man, I say to thee, arise. And he that was dead, sat up, and began to speak. And he gave him to his mother." (*Lk.* 7:11-15).

Left: The Assumption of the Blessed Virgin Mary into Heaven, body and soul. The Bible says of Our Lord, "Thou shalt not suffer thy holy one to see corruption" (*Acts* 13:35), and these words also express God's will regarding His most holy Mother.

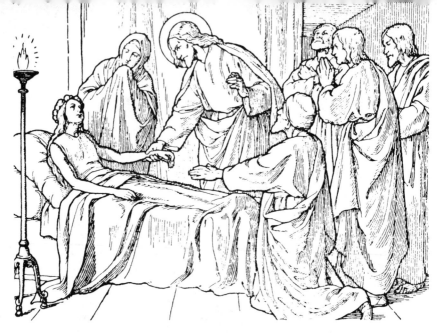

Above: "Damsel, I say to thee, arise!" Our Lord raised the 12-year-old daughter of Jairus, a ruler of the synagogue. He "took her by the hand. And the maid arose." (cf. *Matt.* 9; *Mk.* 5; *Lk.* 8).
Below: "Lazarus, come forth!" Our Lord raised Lazarus from the dead after he had been in the tomb four days. "And presently he that had been dead came forth, bound feet and hands with winding bands." (*Jn.* 11:44). This took place just a short time before Jesus' own death and Resurrection.
Opposite: Jesus raising the daughter of Jairus.

Phillipotaux

Above: St. Ambrose (c.340-397) demanding that the Emperor Theodosius do penance before admitting him to the cathedral at Milan. In Florence, St. Ambrose raised to life a dead boy named Pansopius, whom he had previously freed from an unclean spirit. St. Ambrose converted and baptized St. Augustine; Ambrose was considered by his contemporaries as the exemplar of what a bishop should be—holy, learned, courageous, patient, and immovable when necessary for the Faith. St. Ambrose is one of the original four Doctors of the Church.

Left: The discovery of the True Cross. According to a traditional story, the Empress St. Helena, mother of the Emperor Constantine, went to Jerusalem to find this great relic. Three crosses were found. To determine which was that of Our Lord, each cross was touched to a corpse; when one of the three crosses touched the corpse, the dead man arose, miraculously indicating that this one was indeed the True Cross. (This painting is by Piero della Francesco—c. 1410-1492).

Above: Pope St. Gregory the Great (c.540-604), to whom we are indebted for our knowledge of St. Benedict's life and miracles; St. Gregory devoted Book Two of his *Dialogues* to St. Benedict. In this 13-century fresco St. Gregory is being prompted by the Holy Ghost as he writes. Pope St. Gregory was one of the greatest men in the history of the Church. He is responsible for the conversion of England, and it is to St. Gregory that Gregorian chant is due. He was mainly responsible for the restoration of Rome, which had been devastated by the invasions, pillages and earthquakes of the century before his pontificate. Gregory was untiring in his efforts to ensure that the papacy was the supreme authority in the Church. He is one of the four original Doctors of the Church; he was canonized by acclamation immediately after his death.

Left: St. Benedict (c.480-c.457), who raised two persons from the dead. St. Benedict is the Father of Western Monasticism (never ordained a priest), and one of the greatest saints in the Church. His greatest achievement was the writing of his monastic Rule, which has been adopted all over the western world. This Rule is conspicuous for its moderation and clarity of language. This is one of the oldest portraits of St. Benedict; it is a fresco from the last years of the 9th century, in the crypt of San Crisogono in Trastevere, Rome.

Below: St. Benedict raises to life a monk who had been crushed during construction work on the Monastery of Monte Cassino. *Clockwise, from top left:* St. Benedict warns of the approach of the devil to thwart the work on the monastery; the collapsed building, with a monk crushed to death under the debris (note the devil on top of the wall); the monk's broken body is brought to St. Benedict in a blanket; St. Benedict raises

von Matt

the monk to life. (These pictures are miniatures from *Codex Lat.* 1212 in the Vatican Library, a superb 11th century manuscript made by the monks of Monte Cassino.)
Right: St. Benedict restores a dead child to life. (Picture from *Codex Lat.* 1212, Vatican Library.)

92-11

Above: St. Malachy the Irishman (1095-1148), who raised to life a woman who had died after Malachy decided to delay giving her the Last Sacraments. The saint bitterly lamented his delay; after an all-night vigil, the woman arose alive and cured. St. Malachy was Archbishop of Armagh, worker of miracles, and author of the well-known papal prophecies; his friend, St. Bernard of Clairvaux, wrote his life, stating that the miracles he recounts therein are only a few of those that actually took place. *Left:* St. Bernard of Clairvaux, who raised a blasphemous squire who had been struck dead. Upon being restored by Bernard, the squire reformed his life completely, stating that he had heard his sentence of condemnation and would now be in Hell if Bernard had not interposed. St. Bernard also raised an ecclesiastic. St. Bernard (1090-1153) was one of the greatest saints in the history of the Church, and one of the greatest figures in all history. Though a great mystic and spiritual writer, he also dominated the affairs of western Europe from the age of 25. St. Robert Bellarmine stated, "Bernard has more miracles to his credit than any other saint whose life has been written." (This picture was taken from an ancient bust in the parish church of Fontaines-les-Dijon.)

Above: St. Anthony raising to life an infant with the Sign of the Cross. The child's mother had promised to give the child's weight in grain to the poor if the child were restored to life; thus has arisen the custom called "St. Anthony's Bread"—giving alms to the poor in petition or thanksgiving to St. Anthony. Another extremely dramatic resurrection miracle occurred when St. Anthony raised a dead man to testify to Anthony's father's innocence in a murder trial.

Left: St. Anthony of Padua (1195-1231), great and beloved saint who is credited with a dozen raisings from the dead, as well as with multitudes of other miracles and wonders both during his life and after his death. St. Anthony was canonized within 11 months of his death. He is a Doctor of the Church.

Above: St. Colette (1381-1447) raising a nun who had died without absolution. Colette is also credited with raising a child who had been buried, four grandees, and a number of stillborn infants.

Left: St. Joan of Arc (1412-1431), the Maid of Orléans. She raised a stillborn infant long enough for him to be baptized; this occurred in the village of Lagny-sur-Marn, near Paris. St. Joan was directed by heavenly voices to drive the occupying English out of France; this she did. Nevertheless, she was burned at the stake at age 19. St. Joan of Arc was finally canonized in 1920.

F.B.

92-16

darkened, but this is probably due to the flames and fumes of the innumerable candles and votive lights that have been burned there for over 500 years.

One of the most unique saints of all time was Joan of Arc (1412-1431), *La Pucelle,* the Maid of Orléans. While still in her teens she courageously and successfully led French troops against the occupying English armies; she had been so directed by "voices" of St. Michael, St. Margaret, St. Catherine, and others. Like all great saints, St. Joan was a very balanced personality; allied to her fortitude and fearlessness were gentleness and pity for the suffering.

In early March, 1430, St. Joan arrived at the village of Lagny-sur-Marn, in the direction of Paris. Here she learned of a woman who was greatly distressed because she had given birth to a stillborn son. Some villagers approached Joan and asked for her intercession. The mother prayed only that the child might be brought to life long enough to be baptized and so gain Heaven.

Joan went to the church where the dead child had been laid at the feet of the statue of the Blessed Mother. Young girls of the village were praying by the small corpse.

St. Joan then added her own prayers. The baby came to life and yawned three times. Baptism was hurriedly administered. Then the baby boy died again, and his beautiful spotless baptized soul went straight to Heaven.

RESURRECTION MIRACLES
OF THE BRITISH ISLES AND BELGIUM
Drithelm, Christina the Admirable, and Winifride

"Whether in the body I know not, or out of the body . . ."
—2 Corinthians 12:2

There have been myriad supernatural manifestations and experiences related or claimed by various persons through-out the history of the Church. At times it is hard to deter-mine their reality, or the category to which an individual miracle may belong. As evidenced by the quotation above, even St. Paul could not nail down the exact nature of a real experience—"such a one caught up to the third heaven."

There have been any number of real experiences of canonized saints and genuine mystics who were absolutely convinced of having had real visits to (and not mere visions of) Heaven (though not enjoying the actual Beatific Vision), Hell and Purgatory. In some cases the soul seems to have gone out of the body, leaving it—whether or not in an ecstatic state—seemingly dead. In fact, experienced spiritual directors of certain mystics often must decide whether to call for medical assistance or to wait (medical treatment at the hands of doctors who do not understand "mystical states" is often a torture for a mystic), despite the cries around him that "She is dead!" or "She is dying!"

Once St. Catherine of Siena seemed to be dying, or even already dead. Actually she was experiencing a mystical death. She was cold and immobile. She felt that her soul was separated from her body, and she experienced the extremes of the glory of God and of the terrible punishments of sinners, especially of those who defiled the sanctity of marriage. After her temporary death she told how she had seen the horrors of the damned, and that Christ had then said to her, "Return to earth and point out to men their errors, their danger, their punishment."

Thus, it is demonstrated in the biography of one of the best established saints—written by the very capable Blessed Raymond of Capua—that these apparent deaths and returns to life can really happen. This mystical phenomenon of apparent death and subsequent recovery is of course to be distinguished from the real deaths and resurrections recounted in this book. In these latter cases the person in question is truly dead in the ordinary sense that the decaying process has begun, even if almost imperceptibly. Such experiences in the realms of the other world also differ from the experience of a vision, like that of the three children of Fatima, their feet rooted to earth, who were shown a vision of Hell by the Blessed Mother.

This distinction is significant to one who considers Drithelm and Christina. St. Bede the Venerable (c. 672-735), Doctor of the Church, was one of the most respected historians in early Europe, and the most authoritative one on early English history. That great and learned cardinal, St. Robert Bellarmine, advisor of popes and a powerful reformer, accepts as an established fact Venerable Bede's account of Drithelm, a Northumberland man who returned from the dead. It was an event known all over early England, and it led to many conversions.

Drithelm, who had led a good Christian life, as had his family, died of an illness. Just before interment, he suddenly returned to life, rose, and placed himself in a sitting posture. His family, including his wife and children, who had spent the previous night mourning at his bier, were seized with fear. They all fled except his faithful wife who, though trembling, remained alone with her risen husband.

"Fear not," he reassured her, "it is God who restores to me my life; He wishes to show in my person a man raised from the dead. I have yet long to live on earth, but my new life will be very different from the one I led heretofore." Drithelm proposed to change his life, even though he had always been a very good man. Then he arose and went immediately, in perfect health, to the chapel of the church nearby and prayed there a long time.

Drithelm then told his family he would henceforth live only to prepare for death; he advised each of them to do the same. He divided his property between his wife and children and reserved one-third for himself to give alms. When he had distributed his share to the poor, he went to a monastery where he asked the abbot to receive him as a penitent, as a religious who would be the servant of the others.

Drithelm was given a cell apart, where he lived for the balance of his life—or his second life. He prayed, he labored hard, he did extraordinary penances. He performed rigorous fasts, and would plunge himself into freezing water where he prayed for hours reciting the entire Psalter (the 150 Psalms).

Drithelm also maintained a perpetual silence, and his whole attitude, with downcast eyes and ascetic features, showed a soul fearfully aware of the judgments of God. But he did break his silence to relate what he had seen in the other world, for the edification and help of others. (The entire story can be read in the *Ecclesiastical History* of Bede, or in shorter form in the book *Purgatory* by Father F.X. Schouppe, S.J.). Drithelm said:

> "On leaving my body I was received by a benevolent person who took me under his guidance. His face was brilliant, and he appeared surrounded with light. He arrived at a large deep valley of immense extent, all fire on one side, all ice and snow on the other; on the one hand braziers and caldrons of flame, on the other the most intense cold and the blasts of a glacial wind."

Drithelm went on to tell how he saw innumerable souls

tossed as if by a furious tempest from the side with the freezing cold to the side with the blazing heat, from torture to torture, constantly seeking relief in the opposite extreme, to and fro. He thought the terrible place was Hell, but his guide informed him that it was a special place in Purgatory. In this place were the souls who had deferred repentance to the end of their lives, but had been saved by the mercy of God at the last minute. There in Purgatory they would endure their temporal punishment for forgiven sin. Most of them would do penance there, he understood, until Judgment Day.

Drithelm was also shown terrible scenes of Hell. Tremendous globes and masses of stinking fire rose up from the dark crater of the noisy pit. The souls there were ceaselessly tossed up to the tips of the flames and then sucked downwards as the vaporous flames fell back. Drithelm saw a crew of jeering spirits, demons, dragging into the pit five wailing and weeping souls, among them one who was tonsured, a layman, and a woman.

On the happier side he saw flowery fields, youthful spirits, happy abodes, but that was not Heaven. He came to a place where he heard the sound of sweet singing amid a delightful fragrance and glorious light. His guide told him that Heaven was nearby, but Drithelm did not see it. Then his heavenly guide told him to return to earth. And he ended up in the monastery at Melrose by the bend of the Tweed River.

When Drithelm was asked why he did such great penances as plunging his body into freezing water he would reply, "I have seen penances still more astonishing." Or if they remarked on his austere life, "I have seen it harder!" Even to a broken old age he continued to afflict his body mercilessly. And so he produced a great sensation in England, and many sinners were converted through his graphic accounts and the example of his reparational penances.

There was also a woman who was brought back from the dead to live a long, penitential life. Again one is encouraged to accept the reality of the wonders in this life, that of St. Christina the Admirable, by no less an authority than St.

Robert Cardinal Bellarmine, S.J. Another serious author, Cardinal James de Vitry, had great admiration for Christina.

Christina lived in Belgium at the end of the twelfth century and beginning of the thirteenth (1150-1224). (There is apparently some confusion about other Blessed Christinas, but with the reported endorsement of the two eminent cardinals one would do well to accept the reality of *this* Christina experience.)

When Christina was about to be buried (having died at the age of 32), as her body rested in an open coffin, she arose from it healthy and strong. It is said that the whole city of Trond witnessed this miracle with amazement, and were even more astonished at what she then related:

> "As soon as my soul was separated from my body, it was received by angels who conducted it to a very gloomy place entirely filled with souls. The torments which they there endured appeared to me to be so excessive that it is impossible for me to give any idea of their rigor. I saw among them many of my acquaintances, and, deeply touched by their sad condition, I asked what place it was, for I believed it to be Hell.
>
> "My guide answered me that it was Purgatory, where sinners were punished who before death had repented of their faults, but who had not made worthy satisfaction to God. From there I was conducted into Hell, and there also I recognized among the reprobates some whom I had formerly known. The angels then transported me into Heaven . . ."

In Heaven (again, not the full Heaven of the Beatific Vision) the Lord gave Christina a choice of remaining in glory, or, having been so moved with compassion for the souls in Purgatory, and horror for those in Hell, to return to earth, there to suffer dreadful torments and penances without dying. By such reparational sufferings she would deliver souls from Purgatory and convert sinners away from the road to Hell and toward that of eternal salvation. The Lord told Christina that then, "after having ended this new life, you shall return here laden with merits."

Christina told the people on earth that she had answered the Lord without hesitation: she would return to life on earth. At that instant she arose from her coffin. She warned the people not to be surprised at the extraordinary penances she planned to suffer from then on.

Thenceforth Christina lived without house or fire; she threw herself into burning furnaces, where she survived the torment of the flames. The Lord told her that she would endure great torments without dying from their effects—this would constitute a constant miracle. She prayed in winter in the frozen waters, and on and on.

Cardinal Bellarmine wrote that everyone could see Christina standing in the midst of the flames without being consumed, and covered with wounds, every trace of which disappeared a few moments afterwards—certainly a vivid picture of expiatary suffering against the flames of Purgatory and Hell. (Compare Padre Pio surviving a fever of 125 degrees Fahrenheit that broke the thermometer, the biblical three children in the fiery furnace, or St. Francis of Paola in a furnace.) St. Robert Bellarmine also said that Christina's life, virtues, miracles after her death, and the striking conversions she effected all proved the hand of God in the matter and the truth of her words about the next life.

Christina led this terrible life of penance for 42 years after her restoration from the dead. Her body was preserved in the church of the Redemptorist Fathers at St. Trode.

A young girl in Wales, St. Winifride (also spelled Winifred, Winefride, Guenvrede or Guenfrewid—d. c.650), also presents an unusual case of resurrection. Her father was Thevith, a rich noble second only to the King of North Wales. From listening to the holy priest monk, St. Beuno (Benno, Benow), Winifride conceived the holy desire of consecrating her virginity to God, the heavenly Bridegroom of souls.

She was alone one day in her father's house when a youth enflamed with lust, Caradoc, son of Alan the King of North Wales, came asking to speak with her father, and in the meantime asking her to consent to his wishes. Realizing Caradoc's intentions, Winifride pretended to be distressed that he had found her in her ordinary dress; she told him to wait while she went to her room. She could see that the unhappy young man was nearly wild with his unholy passion. Instead of returning, Winifride fled and ran as fast as she could to the church, where her parents were attending Mass and listening to the preaching of St. Beuno.

When Caradoc discovered that Winifride had fled, he seized his sword and furiously made after her, soon overtaking her. Staring savagely at Winifride, he thus addressed her: "Once I loved you, and desired to hold you in my embrace. You have fled from me when I came to you; you reject the suit I made to you. Yield now to me, or else this sword shall put an end to your life, for I will cut off your head."

Perceiving that no help was coming from the direction of the parish church, Winifride turned to Caradoc and told him, "I am betrothed to the Son of the Eternal King, the Judge of all mankind. No other spouse can I receive; no other will I have while I live. I should outrage Him otherwise. Draw your sword, and exert all your strength and ferocity; but be sure that neither terror nor flattery, promises or threats, will ever draw me away from the sweetness of His love, to Whom my own love and devotion are pledged." The passion of the licentious prince overmastered him; he felt he could never know a moment's rest while Winifride was alive. Drawing his sword from the scabbard, he cut off her head.

When the people discovered what had happened, they were filled with dismay and horror. St. Beuno offered Mass, after which both he and the congregation prayed long and earnestly for Winifride's restoration to life. This immense favor was granted. A fountain sprang from where Winifride's head had fallen, and the place is called Winifride's Well, or the Holy Well in Flintshire.

Winifride served God in a small convent her father built near Holy Well. After the death of Beuno she went to a convent at Gutherin under the direction of the holy Abbot Elerius who governed a double monastery there. She succeeded Abbess Theonia.

Winifride carried her austerities to the utmost degree of endurance, but was always simple and humble, and in speech so beautiful and attractive that people of all ranks came from all parts of Wales to speak with her. She had an amazing ability to banish cares and sorrows and convert sinners; wonderful cures followed her prayers. Elerius often declared that God had appointed Winifride for the illumination of their country.

The writer Leland does not mention the miracle of St. Winifride, but Robert of Salop and others do. Some authors add that a red or white circle was always on her skin about her neck.

Holy Well became a great place of pilgrimage, and over the centuries many miracles have taken place there. On one occasion a man left the body of his little daughter, wrapped for burial, overnight in the church of St. Winifride. The next morning the priest found the child released from the grave-clothes and crawling on the floor; she was too weak to walk upright, but otherwise perfectly well, and she asked to be given some food. Another example: in 1606 Sir Roger Bodenham, Knight of the Bath, was cured of a malady closely resembling a horrible leprosy. He became a Catholic and attested to the miracle, as did many witnesses.

Cardinal Baronius was astounded at all the cures which the Bishop of Asaph, a vice-regent of the Pope for episcopal functions at Rome, had personally witnessed at St. Winifride's Well.

FAMILIES, FOUNDERS, AND SPECIAL GROUPS

14

THE SAINTS RAISE THEIR RELATIVES FROM THE DEAD

Miracles Performed by St. Catherine
of Siena, St. Teresa of Avila, St. Francis
of Paola, Venerable John Baptist Tholomei

"Death is swallowed up in victory."
—1 Corinthians 15:54

St. Catherine of Siena, Virgin and Doctor of the Church (1347-1380), probably would never have made it into the world in our time. The 23rd child of Jacomo and Lapa Benincasa (the 24th and last was Catherine's twin, who did not survive infancy), she was cheerful, intelligent, practical, but also mystical. She was a tertiary of the Dominican Order, and she worked for a crusade against the Turks, for peace between the Pope and Florence, and for the return of the Pope from Avignon to Rome.

St. Catherine's mother, Mona Lapa, who was rather careless about the condition of her own soul, endured a lengthy illness after her husband's death. When Catherine was praying for her mother, the Lord told the holy virgin that it would be better for Lapa to die at that time rather than to live and face all the misfortunes that lay ahead of her. Catherine tried to tell Lapa in a gentle manner to resign herself to God's will.

But Lapa would not hear anything about death. Catherine, mindful of the spiritual carelessness of Lapa, continued to pray ardently to Jesus, but Lapa refused to confess, and one day in October of 1370 she suddenly died. Catherine returned from the church to find her mother dead.

The following account of what then happened is taken

from the life of St. Catherine written by her spiritual director, Blessed Raymond of Capua, O.P. There were present at Lapa's deathbed three women of Siena: Catherina di Ghetto and Angela di Vannino (who later became members of St. Dominic's Third Order of Penance, Dominican tertiaries), and Lisa the sister-in-law of Catherine and daughter-in-law of Lapa. All three were witnesses and all three were living in Siena at the time of Blessed Raymond's writing.

These three heard Catherine cry out: "Lord, my God, are these the promises Thou didst make to me? That none of my house should go to Hell? Are these the things that in Thy mercy Thou didst agree with me, that my mother should not be taken out of the world against her will? Now I find she has died without the Sacraments of the Church. By Thine infinite mercy I beg Thee not to let me be defrauded like this. As long as there is life in my body I shall not move from here until Thou hast restored my mother to me." Oh, the boldness and confidence of the saints!

The three women were ready to perform the traditional preparation of the dead, but they waited because of Catherine's tears and prayers. Then Lapa's body began to move, and her soul returned to her body. She lived to be 89 and lived to see many sorrows, as Christ had forewarned her daughter Catherine.

Blessed Raymond, another saint of the Dominican Order, and one who held high office in it, relates in his life of Catherine many wonders over and above the wonders of her spiritual life and the holiness that made her a great saint and one of the first two women to be declared Doctors of the Church.

Shortly after Catherine's death, a girl made her way to the place where the body was laid out. The girl's face was horribly disfigured, her nose and lip gangrenous, "stinking." She boldly, with heart-stirring trust, touched both Catherine's hands, and apparently pressed her disfigured face against Catherine's beautiful face. Catherine, who with beautiful charity had kissed cancerous patients in life, cured the disfigured girl.

Besides St. Catherine of Siena, the only other woman Doctor of the Church is St. Teresa of Avila (1515-1582). Teresa was a great reformer of the Carmelite Order, a foundress of convents, a great contemplative and author of mystical books, and a most charming Spanish woman. St. Teresa had many ecstasies, was a friend of Sts. John of the Cross and Peter of Alcantara, and had her heart pierced by an angel with a golden arrow, leaving within it a mystical wound of love.

When Teresa was working on her first convent building of the Carmelite reform in November of 1561, her sister Juana and Juana's husband Juan de Ovalles went somewhere with Teresa, leaving the Ovalles' six-year-old son Gonzalo alone at home.

When they returned, a woman was waiting to see Juana, who stopped to speak with her in an anteroom. Her husband Juan, going into another room, found Gonzalo on the floor; he was dead. His desperate efforts to revive the boy were fruitless, and the child remained deathly white.

Juan carried the lifeless body to Teresa, who took him in her arms. Juana, who was with child, was kept unaware of the situation (Juan conveyed a message to the visitor to keep his wife occupied) for fear the shock would harm the unborn child.

With the agonizing servants and the father in the other room, Teresa held the child tightly, covered him with her veil, and prayed that God would spare the parents this anguish. Just then Juana entered, became excited, and asked what was wrong. St. Teresa motioned to her to keep calm, as if it were some insignificant matter. In a few moments Gonzalo began to breathe. He reached out his hand to his Aunt Teresa's face, caressing her. Teresa then handed the boy over to his mother.

Between the time of St. Catherine of Siena and that of St. Teresa of Avila came the life of St. Francis of Paola (1416-1507), one of the greatest wonder-workers in the history of the Church. Francis was so famous that Louis XI of France, suffering from a prolonged ailment, begged Francis to make the journey from Italy in order to cure him. St. Francis taught the king that resignation to God's will was more important than bodily healing. After helping Louis spiritually and preparing him for death (and exerting great influence through the king), St. Francis held the king in his arms as he died a good death.

St. Francis of Paola also had occasion to help his own family—specifically his nephew, Nicholas d'Alesso, son of Francis' sister Brigida. His sister had not consented to allow her son to become a monk, and the lad had died. St. Francis of Paola decided to bargain with his sister over the death and life of the nephew.

When the young man's body was about to be lowered into the grave at Francis' monastery, Francis stopped the grave workers, and instead carried the body to his own room. That same night, after many tears and prayers on the part of Francis, his nephew came back to life. But Nicholas' mother did not know this.

In the morning Brigida came to the monastery church, unaware of what had happened. She wept there in the church over the death of Nicholas, her oldest son. Francis kept the youth hidden away while he spoke to Brigida: "Brigida, if your son should return to life, would you consent to his becoming a religious?" Brigida looked at her brother in his penitential sackcloth robe. Her eyes glimmered with some spark of hope. "If Heaven wants it," she said—bemoaning that it was now too late—"it will be my greatest consolation."

Francis left her, went to his cell, and returned with Nicholas clothed as a monk. His mother, relatives and friends who had come sorrowing to the church greeted him with amazement and great joy.

This and many other miracles were sworn to by numerous witnesses both before the Bishop of Cosenza, and later at Rome during canonical hearings in 1519.

To conclude this chapter we mention the resurrection of the Venerable Angela Tholomei, a Dominican nun who was raised from the dead by her own brother, Venerable John Baptist Tholomei, as her body was being carried to her tomb. While she was dead she had seen torments in the other world, and subsequently she did much penance on earth— thus attesting by her deeds to the truth of her remarkable experience.

15

A FRANCISCAN
CELEBRATION OF LIFE

Resurrection Miracles Performed by
St. Bernardine of Siena, St. John Capistrano,
St. Francis of Paola, St. Joseph of Cupertino,
and St. Peter of Alcántara

*"Peter presented her alive . . . and many
believed."*

—Acts 9:41-42

As the author of this book was born on the feast day of St. Francis of Assisi, and has subsequently been devoted to him, he would definitely be remiss not to include a chapter on some Franciscans who revived the dead. Strangely, there seem to be no reliably accredited miracles of raising the dead attributed to the first Franciscan, St. Francis of Assisi himself. I must apologize if I have done him wrong here, but Francis was "the little poor man" (*Il Poverello*), the founder, and not the same kind of great preacher that some of his sons became—such as St. Anthony of Padua, St. Juan Capistrano, or St. Bernardine of Siena. (For St. Anthony alone the authority Azevedo lists a dozen cases of the dead returned to life.)

Elsewhere in this book, in the chapter on resurrection miracles in the Americas, are given the stories of two other great Franciscan wonder-workers, St. Francis Solanus and Bl. Sebastian of Apparizio.

St. Bernardine (Bernardino) of Siena (1380-1444) was one of the all-time great preachers, often speaking to crowds of up to 30,000. He propagated devotion to the Holy Name of Jesus and devised the symbol IHS for its veneration. He cured many lepers and is credited with raising four persons from the dead. St. Bernardine became the Superior General of those Franciscans called Friars of the Strict Observance. When he began there were 300 in the community; when he died, 4,000. He died preaching on the road.

At Volterre, a bull that had been frightened by the crowd attacked a young man and left him as dead. St. Bernardine made the Sign of the Cross over the body and said, "By the grace of God this young man shall have no hurt! Carry him away." And when they had gone a few paces, the young man arose strong and well.

On one occasion when St. Bernardine was sitting beside a spring, not long before he died, St. Peter Celestine appeared to him, embraced him, and told him he would die at Aquila and there become a patron along with Peter Celestine himself. At St. Bernardine's death there were so many miracles that Siena sent an envoy that collected records of 30 miracles attested to by the magistrates and subscribed to by the chancellor of the city on July 19, 1444.

A short time after the canonization of St. Bernardine, an 11-year-old boy, Blasio Massei, died at Cascia in the Kingdom of Naples. All of his family had a great devotion to the saint. The day after Blasio died, as his body was being carried to the grave, he awoke as if from a dream. He said that St. Bernardine had restored him to life—and not without a special reason, for the child was to tell of the wonders he had seen in the other world.

Holy Scripture relates that at the banquet given for Christ at Lazarus' home, some time after Lazarus was raised from the dead, many attended just to see the resurrected Lazarus reclining at table. One can imagine a similar reaction when the news about Blasio got around. Blasio spoke for a whole month about what he had seen, and he willingly answered questions.

Blasio said that Bernardine had appeared to him at the moment of his death, telling him not to fear, and had told him to observe well what he would see so he could later recount his experiences. He was then taken on a trip through Hell, Purgatory, Limbo and Heaven. As Blasio related his experiences in the other world, he spoke with simplicity, accuracy and an unusual knowledge that witnessed to the truthfulness of his words.

On the visit to Hell, Blasio witnessed great horrors and various tortures suffered by the impure, avaricious, and other sinners. He saw some persons he once knew on earth, including the arrival of two who had just died, B. and F.

F. was damned for keeping ill-gotten goods. His son, who was still alive, heard Blasio's story and knew it to be true; he made restitution, distributed his own fortune to the poor, and became a monk.

In Purgatory Blasio recognized a number of persons, several of whom asked that he inform relatives and friends of their need of prayers and good works to hasten their release. After returning to life, Blasio made direct statements such as:

"Your father has been in Purgatory since such and such a day. He charged you to pay such a sum in alms, and you have neglected to do so."

"Your brother asked you to have so many Masses celebrated. You agreed to do so, and you have not fulfilled your promise. So many Masses remain to be said."

In telling of Heaven, Blasio spoke in particular of the multitudes of angels about the throne of God, and of the Blessed Virgin Mary's great beauty and glory.

St. Bernardine was also one of those saints who were able to sail over water on a cloak—in his case, to pass a river to get to Mantua.

St. John (Juan) Capistrano (1386-1456), friend and companion of St. Bernardine of Siena, at age 26 was Governor of Perugia. He married, but later changed his life and obtained a dispensation to join the Friars Minor, which he did in 1416, studying under St. Bernardine and then being ordained a priest. St. John Capistrano became a great preacher who, together with other Franciscans, revived the Faith in central European countries. He healed the Order of St.

Francis of its dissensions over the interpretation of the Rule of St. Francis. He preached a crusade for the defense of Europe and personally led an army at Belgrade where, with General John Junyadi, he defeated the Turks in a great victory in 1456. The failure of the Turks to capture Belgrade during the ensuing siege saved Europe from being overrun by the Turks. He died a little later, and his tomb graced the town of Villach in Hungary.

John's companion, Nicholas Fara, the first to record the essential information about his cures, reported 200 healings at Vienna. Later, the Bavarian Franciscan, Conrad of Freyenstadt, prepared a full list of Bernardine's miracles, the *Liber Miraculorum.* It contained 2,507 reports of miracles under seven headings: "Raised from the Dead," "Saved from Death," "Blind," "Lepers," "Crippled," etc.

The life of St. Francis of Paola (c. 1416-1507), founder of the Hermits of St. Francis of Assisi ("Minims"), is well documented as that of a super miracle worker—not only a real thaumaturge but also a man who fearlessly counseled kings. Francis is credited with raising at least six persons to life. (See chapter 13 for one of these miracles.) One he raised twice: Thomas d'Yre of Paterna was first crushed by a tree, and later he fell from a steeple.

When another man, the workman Domenico Sapio, was crushed by a huge pine tree, St. Francis prayed on his knees beside the corpse, raised his arms to Heaven and then having risen to his feet, cried out: "In the Name of Charity, Domenico, arise!" (Francis continuously preached *Caritas,* or Charity, the virtue of supernatural love and also one of the names of God.) In the Name of Charity Domenico arose, dusted himself off and, after thanking Francis, returned to work.

Those who worked on St. Francis' monastery building projects were so aware of the great number of astounding miracles performed by the saint that they worked with a calm unconcern unknown on construction projects. But what else could one expect of a saint who cured the deaf, the paralyzed, the dying, who drove out demons, ordered a boulder rolling down a mountain to stop, withstood the heat within a furnace, and held burning coals in his hands in the presence of the papal investigator who was sent to interview him?

After St. Francis of Paola's famed crossing on his cloak over the straits of water from Italy to Sicily, he came to a place called the "Pond of the Hanged." A body had been dangling from the gallows there for three days. With the help of Brother John who was with him, the saint removed the rope, and compassionately gathered the dead man into his arms. He prayed to God, and the revived criminal fell at his knees with an outpouring of thanks.

Wanting to be sure of the subsequent safety of his soul, the hanged man begged Francis to receive him into his order. He became one of Francis' Minim friars and saw many years service of God as a monk.

It is interesting to note that a companion who was with St. Francis at the time, Father Rendacio, refused to interfere in this "legal execution." But sometimes the saints take matters into their own hands, just as Christ often overruled the petty objections of the Pharisees.

At Galeazzo, St. Francis also restored to life the dead son of the Baron of Belmonte. Later, after Francis' death, there were many miracles, including the April 2, 1613 resurrection of the four-year-old Ponger boy who had drowned in a pool at Amiens, France. (April 2 is St. Francis of Paola's feast day—the date of his death, or birthday in Heaven.) And earlier, Francis had helped the King of France to prepare for death, and had influenced events in that country.

It seems fitting to mention also, in the spirit of St. Francis of Assisi himself and his love for all creatures, the revivals of the pet trout, "Antonella," and the pet lamb, "Martinello," by St. Francis of Paola. If St. Francis of Assisi had a tender spot in his heart for even the fierce wolf of Gubbio, it is understandable how Francis of Paola reacted when his innocent pet trout met with a sad fate.

One day Antonella was swimming about the pool, like a good fish should. A visiting priest helping with a religious service saw it, caught it, took it home and began to fry it.

St. Francis missed the trout, and either realizing naturally or else having superior knowledge of what had happened, he sent one of his religious to get it back. When the priest heard this request from the hermit sent by Francis, he was annoyed. He threw the cooked trout on the ground, the impact shattering it into several pieces.

When the hermit returned to St. Francis with the broken pieces, Francis placed them in the pool and prayed: "Antonella, in the Name of Charity, return to life!" The trout at once became whole again and happily began to swim about the pool. Friars and workers witnessed the miracle.

Later, at Bormes, as a guest in the home of the governor, Francis restored to life a cooked fish which his host had prepared for him, not realizing that Francis would hold himself to his very limited personal diet.

On another occasion, from nothing but bones and fleece left and thrown into an oven, St. Francis of Paola called back to life his pet lamb Martinello, which had been recently roasted and eaten by some nearby workmen.

Approximately two centuries later, another great Franciscan, St. Joseph of Cupertino (1603-1663), raised to life a flock of sheep that had been killed by enormous hailstones.

Some may find such miracles straining the economy of God. But the saints, like God, loved all God's creatures and cared for them. St. Francis of Assisi was even careful not to step on an ant. Moreover, such miracles increased the reverence accorded to the words and counsels of the saints who worked them. These "fish" and "lamb" miracles also make it easier to accept the greater miracles the saints worked on God's greater creatures—the miracles of men being raised from the dead. Each miracle, large or small, sparks renewed hope of eternal resurrection someday.

St. Peter of Alcántara was born in 1499 in Alcántara, Spain. He was a friend and spiritual director of St.Teresa of

Avila, and was famous for incredible penances—like sleeping only one hour per night. St. Peter of Alcántara once sped in ecstasy to a mission cross through the air and prayed there a good while, with very bright rays of light being emitted from his person. After his death on October 18, 1562, he appeared to St. Teresa and said, "O happy penance that has merited for me such wondrous glory!"

Around the year 1556 a son of the Count of Osorna, one of the greatest admirers of St. Peter of Alcántara's virtue, fell dangerously ill. St. Peter was sent for, but before he could arrive, the young man died. Seeing a great concourse of persons around the bier, Peter was touched with compassion. (His arrival had brought together a great multitude in hopes of seeing him work some miracle.)

We continue the account in the words of St. Peter's biographer, Father Marchese:

> "Throwing himself on his knees, and raising his eyes to Heaven, Peter prayed to God for a short time, but with inconceivable earnestness . . . No sooner did he arise from his prayer than, without the least intimation of his intention, he threw himself most earnestly on the dead body, placing himself feet to feet, breast to breast, and face to face. Filled with the same spirit that had heretofore animated the prophet Eliseus, he remained for a time in this position, immovable, in perfect silence, addressing his fervent supplications from the depth of his heart to the Author of life. Those present were strangely surprised at the novelty of the spectacle before them, and already were assured within themselves that some wonderful result would soon take place.
>
> "When the corpse colder than marble began to show signs of returning warmth and animation, the holy man withdrew from the body, and at the same instant the youth stretched forth his feet,

opened his eyes, and raised the bier on which he lay exposed. Immediately the Count and the whole assembly, no longer able to contain the excess of their astonishment, cried out with joy and wonder, "A miracle!" "A miracle!" But the youth, who by a supernatural light knew who had restored him to life, quitting his couch, ran to embrace the feet of the saint, whom he humbly thanked for the life God had given him through his prayers."

When all those present prostrated themselves before St. Peter of Alcántara, he endeavored to persuade them that the miracle was the result of their firm faith. He exhorted the young man to thank God for the life restored to him, and to use it as he ought in His service and glory.

The saint then hastened to leave, passing through the crowd "as if he had wings" in order to avoid the people's acclamations and honors. Other people, hearing of the miracle, crowded to the palace of the Count to see the man restored to life, "and when their eyes were satisfied with the truth of the report, they ceased not to thank Almighty God, who worked such wonders by His servant."

After St. Peter of Alcántara's death there occurred further miracles through his intercession—including the raising of six dead persons to life again.

The true accounts given above, magnificent as they are, are nevertheless unknown to most people—including Catholics. They suggest what may yet be discovered with more research on the lives of holy members of the Franciscan Order, as well of the other religious orders of the Church. One can only imagine the dramas that would be unfolded if the accounts of all the dead who have been raised could be known in full detail, in all their divine and human dimension!

16

RESURRECTION MIRACLES PERFORMED BY FIVE GREAT FOUNDERS OF RELIGIOUS ORDERS

St. Dominic, St. Ignatius Loyola,
St. Philip Neri, St. Paul of the Cross,
and St. John Bosco

*"Go and relate to John what you have
heard and seen . . . the dead rise."*
—Matthew 11:4

Founders of religious orders usually remain simple priests. They usually do not become abbots, bishops, or popes. But their works and the influence flowing from their orders are often tremendous. It should be no surprise then, that many of them have unusual spiritual gifts, including the gifts of working miracles and raising the dead. Elsewhere in this book (chapters 8 and 9) we have examined the resurrection miracles of two early founders, St. Benedict and St. Bernard of Clairvaux.

St. Dominic de Guzman (1170-1221) was the founder of the Order of Preachers, popularly known as "Dominicans." This religious Order had such great intellectual lights as St. Albert the Great and St. Thomas Aquinas, and such impressive missionaries as St. Hyacinth and St. Vincent Ferrer.

When Dominic was building St. Sixtus, his first convent at Rome, a noble Roman lady, Guatenia or Tuta di Buvalischi, lost her son. Guatenia was a devoted follower of St. Dominic and had left her son seriously ill at home in order to go and hear St. Dominic preaching at St. Mark's. When she returned home her son was dead.

One can imagine the distress of this mother, how she

blamed herself, how she wept. After a period of initial grief, she was seized with a strong hope in the mercy of God and the intercessory power of Dominic, a saint and friend of God. Guatenia set out on foot with her women servants behind her carrying the cold and lifeless body of the boy.

As the monastery was under construction at that time, there were no enclosure rules, so Tuta walked right onto the grounds. Finding St. Dominic before the door of the chapter house, she knelt at his feet and laid her son before him. Tears, sobs of anguish were her only speech.

Dominic turned aside and prayed a few moments. Then he came back and made the Sign of the Cross over the boy. He took the lad by the hand and raised him up alive. He gave him to his mother.

But Dominic did not raise the boy as he had been—ill; rather, the boy was also healed. This kind of "double miracle" has often occurred when the dead were miraculously returned to life. They were not only saved from death, but also from the illness, disease or wounds that had caused it.

Some Dominican friars witnessed Dominic's miracle and gave testimony of it at the canonical proceedings of the Church. (Such investigations are conducted with exacting care and scrutiny.) Pope Honorius ordered the miracle to be published from the pulpits of Rome.

When Dominic heard of the pope's order, he hastened to him and begged him to rescind it; he feared a deluge of crowds which would force him to flee. The pope listened but did not withdraw the order. Dominic's fears were justified: the Romans so venerated him as a powerful intercessor with and friend of God that they surreptitiously (or even boldly) snipped off pieces of his religious habit as he walked through the streets.

St. Dominic restored other dead persons to life right in Rome, the center of Christendom. When the Dominicans were engaged in construction work on their early convent of San Sisto (St. Sixtus) in Rome, the subsoil concealed masses of old masonry and unsuspected cavities. A serious landslide occurred which left an architect who had been hired by the brethren buried in a cellar under a pile of rubble. By the time he was extricated he was dead.

The Dominicans were greatly distressed, not only because of the death without the Sacraments, but also because strange tales were being circulated among the people about the fledgling order. They feared that the disaster would be interpreted as a sign of God's displeasure with this new religious venture.

Dominic noticed the concern of his disciples. He had the dead body brought to him, and "by the power of his prayer restored the man to life."

This miracle was just one of those entered into the canonical process regarding Dominic. Another such miracle occurred during a ceremony of profession or taking of vows by the nuns at St. Sixtus; there was great excitement outside, and a call for St. Dominic to come out. Lying in the square near St. Sixtus was the mangled body of a young man named Neapolion (Napoleon), nephew of a bishop, Cardinal Stefano of Fossonova (who seems to have been in the chapel at the time).

The young man had been foolishly amusing himself by letting his horse carry him away in a wild race, and he had a serious fall. Father Tancred, prior at the time, later told Blessed Jordan, the second general of the order, that he had urged Dominic to beseech the Lord confidently for young Neapolion. Dominic, motivated by his own compassion and by the urgings of Father Tancred, had the youth's mangled body removed to a room that could be locked. Then he offered Mass, during which witnesses testified that they saw him raised above the ground in ecstasy.

Then Dominic prayed for the young man. At the saint's command—"Young man, in the Name of Jesus Christ I say to you, arise!"—the rider was restored safe and sound to the warmth of life. The early biographers of St. Dominic considered this a miraculous raising from the dead. This miracle was instrumental in bringing into the Dominican Order two of its most famous members, Sts. Hyacinth and Ceslaus, apostles of the North, who were then visiting Rome as canons of Cracow with their uncle, Bishop Ira of Cracow.

At the time of Dominic's miracle of the restored architect, Friar Giacomo de Bella, Roman born, well-known procurator of St. Sixtus, was restored when he seemed nearly dead as he lay in agony after receiving the Last Sacraments. Dominic made everyone leave the room and then, like Eliseus, he stretched himself against the body of the man—holding back, as it were, by the violence of his supplication, the man's departing soul.

Friar Giacomo was restored to health again and rehabilitated in his office of procurator. He recounted this miracle himself at the provincial chapter of Rome in 1243 or 1244.

The founder and first general of a different order was another Spaniard, St. Ignatius Loyola (1491-1556), who gave to the world the original Company of Jesus, or the Jesuits. Ignatius had many supernatural visitations and was accomplished in discerning spirits and fighting the devil. He is famous for his *Spiritual Exercises* which have influenced countless people for centuries. Bartoli's biography of Ignatius gives the history of 100 miracles attributed to the saint.

One time in Barcelona, about 1524 or so, Ignatius was returning from the convent of the Dominican nuns. Passing through the street of Belloc he heard loud cries and lamentations. A man named Lessani (Lasano), in a fit of despair for having lost a lawsuit against his brother, had hanged himself. Ignatius, a practical, active and decision-making man, quickly cut him down.

Efforts were made to revive the man, but they were in vain. Ignatius prayed in tears, sorrowfully lamenting the fact that a man should die in such a manner. The bystanders joined in. Then Ignatius arose and pronounced the Holy Name of Jesus over Lessani. He instantly opened his eyes, came to himself, and expressed sorrow over his action. He then made his confession, received the Sacraments, and soon afterward expired.

This account is taken from the official Acts of Canonization of St. Ignatius Loyola. Bystanders and John Pasquale verified that Lessani had really been dead. The miracle caused a great stir in the area.

A contemporary of Ignatius was St. Philip Neri (1515-1595), "Apostle of Rome" and founder of the Oratory and the Oratorian Fathers. Centuries later, Cardinal Newman would become one of the more famous Oratorians. Philip cured many with just the touch of his hand, and the raising of the dead is attributed to him both during his life and after his death.

Some of his miracles were performed to restore the dying. Giovanni Francesco, age 14, had a pestilential fever and the physicians gave him up. For 17 days he lay like a corpse, never speaking, taking no food, showing no movement; his only signs of life were some warmth in his body and a scarcely perceptible respiration. Philip came and bantered with the mother: "A pretty thing indeed, to let this poor fellow die of hunger—a little wine, please!" Philip gave the boy a few drops between his lips, and he recovered in a few days. It was not the wine, of course; it was the touch of Philip's hand.

Similarly, as in 1560, by the touch of his hand he cured Pietro Vittrici of Parma in the service of Cardinal Boncompagni (afterwards Gregory XIII), who had been given up by doctors as virtually dead. Philip did the same for Maurizio Anerio, who had no speech, hardly any pulse, whose physicians said he could not possibly live. He also revived Lady Ersilia Bucca as she lay near death.

A good friend of Philip was Fabrizio de' Massimi, who once asked prayers for his wife, Lavinia de' Rustici, who was pregnant. She already had five daughters; Philip forecast a son and forenamed him Paolo. Years later, after Lavinia's death, Paolo, then 14, sickened on January 1, 1583 with a fever that went on for 65 days. Every day Philip visited the boy, who suffered his long illness patiently and bravely.

On March 16, a messenger was hurriedly sent to St. Giorolamo to inform Philip that Paolo was expiring and to tell him to hurry if he wanted to see him alive. (The parish priest had given the boy Extreme Unction and then had left.) But the messenger found that Philip was offering Mass and so could not inform him. Before he finished, Paolo died. The father closed his son's eyes, and prepared water to wash the body and linen cloths to wrap it in.

In a half hour Philip arrived. Fabrizio met him at the top of the stairs, weeping, with the words "Paolo is dead."

"And why did you not send for me sooner?"

"We did, but your Reverence was saying Mass."

Philip entered the room. There he threw himself on the edge of the bed. He prayed for seven or eight minutes and his praying was accompanied by the usual palpitation of his heart and trembling of his body. He then took holy water and sprinkled the boy's face; he put a little in his mouth. After this, Philip breathed into the boy's face, laid his hand upon his forehead, and called out loudly, in a sonorous voice, "Paolo! Paolo!"

At that, the boy, as if awakening from a deep sleep, opened his eyes and said, "Father, I forgot to mention a sin, so I should like to go to confession." Philip then made those around the bed retire a while, and, putting a crucifix in Paolo's hand, he heard his confession and absolved him.

When the others returned, Philip talked to Paolo for about half an hour about his deceased mother and sister. The youth answered with a clear distinct voice as if he were in perfect health. The color came back to his face so well that those around him could hardly persuade themselves that anything was wrong. At last Philip asked Paolo if he could die willingly now; Paolo said yes, he could. A second time Philip asked him, and Paolo said, "Yes, most willingly— especially that I may go see my mother and sister in Paradise."

"Go, and be blessed, and pray to God for me," said Philip as he blessed Paolo. Immediately, with a serene countenance and without the least movement, Paolo expired peacefully in St. Philip's arms.

All through this most heartrending experience, Paolo's father Fabrizio was present, along with his two daughters (who later became nuns at Santa Marta), his second wife Violante Santa Croce, the maid Francesca who had attended Paolo in his illness, and several others. In commemoration of this miracle a special feast, La Festa del Miracolo, is cele- brated in the chapel of the Palazzo Massimo on March 16, with a special Mass granted by Pope Pius IX through a decree of the Sacred Congregation of Rites on March 1, 1855.

If Philip could order, through the power God had given to him, a dead person to come back to life, he could also order a living person to die. He had repeatedly visited one of the principal ladies of Rome, who had been ill for a month. One day when she was in her agony and in great distress of mind, he stayed a while to comfort her, and then left to return to the Vallicella. But after having gone some distance he stopped and said to those accompanying him, "I feel con- strained to return to that dying lady."

He found her in the same condition, but they thought she would last until the next day. He sent some persons away, laid his hands on her head and breathed once or twice into her face. He prayed earnestly for her, uttering a few words with great fervor. He then fixed his eyes on her and said in a loud voice which several persons heard, "Soul, I command you, in the Name of God, to depart from this body"; at that instant she died. Philip then told those present that if the lady had remained in that agony much longer she would have run the risk of giving way to certain temptations. On that account he had prayed to God to accelerate her death.

There is also the case of Giovanni Manzoli, about 70 years of age, who when the doctor said he would be dead in one hour, bade a nephew to ask Father Philip to send a priest. Giovanni ordered that he be buried where Father Philip directed. The family prepared mourning garments and sent word to the Compagnia della Misericordia to be ready next day to accompany Giovanni's body to the grave.

The next morning, when several members of the Oratory told Philip that Giovanni was dead, he answered, "Not so, he is not dead, and moreover will not die of this illness." He called in Father Maffei (the priest he had sent to the family), who said, "I went to the home this morning, and I learned that he was dead." Philip replied, "No, Manzoli is alive. Go back and see how he is with your own eyes." Father Maffei did—he found the man alive and fairly well. Apparently Father Philip used his bantering ways to cover up his miracles. Philip also predicted that this old man would outlive Philip—which the man did by some years.

After St. Philip's death, miracles were worked by various relics of his—hair, rosaries, his collar, a picture, etc. Caterina Lozia, wife of Girolamo Martignone, a Milanese, when eight months pregnant delivered dead a premature child with blackened face. The midwife, a woman of great experience, used every possible means to see if the child was really dead, but there was no sign of life. She was sorrowing that no Baptism was possible.

She first cried out to the Madonna for help. Then, remembering that she had some of Philip's hair, she placed it on the corpse, praying, "O St. Philip, ask the Madonna to restore this little babe to life, in order that I may give it Holy Baptism." Immediately the child struggled and came to life. It was baptized Giovanni Pietro and lived only 20 days. In five more days the mother died.

Annibale, two-year-old son of Angelo Gerioni of Tivoli, grew grievously ill. Finally there was no sign of life; he was cold and with no pulse. When the family prepared for the funeral, a friend suggested that the father go to her aunt to get relics she had of St. Philip. She placed them on the child's neck. He opened his eyes, which had been closed two entire days, and was restored to life.

Many have heard of the Passionist Fathers, or perhaps have attended a stirring mission given by them. St. Paul of the Cross (1694-1775) was their priest-founder. Paul was one of the great mystical souls of reparation. He endured terrible sufferings and spiritual trials, but also sustaining consolations like visions of Our Lord and Our Lady. He had visions of souls in Purgatory, who were allowed to come into his cell and tell of their sufferings. At times rays were seen shining around Paul's head.

St. Paul was once working on some soldiers at Portecole in an effort to reform their lives. One not only resisted conversion but also made blasphemous and obscene remarks about the matter. This soldier had been sitting outside on a stone and had been trying to draw a sentinel nearby into conversation and a game of cards. The other remonstrated with him, saying that the holy priest Paul might pass by at any moment.

The other soldier reacted strongly: "I will be as soon converted as that ox returns again to life!" He was referring to the lifeless body of a slaughtered ox that lay nearby. The butcher had already partially flayed it. But at the soldier's unwise and irreverent remark, the ox rose up alive and ran with wild fury at the soldier sitting on the stone. He managed to escape, and the ox hit his own head on the stone where the soldier had been sitting but a moment before. The stone was drenched with blood and the ox "died" there.

At the close of a mission given by Father Paul in Orbetello in September of 1741, a child was gazing out a window at the crowd which was leaving the church. He fell to the pavement and was instantly killed. Medical assistance was called for and life was pronounced extinct.

At that moment St. Paul of the Cross was about to enter a boat to go elsewhere. The bereaved parents ran to the shore and told him of the tragedy. He went back with them and contemplated the corpse of the innocent child. Paul remained silent a little while and then spread his hands over the little body. The onlooking crowd was silent. In a few seconds the child came to life, and Paul restored him to the arms of his parents.

On another occasion, the saint was a guest at the house of

Signori Goffredi, where a hen was served for dinner. St. Paul said, "You have done wrong to kill that poor animal, because with her eggs she was the support of a poor woman to whom she belonged. Let us do an act of charity. Open that window." He then blessed the hen—already cooked, as it was—in the Name of the Father, and of the Son, and of the Holy Ghost. He had hardly pronounced the words when the hen returned to life, was covered with feathers, took wing and went off screaming out the window to the house of her poor mistress, from whom she had been stolen by the man who sold her. This miracle was recorded on oath by an eye-witness. St. Paul of the Cross worked a similar wonder in Fianello of Sabina.

When St. Paul of the Cross was preaching from a platform he would sometimes become too weak to continue, so his guardian angel spoke for him. Once the angel also went, under Paul's appearance, with a flashing sword to threaten an unrepentant sacrilegious sinner of 50 years. The man hastened to confess.

St. Paul of the Cross looked beautiful in death, and afterwards a child born horribly deformed was cured by a mere picture of him—and of course, by virtue of the petitioners' all-important faith.

More recently, St. John Bosco, also known as Don Bosco (1815-1888), founder of the Salesians, is credited with restoring at least two boys to life. In addition to his prophetic dreams, so many miraculous occurrences happened to and around Don Bosco that Pope Pius XI said of his life: "The supernatural almost became natural, and the extraordinary ordinary." When one becomes aware of the many wonders performed by saintly souls of recent times—such as St. John Bosco, St. John Vianney (the Curé of Ars), and Padre Pio (who died in 1968), one finds it easy to accept the miracle accounts from earlier ages also.

In 1866, when Don Bosco was in the area of Florence, a boy lay dead. Don Bosco prayed to Mary Auxiliatrix (Mary, Help of Christians), the other priests joined in, and the boy began to breathe.

A more famous case took place earlier, in 1849. A 15-year-old boy named Charles, who attended the Oratory of Don Bosco, was dying. He called for Don Bosco, but the priest was away. So the parents called another priest, who heard the boy's confession. But still the boy called for Don Bosco before he died.

When the saint returned to Turin and became aware of the death he hurried to the boy's home, asking, "How is he?" The servant questioned responded clearly: "He is dead 10 or 11 hours!" (One report said 24; perhaps what was meant was the length of a day.) But Don Bosco said that the boy was "just asleep," the same words Our Lord had used for Lazarus and the daughter of Jairus. The servant replied that everyone in the house knew the boy was dead and that the doctor had already signed the death certificate.

The servant led Don Bosco to the living room and the sad parents. The mother informed him how Charles had kept calling for him before he died. In the sickroom chamber Don Bosco sent everyone away except the mother and an aunt. The body lay there enshrouded, sewn into a sheet, a white veil over the head, ready for burial. Don Bosco closed the door, prayed for a moment, and cried out: "Charles! Rise!"

The body of the boy within the sheet began to move. The tearful mother and aunt watched in awe. The priest tore away the sheet from the body and removed the white veil covering the face. Charles sighed, stirred, and opened his eyes. He stared at his mother and asked her why he was dressed in the now-torn shroud. Then he noticed Don Bosco and greeted him happily and thankfully.

The boy told the priest how he had needed him, that out of fear he had not told all in his last confession and that he should now be in Hell. Charles told Don Bosco how he had dreamed he was surrounded by a mob of demons who were about to throw him into the flames of a huge furnace when a beautiful Lady had intervened. She told him, "There is still hope for you, Charles! You have not yet been judged."

At that moment he had heard Don Bosco ordering him to rise. The mother and aunt left the room as the boy asked to confess. Then, after his confession, Charles cried aloud for all to hear: "Don Bosco has saved me!" All the mourners rushed into the room to see and hear the story. Few noticed that, despite the boy's liveliness, his body remained deathly cold.

It was a moment when a weighty decision had to be made. The saint remarked on the goodness of God in showing the value of a good confession. But he also asked Charles whether, now that he was ready for Heaven, he would rather go there or remain on earth.

The boy, in the presence of his mother and loved ones, turned his glance away. Tears moistened his eyes. All was quiet expectancy. One can imagine the emotions of all.

"Don Bosco, I'd rather go to Heaven." (At times the wisdom of the saints will rub off onto an ordinary mortal!) Then Charles leaned back, closed his eyes, and once again was quiet in death.

Don Bosco himself told of this event several times during his life. He usually spoke of the priest involved in the third person, using the word "he." But in 1882, not noticing it, he told the story using the first person, "I."

17

RESURRECTION MIRACLES PERFORMED BY LESSER-KNOWN DOMINICANS

Blessed James Salomoni, St. Agnes of Montepulciano,
Bl. Constantius of Fabrino, Bl. Sadoc and Companions,
Bl. Mark of Modena, Bl. Ceslas, Bl. Augustine of
Bugella, Bl. Colomba of Rieti

> *"Jesus Christ, who hath destroyed death."*
> —2 Timothy 1:10

Here are some "lesser lights" in one order, that of the Dominicans—if any saint can be styled a "lesser light." Elsewhere in this book are told the stories of the Dominicans St. Dominic, St. Hyacinth, St. Vincent Ferrer, St. Louis Bertrand, St. Rose of Lima, and of Bl. John Tholomei, who raised his own sister.

This one admittedly selective chapter will illustrate how many death-to-life miracles have been credited to a single order alone. The greatest number of such miracles occurred, of course, in the lives of the great Dominican missionaries. Many times, those saints who were called to preach among great numbers of people, whether non-Catholics to be converted or lapsed Catholics to be renewed, possessed great miraculous powers, including that of recalling the dead to life. But there were also others with more limited performances.

The fact that the Dominicans seem to have the largest number of miracles may be nothing more than the result of the author's particular research sources. But this order does benefit from a long existence, dating from the days of St. Dominic himself (1170-1221)—a long time in which to per-

131

form miracles! Perhaps the long association of the Dominican Order with truth and great learning will augment, for some, the credibility of the miracles claimed for its members. The Dominicans are not so ancient that many miracles might be assigned to the legendary—but neither are they so recent that they have not had time to accumulate an army of saints.

With regard to intellectual endowments, two of the Dominican saints, Albert the Great and Thomas Aquinas, are virtually unrivaled in Christian history (except, of course, by St. Augustine). When "incredible" wonders have been accepted by and constitute a tradition for such learned men, among whom were many great doctors and preachers, one is persuaded to accept them.

The miracles of the lesser-known Dominicans listed here will primarily be limited to resurrection miracles. According to this author's research, neither Albert the Great nor Thomas Aquinas are reported to have revived the dead. But these saints were more of the intellectual and contemplative nature—although Albert, especially as a bishop who traveled often, did move much among the people.

Blessed James Salomoni, O.P. (of Salomonio) was born in Venice of rich and noble parents (c. 1231). He was also known as "of Forli," and died at the Dominican convent there in 1314. Once on a pilgrimage to Rome, when the sacristan with the keys could not be found to let him into the catacombs, Bl. James prayed and touched the iron bar which was fastened by a padlock. The gates instantly opened and he and his party were able to perform their subterranean devotions.

In one short biography of Bl. James Salomoni in a book of Dominican saints (as in most cases for the various saints given there), the chapter closes with the words: "He worked many miracles, both during his life and after his death." The following miracle was recorded only in a fuller account of his life. It proves the point that there are many miracles of the dead being raised that will never be heard of without exhaustive research, remarkable miracles though they may be.

The account of this miracle is as follows: The child Giacomino fell into the Montone River; when he was pulled out, doctors pronounced him dead. The agonized screams of the mother drew a number of people to the scene. Some suggested, "Let us take him to the tomb of Blessed James." They did so, and before the onlooking crowd the lifeless body of the boy came back to life. (Incidentally, Bl. James had a cancer for four years and is a patron of those suffering from this disease.)

St. Agnes of Montepulciano was born in 1268 in the town of Graciano Vecchio near Monte. She freed her convent of noises caused by the devils, dispossessed a man of an evil spirit by the Sign of the Cross and the recitation of the Athanasian Creed, and cured a man who was totally blind.

She was ordered to the Chianciano baths for her health, and while she was there a little child was playing by the waters. There was no one watching him at the time, and he fell in. Later he was found dead, floating on the surface. When his mother found her child dead she was in great grief.

St. Agnes took the little corpse in her arms, went to a place apart, and prayed alone there for a while. All the onlookers waited expectantly. Agnes finally returned with the small body and laid it at the feet of the mother. She took the tiny hand, raised the child from the ground alive, and presented him to his mother.

Agnes also knew the secrets of hearts. Showers of manna fell wherever she prayed. She fasted on bread and water for fifteen years, and slept on the ground. Her ecstacies were frequent, and she was seen to rise in the air to venerate the crucifix on a high wall; meditating on the crucifix flooded her soul with peace and with patience to endure sufferings with calm and courage. The Mother of God placed in her loving embrace the Infant Jesus. Angels brought her communion on several occasions.

This is the same St. Agnes who, when St. Catherine of

Siena was about to stoop to kiss her foot in her coffin, raised it toward her fellow saint so Catherine did not need to bend over—one saint saluting another! St. Agnes' death (April 20, 1317, at age 49) was also followed by many other miracles. Her incorrupt body is preserved in the Church of Santa Maria Novella at Montepulciano, now a place of pilgrimage.

Blessed Constantius of Fabrino (1410) was born to the family named Servoli. As a child he prayed for his sister, then nine years old and suffering from an incurable malady; she was restored to perfect health. He had the gift of prophecy, worked many miracles, and is reported to have raised a young man who had been dead *two days.*

Relatives of the deceased, and others standing nearby, reviled Constantius when they heard him address the corpse: "In the Name of Jesus Christ, arise!" They were accusing him of tempting God—when suddenly the dead man arose! At this they all threw themselves at the feet of Constantius in terror and apology. He gently raised them up and rebuked them mildly: "Never despise the servants of God, and remember Our Lord's promise: 'He that believeth in me, the works that I do he also shall do, and greater than these shall he do.'"

That certainly is a proper answer with regard to many great miracles that seem so incredible to the lukewarm and narrow-minded. One might wish for more of the simplicity of little children—and their discernment—like that of the little children who ran through the streets when Bl. Constantius died on February 24, 1481, shouting, "The holy prior is dead! The holy prior is dead!"

When Bl. Sadoc and his companions were martyred in 1260 at the Dominican convent in Sandomir, Poland, a unique wonder occurred. Before the massacre, letters of gold appeared in the Divine Office book at the beginning of the martyrology passage that was to be read at the conclusion of matins and lauds. The inexplicable entry was: "At Sandomir, the passion of 49 martyrs."

Of course, "passion" signified suffering and death. The

prior, Bl. Sadoc, counted his friars—49 in all! He interpreted the miraculous appearance of these words as a warning of death from the barbarous Tartars who were camped nearby. As the friars sang compline the following evening, a band of the Tartars, traitorously let in the city by some Russians, cut 48 of them to pieces.

One friar fled to the belfry; there he heard a wonderful sound. The mangled bodies of his 48 brethren, though dead, were chanting the sweet melody of the *Salve Regina*. From the midst of the bloody corpses of those ever-devoted children of Mary, those preachers of her holy Rosary, rose those dear words: "Hail Holy Queen, Mother of Mercy, our life, our sweetness, and our hope . . ." which are sung at eventide in monasteries and religious houses throughout the world.

Who can imagine the emotions of the 49th friar in the belfry as he heard the 48 dead martyrs chanting to their Blessed Mother! Already *they* were heroes and saints, welcomed into their reward in another and far more glorious world, even as their voices rose from bodies dead on the field of spiritual combat. Overwhelmed with that beauty, that heroism, and that message, the last friar regained his courage. He descended from the belfry and submitted to the swords of the barbarians; then there were 49 voices raised in singing the *Salve Regina* to the Mother of God. From this miraculous event began the Dominicans' custom of singing the *Salve Regina* at the deathbed of each of the Order's members.

Blessed Mark of Modena (d. 1498) was sent for by a woman who had just lost a son about three or four years of age. "Weep not," said Mark. "Your little one is in Heaven. Do not wish to have him back again, for you would lose him a second time, and in a more distressing manner."

The woman would not listen to Bl. Mark's words of warning, so he prayed. Then he took the child by the hand and cried out in a loud voice: "In the Name of Our Lord Jesus Christ, arise!"

The child immediately sat up, and Bl. Mark restored him

to his mother. But the saint's prophetic words were fulfilled when, ten years later, still a mere youth, the boy died of the plague.

Blessed Ceslas (also spelled Ceslaus; 1184-1242) was kin to, probably a brother of, the great missionary of Poland and Euro-Asia, St. Hyacinth. Ceslas was born to the noble family of the Odrowatz in the family castle near Breslau in Silesia. At Rome with St. Hyacinth, he saw St. Dominic raise the nephew of Cardinal Stephen. They had been traveling with their uncle Yvo Odrovatz, Bishop of Cracow. Dominic made four of that party Dominicans.

Like his brother Hyacinth in a similar situation, Bl. Ceslas once crossed the stormy, swollen and raging River Oder on his mantle, landing a few minutes later on the opposite bank with both mantle and clothes perfectly dry.

Ceslas raised four dead, one of them a boy, the only son of his mother, who had drowned *eight days* earlier.

Blessed Augustine of Bugella (Biella; died 1493) was born of noble parents, the Fangi, in Piedmont. He had the gift of tears, and was often seen levitated in ecstasy. He worked numerous miracles, and was especially able to cast out devils. He once raised to life an infant who had died without Baptism.

We close this chapter with a saint who lived most of her life in the 15th century, dying just after the dawning of the 16th century—Blessed Colomba of Rieti (Umbria, Italy; 1468-1501). At her Baptism a dove hovered over her forehead, whence the name Colomba (dove). Like St. Catherine of Siena, Bl. Colomba undertook an amazing public apostolate of healing, converting sinners, peacemaking, and counselling people (including Pope Alexander VI). She also raised several dead persons to life. Among the other wonders that marked Colomba's life were ecstatic Communions, perpetual abstinence from food, and the immediate cessation of the plague in Perugia after Colomba got the people to dedicate the city to St. Dominic and St. Catherine.

Bl. Colomba was one of the purest souls in the Church in

the 15th century. Her last words were directed to Our Lord: "Come, my Spouse, come. It is time." The relics of Bl. Colomba rest in the Church of St. Dominic in Perugia.

After glancing briefly at these "lesser lights" of Dominican holiness, one soon understands that they are not so "little" after all. This short survey of Dominican saints, along with more famous ones elsewhere in this book, could not possibly detail every miracle of the dead being restored to life by members of that order. But it does provide a fairly comprehensive overview.

It also indicates how many *more* miracles of the dead returning to life might be found in an exhaustive survey of *all* religious orders, especially the large and ancient ones like the great family of Franciscans, or those grouped around a certain Rule, like the rules of Sts. Basil, Augustine, Benedict or Bernard.

One must also take into consideration the humility and reticence of the saints. They often tried to hide many of their miracles. And although some miracles were quite public and soon became well-known, the more private miracles of charity, personal sympathy, or reward for the faith of a single individual petitioner were easier to hide, if only by requiring a pledge of silence from the recipient.

18

RESURRECTION MIRACLES PERFORMED IN THE AMERICAS

St. Rose of Lima, St. Martin de Porres,
St. Francis Solanus, Marianne de Jesus
of Quito, Blessed Sebastian of Apparizio

*"I believe to see the good things of the
Lord in the land of the living."*
—Psalm 26:13

Elsewhere in this book is recounted the resurrection miracle performed by St. Louis Bertrand in South America. But St. Louis Bertrand did not remain in the Americas; he returned to his native Spain. Two saints in this chapter who might have been included in that on Dominican saints, Rose of Lima and Martin de Porres, are grouped here in this chapter with other American saints.

St. Rose of Lima (1586-1617) was the first canonized saint of the New World. She was given the name "Isabel" in Baptism, but everyone called her "Rose" because she was so lovely. She rubbed her face with pepper, or used other means to disfigure herself to discourage the young gallants from chasing her. As her parents opposed her becoming a nun, preferring her to marry, she did work to support them, but still she became a member of the Third Order of St. Dominic. As penance, she wore a silver circlet with studs inside to press on her head like a crown of thorns.

St. Rose looked after the poor, the homeless, children, and the aged. She was a good friend of St. Martin de Porres. When she received Holy Communion, the Dominican provincial, Fr. John de Lorenzano, witnessed an amazing transformation of her face—as if she were already in glory.

Once when news arrived that savage pirates were nearby, St. Rose was praying before the Blessed Sacrament at St. Dominic's; she cut her long skirts to be better able to defend It against any sacrilege. Through Rose's prayers the Blessed Sacrament and the people of Lima were spared from attack. Rose had all kinds of spiritual gifts, worked wonders, and in death her body was simply beautiful, supple and fragrant.

After death she worked more wonders. In October, 1627, the daughter of a poor laborer on the outskirts of Lima was seized with a violent fever and diarrhea. When she died, they placed the body on a straw mattress until the next morning. Everything was ready for her burial, when her mother had an inspiration.

The mother had a piece of a garment of St. Rose, and she placed it on the mouth of her dead daughter. The body had been both cold and stiff, but suddenly the girl opened her eyes. In the presence of her father and several others in the room, she arose from the straw mattress in full vigor and perfect health.

In 1631 Anthony Bran, a servant of Madame Jeanne Barette, had been ill with a fever for three months when he passed away. Those who witnessed his death informed his mistress. When she saw him with no more breath in his body, cold and dead, she sighed. Then looking up to Heaven she said humbly, "God has taken from me this faithful servant who was so useful to me in my affairs and in the management of my household. May His Holy Name be forever blessed."

In making her act of resignation she noticed near the bed of the dead servant a paper picture of Rose. Immediately Madame Barette entreated Rose to protect her in her affliction, and she earnestly begged of Rose to obtain from God the restoration to life of her servant. Confidently she placed the picture of Rose on the corpse.

While the mistress was on her knees praying, along with others in the room, Anthony came back to life. He rose to a sitting position and cried out aloud his thanks to Rose for this great favor. The next day he went to her tomb to thank publicly the Rose of Lima, the First Flower of the New World.

Rose cured many after her death: she saved infants, helped women with difficult childbirth, cured lepers, healed a dying Negress who had been carried to Rose's tomb, and straightened Alphonse Diaz, a cripple who previously could only drag himself around.

St. Martin de Porres (1579-1639), a mulatto who lived nearly twice as long as his friend Rose, brought black and white together then and has done so ever since. When he died, as when Rose passed away, the whole city of Lima and the "most important" people turned out. There were many wonders in Martin's life of charity: the multiplication of food, cures, ecstasies, bilocations, etc. Though he was a Dominican he had a Franciscan love for animals, and was so kind to them as even to warn rodents to leave the monastery when their destruction was being planned.

Martin brought back to life a dead dog, a long-time pet of the Dominican monastery in Lima. The dog had grown quite old, 18 years old, and had become mangy and smelly to boot. The animal was a pet of an older monk of the community, Brother John, who felt it his duty to destroy the dog. He ordered a Negro to do so. The Negro killed it with a blow from a stone that fractured its skull.

The man was dragging off the dead dog to dispose of it when he ran into Brother Martin. Martin reproved him severely, then carried the dog in his arms to his cell and laid it on the floor. As soon as the dog touched the floor it began to move and pulled itself to a sitting position. Then Martin washed the blood and dirt out of the wound and stitched the head together. The dog was cured of both the head wound and the mange. The old monk was very pleased to have his pet back; Martin humbly reproved him, stating that "he had not done well in ordering a companion of so many years to be killed." This story was attested by three witnesses and presented during St. Martin's canonization process.

Wonders seemed to abound in Lima—and why not? In its early days there were four or five saints in that one South American city alone—a glory of and for the Americas!

The author recalls hearing that Martin also raised the human dead, but in his research he has found little mention of this type of miracle. There seems to be only one documented case, that of Brother Thomas. The chief infirmarian called the community to come together because Brother Thomas was dying. Perhaps he delayed too long, because the brother died even as the large community was hurrying through the corridors and hallways.

Before the others arrived, St. Martin leaned over the dead Brother Thomas. He stood up as the brothers entered, and out of humility and a certain fear of being treated as a saint, merely passed off the restoration with a remark that the brethren could return to their cells or occupations, as Brother Thomas had regained his senses.

When St. Martin himself was dying, an illustrious visitor, the Viceroy, Count of Chinchon, was kept waiting a while before seeing Martin. Martin accounted for the delay by waving to a small altar where reposed the Blessed Sacrament, explaining that the Blessed Mother, St. Dominic, St. Vincent Ferrer, and many other saints and angels had been his visitors by the altar in that interim.

Right after Martin's death, Brother Anthony Guitierrez, who had been infirmarian for Martin, was in violent agony, dying of the same fever that had felled Martin. The 23-year-old brother suddenly grew very calm, opened his eyes and said, "This time I shall not die." St. Martin had appeared to him—along with Mary, St. Dominic, and St. Catherine the Virgin and Martyr—and said, "This visit will cure you."

There were other cures, too: that of a child, Francis de Ribera of Lima, who was so near death that he was like a corpse, and of Elvira Moriano, to whose empty eyesocket was restored an eye that had been completely destroyed in an accident.

Father Vincent Bernedo (1562-1619), Dominican, was a

Spanish-born missionary to the New World. Preaching in Spanish, he was understood by Indians who knew only their native Qechua. He raised to life a dead widow about to be buried, and called back to life an Indian lad who had drowned, the son of a poor miner. He healed a cancer victim and an expectant mother in danger of death. When St. Rose of Lima died, Father Vincent Bernedo was carried in spirit to her sickroom, where he witnessed her beautiful departure for Heaven. He himself died two years later.

Many, many miracles took place through the intercession of the Franciscan St. Francis Solanus both before and after his death. From Spain, where he was born in 1549 at Montilla, Andalusia, St. Francis Solanus went to the South American missions in 1589 with other Franciscans. Francis had the gift of tongues, and Indians of various languages understood him. One Holy Thursday he disarmed thousands of angry Indians who were determined to slay Europeans and Christian Indians: he then baptized 9,000 of them. St. Francis Solanus crossed rushing streams on his mantle, gently led a wild bull with his Franciscan cord, and ordered locust swarms away.

After his death in Lima, Peru on July 14, 1610 his body remained flexible, sweet-smelling and as warm as it had been in life, and did not look at all like a corpse. It remained thus until he was buried, three days later; when one of the brothers pulled out some of St. Francis' hairs to keep as a relic, the scalp bled. Numerous miraculous healings took place during the time preceding his funeral. After his death, 800 persons, including physicians, prelates, and high-ranking army officers, presented themselves to testify under oath to the prodigies performed through his intercession.

St. Francis Solanus' miracles especially included sick children being restored to health, but he also restored to life a dead child. On November 8, 1639, years after St. Francis' death, a five-year-old girl named Maria Monroy fell to the ground from the second-story; down with her came an iron latticework which split her skull, destroyed her face, and put out one of her eyes. When she was picked up, she was dead. Her mother was hysterical with shock and grief and no one could calm her.

Then the mother's eyes fell upon an image of St. Francis Solanus above the bed where the dead child lay, and she began to hope. She demanded oil from a lamp burning before Father Solanus' tomb in the nearby church. When it was brought and applied to the little girl's face and head, there was an instantaneous response. The historical records state: "The eye returned to its orbit, the break in the head closed, and little Maria returned to life with the exclamation, 'Jesus, remain with me!'" This miracle quickly became known far and wide, and another wave of cures followed it.

St. Marianne de Jesus of Quito (1618-1645) was another wonder-worker of Spanish America in the New World. Also known as Marianne de Paredes y Flores, she was born at Quito, Ecuador, and became a solitary under the direction of her Jesuit confessor. She practiced the greatest austerities, ate hardly anything, slept for only three hours a night for years, and had the gifts of prophecy and miracles. When an earthquake and epidemic shook Quito in 1645, she offered herself publicly as a victim for the sins of the people. When the epidemic began to abate, she was stricken, dying around age 27. She is known as "The Lily of Quito." On one occasion Marianne's niece, Jane, a mere child, suffered a severe kick by a mule, which fractured her skull and left her dead. Marianne ordered the child to be brought to her room. There she prayed over her and restored her so perfectly that no one could tell where the fracture had been.

Marianne lived with Donna Geromine, who had an Indian man in her service. The Indian was jealous of his wife, and strangled her. He then transported the body some distance away, where he threw it over a precipice. Marianne was shown all this in a vision. She sent a man to the indicated place to find the body and bring it secretly to her room. He did so, and there in her room, through her prayers, Marianne restored the poor woman to life.

Bl. Sebastian of Apparizio (1502-1600) was a Spanish-born Franciscan lay brother of the Province of the Holy Gospel in Mexico. His biography in English was taken from the Italian of Fr. Matteo Ximenez, Observantine Friar, postulator of Sebastian's cause. The English edition of 1848 had a preface by the famous Father Frederick W. Faber. Bl. Sebastian is an example of a comparatively little-known saint who performed many miracles. To concentrate only on those miracles of raising the dead, the following are from cases proposed to the Sacred Congregation of Rites at the judicial examination into Sebastian's heroic virtue; these miracles took place after Bl. Sebastian's death and burial.

The young son of Giovanni Battista Garzia and Maria Rodriguez, playing with other children, came too near a horse, and from its hoof received a violent blow to the temple. He was dashed to the ground, and no sign of breath or other indication of life was noted for over an hour. The parents and others running to the scene prayed to Sebastian. The child rose, perfectly cured, and returned to play with the other children as if nothing had happened.

In Degli Angeli, Nicolo, a slave child of Don Bartolomeo Nabaez, commendatory of the Order of the Holy Ghost, and Donna Caterina Perez, his wife, was pushed by another child in sport. He fell from a high window to a heap of stones below and lay there dead. His mother carried his body to her mistress, who took him into her own arms and prayed: "Apparizio! Brother and saint, since, in taking leave of me shortly before your death, you promised to succor me in my necessities, fulfill your promises now and restore this child." The lady laid a piece of Sebastian's habit on the child's breast and wrapped him in a sheet. Four hours later, while Donna Perez was renewing her prayers to Bl. Sebastian, the child suddenly spoke, asked to eat, and rose up safe and sound with no bruises or injuries from his fall.

An infant, Andreana of Angelopolis, fell into a stream which carried her under several houses; she was found in the water senseless and lifeless. Her parents prayed to Sebastian, and the child was restored to life and perfect health.

The baby daughter of Giovanni Nugnez and Giovanna Dusan died. The parents, who were devoted to Sebastian, put a personal relic of his on the breast of the little girl; she was restored to life.

Maria Rodriguez was obliged to make a journey near her time of delivery. She fell from her horse, and the child in her womb died. Devoted by experience to Sebastian, she prayed to him. Not long afterwards she had a healthy, live delivery.

A child of three, son of Francesco Granado, died from a blow to his temple. Prayers were offered for him and he was touched with a relic of Sebastian. The child returned to life in perfect health before numerous spectators, who afterward gave a deposition on oath, testifying to the facts.

Giovanni, two-year-old son of Giuseppe Hortiz and Maria Salmeron, was killed when a heavy beam fell on him and dreadfully crushed his head. Having heard of other miracles, the parents implored Bl. Sebastian to restore him. After they placed a small piece of the flesh of Sebastian on the corpse, the child began to breathe again. He was not only restored to life, but the broken and mangled head was perfectly healed without even a scar. Giovanni's parents and grandparents bore testimony to this miracle in the process of both beatification and canonization.

A three-year-old daughter of Giovanni Naxara and Eleanora Rodriguez in the district of Nativitos near Degli Angeli had been out in the cold and was benumbed and frozen. All efforts to revive her failed. She was wrapped in a shroud, ready for the grave. Then a lady, Donna Francesca de Ullarte, moved to compassion by the tears of the parents, took a piece of cord that Sebastian had used and placed it on the dead child. The little girl instantly returned to life.

Bl. Sebastian of Apparizio is called the "first road builder in the Americas." His incorrupt body can be seen to this day in the Church of San Francisco in Puebla, Mexico.

19

MORE RESURRECTION MIRACLES
St. Bernard of Abbeville,
St. Stanislaus of Cracow, St. James of Tarentaise,
St. Cyril of Constantinople, St. Peregrine,
St. Philip Benizi, Bl. Peter Armengol, Bl. Eustachio,
St. Gerard Majella, St. Charbel Makhlouf, Padre Pio

"And when they had heard of the resurrec-
tion of the dead, some indeed mocked . . ."
--Acts 17:32

This chapter might be considered a rather "mixed bag" of miracle accounts given in roughly chronological order. A few of the saints presented here are well-known. Some who might seem to belong here have been excluded because the records of their miracles seem to have confused less trustworthy accounts with fact. Many in this somewhat questionable category are nevertheless included in an appendix, lest some saints or friends of God (and God!) be robbed of a glory due them.

St. Bernard of Abbeville (1046-1117)—not the great Bernard of Clairvaux—was called to an infirmary where a young nun, actually a novice, lay dead. It was harvest time and she had been knocked down by a very heavy cart drawn by ten bullocks. The wheels had run over her and she had been terribly crushed. Bernard laid his hands on her and bade her arise. She did—and without the least trace of the accident. This story is reported from a life written (1137-1148) by Geoffroy le Gros, one of Bernard's disciples.

St. Stanislaus, Bishop of Cracow and martyr (July 26, 1030—May 8, 1079) is surely one of the greatest—if not the greatest—of the patrons of Poland. Born Stanislaus Saze-

panouski in Sezepanou, in what was then the diocese of
Cracow (lately the archdiocese of Cardinal Wojtyla, to
become Pope John Paul II), he had great difficulties with
Duke Boleslaw, who had become the cruel King Boleslaw II
of Poland. He prayed for the king and pleaded tearfully with
him to better his life—but to no avail.

It is generally conceded that there were disputes with the
king over property claimed by the Church. Boleslaw was
also hostile to the saint because of his preaching and holiness. The king conspired with the heirs of one Peter Miles,
who had been dead for three years. Before he died he had
sold a certain piece of property to the Church. But the conspirators claimed that Stanislaus possessed it for the Church
by fraud, and they brought the saint to court on this false
charge.

St. Stanislaus asked the judge for a three-day delay, after
which he would produce the dead man himself as a witness
to the right of the Church to possess the property. His request was granted, although the saint was laughed to scorn
by some, particularly his enemies. St. Stanislaus then prayed
and fasted for three days (and it is likely others may have
done the same along with their holy bishop).

On the third day the court reconvened. After Mass
Stanislaus led a procession to the graveside of Peter Miles.
Stanislaus prayed before the grave. Then he had the grave
opened; there before them lay nothing but the bones of Peter
Miles, deceased three years.

Stanislaus then touched the bones of Peter with his
episcopal crozier, and in the Name of Christ, ordered the
dead man to rise. Before the awed clergy and crowd the
bones suddenly reunited, became covered with flesh, and
Peter Miles came forth from the grave.

Peter took the hand of Stanislaus and they proceeded to
the trial. There Boleslaw waited with his "witnesses" in expectation of securing "restitution" of the property, and dis-
gracing the holy bishop. In amazement and consternation
king and plotters watched as the Bishop and Peter Miles en-

tered the court, followed by a reverent but excited crowd.

"Behold Peter!" spoke the saintly Bishop. "He comes to give testimony before you. Interrogate him. He will answer you."

Amidst the stupefaction, awe and—one suspects—the frightened consciences of king and conspirators, Peter affirmed before the court that he had been paid for the contested property. He then turned to his terrified relatives and reproached them for their evil plans, exhorting them to do penance. St. Stanislaus was acquitted.

Then occurred something that has happened more than once in similar raisings from the dead. St. Stanislaus, no doubt inspired by the Lord to impart a good lesson to the crowd, offered Peter the opportunity to remain alive a few more years if he so desired. But Peter replied that he would rather return to Purgatory and to the surety of eternal salvation—but he did ask for prayers.

Then Stanislaus and a vast crowd (no doubt with more added from the court scene) accompanied Peter Miles back to the place of burial. There he lay down in his grave and composed himself. His body fell to pieces and his bones lay there exactly as they had been when the grave was opened.

There are those who may find such a miracle hard to believe. But there have been others similar to it: St. Anthony was transported to Lisbon to have a dead man clear his accused father, St. Francis Xavier raised a man long dead to confound his hard-hearted listeners, and St. Vincent Ferrer raised someone to proclaim him (Vincent) as the "Angel of the Apocalypse."

With God *all* things are possible. Why limit the Creator of all the marvels of this vast universe? This Creator seems especially pleased to work great miracles through His saints for the good of the faithful, for the conversion of pagans and sinners, for the confounding of His enemies, and for the glory of His saints, the glory of His Church, and His own glory.

When some of Boleslaw's minions refused to kill Stanislaus, he dispatched the saint with his own hand as

Stanislaus was saying Mass, offering the Holy Sacrifice in the chapel of St. Michael in a suburb of Cracow. The saint is often depicted with a sword, and is invoked in battle. King Boleslaw was forced to flee, and reportedly spent his last days as a penitent in a Benedictine abbey at Osiak, Hungary.

The story of St. James of Tarentaise accents the beauty of Christian friendship and the humanity of the saints. St. James had been on a missionary tour when he returned to find that a very dear friend of his had died. He went to the grave where his friend had been buried while he was away. There he shed such tears that the friend came back to life. This story was recorded by Pope Callixtus II (d. 1124), who wrote the life of St. James before he (Callixtus) became pope. The pope was the fifth son of Count William of Burgundy; thus Tarentaise, in the Department of Savoie (Savoy), was not a great distance away from his ancestral home.

There are two accounts of the dead being raised which seem to apply to the same St. Cyril (1191-c.1235) who was Superior General of the Carmelites and had been prior at Mt. Carmel. Information is vague about St. Cyril, who has also been styled "of Constantinople."

On one occasion, when St. Cyril once gave a blind man a coin, the man realized that the giver was Cyril of holy reputation and applied the coin to his blind eyes. His sight returned. Inspired to live a better life, he went immediately to a monastery, where he was refused admittance because the prior was away. Perhaps heart-broken at the refusal, the man died of an illness a few days later. He was brought back to life by the prayers of St. Cyril.

After Cyril had passed away, a young man coming from Cyprus to the Holy Land died aboard ship. The pilot of the vessel asked the nearby monks, the Carmelites, in charity to bury the body. They laid it out on the tomb of their late superior, Cyril, until a suitable grave could be dug for the dead voyager (a pilgrim, one assumes). But as the body touched the tomb of the saint, it immediately came to life, and the young man cried out: "Cyril has restored me to life and reserved me for a better!" He joined the Carmelites and lived for another 12 years. Perhaps it was all a reward for seeking the Holy Land.

St. Peregrine Laziosi (1265-1345) is known as "The Cancer Saint." He suffered from cancer in his right leg for several years. When the doctor recommended amputation, Peregrine spent the night before the scheduled operation praying before a picture of the crucifix. He saw Our Lord, in a vision, descend from the cross with an outstretched hand. The next morning he was perfectly cured; there was no trace of cancer! St. Peregrine is also reported to have raised the dead on more than one occasion.

St. Philip Benizi (1223-1285) died at 52, after 18 years as the fifth General of the Servite Order. He was so highly regarded for his holiness and ability that in 1268, on the death of Pope Clement IV, he was proposed as a candidate for the papacy. Philip fled and hid in a cave until a new pope was elected. Angels sang at his death, a fragrance spread through the house of his death, and for six days in the August heat amid the press of crowds his body remained incorrupt.

Some saw a light, a brightness about his dead countenance. His funeral was delayed when miracles began occurring near his body, which was laid out in the Church of St. Mark. Twenty-eight miracles were recorded in the process drawn up on the spot. It began when the daughter of a notary in Todi (where he died) was carried in on a litter and placed by St. Philip's body. She had lost the use of both her feet and her right hand.

The girl simply touched the body of Philip, and then she immediately stood up with full use of both feet and hands. After that, the authorities (as has happened with many other deceased saints) simply had to delay the funeral for about a week. After the girl's miracle, a stooped Servite religious took heart and was cured in a similar manner. A man born blind in the neighborhood of Todi gained his sight by kissing the saint's feet. And a madwoman, who had been falling into all sorts of frenzies, was cured.

Along with these and other miracles as Philip's body lay in the church, a woman from Todi came in with a dead child, mangled and gnawed. The child had been left alone in her cottage home; she went outdoors by herself, and was attacked by a wolf. The wolf had already devoured part of her body when the mother returned. Courageously and with fierce emotion, she snatched the body away from the rapacious wolf.

This woman possessed not only courage, but also great faith; she carried the bleeding trunk of the little girl to the church and placed the partially devoured corpse close by the side of Philip's incorrupt body. The girl was not only restored to life, but came to life again with all her members intact.

Even a pair of slippers can have the power of their owner. A pair of slippers had been given by St. Philip to a friend of his. They were later thrown into a conflagration in the home of the friend, and they extinguished the fire; not a mark was visible on the slippers. Philip was a missionary preacher who worked miracles throughout Europe; he was also noted as a peacemaker in Italy.

In the fourteenth century there was a miracle involving Bl. Peter Armengol (c.1238-1304), a converted robber captain. In his new life of charitable zeal, at one time he was attempting to arrange a ransom deal for 18 Christians held captive by the Moors; one account says he offered himself as hostage while waiting for the ransom money to arrive, Peter, in the new-found enthusiasm of his conversion, preached Christ to the Moors.

The Moors did not respond favorably to Peter's efforts. They hanged him. He had been hanging there for six days when his friend Florentin arrived with the ransom money. Florentin, in great shock and grief, was amazed to hear the body speak to him, saying that he, Peter, was alive through the intercession of the Blessed Virgin Mary. In the presence of many witnesses Florentin cut Peter down, alive and well.

Bl. Giorcanni Tomaso Eustachio, Bishop of Larino (b. March 7, 1575), was a member of the Oratorian Fathers. The bishop not only predicted the birth of a child and the name he was to be given at birth, but also ended up saving the child when he was born.

Later, there was another prediction. A certain mother was without children for many years. Father Eustachio predicted that she would have a child, and that the child would be a boy and would be named "Charles." The mother said that name would never be given if she did have a child, because there was a prominent member of her family who would resent anyone else having the same name. Then that relative died, and a child was born. But at birth the child showed no signs of life; for upwards of an hour there was no breath, no movement.

They sent for Father Eustachio, who came in haste. He invoked the Names of Jesus, Mary and Joseph. Father Eustachio called the infant by the prophesied name of "Charles," and the child came to life in perfect health. The bystanders were filled with astonishment and joy. Proofs of this miracle still exist in Naples and were part of the evidence in the beatification process of Blessed Eustachio.

Bishop Eustachio also predicted that Cardinal Matteo Barberini would soon become pope. The Cardinal replied that he was not mature enough—but soon afterward he was elected pope. Prophecies made and miracles worked often go together in the lives of the saints.

St. Gerard Majella (1726-1755) was a Redemptorist lay brother whose miracles reach into fairly recent times. He had powers of discernment of spirits, bilocation, control over nature, and was a regular wonder-worker.

Near Liege around 1896 an infant had died without Baptism. The physicians considered her dead. The mother prayed to the deceased St. Gerard, bargaining with him that if he brought the child back to life she would name it Gerard at Baptism. The child returned to life.

There was another case about the same time in which a

nine-month-old baby drowned. The child remained blue and cold for an hour despite attempts to resuscitate it. The mother prayed to St. Gerard. The child opened its eyes and began to laugh.

St. Gerard is a special patron of mothers, particularly those in pregnancy, and of mothers of infants. The above miracles are only two of the many that occurred around the times of his beatification and canonization, in 1893 and 1904. Others considered by the Pontifical Commission included that of a young girl in her agony who was cured, and of a boy, 15, who was fatally ill.

Even more recently, the raising of the dead is attributed to St. Charbel (Sharbel) Makhlouf, the Lebanese Maronite rite Catholic monk (1828-1898). Somehow a baby two years old drowned. When the mother found it, the child was asphyxiated, purple-hued, obviously dead. She hastened with it to the tomb of St. Charbel, and there it was restored to life. St. Charbel is credited with hundreds of other miracles.

As late as the 20th century, Padre Pio (1887-1968) is now known the world over for the many extraordinary events in his life, including the stigmata, the wounds of Christ, which he bore for 50 years. A fellow Capuchin, Father John A. Schug, tells in his book (*Padre Pio*) of a young Spanish-speaking mother from Guayaquil, Ecuador, who spoke to him when he was preparing for Mass at San Giovanni Rotondo, where Padre Pio had died.

The lady told him how her son had been killed in an automobile accident. She claimed that Padre Pio had brought him back to life and that she had a dossier of proofs from doctors and the parish priest. Father Schug was unable to learn more; he had to offer Mass and he then became occupied with another Mass for a pilgrim group from Ireland. Later, he searched for the lady but could not find her. Such a miracle, however, would not be unexpected for Padre Pio, who had a great number of charismatic gifts including bilocation, prophecy, healing powers and the reading of hearts.

20

A POSTSCRIPT TO CHAPTER 15 —

MORE RESURRECTION MIRACLES PERFORMED BY FRANCISCAN SAINTS

St. Margaret of Cortona, St. Felix of Cantalice, St. Rose of Viterbo, St. Pacific of San Severino, and Others.

> *"I am the resurrection and the life: he that believeth in me, although he be dead, shall live."*
>
> —John 11:25

Earlier in this volume the author stated his conviction that if more exhaustive research were done, many other instances of the dead being miraculously restored to life would be found. Just recently a splendid volume came into my hands and amply proves the point. The book is called *The Franciscan Book of Saints,* by Marion Habig, O.F.M., and it recounts a good number of resurrection miracles which I had not discovered in all my previous research.

One can only surmise that if, for example, an extensive compilation of Benedictine saints were available, many other cases besides those of well-known Benedictine saints might surface—from a religious order about 700 years earlier on the scene than that of St. Francis of Assisi!

For the most part this chapter is a simple listing of some resurrection miracles culled from *The Franciscan Book of Saints.* It will suit our purpose best to present these holy workers of great miracles in the order of their feast days. Please note that all are not canonized saints; some are only venerated in certain localities, and some are venerated only within the Franciscan Order.

Blessed Agnes of Prague (1205-1282), who was the daughter of Primislaus Ottokar I, King of Bohemia, and whose mother was an aunt of St. Elizabeth of Hungary, refused marriage offers from King Henry III of England and Emperor Frederick II of Germany. She became a Poor Clare, had the gift of miracles, and recalled to life the deceased daughter of her brother. (Feast Day on March 2).

St. Margaret of Cortona (1247-1297) left home at age eighteen because of harsh treatment by her stepmother. She led a scandalous life for nine years as the mistress of a young nobleman and she bore him a son. One day the nobleman did not come home; his dog returned and led Margaret to the blood stained corpse of her paramour in the forest. She subsequently made a public confession of her sins in the church at Cortona, changed her life, and became a great penitent. She secured the release of many souls from Purgatory, confronted demons, cured the sick, and restored a dead boy to life. At Cortona, Italy, her body is incorrupt to this day, and at times it emits a fragrant odor. (Feast Day on May 16).

St. Felix of Cantalice (1515-1587) was born in Cantalice in the lovely valley of Rieti, Italy, of pious peasant parents. He miraculously escaped death when unruly oxen dragged a sharp plowshare across his body. He was devoted to the Blessed Sacrament in long night vigils, and the Blessed Mother once appeared to him and placed the Child Jesus in his arms. He cured the sick with the Sign of the Cross and restored a dead child to life and gave it back to its mother. (Feast Day on May 18, the day he died in 1587 with a vision of Mary welcoming him to Heaven).

Bl. Andrew of Spello was a parish priest in Spello, not far from Assisi. He joined St. Francis at age 44, and was present at his death in 1226. He once brought down rain in a drought and he worked unusual miracles. The Christ Child appeared to him as a beautiful Boy. Bl. Andrew also restored dead persons to life. (Feast Day on June 9).

Born in a palace in 1374, Bl. Angelina of Marsciano was the daughter of a duke, and married a devout man at her father's insistence. The couple, however, lived together in perfect continence. When she became a widow, many young noblewomen followed her as virgins. This stirred up hostility even to the point of the King of Naples planning to burn her as a heretic. She presented herself, and was unharmed by burning coals held in the folds of her cloak to prove her innocence. Several days afterward she brought back to life the son of a prominent family. She became a prioress at 20 and founded 15 convents. Bl. Angelina died on July 14, 1435. (Feast Day on July 13).

St. Rose of Viterbo, a city in Romagna, Italy, lived from 1235-1252. As soon as she could walk she wanted to go to church, and loved to pray in quiet places. When an aunt died, the weeping of relatives stirred the small child's heart to deep sympathy. Rose was then only three, but she prayed in silence with her eyes raised heavenward. She touched the body of her dead aunt with her small hand and called the corpse by name. The eyes of the dead woman opened; she was alive again! She happily embraced her little niece. Christ once appeared to Rose on the cross, crowned with thorns and bleeding from all His wounds. Rose's body remains incorrupt to our day. (Feast Day on September 4).

St. Pacific of San Severino was born in 1653 in the town of that name in Ancona, Italy. As a boy he was once falsely accused of permitting a wine barrel to empty itself. He was vindicated when the barrel miraculously became full and the cellar floor became dry. As a priest offering Mass he was often in ecstasy, his face radiant. He cured the sick, foretold the future, and after his death on September 24, 1721, among many other miracles, two dead persons were restored to life through the application of his holy relics. (Feast Day on September 24).

Bl. Jane of Signa was born in 1244 in Signa, not far from the famous city of Florence. She was a shepherdess. Her flock was miraculously protected in a storm. Kneeling on her cloak she crossed the swollen Arno river more than once. She worked miracles in her life such as restoring sight to a blind man and restoring life to a dead child. She died on November 9, 1307. (Feast Day on November 16).

Bl. Berthold of Ratisbon was born around the year 1220. He became the greatest preacher of Germany in his time, his outdoor audiences sometimes numbering up to 100,000 people. He had the gift of prophecy. Once at Ratisbon Berthold spoke so powerfully against the sin of impurity that a woman of sinful life became so contrite that she fell dead. At Berthold's prayer she was restored to life and made a sincere confession. Berthold so influenced such sinners that the people of Ratisbon built a chapel and convent for these penitents. He died at Ratisbon on December 13, 1272. (Feast Day on December 19).

The Servant of God, Herman of Gersthagen, was born at Muehlhausen, Thuringia, Germany in 1224. He was a very humble friar who evangelized the regions of northern Germany. He was noted for the souls he restored to spiritual life through the Sacrament of Penance. There were many signs and wonders in his life and after his death. Through Herman nine blind persons received their sight, three mutes regained speech, many sick were cured and, to crown his miracles, Herman raised several dead persons to life. He died in 1287. No feast day is as yet given for him.

From the above accounts one can see that, at the minimum, they include about 15 persons restored to life. It is impossible to ignore all these voices raised from the dead that testify to the reality of what is considered the greatest miracle of all, the raising of the dead to life.

Great Missionary Wonder-Workers

21

RESURRECTION MIRACLES PERFORMED BY THREE GREAT DOMINICAN MISSIONARIES

St. Hyacinth, St. Vincent Ferrer, and St. Louis Bertrand

"And with great power did the apostles give testimony of the resurrection of Jesus Christ."

—Acts 4:33

Here are three Dominican saints who together have been credited with around 100 miracles of the dead raised to life. Their lives involved the sort of missionary vocation and works that accomplish those grace-filled and prophetic words of Christ: "The kingdom of heaven is at hand. Heal the sick, raise the dead, cleanse the lepers, cast out devils: freely have you received, freely give." (*Matt.* 10:7-8).

There are many who do not realize that these charges were literally fulfilled by the Apostles—and later by other apostolic missionaries. Besides the three missionary saints named in the title above, one could also bring up St. Bernard of Clairvaux, St. Francis Xavier, St. Dominic and St. Francis of Paola—and many other saints whose stories are found in other chapters of this book. In other words, such deeds or works were to be the *norm* of great missionaries, and it is more reasonable to expect miracles—including the raising of the dead—than not to expect them.

One should not be overly eager to deny accounts of great miracles even by very early missionary saints, such as St. Patrick or the early evangelizers of Gaul, simply because "historical" records are lacking. Great miracles of healing and raising from the dead have been common in the lives of those great missionaries whose activities *have* been recorded in detail. Hence, it is not unreasonable to assume that these miracles were also worked by missionary saints for whom there are no exact records or precise details. Lack of details, even the presence of confusing details, does not negate the reality that underlies long traditions; these traditions accord well with the norm of what is expected in the lives of great missionary saints.

St. Hyacinth (c.1185-1257) was a nobleman who came into the world at the castle of Lanka near Breslau, Silesia, Poland. He was a young canon of Cracow on pilgrimage to Rome with his uncle Ivo, the Bishop of Cracow, at the time St. Dominic founded the Dominican Order. He witnessed Dominic rearranging the broken limbs of Neapolion, the dead nephew of Cardinal Stephen, and then bringing him back to life.

Later, St. Hyacinth's own life became an almost uninterrupted series of miracles. He even crossed the turbulent Vistula River on his cloak, with his companions trustfully doing likewise. His missionary apostolate took him to many lands, including Scandinavia, Prussia, Lithuania, Russia, Tartary, Tibet, and even to the borders of China. St. Hyacinth is venerated as an apostle of Poland, and he is known as "the Polish St. Dominic" because he established the Dominican Order in Poland.

St. Hyacinth is credited with traveling 25,000 miles on his evangelizing journeys, and in those days it was often on foot. He worked many miracles along the way. He is an obvious example of missionary activity, holiness, and great works going together in the manner of the Apostles.

St. Hyacinth received the special help of the Blessed Virgin Mary in much of his work. At the beginning of his apostolate he had a vision of her in which she promised him that he would obtain all he asked through her intercession. Apparently Hyacinth often asked, and Mary often obtained.

On one occasion during a Tartar invasion, St. Hyacinth

rushed into the burning convent chapel to remove the Blessed Sacrament and hide It as protection against desecration. At that moment he heard the voice of Our Lady telling him not to leave her statue behind to be desecrated. The statue was large and heavy and St. Hyacinth didn't know if he could do this, but Mary assured him, "I will lighten the load." Carrying the Blessed Sacrament in one hand and the statue in the other, St. Hyacinth escaped from the burning convent, and then walked dry-shod across the Dnieper River. At the altar the day before he died, St. Hyacinth had a magnificent vision of the Blessed Mother, who gave him a crown from her own head.

The Vistula River of the miraculous cloak crossing was also the scene of another miracle of Hyacinth. He was about to cross the river on his way to celebrate the translation of the relics of St. Stanislaus, former Martyr-Bishop of Cracow and patron of Poland. (Hyacinth himself was Bishop of Cracow at the time.) As he stood by the river, a woman brought before him the lifeless body of her son, saying, "I am a widow, and this is the body of Peter, my only son. He was drowned last evening, but the body has just been recovered. I beseech you, Venerable Father, to have mercy on me and help me."

Hyacinth, deeply moved and with tears filling his eyes, approached the lifeless corpse. He took the youth's hand, saying: "Peter, may Our Lord Jesus Christ, whose glory I preach, restore you to life through the intercession of the Blessed Virgin."

Peter instantly arose. He thanked God and His servant Hyacinth. When Hyacinth later returned to his convent in Cracow, the mere touch of his hand cured a paralytic, and he restored a dying woman to perfect health.

His last miracle before dying was similar to the raising of the youthful Peter. Primislava, a noble lady, sent her only son, Wislaus, to invite Hyacinth to preach to her vassals on the Feast of St. James. On the way home, Wislaus drowned in the river Raba. Word was sent to his mother. She arrived on the scene at the same time as Hyacinth and his companion.

"O Father," Primislava cried out as she threw herself at Hyacinth's feet, "what have I done to deserve this? My son, whom I sent to invite you, is drowned! You can help me if you will!"

Hyacinth was moved by her sad situation and her strong faith. The scene echoed those in the Gospel where one finds the words, "Lord, if you will," and the responding "I will."

"Be of good heart! You shall see the glory of God," Hyacinth consoled her. He said a fervent prayer, and suddenly the missing corpse of the youth appeared before the mourners. Awe seized them all. They gaped at this miraculous recovery. (St. Peter and the Apostles, too, more than once made a great catch from the silent sea.)

"Blessed Hyacinth," cried the mother, "your prayers have recovered his body; they can restore his life!"

Hyacinth advanced to the corpse, touched the still body, and said, "Wislaus, my son, may Our Lord Jesus Christ, who gives life to all things, resuscitate you." Wislaus arose full of life. The crowd of people who were gathered at the site joined in praise to God.

Just as St. Hyacinth was famous for many great miracles during his life, many more were claimed through his intercession after his death, including the restoration of the dead. According to the *Acta Sanctorum,* "The mere enumeration of Hyacinth's miracles fills thirty-five pages." The bull (papal document) of his canonization, issued April 17, 1594, declared his miracles to be "almost countless."

If that seems exaggerated, note that the commission appointed by the Church to scrutinize St. Hyacinth's life and works ended with a report that "in Cracow alone fifty dead persons had been raised to life, and seventy-two dying persons restored to perfect health." Note the distinction between "dead" and "dying"; they knew the difference.

What fascinating stories must be concealed behind those words, "fifty dead persons in Cracow alone!" The details of each individual account would make quite a book. Here will be mentioned but one of them.

Shortly after Hyacinth died, the corpse of a young man who had just met death in an accident was brought to Hyacinth's tomb. Simply touching the corpse to Hyacinth's tomb restored the dead man to life. And after that, the miracles simply multiply and multiply.

Another of the great thaumaturges of history was the Dominican St. Vincent Ferrer (1350-1419). He moved in the limelight before both ordinary people and the great of the world. He once converted 10,000 Jews at one time by marching right into their synagogue and preaching to them; the Jews turned their synagogue into a Catholic Church.

So great a missionary was St. Vincent Ferrer that he can only be compared to the 12 Apostles. His accomplishments were incredible and rare in the whole history of the Church; his life story contains one amazing story after another.

When St. Vincent Ferrer was 46 years old, suffering from a grievous illness, Our Lord appeared to him, accompanied by St. Francis and St. Dominic; Our Lord said to Vincent, among other things, "Arise, then, and go to preach against vice; for this have I specially chosen thee. Exhort sinners to repentance, for My judgment is at hand." Our Lord told St. Vincent that his preaching before the coming of Antichrist would be for mankind a merciful occasion of repentance and conversion.

During this vision St. Vincent was immediately cured. Two years later, in 1398, he was given permission to begin his apostolate of preaching. St. Vincent travelled all over western Europe preaching penance, attracting enormous crowds, and followed by thousands of disciples. He converted St. Bernardine of Siena and Blessed Margaret of Savoy. Vincent had the gift of languages; preaching in his Valencion idiom, he was understood wherever he went; and in conversation he spoke French, Italian, German or English as fluently as his native tongue.

St. Vincent Ferrer identified himself as "The Angel of the

Judgment" and preached as if the end of the world were near. Some would say that since it did not end, Vincent, at least in that respect, failed as a prophet. It would seem there is a simple answer: All such prophecies or predictions by individuals are contingent upon reform and penance. Through Vincent's thunderous words and the results of his preaching, the end of the world was simply delayed again. Many who are informed in the ways of God, of prophecy and reparation, believe this has probably happened more than once in the history of the world. To cite a lesser example: Jerusalem was spared again and again before its final destruction by the Romans.

Some would consider it a conservative estimate that St. Vincent Ferrer converted 25,000 Jews and 8,000 Moors; his total number of conversions was around 200,000 souls— among them Moors, Jews, heretics, and apostate Catholics. At Toulouse he spoke on the Passion for six hours without a break before a crowd of 30,000 at the packed Place St. Etienne. When he cried out, "Arise ye dead, and come to Judgment!" the whole crowd fell on their faces begging for mercy.

Learning about the many other wonders of St. Vincent makes it easier to accept the accounts of his death-to-life miracles. The *Acta Sanctorum* records 873 miracles performed by the saint, but there were actually many more. In 1412 Vincent himself told a crowd, "God has wrought in His mercy, through me a miserable sinner, three thousand miracles." After that Vincent lived seven more years, which was a period of even greater miracles.

The Bollandist hagiographers tell of 70 persons who were delivered from diabolical possession by St. Vincent Ferrer. He had such power over devils that it was often enough for him to touch a possessed person for him to be freed; at other times, a possessed person would be freed from the devil merely upon going to the same region where Vincent was— or even simply when Vincent's name was pronounced.

St. Antonius (Antoninus), Archbishop of Florence,

another learned Dominican about 30 years old when Vincent died, stated that St. Vincent had raised 28 persons from the dead. But others claimed that St. Antonius' estimate fell far short of the actual number raised. Perhaps there is some confusion in distinguishing those Vincent personally raised during his life and those raised through his intercession after his death. The author Fr. Andrew Pradel states that St. Vincent Ferrer "resuscitated more than 30 persons during his lifetime."

Near Palma of Majorca St. Vincent Ferrer stilled a storm in order to preach from a wharf. At Beziers he stopped a flood. At the gates of Vannes he cured a great number of the sick. At Guerande he delivered a man possessed by the devil and more dead than alive. In France he had the British victors at Caen praying together with the defeated French for a sick man, who was then cured—and all of them, enemies or not, shouted for joy. At Leride he cured a cripple in the presence of the king.

St. Vincent Ferrer is often pictured with wings. Multitudes of people have witnessed him, in the middle of preaching, suddenly assume wings and fly off to help some suffering person; he would return in the same manner and continue preaching. On some occasions, when St. Vincent was exhausted, he would commission somebody else to go perform miracles instead; the helper would then do so.

Vincent once said to a novice, Alphonso Borgia, "You will become pope and will canonize me." And years later that novice, then Pope Callixtus III, did exactly that. Vincent also told St. Bernardine of Siena that he (Bernardine) would be canonized before himself—and so it happened. Once a mute woman signed to him, and then she spoke, asking for speech and bread. He promised her bread, but took back her speech, saying that she would make ill use of it. He made beautiful an ugly woman who had been beaten by her husband for her looks.

One must never mock the gifts God has given to His saints. As has happened in similar cases, on one occasion a boy pretended to be dead, while his friends snickered. St. Vincent leaned over and shook—a corpse! Vincent said: "He pretended to be dead to amuse you, but evil has come upon him; he is dead!" A cross was erected to commemorate the event. Happenings like that can save many souls by instilling in them a healthy fear of the Lord.

At Pampeluna an innocent man had just been condemned to death. St. Vincent knew of his innocence and pleaded for him, but in vain. As the grim procession led the poor man to the scaffold, they met another procession, that of a man already dead. The corpse was being borne on a stretcher to the burial place. Vincent seemed to have a sudden inspiration. He stopped suddenly and addressed the corpse:

"You no longer have anything to gain by lying. Is this man guilty? Answer me!"

The dead man sat up, then spoke the words: "He is not!"

As the man began to settle down again on his stretcher, Vincent offered to reward him for his service. He gave him the opportunity of remaining alive on earth. But the man responded, "No, Father, for I am assured of salvation." With that he died again as if going to sleep, and they carried his body off to the cemetery.

In another miracle credited to Vincent, the Venerable Father Micon is reported as claiming that a number of witnesses, gathered at Lerida before the Church of St. Jean, saw Vincent encounter a corpse there. With the Sign of the Cross Vincent returned the corpse alive to its feet. The Fathers of the convent at Calabria gave guarantees of this miracle.

In another report a priest judged a child to be dead. The child's whole body was mangled and broken. A vow was made, and the child was restored to life. It is not known for certain whether this is the same child as that in the following miracle.

Fifty years after Vincent's death, young Jean de Zuniga, son of Don Alvar de Zuniga, Duke of Placensia and Arevola, and of his Duchess, Leonor de Pimentel, died at the age of 12. The Duchess' confessor, Jean Lopez de Salamanque, O.P., counseled the noble lady to invoke his fellow Dominican, the newly canonized Vincent Ferrer.

The mother made a vow to build a church and convent in St. Vincent's honor. As soon as she had formulated her vow, the boy came back to life. This boy became the Grand Master of Alcántara, the Archbishop of Seville, and a Cardinal. The Duchess became very devoted to Vincent and fervently desired that his life, virtues, and miracles be written about. When a grand ceremony was held at the newly finished cathedral, the Duke and Duchess presented their son, and the raised boy then understood all about his resuscitation.

On the feast day of St. Vincent Ferrer at that same cathedral, the scheduled preacher became ill and did not appear. But a wonderful, charming, unknown preacher appeared from nowhere—and mysteriously disappeared after giving his sermon. Many believed it was Vincent repaying the honors given him.

There are two different accounts of either the same or very similar miracles. In one account Vincent summoned a dead man on the way to burial to attest that Vincent was the "Angel of the Judgment." In another account, it was a woman who was summoned. (Since Vincent performed a great number of miracles of many kinds, it is possible, even if unlikely, that he performed this action on more than one occasion.)

On an occasion when St. Vincent was preaching to thousands at Salamanca, he suddenly stopped and said: "I am the Angel of the Apocalypse and am preaching Judgment!" Then he directed: "Some of you go near St. Paul's Gate, and you will find a dead person borne on men's shoulders on the way to the grave. Bring the corpse hither, and you shall hear the proof of what I tell you."

The men went on their errand, the multitude waited, and soon the bier was brought with a dead woman upon it. They raised the litter and set it up so all could see. St. Vincent bade her return to life, and the dead woman sat up.

"Who am I?" Vincent asked her.

She answered: "You, Father Vincent, are the Angel of the Apocalypse, as you have already told this vast assembly."

In the case of the woman, after her testimony she died again. In the almost identical account of the man, Vincent asked him which was his preference, to live or to die again. The man asked to live, and St. Vincent responded, "Then be it so!" The man is reported as having lived for many more years.

Another miracle seems to involve either a Jew or Jewess. (Recall that Vincent converted 25-30,000 Jews. It is reported that at a church in Vera Cruz a host of little white crosses once fell upon the Jews in the congregation.)

There was a rich Jew of Andalusia, named Abraham, who began to leave a church in anger while Vincent was preaching. The Jew did not like what he was hearing. As some people at the door opposed his passing through, St. Vincent cried out: "Let him go! Come away all of you at once, and leave the passage free!" The people did as he ordered, and at the instant the Jew left, part of the porch structure fell on him and crushed him to death.

Then the saint rose from his chair and went to the body. He knelt there in prayer. Abraham came to life, and his first words were: "The religion of the Jews is not the true faith. The True Faith is that of the Christians."

In memory of this event the Jew was baptized Elias (in honor of the prophet who had raised the boy from the dead). The new convert established a pious foundation in the church of the "accident" and the miracle. Bishop Peter Ranzano's account was used for this version of the miracle.

In the other version, the person involved was a wealthy Jewess, and the place is given as the church in Ecija, Palm Sunday, 1407. As in the miracle of the dead man or woman who declared Vincent to be the Angel of the Judgment, it is of little consequence which of the two accounts is the more accurate; the basic story should be accepted as authentic.

The father of a certain child had given Vincent lodging while he was on a missionary journey. His wife, a virtuous woman, suffered from bad attacks of nerves, and at times was close to madness. Upon his return from hearing one of Vincent's sermons, the father came upon a terrible tragedy. His wife had gone mad, cut their small son's throat, then chopped up the boy's body and roasted a portion of it, which she then attempted to serve her husband.

When he realized what had happened, the man fled in horror and disgust to St. Vincent Ferrer. Vincent told him that—as in the case of the crushed Jew—the tragedy would be for the glory of God. St. Vincent went with the father back to the home and prayed as he gathered the bloody pieces together. He said to the father: "If you have faith, God, who created this little soul from nothing, can bring him back to life."

Vincent knelt and prayed. He made the Sign of the Cross over the reassembled body. The pieces became united together, the body came to life again, and Vincent handed over to the father a living child. This event is depicted in a painting by Francesco del Cossa in the New Picture Gallery in the Vatican.

Bishop Ranzano claimed this as one of the miracles submitted in the canonization process for St. Vincent Ferrer. These are not mere "myths," "legends," or "symbols." As Chesterton has observed, "historians" are willing to accept uncritically all kinds of minor details, places, names, and ordinary events from the chronicles about the saints, yet they want to eliminate arbitrarily what is preternatural, supernatural, or miraculous in these lives. How can such historians consider themselves "critical" thinkers—especially when the preternatural events they reject have been related by competent, reliable men?

Remember, the above miracle is not without some real, though lesser, counterparts. St. Francis of Paola restored a lamb from its mere bones and fleece, and in the palace of the King of Naples he revived an already-cooked fish; also, St. Philip Benizi restored a child partially devoured by a wolf.

A similar wonder was worked for a young man who was

with his parents in a group of pilgrims on their way to the famous shrine of Santiago (St. James) de Compostella in Spain. They stopped at La Calzada, where the young man was falsely accused and hanged. The poor bereaved parents continued their pilgrimage, and on their return journey were astonished to find their son still alive eight days later. Perhaps it was a reward for their tears and for faithfully continuing on to the shrine in hope, rather than succumbing to rebellion and grief.

But the story goes beyond this wonder. When the lad's mother rushed to tell the magistrate (he was at dinner), the magistrate said, "Woman, you must be mad! I would as soon believe these pullets which I am about to eat are alive as that a man who has been gibbeted for eight days is not dead." At his words the pullets on the dish rose up alive. There was a great procession with the live birds to the shrine of St. James at Compostella. The Bollandists relate this miracle, as do many other authors. And there have been other miracles similar to it.

Of course, one cannot be credulous and believe everything one hears, but Christ did tell us to expect great wonders to be worked through faith, especially by His missionary saints. One should note, too, that none of these miracles was performed for mere sensationalism, which the saints avoked. They were worked for various good purposes, including the strengthening of faith. As St. Vincent told the bereaved father, miracles are worked for the glory of God. This was also stated by Christ at the grave of Lazarus, and to His Apostles. The saints' powers are of course limited by God, to whom all power belongs. Otherwise, with unrestricted powers, the saints could be "as gods."

The hagiographer Henri Gheon relates that Père Fages, a patient researcher, found and visited the house of the last related miracle of Vincent. He described the room, the placement of the oven, and the lower room, where a part of the child was served at table. The place had not changed since the fifteenth century. A chapel stands there now and two inscriptions, one inside and one out, attest to the truth of the miracle.

St. Vincent Ferrer died at Vannes, Brittany, France in 1419, and the canonical process at Vannes brought to light an incredible number of wonders—including a surprising number of resurrections from the dead. In the French work, *Histoire de St. Vincent Ferrier* by Père Fages, O.P., are a number of accounts of the dead raised through St. Vincent. Recall, too, that St. Antonius, O.P., contemporary of Vincent, said he raised 28 from the dead, and that others claimed this count fell far short of the real number.

There was still another extraordinary Dominican missionary, St. Louis Bertrand, born in Valencia, Spain on January 1, 1526. In Spain, a nobleman whom Louis had rebuked for his licentious life drew his arquebus on Louis when he met the saint on the road. Louis prayed and made the Sign of the Cross over the drawn weapon; it turned into a crucifix, with its bottom taking the shape of the stock of a gun (as can be seen in some artistic representations).

Louis was to return to his native country as a second Vincent Ferrer after his mission tours in Spanish America, where he converted thousands.

In South America Louis raised a dead woman in the city of Carthagena (in present-day Colombia), the slave port where St. Peter Claver, S.J. also labored. There is also an account (perhaps another version of the same event) of a girl in South America raised to life by the application of a rosary. St. Louis often hid his miracles under the veil of Mary's intercession.

His miracles in South America continued even after his death. In Xativa a little boy died after a severe illness. All the usual signs of death were present. The mother had been to confession to St. Louis when he was alive and preaching in the cathedral. "O Father Louis," she cried, "help me; I implore you to restore my child to me!" She prayed in anguish for a quarter of an hour. Then her husband noticed that the pallid cheeks of the dead child were reddening; he came back to life and to good health. The parents made a pilgrimage of thanks to Louis' tomb at Valencia, presenting offerings. This boy was still living in 1596.

In 1647 John Baptist Ramirez moved from Valencia to Chelva to avoid the plague. But his three-year-old son, having often been seized with a violent fever, died there. When the child had been dead for two hours the parents placed an image of St. Louis on his body. They prayed, and the boy opened his eyes, asked for food, and was restored to perfect health.

After St. Louis returned to Spain he worked many miracles. In his life he held high offices in his order: novice master, prior, and master general. He had the gift of prophecy.

In one biography of St. Louis there is a one-line report on the multiple miracles worked through his intercession after his death; in it there appears the phrase, "including at least thirteen dead brought back to life." *Thirteen dead!* Nevertheless, in another (popular) biography of St. Louis Bertrand, only one such miracle is given. One can only conclude that many of the miracles of the saints have not found their way into their biographies. Further research is needed in order to uncover these wonders.

St. Louis Bertrand went to America in 1562, returned in 1569, and died at Valencia in 1581. Pope Clement X canonized him in 1671.

To summarize the resurrection miracles of these three great Dominican *missionaries,* laborers in the footsteps of the Apostles: St. Hyacinth was credited with at least 50 dead restored to life, St. Vincent Ferrer with at least 28, and St. Louis Bertrand with at least 15. Surely no one can explain away all of these—all performed by the power of the Infinite God.

"Why wonder you at this? Or why look you upon us as if by our strength or power we had made this man to walk? The God of Abraham . . . hath glorified his Son Jesus . . . And in the faith of his name, and the faith which is by him . . ." (*Acts* 3:12-13,16).

22

RESURRECTION MIRACLES PERFORMED BY GREAT JESUIT MISSIONARIES
St. Francis Xavier, St. John Francis Regis, St. Andrew Bobola; Other Jesuit Resurrection Miracles: St. Francis Jerome, Brother Antony Pereyra

"Many wonders also and signs were done by the apostles in Jerusalem and there was great fear in all."
—Acts 2:43

Most definitely to be included in this section are three great Jesuit missionaries, particularly St. Francis Xavier (1506-1552), who is considered to have been the greatest missionary since St. Paul. He is known as the "Apostle of the Indies," and the "Apostle of Japan."

In about ten short years (1541-1552) Francis did the work of a thousand individual missionaries, spreading the Catholic Faith from Goa (Portuguese territory in western India), over South India, Ceylon, Bengal, Cape Comorin, the Moluccas, Spice Islands, Malacca, and through the China Sea to Japan where he died—alone except for one companion, a Chinese youth named Antiry, on the Japanese island of Sancian, waiting for a ship to China. On his journeys St. Francis Xavier converted hundreds of thousands, and the impact of his work lasted for centuries.

Those exotic lands were vastly different from the Basque country of his native northern Spain and the Xavier Castle on the fertile mountain slope overlooking the Aragon River. There in the Kingdom of Navarre, Francis Xavier had been born in 1506, the youngest of the six children of the Chancellor of Navarre, Don Juan de Jassu (a doctor of law), and the very beautiful Donna Maria Azpilcueta y Xavier.

Francis Xavier's was a brilliant and attractive personality. As a student and lecturer at the great University of Paris, he came under the influence of St. Ignatius Loyola. Francis was among the first seven to take their vows in the fledgling Society of Jesus founded by St. Ignatius; he was later the last to make the famed *Spiritual Exercises* of St. Ignatius. If Francis had remained in Europe and the universities he might have become famous as a great teacher or doctor of the Church, judging by the promise of his already brilliant accomplishments.

At that time it came about that King John III of Portugal asked the Pope to send six members of the new society to do mission work in Asia. He wanted them to leave in the royal galleon of the Governor of Portuguese India in April, 1541. Ignatius could spare only two Jesuits, and one of them, Bobadilla, became seriously ill with a severe fever at the last minute. It was apparently with dismay on the part of both Ignatius and Francis that the latter became the substitute.

Then and there the history of the Church and its missions was changed by the workings of Divine Providence. So often it seems that there is a "sacrifice of brilliant talents"; the ability to teach metaphysics in university classes and the meticulously acquired knowledge of Greek and Latin give way to the simplest form of catechism, as a missionary instructs the children, pagans, and cast-offs of many distant places, returning again to language study as he struggles with the idioms of foreign dialects. But God knows what He is about.

Due to inclement weather it took the packed galleon of 900 passengers 13 months to complete its voyage. It arrived at Goa in May, the month of Mary, 1542. There St. Francis Xavier spent five months before traveling on to Cape Comorin. In Goa he preached, cared for the sick and for prisoners, taught children, and endeavored to bring Christian morality to the Portuguese there, particularly denouncing the concubinage which was so prevalent among them.

Besides his numerous cures, there were many other wonders in St. Francis' life: gifts of tongues, predictions, bilocation, calming a storm at sea, and more. Francis had been "all things to all men"; he was known and loved (and sometimes hated) by great and small in all walks of life. Perhaps the greatest wonder of all is the fact that he baptized 100,000 with his own hand. That remarkable right arm is still preserved and venerated.

Apropos of miracles of raising the dead, Butler speaks of four such events which occurred in one period alone, according to the canonization process. Those four resurrections were those of a catechist bitten by a venomous snake, a child drowned in a pit, and a young man and a young girl dead of pestilential fever.

On the Fishery Coast, St. Francis Xavier worked enough miracles to fill a large volume. Once when he was about to begin Mass in a small church at Combutur, a crowd entered with the corpse of a boy who had been drowned in a well (perhaps the "pit" mentioned by Butler). His mother threw herself at the feet of St. Francis—who was also the one who had baptized this child. She implored him to restore the boy to life. Francis said a short prayer, took the dead child by the hand, and bade him arise. The child rose and immediately ran to his mother.

There was a pair of youths who accompanied Francis as catechists. During the night one of them was bitten in the foot by a "cobra da capello." In the morning the youth was found dead. Francis took some saliva from his own mouth, touched the foot of the poisoned catechist, made the Sign of the Cross over him, took him by the hand and bade him arise in the Name of Jesus Christ. The youth responded immediately and was able to continue the missionary journey at once. It was as simple as if he had just gotten up from sleep, instead of having been restored to life itself. This is probably the miracle of the "venomous" serpent given without details by Butler.

It is important to note that the chroniclers attribute to St. Francis other resurrections of the dead in that part of the country. Only the Lord knows how many Francis actually recalled from the dead in all his missionary life, laboring night and day. Large numbers could be expected when one recalls that he was the greatest missionary since St. Paul, and if one considers how many of the dead have been raised by other great missionaries.

Further, it is stated in the processes concerning Francis that one of the children he often sent among the sick in his name raised two dead persons to life. The Christian "children" of St. Francis worked many prodigies. One is reminded of the helpers St. Vincent Ferrer commissioned to continue working miracles for the multitudes during the times when the saint himself was exhausted.

The following miracle of St. Francis Xavier is recorded in the *Relatio* documented in the time of Pope Paul V. In the streets of Mutan, Francis met a funeral procession bearing the body of a youth who had died of a malignant fever. According to the custom of that area, the body had been kept for 24 hours wrapped in a shroud. Like Jesus with the widow of Naim, Francis pitied the bereaved parents; they pleaded with him.

The saint knelt down, raised his eyes to Heaven, and prayed to God for the lad's life. Then he sprinkled the covered corpse with holy water and ordered the funeral shroud cut open. When the body was visible, Francis made the Sign of the Cross over it, took the youth by the hand, and bade him in the Name of Jesus to live.

The youth rose up alive, and Francis gave him to his parents in good health. The crowd marveled and praised the holiness of Francis. The youth's parents and friends, in gratitude and memory of the deed, erected a great cross on the spot and held a festival there.

At another time, St. Francis was preaching at Coulon, near Cape Comorin in Travancore at the southern tip of India opposite Ceylon (Sri Lanka). This was a seaport, a rough town where many Christians dishonored their name. Francis, while preaching in the Portuguese church there, felt baffled and stymied by the wall of obstinacy he met in his hardhearted listeners.

Now it happened that a man had been buried in the church the day before. St. Francis stopped preaching; he prayed to God to honor the Blood and the Name of His Son and to soften the hearts of the congregation. Then he directed a few men to open the nearby grave of the man who had been buried the day before. He had prayed in tears, and now he accompanied his directions with the burning words of holy eloquence. He told the congregation how God was pleased even to raise the dead in order to convert them.

When they opened the tomb and brought out the body, it was already giving off a stench. On Francis' orders they tore apart the shroud—to find the body already beginning to putrefy. Francis expressed his desire that they should all take note of these facts. (They could hardly escape them!) Then the saint fell on his knees, made a short prayer, and commanded the dead man, in the Name of the Living God, to arise.

The man arose—alive, vigorous and in perfect health! The onlookers were filled with awe. Those who needed it fell at the saint's feet to be baptized, and a large number of people were converted because of this miracle.

The two miracles above were accepted by the auditors of the Rota as resting on incontrovertible evidence from two witnesses, Emanuel Gago and Joam Audicondam, as well as from one "dead" person himself. These great miracles led almost the entire kingdom—except for the king and a few of his courtiers—to become Christians within a few months. And as Father Coleridge points out in his two-volume life of St. Francis Xavier, "We must take these miracles as but specimens."

Why would God grant anyone the power to perform such great miracles? This becomes easier to understand when one appreciates the immense number of souls converted by St.

Francis Xavier. Within about a year he had established up to 45 Christian communities in the area. It is hard to conceive of such mass conversions, whether by Francis Xavier or by any missionary apostle, without great and numerous wonders to testify to the truth of the apostle's words. Our Lord used His own miracles as signs that testified to His Messiahship and Kingdom. His wonders proved that He was, indeed, the Son of God sent by the Father. He ordered His disciples to work similar miracles with generosity, and promised that they would work even greater wonders than He had.

Man is inclined to measure miracles by his own limited standards and abilities. But for God, of course, the "great" and the "small" miracle are equally easy. Yet it somehow seems more wonderful when (as with Lazarus) someone who has been dead for days is raised, rather than one who has very recently died. But death is death—whether it has lasted a minute or a week—and the wonder of restoration is equally marvelous in either case.

At Malacca St. Francis Xavier worked a miracle for someone who had been buried for several days. When Francis was away from the town, the daughter of a recently baptized woman died. The mother had sought Francis everywhere while the girl was still ill. When this earnest parent learned that Francis had returned, she was full of the simple faith that Francis, whom she was convinced could have healed her daughter—as he had cured people *en masse*—could just as easily raise the girl from the dead. As Martha said to Jesus, "But now also I know that whatsoever thou wilt ask of God, God will give it thee." (*John* 11:22).

When the mother found St. Francis she threw herself at his feet, and like Martha and Mary, exclaimed that if he had been there her daughter would not have died; nonetheless, nothing was difficult for God, and she knew that Francis, with his prayers, could return her to life. As Jesus had marveled at the faith of the Roman centurion and the Syropheonician woman, St. Francis Xavier marveled at the faith and confidence of this recent convert.

Since the mother seemed so worthy of such a favor, Francis prayed for God to grant her this consolation. Then he turned to the mother and told her to go to the grave; her daughter was alive. Hopeful, fearful, not disbelieving, but because Francis had not offered to come himself to the tomb, she answered simply that the girl had been *three days buried.* But St. Francis had measured her testing tolerance.

She questioned St. Francis no further; with shining faith she ran rejoicing to the church where her daughter had been buried. At the burial place the mother, together with many other witnesses who had hurried there with her, had the stone raised from the grave. The dead daughter, buried three days, came out alive! As with the raising of Lazarus, no one could doubt the verity of such a miracle.

One must admire the tenacious faith of this newly converted woman. Such strong faith is seldom found. The great faith and wisdom of the apostle met and matched the faith of the mother, when he asked her to go to the tomb alone.

This power of raising the dead from a distance seems to have been a special charism of St. Francis Xavier. In Japan, at or near Cagoxima, a pagan nobleman lost his only daughter. He was greatly grieved. Some recent Christian converts, sympathizing with him, recommended that he seek help from the God of the Christians and the prayers of the "great teacher of the Portuguese." The father went to St. Francis and cast himself at his feet. He was so choked with emotion he could not speak. But the saint understood.

St. Francis went into the little oratory where he offered Mass. His helper, Joam Fernandez, went along with him. After Francis prayed for a few moments he came out and told the anxious father to go, that his prayers were heard. That was all Francis said, so the nobleman turned homeward, hurt and grieved.

But on his way a servant met him and joyfully told him that his daughter was alive. Next, the girl herself came running and threw herself upon her father's neck. She informed her father that when she had breathed her last breath, immediately two horrible demons had seized her. They were about to hurl her into Hell when two venerable men came to her rescue. The next moment she found herself alive and well.

When the girl's father brought her to St. Francis Xavier's house she identified Francis and Fernandez as her two deliverers. Father and daughter were subsequently instructed and baptized.

Another miracle occurred when Francis was on a ship, the *Santa Croce,* going to San Chan. A Musselman's five-year-old son fell overboard at a time when the ship was running fast before the wind. It was impossible even to attempt to save him. The father had been in despair for three days when he chanced upon Francis on the deck. Francis somehow—for the glory of God?—had not heard of the tragedy. He asked the father if he would believe in Jesus Christ if his child were restored. (A small child, overboard in the sea for three days, miles behind the ship, and Francis confidently asks such a question!) The man said he would believe.

A few hours passed, probably while Francis was praying. Suddenly the Musselman met his child, bright and joyous, running to him on the deck. The father and his entire family were baptized.

"For, Amen I say to you, if you have faith as a grain of mustard seed, you shall say to this mountain, Remove from hence hither, and it shall remove; and nothing shall be impossible to you." (*Matt.* 17:19). The "mountain" may represent the great obstacle of unbelief to be overcome. A mustard seed is very, very small. Suppose one's faith were the size of a watermelon seed . . . or a coconut . . .?

In Japan at Cagoxima, Francis blessed the swollen body of a deformed child, making it straight and beautiful. And that expresses well the objective of the saints: to make all men straight and beautiful in the eyes of God.

Among his later miracles, Francis raised to life a young pagan woman "of some quality" who had been dead a whole day. At Malacca he restored to life a young man, Francis Ciavos, who later became a Jesuit.

St. Francis Xavier died on December 3, 1552, at the age of 46. Before his burial, the coffin was filled with lime—two sacksfull beneath the body and two over it—in order to hasten decomposition so that at some future time the bones could be easily transported to India. Ten weeks later, when the saint's body was exhumed to be taken to Malacca, it was found to be perfectly incorrupt!

Only 12 years after he had first embarked on his missionary journeys, the body of St. Francis Xavier was brought back to Goa in veritable triumph. Around the saint's body miracles were recorded every day of that autumn and winter.

When his remains were temporarily placed in the chapel of the College of St. Paul on March 15, 1554, several blind were cured, as also were paralytics, those with palsy, etc. Francis had been the special envoy of both the Holy See and of King John III of Portugal; on the order of the King a verbal process was made with the utmost accuracy, in Goa and in other parts of India; in it, accounts were taken of many miracles wrought through St. Francis Xavier.

Today the body of St. Francis Xavier is dry and shrunken, but there is no corruption. Many parts of the body, notably the right arm mentioned above, have been removed and sent to various places as most precious relics. In 1974-75 the body of the saint (in a glass case) was exhibited for viewing and veneration for a six-week period. (See photograph in *The Incorruptibles,* by Joan Carroll Cruz.) Today it rests in a silver reliquary in the Basilica of Bom Jesu in Goa, India.

Another great Jesuit missionary saint was St. John Francis Regis, S.J. (1597-1640), whose mission territory was southeastern France. In his lifetime he brought thousands back to the Catholic Faith. It is summarily stated that he raised a dead person to life. He also converted many prostitutes.

St. Andrew Bobola was a famous Jesuit missionary who was martyred in 1657. Of his tortures and martyrdom the Sacred Congregation of Rites observed: "Never was so cruel a martyrdom reviewed by this Congregation." Miracles by the hundreds were attributed to him and verified. In 1702, nearly 50 years after his death, after two extraordinary apparitions of St. Andrew in which he requested the transfer of his body to a separate burial place, the body, torn by wounds, was found incorrupt, the wounds fresh—and the members flexible. Miracles began—even resurrections of the dead.

Poland's turbulent history slowed St. Andrew's canonical process, but when the Congregation discussed and approved new evidence, four more volumes were added to the five already prepared for beatification. In 1710, due to the miraculous escape of Prince Michael Wisnoyeki of Lithuania (friendly to Poland and imprisoned by the Russians) and of other notables, various nobles came to St. Andrew Bobola's tomb. There were many favors and striking cures.

Two of these miracles stirred increased devotion to Andrew Bobola. Peter Gluszynski, a captain of the military in the Pinsk area, who was gravely ill, did not wish to invoke St. Andrew. He did not believe in the miraculous power of the new wonder-worker. "Until Bobola performs a miracle I shall not believe in his power." Nevertheless, he was cured. But on the morning of February 1, 1711, the maid who came to awaken Peter's nine-year-old daughter Anne for school found her dead. She was stretched out on her small bed, cold, lifeless, with her eyes staring from their sockets. She had been in perfect health.

Terrified by the sudden end, her parents and friends tried to revive her, but there was no pulse, no breath—only a stilled heart. The family members gathered around her bier and prayed. They sent for a priest of the Latin rite, but he was away, so a priest from the Greek rite Catholic Church came and began the ritual prayers.

But the parents were doing their own praying: "O God, one in Three Divine Persons, if Thou dost wish to glorify Thy Jesuit servant, Andrew Bobola, perform a miracle in our house, and restore to us our child alive through the merits of Thy servant who is venerated by men."

While the priest was reciting the words, "The child is not dead but sleeping," Anne moved her head, recovered her senses, and was soon able to walk.

The second case occurred a few days later at Pinsk. After 20 days of sickness, a girl of four died. Her father set out to order a coffin and have a grave dug. But he first turned to the tomb of St. Andrew to obtain resignation to bear his bereavement and this emptiness in his life. It was then that his child suddenly came to life.

It happened that the Gluszynski family came to Pinsk in thanksgiving and was given hospitality by the second family. They all went together to venerate the body of their heavenly benefactor, St. Andrew Bobola.

In 1808 Andrew's body was found to be incorrupt in its tomb. It was tranferred from Pinsk to Plock. A notary and priests witnessed the fact of its incorruption. In two years, 1808-1810, at St. Andrew's tomb in Plock, there occurred 34 miracles and favors. The first was the sight instantly restored to Praxedis Fiordova, who had been blind for three years. By 1813 more than 60 favors had been approved and put into a chronicle, including the cure of a woman who had been blind since 1805. St. Andrew also appeared with dramatic prophecies of Poland's future following a great battle which was to take place.

A letter from the Bishops of Poland to Pope Benedict XV, dated July 28, 1920 speaks of graces won by St. Andrew Bobola in the eighteenth century: "The acts of the process formulated during the pontificate of Benedict XIV count more than 350 favors and miracles sworn to and proven. Besides the extraordinary preservation of his body, there are eleven instances of people raised from the dead, more than fifteen instances of restoration of sight to the blind . . ." etc., etc.

How easily it is said—11 raised from the dead! Consider, though, the dramas of 11 individual stories! The Jesuit Order is still less than 500 years old, and yet so many mira-

cles have already been performed by Jesuits. After hearing
of saints like St. Francis Xavier and St. Andrew, one wonders how many more marvels might be discovered by exhaustive research into the lives of *all* the holy members of
the Society of Jesus.

A lesser-known Jesuit saint and wonder-worker is St. Francis (of) Jerome. Saint Francis Jerome, whose real name is
Francis di Geronimo (Hieronimus), lived from 1642-1716.
When insolent people interrupted his preaching in open
spaces, horses and oxen pulling carriages and carts would
kneel down. Fishermen loaded their nets and boats with
miraculous catches after St. Francis Jerome's intercession.
Even a lava flow from Mt. Vesuvius came to a halt at his
prayers and those of the populace.

Francis wanted to be a missionary to far-off lands, but his
superiors established him for life as the regular preacher at
the Gesu Nuovo church in Naples, and the surrounding
area. Because of the great crowds—up to 10,000 per sermon—he often spoke outdoors. He did not hesitate to hold
up a skull to move his hearers, or to bare his shoulders and
use the discipline on himself to remove their resistance and
move them to repentance. And every Tuesday he spoke
about Mary at the Church of Santa Maria.

The nephew of Pompey Prudente gives an account of the
death and resurrection of Pompey, a capable physician of
Naples. St. Francis had been sent for, but Pompey died
before his arrival. When the saint did arrive, he knelt down
and began the Litany of Our Lady. When he got to the
words *Sancta Maria,* he took his crucifix from his breast, got
up, and with a fiery countenance, cried out three times in a
loud voice: "Pompey, in the Name of Jesus Christ and San
Ciro, I command you to answer me!" At the third command,
Pompey opened his eyes and asked, "What do you want with
me?"

"We want you to remain with us." The saint turned to the
bystanders, exclaiming: "What a good God is ours! Praised
be His Holy Name for evermore!" He then continued with

the Litany of Our Lady and blessed the doctor with the relic of St. Ciro. The doctor was alive and well. (One suspects that St. Francis Jerome covered up his miracles with St. Ciro as the Curé of Ars covered his with St. Philomena.)

Another miracle of St. Francis Jerome concerns a dead child whose body had been abandoned by its mother. On one of the last days of the Carnival in Naples, a woman named Marie Alvire went to the Church of the Gesu where the Blessed Sacrament was exposed (one assumes she wished to make reparation for the sins committed during Carnival time). Marie saw Father Francis Jerome kneeling in prayer a short distance from his confessional. He beckoned to her to come, and said, "Go to my confessional and you will find a baby left there. I think she is asleep; please take her up and bring her to me."

This was the saint's way of covering up, or establishing hope. It reminds one of the words of Our Lord before He raised Lazarus: "Lazarus our friend sleepeth." (*John* 11:11). But the child was truly dead. The mother, named Francesca, who had abandoned her child, knew very well that it was dead. Marie found the tiny body wrapped in a shroud, with stiff little limbs and a face as white and cold as marble. ("Then therefore Jesus said to them plainly: Lazarus is dead."—*John* 11:14).

"Father . . . the poor little creature is dead, as you can plainly see."

The saint said no, and he bade Marie loosen the cloths that bound the child's arms to its sides. He laid his hands on the child's head, made the Sign of the Cross on her forehead, lips and breast. Stroking her face with a caressing gesture, he called her name: "Teresella!" To Marie's astonishment, the closed eyes opened, the rigid features relaxed, and the color began to return to the child's pale cheeks. The saint said with a smile, "Did I not tell you that she was only asleep? Now raise her head a little, and we will give her some water." The priest then opened the baby's lips with his finger and put a few drops of the water of San Ciro into her mouth. Marie, who still had the baby in her arms, noticed that it had two teeth above and two below.

The saint then told Marie to put the baby back where she had found it. She was then to go to another confessional, where she would see a veiled woman kneeling and crying bitterly. Marie was to tell her, "Francesca, go to Father di Geronimo; he wants you."

When Marie fulfilled her errand, Francesca said to her, with some surprise and annoyance, "How does Father di Geronimo know me, and what does he want with me?" Nevertheless, Francesca obeyed; Father Francis asked her why she was weeping and why she did not take her little daughter out of the confessional where she had left her. Francesca replied that she was weeping over her sins, and that she had no children.

"Go to my confessional and you will see whether it is true that you have no child."

Francesca obeyed, and at the confessional the child stretched out her tiny hands, calling aloud, "Mama, mama!"

"Teresella, my darling, you are alive!" cried the delighted mother. Francesca hastened back with her baby to Father Francis, and explained how Teresella had sickened days before and finally died. She, a poor widow, had no means for a funeral, so she had prepared the body for burial and left it early in the morning in the confessional, hoping the Fathers would give it a Christian burial. Francis Jerome gave Francesca a generous alms and exhorted her to go to confession.

This miracle is recorded in the life written by A. M. Clarke (Benziger, 1891). This was the sort of miracle concerning which St. Francis Jerome asked witnesses to say nothing until after his death.

Here we also mention a very sobering incident involving St. Francis Jerome which is described in another chapter (p. 239). A woman of sinful life had died suddenly; with a crowd of people the saint entered the house of the dead woman and called out to her: "Catherine, where are you now?" Catherine's eyes opened and a sepulchral voice

Right: A statue of Blessed Margaret of Castello (1287-1320), blind, hunchbacked and crippled, who worked many miracles including raising a man and two children to life again. (*Statue by Tony Moroder.*)

Below: Princess St. Elizabeth of Hungary (1207-1231) saving the life of a child who had fallen down a well. St. Elizabeth raised three young children, a youth, and a stillborn infant. Married around age 14, she was deeply in love with her husband; she bore four children before being widowed six years after her marriage. St. Elizabeth showed great tenderness toward the poor, assisting multitudes. She died before age 24. (*Painting by Piero della Francesca, c.1410-1492; from the predella of the Perugia altarpiece.*)

88-1

Above: St. Catherine (Karin) of Sweden (1331-1381) in heavenly glory. Catherine was the daughter of St. Bridget of Sweden; she raised two men from the dead. Catherine was married about age 14, but she persuaded her husband to join her in making a vow of perpetual chastity. Later she joined the religious order her mother had founded. (*Painting by Atilio Polombi, 19th c.*)

Right: St. Bridget of Sweden (1303-1373), who is said to have raised two or three persons who had been pronounced dead. St. Bridget is best known for writing her *Revelations.* She bore eight children, and after her husband's death founded the Brigittine Order.

Sᵗᵉ **BRIGITTE**
Canonisée par Erasme.

188-3

St. Bede the Venerable (c.672-735), who recorded the account of Drithelm's death, visit to Hell, Purgatory, Limbo and the vicinity of Heaven, and of his return to life and subsequent life of severe penance. This event became known all over England; it led to many conversions. Venerable Bede is best known for his *Ecclesiastical History of the English People;* he is considered the "father of English history." Venerable Bede is the only English Doctor of the Church. (*Illumination from Bede's* Life of St. Cuthbert, *late 12th c.)*

Upper: Holywell, or St. Winifride's Well, in Flintshire, Wales.
Lower: Chapel over the Well. According to centuries-old tradition, St. Winifride (d. c.650) was beheaded by young Prince Caradoc when she refused to conform with his lustful desires or to marry him. A fountain, Holywell, sprang up where her head had fallen. Her head was restored, she became a nun, and she lived for a number of years. Holywell became a tremendous place of pilgrimage and many, many cures have been reported there over the centuries, as well as at least one raising of the dead.

CHARITAS

Above: St. Francis of Paola (1416-1507), who raised his dead nephew so that he could become a monk (the nephew's mother had refused permission for this). St. Francis of Paola's life is full of miracles.
Right: St. Teresa of Avila (1515-1582), who raised her dead six-year-old nephew, Gonzalo. St. Teresa was a great reformer of the Carmelite Order, a foundress of convents, a contemplative and author of mystical books and a Doctor of the Church—as well as a most charming woman. She is one of the greatest saints in the Church, and is known as "the glory of Spain."

Art Catholique, Paris/Schamoni

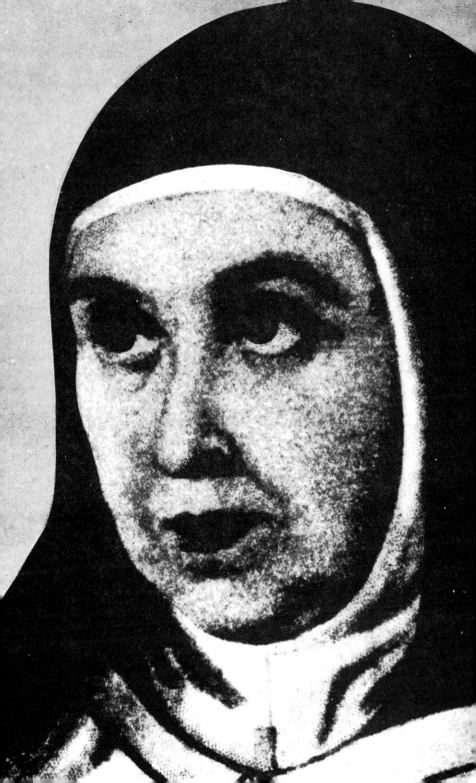

Upper: Famous 14th-century portrait of St. Catherine of Siena (1347-1380). Through Catherine's ardent prayers, her mother, Mona Lapa, returned to life; a spiritually careless woman, she had died without receiving the Last Sacraments. St. Catherine pleaded with God; He heard her prayer.
Lower: St. Catherine receiving the stigmata.

R. Washbourne

St. Bernardine of Siena (1380-1444) and the IHS symbol he devised for veneration of the Holy Name of Jesus. St. Bernardine is one of the all-time greatest preachers, often speaking to crowds of up to 30,000 (without a microphone, of course). He raised four persons; and through his intercession the boy Blasio Massei came back from death to relate what he had seen in Heaven, Hell, Purgatory and Limbo.

Left: St. Domini (1170-1220), who is known t have raised three persons from the dead, as well as one wh was nearly dead. St. Domini founded the Order of Preach ers (Dominicans), which im mediately took off and grew a a phenomenal rate and soo produced some of the greates saints in the Church, includin St. Thomas Aquinas, St Catherine of Siena, and St Vincent Ferrer. (*Portrait b Fra Angelico.*)

Upper right: St. Dominic call young Neapolion back to life Neapolion had been killed b falling from a horse. Domini offered Mass, prayed for th young man, and then com manded him: "Young man, i the Name of Jesus Christ, say to you, arise!" Neapolio arose.

Lower right: St. Dominic save some English pilgrims from drowning in the Garonn when their overcrowded ferr sank; St. Dominic's praye brought them to the surface.

St. Ignatius Loyola (1491-1556), who brought back to life a man named Lessani, who had hanged himself after losing a lawsuit. Ignatius cut him down, but efforts to revive him failed. Ignatius prayed in tears, sorrowing that a man should die in such a manner. Then he arose and pronounced over Lessani the Holy Name of Jesus; Lessani opened his eyes, came to himself, and expressed sorrow over his action. He then made his confession and received the Sacraments, and soon afterward expired. This account comes from the official acts of canonization; the miracle caused quite a stir in the area. St. Ignatius is the founder of the Society of Jesus, the Jesuits.

St. Philip Neri (1515-1595), who raised the 14-year-old boy Paolo Massimi. When he came back to life, the boy told Philip, "Father, I forgot to mention a sin, so I should like to go to confession." After the confession, Philip spoke to Paolo for about a half hour, and then the boy expired serenely in the saint's arms. On March 1, 1855 Pope Pius IX granted a special Mass Proper to commemorate this event every March 16 in the chapel of the Palazzo Massimo. After St. Philip Neri's death, two dead children came back to life through his intercession; the saint also performed numerous other miracles. He founded the Congregation of the Oratory, the Oratorians.

St. John Bosco (1815-1888), the friend of youth, who raised at least two boys from the dead. The most famous was the raising of a 15-year-old boy named Charles in 1849. The boy stated that he would have gone to Hell, but a beautiful Lady had told him there was still hope for him. After coming back to life and then making a good confession to St. John Bosco, Charles chose to die again, now prepared to meet his God. St. John Bosco founded the Salesians.

St. Paul of the Cross (1694-1775), who raised to life a child who had fallen out of a church window to the pavement below and had been pronounced dead. He also gave life back to a hen which had been stolen from a poor woman and subsequently cooked and served at table. On another occasion a slaughtered ox returned to life in response to a blasphemous sinner's boast: "I will be as soon converted as that ox returns again to life!" St. Paul of the Cross founded the Passionist Order.

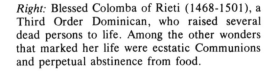

Left: Father Vincent Bernedo (1562-1619), Spanish Dominican missionary to South America, who raised to life a dead widow about to be buried, and called back to life an Indian boy who had drowned, the son of a poor miner.

Right: Blessed Colomba of Rieti (1468-1501), a Third Order Dominican, who raised several dead persons to life. Among the other wonders that marked her life were ecstatic Communions and perpetual abstinence from food.

sounded, as though coming from beneath the house: "In Hell! In Hell!" People fled in terror. Having received this testimony to the eternal damnation of an immortal soul, St. Francis Jerome exclaimed with great emotion: "In Hell! God Almighty! God most terrible! In Hell! In Hell!" Many conversions followed this incident; it was recorded during St. Francis Jerome's canonization process.

Besides the great, well-known missionaries, there are simpler, and often unknown members in any large religious order. In 1599 Brother Coadjutor Antony Pereyra, S.J. suffered a mortal malady on the island of St. Michael in the Azores. After receiving the Sacraments, the brother's body became cold. However, as there seemed to be some almost-imperceptible sign of life in a very faint beat of the heart, they did not bury him. By the third day there were evident signs of decomposition.

But on the fourth day Antony opened his eyes, breathed, and spoke. Under obedience, the brother related how his soul had been separated from his body. His guardian angel and St. Anthony of Padua had saved him from some demons rushing upon him. He also saw the delights of Heaven and the crown yet to be won by him. He witnessed terrible scenes of Hell. He saw the abyss of flames violently burst forth and flare upward as the new material of arriving souls was fed to it. He heard himself consigned to the fires and agony of Purgatory.

Brother Antony was then allowed to return to earth, and his soul returned to his body. For long afterwards Antony performed terrible penances, suffered much illness for 46 years, and died in 1645 in the odor of sanctity.

23

RESURRECTION MIRACLES PERFORMED BY ST. PATRICK, APOSTLE OF IRELAND

*"He that eateth my flesh, and drinketh
my blood, hath everlasting life: and I will
raise him up in the last day."*
—John 6:55

It has been said that St. Patrick (c.389-c.461) performed a thousand miracles. And why not? Many more (40,000) were prudently attributed to St. Vincent Ferrer, the Dominican missionary and "Angel of the Judgment."

Moreover, the author knows of no saint for whom there are claimed so many *resurrection* miracles during one apostolic lifetime as for St. Patrick; there were as many as 39 of these wonders. Thirty-three are mentioned in one specific report:

> "For the blind and the lame, the deaf and the dumb, the palsied, the lunatic, the leprous, the epileptic, all who labored under any disease, did he in the Name of the Holy Trinity restore unto the power of their limbs and unto entire health; and in these good deeds was he daily practiced. Thirty and three dead men, some of whom had been many years buried, did this great reviver raise from the dead, as above we have more fully recorded."

The above is quoted from *The Life and Acts of St. Patrick,* translated from the original Latin of Jocelin, Cistercian monk of Furnes of the 12th century, by Edmund L. Swift,

Esq., Dublin, 1809. A writer that far back probably had sources not available 800 years or more later. Paul Gallico (in *The Steadfast Man*) wrote the following concerning the value of tradition: "Tradition is sometimes more to be trusted than written records, and particularly in a country such as Ireland, where in the early days there was no written record and history was handed down by the poets in the form of sagas, and memory was cultivated far beyond what it is today. In pre-Christian Ireland every educated man's head was the storehouse for the archives of the nation."

St. Patrick was a great missionary bishop who converted a whole land from paganism, overturning the religion of the druids. He consecrated 350 bishops, erected 700 churches, and ordained 5,000 priests. In less than 30 years the greater part of Ireland was Catholic; St. Patrick so consolidated it in the Christian faith that during the Protestant Revolt Ireland was almost unique in its preservation of the Faith. Even to-day, people speak of "the faith of the Irish."

It is hard, indeed impossible, to comprehend such a vast and enduring transformation without the visible support of God through great works and wonders. But that is what Christ promised to His Apostles, and it has been historically demonstrated in the well-attested lives of His great missionary saints.

St. Patrick himself has personally attested to some of these signs and wonders: "And let those who will, laugh and scorn—I shall not be silent; nor shall I hide the signs and wonders which the Lord has shown me many years before they came to pass, as He knows everything even before the times of the world." This seems to apply in particular to his prophetic dream-visions.

In his *Letters* (as in his *Confessions* and his *Letter to Coroticus*), Patrick wrote such things as: "I was not worthy . . . that He should bestow on me so great grace toward that nation." And: "I baptized in the Lord so many thousands of persons." And: "that many people through me should be regenerated to God." Patrick also wrote: "that I might imitate, in some degree, those whom the Lord long ago foretold would herald His Gospel, for a witness to all nations before the end of the world." St. Patrick indicated that the Holy Spirit was within him, and he compared himself with St. Paul in a reference to the "unspeakable groanings" of the Holy Spirit.

Further, the ancient author quotes from a reputed "epistle" (letter) of St. Patrick to a friend in a country beyond the sea:

> "The Lord hath given to me, though humble, the power of working miracles among a barbarous people, such as are not recorded to have been worked by the great Apostles; inasmuch as, in the Name of Our Lord Jesus Christ, I have raised from the dead bodies that have been buried many years; but I beseech you, let no one believe that for these or the like works I am to be at all equalled with the Apostles, or with any perfect man, since I am humble, and a sinner, and worthy only to be despised."

Perhaps because of rumors and his fame St. Patrick was trying to put things in proper perspective. The word "humble," in his usage, probably meant "lowly" or "insignificant." The author of the ancient manuscript observes that he admired the greatness of Patrick's humility more than his raising of the dead. Patrick himself knew well that his abundance of charismatic gifts (given by God for the glory of God and the benefit of others), far from making him holy, could be a great liability.

Despite his limited number of references to his own greatness, and despite their modesty, it is obvious to anyone familiar with great missionary saints that the spiritual greatness indicated above and displayed in Patrick's life would also call for the marvelous gifts often accompanying such apostles—the most common of which is the working of numerous miracles, including the raising of the dead.

Anyone can gather from his writings, and also from the results of his apostolate of 20-30 years, that St. Patrick was a resolute, steadfast "iron man"; he was a bishop who established monastic discipline in a pagan land, who apparently baptized hundreds of thousands, who converted princes and turned pagan princesses into virgin nuns, who converted the worshipers of idols and the sun and impure things, and who organized and built many churches, leaving behind priests to care for souls. These were the tremendous and enduring accomplishments in one apostle's missionary lifetime.

St. Patrick's was an achievement unique in history. Thus it would seem to be a moral certainty that St. Patrick raised the dead on several occasions. This chapter has been cut down from an originally much longer manuscript-chapter on his reported raisings of the dead, because of the lack of historical records on these matters. Herein are presented only the best substantiated cases.

Since St. Patrick is claimed to have worked 33 resurrection miracles, it seems a moral certitude that he truly must have worked at least a good number of such wonders, even if the count of 33 may not be exactly accurate. (Some details may be confused, and thus two slightly different accounts could actually refer to the same event.) It is only fair to report at least several of these.

One day St. Patrick came to a place called Fearta. On the side of the hill two women had been buried. Patrick ordered the earth removed; in the Name of Christ, he raised them up. The two proclaimed that their idols were vain and that Christ was the true God. Along with the women, many bystanders were baptized. As the ancient writer observes, Patrick not only revived these two from a double death (both temporal and eternal death), but by this miracle he gave spiritual resurrection to many other souls.

When Patrick came to Dublina he prophesied how great that small village would someday become. He also caused a fountain to spring up there. It happened that in the region nearby, the young son of the king lay dead in his chamber. The sorrow over his death was compounded when it was learned that his sister, who had gone to bathe in the neighboring river, had drowned in midstream. Her body was finally found resting on the riverbed, and was laid out beside that of her brother. Tombs were prepared for both according to pagan custom.

At this sorrowful time the rumor spread that Patrick of Ardmachia (Armagh), who in the Name of the Unknown God had raised many that were dead, had arrived in the village. The king, Alphimus, promised that he, his nobles, and the whole "city" would be baptized into the new faith if his two children were restored. Patrick, seeing the opportunity for a great gain of souls, raised them both to life.

By the physical resurrection of the prince and princess, the spiritual resurrection of the whole area from the darkness of paganism and idolatry was accomplished. And the temporary resurrection of bodies (that is, until they died again) gave a promise of eternal life in Heaven and of the resurrection of the body on Judgment Day.

After the raising of this royal brother and sister, churches were built and tributes appointed to Patrick as their patron, that is, as the first Archbishop (or Bishop) of Ardmachia. It is reputedly from the revived Princess Dublina that the present great city of Dublin got its name.

In the country of Neyll, a King Echu allowed St. Patrick to receive his beloved daughter Cynnia as a nun, though he bewailed the fact that his royal line would thereby end without issue. The king exacted a promise from Patrick not to insist that he be baptized, yet to promise him the heavenly kingdom. Patrick agreed, and left the matter in the hands of God.

Sometime later King Echu lay dying. He sent a messenger to St. Patrick to tell him he desired Baptism and the heavenly kingdom. To those around him the King gave an order that he not be buried until Patrick came. Patrick, then in the monastery of Saballum, two days' journey away, knew of the situation through the Holy Spirit before the messenger even arrived. He left to go to the King, but arrived to find Echu dead.

St. Patrick revived the King, instructed him, and baptized him. He asked Echu to relate what he had seen of the joys of the just and the pains of the wicked, so that his account could be used for the proving of Patrick's preaching. Echu told of many other-world wonders and of how, in the heavenly country, he had seen the place Patrick had promised him. But the King could not enter in because he was unbaptized.

Then St. Patrick asked Echu if he would rather live longer in this world, or go to the place prepared for him in the heavenly kingdom. The King answered that all the world had was emptiest smoke compared to the celestial joys. Then having received the Eucharist, he fell asleep in the Lord.

There was a prince in Humestia who was baptized. Later he expressed unbelief about the doctrine of the Resurrection. After St. Patrick quoted various texts from the Scriptures, the prince said that if Patrick would raise his grandfather, by then buried many days, he would believe in that Resurrection which Patrick preached.

Patrick signed the tomb of the grandfather with his staff, had it opened, and prayed. A man of very great height, but not as big as a "giant" who had recently been raised from a huge tomb by Patrick, came forth from the tomb. He described the torments that went on in Hell, and was baptized. He received the Eucharist, and retired again to his former sepulcher and "slept in the Lord." After witnessing this miracle none doubted the truth of the Resurrection.

On another occasion a band of men who hated St. Patrick falsely accused him and his companions of stealing, and sentenced them to death. Patrick raised a man from a nearby tomb and commanded him to witness to the truth of the case, which the resurrected man did. He protested the innocence of Patrick and his companions and the deceit of the evil ones. In the presence of all, the resurrected man also showed where the alleged stolen goods—some flax—were hidden. Many of those who had conspired for the death of St.

Patrick now became his converts.

It is interesting to note that each of the miracles related here was aimed at establishing truth, besides doing good to various individuals. Here is a final example.

An evil man named Machaldus, and his companions, who placed on their heads certain diabolical signs called "Deberth," signifying their devotion to Satan, plotted to mock St. Patrick. They covered one of their group, Garbanus, with a cloak as if he were dead. Garbanus, though in perfect health, was placed on a couch as if laid out in preparation for burial. The men then sent for Patrick, asking him to raise the covered Garbanus from the dead. This was a fatal mistake.

St. Patrick told them it was with deceit, *but not with falsehood,* that they had declared their companion dead. Disregarding their entreaties, Patrick went on his way, praying for the soul of the derider.

Then, uncovering their friend, the plotters found Garbanus not feigning death, but actually dead! Contrite of heart, they pursued St. Patrick; they obtained pardon and were baptized. At their entreaty, St. Patrick also revived the dead Garbanus.

The same once-evil Machaldus became a great penitent, a bishop eminent in holiness and miracles, and became known as "St. Machaldus."

Patrick also once raised to life a dead horse belonging to the charioteer of Darius. He also restored to the charioteer the health he had lost after accusing Patrick of killing the horse.

One wonders why men question and marvel so at the "miracles of the saints" as if these were really *their own* miracles? If one thinks of these wonders as being primarily the miracles of God, which they are, why marvel? They are not "miracles" for God; for Him they are quite "ordinary" actions.

In the appendices at the end of Jocelin's *Life of St. Patrick,* in the *Selections from the Elucidations* of David Rothe, sometime bishop of Ossory, that bishop quotes another learned bishop: "Credulity may enter even the most virtuous mind; but when eminent men decline from this readiness of belief they fall into the opposite error, and become incredulous, while there is little fault in credulity, but much in incredulity."

Let no one doubt that the Lord gave to the humble Patrick the gift of raising the dead to life—for the glory of God, the proof of the True Faith, and the salvation of countless souls.

THE BLESSED VIRGIN MARY

24

RESURRECTION MIRACLES PERFORMED THROUGH THE INTERCESSION OF OUR LADY OF CZESTOCHOWA AT JASNA GORA, POLAND

"And the wine failing, the mother of Jesus saith to him: They have no wine. . . . His mother saith to the waiters: What-soever he shall say to you, do ye. . . . And when the chief steward had tasted the water made wine . . . [he] calleth the bridegroom, and saith to him . . . thou hast kept the good wine until now."
—John 2:3-10

Pope Pius XI, who had been Apostolic Nuncio to Poland, secured a beautiful copy of the image of Our Lady of Czestochowa and placed it in a Vatican chapel as a memento of his stay in Poland. During World War II, Polish pilots with the British Royal Air Force kept an image of the same Lady of Czestochowa, patroness of their native land, in a little shrine in a hangar of their bomber squadron.

The Madonna's face is dark, and the picture is therefore often called the "Black Madonna." It has two scars on it: In 1430 a sacrilegious swordsman of the heretical Hussites slashed at the original picture. There is also a scar on the throat from a Tartar's arrow in an action at the castle of Belz. When an artist during the reign of Jagiello retouched the portrait, these scar marks always reappeared, despite his expert attempts to efface them. Apparently Our Lady wants man to remember her sorrows and to recall that she is a Mother who understands sorrow and suffering.

Thus the national shrine of Poland at Jasna Gora (Bright Hill) is much older than Fatima, Lourdes or even Guadalupe. The full history of the famous miraculous picture is not known. Ladislaus installed it in its present location—the Church of the Assumption—on August 26, 1382, the Wednesday after the Feast of St. Bartholomew. On that day he signed an official document ordering the erection of a convent, cloister, and church on Jasna Gora, the Bright Hill.

Ladislaus later brought in the white-robed Pauline Fathers to take charge of the shrine, and they have guarded it ever since. The miracle stories that follow were culled from the accounts of the many wonders that have been effected through the intercession of Our Lady of Czestochowa, as preserved by the Pauline Fathers at Jasna Gora.

This famous Marian shrine is in the Archdiocese of Cracow, the see city of Pope John Paul II when he was the Cardinal Archbishop there. When the Pope visited Poland in 1979 the Poles poured into Jasna Gora, as did many other pilgrims from far-off places. The shrine is intimately connected with the faith of the Polish people and their patriotic loyalty as one nation, a *Catholic* nation despite its puppet Communist leaders whose power is enforced by Soviet tanks.

This special chapter on one great Marian shrine should suggest what dramatic miracles might be found if lengthy investigations were made into other, and even more ancient, Marian shrines—not to mention shrines of Our Lord and of great saints.

In 1517, a Polish child named Samuel died. He was the son of Stanislaw and Anna Wadzic of the town of Husiatyn in the county of Kamienicki. The child's body had been twisted by the excruciating pain he suffered. He died on a Saturday, the day dedicated to Mary, so his mother Anna fell on her knees in tears, offered the cold corpse to the Blessed Virgin Mary, and made a solemn promise to make a pilgrimage to Jasna Gora.

After a night of sorrowing by the casket, Stanislaw went to the church on Sunday morning to make the necessary funeral arrangements, while Anna continued to pray. When the father returned home he learned that the deathly pallor had suddenly left the corpse, rigor mortis had given way to normal reflex action, the boy had opened his eyes and, smiling, had reached out his arms from the casket. Stanislaw beheld his healthy son in his wife's arms!

In thanksgiving, the happy family made the pilgrimage the next day to Jasna Gora. They brought with them two candles the size of their resurrected son, to be burnt before the miraculous image of the Madonna of Czestochowa.

In the year 1564, a group of teenagers in the peaceful village of Zborow in the county of Kalis conducted a mock trial. The make-believe villain, Valentine Zeroniski, son of the town solicitor, was duly condemned and, with the help of his friends, hanged from a tree limb. They all thought him a very good actor, for he even kicked his feet as if it were for real.

But their pleasure at his performance turned to terror when they saw his face grow pale and turn a purplish hue. Fearfully, they tried to release him, but their boyish strength was insufficient. They fled their play-acting gallows, and overwhelmed with fear of punishment, told no one. The body hung, slightly swaying from the limb.

When the six o'clock Angelus bell had rung and darkness had fallen and Valentine had not returned, his parents went calling and searching. Late at night, by the light of lanterns and tapers, they found their dead son hanging from the branch of a willow tree. They took the body down, but all their efforts at resuscitation proved fruitless.

The parents fell on their knees and pleaded to the Madonna of Jasna Gora for mercy on their son. That compassionate Mother, who had once held the dead corpse of her own Son on her knees, responded to their plea. Valentine opened his eyes wide. He looked about, and then rose up alive and well. A fresco on the ceiling of the chapel at Jasna Gora recalls this miracle.

An incident which took place in 1598 concerns a little girl

named Ema, two years old, the daughter of Maciej and Jadwiga Klimczak, residents of Kazimierow. One day when Ema's parents had left her in the care of a babysitter, the latter set the child on the sill of a high open window where, from her high perch, Ema looked about happily at the entrancing countryside. But in a moment of forgetfulness, the sitter stepped away from the child—who lost her balance and fell. When the terrified sitter rushed down to the ground, Ema was dead.

When the parents returned they were torn between sorrow and anger. But they had to face reality, so they dressed Ema in white burial clothes, put a green wreath resembling a crown on her head, and placed a holy card of the image of Our Lady of Czestochowa in her small hand. Thus, with heavy hearts, father and mother began their vigil.

Their eyes were centered on the picture in their daughter's small hands. Suddenly the parents seemed to have a special flash of inspiration that made them both cry out together: "The Lady of Czestochowa! In her goodness she brought so many others back to life. She will help us! She will not refuse our plea and supplication!" (Note that in the sixteenth century, the Polish recognized Mary's great power of raising the dead because of her *past* interventions in this regard.)

The father and mother placed the little casket in their wagon and started for Jasna Gora. The sun shone on them by day and the moon by night, but the once-bright eyes of Ema remained closed. Two, then three days passed, as they journeyed on. Mother and father were mostly silent, like their child's body, except for their audible prayers.

The fourth day arrived, and only half the journey to Our Lady's shrine had been covered. Still they held the reins, guiding the wagon steadily ahead. The eyes of Maciej and Jadwiga were almost closed from so many tears and sleepless nights. Then—suddenly—the body of Ema began to move; her eyes opened, and she rose up alive and well! The overjoyed parents continued on to the shrine in order to thank the Blessed Lady of Jasna Gora.

One cannot help but admire such faith, and its reward. How much faith like that is found in the West today?

In 1625 a lengthy trial in Warsaw ended with the sentencing to death by drowning of one Anna, daughter of the peasant Bartlomiej and his wife Jadwiga. Anna had been sent to Warsaw to work and help her parents with their expenses.

Anna had been a good country girl, and she became a good servant in Warsaw. But unfortunately, she fell in with a man whom she thought sincere. Anna became pregnant, but the man would not marry her. With her baby born out of wedlock, and filled with shame, fear and despair, Anna threw the child out the window onto the bank of a nearby river. She was tried and sentenced to death.

When the judges sent the chaplain to prepare the condemned girl for death, the priest found her sincerely contrite; he recommended that she place herself under the protective care of Our Lady of Czestochowa.

On the day set for her execution, a curious crowd followed Anna to a bridge over the Vistula. They saw the executioner tie a huge stone to Anna's legs to make sure she would remain submerged in the deep river.

There stood Anna, still young, full of vigor, eager to live, but doomed to death because of one fatal mistake, one moment of despair. She fell on her knees before the assembled people, wept bitter tears, and declared before the crowd her sorrow for her crime. She begged God's forgiveness; then she begged Our Lady of Czestochowa for help, and in return she vowed to reform her life.

But the executioner had to do his duty despite sympathy from the crowd, so he threw Anna into the river. As she struck the water she uttered a shrill cry; the crowd stared silently and in awe as the waters closed over her. Then the river flowed on as peacefully as before.

Some witnesses stayed there nearly a half hour as the Vistula flowed on toward the sea. They seemed fascinated, looking at the waters, knowing the young girl was down there, weighed down by the heavy stone. Suddenly there was a murmur, and then an outcry! In the distance the onlookers saw the surface of the river break as the form of a girl shot up from the depths! She swam toward the shore with ease and clambered up onto the bank. Anna had survived!

Anna explained to the astonished witnesses, who had rushed over to her, that as she rested on the bottom of the muddy river, Our Lady of Czestochowa had appeared to her. Our Lady had removed the stone attached to Anna's legs and had ordered her to swim to the shore.

The judges and all those present fell to their knees in praise and thanksgiving to Mary for the miracle. Later Anna, her mother, and many of the witnesses to the miracle went to Jasna Gora and made a solemn deposition there. They returned to their homes to lead exemplary lives.

In 1643 two miners, Jan Wieliczko and his son Wawrzyn, carrying their tools, began to descend together on a single rope down the 60-foot shaft of a small mine they operated. The rope broke and they fell to the rocky bottom far below. The mountaineers of the area assembled and, after much difficulty, brought the two bodies, crushed and mangled, to the surface.

Though all seemed beyond any human aid, the people did not despair. With the simple faith of the Polish, they fell on their knees and implored Our Lady of Czestochowa for mercy. Suddenly the two men stood up, healthy and well. All raised their voices to sing the praises of the Blessed Mother. ("If you have faith as a grain of mustard seed . . .")

In 1680 the townspeople of Nowograd heard the local church bell tolling for the burial that morning of Judge Mikolaj Grocholski. He had died after a long and painful illness. The judge was much loved, and, according to the Polish custom, his grave was decorated and a buffet lunch prepared for the mourners. But when the pallbearers raised the coffin for the hearse, the judge sat upright in his coffin!

At first everyone fled in fear, but then, seeing that he was real flesh and blood and not an apparition or ghost, they returned and questioned him. His Honor explained: "When

I was dying and could not confess my sins because I had lost my power of speech, although I was still conscious, I raised my heart to God, and begged the Madonna of Czestochowa to restore my health and life, making a promise to visit Jasna Gora. Now I have come back with her help to confess my sins and do penance for them." All were greatly impressed, and the funeral buffet turned into a joyful banquet.

But the judge procrastinated on fulfilling his promise to visit Jasna Gora, and became seriously ill again. When the final moments seemed at hand, he again turned to Mary, contrite and begging for another chance. That night he received an inspiration, or warning, not to delay, and the next morning he rose from bed well and healthy. He immediately left to fulfill his vows at Mary's shrine.

Not long after this a friend of the judge, a knight, John Kozlowski, while participating in military maneuvers, was thrown at high speed when his charger stumbled; he died of a broken neck. When the judge heard of the tragedy he traveled six hours to arrive at the place of the knight's death. The judge fell on his knees beside the body, and with his eyes fixed on one spot, prayed to his heavenly benefactress: "O Lady of Jasna Gora, just as you have brought me back from the dead to serve you, please restore him to life so that he, too, can wait on you, just as I." All present joined in beseeching the Blessed Virgin Mary.

Before the eyes of the entire audience, Sir Kozlowski, knight of Poland, arose. As becomes a knight, he was able to go on a steed to thank Our Lady of Jasna Gora.

Szymon Wruszewski, a citizen of White Russia, became mortally ill in Lent of 1628 and died on Holy Thursday morning. As his family wanted to give him a solemn funeral, they postponed the funeral until after the joyful celebrations of Easter. But with the Resurrection on their minds, the family also prayed that the Lord who had arisen after a Good Friday death might also raise Szymon, through the intercession of His Holy Mother Mary.

On Holy Saturday, after the *Gloria* bells had rung out and

the last rays of sunset were leaving the horizon, Szymon arose from his casket. All sang the praises of God and Mary; the Resurrection *Alleluias* of Easter had never carried such meaning, nor had they ever been sung with such spontaneous enthusiasm.

In 1674, Stefan, a son of Malgorzata Zloczewska became seriously ill, and his mother vowed a donation of a gold memento to the shrine at Jasna Gora if Our Lady of Czestochowa would heal him. But Stefan died. However, the mother was not discouraged by his death; she considered this a further test of her persevering confidence in Mary, and she continued to pray.

By and by the mother heard the excited voice of the nurse who was watching over the corpse. The nurse was crying that Stefan's eyes were moving, his color was returning, and he was coming to life. The mother rushed in and cried out: "Stefan is alive!" Her son had been brought back to life.

On February 8 of 1720 a priest by the name of Michael Pruszynski, Canon of Kijow, pastor of Toporow, in the deanery of Bielski and the diocese of Luch, departed this world. Remarkable occurrences followed. Later that year (on June 14, 1720), very much alive, he made a deposition under oath before witnesses as to what had happened four months earlier.

The priest told how he owed his vocation to Mary, how he had grown ill in recent years, had become paralyzed, deaf and blind, and was like a living corpse. Knowing his demise was near, he made his last will. As he was informed later by the three priest witnesses, he died later that day, February 8, 1720.

They placed him in the prepared casket, dressed simply in his white priestly alb. He was carried in the closed coffin to a cold dark room where normally he should have frozen completely. (Poland in February!) Father Michael said that while he lay within his coffin, the venerable patriarch of the Pauline Fathers, St. Paul, appeared to him, took him by the right hand, and said, "Arise, and go pay your respects to the

Madonna of Czestochowa, because it is by her grace and intercession that you are rising from the dead."

As St. Paul disappeared with the words, "Jesus and Mary of Czestochowa," Father Michael, from within the coffin, began to call for help. Turmoil ensued; some fled, while others pulled at the boards sealing the casket. When he was released, the priest first asked for St. Paul, but the saint was gone. Father Michael then realized he had spent a whole day in freezing cold dressed only in a thin alb. Yet his body was warm and normal in every respect.

Despite protests, Father Michael left at once for Jasna Gora, a distance of 70 miles. On his return he brought a beautiful portrait of Our Lady of Czestochowa. It was placed in the church and many of his parishioners received graces and blessings through it and through the Lady it represented.

In 1747 an infant named Jozefa Magdalena, just a few months old, daughter of Antoni and Anna Karwat of Salicia, became ill and died. All night the mother wept over the baby's lifeless body, praying to Mary of Jasna Gora to restore her child. Friends and relatives began to scold her: "You expect the Blessed Mother to resurrect your child. You are not worthy of it. Stop your lamenting and give to the earth that which belongs to it."

The mother, unnoticing, seemed to have a sudden inspiration. She stood up facing the assembled mourners and said, "You do not understand me! If my child does not come to life here, I am taking her to Czestochowa, and there for sure the Blessed Mother will restore her life and health." With that the mother picked up the miniature basket with the small stiffened corpse, and getting into a wagon, began to pray in audible tones. But the Blessed Mother did not delay longer; she restored the child then and there. Then all the witnesses cried out, "A miracle! A miracle!"

In 1748, a nursemaid took her small two-year-old charge, Anna Gorniakowna, for a walk on the outskirts of the town of Lancuc. It was a beautiful spring morning, and as Anna ran about, she discovered a cave. The child took advantage of the momentary inattention of her attendant and playfully hid within the grotto. Without warning, there was a sudden landslide, and the sandy walls of the cave closed in on Anna, completely burying her.

The nursemaid ran frantically yelling for help. Responding workers labored for over two hours before they reached the little body, bruised, cold, purple-hued, dead. The mother—in great anguish yet with great faith—took the small corpse toward the church of the Dominican Fathers. Friends and relatives tried to stop her, protesting, "What are you doing? The girl is already dead. At least place her in some kind of casket."

"Let me go," she replied firmly, "because I am sure that Mary of Jasna Gora will restore her to me alive."

The mother ran into the church and placed the child in the care of Mary, promising to visit Jasna Gora in homage and thanksgiving. Anna opened her eyes and smiled. The mother went at once to the shrine of Our Lady of Czestochowa.

In 1749, in the vicinity of Kleczur, Ewa Wozniacka, a professional nursemaid, took little Janek (or Jasio?) along the bank of a river. Ewa was distracted momentarily, and Janek slipped and plunged into deep water where a strong undertow pulled at him. Hearing the splash, Ewa ran to the spot, but could only watch the little boy disappear beneath the turbulent water. Fearing punishment, Ewa ran away.

A woman passing by had witnessed the entire tragedy and ran to inform the mother, who raced to the scene, followed by many others. Again and again in the ensuing search the dragnets came up empty. Finally, after a long period of diving and dragging operations, the icy, water-soaked body of the boy was brought to shore.

The mother fell on her knees, her tears dropping on the limp body, and offered her child to the Queen of Jasna Gora. The heavenly Mother had pity on her; Janek opened his eyes, smiled, and cuddled to the breast of his mother.

In the history of the Church there have been many miracles involving the raising of the dead—even of three or more persons raised at one time. But seldom has one encountered a revival from the dead that began so tragically and ended so joyously as the following miracle of Our Lady of Czestochowa.

In 1540 a really gruesome event left a lasting memory among the inhabitants of Lublin, a few miles from Jasna Gora. Marcin Lanio, operator of a large slaughterhouse, went to town on a shopping tour. His wife, Malgorzata, left her kitchen momentarily to borrow some yeast from a neighbor. She needed it for the batter she was about to bake in her large oven.

Malgorzata left her two youngsters at home; Poitrus, only four, who had often watched the butchers slaughter the livestock in the yard, decided to imitate them. In his childish mind the nearest and most convenient victim would be his little brother Kazio, age two, sleeping peacefully in a nearby crib.

Without realizing the consequences of such an action, Poitrus took a sharp knife and slashed the throat of his oblivious innocent brother. Seeing the blood gush out, Poitrus realized that something bad had happened, and overcome with fear and dread of punishment, he hid inside the large baker's oven left open by his mother.

Within a few moments the unsuspecting mother returned, and not hearing the children, assumed they were both asleep. She finished preparing the batter and started the log fire in the oven in which Poitrus lay hidden. Poitrus, poor child, suddenly realizing his terrible predicament, began to scream in agony.

The poor mother's blood froze: Realizing where the boy was, she finally managed to pull him out, but the boy had already suffocated in the smoke-filled oven; he lay lifeless in her arms. As the mother looked about, paralyzed at this sudden tragedy, her eyes fell upon her other son, lying slain and blood-soaked in his crib.

The double shock was too much for the poor woman. She

became demented, struck her head against the wall, pulled at her hair, tore her clothes to shreds, and became like a madwoman.

Her unsuspecting husband, Marcin, walked in on this dreadful sight. When he saw his wife in that condition between the two corpses of his sons, he did not pause to think, but in great emotion, and apparently thinking she had killed them both, he grabbed a nearby axe and crushed her skull with one blow.

After a little while Marcin's mind cleared. He realized what he had done, and dreadful fear and remorse seized him. In the meantime neighbors and friends were gathering with mixed emotions, and some with pious advice. Marcin seemed to have a heavenly inspiration, and he turned from despair to hope in Our Lady of Czestochowa, to whom he had always been devoted.

By now all the neighbors had arrived, standing in shock and amazement at the triple tragedy. Their astonishment grew as Marcin silently and determinedly loaded the three corpses onto a wagon, made the Sign of the Cross, and turned the horses toward Jasna Gora. Some watched in fear, others in tears.

Marcin journeyed on silently toward Jasna Gora, with people assembling along the roadside as they saw or heard of the strange sight of a man with three dead persons, apparently his own wife and sons, in an open wagon. As Marcin came to the shrine, several kind persons improvised three caskets and carried them into the chapel. Marcin remained at the door, prostrate, pleading with the entering faithful to pray to the Madonna for his family. Perhaps he felt too guilty to go inside.

Inside the shrine, Blessed Stanislaw Oporowski, a devout priest, was conducting Benediction of the Most Blessed Sacrament. The portrait of the Black Madonna, high above the main altar, seemed to glow with heavenly splendor. Blessed Stanislaw and all the congregation joined in supplications for the poor husband and his family. The three dead persons laid out before all—the mother and two little boys—were a piteous sight.

All the congregation sang the Blessed Mother's hymn, the *Magnificat*. A supernatural feeling penetrated the chapel. At the words, "Because He that is mighty hath done great things to me, and holy is His Name," a shock came over the congregation.

The three lifeless corpses came to life and slowly rose from their places.

For a moment there was a seemingly age-long silence. Then came a spontaneous outburst, and all joined in a thanksgiving hymn to the Madonna. Husband, wife, and children had a marvelous reunion.

Soon the fame of this tremendous miracle spread worldwide. The Emperor ordered a true copy of the miraculous portrait of Our Lady of Czestochowa to be made and placed in the Cathedral of Vienna. Copies of this portrait should also be placed in many home shrines and in public places. Just as the Poles (many in America) love Our Lady of Jasna Gora, so should everyone love her.

If the faith of the Poles were imitated by others, there might well be many more miracles like those which gave splendor to Jasna Gora, the Bright Hill sanctuary of Our Lady of Czestochowa.

25

RESURRECTION MIRACLES OF THE BLESSED VIRGIN MARY IN THE AMERICAS

Our Lady of Itati (Argentina), Our Lady of Guadalupe (Mexico), Our Lady of San Juan (Texas, U.S.A.)

> *"And this is the will of my Father that sent me: that every one who seeth the Son, and believeth in him, may have life everlasting, and I will raise him up in the last day."*
> —John 6:40

The Blessed Virgin Mary is credited with the raising of the dead in more than one of her shrines, although there apparently have been no documented resurrections of the dead at such famous modern shrines as Lourdes in France or Fatima in Portugal, or at Banneux and Beauraing in Belgium.

An early American shrine of Our Lady was established in Argentina, at Itati, near Corrientes. It began in 1615 with an ancient wood carving of the Virgin. Around the year 1900 it was moved from Itati to Corrientes, about 40 miles away.

It once happened that a young son of Maria Salinas from Vera, Rodrigo, died suddenly. A cousin, Maria de Velazco, daughter of Martin Sanchez, came to take him away. In front of many people she tied a ribbon, especially dedicated to the devotion practiced in honor of Our Lady of Itati, to the boy's head. The boy came to life again fully restored and healed.

A second instance at the same shrine involved a dead Indian who had been bitten by a poisonous snake. When the sacristan, Juan Guayamaro, tied a ribbon of the devotion to the dead Indian's head, he too came alive.

Most North Americans are unfamiliar with the many shrines south of the Rio Grande and the miracles that have been worked at holy places throughout Mexico and in other countries of Central and South America. In those old and large Catholic populations, although many areas lack priests and sometimes the faithful are not well instructed, the vast extent of the spread of Catholicism and the numbers of Catholics argue for the likelihood of a certain number of supernatural manifestations.

Our Lady of Guadalupe has been Queen of all the Americas since 1531. Few Americans have been to Guadalupe, in Mexico City, where Mary's apparitions to Juan Diego took place 450 years ago. In that year there occurred (to the best of the author's knowledge) the very first instance in the New World of a man returned from the dead through the intercession of the Blessed Virgin Mary.

In December of 1531 Our Lady appeared to the Indian, Juan Diego, and asked for a chapel to be built in her honor. As a confirming sign to convince Bishop Juan de Zumárraga, Mary not only produced for Juan miraculous Castilian roses on the barren hillside of Tepeyac (then it was open countryside, now it is a suburb of Mexico City), but also added one of the most remarkable miracles of all time. On Juan's tilma—the cape-like garment worn by the Aztecs at the time—she miraculously imprinted a beautiful image of herself. A third confirming sign was the cure of Juan Bernardino, Juan Diego's uncle, who had been gravely ill.

Bishop Juan de Zumárraga accepted the signs—the roses, Juan Bernardino's cure, and the portrait, a "painting" no artist can explain—and he arranged a festive celebration for December 26, 1531. There was to be a grand procession to conduct the holy image from his chapel to the shrine chapel that had been hastily constructed in only two weeks.

Present on this historic occasion were Hernando Cortez, the conqueror and ruler of Mexico, and many notables of this new and great possession of Spain. When the procession arrived at the chapel, a Mass was celebrated with the conquistador conquerors and the native conquered embracing before the altar. Then and there the seeds of a new nation were sown—a nation that would eventually be known as Mexico.

During the procession outside, as some of the Indians celebrated with native musical instruments and symbolic dances, one Indian was accidentally—and fatally—shot in the neck with an arrow. With grief interrupting their joy, but also with hope in their wonderful Queen, the people brought the dead Indian to the new shrine and laid him down there.

They removed the arrow and confidently implored Our Lady to restore him to life. The Blessed Mother did so, and the Indian got up on his feet. Then the jubilation was even greater than before, as everyone praised God and Mary with great joy. Subsequently a large painting was made depicting many of the prominent figures participating in the festival, including the resurrected Indian. This painting can be seen today in the Basilica of Guadalupe, where great numbers of pilgrims also venerate the miraculous image of Our Lady of Guadalupe.

According to the laws of nature, the unique image of the Virgin on coarse cactus cloth should have disintegrated centuries ago, especially since it has been exposed to the open air for many years. Another marvel: it has been scientifically demonstrated that the the eyes of the image of Our Lady contain the reflected image of Juan Diego, as would be the case with a photograph but not with a painting (See *The Wonder of Guadalupe* by Francis Johnston.).

Because of the miraculous image, its symbolism, and the accompanying miracles, over nine million of Mexico's Indians were converted to Catholicism within a short time. This was a mass conversion that seems unparalleled in history; it is perhaps the greatest miracle of all in North America. It occurred at the same time that five million souls in Europe left the True Faith to follow the Protestant Revolt.

Mexico's northern neighbor, Texas, also possesses a miraculous image of the Blessed Virgin Mary. On April 27, 1980, the new edifice of the shrine of Our Lady of San Juan was dedicated in Hidalgo County, near Brownsville. Cardinal Madeiros of Boston attended, as did a large crowd of clergy and faithful. It had taken five years to build.

At the old shrine, around the year 1683, a child who had been killed in an accident was restored to life through prayers to Our Lady of San Juan, because of her miraculous image there.

— PART THREE —

OTHER WONDERS: FURTHER SIGNS OF IMMORTALITY

" . . . He [Christ] will come at the end of the world; He will judge the living and the dead; and He will reward all, both the lost and the elect, according to their works. And all these will rise with their own bodies which they now have, so that they may receive according to their works, whether good or bad; the wicked, a perpetual punishment with the devil; the good, eternal glory with Christ."

—*The Fourth Lateran Council*
1215

26

REVIVALS OF THE DYING
RIVAL THE RAISING OF THE DEAD

"Like unto them that go down into the pit."

—Ps. 142:7

The skeptic Emile Zola once went to Lourdes, reportedly saying that if he saw one cut finger healed he would believe. It happened that while he was there a woman whose face was terribly disfigured from lupus was cured. A doctor at the shrine presented the case to Zola, saying that the latter had received more than he had asked for. Yet Zola went away saying it could not be (supernatural), simply because it could not be. He had been given a singular grace and privilege and he tried to explain the wonder away.

In 1903 a Dr. Alexis Carrel went to Lourdes to prove its miracles either true or false. This young French scientist had an open mind. On the train carrying the sick to Lourdes there was a woman (Marie Bailly) so desperately ill that, as a doctor, Carrel thought she should not be there at all. Worse, he feared that they would try to put her, in her condition, into the bath of the spring's "miraculous" water. Her stomach was greatly distended with her disease. Lying on her stretcher she looked like a woman in late pregnancy.

After the bath the woman was wheeled near the grotto where Mary had appeared, and Dr. Carrel, standing a little distance away, observed her. He noticed her color changing, and then the big maternal-like rise of the blanket over her stomach quickly lowered. The humped area dropped until her body had the flat appearance of a woman in normal condition.

Along with other doctors, Carrel examined her at the Lourdes Medical Bureau. She was completely cured. Carrel went over to the church and wept.

Some older doctors at Lyons, France, told Carrel that if he were known to sympathize with the manifestations reported at Lourdes he would not get far in medical circles. But Carrel was an honest scientist, and he did not try to deny his experience at Lourdes. Carrel left Lyons for the United States, joined the Rockefeller Institute for Medical Research, and became America's first Nobel Prize winner in science (1913).

In the physical and material order, as Zola seems to have recognized, the immediate healing of a cut finger is as impressive as a cure of a person in his final agony or a raising from the dead, because these feats are all equally impossible for nature or the scientific powers of man. Science, of course, can heal wounds and cure some of mankind's ailments. But science must use *some visible means,* and such means of effecting cures take time. However, a healing—in any age—for which no natural explanation can be found is most reasonably attributed to a supernatural power at work.

There are many, many well-documented cures on record at the Medical Bureau of Lourdes, France. Three of the most famous cures effected by Our Lady of Lourdes are those of Pierre De Rudder, Gabriel Gargan, and Jack Traynor.

Pierre De Rudder, a farm laborer of Jabbeke, Belgium, suffered a lumbering accident in 1867 which crushed his left leg and broke its bone. The two ends of the broken leg bone, about an inch apart, could be seen through the open wound; there was no sign of healing. The leg could thus be turned in any direction, and could almost be folded in half. In addition, the bandage was constantly wet with blood and offensive matter given off by the open wound; the odor was insupportable. Doctors recommended amputation of the leg, but Pierre De Rudder refused, even though he was in pain every waking moment. This situation continued for eight years, and numerous people witnessed the terrible condition of the leg.

In 1875, Pierre undertook a pilgrimage to the shrine of Our Lady of Lourdes at Oostakker, near Ghent, Belgium, where the grotto is modeled after that of Lourdes. There, praying in front of the grotto, he felt a strange sensation and agitation. He arose, completely cured. Medical examination revealed that the leg was healed, closed up, and completely normal except for scars. An examination of the bone itself after De Rudder's death showed a one-inch-long piece of new bone connecting the pieces that had been severed. This piece of bone, unaccountable on natural grounds, had apparently been created instantaneously as Pierre De Rudder prayed to Our Lady at the Lourdes grotto of Oostakker on April 7, 1875.

A second case was that of a French postal worker named Gabriel Gargam, who was paralyzed from the waist down in a train accident. He then developed gangrene in both feet (the feet were black, and when they were rubbed, the skin came off and pus oozed out) and he became unable to speak out loud. The railway company agreed to pay Gargam a pension for life, conceding that he had become "a veritable human wreck, whose intelligence alone has remained unimpaired."

Although Gargam had not been in a church for 15 years, he acceded to his mother's urging to make a pilgrimage to Lourdes. He arrived there on August 20, 1901; at that time he was 32 years old. He went to Holy Communion with little faith, but as he received the Host he was seized with a great longing to pray, and his faith suddenly returned; he loved God with his whole heart and laid his life at Our Lady's feet.

Later that day, at the Blessing of the Sick with the Blessed Sacrament, Gargam found that he was able to arise to take several steps. The next day he was able to walk normally, though he still had no leg muscles. The gangrene was completely gone, leaving only scars. All the doctors in the Medical Bureau, both believers and unbelievers, agreed that Gabriel Gargam had been cured, although his case had been medically incurable. Subsequently Gabriel spent every summer at Lourdes as a brancardier, or attendent for the sick.

He had his disability pension from the railroad discontinued.

A third case was that of Jack Traynor, an Englishman from Liverpool whose service in World War I had left him with his right arm paralyzed and its muscles atrophied, and with his legs partially paralyzed. He was also epileptic, sometimes suffering three fits per day. An operation to remove shrapnel left him with a hole in his skull an inch wide, through which his brain's pulsations could be seen. The hole was covered with a silver plate. The British War Pension Ministry considered him completely and permanently disabled and granted him a 100% pension for life.

After suffering for close to ten years, Jack Traynor decided to join a pilgrimage to Lourdes in July of 1923. The trip proved extremely trying, and he arrived in Lourdes in miserable condition. The brancardiers hesitated to take him to the baths for fear he would die on the way there, but Jack insisted. In the bath his paralyzed legs became suddenly agitated, and during the Blessing of the Sick with the Blessed Sacrament the same sensation arose in his arm, which had been "dead" since 1915. Traynor attempted to rise from his stretcher, but the attendants knew he was an obstinate pilgrim and apparently feared he was going to create a scene. Traynor was given a hypo. It was not until the next morning, after the injection had worn off, that it became obvious he was cured. He jumped out of bed, pushed aside two brancardiers, and ran to the grotto in his night clothes to thank Our Lady, with the brancardiers racing after him!

The story of Jack Traynor's cure was reported in the Liverpool newspapers, and he was welcomed home by the Archbishop and crowds of people at the train station. Doctors conducting a medical examination concluded that new nerves and muscles must have been created in Traynor's previously atrophied and skeleton-like arm. The only trace of its former condition consisted in the fact that the right forearm was a little less thick than the left forearm. His paralysis and epileptic fits had suddenly and completely disappeared, showing that his brain injury had been repaired.

In addition, the hole in his skull closed up, leaving only a slight depression.

Jack Traynor went to work in the coal and hauling business, which involved lifting 200-lb. sacks of coal. Nevertheless, the British War Pension Ministry refused to cancel his pension, as he had been declared incurable. Like Gabriel Gargam, Jack Traynor served as a brancardier at Lourdes. His cure resulted in a great number of conversions in Liverpool. (Further details on these cures are available in *After Bernadette: The Story of Modern Lourdes,* by Don Sharkey.)

Some cures are almost as remarkable as resurrections from the dead. While the raising of a dead person back to life is actually a greater miracle than a cure, some cures have involved more extensive "repairing" of the human body than does a raising from the dead.

Consider the case of a child who has been drowned, or of a person who has been asphyxiated, while otherwise perfectly healthy. In a way, restoration to life in such cases may seem less wonderful than the case of a dying person, immense with tumors, liquids, pus, decayed cells, etc., who is cured. All that matter is suddenly removed, and the entire burdened system is restored completely whole through a miraculous cure.

Where did all that matter go? Immediate absorption by the body itself would kill the person because of the impossible burden placed upon the heart and because of uremic poisoning.

Or consider the cures of dying persons whose bodies are in the opposite condition: skeletal, or full of "holes," fistula, deep wounds, or missing bone. In such a case, all that is missing is instantly restored, whole and entire. This involves a new and immediate generation of tissue or a "creation" to fill in parts of the decimated body.

In a way, this filling-in is more wonderful than a "whole" corpse, such as that of a drowned person, being brought to life. Such a cure is also a matter of "new life."

The case of a healthy body suddenly dead and restored to

life is something like that of an otherwise good car inoperative because the battery is "dead," and perhaps having a disconnected small wire. The case of a dying person with so much missing, damaged or mangled is like that of a car that still has some power in the battery, but needs serious and costly repairs that will take much more time than recharging or slipping in a new battery and perhaps connecting a wire.

If nature tried to heal instantly or rapidly such a diseased dying person as described above, the person, far from being healed, would actually be destroyed. Emaciated concentration-camp victims, when freed, at times have died by simply eating too much at once. For the riddance of excess matter or the repletion of lost body tissue, an element of time is necessary.

So when doctors have considered certain patients to be as good as dead, or in their last agony from various wasting diseases or from deep wounds or lesions, or missing organs and parts, such immediate cures are of a very high supernatural order. They are almost parallel to actual raisings from the dead. Such cures of the *dying,* of course, are more numerous than those of the actually *dead* being raised. Their listing among miracles also accents the distinction made between *dying* persons cured and *dead* persons raised.

Thus a Church commission report concerning miracles attributed to St. Hyacinth stated: "In Cracow alone fifty dead persons [were] restored to perfect health." Note the differentiation between "dead" and "dying." Perhaps the commission's distinctions will reveal something to those "critics" who do not believe that intelligent men usually know whether someone is dead or near death.

There are many cases of persons brought back from death's door over the years that go unrecorded. Often there is no more notice than a change noted on the patient's chart, and a priest will be told, especially by non-Catholic doctors, that there has been a surprising change, or a reverse of trend in a critical or despaired-of case, after the priest's anointing of the patient.

Yet one seldom hears of the Church—or anyone else—bothering to obtain affidavits about such recoveries. The power of the anointing in the Sacrament is just taken for granted. As St. James wrote: "Is any man sick among you? Let him bring in the priests of the church, and let them pray over him, anointing him with oil in the name of the Lord. And the prayer of faith shall save the sick man: and the Lord shall raise him up: and if he be in sins, they shall be forgiven him." (*James* 5:14-15). It is also a fact that many cures have been worked through the Holy Eucharist.

Following are a few miraculous cures that practically amount to a snatching from the grave.

Sister Magdalen Arnaul, a nun at Le Puy, France, was dying, her body monstrously swollen from dropsy and palsy. Her physicians declared she would not live a half hour. A relic of St. John Francis Regis, the Jesuit missionary into the mountain regions of France, was applied to her stomach. In the presence of 14 eyewitnesses she was instantly cured. Certainly that is as miraculous as coming back from the dead, with death less than a half hour away.

What happened to all the noxious fluids associated with that monstrous swelling? This author had a dear sister, a nun, dying of cancer of the stomach, patient as a saint. But her abdomen was horribly distended and hard toward her last days, and near the end her eyes were rolling back and forth. Imagine being a personal witness to such a terrible situation, and then seeing a sudden metamorphosis to a normal healthy condition, a complete cure! Such was the case with Sister Magdalen. What about all the new cells that had to be instantly replaced in such a diseased body? And what about—as has happened in some established miracles—new and healthy organs instantly replacing severely damaged ones?

An awareness of these points may enhance appreciation of the greatness of such miracles from a medical point of view. What actually happens is a sort of "new creation"—physical, of course. After the instant destruction of all the old, dead, decayed, malignant cells and matter, there is an instant replacement or filling out of the body with healthy new cells, tissues, blood vessels, nerves, etc.

What a wonder to behold! Such miracles may be even more astonishing to doctors, who know the physiological factors involved, than to ordinary believers. No one should find such miracles beyond credibility, for they have happened again and again in the Church of the supernatural, the Holy Catholic Church. Any honest investigator can determine that.

There are two examples concerning near-death where a modern American saint was invoked. One of the miracles accepted by the Church in the process of Bishop John Neumann (1811-1860) being declared a saint was that of a dying child, Eva Benassi, being wonderfully healed in Italy in 1923. A second miracle from Bishop Neumann's process was that of Kent Lenahan, who was dying in July of 1949. He had been crushed and pinned between a utility pole and a car. His skull had been crushed, one of his eyes was protruding, and he had a very high fever. A piece of Bishop Neumann's cassock was put near him as he lay in the hospital. In the middle of the night he was found sitting up on the side of his bed. He subsequently became a champion weight lifter in Pennsylvania.

Consider another modern saint, Pope Pius X (1835-1914). Few know of the many miracles he quietly worked during his lifetime. Two nuns, both dying of cancer, were granted a private audience with him. When the nuns came in to see him they were looking desperately ill and weak. When they returned to friends who were anxiously awaiting them in the antechamber, the friends nearly reeled with shock and wonder, for both nuns were glowing with health. Outside in St. Peter's Square, the cab driver who had brought the nuns would not believe they were the same women—and he refused the fare. In a similar case, a mother superior of an orphanage was dying in India. When Pius X telegraphed her his blessing, she was healed. And there were other long-distance cures through this holy Pope. (Anyone desiring to check on the scientific testing of such miracles—medical terminology, etc.—can refer to the records of the canonical process of the saints' beatification and canonization.)

A number of saints, like St. Martin of Tours, healed lepers in an advanced state of that terrible disease. Think what was physically involved in that immediate transition from a "living death" to a living life! Biblical accounts of the cure of leprosy usually relate that the leper's flesh became like that of a little child. This is because the flesh had been created anew, without wrinkles or any of the defects of age.

St. Augustine writes of a child playing in the square of the church in the village of Ardurus where there was a shrine to St. Stephen. A cart drawn by oxen left the road and a wheel ran over the child, crushing him. As he was breathing his last, his mother snatched him up and placed him on the altar of the shrine. He not only returned to consciousness, but showed no sign of the injury he had just received.

St. Catherine of Siena (1347-1380), Virgin and Doctor of the Church, was a young woman of many wonders. In 1374 a plague epidemic struck Siena; in those days, plague could decimate an area. The founder and head of the Misericordia Hospital, a nobleman of Siena by the name of Matteo Cenni di Fazio, lay in bed, shaken by convulsions; his fever was high and he was very pale. Catherine came to his room and said, "Get up, sir, this is no time to be lying in bed!" Matteo arose immediately, cured, and apparently saved from approaching death.

St. Catherine cured her own director, Blessed Raymond of Capua, of the same plague even as he was preparing for the terrible death it would bring. There was also a holy hermit, Santi, living near Siena in a cave. He, too, caught the dreaded pestilence. Catherine had him brought to the city. He was dying; in his breathing she could hear the death rattle, but she ordered, "I command you, in the Name of Our Lord Jesus Christ, not to die." He was cured, and he got up and ate. He attended Catherine's death only six years later, and considered that he had not so much been cured as brought back to life.

There are many other instances that could be related from the lives of the saints and the records of Catholic shrines like Lourdes where people dying from all kinds of diseases or injuries were instantaneously restored to perfect health. There are well nigh endless such cases of dying men, women, and children either burdened with excess matter and liquids, or emaciated, skeletal and "eaten out," or with cavernous wounds, whose immediate restoration to health is a super-miracle that is *impossible* to nature.

Finally, there was a case involving St. Hilarion (c.291-c.371), in which it is uncertain whether the subjects were in an advanced dying condition, or actually dead. St. Hilarion (abbot) was a hermit monk at Tabatha, five miles from Gaza. St. Jerome, not far removed from Hilarion in time and in the same Palestine, recorded in his *Life of St. Hilarion* an account of three boys whom St. Hilarion saved from dying—or death.

These were not his only miracles: Hilarion had already told a woman barren after 15 years of marriage to have faith—and a year later he saw her with a son. Hilarion performed other wonders; he drove a demon out of the rich man Orion, who subsequently wanted to give rich gifts, at least to the poor. At Facida, near Rinocorura in Egypt, he cured a woman who had been blind for ten years. To help destroy the worship of Marnas, the great idol of Gaza adored by Duumvir of Gaza, Hilarion enabled the horses and chariot of the Christian Italicus of Majuma to "fly" ahead of the others in a chariot race, thus vanquishing both Duumvir and his false god.

It happened that Elpidius, later a praetorian prefect, well-known and honored by fellow Christians, was returning home with his wife Aristaenete and their three children after a trip to the great St. Anthony of Egypt. In Gaza, the three sons became seriously ill with what the physicians said was the incurable semitertian ague. In St. Jerome's words, "The distraught mother was crushed with grief and ran from one to the other of what seemed to be the corpses of her three children, not knowing which one to mourn for first."

Hearing there was a monk in the nearby desert, Aristaenete immediately set out with eunuchs and maidservants. It was only with difficulty that her husband persuaded her to ride on an ass. When she found Hilarion, she cried out, "I beseech you through the most merciful Jesus Our Lord, through His Cross and His Blood, that you restore to me my three sons, that the Name of the Lord Our Saviour may be glorified in the city of the Gentiles, and that His servant may enter Gaza and overthrow the idol, Marnas." Hilarion refused, saying he never left his cell nor entered even a small village, much less the city. The mother prostrated herself in desperation: "Hilarion, servant of Christ, give me back my children; Anthony watched over them in Egypt, you must save them in Syria."

Those present wept; Hilarion wept too, but he still said no. Aristaenete persisted until Hilarion promised he would enter Gaza quietly, after sundown. When he came into Gaza he stopped at the bedside of each child. He looked with sadness at the "feverish" body of each and called upon Jesus. Perspiration broke from each one, and within the hour they all took food. They blessed God and kissed the hands of Hilarion.

Because of this miracle many people came from Syria and part of Egypt beside Palestine; many believed and became monks. During his life St. Hilarion moved from country to country five times, trying to escape the people who constantly sought him out because of his holiness and his miracles.

Now, these three youths may have been merely dying, for the account mentions feverish bodies. But a very good researcher of the last century, translating the Latin *Vita St. Hilarionis Eremitae* by St. Jerome, says plainly that the three "sickened and died." And the same researcher concluded the account with the words: "The three sons who were dead arose, and were led to their mother." Critics may argue over texts and translations. Actually, the account in the twentieth-century translation (in a Fathers of the Church series) is not altogether clear or consistent. First the distraught mother runs from one to another of her sons, who "seemed to be corpses." Also, she is described as "not knowing which one to mourn for first." Later, the bodies are "feverish."

One scarcely "mourns" for ill but living children. Further, a mother with sons who are dying, or so near death that they look like corpses, is not likely to leave them at that supreme moment and go miles away with perhaps her whole household of eunuchs and maids (the family was not at home, remember, but traveling, probably with a reduced staff) to seek out a hermit.

Then, at the feet of the holy Hilarion, she begs "that you restore to me my three sons"; again, she pleads, "Give me back my children!" These terms certainly seem to refer to sons dead and lost as far as this life goes. And when Hilarion looks at each "feverish" body, it seems wonderful that "perspiration" breaks out.

Finally, while there is nothing unusual about "feverish" bodies breaking out in "perspiration," it would be remarkable for perspiration to break out from cold bodies that had been dead for hours while the mother made a journey into the desert and back. Nor does it seem that a miracle like the raising of three sick boys would attract such a number of people from far-flung places—but three boys of a prominent family who were raised from the dead would certainly attract a crowd. And it should be borne in mind that this miracle was one of Hilarion's early miracles, performed before his fame had become established on account of other wonders.

In any case, it can certainly be affirmed that many cures of the sick and dying, involving—as they do—the creation of new body parts or repair (partial recreation) of existing parts, are also a form of "resurrection miracle." Like actual raisings from the dead, they too affirm the creative power of God, who alone has made all things, both visible and invisible.

27

VISITS TO AND FROM
THE OTHER WORLD

"Unto the hope of life everlasting,
which God, who lieth not, hath promised
before the times of the world . . ."
—Titus 1:2

There have been many instances in history of visits to earth by spirits from the other world. There have also been mysterious visits of persons living in this world, or of their souls or spirits, to realms of the other world. These mysterious visits should serve as further proof to any reasonable person of the reality of another world, of Heaven and of Hell. For a Christian who believes in the supernatural, there can be little doubt that the supreme God in control of Heaven and Purgatory can allow occasional visits from their inhabitants to the brethren on earth.

Although visits from inhabitants of Hell will not be covered here, it is true that various persons have suffered from visits—and attacks, even physical attacks—from the devil. This happened to the Curé of Ars and to St. Louis De Montfort. Witnesses at St. Louis De Montfort's beatification investigation testified that during his life they had heard him struggling with the devil; they had heard the sound of fist blows as well as the swish of whips. This testimony was backed up by the saint's words on his deathbed, apparently spoken to the devil: "In vain do you attack me; I am between Jesus and Mary! I have finished my course; all is over. I shall sin no more!" It can be surmised that the devil was enraged by the large numbers of souls which these two zealous priests snatched from his hands and won for

Heaven. The devil once admitted to the saintly Curé of Ars, "If there were three such priests as you in the world, my kingdom would be destroyed."

The visits to earth by angels or by deceased human beings are usually referred to as "apparitions." (The word "ghost" can give a wrong impression.) The persons visited are usually saints and chosen souls, but at times they are very "ordinary" people. The visiting parties are usually Our Lord, the Blessed Mother, the angels and saints—very holy people; but again, sometimes they are "ordinary" people, such as souls from Purgatory.

Of course Jesus and Mary are in a special class because they have possessed their glorified bodies in Heaven since the Ascension of Christ and the Assumption of Mary. Except for Henoch and Elias, all others in Heaven or Purgatory are bodiless souls—although there is some speculation that St. Joseph may also have his body in Heaven.

Visits from persons in the other world are not matters of faith—that is, Catholics are not obliged to believe in a particular apparition. They are placed in the same category as private revelations—which, indeed, often accompany such heavenly visitations. Yet well-substantiated apparitions are worthy of credibility, particularly such great appearances as those of Our Lord to St. Margaret Mary concerning devotion to His Sacred Heart, and those of the Blessed Virgin Mary at Lourdes and Fatima.

There have also been many apparitions of angels, who have no bodies but who appear in human form (as they did to Abraham and Lot) to provide practical evidence of their actual presence. St. Michael reputedly appeared at Monte Gargano to the Bishop of Siponto and on Mont Saint Michel off the coast of France. The Angel of Portugal appeared to the three children of Fatima, and angels also appeared to St. Gemma Galgani and to Pere Lamy. In our own time, Padre Pio saw his guardian angel, as had St. Frances of Rome in the 15th century, Anne Catherine Emmerich in the 19th, and Cecy Cony (a little Brazilian girl who later became a nun,

Sister Maria Antonia) in the early 20th century (1900-1939).

The saints, too, have often appeared on earth—usually to other holy persons, but occasionally to all sorts of ordinary people. In an apparition, such a person's presence or communication is made obvious together with his body as it was known on earth. It is a manifestation of a "person" who is temporarily bodiless, living as a disembodied soul in expectation of the resurrection at the end of the world.

Whatever the method or means by which God allows saints or others to appear in apparitions, the recipients of such "visions" experience and refer to them just as if the person appearing were actually there in his body; the apparitions are usually radiant and accompanied by a strong but soft and beautiful light unknown to earthly experience. There is something unforgettable about genuine apparitions. Good spiritual directors can differentiate the real thing from illusions or hallucinations.

St. Teresa of Avila was allowed to see many souls for whom she had prayed as they were being released from Purgatory and were on their way to enter Heaven. A deceased religious appeared to St. Louis Bertrand of the Order of Preachers. Many souls appeared to St. Margaret of Cortona. St. Mary Magdalen de Pazzi saw a deceased fellow religious who was granted the privilege of spending her last hour of purgatorial satisfaction in adoration before the Blessed Sacrament. That completed, St. Mary Magdalen saw the sister depart joyfully for Heaven.

There have been many apparitions of St. Joseph, the husband of the Blessed Virgin Mary, one of which was to St. Teresa of Avila. He has always been a great patron of the Carmelites. St. Joseph also appeared to Emilie de Vealar, foundress of the Sisters of St. Joseph of the Apparition.

St. Maurice appeared to Venerable Benoite Rencurel, a shepherdess, when Benoite was eating her lunch and saying the Rosary.

St. Albert the Great, Dominican, Doctor of the Church, immediately after his death appeared to Gottfried von

Duisberg, his confessor, saying, "I am very happy," and spoke at some length of the splendor and glory surrounding him. He also appeared to a Cistercian abbess he had befriended, again speaking at length and ending with, "These are the marvels which I now contemplate with my own eyes." Albert further appeared to St. Mechtilde and to Theodoric the Lector at Triers.

St. Albert's fellow Dominican and Doctor of the Church, St. Catherine of Siena, was not alone when she received the wedding ring of mystical espousal to Christ. Also present were the Blessed Mother and Sts. John the Evangelist, Paul, and Dominic. This group has been beautifully depicted in art.

St. Jane Frances de Chantal, founder of the Visitation Order and spiritual daughter of St. Francis de Sales, Doctor of the Church, appeared to Jeanne DuHoux, mystic and Visitation nun, and taught her the practice of holy abandonment to God.

More contemporary appearances have also been seen: St. Gabriel of the Passionists appeared to St. Gemma Galgani, and St. John Berchmans appeared to a sick young novice, Mary Wilson, at the Sacred Heart convent at Grand Coteau, Louisiana, and cured her. St. Dominic Savio appeared to St. John Bosco and told the latter how much he, Dominic, had been consoled at the point of death by the Blessed Mother.

In the nineteenth century Our Lady, St. Joseph, and St. John the Evangelist were present in the tableau apparition at Knock, Ireland. And in the twentieth century St. Therese the Little Flower appeared to the stigmatist Therese Neumann and Sister Elena Aiello. Sister Aiello also saw an apparition of St. Rita of Cascia. And it is well-known that Padre Pio (died 1968) has appeared to a number of living persons.

An actual listing of the number of such apparitions would be virtually endless. These appearances testify to the reality of the glory of these saints, real "immortals" from another, better world. Their halos are promises of the eventual restoration of their bodies at the General Resurrection. These accounts should confirm our faith and strengthen our hope.

There have also been visits in the opposite direction: Visits of mortals to Purgatory, Hell and Heaven. Of course, one's soul never enters the real Heaven of the Beatific Vision except to remain forever. Even if one were lifted up to the "Third Heaven," as St. Paul was, it would not be to the Beatific Vision itself. The closest mortal man can come to that is a "partial" sight of God, or a very deep spiritual experience, as happened to Moses and Elias.

Those whose souls have been allowed to visit Heaven often describe it in terms of figures and scenes familiar to earthly sense faculties. The privileged persons see paradise gardens, hear glorious choirs of saints and angels (in human form) singing ineffable songs, and smell celestial fragrances. They especially see Jesus (in His humanity) and the Blessed Virgin Mary in great beauty and splendor. They experience great joy, and hate to "return" to earth again.

Of course the experience of Heaven goes much deeper than the sense level. The primary joy of Heaven comes from the vision and love of God. (See *The Happiness of Heaven,* by Fr. J. Boudreau.) This is difficult for our earthly minds to understand; nevertheless, those who have received the gift of contemplation experience a true foretaste of the union with God as experienced by the blessed in Heaven. (For a clearer idea of the presence of God in infused contemplation as great mystics have felt it, one should investigate Father Poulain's famous and as yet unrivaled work, *The Graces of Interior Prayer.*)

The day before St. Hyacinth died, while kneeling at the altar he saw a brilliant light come down from Heaven. On the light's great beam there descended a long procession of bright angels who escorted Our Lady as their Queen. They prostrated themselves around the altar until the Holy Sacrifice ended.

Then Our Lady motioned to Hyacinth and said, "Behold," and at that instant the heavens opened. Hyacinth saw Mary advance in majesty to the throne of the Most High. There was a great silence while the Eternal Father placed upon her head a crown of flowers and stars. Mary then turned to St. Hyacinth and said, "Behold, Hyacinth! This crown is for you." Then the vision ended.

St. Anthony of Egypt, the great hermit, saw St. Paul the first hermit (not the Apostle) being carried to Heaven by the angels after his death. Anthony also saw Paul being given a place in Heaven among the prophets and Apostles. For the most glorious visions of Heaven, with its multitudes of bright angels and saints, the ultimate source is of course the last book of the Bible, the *Apocalypse* of St. John.

Blessed Jordan, a superior of the Dominicans, was favored with a vision in which he saw Mary Queen of Heaven escorted by a multitude of angels and two princesses of Paradise. They were bringing food to the brethren, and Mary served them with her own hands.

Anna Maria Lindmayr (1657-1726), after seeing the sins and follies of the whole world, suddenly saw the Most High God. Before Him knelt a woman beseeching the all-holy God and praying earnestly for the sinful world.

Blasio Masseo, a boy who was taken to Heaven after his first death and who then returned to life, was impressed by the immense multitudes of angels that surrounded God's throne, and was awed by the inexpressible beauty of Mary, who ranked above all the heavenly choirs. (cf. p. 112).

The Venerable Anne Catherine Emmerich (1774-1824) was privileged to visit Purgatory in spirit. There she saw the sufferings endured, the workings of indulgences, and the pains of Protestants, who suffer much more in Purgatory than do Catholics, because no one prays for them or offers Masses for them. Anne Catherine Emmerich also visited Heaven, where she saw all kinds of supernatural wonders. During her lifetime she saw visions of many, many saints.

In fact, Anne Catherine Emmerich's entire life is one continuous fabric of supernatural visions and experiences. She narrated these to Clemens Brentano, and her fascinating life has been written up based on Brentano's notebooks (*The Life of Anne Catherine Emmerich,* by Fr. Carl Schmöger). A reading of this two-volume work will powerfully strengthen a Catholic's faith, for this saintly mystic was privileged to *see* the manifold truths of the Faith which the rest of us simply have to accept on faith.

St. Lydwine of Schiedam's visits to the other world were remarkable even among saints. She often saw Heaven as a great festal hall in a palace, with crystal and gold goblets, and with Jesus and Mary presiding over a love feast with the elect at the tables. More often Lydwine ran, under the care of her guardian angel, in a beautiful garden of Eden with marvelous trees and flowers. Along the lovely paths the saints would sing of the glories of God as on a beautiful eternal springtime morning. Lydwine's angel would help her over great clumps of roses and lilies.

St. Frances of Rome, foundress of the Oblates of Mary, visited both Hell and Purgatory, as did St. Lydwine. St. Teresa of Avila was shown the place in Hell that would be hers one day if she did not reform her life. Such salutary visions have been granted to a number of persons.

The saints always preach mercy, but often a tangible reminder of the immutable justice of God is also necessary in order to jolt people. St. Francis Jerome, preaching in a bad quarter of Naples, heard of the sudden death nearby of a sinful courtesan. With a crowd he entered her house and called to the dead woman, "Catherine, where are you now? Answer me!"

Catherine's eyes opened, her lips moved, and a sepulchral voice, as if from below the room, sounded on the ears of all: "In Hell! In Hell!" People fled. The saint came away exclaiming with great emotion, "In Hell! God Almighty! God most terrible! In Hell! In Hell!"

Many conversions followed that report from the nether world. As is so often the case, the Lord drew good out of evil. This miracle was reported during the canonization process of St. Francis Jerome.

The three children of Fatima were shown a vision of Hell by the Blessed Virgin Mary (who supported them during the terrible experience). Their vision was as real as if they were right there with the damned souls tossing about. It was an experience that utterly changed their lives, which afterward included the performance of great acts of penance and self-denial seldom heard of in little children. (See page 261).

St. Mary Magdalen de Pazzi visited the dungeons and prisons of Purgatory. St. Lydwine, conducted to Purgatory by her angel, saw there souls she knew. In one special case where she had helped a soul through Purgatory she saw the heavens opening for him as he went into glory. Blessed Catherine de Racconigi went to Purgatory and brought back an agonizing wound from a mere spark that had fallen on her cheek.

Here we also mention the scourgings by angels that were administered to St. Jerome, to Heliodorus (*2 Mach.* 3:25-29), and possibly also to Edelard (*Purgatory Explained,* p. 201)—as also the thigh of Jacob, which shrunk when touched by the angel with whom he had wrestled. (*Gen.* 32:25, 32). It is also prophesied that the future "Great Monarch" will receive a wound in his leg from an angel.

Finally (though many more stories could be recounted), St. Catherine of Genoa had many experiences concerning Purgatory and the souls there. She recorded them in her famous book, *Treatise on Purgatory,* which is still read today.

For those who desire more detailed knowledge about Purgatory, visits to and from Purgatory, and associated wonders, *An Unpublished Manuscript on Purgatory* and Father Schouppe's *Purgatory—Explained by the Lives and Legends of the Saints* are invaluable sources. In the latter, one will find stories of Purgatorial visitations and revelations from the lives of St. Margaret Mary, St. Teresa of Avila, St. Bridget of Sweden, St. Gertrude The Great, St. Francis de Sales, St. Catherine of Genoa, St. Magdalen de Pazzi, St. Lydwine of Schiedam, St. Margaret of Cortona, St. Thomas Aquinas, and the Curé of Ars. This chapter has indeed presented only a sampling.

28

MIRACULOUS BODILY PHENOMENA IN THE LIVES OF THE SAINTS— A PREVIEW OF THE RISEN BODY

"In a moment, in the twinkling of an eye, at the last trumpet: for the trumpet shall sound, and the dead shall rise again incorruptible: and we shall be changed. For this corruptible must put on incorruption; and this mortal . . . immortality."
—1 Corinthians 15:52-53

It is reported of Padre Pio that in his sufferings he sometimes hit temperatures of 120-125 degrees that broke thermometers. A burning candle held near St. Bernadette's arm while she was seeing the Blessed Virgin Mary brought no reaction. Certain Catholic mystics have been called "salamanders" because, like the mythical animal, they suffered and survived intense heat. Some mystics have "died" again and again without dying.

The three children of the Old Testament survived their enclosure in the fiery furnace, and St. Francis of Paola worked in a blazing furnace without harm. St. Christina survived similar and worse fires. St. John of God emerged unscathed after returning again and again to a terrible hospital fire to lead many patients to safety. The bodies of these saints in their miraculous experiences were more like impervious spirits than flesh and blood.

St. Maur ran on the water of a lake to rescue Placid. Other saints, like Francis of Paola, Raymond of Pennafort, and Hyacinth, used their cloaks to sail good distances over water. They were seemingly weightless. Still others, like the prophet Habacuc or St. Anthony of Padua, were miraculously transported over great distances. And there are many marvelous cases of the spiritual phenomenon of bilocation.

To search the lives of the saints is to find numerous wonders and extraordinary gifts. These give us some idea of the qualities that will belong to the resurrected spiritualized bodies of the just on Judgment Day. The supernatural or preternatural realities witnessed on earth support the promises of God for the future life.

It is one of the great works and glories of God that He can take a creation of His that is material or "animal," in that man has a body, and by giving it a soul, elevate that material creature to a state similar to that of the pure spirits; the Scriptures state that man is "a little lower than the angels."

Yet the spiritualized bodies of the blessed in Heaven after the resurrection will be gifted with qualities and powers no human body in its earthly state could exhibit. Man's body then will still be truly human, but it will be relieved of many of its present lowly functions, embarrassments, and limitations.

Food and drink are basic necessities common to any physical being. But in Heaven there will be no eating or drinking, as we now understand these actions. Nevertheless, all man's senses will be gratified in Heaven—though not by corruptible objects. Many saints lived for years without food—an anticipation of the life of Heaven.

St. Lydwine of Schiedam (1380-1433) lived without any food, or at certain times with very little. St. Catherine of Siena (1347-1380) did without food except for the Eucharist for years, as did many others for long periods: St. Angela of Foligno, St. Colomba of Rieti, and St. Peter of Alcántara. More recently, Therese Neumann (1898-1962) went over 30 years without food or water, except for the Blessed Eucharist. And Alexandrina Maria da Costa went from March 27, 1942 until her death on October 13, 1955, with only the Eucharist as daily food.

Neither Therese nor Alexandrina had any ill effects from

their abstention, nor did they have the usual bodily eliminations. Alexandrina was bed-ridden, but Therese Neumann engaged in her regular day-to-day activities. In fact, she steadily gained weight and became quite heavy despite her proven abstinence, so that her weight pattern matched that of her relatives. Truly, "not by bread alone doth man live," but by the Lord God—in a holy consecrated wafer that is His own Flesh!

Sleep is also a necessity for man. Like food and drink, without it man cannot survive for long. Saints like Peter of Alcántara (friend of St. Teresa of Avila) functioned with very little sleep, perhaps less than one hour in 24. St. Catherine de Ricci slept one hour a week. Others, like St. Catherine of Siena, Christina the Admirable, and St. Colette needed very little sleep. These saints were very active and were often burdened with heavy trials and sufferings.

Concupiscence of the body is something that troubles many good people, along with St. Paul, who bewailed a sting of the flesh and the pull of lower nature against the law of the spirit. But there have been saints like St. Thomas Aquinas who, for his heroic resistance to temptation against purity (a harlot sent by Thomas' family members to break his resolve to join the Dominican Order), was girded by an angel with a miraculous cincture which preserved him from temptations of the flesh for the rest of his life. There have been similar gifts of control over various other human temptations. This gives a preview of Heaven, where the flesh will no longer war against the spirit, and the integrity of human nature will be perfectly restored.

Levitation often accompanies ecstasy. Innumerable saints have been levitated to heights, thus defying the law of gravity. St. Teresa of Avila used to beg her fellow nuns to hold her down so she would not be embarrassed before the others. St. John of the Cross twisted bars of an iron grille in a convent as he resisted being drawn upwards. St. Francis of Assisi went so high he disappeared from sight. St. Joseph of Cupertino would hover near the ceiling of the chapel, and he "flew" in the air so often that he is now the patron of those who fly. "Floating" or "flying" are terms sometimes applied to such movements.

Transportation in miraculous ways impossible to ordinary mortals has also occurred among the saints. There is "mobile ecstasy," where saints have run above the ground rapidly or skipped the steps going up stairways. The saints were sometimes transported over long distances, as when St. Anthony of Padua was journeying from Padua in Italy to Lisbon in Portugal to help his father who was facing trial; St. Anthony suddenly found himself in Lisbon. Other saints have had similar experiences, such as a priest going on a sick call to another village and arriving there impossibly fast and without any tracks in the snow.

In addition, some saints in ecstasy have become so light that they could be easily moved with a mere push of the finger. On the other hand, some saints have become incredibly heavy, far beyond their normal weight. This happened to Agnes, the sister of St. Clare of Assisi, when several of her male relatives tried to remove her from the convent she had run away to join under cover of night.

Bilocation is perhaps one of the most mysterious wonders of all. Yet many saints have bilocated and continue to do so even today. There are such claims for more than one person living at the time of this writing. A few of the saintly persons who are known to have bilocated are St. Alphonsus Liguori, St. Anthony of Padua, St. Martin de Porres, Venerable Mary of Agreda, and Padre Pio.

For example, on one occasion St. Anthony of Padua was preaching from a pulpit when he stopped short, sort of reclined easily, and remained in that position for some time. The people, knowing of the wonders that surrounded St. Anthony, did not disturb him. After a good while he came to himself and resumed his preaching. In the meantime, St. Anthony had been present at another Mass, at which he had promised to participate, but which he had temporarily forgotten about.

St. Catherine of Siena would often experience a swoon in which her soul seemed to have left her body, leaving the body apparently dead. Some time later, she would return to normal. Therese Neumann often experienced a similar phenomenon.

Penetrating locked doors or other material substances has also been done by the saints. St. Rita of Cascia was a widow who had tried a number of times to enter a convent as a religious but was refused because of her age. Finally, a few of her patron saints—St. Augustine, St. John the Baptist, and St. Nicholas of Tolentino—took her in the middle of the night and placed her right within that convent, all the doors of which remained locked. The sisters then saw the hand of God and accepted Rita into their convent.

This miracle was like Our Lord miraculously appearing in the midst of the Apostles on Easter Sunday when the doors were locked, or emerging from His sealed tomb. St. Raymond of Pennafort had a similar experience with locked doors, and there is a person alive at this writing who is believed to have "passed through" a locked door.

These are obviously great miracles. The ordinary person would gain only bruises should he try to go through a brick wall or negotiate the hard timber of a closed door. This shows how the Lord can "exalt" the human body to operations above its natural abilities, without destroying the body which is being exalted.

Healing and the curing of all possible diseases, hurts, wounds and other disabilities are common in the lives of the saints and even after their deaths (sometimes through the application of their relics). These restorations forecast how, at Judgment Day, the raised bodies of the just will be free of any physical sickness, blemish, injury, malformity or bodily ailment.

The incorruption of the bodies of many of the saints, the bodies often remaining fragrant, supple, and undecayed against all the normal laws of death, is another dramatic indication of the ease with which God will be able to raise the body on Judgment Day. If God created the creature, man, out of nothing, He surely can restore him.

Two of the most remarkable cases are those of St. Bernadette Soubirous, who died in 1879, and St. Catherine Labouré, who died in 1876. St. Bernadette's body rests in a glass case in her convent in Nevers, France, visited by thousands of pilgrims every year. St. Catherine Labouré's body rests in a glass case in the chapel of the motherhouse of the Sisters of Charity at 140, rue du Bac, in Paris. In 1986 there are sisters at this convent who remember the exhumation of St. Catherine Labouré's body in 1933. They describe the body as having been so flexible and supple that the arms and legs could be moved freely, like those of a living person. (The book entitled *The Incorruptibles* treats of 102 cases of incorruption, and there have been many more.)

There have been many instances of the restoration, strengthening, elevation and transformation of man's superior or spiritual faculties—of his memory, intellect, and will. For some very brief examples: the wisdom given to Solomon, the intellectual gifts given by Our Lady to St. Albert the Great (and subsequently taken away before the saint's death because he had chosen human rather than divine knowledge), the practical intuition into the state of hearts of the Curé of Ars and Padre Pio, and the prophetic knowledge of Blessed Anna Maria Taigi—not to mention the sublime wisdom and expansion of the soul in infused contemplation.

Lives of the saints and other holy persons are full of such wonders. The point is that if one assembles together all these various gifts found individually in God's holy ones, he will find no difficulty in seeing how the bodies of ordinary mortals will possess similar qualities in a unified whole on Judgment Day.

In *First Corinthians* St. Paul says, "It [the body] is sown in corruption, it shall rise in incorruption. It is sown in dishonor, it shall rise in glory. It is sown in weakness, it shall rise in power. It is sown a natural body, it shall rise a spiritual body." (*1 Cor.* 15:42-44).

After the resurrection on Judgment Day, the bodies of the just will take on the properties which naturally belong to spirits, not to bodies—yet they will remain true bodies. This will be a perfection, not a deprivation, of bodily nature. Our Lord told St. Thomas to touch His glorified body after His Resurrection and, moreover, to put his hand into the wounds made in His body by the nails and by the thrust of the spear. He said: "See my hands and feet, that it is I myself; handle and see: for a spirit hath not flesh and bones, as you see me to have." (*Luke* 24:39). These wounds proved that He had a real human body—His own body. Yet Our Lord restrained the full light and splendor that would radiate from Him in Heaven.

There are four qualities that theologians generally attribute to a glorified body: impassibility, subtility (subtlety), agility, and clarity.

Impassibility means that the body will no longer be able to suffer any physical evil. Weariness, weakness, frailty, exhaustion, sorrow, disease, injury, discomfort from heat or cold or hunger and thirst, pain and death—all these will be no more. Every risen body of the just will be strong, healthy, robust, virile, in the bloom of perfect health. It will be integrated in a more wonderful way than any top athlete's, even at the peak of his physical maturity. "And death shall be no more, nor mourning, nor crying, nor sorrow shall be any more." (*Apoc.* 21:4). The risen body will be absolutely perfect and eternally incorrupt, as well as spiritualized and glorified.

The body of St. Charbel Makhlouf, Lebanese monk and hermit, remained incorrupt from his death in 1898 until his beatification in 1965. The body was soft and supple, and the flesh was of natural color; it used to bleed when cut, and it "perspired" a fluid years after Charbel's death. Charbel was called "the living dead saint." If the dead body of St. Charbel did not suffer the effects of death for 67 years, what then will the omnipotent God be able to do for risen bodies on Judgment Day? (Needless to say, thousands of miracles have been worked through St. Charbel.)

Subtility refers to the lightness and spiritual quality of the risen body. "It is sown a natural body, it will rise a spiritual body." (*1 Cor.* 15:44). This comes about because of the body's perfect subjection to the soul. But though it takes on the qualities of spirit, it remains a body. St. Thomas says that the risen body is subtle through completest perfection of bodily nature, and not through lack of that nature.

The third quality of the glorified body will be agility. "It is sown in weakness, it shall rise in power." (*1 Cor.* 15:43). This is another quality which properly belongs to spirits. The Creator has given man lordship over His lower creations on earth. But what is in store for man beyond this world and this life? The body will be so perfectly under the dominion of the soul as its mover that the person will be able to move almost instantaneously, and without labor, and will be able to move other bodies with a like velocity. With the gift of agility, spiritualized bodies will find no difficulty in traversing great distances in an instant. The body will become a perfect instrument, alert and quick to obey the soul.

There have been similar qualities miraculously given to the bodies of saints on earth. Such bodies were free from the usual weight of matter caused by the gravitational pull of the earth. Or they defied the nature of water, as when Hyacinth or Ceslas crossed rivers on their cloaks. Or they levitated, like Joseph of Cupertino, whose body, though far heavier than air, floated as if lighter than air.

It is said that St. John of the Cross, when offering the Holy Sacrifice of the Mass, had to do violence to himself to avoid levitating. He would bite the chalice in order to prevent this—like a person will bite his lips to avoid crying. The teeth marks can be seen on this chalice yet today. Likewise, St. Philip Neri had to hurry through Mass in order to avoid levitating.

Some scientists and explorers would give their lives—and

in some cases perhaps also their souls—to accelerate the speed of travel into far-off regions of space. Yet the littlest old lady, or some good small child, who was obedient and faithful to God, will be able to do infinitely more after Judgment Day than all the Cape Kennedys and Soviet launching pads can today, because of the agility of their spiritualized bodies.

On earth, the body is slow and sluggish in responding to the commands of the soul, and often it is rebellious. The body may even enslave the soul if the soul surrenders to physical urges. But in Heaven the dominion of the soul and spirit will be absolute over an obedient and totally responsive body.

Some of the saints performed wonders of abstinence from food and drink, extreme penances, and various heroic acts of self-denial, as evidenced by their continual labors and in the terrible trials they underwent. But all this will seem miniscule compared with the powers they will possess and exercise in their spiritualized and glorified bodies.

Obviously, one cannot know all that is in store for the blessed when they enter into eternal union with the all-generous God who has much more than the entire universe at His disposal. No one knows what the triumphant faithful may perform in the matter of supervising the material universe. St. Paul said, "Eye hath not seen, nor ear heard, neither hath it entered into the heart of man, what things God hath prepared for them that love him." (*1 Cor.* 2:9). Though lost in the contemplation of the Beatific Vision, the blessed will not be "frozen" in Heaven, but will enjoy the perfect exercise of all their powers of body and soul. (*The Happiness of Heaven,* by Fr. J. Boudreau, gives a good description of the wonderful joys and holy pleasures in store for the blessed.)

The fourth quality of the risen body is clarity. "It is sown in dishonor, it shall rise in glory." By clarity is signified glory, resplendent radiance, and beauty. The beauty of the beatified soul will flow over and communicate itself to the body. St. Thomas says that the glory of the soul will shine through the body even as a glass vessel shows the color of that which is contained within it. The degree of each saint's bodily glory will depend on the degree of glory of his soul, and this will depend on his degree of merit before God.

This quality of the glorified body was shown forth by Our Lord on Mount Thabor when He "was transfigured before them. And his face did shine as the sun: and his garments became white as snow." (*Matt.* 17:2). This was even before Our Lord's Passion and Resurrection; His purpose, at least in part, was to encourage His Apostles to believe in Him and to persevere through the dark days of Good Friday and the sepulcher because of the glory of the future which they had glimpsed. In Heaven, like St. Peter at the Transfiguration, the elect will exclaim before the glorified Christ, "Lord, it is good for us to be here!" (*Matt.* 17:4).

Our Lord once showed St. Catherine of Siena the soul of a woman named Palmerine, whom Catherine had saved from Hell by her prayers and fasting. This soul, though suffering in Purgatory, was yet exquisitely beautiful. St. Catherine's biographer, Bl. Raymond of Capua, states: "It was so brilliant that she told me she could find no words capable of expressing its beauty. It was not yet admitted to the glory of the beatific vision, but had that brightness which creation and the grace of Baptism imparts." If such is the radiant splendor of a soul in Purgatory, what will be its radiance in Heaven? And this soul will render the risen body likewise glorious and radiant.

Impressed as one may be with the powers of agility, such as levitation, bilocation, or other miraculous transport to far places, these abilities may seem quite unremarkable in Heaven compared to the glory, the clarity, of the risen body. After all, the light and splendor of the sun are more impressive than its movement.

There have been many instances of saints or other holy persons, particularly contemplative ecstatics, who have been seen with light, halos or aureoles around them. Sometimes the light has flooded the room of the person in ecstasy, calling attention to the graces he or she would have preferred to keep hidden. At other times witnesses have seen a light falling in a shaft upon them or radiating from their figures.

When Moses came down from Mount Sinai his face shone so brightly that two horns of fire seemed to come from his head. The people were awed, and the Bible says that to hide this radiance Moses had to wear a veil. So also have saints in ecstasy or levitation appeared gloriously radiant, as when St. Bernadette saw Our Lady in the grotto of Massabielle at Lourdes. St. Philip Neri was often raised in ecstasy and surrounded by light. King Ferdinand I of Naples saw St. Francis of Paola elevated in light when the saint was in the King's palace.

Many saints who were granted visions of Our Lord or the Blessed Virgin Mary claimed that the light surrounding the heavenly visitor was more brilliant than that of the sun. Nevertheless, the witnesses were saved from blindness by a special softness of that celestial light. By a special divine dispensation, the glory of Christ's soul did not overflow into His body from the first moment of His conception; this was so that He might fulfill the mysteries of our Redemption in a passible body.

Sometimes the face of a saint or holy person is transfigured, like that of St. Benedict Joseph Labre, to appear like that of Christ. St. Catherine of Siena was also thus transfigured. There were what seem to have been such transfigurations in the lives of two persons still living at this writing. If this can happen on earth, what then will be the appearance of the blessed in their glorified bodies, remade according to the pattern of Christ's glorified body? "Now not I, but Christ liveth in me." (*Gal.* 2:20).

Some saints have become radiant and beautiful as they lay dying, seeming to be in the flower of youth despite their aging, emaciated, or tortured bodies. St. Francis of Assisi, St. Dominic, St. Anthony of Padua, St. Teresa and St. Rose of Lima are but a few of those so glorified. St. Francis

Xavier, the exhausted missionary, had a beautiful appearance in death. St. Catherine de Ricci's face glowed; her body was radiant and gave off a perfume. St. Louis Bertrand's entire body shone at death like pure crystal and, like those of many other saints, remained incorrupt.

"Our Lord Jesus Christ will reform the body of our lowness, made like to the body of his glory, according to the operation whereby he is able to subdue all things unto himself." So claimed St. Paul in Philippians (3:20-21).

Perhaps one of the most remarkable cases was that of St. Lydwine of Schiedam, who had been wasted by plague and who had suffered so many ailments that her body seemed to be held together only by her clothing. This saint at death became as fresh and fair as if she were a girl of 17, smiling in her sleep. Lydwine had also been disfigured by a cleft in her forehead, which disappeared completely at her death, giving way to a serene and beautiful appearance. And a similar wonder: The nuns who prepared the body of St. Therese the Little Flower for burial stated that she seemed no older than 12 or 13 years old, although she died at age 24 after terrible physical and spiritual sufferings.

Some saints, tortured and martyred, disfigured and beheaded, cut to pieces by swords or mangled by wild beasts, seemed to have ended their lives in humiliation, disgrace, and utter destruction before their merciless tormenters. In some cases, martyrs were temporarily healed by God to testify to the truth of their faith and to glorify God. Usually this has not happened; but on Judgment Day the roles shall be reversed: the persecuted shall judge their persecutors. Then shall the saints appear totally different from the way they looked in those last bloody scenes on earth. Then will they shine in glory, and their enemies will shudder with shame. The risen bodies of the saints will then be comely and beautiful, strong and supple, perfect, radiant, and glorious.

No *person* ever dies. Once a soul has been created, it can never die, but will live forever, in either great joy or in terrible misery. Only the body dies, because the soul must leave a physical instrument in which it can no longer operate. At "death" the indestructible soul goes right on living either in Heaven, Hell, Purgatory, or possibly in Limbo, and it is the saved soul that shall reclaim a resurrected and glorious body on the day of Christ's Second Coming.

Will spiritualized bodies perform their usual physical functions? St. Paul says, "Meat for the belly, and the belly for the meats; but God shall destroy both it and them." (*1 Cor.* 6:13). A spiritualized body will have no need of earthly material food or drink. Nevertheless, the blessed will somehow be rewarded in all their senses—including taste and smell.

Regarding sex and marriage, although reason could tell us that there will be no marriage or sex in Heaven, Christ's words were very specific on the subject: "For when they rise again from the dead, they shall neither marry, nor be married, but are as the angels in heaven." (*Mark* 12:25). In a word, marriage was given as a passing institution to increase and multiply human beings on earth. Its purpose is not just to populate an impermanent world, but to populate the eternal kingdom of God in Heaven. Hence the horror of those sins that prostitute the nobility and preciousness of a holy use of sex in marriage, perverting the plan of God.

Neither God the Infinite Spirit, nor the multitudinous angels, who are finite, limited spirits, have either bodies or sex. But they enjoy a happiness superior to all physical pleasures, even as spirit is superior to flesh. Nevertheless, man's elevated life in Heaven will not exclude a special love or friendship forever between those who were husband and wife on earth.

God's elect will enjoy a glorious life in the hereafter with resurrected, spiritualized and glorified bodies. But the physical body, which so occupies human attention on earth, in eternity will be more like a setting for the scintillating jewel of the soul. A setting can be beautiful, but the precious stone it holds is much more valuable and entrancing. In eternity the soul will sparkle with its superior strength and comeliness, in the beauty and the grandeur of its intellectual and volitional endowments, and in its great joy in the perpetually present Beatific Vision, from which flow all its other joys. And this great happiness will never end.

Then it will be the soul that will rightly have first place. The body will assume its proper submission to the soul in perfect harmony. Men will commune with each other, with angels, and every man will commune with God. In the eternal embrace, the finite but wonderful soul of man, reunited in perfect harmony with the body in rectification of the tragic sin of Adam, will be face to face with the Infinite Spirit. Man will once again be able to walk with God in the garden of Paradise.

In the meantime, let us make the very best use of the time given to us in this our earthly sojourn, this transitory pilgrimage which is, in truth, but a passing moment compared to eternity. All the wonders of Heaven will be ours if—and only if—we have been faithful to the law of God here on earth.

Pray for us, O holy Mother of God, that we may be made worthy of the promises of Christ!

29

POST CLINICAL-DEATH
RETURNS TO LIFE

"And they that have done good things,
shall come forth unto the resurrection of
life; but they that have done evil, unto the
resurrection of judgment."
—John 5:28-29

In recent years attention has been drawn to cases in which hospital patients or accident victims have returned from an "other-world" interlude or experience after having been pronounced clinically dead. In this chapter we will examine this phenomenon, and then analyze it in light of the teachings of the Catholic Church. We do not judge Catholic teaching by reports of after-death experiences; rather, we judge these reports by Catholic teaching. All the teachings of the Catholic Church are guaranteed by Almighty God, who can neither deceive nor be deceived, whereas the truth of these after-death experiences rests simply on human testimony and human judgment (and could possibly involve the deceit of the devil, the Father of Lies).

Some of these post clinical-death experiences have been marginal cases of near death, but quite a few statements have been gathered from persons who, like their medical attendants, thought themselves really dead. These people heard the doctors or others declare them dead. They watched events from a "spiritualized" body of their own hovering nearby, not from their "dead" physical body. They observed their own dead body and the action and conversation surrounding it.

There is the usual doubt and skepticism, especially among

"scientists," as to how scientific certainty can be obtained about such experiences. Scientists love "controlled" experiments, but things spiritual, issues of after-death experiences, do not easily conform to laboratory specifications. Adding to the difficulty is the tendency of the once "dead" person to become silent about what he saw, after hearing disparaging remarks and expressions of disbelief from family and friends. Despite these handicaps, some doctors have been researching such cases, and others are growing more cognizant of these post clinical-death phenomena.

Post clinical-death experiences are not instances of spiritualism, of people seeking contact with the departed against the laws of God and the Church. The experiences were not asked for and were frequently unexpected and sudden, as in deaths from heart attacks, strokes, and accidents. One of the better books on such accounts is Raymond A. Moore, Jr.'s *Life After Life.*

These accounts have many common elements: experiencing another dimension of being, hearing that one is dead, an uncomfortable ringing or buzzing noise, a feeling of peace or warmth. Also common is the sensation of going through a dark tunnel, and realizing one is outside his physical body but in possession of a "spiritualized body" from which he can observe his own "dead" body from a distance (usually from a hovering position), seeing and knowing what is going on in the area of that body.

These "dead" people are usually met by deceased relatives and friends who seem to want to be welcomers or helpers. But the big experience is meeting some "being of light," a being which is seen as a small light which gradually enlarges to become very bright. This being is warm and personal, comforting and reassuring yet questioning, not condemning but making one evaluate his life in a panoramic, instantaneous, complete, and incredibly vivid and visual memory review. Some consider this "being of light" to be Christ or an angel, or some other spiritual figure in accord with the person's religious beliefs.

The "dead" person usually confronts some boundary line or other limiting obstacle to his progress into this other world. The stopping point may be a door, a fence, a mist, or a simple line. It is then made known to him that he must return to earthly life.

Some resist this return. Others, feeling some duty or obligation, such as mothers with young children, feel they must return, even if regretfully. When these persons return to earth, they relate their experiences, convinced that they had no personal part in making them up, and that they were not hallucinations. However, when they meet with doubts, rebuffs, or mockery, they tend to become silent.

The other-world experiences of these people have a great impact on their subsequent lives, often bringing about a deepening, and influencing them to live better lives, to love and help others. One of the most beneficent effects is that they no longer fear death, but anticipate it as a pleasant experience; yet none would favor suicide to attain it. (In one reported case of a suicide returning, the suicide did not have a pleasant experience on the other side.)

The above is a brief review of some of the findings of Raymond Moore as presented in the above-mentioned book. Of course, there are variations among post clinical-death experiences, and further explanations are needed for a more complete accounting. Yet many others know of or have had similar experiences.

Interestingly, most such accounts, especially those in Moore's book, give a very comforting and pleasant view of death. It would seem that most of these people interviewed were basically good people. No doubt to some, on their own admission, it was gently but clearly pointed out by the being of light that they should change or amend their lives.

One must consider, of course, that none of these people was dead permanently, or even dead for any considerable time, and they were all allowed to return to earth. Obviously these modern "returners" did not meet their Judge for a final sentence of reward or punishment. Nor were they shown either a heavenly crown marked with their name or the place in Hell that might yet be theirs. And there have been none like the unfortunate woman who replied in answer to St. Francis Jerome's questioning: "In Hell! In Hell!"

Perhaps some clinical-death patients who learned that their sins did merit a frightening Hell were too ashamed to admit it, while it was easy for those whose spiritual state entitled them to more pleasant experiences to share them with others. (One must not forget, however, those who received a gentle, even loving, warning, or even a strong and urgent one—a warning of mercy, it would seem—to make some changes in their lives before their next, and probably final, death and judgment.)

There are, admittedly, a few reports of post clinical-death experiences of persons who believed they experienced Hell, and in one case an "angel of darkness." Others give an explicit reference to a Heaven or Hell. Dr. Maurice Rowlings, author of *Beyond Death's Door,* makes a good point in observing that people tend to forget or put out of their minds unpleasant "death" experiences. When such persons are questioned some time later, they actually will not recall them. Thus, it is obviously much more valuable to interview such "dead" persons as soon after their "return" as possible. Perhaps more extensive findings and more immediate questioning will give more balance to a largely lopsided report of uniformly pleasant experiences. Dr. Rowlings also points out that there is a possibility of deceit from the false angel of light.

This is indeed true. Satan could deceive a person into believing he is experiencing clinical death when he has not actually died at all. Death is presented as merely a rosy experience. The devil's real purpose, of course, would be to betray the person, to lure him to a final defeat on the occasion of his actual and permanent death, when he is judged and the state of his soul is settled once and for all.

The wise and learned Father Schouppe, who collected so many accounts of apparitions by souls in Purgatory, likewise issues a warning with regard to possible tricks by the devil, the Father of Lies. Father Schouppe states that when a person who has led a wayward life appears after death and claims to have been saved at the last moment, and states that he or she is suffering in Purgatory, it is wise to be wary. One can hope that the person did indeed make a last-minute conversion, but one cannot be at all certain about this. And one must not thereby become complacent about the ease and frequency of deathbed conversions. The evil spirit desires to make us complacent about our salvation, and apparitions from souls who are actually in Hell, promoting presumption on God's mercy, may well be one of his wicked schemes to promote laxity and thus draw more souls down into everlasting Hell.

The evidence from post clinical-death experiences seems off-balance in that death, on the whole, appeared to be quite a pleasant experience. It seems strange that "souls"—even those of the Christians—coming back from clinical-death experiences seem to learn nothing of Purgatory or Hell, experiencing only a state vaguely resembling Heaven—or perhaps more accurately, Limbo. There may be reasons for such an off-balance and incomplete picture of the afterlife, but those reasons have yet to be explained.

One cannot fail to notice that these after-death experiences seem very subjective; they seem to conform to each individual's personal religious beliefs, thereby affirming one of the most popular religious errors of our time: It doesn't matter what church you belong to as long as you are a nice person. Those who did not know of Christ and His Church, the one way of salvation for all men (at least by Baptism of desire), were not informed of their error and of the necessity of joining themselves to Christ by becoming Catholics. In this respect the "being of light" is disregarding the practice of Our Lord Himself, who insisted that all men follow His authoritative divine teachings—as well as the practice of all the Catholic saints of 20 centuries. Recall that St. Vincent Ferrer even raised a man from the dead to testify as to which religion was the true religion. The "being of light," on the other hand, refuses to shed the light of the True Faith on non-Catholics, apparently choosing to leave them in darkness. Does this seem like the work of a holy angel or saint from Heaven?

Or, does it seem like a subjective experience undergone by a still-living person who is viewing reality in accord with his or her own "lights"?

Further, in these "after-death" experiences no importance seems to be given to the all-important question of whether a person is in the state of friendship or of enmity with God— that is, whether or not he is in the state of sanctifying grace. The state of sanctifying grace, as we know from divine revelation, is the absolutely necessary "ticket to Heaven" (as well as the only path to true happiness on earth.) In after-death experiences the whole issue of the person's relationship with God seems to be completely disregarded by all concerned—the "dead" person, the "being of light," and anyone else the "dead" person meets in the world beyond.

The implication is either that one's relationship to God is not important—or, that almost everyone is in the state of grace and therefore needs no admonition as to the state of his soul. Is this a realistic assumption?

Remaining in the state of grace (presuming a person has *received* sanctifying grace in the first place, through Baptism, or possibly Baptism of desire) is not easy, especially for an adult living in today's seductive world. It is not even easy for Catholics, who have the Church to guide them to salvation, and who have the Sacrament of Penance to cleanse them from sin and restore them to God's friendship. And speaking on the practical level, perhaps many Catholics today may not be in the state of grace, because they have fallen into mortal sin and have neglected to confess their sin and obtain God's forgiveness in the Sacrament of Penance.

Non-Catholics have an even harder time. Since they do not have the Sacrament of Penance, their way to the forgiveness for mortal sin must be that of *perfect contrition*, that is, contrition based on love of God and sorrow for having offended Him. (In the Sacrament of Penance, *imperfect contrition* is sufficient—even for the forgiveness of mortal sin—that is, contrition based on fear of God's punishments, especially Hell). But perfect contrition can well be difficult. Thus we may well fear that very many non-Catholics do not have their sins forgiven by God and thus are not in the state of friendship with Him.

Like faith, contrition is a gift of God. It is also an act of the human being, and it is the necessary condition for the sinner to obtain forgiveness from God and thus return to God's grace if he has had the grievous misfortune to commit a mortal sin. To be real, contrition (both perfect and imperfect) must be sincere and must proceed from the will, rather than being a passing mood or emotional experience. One must also renounce *all* mortal sins, as well as recognize sin as the greatest of all evils and be willing to make amends accordingly. Without these dispositions there is no true contrition. This must all be taken seriously if one desires forgiveness. We cannot expect God to forgive a sinner (even in the Sacrament of Penance) who is not really repentant.

Is true sorrow common and easy for a worldly-minded person? No. Thus it is not wise to assume that most people, including even lax Catholics and non-Catholics, are in the state of grace. Yet the "being of light" issues no warnings to the "dead" person to examine his soul to see if he is in the grace of God.

On the other hand, St. Bernard of Clairvaux raised from the dead a man who claimed that he would now be in Hell had not St. Bernard interposed. And St. John Bosco raised a dead 15-year-old boy who said he would have been condemned to Hell; he had "dreamed" he was surrounded by a mob of demons who were about to throw him into the flames of a huge furnace. But a beautiful lady intervened and told him, "There is still hope for you, Charles! You have not yet been judged." At that moment he heard St. John Bosco ordering him to rise. Charles arose, made a good confession, and

then died again. See how, in these well-authenticated resurrection miracles performed by the saints, the state of the person's soul before God is all-important. Why is it given little or
no attention in contemporary "after-death" experiences?

Further, a person in the state of mortal sin does not have
the spiritual protection of the Blessed Trinity dwelling within his soul; in fact, he is at enmity with God and has put
himself under the power of Satan. Is not such a person wide
open to deceit by the Father of Lies during an "after-death"
experience?

Here it is well to cite the opinion of a true Catholic
mystic, Venerable Anne Catherine Emmerich (1774-1824),
with regard to preternatural experiences; Sister Emmerich
herself had countless visions and mystical experiences
throughout her life. She states: "Now, for all who are not in
living union with Jesus Christ by faith and grace, nature is
full of Satan's influence." (*Life of Anne Catherine Emmerich*,
Vol. 1, p. 366). Anne Catherine Emmerich was speaking
particularly of mesmerism and clairvoyance; this saintly nun
saw clearly the power which the devil has over people who
put themselves into this dangerous preternatural state. But
her warning can well be applied to other forms of preternatural communication also—like "after death" experiences.
And although "after death" experiences are apparently not
something that is sought after by the persons involved,
nevertheless the same cautions apply.

How different from these experiences are the many cases
of returns from the dead (long after clinical death) which
one reads of in the lives of the saints. How different, also,
are the salutary warnings of God's justice which souls in
Purgatory have brought when they appeared on earth. God
allowed these returns and apparitions to reveal His justice as
well as His mercy in dealing with immortal souls. Some of
the frightened recipients of visits from Purgatory, in fact,
would rather have done without them, at least at first.

In earlier times, in many cases when early missionary
saints were surrounded by pagans, or were attempting to

convert whole countries, they called upon the dead they raised not only to tell of the joys of Heaven, but also to relate vividly the pains of Purgatory and the horrors of Hell. If God, who is in absolute control on the other side (where men's wills cannot further oppose His), sent even pagans back from the tomb to describe the realities of Hell, then it seems strange that He does not send today's returners-to-life back with this mission.

It also seems strange that the recent accounts of post clinical-death "return" experiences, where the actual deaths might easily be challenged, are accepted so readily as being some new, *modern* experience, when the wealth of the Church's centuries-old history contains myriad well-documented accounts of other-world contacts. And these other-world contacts recorded in Catholic history—experiences which proceeded from a true, objective, supernatural other world, and which were not initiated here on earth—give a very balanced and complete picture of life in the realms of everlasting life. They confirm clearly that there *is* a real, well-defined Heaven, but also a Purgatory and a Hell. The latter is a terrible reality—one we cannot ignore as impossible for us. And Purgatory is a place of real and terrible suffering, where even saintly souls must expiate their sins and faults. As Our Lord said, "Amen I say to thee, thou shalt not go out from thence till thou repay the last farthing." (*Matt.* 5:26).

Contemporary Christians, however, prefer a crossless Christianity and a painless society. Catholics rarely hear a sermon on Hell. Some may speculate that the "being of light" understands the psychology of today, where even Christians like to hear much of pleasure and little of penance, much of a heavenly place, but none of a hellish one— and so he only gently warns some of these post clinical-death persons of a final test.

But I wouldn't bank on the success of that approach! It is better to have a clear vision of Heaven, Hell, and Purgatory. That is the way the Lord and His saints presented it, even for pagans. Though He was Love Incarnate, Jesus gave extremely severe warnings about Hell. For example,

> "And if thy hand scandalize thee, cut it off: it is better for thee to enter into life, maimed, than having two hands to go into hell, into unquenchable fire: where their worm dieth not, and the fire is not extinguished. And if thy foot scandalize thee, cut it off. It is better for thee to enter lame into life everlasting, than having two feet, to be cast into the hell of unquenchable fire: where their worm dieth not, and the fire is not extinguished. And if thy eye scandalize thee, pluck it out. It is better for thee with one eye to enter into the kingdom of God, than having two eyes, to be cast into the hell of fire: where their worm dieth not, and the fire is not extinguished." (*Mark* 9:42-47.).

Our Lord tells us that the gate to Heaven is narrow—"and few there are that find it"! (*Matt.* 7:14; see also *Matt.* 22:16 and *Luke* 13:24). Contemporary accounts of returns from the other world, however, seem to intimate that Heaven is open to almost everyone, with little attention being paid to one's service of God—or negligence toward Him—on earth. On the contrary, Our Lord tells us that those who neglect to aid their neighbor in need will hear the dread sentence: "Depart from me, you cursed, into everlasting fire which was prepared for the devil and his angels. . . . And these shall go into everlasting punishment: but the just, into life everlasting." (*Matt.* 25:41, 46).

Fear of Hell did a lot to get many people into Heaven in the past. One doubts that just talking about Heaven will keep everybody out of Hell!

Consider the Blessed Mother's apparitions at Fatima in 1917. She did not think it amiss, or "bad psychology," to show the three children of Fatima—at the tender ages of seven, nine, and ten—a terrible vision of Hell and the vast multitude of souls falling into it. Such a vision changed many lives; and those little children, largely because of that experience, became self-sacrificing, penitential, and saintly.

On that July 13, 1917, the Blessed Virgin Mary opened her hands on the three children, and the light streaming from them seemed to penetrate the earth; the three children beheld a vision of Hell. Lucia cried out in terror, calling upon Our Lady. "We could see a vast sea of fire," she revealed many years later. Lucia described the vision:

> "Plunged in the flames were demons and lost souls, as if they were red-hot coals, transparent and black or bronze-colored, in human form, which floated about in the conflagration, borne by the flames which issued from them, with clouds of smoke falling on all sides as sparks fall in a great conflagration without weight or equilibrium, amid shrieks and groans of sorrow and despair that horrified us and caused us to tremble with fear. The devils could be distinguished by horrible and loathesome forms of animals, frightful and unknown, but transparent like black coals that have turned red-hot." Full of fear, the children raised their eyes beseechingly to Our Lady, who said to them with unspeakable sadness and tenderness: "You have seen Hell, where the souls of poor sinners go. In order to save them, God wishes to establish in the world devotion to my Immaculate Heart. If people do what I ask, many souls will be saved and there will be peace."

Little Jacinta, in particular, was powerfully struck by Our Lady's revelations on the poor sinners who are condemned to Hell for all eternity. She would exclaim, "Oh, Hell! Hell! I am so sorry for the souls who go there!" And thus motivated, she prayed and made sacrifices continually.

Our Lady said at Fatima, "Many souls go to Hell because

there is no one to pray and make sacrifices for them." On the other hand, there are probably many, many souls in Heaven and Purgatory today because of Our Lady's warnings at Fatima—because innocent Jacinta and Francisco, and many "ordinary" Catholics, heeded the Blessed Virgin's words.

As stated above, today's post clinical-death accounts seem "selective," almost always pleasant, whereas the experiences well-verified in the long history of the Church are much more trustworthy—especially those connected with canonized saints.

In any case, one should be extremely cautious in accepting contemporary accounts of post clinical-death experiences. The Church is always wary of other-world contacts or experiences. She remembers well the injunction of the Apostle Paul to test the spirits. In these matters it is necessary to have the guidance of the Church, and the advice of one of her priests well-trained in the discernment of spirits. This is very important, both for attaining a balanced mind in this life and eternal salvation in the next.

— PART FOUR —

CONCLUSIONS

"I confess one baptism for the remission of sins, and I hope for the resurrection of the dead, and the life of the world to come. Amen."

—*Creed of the Council of Trent*
1564

30

MIRACLES AND THE PLAN OF GOD
A Look at the Facts

"But they going forth preached every-
where; the Lord working withal, and con-
firming the word with signs that followed."
—*Mark* 16:20

As was noted in the beginning, this volume is not intended
to be either an encyclopedia of all the miracles of the dead
who have been raised, or a scientific work with detailed
documentation and critical comments. Such aims would involve too extensive a volume and defeat its actual purpose: a
popular work for the the average, not scholarly, reader.

For those who desire more detailed and critical treatment
of miracles, an extensive bibliography has been provided.
Three volumes, those by Aradi, Leuret and Bon, and
Monden, are particularly excellent. In the latter two especially, one will find complete case records of cures with all the
minutiae of medical diagnosis, progress of diseases, cure
reports, scientific terminology and professional statements.

This book was also not written to provide the titillations of
sensationalism—although curiosity may well be the first motive that prompts many readers to pick it up. Admittedly,
resurrection miracles are sensational. When Our Lord lived
on earth and worked His great miracles, He knew that some
would seek only their sensational aspects, refusing to take
the next step and put their faith in Him and His words. Yet
He continued to perform miracles for the good of those who
would accept them properly, even to the raising of Lazarus
and His own Resurrection from the dead. But Christ would
not put on a circus show for the Tempter (a leap from the

pinnacle of the Temple), nor would He perform a "magic trick" for King Herod and his curious but faithless court. Neither would He come down from the cross on Calvary, as some of the irreverent onlookers urged Him. Our Lord's every miracle was completely in accord with the will of His Father in Heaven.

What, then, *is* God's purpose in performing miracles?

Miracles are performed for the glory of God and the good of men. The famous 19th-century Catholic mystic, Anne Catherine Emmerich, saw visions of Our Lord performing His miracles. Though these constitute *private* revelations, not binding in faith, they are valuable for the light they shed on the life of our Saviour. Sister Emmerich says that Our Lord always made His manner of curing correspond to the special needs of the recipient: "As every malady of the body symbolized some malady of the spiritual order, some sin or the chastisement due to it, so did every cure symbolize some grace, some conversion, or the cure of some particular evil." (*The Life of Christ,* Vol. 2, p. 229).

Miracles also provide proofs for the truth of the Catholic Christian Faith. Vatican Council I (1870), in fact, addressed this very point in its chapter on Faith:

> "Nevertheless, in order that the obedience of our faith might be in harmony with reason, God willed that to the interior help of the Holy Spirit there should be joined exterior proofs of His revelation, to wit, divine facts, and especially miracles and prophecies, which, as they manifestly display the omnipotence and infinite knowledge of God, are most certain proofs of His divine revelation, adapted to the intelligence of all men." (Chapter 3).

Further, Vatican Council I issued two canons, or solemn dogmatic statements, on the value of miracles for our faith:

III. If anyone shall say that divine revelation cannot be made credible by outward signs, and therefore that men ought to be moved to faith solely by the internal experience of each, or by private inspiration, let him be anathema.

IV. If anyone shall say that miracles are impossible, and therefore that all the accounts regarding them, even those contained in Holy Scripture, are to be dismissed as fabulous or mythical, or that miracles can never be known with certainty, and that the divine origin of Christianity is not rightly proved by them, let him be anathema.

As Our Lord said, "The works themselves, which I do, give testimony of me, that the Father hath sent me." (*John* 5:36). And also: "If I do not the works of my Father, believe me not. But if I do, though you will not believe me, believe the works: that you may know and believe that the Father is in me, and I in the Father." (*John* 10:37-38). And when questioned by St. John the Baptist's followers as to whether He was the One to come, Our Lord answered by pointing out His miracles; He told them to report to John that "The blind see, the lame walk, the lepers are cleansed, the deaf hear, the dead rise again, the poor have the gospel preached to them. And blessed is he that shall not be scandalized in me." (*Matt.* 11:5-6; also *Luke* 7:22). Finally, we recall St. Peter's description of Our Lord, spoken on the first Pentecost: "Jesus of Nazareth, a man approved of God among you, by miracles, and wonders, and signs . . ." (*Acts* 2:22).

Vatican Council I also set forth the following additional reason for believing the teachings of the Catholic Church:

Nay, more, the Church itself, by reason of its marvellous extension, its eminent holiness and its inexhaustible fruitfulness in every good thing, its Catholic unity and its invincible stability, is a great and perpetual motive of credibility, and an irrefutable witness of its own divine mission. (Chapter 3, "Of Faith").

Thus, in addition to miracles, the Church's claim to be the One True Church of God is also testified to by the holiness and worldwide unity of her teachings, by her manifold works of charity, by her innumerable consecrated virgins—who have made a holocaust of their lives by the vows of perpetual poverty, chastity, and obedience—and by her saints.

These are all facts which a person can *see,* even before he makes the act of faith. These facts convince the honest inquirer that the claims of the Catholic Church are indeed credible, and that he should take the next step and embrace all the teachings of the Catholic Church. These teachings must *all* be accepted, since the Church conveys them to us from God Himself. The Christian accepts them not on any human authority, but on the authority of God, who can neither deceive nor be deceived.

It is this total act of faith that God desires from every soul. By this act the soul renders to its God the homage of the intellect, the obedience of the mind (which is just as necessary for salvation as is the obedience of external acts). In His divine truthfulness God does not allow the soul to pick and choose what it wishes to believe (a practice which is well described by the term "cafeteria Christianity"). The act of faith is a supernatural act, essentially a gift of God, and impossible without His grace. By this act man offers to God a free obedience inasmuch as he concurs and cooperates with God's grace, when he could resist it.

But the assent of faith is by no means a blind impulse. God does not fail to provide the potential believer with abundant motives for making this all-important act of faith. Among these motives are miracles, which, "as they manifestly display the omnipotence and infinite knowledge of God, are most certain proofs of His divine revelation adapted to the intelligence of all men."

The gift of working miracles is one of the *extraordinary* gifts of the Holy Ghost; it is mentioned by St. Paul in *1 Corinthians* 12:9-10 among several other extraordinary gifts. These gifts—known as *charismata,* or graces *gratis datae* (gratuitously given)—are distinct from the seven gifts of the Holy Ghost which all Christians receive in Baptism and which remain in the soul so long as a person is in the state of grace—that is, while the Blessed Trinity is dwelling in the soul. These seven gifts, enumerated in *Isaiah* 11:23, are Wisdom, Understanding, Counsel, Fortitude, Knowledge, Piety, and Fear of the Lord.

As a person becomes holier, through the practice of the Christian virtues—especially faith, hope and charity—he comes to live more and more in accord with these seven gifts. These gifts have traditionally been compared to seven sails on a ship, enabling the Christian to catch and profit by the breathings of the Holy Ghost. Unfortunately, in very many Christians, these seven gifts remain dormant, with the person therefore living a stunted Christian life. And if a person has the misfortune to commit a mortal sin, these gifts immediately leave the soul, along with the indwelling Father, Son, and Holy Ghost. God and His gifts do not abide in a soul in the state of mortal sin.

The seven gifts of the Holy Ghost are therefore intimately connected with sanctity of life; they are possessed by all Christians in the state of grace. Though they are completely and sublimely supernatural, they are part and parcel of the way of holiness prescribed by God for every Christian.

The *charismata,* on the other hand, are special and extraordinary powers vouchsafed by God to only a few, and primarily for the spiritual good of others rather than of the recipient. Thus, although the grace of miracles is very often a sign of sanctity in the miracle-worker, this is not *necessarily* the case.

Miracles are usually required as evidence in the beatification and canonization investigations of saints, as proofs of their sanctity. Yet more important than miracles is evidence

of holiness in the life of the person who is under consideration for beatification or canonization. The "bottom line" in
such an investigation is the answer to the question: Did he
practice the Christian virtues—especially Faith, Hope, and
Charity—to an heroic degree? Pope Benedict XIV explained that miracles alone are not sufficient to prove a person's sanctity—indeed, it is even possible for a person who is
in the state of mortal sin to perform miracles:

> "It is the common opinion of theologians that the
> grace of miracles is a grace *gratis data,* and
> therefore that it is given not only to the just [those
> in the state of grace], but also to sinners [those in
> the state of mortal sin], (though only rarely).
> Christ says that He knows not those who have
> done evil, though they may have prophesied in
> His name, cast out devils in His name, and done
> many wonderful works. [*Matt.* 7:22-23]. And the
> Apostle said that without charity he was nothing,
> though he might have faith to remove mountains."
> (Treatise on Heroic Virtue, III, 130).

Yes, it is true that there have been miracle-workers who
were not sent by God—like Simon Magus (*Acts* 8:9), Elymas
the magician (*Acts* 13:8), and Pharaoh's magicians (*Exodus*
7:10-12, 22; 8:7). It should also be remembered that Our
Lord warned us: "For there shall arise false Christs and false
prophets, and shall show great signs and wonders, inasmuch
as to deceive (if possible) even the elect." (*Matt.* 24:24).

Thus, holiness of life, as evidenced by a person's practice
of the Christian virtues, and by the flowering of the seven
"ordinary" gifts of the Holy Ghost in his life, is infinitely
more important than the extraordinary charismata, splendid
though these may be. Both types of gifts have been evident
throughout the centuries in the lives of the Catholic saints.

And in the life of Our Lord Jesus Christ there was evident,
in addition to most striking miracles, holiness of life and of

teaching, fulfillment of the Old Testament prophecies, divine authority, and complete truthfulness. Together these provide abundant evidence for believing in Him.

The Resurrection of Christ is a matter of historical record. However, those so-called—and often ivory-tower— Scripture scholars, exegetes, theologians and other writers who deny biblical miracles, mythologizing them or turning them into mere "symbols," should consider that the many well-attested miracles of later centuries are themselves a testimony to the miracles of Christ. If the humble servants of the Master can work such wonders over the Christian centuries, then surely the very Son of God, He who is claimed as the source of power for these many resurrections, could and did work authentic miracles Himself. The miracles of Christ were not "symbols" thought up by some "ruminating" early community, but actual deeds testified to by actual witnesses.

Further, the miracles of Christ's Apostles, and later on those of His missionaries, saints, and lesser holy ones, fulfill both Christ's orders to work miracles and His prophecy that His servants would work even greater wonders than He had worked—not because they would have any greater powers than the Master, but because they would have a longer time and more occasions to exercise them in public ministry than He did. "Amen, amen I say to you, he that believeth in me, the works that I do, he also shall do; and greater than these shall he do." (*John* 14:11-12).

Anne Catherine Emmerich, mentioned earlier in this chapter, says that Our Lord performed His more astounding and more prodigious miracles only in the presence of pagans. She even stated: "The miracles of the Apostles and of saints that came after them were far more striking than those of Our Lord and far more contrary to the usual course of nature, for the heathens needed to be strongly affected, while the Jews needed only to be freed from their bonds." In fact, Sister Emmerich states that Our Lord's miracles were usually not spectacular and instantaneous—though He could well have performed them in that manner. But they were not intended as spectacles; rather, "they were works of mercy, they were symbolical images of His mission . . . As He desired man's cooperation in the work of his own Redemption, so did He demand from those that asked of Him a miraculous cure their own cooperation by faith, hope, love, contrition, and reformation of life." (*The Life of Christ,* Vol. 2, p. 229).

In a word, the miracles of God's saints reinforce our faith in, and indirectly prove the authenticity of, the Gospel miracles. And one need not have been present when Christ worked His miracles to accept the testimony of the thousands who have died in defense of their belief in those miracles.

One *can* examine the contemporary records of the Medical Bureau at Lourdes or at Fatima. One can be present at sessions of twentieth-century canonical commissions of the Church that examine and authenticate hundreds of modern-day miracles in the processes of beatification and canonization of saints. All these wonders, both ancient and modern, hang together in one living, continuous Catholic Church, and they strengthen the credibility of each other.

They show the unity of the Church over the ages, for no other religion can show such a great and constant tradition of miracles.

These miracles show the holiness of the Church, for the power to work miracles is given only by God, and usually only to His holy instruments, the saints.

They show the catholicity or universality of the Catholic Church because they have been worked all over the world for a period of 20 centuries, among all peoples: for peasants and princes, by pope, bishop, abbot, priest or religious; by man, woman or even child saint.

These miracles show the apostolicity of the Church, for they involve gifts and wonders common among the Apostles, in fulfillment of Our Lord's prophecy to His Apostles.

In a word, these outstanding miracles are wonderful proofs of the truth of the Catholic Church. Any claims to similar wonders outside the Church cannot be authenticated as such, or if there is some rare case granted because of God's mercy, it would be an exception. At times, too, there have been so-called raisings from the dead in tawdry circumstances that make one uncomfortable—unnatural, unholy results of witchcraft and diabolical orgies.

An account of one such diabolical "raising of the dead" was given by Frederick Kaigh, an English physician who witnessed it, in *Witchcraft and Magic of Africa;* it was summarized by Edward Connor in *Prophecy for Today* (page 129) under the heading: "Can the Devil Raise the Dead?" In this account, an African chief was raised (in order to name his murderer), apparently through the words and actions of a witch doctor. The raising took place at night, and it involved strange preternatural phenomena; at the end of the ceremony the chief walked off down a lane in the moonlight and was seen no more. The accused murderer was found unexplainedly dead the next day.

Edward Connor comments: "Despite the impressiveness of the occurrence, it will be apparent that the chief was not returned to life in the sense that Christ gave life back to Lazarus or the widow's son. In true restorations, the person raised from the dead continues a normal life among men. In false restorations, there is no evidence that the soul has been restored to the corpse in anything like its true natural relationship, nor even any evidence that the spirit using the corpse is the soul which originally animated it."

On the other hand, one should note the "naturalness" of the miracles of the saints. Despite the variety of circumstances in these miracles, the actions of the participants in these scenes are true to life. There is nothing that smacks of contrivance or invention. We recognize the feelings of the people involved.

Resurrection miracles have been worked in widely varied circumstances and among different peoples from many lands: of various races, tongues and nations the world over. The recipient may be an infant—especially an unbaptized one—a child or youth dead from drowning or some other accident or disease, a young woman, a father, a wife, a knight, a prince, a priest or religious. Each case has its own interest.

These miracles nearly always involve a saint or very holy person, and/or the prayers of many people. If miracles, particularly miracles of the dead being raised, were reported to be performed by any Tom, Dick or Harry, there would be reason to doubt. But who can be trusted more than the saints, especially when their miracles have been reported by other saints, as St. Gregory related stories of miracles performed by St. Benedict, and Antoninus related those of St. Vincent Ferrer.

Saints, one should remember, have spiritual powers of discernment not possessed by ordinary Christians. Saints are also totally honest and truthful; when it comes to holy things or the honor of God and the Church, it is much safer to trust the discernment and truthfulness of the saints than that of some scientists. Of course, there are many open-minded scientists who readily acknowledge possibilities beyond their own area of expertise.

Divine miracles are worthy of the holiness, goodness, and justice of God. They also illustrate the teachings of Jesus Christ. For example, Our Lord's multiplication of loaves (*John* 6), miracle at Cana (*John* 2), and cure of the paralytic give a hint of His sacramental powers: to feed the whole Church with His Body and Blood, to change the natural institution of marriage into an inseparable supernatural bond, and to forgive sins. The raising of the dead signifies the souls, rising from sin to the life of sanctifying grace. Thus the miracles of Christ have an intimate connection with His life and supernatural teachings. This is also true of the miracles of the saints.

There have been many resurrected persons whose lives were utterly changed—by conversion, by repentance, by reparation, by holiness. These changes in way of life constitute one of the most cogent arguments that a momentous event actually occurred to these people. Both trees and human beings will reach upward and grow toward the Sun that has given them light and life.

In certain special cases, persons who returned from the dead were given very special missions, as were Drithelm of Northumbria, St. Christina the Admirable, and the boy Blasio. Others, particularly pagans raised from the dead, had their own unique part to play in the labors of the great missionaries of the early Christian centuries. They became an adjunct of the apostolate of the saints. They affirmed the truth of the saints' teachings, identifying them as messengers of the one true God, and thus they helped to lead thousands of others to the Faith. They were the greatest walking communication miracles of all, these persons not merely revived from sickbeds, lameness or paralysis, but returned from the funeral bier, or the sepulcher! Their constant narration of their resurrection experiences and their adventures in the other world or worlds—Purgatory, Hell, and Heaven—made a profound impression and altered the lives of many for the better.

These great miracles, along with innumerable "lesser" ones such as cures, enhanced the dignity of the special instrument of God, the miracle-working missionary, preacher, abbot, bishop or pastor. They compelled reverence for his person and office, credibility for his claims, and receptiveness for his teaching and counsel. The pagans soon learned that such men would rather die than lie. Thus the testimony of the converted would inspire belief in the minds and hearts of later generations.

Many of these miracles have been either worked or vouched for by some of the holiest persons and greatest minds in history. It is utter foolishness, bias, unscientific scholarship and uncritical research to accept the secular historical facts recorded by such authors as Venerable Bede *(Ecclesiastical History of the English People)* or Pope Gregory the Great *(Dialogues)* and to reject, debunk, mythologize or smile patronizingly over the miraculous or supernatural events concurrently recorded in those works. If the accounts of miracles are rejected, why should the other accounts be accepted? But if the "secular" accounts are acceptable, why not then the miracle accounts in the same historical work?

What is needed today is another Gilbert Keith Chesterton to make certain prejudiced historians acknowledge and laugh at the absurdity of their own objections and omissions. In his *Life of St. Francis,* Chesterton observes of such men:

> "I have never been quite clear about the nature of the right by which historians accepted masses of detail from them as definitely true, and suddenly denied their truthfulness when one detail was preternatural—I am puzzled about why the skeptics are not more skeptical."

In his masterpiece entitled *Orthodoxy,* Chesterton further comments:

> "Somehow or other an extraordinary idea has arisen that the disbelievers in miracles consider them coldly and fairly, while believers in miracles accept them only in connection with some dogma. The fact is quite the other way. The believers in miracles accept them (rightly or wrongly) because they have evidence for them. The disbelievers in miracles doubt them (rightly or wrongly) because they have a doctrine against them."

A critical attitude is good, but actually the most *reasonable* attitude consists in believing the testimony of trustworthy witnesses. This is also the approach of true humility. A wise bishop once commented on the miracles of St. Patrick and the acceptance of miracles in general:

> "Credulity may enter even the most virtuous mind; but when eminent men decline from this readiness of belief they fall into the opposite error,

and become incredulous; while there is little fault
in credulity, but much in incredulity."

Of course, if one does not believe in God, he is simply a
fool, according to Sacred Scripture, that best-seller of all
time and in the entire world. In denying the existence of a
Creator, one must even fly in the face of reason! But if one
admits a God, a Creator, there should be no problem at all
in accepting that an exalted pre-eminent Being can employ
powers that are natural to Himself, even if they are
miraculous to man. This involves something that is "supernatural" only in relation to man's nature. It is "above" man's
limited six-foot mental faculties and bodily powers. As Bon
and Leuret put in in their *Modern Miraculous Cures,* "Miracles are only marvels at man's level. At God's level they are
ordinary actions."

To further illustrate this ease of divine operation, one
might note that it is as simple for God to work a miracle as it
is for an electrician to put power through a copper wire by
flicking a switch, or for an aviator to lift a dog off the earth
in his jet plane. The copper by itself could never light up a
lamp, nor could a dog fly through the air unassisted by the
superior being, man.

Both the copper and the dog—one might fancy!—at the
end of such a day's events, could return to their fellow pieces
of copper in the mine or to the hounds in the countryside
and relate their marvellous "miraculous" experiences, so
outside and above the natures of animal or mineral.

Well, those things which are miracles to man, in his
human nature, are quite natural and effortless to God in His
divine nature. But because they are above our human
nature's abilities, man makes much ado about them. So "the
fool" accepts the electricity in the copper and the dog flying
in the plane, but rejects the miracles of God. But it should
be obvious that one can be raised in wondrous ways above
his own level.

But perhaps the dissenters can be helped by means of

their own "show me" attitudes, by the working of their faculties of reason—in a word, by dealing with facts. For no matter what one believes or disbelieves he can always look to the facts. Even if a man refuses to believe in God, even if he is a pagan with a pantheon of gods (and the latter is the more honest and humble of the two in admitting powers superior to himself), he must come, as the Christians did long ago, to the bar of reason and the admission of facts.

Now, in this book alone there are listed or described around 400 cases of the dead being raised. And exhaustive research would certainly turn up a lot more. But limiting the discussion to these 400 cases, the first thing is to ascertain the *fact* that deaths actually occurred.

Included in the cases detailed herein were men (or women or children) who had been dead for as long as 24 hours or even several days, persons who had drowned hours or days before the bodies were recovered, and of others who had been hanged by the neck for days or even a week. There were others who had suffered violent deaths, having been thrown from horses, crushed under wheels, fallen from great heights or buried by falling walls, debris, or landslides; some had dropped into a mine shaft or plunged into a well. Finally, there were those who had been sealed in a coffin, wrapped in shrouds and actually buried under earth or stone, some for long periods of time.

There are those who will say: Yes, but those people in bygone days did not always really know when someone was dead; they did not have the scientific know-how and medical technology of today to judge whether a person was actually dead. Granted, there *may* have been a *few* cases in which a person was mistakenly judged to be dead. But to assume that people in other ages did not generally know how to determine the state of death is simply preposterous.

In ages past, as in some underdeveloped nations today, death often came at an early age. Furthermore, it occurred at home, rather than in a far-off hospital, and people were very familiar with the sight of it. Older members of a community, as well as physicians, were often close to death and were quite able to determine it. If there was any doubt, they would certainly err on the side of life, waiting as long as possible to declare the person dead. Certification was often required, even as it was required for Christ on the cross. To think that people regularly buried their loved ones alive is ridiculous.

One factor common to many resurrection miracle accounts is the fact that the miracle-workers were usually priests. Other than doctors, who is it who has the most experience with the sick, dying, and dead? It is the priest. The parish priest or hospital chaplain, especially in time of war or plague, is constantly found with the dead or dying, either at the bedside or at some site of recent death (such as a street accident). Often the state of the person is clear to all.

At other times the priest, because of his responsibility for the administration of the Sacraments, has to make a judgment as to whether or not the person is actually dead. Now, throughout history, the priest was often the most educated man—or one of the few educated men—in the parish. And in the past, as today, the priest had to decide whether to administer absolution, anointing, or Baptism *conditionally,* depending upon his judgment of whether death had occurred. So the fact that most miracles of raising the dead were performed by very *experienced* priests, bishops or great missionaries, men well educated and familiar with sickness and death, further substantiates the reality of the raised having been really dead before they were raised.

In those miracles where the *dying* were restored to perfect health, it is sometimes claimed by skeptics that the patients, physicians, and priests involved could not distinguish between those who were simply sick and those who were critically ill. Ridiculous! And it is perfect nonsense to suppose that dead corpses were raised by hypnosis or mass hysteria—or that a drowned infant or mangled corpse arose by autosuggestion! There is a limit even to foolishness.

There is a further point to support the fact that death had

actually occurred in the miracles related. As noted earlier, the saints usually have gifts of discernment beyond those of ordinary mortals. Moreover, some have had quite a few charismatic gifts—discernment of spirits, and unusual knowledge of those present or absent, living or dead, of past and future events, etc. Who, then, is better equipped than a saint to discern the real state of one considered dead, for whom the saint prays and appeals to God for restoral to life? Who could better determine life or death than one who was familiar with the condition and needs of that soul whose eternal fate was at stake? And who could tell better than the saint whether a true power of God was being exercised through them? "There are more things in this world than are dreamt of in thy philosophy, Horatio!"

Thus, it should be clear that the saints are well able to discern death and miracles, though scientists are better at diagnosing particular diseases. And sometimes, it is in the scientist's purview to document that somehow, inexplicably (and miraculously), the disease is gone! To each his own.

And finally, someone may say: Sometimes the saints referred to the "dead" person as being "asleep." Yes, perhaps in two or three cases in this entire book. But so did Our Lord first say of Lazarus. So is it said of the dead: "those who are asleep in the Lord." It is a phrase that permits a double interpretation: it is suited to console and raise hope in the mourners, who then have more insight as to the meaning of a temporary death; the phrase also seems to serve some saints as a way to hide their miracles, distracting attention from their own greatness.

So, too, when a miracle-worker uses some oil or water (not the *oleum infirmorum* of the anointing of the sick), or when he appeals to San Ciro or St. Philomena or some other saint, one can suspect a cover-up for his own miracles, a warding-off of the adulation he fears. Such oil or water, as the scientists could demonstrate, has no therapeutic value in itself.

Relentlessly pursuing facts, the strict inquirer and the

St. Agnes of Montepulciano (1268-1317) holding the Infant Jesus. This saint raised to life a child who had drowned and whose body had been found floating in the water. Many other wonders also accompanied St. Agnes' life; for instance, the Mother of God placed the Christ Child in her arms, and angels brought her Holy Communion on several occasions.

St. Rose of Lima (1586-1617) holding the Christ Child. Through St. Rose's intercession after her death, two dead people were raised to life— and many sick people were cured, women in difficult childbirth were assisted, lepers were cured, and infants were saved. St. Rose's heroic penances and gift of contemplation culminated in her mystical marriage to Our Lord; He said to her, "Rose of My Heart, be My bride." Our Lady called her "Rose of St. Mary," and permitted her to embrace the Christ Child.

St. Martin de Porres (1579-1639) of Lima, Peru, who raised to life a fellow monk and also a dog. Of illegitimate birth, Martin was the son of a white father and a black mother. He became a Dominican lay brother and was known for his miracles, his great charity to the poor, and his kindness to animals—with whom he was literally "on speaking terms."

B. SEBASTIANI

Left: Blessed Sebastian of Apparizi (1502-1600), Spanish-born Franciscan lay brother and missionary to Mexico, who after his death obtained the resurrections of eight children. His incorrupt body is enshrined in the Church of San Francisco in Puebla, Mexico.

Below: Saint Francis Solanus (1549-1610), Spanish Franciscan missionary to South America, through whose intercession a five-year-old girl named Maria Monroe was brought back to life and healed after a terrible fall which had split her skull, destroyed her face, and put out one of her eyes. St. Francis Solanus is called "the Wonderworker of the New World." After his death and interment it was suddenly and sorrowfully realized that no portrait of the saint had ever been made; the Viceroy of Lima therefore ordered the body disinterred for a portrait. The body's horizontal position caused the disarrangement of the capuche.

Opposite: St. Marianne de Jesus of Quito, Ecuador (1618-1645), who brought back to life her niece, whose skull had been fractured when she was kicked by a mule, as well as a woman who had been strangled and then thrown over a cliff by her jealous husband. St. Marianne lived as a solitary under a Jesuit spiritual director; she practiced the greatest austerities, ate hardly anything, slept for only three hours a night for years, had the gift of prophecy, and performed miracles. She is known as "the Lily of Quito."

Above: St. Philip Benizi (1223-1285), fifth General of the Servite Order. At his death, when his body was laid out in church before burial, a woman brought in the dead and partially devoured body of her little girl, who had been attacked by a wolf. The woman placed the body near St. Philip's body, and the child was restored with all her members intact. Here St. Philip Benizi is pictured in the cave he fled to when there was talk of electing him pope upon the death of Clement IV; note the triple tiara, in which he is obviously not interested, at bottom right.

Left: St. Stanislaus of Cracow (1030-1079), Bishop and martyr. This early 14th-century fresco in the Church of St. Francis in Assisi apparently depicts St. Stanislaus' miraculous raising of a certain Peter Miles in order to clear Stanislaus of a false charge; the saint was acquitted. He then gave to Peter Miles, whose soul had come from Purgatory, the choice of returning there or of living a few more years; Peter chose Purgatory and the certainty of eternal salvation. Then he lay down in his grave, his body fell to pieces, and his bones lay there exactly as they had been when the grave was opened.

Above: St. Peregrine (1265-1345), who is reported to have raised the dead on more than one occasion. St. Peregrine is the patron of cancer victims; for several years he suffered from cancer in his right leg. The night before a scheduled amputation, as he was praying before the crucifix, he saw Our Lord descend from the Cross and stretch out His hand. The next morning St. Peregrine found himself cured; there was no trace of cancer.

Left: St. Felix of Cantalice (1515-1587), Franciscan saint who restored a dead child to life and gave it back to its mother.

Right: Saint Gerard Majella (1726-1755), Redemptorist lay brother who raised two infants, one of whom had died without Baptism. St. Gerard is a patron of mothers, particularly those in pregnancy, and of mothers of infants.

Left: Saint Charbel Makhlouf (1828-1898), Lebanese hermit, through whose intercession a two-year-old child who had drowned was returned to life; St. Charbel is also credited with thousands of other miracles. His body remained incorrupt until 1965.

Left: Padre Pio (1887-1968), Franciscan stigmatist and miracle-worker, through whose intercession a dead man is reported to have been raised.

Right: Therese Neumann of Konnersreuth (1898-1962), Bavarian mystic and stigmatist who experienced the Passion and death of Christ hundreds of times during her life. After experiencing the death of Christ, Therese would show no signs of life for about 45 minutes, but then would gradually return to normal.

St. Vincent Ferrer (1350-1419) preaching to the Moors; in his lifetime he converted 8,000 Moors, 25,000 Jews, and a total of 200,000 souls. This great Spanish Dominican performed an estimated 40,000 miracles, including the raising of at least 28 persons from the dead. On one occasion he raised a person to testify that he, Vincent, was "the Angel of the Judgment"; he raised another to testify to the innocence of a condemned man; and on another occasion he raised a Jew named Abraham, who then testified: "The religion of the Jews is not the true faith; the True Faith is that of the Christians." On still another occasion, St. Vincent Ferrer restored to life a dead child who had been chopped up, roasted, and served by its mother in a fit of madness. Vincent Ferrer is one of the greatest saints in the entire history of the Church—yet he is almost unknown.

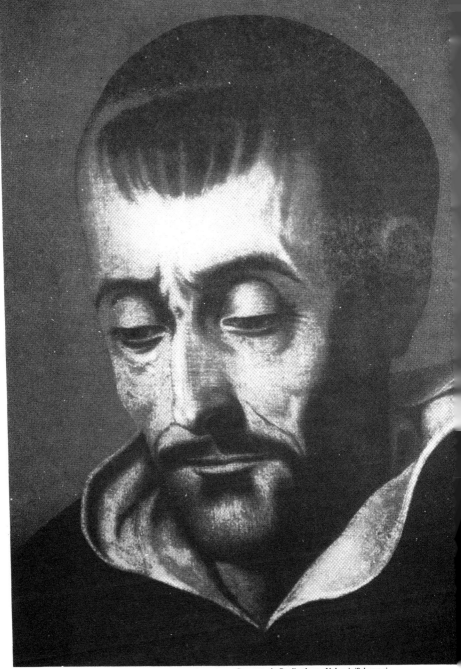

Convento de Predicadores, Valencia/Schamoni

St. Louis Bertrand (1526-1581), great Spanish-born Dominican missionary to South America who is credited with at least 13 persons raised from
the dead through his intercession after his death, in addition to two he
raised during his life. St. Louis Bertrand traveled all over the Caribbean
area and became known for prophecies, miracles, and the gift of tongues.

St. Hyacinth (c. 1185-1257) crossing the Dnieper River on his cloak, carrying the Blessed Sacrament and a statue of Our Lady to save them from desecration at the hands of the invading Tartars. He raised to life 50 dead persons in Cracow alone, as well as restoring 72 dying persons to perfect health. The bull of St. Hyacinth's canonization declared his miracles to be "almost countless." St. Hyacinth is called "the Polish St. Dominic" because he established the Dominican Order in Poland; he traveled 25,000 miles on his evangelizing journeys, much of this on foot.

Right: St. Francis Xavier (1506-1552), "Apostle of the Indies" and "Apostle of Japan." This great Jesuit saint is considered to have been the greatest single missionary since St. Paul. In ten short years he converted hundreds of thousands, and the impact of his labors lasted for centuries.

Left: St. Francis Xavier; this picture is apparently portraying the incident when the saint raised a boy whose dead body had been wrapped in a shroud for 24 hours. St. Francis Xavier made the Sign of the Cross over the body, took the youth by the hand, and bade him in the Name of Jesus to live.

Left: St. Isaac Jogues (1607-1647), Jesuit missionary to the Hurons and Iroquois and the leader of the heroic eight "Jesuit Martyrs of North America." His picture is included here not for having raised the dead (we are not aware of any resurrection miracle attributed to this saint), but to point out the terrible tortures and bodily mutilations suffered by some of the servants of God, and to call to mind that these bodies will arise resplendent and whole on the last day. The Iroquois tortured St. Isaac Jogues for a year, cutting off some of his fingers. He escaped, and by a special dispensation from the Pope was allowed to continue saying Mass. He then set out again for Iroquois territory, but was tomahawked and beheaded near Albany, New York. The Jesuit Martyrs of North America were canonized in 1930.

Lower left: St. John Francis Regis (1597-1640), Jesuit missionary in southeastern France, who raised a dead person and brought thousands back to the Catholic faith.

Lower right: St. Francis Jerome (1642-1716), Jesuit preacher who raised to life a man and a baby.

Opposite: St. Patrick (c. 389-c. 461), Apostle of Ireland, who is said to have raised as many as 39 persons, including some who had been buried for many years. He consecrated 350 bishops, erected 700 churches, and ordained 5,000 priests. After 30 years of St. Patrick's missionary labors, the greater part of Ireland had become Catholic. St. Patrick's was a tremendous achievement, equalled by few saints in the entire history of the Church.

284-16

Left: Our Lady of Czestoch~~owa~~, ~~th/ou~~ whose intercession 17 persons a~~re~~ ~~to~~ ~~u~~ have been raised from the dead ov~~er~~ ~~cen~~ turies. The famous shrine of Our ~~La~~ Czestochowa is located in the dioces~~e~~ Cracow, Poland, on Jasna Gora (Bright ~~H~~
Below: Our Lady of Guadalupe (Mexic~~o~~ 1531 the Blessed Virgin Mary miracul~~o~~ imprinted this picture on the *tilma* or cloa~~k~~ an Indian named Juan Diego. Science determined that it could not have b~~een~~ painted; furthermore, it has the cha~~rac~~ teristics of a photograph.

Marianas-~~~~

The raising to life of an Indian who had been accidentally shot with an arrow during festivities attending the transfer of the miraculous image of Our Lady of Guadalupe to its first chapel (December 26, 1531). The Indian's body was laid before Our Lady's image, and the people prayed for a miracle. Their plea was granted. (*Original painting in the Basilica of Guadalupe.*)

Left: Saint Louis De Montfort (1673-1716), who had to suffer physical attacks by the devil; witnesses at his beatification investigation stated that they had heard the commotion from these struggles, including the sound of fist blows and the swish of whips. St. Louis De Montfort is the Apostle of Mary, who in his *True Devotion to Mary* showed how the shortest and surest way to Jesus is through the Blessed Virgin Mary.

Generelat, Rome/Schamoni

Conteri/Schamoni

Right: St. Catherine of Genoa (1447-1510), famous mystic whose *Treatise on Purgatory* records the revelations she received. She also wrote *Dialogue between the Body and the Soul.* Catherine was married at age 16 to a man who proved to be shiftless, unfaithful, and a spendthrift. He then reformed his life, and the couple agreed to live in continence. They devoted themselves to an intense spiritual life and to work in the Pammetone hospital. St. Catherine was widowed at age 50 and died around age 63.

Right: The Curé of Ars, St. John Vianney (1786-1859), who was subjected to continuing physical attacks by the devil over a 30-year period. St. John Vianney heard confessions 13-17 hours per day, and converted thousands of sinners in his lifetime. The devil once revealed to him that if there were three such men as himself on earth, his (Satan's) kingdom would be broken.

Ed. Lescuyer et fils, Lyon

Left: Anne Catherine Emmerich (1774-1824), Augustinian nun, mystic and stigmatist, who was privileged to see visions of Heaven and Purgatory. Sister Emmerich was the greatest visionary in the history of the Church; she received innumerable revelations on all aspects of the Catholic Faith. Anne Catherine Emmerich had the use of reason from birth, and for the last 12 years of her life took no food except Holy Communion.

Right: Our Lady of Fatima, Portugal, who on July 13 of 1917 showed a most terrifying vision of Hell to little Jacinta and Francisco Marto, ages 7 and 9—along with their 10-year-old cousin, Lucy. Our Lady told the three children: "You have seen Hell, where the souls of poor sinners go. In order to save them, God wishes to establish in the world devotion to my Immaculate Heart." Our Lady also said, "Many souls go to Hell because they have no one to make sacrifices and pray for them."

Left: Saint Dominic Savio (1842-1857), who after death appeared in glory to his teacher, St. John Bosco; his motto in life had been "Death but not sin." Dominic told St. John Bosco that the thought that had sustained him the most at the hour of death was that of the assistance of the Blessed Virgin Mary.

Right: Jacinta Marto (1910-1920), Fatima seer whose heart was torn in agony by the thought of poor sinners falling into Hell. Jacinta constantly prayed and made sacrifices for the salvation of sinners. She said, "If men only knew what awaits them in eternity, they would do everything in their power to change their lives." Also, referring to Hell, "So many go there. So many." Jacinta died alone in a hospital, suffering intensely for sinners; all that afternoon she had been heard wailing of the lost in Hell and pleading with God to accept her pain as penance for hardened sinners. When the night nurse found her dead, there were tears of blood on her little cheeks.

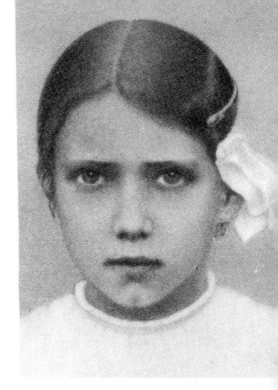

Left: Francisco Marto (1908-1919), brother of Jacinta, who was consumed by the desire to console Our Lord, so offended by sins. Our Lady promised to take him to Heaven, but she stated that first he must say "many Rosaries."

Mella

Pope St. Pius X (1835-1914), who performed various long-distance cures, such as the cure of the mother superior of an orphanage who was dying in India; when Pope Pius X telegraphed her his blessing, she was healed.

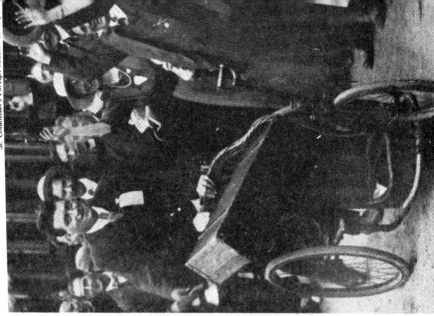

Jack Traynor just before leaving on his visit to Lourdes in 1923, and jubilantly returning home after his remarkable cure. Due to war injuries, his right arm had been paralyzed, with the muscles atrophied, his legs had been partially paralyzed, he had become epileptic, and he had an inch-wide hole in his skull from an operation to remove shrapnel. The British War Pension Ministry considered him completely and permanently disabled and granted him a 100% pension for life. All these serious infirmities were healed at Lourdes, and Traynor subsequently went into the coal and hauling business, which involved lifting 200-lb. sacks of coal. His cure resulted in a great number of conversions in Liverpool.

Next page: The resurrection of the body at the end of the world.

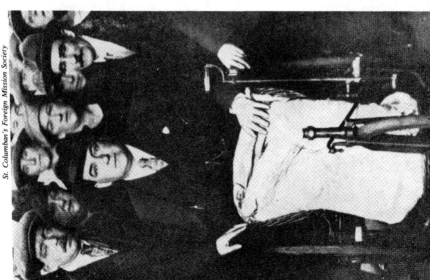

dubious doubter will find that evidence accumulates rapidly. Christians in the latter part of the twentieth century have easy access to huge piles of accounts of genuine miracles, which continue to increase. Consider, for example, the number of miracles authenticated at Lourdes alone (under strict medical examinations, with cures of nervous and psychosomatic disorders being excluded), or the cosmic miracle of the spinning sun at Fatima in 1917.

Modern man has the benefit of this vast store of wondrous works of God, brought about in His Church and through His saints. That was not the situation for those living in the early centuries. Today the evidence can be examined and the results of that search can edify, console, and convince an honest searcher of the greatness of God and the power of His Son.

But even for His first listeners, and also in early Christian times, Christ worked many and great miracles. The Jews were already established in their God-given faith; the pagans had never heard of the One True God or of Christ—in a sense both were entitled to great miracles authenticating the divine authority of Christ, so that they could reasonably accept His Faith with its demands and its eternal consequences.

St. Irenaeus (c. 125—c. 203), the first great Catholic theologian after St. John and St. Paul, wrote that miracles, including the raising of the dead, were frequent occurrences in the early Church. Regarding the magicians of his time, he states that "they cannot give sight to the blind nor hearing to the deaf, nor put to flight demons; and they are so far from raising the dead, as Our Lord did, and the Apostles, by prayer, and as is most frequently done among the brethren, that they even think it impossible." (*Adversus Haereses,* II). St. Justin Martyr (died 167), outstanding apologist, also testified that the gift of miracles and the casting out of demons were frequent in the Church of his day. So one must not jump to the conclusion that miracles were rare, or that they did not exist, in those early centuries. God grants more

miracles when there is more faith, and there was more faith
and less unbelief in those early times.

Nor is the power of miracles lessened in the Church today. Then why do we not hear of such miracles today? In
many instances, faith has decreased. "And he wrought not
many miracles there, because of their unbelief." (*Matt.*
13:58). The mustard seed of faith is the lever needed to
move any mountain or obstacle. Now death is the greatest
"mountain" to be overcome. Where holiness and faith increase, and where there is need, as for the pagans, miracles
in general will increase, including the raising of the dead.

It is a fact, then, that human beings, objectively dead,
have been restored to life through other human beings, instruments of God—usually saints. And this historical,
universal, and continued phenomenon is found only in the
Holy Catholic Church. God works this miracle in and of the
Catholic Church in order to endorse its divine origin and its
divine message.

Further, we know that if creature instruments of the Creator can work such wonders, it was certainly no problem for
Christ, the Eternal Word, co-equal with the Father, to raise
Lazarus or to perform any other miracle when He was on
earth. Here is where demythologizing exegetes and
"ruminating faith-community" theologians stumble over the
mustard seed of faith and against God's power.

And if the miracles of today successfully withstand the
probings of the Lourdes Medical Bureau, if the miracles examined in canonical processes can bear the scrutiny of outstanding scientists, why should one fear that the miracles of
Christ or those of yesterday's saints would not have? It will
pose no problem, likewise, for Christ to raise all human
beings on the Last Day. The same God who has created
billions can easily re-create or restore the bodies of billions.

As St. Paul says in *Hebrews,* Our Lord came "that through
death, he might destroy him [Satan] who had the empire of
death." (*Heb.* 2:14). But St. Paul also says a little later on
regarding some people, "And we see that they could not

enter in, because of unbelief." (*Heb.* 3:19).

As Vatican I stated, miracles in the Church are signs by which she is lifted up as a sign to the nations and proven to be the One True Church of God. And as Monden observes, "The miracle makes use of a language which is equally clear to the men of every age." For that reason, the miracles of Christ, those of the saints, and those in the Church today are all interchangeable. The authenticity of the one vouches for the authenticity of the other, and the authenticity of all holds them all together as one great sign from God.

31

THE RESURRECTION OF CHRIST:
THE BASIS OF OUR FAITH

*"Now God hath both raised up the
Lord, and will raise us up also by his
power."*

—1 Corinthians 6:14

The Resurrection of Jesus Christ was the turning point in
human history and is the basis of the Christian Faith. It
completed the work of man's salvation and redemption by
which "the gates of Heaven," closed since the sin of Adam,
were again opened. The Passion, death and Resurrection of
Our Lord constitute the most momentous event in the history of the world.

St. Paul summed it all up when he stated: "And if Christ
be not risen again, then is our preaching vain, and your faith
is also vain . . . And if Christ be not risen again, your faith is
vain, for you are yet in your sins." (*1 Cor.* 15:14, 17). Thus
the Resurrection of Christ is the basis of our faith. If it did
not happen, Christianity is based on a lie and we have no
hope of our own resurrection.

The fact of the Resurrection is so important that St. Peter
declared that the characteristic of an Apostle was to be a
witness to it. When the followers of Christ were gathered
together to choose someone to replace Judas, St. Peter stated
that from among the men who had known Jesus, "one of
these must be made a witness with us of his resurrection."
(*Acts* 1:22). The writings of St. Paul contain numerous
references to the Apostles' preaching the Resurrection of
Christ—in Jerusalem (*Acts* 3:15; 4:10; 5:30; 10:40), at Antioch (*Acts* 13:30 ff.), at Athens (*Acts* 17:31), at Corinth (*1*

Cor. 15), at Rome (*Rom.* 6:4-5), and in Thessalonica (*1 Thess.* 1:10).

The Resurrection of Christ from the dead was possible only because He was both divine and human. He was the Second Person of the Blessed Trinity from all eternity, but He had also taken to Himself a human nature in the womb of the Virgin Mary, by the power of the Holy Spirit.

Jesus could suffer and die in His human nature, but because He was a Divine Person, all that He suffered had a divine value that purchased universal redemption for all mankind. All men would not make use of that redemption, so all would not be saved, but Christ had made salvation *available* to all.

God's perfect wisdom expressed itself in the way He planned and arranged the entire Incarnation and Redemption. Our Lord might have appeared suddenly, with great display, as a full grown man. He could have saved humanity in some other, easier manner.

But this would have prevented man from having many wonderful blessings of Divine Providence. Moreover, there would likely have been allegations that it was just a spirit or apparition that had appeared on earth in such a brief redemptive action, and not really the true God-Man. Indeed, even with His long life to prove His humanity, there were early heresies denying the fact of Our Lord's real, true human nature.

But the full Christmas story of a real Babe, of Herod's swords being aimed at His infant head, of His long family life at Nazareth amidst flesh-and-blood cousins or "brethren," and of His final three years of open public ministry, solidly established the fact of His genuine human nature. Thus His familiars could ask, "Is not this the carpenter's son?" (*Matt.* 13:55). And Jesus could say, "The Son of man came eating and drinking, and they say: Behold a man that is a glutton and a wine drinker, a friend of publicans and sinners." (*Matt.* 11:19).

It is obvious, then, that both Jesus' fellow townspeople of

Nazareth and His irreverent enemies were convinced that He was human: "because that thou, being a man, makest thyself God." (*John* 10:33). Because His enemies considered Jesus a mere man, they crucified Him for His "blasphemy." But because He was God, He rose by His own power.

Our Lord Himself provided the proof for His divinity: the Old Testament prophecies fulfilled in Himself, His mighty works, His absolute innocence, His Lordship of the Sabbath, and His supreme power over all nature as manifested in His miracles. Moreover, He cast out those archenemies of God and man, the fallen angels, the demons. He performed all His miracles and forgave sins in His own name and by His own power.

He sealed His claim with the sublime words, "Before Abraham was made, I am" (*John* 8:58)—as well as with many other words testifying to His divinity. When He finally expired on the cross, the centurion, a witness for Rome, exclaimed, "Indeed this was the Son of God."

Our Lord spoke of Himself as a man who had a human nature that could be destroyed—and yet triumph over that destruction. He prophesied His own death and Resurrection. "Destroy this temple," He said, speaking of the temple of His body, "and in three days I will raise it up." (*John* 2:19). An incredulous generation would be given only one last, final sign, that of Jonah coming out of the belly of the whale after three days. And He spoke even more specifically: "From that time Jesus began to shew to his disciples that he must go to Jerusalem, and suffer many things from the ancients and scribes and chief priests, and be put to death, and on the third day rise again." (*Matt.* 16:21; cf. also *Matt.* 26:32).

The Bible also makes many other references to the Resurrection of Christ. Sometimes it is stated that God raised Him from the dead (cf. *Acts* 3:15), and sometimes it is stated that He "is risen" (cf. *Matt.* 28:6-7), thus showing forth both natures of Christ: as man, Our Lord was raised by God; as God, He arose by His own power. Referring to His own divine power, He said: "I lay down my life, that I may take it again. No man taketh it away from me: but I lay it down of myself, and I have power to lay it down: and I have power to take it up again. This commandment have I received of my Father." (*John* 10:17-18).

Because Christ was man, the Son of Man, He was going to suffer and die. Because He was God, He was going to rise from the dead. It is ridiculous to conceive of a God-Man remaining dead!

Jesus planned way ahead that there would be no doubt that it was His true physical body that was involved in the Good Friday crucifixion, that it was His flesh and blood that lay wrapped in a shroud in the tomb borrowed from Joseph of Arimathea, and that it was with His own body that He arose on Easter morning.

So He came to His Passion, to thorns that pressed about His human brow, to scourges that rent the flesh of His human body. And red, red blood flowed from His wounds. He was fixed to the cross with real iron nails that made real holes in real hands and feet. He refused wine with gall that would have acted as a pain reliever, but He took wine at the last moment.

His enemies, thinking they had a mere man nailed to the wood, and forgetting His great deeds, or blinding themselves with obstinate pride, jeered: "If Thou be the Son of God, come down from the cross." The same words might the devil have spoken, realizing at last that this was his most terrible mistake of all, to have Jesus crucified and *not* come down. "Come down!" he might have frantically yelled, or inspired others to shout. For it was clear that Christ's real triumph would be in remaining on the cross. The scheming of the Jewish leaders was working out according to the plan of God, for His glory and the salvation of man.

No, Christ would not come down from the cross, though many others had rejected their God-given sufferings. And there would subsequently be many false or weak Christians who would walk away from the sufferings of martyrdom for temporary relief or earthly favors. No, Our Lord's death was the goal and purpose of His whole life and mission, a victory over sin, the demons, the grave.

When at last He expired with the words "It is consummated," in accord with His Father's will, the human body that hung there upon the wood was really dead.

However, God wanted everything to be completely certified by historical records, to *show* that His Son was really dead. Joseph of Arimathea, perceiving—perhaps against all his hopes—that Jesus was dead, went to Pilate and asked for the body. Pilate, thinking of the responsibility of his position and fearing further trouble from the Jews, wanted to be sure Jesus was dead.

The Jews, too, wanted the three "criminals" on the crosses officially declared dead. It was the eve of the preparation day for the great Sabbath, and they did not want that day, which began at sunset, to be profaned by unburied bodies. (What a fine, pious scruple—rather than profane the Sabbath, to batter the body of the Son of God in order to hasten His death!) So the soldiers went to break the legs of the three crucified men so they would die quickly and the bodies could be removed.

They found the two thieves still alive, and broke their legs. How Mary His Mother must have trembled in her heart as she saw the soldiers smash their legs—sympathizing with them in their agonies, praying that her Son would be spared this barbarity. There was a Scriptural prophecy: "You shall not break a bone of him." And another: "They shall look on him whom they pierced." (*John* 19:36, 37). The soldiers saw that Jesus was dead, and did not break His legs.

However, the Roman centurion in charge had a responsibility. So that there would be no doubt, the report to Pilate included one final proof of death: One of the soldiers (traditionally called "Longinus") "with a spear opened his side and immediately there came out blood and water." (*John* 19:34). St. John, Apostle and Evangelist, was standing there with Mary, and he attests to this truth. So there can be no doubt that this Man on the cross was dead, the last blood and water (or fluid) having trickled from His body.

Now when brave and bold Joseph of Arimathea secured the body of Jesus, after Pilate had summoned the centurion for his report of death, a little group made haste to bury their Lord before sundown. Joseph had offered his own new tomb hewn out of rock, a tomb in which no one had ever been buried, in the garden near Calvary. Nicodemus came with a mixture of myrrh and aloes, about a hundred pounds in weight. Jesus' friends hurriedly anointed His body, the women planning to come back after the Sabbath to honor Jesus lovingly with a more complete service.

Joseph's was a good-sized tomb, that of a rich man, and within it they laid Jesus on a "table," or slab of rock; then they helped Joseph roll a huge stone across the entrance. Then they all hastened homeward to observe the Sabbath.

The Jews, telling Pilate of Jesus' prediction that He would rise again after three days, asked for a guard to be stationed at the tomb, lest His disciples steal the body and say Jesus was raised from the dead. Pilate agreed, gave them a guard, and ordered a seal placed on the tomb.

The action of the Jews is one more illustration of how God makes use of the folly and evil intentions of men to confound their plans and further His own designs and glory. Here was established a guard composed of soldiers of the greatest and most famous human power in all history, the Roman Empire. Here, one might say, stood the power of the Roman Emperor—his soldiers, his seal. It was all there to assure that Jesus' body would stay in that tomb and that there would be no human tampering with it.

How naive can men be! But there was indeed one thing that all these various men did know for sure: they were guarding a *dead* body.

But lo! On Sunday morning there was a mighty earthquake, and the angel of the Lord, resembling a flash of lightning with his garments as dazzling as snow, rolled the stone back and seated himself upon it. His action seemed to declare that the stone which was guarding death, as well as the power of the Roman government, was ingloriously sat upon and conquered.

At the appearance of this shining angel "the guards were struck with terror, and became as dead men." The angel had not flashed down to let Jesus out; the angel came to show that He was already gone, already risen. Just as Jesus' risen, spiritualized body would pass through the cenacle room with its locked doors later that day, so Our Lord had already passed through the sealed tomb with ease.

At daybreak, Mary Magdalen, Mary the mother of James, and Salome hurried to the tomb with perfumed spices to complete the anointing of Jesus' body. They were wondering: "Who shall roll us back the stone from the door of the sepulchre?" (*Mark* 16:3). It was a huge stone, and even the three of them would not be able to slide it along its trench.

When the women arrived they saw that the stone was rolled back and that the tomb was empty. Then the angel addressed them: "Fear not you; for I know that you seek Jesus who was crucified. He is not here, for he is risen, as he said. Come, and see the place where the Lord was laid." (*Matt.* 28:5-6). Here was angelic, supernatural testimony to the Resurrection of Jesus Christ.

As the women spread the news, there were a number of visitors to the empty tomb that first Easter Day. Mary, the Mother of Jesus, is not mentioned among these visitors. Most writers in the Church agree that Jesus visited her first, privately. Mary did not go to the empty tomb, or at least she did not rush to it as the others did, because she remembered and believed Jesus' words that He would rise.

Simon Peter and John raced there, though; Peter entered the tomb and noticed the wrappings of Jesus' body on the ground, and the head cloth rolled up in a place by itself. John attests that he too saw and believed. Perhaps the body cloth or shroud and wrappings were left as if a body had simply passed through them.

Jesus made a special appearance to Mary Magdalen and to another or other women. The women clung to the feet of

Jesus as if to make sure He was real; they did not wish to let Him go. This Gospel detail shows the reality of Our Lord's risen body, which was not a "ghost" or an apparition. It was a real, physically tangible body.

There are variations among the four Gospel accounts of the events after the Resurrection of Jesus, but they all make the same point: He was there, He was real, He spoke and walked and "broke bread" with His faithful followers. The acounts are well known from the Easter liturgy. Well-known, too, is the account of how Jesus walked along with the two disciples on their way to Emmaus, as well as the accounts of His appearances to the Apostles and others—on one occasion including five hundred of the faithful gathered together. (St. Paul stated later that many of those witnesses were still living at his writing.)

When the two from Emmaus had rushed back to tell of meeting Jesus, they were greeted by the eleven and others: "The Lord is risen, indeed, and hath appeared to Simon." (*Luke* 24:34). And even as they were talking, Jesus Himself appeared to them all. "Peace be to you; it is I, fear not." (*Luke* 24:36). But they were near panic, thinking they saw a ghost; Jesus asked them why they were disturbed. He knew how to calm them. He said, "See my hands and my feet, that it is I Myself; handle and see: for a spirit hath not flesh and bones, as you see me to have." (*Luke* 24:39). And Our Lord showed them His hands and feet with the wounds that no longer bled, for He now had a risen, spiritualized body, though it would be fully glorified only in Heaven.

As some were still incredulous with joy and wonder, He said to them, "Have you here anything to eat?" Jesus was always the practical instructor, the perfect psychologist. "And they offered him a piece of broiled fish and a honeycomb. And when he had eaten before them, taking the remains, he gave to them." (*Luke* 24:42-43). They could see that He had eaten. There was no mistaking; they could see that the part He returned to them was still the same food.

On the first Easter Sunday evening Thomas had been absent when Jesus appeared to the Apostles, and later he would not believe their account. So, in that same room a week later, Jesus, appearing again, said to the doubter, "Put in thy finger hither, and see my hands; and bring hither thy hand, and put it into my side; and be not faithless, but believing." And Thomas exclaimed, "My Lord and my God!" One might say that Our Lord bent over backward to give every possible proof of His having risen with His real body. He knew it was a tremendously important fact to establish—and He established it superbly.

Nevertheless, the Jewish leaders persisted in their unbelief, their obstinate refusal to see the truth, even after the sepulcher guards had gone into the city and reported to the chief priests all that had transpired at the tomb. The priests got together with the elders, who bribed the soldiers to say that the disciples had come by night and stolen the body of Jesus while they were sleeping. The Jews told the soldiers that if they got into trouble with Pilate over the open tomb and the missing body the Jewish leaders would straighten out the matter with Pilate—which probably meant a big bribe, or some notable concession to him. As St. Matthew said later, the soldiers accepted the bribe, and the false account of what had happened was still circulating among the Jews of his time. (*Matt.* 28:15).

Anyone who has been a soldier, or is familiar with military life and discipline, knows what a preposterous plot the Jews and guards engineered. A soldier on important guard duty is subject to death for sleeping on his post; he would never confess to such negligence unless he was assured of protection by higher authority.

As St. Augustine, with his trained, logical mind, observed centuries ago: What kind of witnesses are sleeping witnesses? This is a contradiction in terms. If they were asleep, what could they witness to?

Nevertheless, in the name of history, some people attempt to destroy history, as in the name of truth or of Christian faith some so-called theologians today attempt to destroy even the basic truths of the Faith.

The unbeliever, fixed in his preconceived, false position, can always find an excuse for not believing, even when he is faced with arguments that would be incontrovertible for the average sane man. That is why Jesus told some of the Pharisees that they were hopelessly blind, and that if they persisted in that blindness they would die in their sins.

To further instruct His Apostles and to let all know that He had undoubtedly risen from the dead, Jesus appeared frequently during a 40-day period to His disciples and others, and He often ate with them.

In the years that followed, the continuing response of the Apostles and disciples to Our Lord's Resurrection, and also the response of their hearers—as well as the reactions of the Jewish leaders, all provide proof for the reality of this historical event.

The Apostles had nothing earthly to gain, and they had everything to lose, by preaching something so contrary to what the authorities wanted to hear as was the doctrine of the Resurrection of Christ. In fact, all but St. John suffered martyrdom for their testimony to Our Lord's life, words, and Resurrection.

Although the 12 Apostles scattered throughout Europe, Asia, and northern Africa (rather than sticking together for mutual psychological support like, for example, various modern cult groups), not one of them tired of the battle and defected, confessing that the Resurrection story had been made up. Eleven of the 12 gave their lives for this extraordinary story of a Man who had come back from the dead and who had promised that all His faithful followers would likewise rise again after death.

Also, the fact that thousands of Jews and Gentiles, having heard the Apostles' teaching, firmly believed in their message, further substantiates the evident factuality of the Resurrection account. These followers, too, suffered torture and martyrdom by the thousands in support of the "new" religion, a religion based on the fact of the Resurrection of

Jesus Christ. It has well been said that the rise of the Catholic Church amid such terrible opposition and persecution, without the Resurrection, would have been an even greater miracle than the Resurrection itself!

Totally inadequate to explain the growth of the Church is that ridiculous theory of the modernists, i.e., that the "resurrection" of Christ was not a historical reality, but rather a spiritual event which took place in the minds and hearts of the Apostles. People do not suffer and die by the thousands and millions for a spiritual experience which took place in somebody else's mind!

True, there have been cases of charismatic figures misleading large numbers of people, to their own destruction. But the 12 Apostles were ordinary men—slow to understand, slow to believe. Several of them had been fishermen. The power of their message did not come from their own talents or their own personal charisma. And the Resurrection account had to "compete in the open marketplace" of beliefs in Jerusalem, Antioch, Corinth, Rome, and many, many other sophisticated cities, as well as among hard-nosed common-sense country folk—yet it won acceptance everywhere.

Furthermore, the leaders of the Synagogue have provided their own unwilling testimony by their failure to come up with any good alternative explanation for the fact that Jesus' body was missing from the tomb. (This fact they did not even attempt to deny.) As mentioned above, their "witnesses" claimed to have been asleep at the time of the event in question! And the guards were apparently not punished, as would have been the case if Our Lord's body had actually been stolen.

Neither during nor after Jesus' life on earth did the Synagogue leaders give evidence of being disinterested seekers after the truth regarding His words and deeds; they were interested parties. They felt it was to their own advantage to squelch the religion of Christ, which was drawing away support in droves from their own (now superseded) religion.

But despite their efforts, they failed to squelch it.

The Jewish leaders' lack of sincerity is shown in their reaction to Sts. Peter and John after the former had cured a lame man. The Jewish leaders said among themselves:

> "What shall we do to these men? for indeed a known miracle hath been done by them, to all the inhabitants of Jerusalem: it is manifest, and we cannot deny it. But that it may be no farther spread among the people, let us threaten them that they speak no more in this name [that of Jesus of Nazareth] to any man...." (*Acts* 4:16-17).

Sts. Peter and John answered that they must continue to "speak the things which we have seen and heard [regarding Christ]." (*Acts* 4:20). St. Peter was eventually crucified for sticking to his story. (In response to his request, he was crucified head downward, as he felt unworthy to be crucified in the same manner as his Lord.)

Much more honest was the attitude of the wise Pharisee Gamaliel. Gamaliel, recalling other religious leaders who had recently arisen, only to be soon forgotten, gave the following advice to his fellow members of the Jewish council:

> "And now, therefore, I say to you, refrain from these men, and let them alone; for if this council or this work be of men, it will come to naught: but if it be of God, you cannot overthrow it, lest perhaps you be found even to fight against God." (*Acts* 5:38-39).

With the benefit of 20 centuries of hindsight, those of us living today (even those without faith) can see that the stupendous and wondrous teaching that Christ is risen and that His faithful followers shall also rise again has indeed been confirmed by God. The Catholic cathedrals, churches and chapels which testify to this doctrine are to be found throughout the world. Every one of these churches, sheltering the true risen God in its tabernacle, is the fulfillment of the ancient Temple of Jerusalem. The poorest Catholic chapel, literally containing Almighty God Himself in the Blessed Sacrament, infinitely surpasses that magnificent temple, which despite its splendor was only a prefigurement of the Tabernacles of the holy Catholic Church.

Believers in the risen Christ, adorers of His holy Body and Blood present among us, are to be found among every type of people—both eastern and western; educated and uneducated; white, black, and yellow. The Faith is not a local phenomenon. All over the world people have testified with their lives to the truth of the religion of Jesus Christ. Time itself has been divided into two eras, B.C. and A.D., because of the momentous events which took place in Jerusalem 2000 years ago.

The Jews continue to disbelieve (very many even losing faith in their own religious traditions), though even among these people there has been a steady stream of conversions to the religion of Jesus Christ. Among the most famous are Fathers Theodore and Alphonse Ratisbonne, Father Hermann Cohen, Edith Stein, and Father David Goldstein. Worthy of mention is the fact that in 1917 there was formed a "Catholic Guild of Israel" for the conversion of the Jewish people to the True Faith; many of its members were Catholics of Jewish descent.

When Jesus finally ascended into Heaven from Mount Olivet, two angels assured those who were watching that He would similarly return, in clouds of glory. (In the Scriptures, and throughout Old Testament history, the cloud signified the presence of God.) The God-Man had gone to His glory to sit at the right hand of the Father. But we know that one day, just as He promised, He will come back to judge the living and the dead.

32

ARMAGEDDON, THE VALLEY OF JOSAPHAT, AND THE GENERAL JUDGMENT

> *"And the sea gave up the dead that were in it, and death and hell gave up their dead that were in them; and they were judged every one according to their works."*
>
> —Apocalypse 20:13

Near Megiddo of ancient Israel there is a plain called Esdraelon. Near the plain is the Mountain of Megiddo. From the Hebrew *"har-meghiddo,"* to designate the mount, comes the word "Armageddon." There many vital battles were fought throughout the history of the Holy Land. The site and the name have become the apocalyptic symbol for the final great battle to be fought toward the end of the world. St. John wrote in the Apocalypse:

> "For they are the spirits of devils working signs, and they go forth unto the kings of the whole earth, to gather them to battle against the great day of the Almighty God. Behold, I come as a thief. Blessed is he that watcheth . . . And he shall gather them together into a place, which in Hebrew is called Armagedon." (*Apoc.* 16:14-16).

This great conflict is to be one of the signs of the approaching end of the world. However, it is not clear whether this means the *final* end. Satan will be cast into the abyss for a "thousand years," apparently after the time of the Antichrist. Then it is written that Satan will be loosed again for "a little while."

> "And when the thousand years shall be finished, Satan shall be loosed out of his prison, and shall go forth, and seduce the nations, which are over the four quarters of the earth, Gog, and Magog, and shall gather them together to battle . . . And there came down fire from God out of heaven, and devoured them; and the devil, who seduced them, was cast into the pool of fire and brimstone, where both the beast and the false prophet shall be tormented day and night for ever and ever." (*Apoc.* 20:7-10).

So it seems that first there will be a great battle at the time of the Antichrist, when he and the false prophet will be cast into Hell. Then, after the "thousand-year" period when Satan is bound and Christ is reigning, the dragon will be released for a "little while," and the last great contest between evil and divine powers will take place. Then shall come the Final Judgment, the triumph of the Lamb, the establishment of a new heavens and a new earth, and the eternal era of the heavenly Jerusalem assembled before the throne of God and the Lamb.

According to the prophet Joel, the Valley of Josaphat will be the place where Christ will judge all the nations. The third chapter of the Book of Joel states:

> "I will gather together all nations, and will bring them down into the valley of Josaphat: and I will plead with them there for my people, and for my inheritance Israel, whom they have scattered among the nations, and have parted my land. . . . Let them arise, and let the nations come up into the valley of Josaphat: for there I will sit to judge all nations round about." (*Joel* 3:2, 12).

The Valley of Josaphat has been identified with the Valley of Cedron (Kedron) since the time of Eusebius (265-340 A.D.), but that is only an opinion. The Valley of Cedron is east of Jerusalem. Joel says both "bring them down" and "come up." To get to Cedron one must first go *up* to Jerusalem, then *down* into the Valley of Cedron, where there was the sepulcher of Josaphat. The valley passes between the eastern walls of the city and Mount Olivet. Many pilgrims walk down there (as the author has done), past the shrine church of the tomb of the Blessed Virgin Mary's Assumption, to the Garden of Gethsemani. The brook Cedron is usually dry. Our Lord crossed it on the night of His betrayal to go to the garden of His agony. (According to the visions of Anne Catherine Emmerich as described in her *Life of Christ,* the soldiers who captured Our Lord in the Garden of Gethsemani dragged Him through the Cedron; it was filled with water.) Some think the name "Cedron" means the "Valley of Cedars."

The Cedron Valley is much longer than it seems when seen from Mount Olivet. It runs for about three miles, beginning about a mile and a quarter north of Jerusalem. After it passes the familiar Mt. Olivet spot and St. Stephen's Gate (where it is 100 feet deep—and at the latter point, about 400 feet wide) it turns sharply southeast and wanders off to the Dead Sea. Actually it is not a very small area.

However, the Valley of Josaphat may be only a symbolic name for the actual gathering place of all mankind for the General Judgment. Interestingly, when the author was in Jerusalem in 1979 and walked about this spot, the well-informed Palestinian guide pointed out the many tombs of the Jews there and said that Jews desire to be buried there because they believe that on Judgment Day the valley will split and all the dead will come forth from their graves.

The events of the actual Judgment Day assemblage are provided in the Gospel accounts in Our Lord's words: the great disturbances in nature, the trumpets sounding, the angels gathering every human being, the Saviour coming on the clouds in majesty.

That Christ would appear in Judgment near Jerusalem, the holy city, seems reasonable. Jerusalem not only represents Heaven, but it was there that Our Lord wept over the city "that killeth the prophets." Since the enemies of God are then to be judged by Christ along with the Apostles and other holy ones, then the valley where the Son of Man was betrayed and seized seems a very suitable assembly place.

The rather inane statement has been made that the Valley of Josaphat does not offer much room for the judgment of the billions who will be assembled on that awesome and rewarding day. That argument is as ludicrous as a claim that the Blessed Mother's body could not have survived its ascent through the rarefied air when she was assumed into Heaven! The Lord's powers surely preclude the necessity for oxygen masks!

Judgment Day, of course, will not be the first time that the dead arose in Jerusalem. When Our Lord died the earth quaked, the temple curtain and the rocks were rent, and "many bodies of the saints that had slept arose, and coming out of the tombs after his resurrection, came into the holy city, and appeared to many." (*Matt.* 27:52-53).

We must distinguish between the Particular Judgment, which every person faces at death, and the General Judgment, which will take place at the end of the world. The Church teaches that there will be a Particular Judgment at which the souls of the deceased will be sent to Heaven, Hell, or Purgatory (or possibly Limbo), though this doctrine is not expressly taught in the Scriptures. But it is clearly implied in the Biblical passages which refer to the immediate reward or retribution after death—for instance, in the story of Dives and Lazarus, and in the case of the Good Thief. ("This day thou shalt be with Me in Paradise!") The Judgment which is set forth in the creeds, however, is the final or General Judgment.

It is at this latter judgment that all the thoughts, words, and deeds of every man will be manifest to the whole world.

At this time the wicked will see clearly how they have wasted their lives; their pride and riches have passed away like a shadow. Seeing the salvation of the elect, they will say to themselves: "We fools esteemed their life madness, and their end without honor. Behold how they are numbered among the children of God, and their lot is among the saints." (*Wis.* 5:4-5). Then will the bodies of all the dead rise—those of the elect, or saved, to enjoy eternal glory, and those of the damned to endure eternal torment. Purgatory will no longer exist.

The prophet Ezekiel, at the time of the Babylonian Captivity of the Jews, had a great vision of the plain of dry bones; he watched as all the bones reassembled with dramatic movements and came to life as an army. (*Ezech.* 17). This imagery was intended to prophesy the restoration of the destroyed nation. However, it is also applied to the general resurrection of the dead, for He who gave life the first time can certainly give life the second. (There is, or at least there was, among the replicas of Holy Land shrines at the Franciscan Monastery in Washington, D.C., a striking mural of Ezekiel's vision of the dry bones.)

Many authorities believe that Henoch and Elias, who apparently never died, will return alive to the holy city in the latter days. Elias went up in the fiery chariot (*4 Kgs.* 2:11; *Mal.* 4:5-6; cf. also *Matt.* 17:10-12; *Mark* 9:11), and Henoch walked with God and was seen no more (cf. *Gen.* 5:24; *Heb.* 11:5; *Jude* 14-15). There they will fight the Antichrist and his false prophet, be slain, and after lying dead in Jerusalem for three days, will come to life again.

The most important thing at the General Resurrection will not be the place or manner of assembling. The crucial question when those trumpets blow and the angels gather the dead from land, sea and space is on which side of Christ an individual will be placed. As the Lord comes with His standard of the cross glowing and His wounds shining, "to judge the living and the dead," will one be living among the sheep on His right hand, or dead forever among the goats on His left?

Judgment will be decided on the state of the soul, no matter whether the individual died long ago in the days of Abel, or was taken up alive on the Last Day. The important factor will be whether that person died in the state of grace, whether he loved God and assisted Christ in his unfortunate neighbor. As St. John of the Cross says, in the end "we shall be judged by love."

The good then will enter into the joy of the Lord, in their glorified bodies. The bad, rising with their horrible deformed bodies, will hear those terrible words from a just Saviour whose salvation they resisted: "Depart from me, you cursed, into everlasting fire which was prepared for the devil and his angels." (*Matt.* 25:41).

In the last few chapters of the Apocalypse (Revelations) one will find a good symbolic picture of the heavenly happiness of the saved and the eternal hellish misery of the damned. The symbolic language regarding the beautiful golden city is used because, at present, human language is unable to express the superior joys and happiness that God has prepared for His elect. "Eye hath not seen, nor ear heard, neither hath it entered into the heart of man, what things God hath prepared for them that love him." (*1 Cor.* 2:9).

Let every soul spare no pains to make sure that on that Last Day he is numbered among those admitted to the Kingdom of Heaven, and not among those rejected forever from the face of their God and Saviour. We were created for Heaven, and if we miss our eternal destiny it may well be said of us: "It would have been better had he never been born." Those admitted to the Kingdom of Heaven, however, will praise God eternally for having created them and for having saved them. Bless the Lord, O my soul, for His mercy endures forever!

33

THE RESURRECTION OF THE BODY AT THE END OF THE WORLD

"For the hour cometh, wherein all that are in the graves shall hear the voice of the Son of God. And they that have done good things, shall come forth unto the resurrection of life; but they that have done evil, unto the resurrection of judgment."
—John 5:28-29

In this last chapter we will review some of the things covered in this book—to strengthen our faith in Christ, in Christ's holy Catholic Church, and in the General Resurrection which will take place at the end of the world. Further, the wonders described herein fill out the Christian's mental picture of his hoped-for end, and of the glorious state of the elect that will come at the final Resurrection and Universal Judgment. We will also bring forward a few other points with regard to this most important future event.

Throughout history there have been those who reject the doctrine of the resurrection of the body. Among these are those who see the body as the prison of the soul and who therefore desire to escape from it at death. Others, such as the Gnostics and Manichaeans, believe that matter is evil in itself, and thus see no good in a resurrection of the body. And of course there are those who do not even believe in the immortality of the soul (even though this is a truth that can be proven by reason alone, without divine revelation).

The Bible states that when St. Paul preached to the Athenians regarding the resurrection of the dead, "some indeed mocked." (*Acts* 17:32). Almost four centuries later, St.

Augustine stated that "No doctrine of the Christian Faith is so vehemently and so obstinately opposed as the doctrine of the resurrection of the flesh." (*In Ps. 88,* sermo 2, n. 5).

Indeed, it is true that a resurrection of the body *as it exists on this earth* would be a hindrance. This body cannot keep up with the powers of the soul, intellect and will. For example, a person cannot move nearly as fast as he can think, and his body provides many obstacles to the carrying out of his desires—for example, the need to eat and sleep. And this is even truer of a body that is diseased, injured, in pain—or which has either not yet reached, or has passed beyond, the youthful vitality of its prime. Plus, the body provides an entrance to many temptations of the flesh, making it necessary for a virtuous person to be constantly vigilant, and often to engage in "battle" with his own inclinations.

But the risen bodies of the just (not the risen bodies of the damned) will no longer present these drawbacks to the soul. Possessing the four qualities of 1) impassibility; 2) subtility (subtlety); 3) agility; and 4) clarity—also called "glory" or "brightness," the body will be 1) immune from all pain; 2) like a spirit—without, however, ceasing to be a true body; 3) able to move with the speed of thought; and 4) free from anything deformed, and filled with beauty and radiance because the beauty of the transfigured soul overflows onto the body. The degree of a person's glory will depend upon the degree of his merit.

Thus the souls of the elect after the resurrection will have perfect dominion over their glorified bodies. Such a body will be no drawback to the soul; soul and body will be intimately united and will work together in perfect harmony.

It is most fitting that the human body rise again; its perpetual separation from the soul would seem unnatural. Since the body has been the partner of the soul in the person's sins and virtues, it is just that it share in the soul's reward or punishment. The soul and body belong together, and the soul's happiness is completed by reunification with its body, now perfected and filled with every good. Even in this life God preserved the body of Jonas in the belly of the whale, of the three young men in the fiery furnace, of Daniel in the lions' den, and the bodies of Henoch and Elias (which did not die but were carried up to Heaven); and then there were the bodies of Lazarus, the daughter of Jairus, and the widow's son, whom Our Lord raised from the dead.

Sometimes the question arises: How will the dead be able to arise with their own bodies, since the matter on this earth has been recycled over and over again over the centuries? Indeed, the material elements which compose the bodies of those living today may well have also been part of the bodies of other human beings who lived years ago. On resurrection day, whose body will get those elements? And what about the case of cannibalism, where one person consumes another human being's flesh?

At first glance this may seem like a formidable problem. It is definitely not a *new* problem; this and other objections to the doctrine of the resurrection of the body were discussed by theologians centuries ago. Although no one can explain just how it will happen, we know that on the last day it will not matter at all that the minerals of John's dead bones have been reabsorbed into the earth, eventually becoming part of James' living body. Scientists claim that a person gets a complete new suit of skin every seven years— but he does not thereby lose his identity of body.

St. Thomas states that if there were not a material identity between the body in this life and the risen body, we ought to speak not of the *resurrection* of the body, but of the *assumption* of a *new* body. Certainly the "mechanics" of giving us back the same bodies as we had on earth will present no difficulty to the omniscient and all-powerful God who created them *ex nihilo*—"out of nothing"—in the first place.

The life of Heaven is not to be conceived as a static life—still less does it carry any trace of boredom. There is no sluggishness or weariness there; on the contrary, the elect are full of energy and vigor. All is life and activity in Heaven. The intellect, will, memory, imagination, senses, and all the members of the risen body will be engaged in holy activity. "Our union with God in the beatific vision, far from destroying the activities of our nature, will rather increase and perfect them . . . Our faculties will receive supernatural powers, which will give to our nature its highest degree of perfection and similitude to God, who is all activity." (*The Happiness of Heaven,* by Fr. J. Boudreau, S.J., p. 107-112).

What age will the risen body be? Theologians commonly teach that the bodies of the elect will arise in the bloom and vigor of youth. St. Thomas Aquinas states that since in childhood the body has not reached its full perfection, and in the aged it has already receded from its full perfection, therefore the bodies of the just will be at the age of youth. This perfect age has often been speculated to be 33, the age at which Our Lord rose from the dead. On the other hand, the Blessed Virgin Mary has been younger than this in some of her apparitions; for example, St. Bernadette said that Our Lady was "very young," as well as very beautiful. In any case, the body will be at the perfect age, whatever age that may be.

The damned, too, shall rise again—but not to eternal glory. As stated by the Fourth Lateran Council (the 12th ecumenical council of the Church, convoked in 1215): "He [Christ] will come at the end of the world; he will judge the living and the dead; and he will reward all, both the lost and the elect, according to their works. And all these will rise with their own bodies which they now have so that they may receive according to their works, whether good or bad; the wicked, a perpetual punishment with the devil; the good, eternal glory with Christ." Our Lord Himself stated that they that have done evil shall come forth unto "the resurrection of judgment." (*John* 5:29).

Thus the bodies of the damned will endure perpetual

torment for sins; they will be punished forever. Our Lord referred to Hell thrice in succession as a place "where their worm dieth not, and the fire is not extinguished." (*Mark* 9:43, 45, 47). We may well assume that the damned will wish their bodies had *not* risen, to partake of the tortures of Hell. St. Augustine says that their very incorruptibility is an incorruptibility of continuous corruption. This is the terrible place which, rather than go there, it is far better to pluck out one's hand or foot or eye.

But just as the damned will suffer in all their senses, so will the elect experience pure and exquisite pleasures in all their senses. The body, which shared so intimately in the soul's journey to salvation, will be rewarded along with it. Here will the bodies of the martyrs who suffered so terribly be recompensed. Here will the elect be rewarded in their bodies as well as in their souls. Thus God's justice and mercy extend not only to the soul, but also to the body.

In this book we saw the many resurrection miracles which have occurred over the centuries, miracles which are a continuing testimony to the doctrine of the resurrection of the body at the end of the world. Added to these miracles we saw that there have been many cases of the *dying* being restored to perfect health (such events being just on the borderline of being actual resurrection miracles).

Also, we saw that there have been other types of miracles than those of raising the dead—works that seem equally, or in a way even more wonderful, than the raising of a recently dead, fairly intact body. These include the seemingly impossible act of the immediate ridding of a seriously sick body of all harmful excess matter—tumors, dropsy liquid, dead cells, pus and other poisons—without *killing* that body of strain.

Then we saw the obverse side of that medical coin: the immediate rebuilding of an emaciated or dehydrated body, or one whose tissues have been eaten away, the restoration of decimated cells, or even of whole missing organs or parts of bones (up to three centimeters of missing bone), or the filling out of a deep cavity. These recoveries are simply impossible according to the laws of nature. They could not happen instantly without destroying the body. In the first instance, uremic poisoning would result from rapidly absorbing so much toxic matter, and in both cases the heart would be unable to function under the strains imposed by such rapid change. All these wonders make it easier to see the credibility of the doctrine of the Resurrection on the Last Day.

Further, a great number of unusual gifts, charisms, and supernatural wonders were seen among various saints while they were still alive on this earth. These gifts, or at least some of them, showed that it was only God who could have sustained these saints from death under the circumstances. These gifts also show how easy it will be for the spiritualized bodies of the blessed to have similar endowments and capacities on Judgment Day.

Many saints or holy persons could survive long periods of time without food or drink, except for Holy Communion, the Bread of Life—a wonder that is restricted to saints and other holy souls of the Church. There were other gifts: The saints' bodies were often immune to the effects of fire, extreme cold, or other mortal enemies of mere flesh and blood according to the usual vulnerabilities of our material human nature.

We saw also the gifts of ecstasy, levitation, miraculous mobility and transportation, and of bilocation—all of which, if attempted on one's own (an impossibility), would only lead to injury or death. For example, Simon Magus, the Magician, attempted to "fly" or leap from a great height, and was immediately dashed to the ground. There is a great difference between the audacity of daring to attempt the impossible by one's human powers and the humility of the loving, contemplative saint whom God lifts up in levitation.

These various gifts defy all the laws of nature concerning matter and gravity, time and place. They show how easy it is for God, the Author of nature, to elevate nature. And especially, they show how well the Lord rewards supernatural faith or love.

There were still other gifts given to or wonders worked for the bodies of the saints, those men and women of mortal dust whose bodies nevertheless remained incorrupt at death, sometimes for centuries. Sometimes corpses which at the time of death were emaciated, diseased and "wrecked," became immediately youthful again: serene, beautiful, even radiant and giving off a lovely fragrance. Merely touching these bodies was often enough to effect a miracle.

Even in their lifetime on earth, many saints were seen with a brilliant light about them that filled their cells or rooms at night, or with aureoles or nimbuses that surrounded their heads or bodies with wondrous beauty.

Besides the experiences of the living saints and the wonders that have occurred at their graves, we saw that there have been innumerable apparitions of Christ, Mary, the angels and saints given to persons yet on earth—often to other, still-living saints. These appearances or apparitions add convincing evidence (even though they were private experiences or revelations) for the immortality of the souls of those who appeared, for the reality of the resurrected bodies of Christ and Mary, and for the real existence of Heaven in the other world.

In reverse, the visits of saints or holy persons from earth to Purgatory and Hell give evidence for the actual existence of those places. And the fact that the saints' experiences there influenced them to lead, on their return to earth, even more holy and penitential lives, adds further convincing evidence. Moreover, glimpses of Heaven, sometimes granted even to deceased pagans who were subsequently raised from the dead, provided holy incentives for living good Christian lives in hopes of gaining Paradise for all eternity.

In brief, all these wonders enable one to see the ease with which, on Judgment Day, the elect will be raised from the dead and blessed with the many gifts and qualities of spiritualized bodies.

Finally, we saw that in the latter days, Henoch and Elias (having never really died) are expected back on earth at the time of the Antichrist to fight the battles of the Lord. One of the final great battles, although apparently not the very last, will be fought at Megiddo (though that place name may be only symbolic of the actual conflict). Then later will come Judgment Day, which, according to one tradition, will take place in the Valley of Josaphat near Jerusalem—although that, too, may be a symbol for the actual gathering.

On the last day, then, there will be a final assembly, with the trumpets of the angels and the separation of the "sheep" from the "goats." Then, after the Judgment at this Second Coming of Christ, the procession of the blessed in their glorious spiritualized bodies will wend its way up to the new and heavenly Jerusalem, the Golden City where the Lamb is the Light thereof. Then too will sound, because of the terrible necessity of justice, the awful final dismissal of the damned: "Depart from Me." And in their risen bodies, bodies destined to suffer excruciating pains for all eternity, the damned will plunge into the eternal abyss of the demons in Hell, "where their worm dieth not, and the fire is not extinguished."

But as a beacon of hope for all mankind on earth, we saw the solicitude of Mary, the Sorrowful Mother, toward her desolate children. This hope is manifest in the miracles of the dead who were raised at some of her shrines, especially at the shrine of Our Lady of Czestochowa at Jasna Gora in Poland.

We also read of the wonderful life of the blessed, and of how their spirits will reign completely over their purified, spiritualized, completely submissive bodies. We saw that according to Our Lord's words (and also according to reason), at the end of the world, marriage (and carnal marital pleasures) will be no more, its institution having been a passing thing primarily to populate earth, to offer an opportunity for billions to merit eternal life.

We recalled now and then that while treating so much of raised bodies, we by no means meant to neglect those much greater wonders that were often concurrent with the raising of the body: the spiritual wonders of the conversion of souls, the reformation of life, the receiving of the supernatural life of sanctifying grace, and growth in sanctity. In a word, the *lives* of the saints, not their miracles, were the greatest wonders of all. "Be ye perfect as your heavenly Father is perfect."

And in eternal Paradise the joys of the spirit will be much higher than those of the body. The gifts of agility, mobility, and all the other "physical" wonders occasioning pleasure in their exercise, will be minor compared to the more elevated spiritual joys of the soul. There will be contemplation, peace, love, the company of the multitudes of angels and saints, the presence of Jesus and Mary and their love and friendship, and the utter beatitude of being lost in rapture before the Beatific Vision—the vision of the supreme and sublime Blessed Trinity, the Triune God.

Thus we can rejoice in hope "as we await the redemption of our bodies." For we know that then, "Lo! . . . we shall all be changed." "Therefore shall they receive a kingdom of glory and a crown of beauty at the hand of the Lord."

Indeed, on that day the Lord might say, not only of the resurrected body, but of the whole person in every part of his or her being: "Thy faith hath made thee whole!"

And so we cry with St. John in the Apocalypse: "Amen! Come, Lord Jesus!" On that glorious day all the elect will be able to proclaim triumphantly: "Death is swallowed up in victory. O death, where is thy victory? O death, where is thy sting?" (*1 Cor.* 15:54-55).

Amen, Lord Jesus! Amen!

— APPENDIX —

Less Well-Authenticated
Resurrection Miracles

In my research for this volume, I came across a number of claims for restorations from the dead that I chose not to include in the body of this book since there is less evidence for them. Further research might establish some of these claims beyond a doubt, or at least provide stronger evidence for them. Some others, mostly in the early centuries, may belong more to the "legendary" classification.

I would not be so bold as to disclaim any one of them as outright frauds, deceits, or pious fictions, but neither can I present them as true resurrections from the dead without having more concrete documentation. But lest I rob God or some saint of what is due, I will list these cases. They will be given more or less chronologically, with the basic minimum of information (though in many cases there are full anecdotes or stories surrounding them, many of which seem very lifelike in their narration, as well as varied and inspiring).

Perhaps this listing will encourage other authors to do more research, or to "defend" some friend or patron of theirs. Where it is possible, dates and sources will be given in the listings. Some of these sources would certainly be considered sufficient by many readers.

St. Michael the Archangel (we shall be pardoned for not giving his dates!), after being appealed to by Mulhoares, King of Dacia who had lost his children, obtained twins for the royal pair. But later, the twins, too, dying, Mulhoares placed the bodies before the archangel's altar. St. Michael restored the twins to life, presented the prince-angel of the kingdom to the king, and also restored the king himself to health. (Fr. Paul O'Sullivan, O.P., *All About the Angels.*)

Resurrection miracles are claimed for St. Anne, mother of the Blessed Virgin Mary and grandmother of Our Lord, by the famous and learned abbot John Trithemius (1462-1516). Trithemius lists many different favors which St. Anne obtains, assuring his readers that God has given her the power to aid in every necessity, spiritual and temporal, and that He grants all she asks. He states: "St. Anne has rescued many from imminent death; yes, through her intercession the dead have, in several instances, been restored to life. Those who worthily venerate St. Anne can obtain aid in every necessity through her mediation." The abbot affirms that he himself has obtained many a favor through this saint; he tells his readers that "No one knows, no one believes, how many favors God confers on lovers of St. Anne." Trithemius' trust in St. Anne is confirmed by the great St. Teresa of Avila, Doctor of the Church, who said: "We know and are convinced that our good mother St. Anne helps in *all needs, dangers, and tribulations,* for Our Lord wishes to show us that He will do also in Heaven what she asks of Him for us." (Benedictine Sisters of Clyde, Mo.: *Good Saint Anne—Her Power and Dignity.*)

St. John the Evangelist, according to the ecstatic-visionary experiences of Therese Neumann, is credited with raising two dead men to life in Smyrna. This was a locale where Greek was spoken, and Therese heard the multitude acclaim John's dramatic action, shouting in Greek: *Zosin!—"They are alive!"* (Johannes Steiner, *Therese Neumann.*)

St. Julian, Bishop of Mans (d. 117), converted many through his raising of the dead. Not long after he arrived at Mans, a prominent pagan citizen challenged him: "If now you could raise this lad [his son] from death, I would confess Jesus Christ, whom you preach . . . and would renounce at once the gods I now worship." Julian did so.

At Champagne, Julian met a funeral procession, and challenged the father of Jovian, the dead youth, to believe in the true God if Julian would raise him. The son was raised, and the father confessed: "The God of Julian is indeed the true God!"

Invited to the house of a pagan woman, Pruila Leguilla, Julian found that her son had just died. He restored him, and as with the other restorals to life, there were many conversions. (These accounts of St. Julian are referred to by D. Piolin in his 10-volume *Histoire de l'Église du Mans*. I see no reason not to accept them as authentic miracles, typical of holy missionary bishops among pagans, just because they occurred so early.)

It is reported that the Emperor Diocletian (284-305) attempted to have St. George of Cappadocia poisoned by the magician Athanasius, but the effort failed. When Diocletian expressed surprise at the failure of the poison, St. George said, "The God whom I adore can not only preserve life, He can also restore it." St. George led the emperor to a cemetery where he called out of a tomb in a cave a dead man, who arose in his burial clothes. But the emperor, who had promised to believe if the dead man came to life, reneged and attributed the revival to magic, though his own magician said this would be impossible. (This account reputedly from Pasicrates, an eyewitness to the miracle and close friend of St. George).

St. Nicholas of Bari (Bishop of Myra or Mira) lived in the fourth century; there are few authentic records of his activities, and there may be some confusion with another Nicholas. But tradition has been so strong, and his name has been left to so many places and churches, that the common story that St. Nicholas raised three children from the dead may well be true. They are said to have been killed by a wicked innkeeper. A painting in the Church of St. Goar, Germany, recalls the story.

St. Germanus (380-448, Ravenna), Bishop of Auxerre, was first a duke and later was made a reluctant bishop. He changed his life pattern, and he and his wife, the noble lady Eustachia, lived as brother and sister. At or near Ravenna he raised the dead son of Volusian, chancellor or secretary to the patrician Sigisvullus. This Germanus seems to have been the same saintly bishop who was influential in the life of St. Patrick.

St. Patrick (c. 389 - c. 461), Apostle of Ireland, is credited elsewhere in this book with what I call the moral certainty of having raised several dead. Readers who would like to read other detailed accounts of more of those reported miracles should read *The Life and Acts of St. Patrick,* by Jocelin (Swift's translation from the twelfth century Latin, Dublin, 1809). I hope more historical documentation will someday be unearthed about Patrick.

St. Brigid of Ireland, of the same period, has been credited with all sorts of miracles, among which I would imagine are claims for her raising the dead. Considered a thaumaturge, no doubt she did work many wonders, but again, more historical records are necessary. (Perhaps Bollandus, *Acta Sanctorum* might throw more light on the subject.)

St. Genevieve of Paris (423-512), patroness of France, is credited with many miracles, including raising the dead. As Genevieve was a great saint with a great tradition, I can believe it. (Monsignor Guerin, *Vies des Saints,* 1880.)

St. Zanobi (d. 407), Bishop of Florence, is credited with raising five persons, one the son of a noble lady passing through Florence on pilgrimage to Rome. Another was a young man being carried to his grave in the faubourgs of the city, whose parents begged the same compassion which Zanobi had shown the mother above. The third was another saint, Simplicius, envoy of St. Ambrose, who had fallen from his horse over a precipice and lay badly mangled below. He was not only restored to life, but also healed so that there were no reminders of the accident. The fourth was a small child of a noble family who had been run over by a carriage while playing before St. Saviour's Cathedral. Sts. Crescentius and Eugenius, who were also present, prayed too, and the child was restored to life and perfect health, as if the interlude of only a dream had passed. The fifth instance occurred when Zanobi directed St. Eugenius to sprinkle his

(Eugenius') father, who had died without the Sacraments; the man came back to life. (John Tortel, Archpriest of Arezzo, *Life of St. Zanobi,* 1433.)

St. Severin (d. 482) restored a dead woman who was laid outside the door of his cell. The people said, "We know that God hears you, and if you ask, He will deny you nothing." Severin restored her to life, saying, "Know that this miracle is not due to my merits, but to your faith. Only believe and nothing is impossible with God." (*Les Petits Bollandistes,* vol. i, p. 219).

St. Germanus of Scotland (fifth century) left the city of Bayeux in anger when the governor refused to release 24 prisoners, but then returned and raised a dead man to life— which led to the eventual release of the prisoners. (Corblet, *Hagiographie d'Amiens.*)

St. Severinus (or Severin, d. 511), after an all-night vigil at the bier of the dead priest Silvinus, ordered the dead man to speak to the brethren, in the Name of God. When Silvinus opened his eyes, St. Severinus asked if he wished to return to earthly life; the priest replied with some annoyance, "Keep me no longer here, nor cheat me of that everlasting rest which those who sleep in the Lord enjoy." Then the priest died again. (Eugippius, *Life of St. Severin.*)

St. Avitus (d. 530), abbot of St. Mesmin, was called from a forest to one of his religious, who had been brought to the church after dying on the road. He had asked not to be buried before the abbot had seen him. At the church Avitus restored him to life, and the resurrected monk took part in chanting a service. St. Lubin, Bishop of Chartres, reportedly said he was told of this revival by the resuscitated man himself. (*Les Petits Bollandistes,* vol. vii, p. 110.) I do not find it easy to disclaim such an account.

When St. Eleutherius (d. 531) was young, the daughter of the pagan governor of Tournai one day at Blandain avowed a violent passion for him. As he rebuked her and ordered her out of his presence, she fell dead. Her pagan father promised conversion if the girl was restored. Eleutherius, after days of fasting and praying, ordered the stone rolled away from her grave, crying out, "Damsel, I command you in the Name of Christ, come forth!" She did so, and was baptized. (*Les Petits Bollandistes,* vol. ii, p. 600.) Attwater seems to consider the raising of the governor's daughter a "fiction." On the other hand, the cathedral and its records burned in 1092, so one cannot know what evidence the records may have contained.

St. Maurus (or Maur, 512-584), a disciple of St. Benedict, is known as the man who ran on top of the water to save the youth Placid; during the construction of the monastery of Bertulfe, he was faced with the corpse of this eight-year-old boy, mangled and bleeding profusely from several areas. The son of Florus, the Viscount of Austrasia, he had fallen from a high scaffolding upon a heap of stones. At Maurus' Sign of the Cross over him he arose perfectly restored. I agree with the overjoyed father of the lad, who exclaimed: "O Father, you are indeed a worthy disciple of St. Benedict!" While doubt has been cast on this miracle, why should not such a holy disciple of Benedict be able to perform such a wonder? (Odo of Glanfeuil, *Life of St. Maur,* 868.)

St. Germanus of Paris (496-576), Bishop, reportedly brought back to life Attila, a favorite of Childebert, King of France. (Fortunatus or Fortunat, Bishop of Poitiers, *Lives of the Saints.*)

St. Severus (sixth century) was called to absolve a dying man, but he delayed a bit, pruning a vine. When he finally arrived, he was horrified to find the man dead. Blaming himself for the "murder" of the man's soul, he threw himself on the earth and wept. The man was restored, to the holy priest's great joy and thanks. The man lived seven days and then died better prepared. (*Propre de Trèves.*)

St. Gildas the Wise (494-570) restored Trifina, daughter of Guerech, who was murdered when her husband, the evil Conomor, discovered she was with child (even though it was his child). Gildas restored this princess to life; also, her son was born safely and named *Trech-meur* or "Death-won."

(*Les Petits Bollandistes,* vol. ii, p. 106.)

St. Galla (sixth century) was a Roman widow who restored her maidservant to life when the latter fell and hurt herself severely on the way to get water; she had been adjudged dead by all. Galla's prayer was, "O Lord, heal her!" When her handmaiden arose, all the witnesses joined in exclaiming, "See, what mighty power the Lord and Saviour has committed to His saints!" (*Les Petits Bollandistes,* vol. ii, p. 199.)

When the funeral procession of St. Virgilius, Bishop of Arles (d. 610), arrived at his grave site, another procession also hurried to the site, escorting the body of a young girl, the only child of her widowed mother. These people implored the clergy to let the girl's dead body touch that of the deceased saint. The *Kyrie eleison* was intoned, a thousand voices joined in, and at its seventh repetition, the young girl rose to her feet. There was a thrilled second of silence, and then a spontaneous shout of joy and a hymn of praise. The crowd pressed around the young girl in a triumphant march, the girl exclaiming: "O blessed Bishop, O good and holy pastor! How I am your debtor! How powerful your merits! Well have you shown your inheritance to eternal life in giving me back to life!" The burial of Virgilius became a scene of Gospel awe and jubilation. (Dinet, *Saint Symphorien d'Autun.*) I see no reason to believe that such a story is a fabrication.

St. Valery of Luxeul (d. 619), when once at Gamaches, braved executioners to cut down the hanged body of a criminal condemned by the nobleman Sigobard. He prayed, and the hanged man stood on his feet alive and with all his strength restored. But despite Valery's pleas, Sigobard ordered the man hanged again. Valery cried out: "You have already punished him with death for his offenses, and cannot in justice punish him twice for the same crimes. God has given him a new life, and in this new life he is yet innocent!" Sigobard surrendered before the force of this logic and let the man go free. He lived for many years, and a chapel marks the spot of his double restoration—to life and to liberty. (Besançon, *Les Saints de Franche Comté*, 1854.)

St. Gertrude of Nivelles (626-659), abbess of a monastery near Brussels, was instrumental after her death in the revival of a dead child who had fallen into a well. The body was laid on the tomb of the saint, and while the mother did not believe Gertrude could do anything, a nun cried out: "O great saint, make manifest now the power of your merits!" At the nun's words the dead child came back to life. (Surius, *Lives of the Saints*; this is a different St. Gertrude from the famous 13th century mystic, St. Gertrude the Great.)

St. Amandus, (594-684) Bishop, entered a court at Tournai and pleaded with the governor, Dotton, for the custody of a brigand deservingly condemned to death. But the executioners hanged the criminal and watched until he was dead. Amandus came secretly at night, cut the criminal down, brought him to his cell, prayed over him, and restored him to life. The man was amazed to find himself alive in the cell of the traveling bishop, who told him to return home and sin no more. At news of the miracle, crowds came for Baptism, monasteries rose at Gand and on Mount Blandin, and a whole people was spiritually born—in a day, as it were. (Menjoulet, Vicar-general of Bayonne, *St. Amand, Apôtre des Basques*.) Again, in view of the miracles of later, well-established saints, is there any reason to reject such a miracle as this one performed by a zealous missionary apostle? (The old *Catholic Encyclopedia* remarks that Amandus "calmed a sea.")

St. Austrebertha (630-704), Abbess of Parilly, was disliked for restoring discipline to her convent. Her fellow sisters gave her poisoned food, but she survived. The devil took advantage of the spiritual situation and shook the convent building. As the terrified sisters began to flee, St. Austrebertha forbade them to move; one who disobeyed was crushed to death under a fallen part of the building. When the mangled corpse was dug out and placed in the infirmary, the saint anointed the dead sister with a little blessed oil, and she came back to life. (Surius, *Lives of the Saints,* vol. 1.)

St. Attalus (d. 627), Abbot of Bobbio, near Genoa, was first with St. Columba at Lexeuil; he left with Columba when the latter was expelled and founded the monastery at Bobbio. There Attalus succeeded Columba as abbot. A certain monk of Bobbio, following the custom of orthodox Catholics, did not salute the passing king of Lombardy, Ariowald the Arian; Ariowald had the monk assassinated. Attalus restored the monk to life, and the devil subjected the murderer to horrible torments, from which, in the end, Attalus delivered him. Attalus restored another monk who, while endeavoring to wipe out the remnants of paganism in Tortuna, had been thrown into a river with great stones piled on him. (Jonas, a Scotsman and disciple of the saint, *Life of St. Attalus.*) Again, just because a cloud has been thrown over the lives of many saints of early centuries or over their biographies, particularly those by French authors, is there any reason to deny such miracles performed by a companion saint of the great Columba?

St. Fursy (d. 650), of royal blood, monk, hermit and monastery builder, raised the bodies of his cousins, twin daughter and son of King Brendin of Ultonia (Ulster, Ireland), who had been buried at sea and washed ashore near St. Fursy's hermitage. (*Les Petits Bollandistes,* vol. i, p. 401. Msgr. Guerin claimed the life of St. Fursy was written by a contemporary and published by Surius, J. Bolland, and Mabillon, abstracted by Venerable Bede, and written up by Abbot Corblet in *Hagiographie du Diocèse d'Amiens,* vol. ii, p. 260. All this would seem to verify this double miracle, at least in substance.)

St. Cuthbert (c. 634-687), Northumbrian-born wonderworker of early Britain, was consecrated a bishop, although he would have preferred to remain a monk and abbot of Lindisfarne. He is credited with reviving an apparently dead boy with a kiss and with healing a girl, dying in terrible pain, by anointing her with oil. In this particular case there is a question as to whether the boy was at the point of death or actually deceased. Other miracles are also attributed to St. Cuthbert; he was called the "British Thaumaturge." (*Acta Sanctorum*; Bede's *Ecclesiastical History of England*.)

St. Wulfran (647-720), Archbishop of Sens, entreated King Radbod to forbid the hanging of the young lad Ovon as a sacrifice to the Frison gods. When Ovon nevertheless was hanged on a gibbet and strangled to death, Wulfran prayed to God to magnify His Name before the idol worshipers and confound their false gods. After two hours of his prayers the rope suddenly broke. Ovon's body fell to the ground, and Wulfran ran to the spot crying, "Ovon, I command you, in the Name of Jesus Christ, stand up!" He did, and many Frisons were converted. (L'Abbé Corblet, *Hagiography of the Diocese of Amiens*.)

St. Poppo (978-1048) was on his way to see the Emperor Henry when he noticed in a thicket a wolf with a shepherd in its jaws. He pursued it and found the poor shepherd in a swamp, mangled and dead. The saint prayed on his knees, restored the shepherd to life, and then the two had breakfast together. To the end of his days the shepherd carried a scar on his neck from the wolf's teeth, and the town of Stavelot (where the saint was abbot) had a wolf in its coat of arms in memory of the miracle. (Everheilm, who wrote the *Life* in Bollandus, vol. iii, p. 251, claimed he was told of this miracle by St. Poppo himself.)

Among other saints credited with raising the dead, for whom I have no definite dates, are St. Guido, the abbot, who raised the monk Martin at the monastery of Pomposa; Melanius, who raised the son of an old man at Vannes, which helped to effect the conversion of the area; Sacerdos, Bishop of Limoges, who called his father Laban back to life when he had died without the Sacraments; and Tiburtius, who raised a young man who had fallen from a great height and was about to be buried by his parents. (*Acta Sanctorum* of the Bollandists; Dom Lobineau, a contemporary, *Life of St. Melanius*; Pergot, *Life of St. Sacerdos; Life of St. Sebastian*, respectively.)

I believe that many other cases of similar reported miracles could be added to the above listing. And I would never want to be interpreted as denying the reality of any particular miracle reported in this appendix. Some might be considered "legendary"; some I would have preferred to research further for more certainty, but one must bow to the limits of time. And I believe my aims have been more than realized in the large number of miracles reported in the main part of this book.

Finally, I hope others will be led to continued and fuller research, both to settle more conclusively some of the critical problems, and also to bring forth many more authenticated miracles of the dead being restored to life. Our times need the hope and jubilation that comes from the certainty that there will be an eternal resurrection, a certainty well supported by all these many resurrection accounts—but most of all, a certainty based upon the Resurrection of Our Lord Jesus Christ from the dead, by His own power, to reign in Heaven forever and ever and ever. Amen.

— SELECTED BIBLIOGRAPHY —

General Works

Acta Sanctorum (January to October), 54 volumes. Paris and Rome, 1868.

Aquinas, Thomas. *Summa Theologica.* Transl. by Fathers of the English Dominican Province. New York: Benziger Bros., 1948.

Aradi, Zsolt. *Book of Miracles.* New York: Farrar, Straus and Cudahy, 1956.

Venerable Bede. *Ecclesiastical History of the English People.* Edited by Bertram Colgrave and R. A. B. Mynors. New York: Oxford University Press, 1969.

Brewer, E. C. *A Dictionary of Miracles.* J. B. Lippincott Company. (Republished by Gale Research Company, Book Tower, Detroit, 1966.)

Budge, Ernest A. Wallis. *Stories of the Holy Fathers,* including "The Paradise of Palladius." (Translated from the Syrian of Ânân Îshô.) New York: Oxford University Press, 1934.

Butler, Alban. *Lives of the Saints,* 4 volumes. New York: D. and J. Sadlier, 1846.

Butler, Alban. *Lives of the Saints.* Edited by Herbert Thurston, S.J. and Donald Attwater. London: Burns & Oates, 1956.

Catholic Encyclopedia, The. New York: Robert Appleton Company, 1909.

Catholic Encyclopaedic Dictionary, The. Donald Attwater, general editor. New York: Macmillan, 1931.

Cruz, Joan Carroll. *The Incorruptibles.* Rockford, Illinois: TAN Books, 1974.

Delaney, John J. *Dictionary of Saints.* Garden City, N.Y.: Doubleday, 1980.

Delehaye, Hippolyte (Bollandist). *The Legends of the Saints.* New York: Fordham University Press, 1962.

Dogmatic Canons and Decrees (of the Council of Trent, etc.). New York, Devin-Adair, 1912; Rockford, Ill.: TAN Books, 1977.

Dominican House of Studies (Novices). *Dominican Saints.* Washington D.C.: Dominican House of Studies, 1921.

Dominican Saints. London: Kegan Paul, Trench & Trubner, 1901.

Dorcy, Sr. Mary Jean, O.P. *St. Dominic's Family: The Lives of Over 300 Famous Dominicans.* Dubuque, Iowa: Priory Press, 1964; Rockford: TAN Books, and Washington: Dominicana Publications, 1983.

Fathers of the Church Series. Edited by Roy J. Deferrari. New York.
Writings of St. Justin Martyr (vol. 6).
Writings of Sulpicius Severus (vol. 7).
St. Augustine, *City of God,* Books XVII-XXII. (vol. 24).
Early Christian Biographies (vol. 15), including: Paulinus, *Life of St. Ambrose;* St. Athanasius, *Life of St. Antony;* Possidius, *Life of St. Augustine;* St. Jerome, *Life of St. Paul; Life of St. Hilarion.*
Eusebius, Pamphili. *Ecclesiastical History,* Books 1-5 (vol 19); Books 6-10 (vol. 29).
St. Gregory the Great. *Dialogues* (vol. 39).
St. Gregory of Nyssa. *Life of St. Macrina* (vol. 58).

Foley, O.F.M., Leonard. *Saint of the Day,* 2 volumes. Cincinnati: St. Anthony Messenger Press, 1974.

Gillet, H. M. *Famous Shrines of Our Lady.* Westminster, Maryland: Carroll Press, 1950.

Goodier, S. J., Alban. *Saints for Sinners.* London: Sheed & Ward, 1931.

Habig, O.F.M., Marion A. *The Franciscan Book of Saints* (revised edition). Chicago: Franciscan Herald Press, 1979.

Hardon, John A., S.J. *Modern Catholic Dictionary.* Garden City, N.Y.: Doubleday, 1980.

Jesuit Fathers of St. Mary's College. *The Church Teaches* (Documents of the Church in English translation). St. Louis: B. Herder Book Company, 1955. Rockford, Ill.: TAN Books, 1973.

Jesuit Fathers, English Province. *Companions of Jesus* (Spiritual Profiles of the Jesuit Saints and Beati). London, 1974.

Knowles, Leo. *Saints Who Changed Things.* St. Paul: Carillon Books, 1977.

Knowles, Leo. *Saints Who Spoke English.* St. Paul: Carillon Books, 1979.

Leuret, François, and Henry Bon. *Modern Miraculous Cures, A Documentary Account of Miracles and Medicine in the 20th Century.* New York: Farrar, Straus and Cudahy, 1957.

Levy, Rosalie Marie. *Heavenly Friends.* New York: St. Paul Editions, 1958.

New Catholic Encyclopedia. New York: McGraw Hill Book Company, 1965.

New Catholic Dictionary. Corde Pallen, John J. Wynne, S.J., gen. eds., under the auspices of the editors of *The Catholic Encyclopedia.* New York: Universal Knowledge Foundation, 1929.

Newman, John Henry (Cardinal). *Two Essays on Biblical and Ecclesiastical Miracles.* New York: Longmans, Green & Company, 1901.

Ott, Dr. Ludwig. *Fundamentals of Catholic Dogma.* Trans. by Patrick Lynch, ed. in English by James Canon Bastible. Cork: Mercier Press, Ltd., 1955; Rockford, Ill.: TAN Books and Publishers, Inc., 1974.

Petits Bollandistes, Les (vies de saints). 15 volumes plus 3 supplements. Paris, 1874.

Poulain, A., S.J., *The Graces of Interior Prayer,* first English edition, 1910. Reprint of enlarged edition, Westminster, Vermont: Celtic Cross Books, 1978.

Proctor, O.P., editor. *Short Lives of the Dominican Saints.* London: Kegan Paul, Trench & Trubner, 1901.

Steinmueller-Sullivan. *Catholic Biblical Encyclopedia,* New Testament and Old Testament Volumes. New York: Joseph F. Wagner, Inc., 1959.

Widdowson, Gregory. *An Outline of Lay Sanctity.* Huntington, Indiana: Our Sunday Visitor Press, 1979.

Individual Biographies

Albert, S.M., O.P. *St. Albert the Great.* Oxford: Blackfriars Publications, 1948.

Alphonsus, Sister Mary, O.SS.R. *St. Martin de Porres.* New York: St. Martin Guild, 1966.

Anderson, Robin. *St. Pius V: His Life, Times, and Miracles.* St. Michael's Press, 1973; Rockford, Illinois: TAN Books, 1978.

Bacci, Fr., of Rome Oratory. *The Life of St. Philip Neri, Apostle of Rome, and Founder of the Congregation of the Oratory,* 2 vols. Edited by F. I. Antrobus. London: Kegan Paul,

Trench & Trubner, 1902.

Bardi, Msgr. Giuseppe. *St. Gemma Galgani.* Translated from Italian by Margherita M. Repton. Boston: St. Paul Editions, 1951.

Bernard of Clairvaux. *The Life and Death of Saint Malachy the Irishman.* Translated and annotated by Robert T. Meyer. Kalamazoo, Mich.: Cistercian Publications, 1978.

Bonniwell, William R., O.P. *The Story of Margaret of Metola.* New York: P. J. Kenedy, 1952. New edition, *The Life of Blessed Margaret of Castello.* Rockford, Illinois: TAN Books, 1983.

Cavallini, Giuliana. *St. Martin de Porres, Apostle of Charity.* Translated by Caroline Holland. St. Louis: B. Herder Book Company, 1963. Rockford, Illinois: TAN Books, 1979.

Clarke, A. M. *The Life of St. Francis di Geronimo.* New York: Benziger Brothers, 1891.

Coleridge, James, S.J. *Life and Letters of St. Francis Xavier,* 2 volumes. London: Burns & Oates, 1902.

Cristiani, Msgr. Leon. *St. Joan of Arc, Virgin-Soldier.* Translated from the French by M. Angeline Bouchard. Boston: St. Paul Editions, 1977.

Curley, Edmund F. *Battlefield Dropout: Life of St. Camillus.* Huntington, Indiana: Our Sunday Visitor Press, 1975.

de Robeck, Nesta. *St. Elizabeth of Hungary,* Milwaukee: Bruce, 1954.

Desmond, Cecilia. *Bl. James Salomoni.* Boston: St. Paul Editions, 1971.

Dorcy, Sr. Mary Jean, O.P. *St. Dominic.* St. Louis: B. Herder Book Company, 1959. Rockford, Illinois: TAN Books, 1982.

Eid, Chor-Bishop Joseph, D.D., Ph.D. *The Hermit of Lebanon, Blessed Sharbel,* third edition. Fall River, Massachusetts: St. Anthony the Desert Church, 1965.

Fages, Le Rd. Père, O.P. *Histoire de St. Vincent Ferrier, Apôtre de l'Europe.* Paris, 1893.

Fullerton, Lady Georgiana. *Life of St. Frances of Rome.*

Gallagher, Louis J., S.J., and Paul V. Donovan, Ll.D. *Life of St. Andrew Bobola, S.J., Martyr.* Boston: Bruce Humphries, 1939.

Gallico, Paul. *The Steadfast Man* (St. Patrick). Garden City, New York: Doubleday & Company, 1958.

Genelli, S.J. *Life of St. Ignatius Loyola.* New York: Benziger, 1917.

Gheon, Henri. *Martin of Tours.* Translated by F. J. Sheed. New York: Sheed & Ward, 1946.

Gheon, Henri. *St. Vincent Ferrer.* Translated by F. J. Sheed. New York: Sheed & Ward, 1939.

Giordani, Igino. *St. Catherine of Siena.*

Boston: St. Paul Editions, 1975.

St. Gregory the Great. *Life and Miracles of St. Benedict* (Book Two of the *Dialogues*). Collegeville, Minnesota: Liturgical Press.

Huysmans, J. K. *St. Lydwine of Schiedam.* London: Kegan Paul, Trench & Trubner, 1923; Rockford, Illinois: TAN Books, 1979.

Jocelin, Cistercian of Furnes. *The Life and Acts of St. Patrick.* Translated from Latin by Edmund L. Swift. Dublin, 1809.

Lappin, Peter. *Give Me Souls: Life of Don Bosco.* Huntington, Indiana: Our Sunday Visitor Press, 1977.

Life of St. Peter of Alcantara, The. (Oratorian series: Modern Saints and Servants of God). London: Richardson and Son, 1856.

Life of St. Philip Benizi. (Oratorian Lives of the Saints). London: R. Washbourne, 1874.

Life of St. Rose of Lima (Introduction by F. W. Faber). London, 1847.

The Life of St. Winefride, Virgin and Martyr. Based on the acts compiled by the Bollandist Fathers. Edited by Thomas Swift, S.J. London: Burns and Oates Ltd., 1888.

Lives of Frs. Talpa & Ven. Fr. Eustachio of Naples Oratory and G. Prerer of Turin Oratory. New York: Edward Dunigan & Brothers, 1851.

Luddy, Ailbe J., O. Cist. *Life and Teachings of St. Bernard.* Dublin: M. H. Gill & Son, 1937.

Maeneil, Eoin, D. Litt. *St. Patrick.* Dublin: Clonmore & Reynolds, 1964.

Mary Francis, Sister, Poor Clare. *Walled-in Light—St. Colette.* New York: Sheed & Ward, 1959.

McGratty, Arthur R., S.J. *The Fire of Francis Xavier.* Milwaukee: Bruce, 1952.

Papasogli, Giorgio. *St. Teresa of Avila.* Translated from Italian by G. Anzilotti. New York: St. Paul Editions, 1959.

Paredi, Angelo. *St. Ambrose, His Life and Times.* Translated by M. Joseph Costelloe, S.J. South Bend, Indiana: University of Notre Dame Press, 1964.

St. Patrick. *Confessions* and *Letter to Coroticus.*

Pius of Spiritus Sancti, Fr. *St. Paul of the Cross, Passionist Founder.* New York: P. J. Kenedy.

Pradel, Rev. Andrew, O.P. *St. Vincent Ferrer of the Order of Friars Preachers: His Life, Spiritual Teaching, and Practical Devotion.* Transl. by Rev. T. A. Dixon, O.P. London: R. Washbourne, 1875.

Ratisbonne, M. L'Abbé. *Life and Times of St. Bernard.* New York: D. & J. Sadlier & Company, 1855.

Redemptorist. *Life of St. Gerard Majella.* Boston: Redemptorists, 1907.

Royer, Fanchón. *St. Francis Solanus: Apostle to America.* Paterson, N.J.: St. Anthony Guild Press, 1955.

Schug, John A., O.F.M. Cap. *Padre Pio.* Huntington, Indiana: Our Sunday Visitor Press, 1976.

Simi, Gino, and Mario Segreti. *St. Francis of Paola: God's Miracle-Worker Supreme.* Rockford, Illinois: TAN Books, 1977.

Spadafora, Msgr. Francesco. *Incredible Life Story of Sister Elena Aiello.* Translated from the Italian by Msgr. Angelo R. Cioffi. Brooklyn: Theo. Gaus' Sons, 1964.

Steiner, Johannes. *Therese Neumann.* Staten Island, N.Y.: Alba House, 1967.

Stoddard, Charles Warren. *St. Anthony, the Wonder-Worker of Padua.* Notre Dame, Ind.: The Ave Maria, 1896; Rockford, Illinois: TAN Books, 1971.

Trochu, Abbé Francis. *The Curé d'Ars, St. Jean-Marie Baptiste Vianney.* London: Burns, Oates & Washbourne, 1927; Rockford, Illinois: TAN Books, 1977.

Vicaire, M. H., O.P. *St. Dominic and His Times.* Translated from French by Kathleen Pond. New York: McGraw Hill Book Company, 1964.

Ward, Maisie. *The People's Preacher, San Bernardino.* St. Louis: B. Herder Book Company, 1914.

Wilberforce, Fr. Bertrand, O.P. *Life of St. Louis Bertrand.* London: Burns & Oates, 1882.

Wilms, O.P. *As the Morning Stars* (Life of St. Dominic). Translated from German by a Dominican Sister. Milwaukee: Bruce, 1956.

Ximénez, Fr. Matteo. *Bl. Sebastian of Apparizio, Franciscan Lay-Brother.* London: Th. Richardson & Son, 1848.

Other Works

Arendzen, J. P. *Purgatory and Heaven.* New York: Sheed & Ward, 1951; Rockford, Illinois: TAN Books, 1972.

Boudreau, Fr. J., S.J. *The Happiness of Heaven: The Joys and Rewards of Eternal Glory.* Baltimore, John Murphy, 1872; Rockford: TAN Books, 1984.

Bouix, Marcel, S.J. *Apparitions of Our Lady of Lourdes.* New Orleans: Th. Layton, 1879.

Emmerich, Anne Catherine. *The Life of Jesus Christ and Biblical Revelations* (4 vol). From the Journals of Clemens Brentano. Bruges: Desclee de Brouwer, 1914; Rockford, Ill.: TAN Books, 1979.

Glories of Czestochowa and Jasna Gora, 5th edition. Worcester, Massachusetts: Our Lady of Czestochowa Foundation, 1975.

Handbook on Guadalupe. Kenosha, Wisconsin: Franciscan Marytown Press, 1974.

Kübler-Ross, Elisabeth. *On Death and Dying.* New York: Macmillan, 1969.

Lamberty, Sister Marietta, S.S.C. *The Woman in Orbit* (Marian feasts, apparitions, shrines). Chicago: Lamberty Company, 1966.

Lassère, H. *Our Lady of Lourdes.*

Marnham, Patrick. *Lourdes: A Modern Pilgrimage.* New York: Coward, McCann and Geoghegan, Inc., 1981.

McCann, Dom Justin, O.S.B. "The Resurrection of the Body," in *The Teaching of the Catholic Church,* arranged and edited by Canon George D. Smith. New York: MacMillan, 1955.

Monden, Louis, S.J. *Signs and Wonders.* New York: Desclee Company, 1966.

Moody, Raymond. *Life After Life.* New York: Bantam Books, 1976.

O'Sullivan, Fr. Paul, O.P. *All About the Angels,* seventh edition. Clovis, California: Christian Renewal Press, 1976.

Rawlings, Maurice S., M.D. *Beyond Death's Doors.* Nashville: Thomas Nelson, 1978.

Reparation Society of the Immaculate Heart of Mary. *An Unpublished Manuscript on Purgatory.* Baltimore, 1967.

Sanchez, Rev. Benjamin Martin. *The Last Times.* Opus Reginae Sacratissimi Rosarii.

Schamoni, Wilhelm. *Das Wahre Gesicht der Heiligen.* Stein am Rhein: Christina-Verlag, 1966.

Schouppe, F.X., S.J. *Purgatory: Explained by the Lives and Legends of the Saints.* Originally published in 1893. Reprint, Rockford, Illinois: TAN Books, 1973.

Sharkey, Don. *After Bernadette: The Story of Modern Lourdes.* Milwaukee: Bruce, 1945.

Wolter, Allan B., O.F.M. "The Recognition of Miracles." *Philosophical Studies in Honor of the Very Rev. Ignatius Smith, O.P.,* pp. 233-256. Edited by John K. Ryan. Westminster, Maryland: Newman Press, 1952.

If you have enjoyed this book, consider making your next selection from among the following...

Prices guaranteed through June 30, 1987.

Prophecy for Today. Edward Connor 3.00
What Will Hell Be Like? St. Alphonsus Liguori .... .40
A Year with the Saints. Anonymous 5.00
Saint Michael and the Angels. Approved Sources 3.50
Dolorous Passion of Our Lord. Anne C. Emmerich 10.00
Modern Saints—Their Lives & Faces. Ann Ball 10.00
Our Lady of Fatima's Peace Plan from Heaven. Booklet .... .40
Divine Favors Granted to St. Joseph. Pere Binet 3.00
St. Joseph Cafasso—Priest of the Gallows. St. J. Bosco 2.00
Catechism of the Council of Trent. McHugh/Callan 15.00
The Foot of the Cross. Fr. Faber 10.00
The Rosary in Action. John Johnson 5.00
Padre Pio—The Stigmatist. Fr. Charles Carty 8.50
Why Squander Illness? Frs. Rumble & Carty 1.50
My God, I love Thee! (100 cards). St. Augustine 4.00
The Sacred Heart and the Priesthood. de la Touche 5.00
Fatima—The Great Sign. Francis Johnston 6.00
Heliotropium—Conformity of Human Will to Divine. 8.50
St. Rose of Lima. Sister Alphonsus 8.00
Charity for the Suffering Souls. Fr. John Nageleisen 10.00
Devotion to the Sacred Heart of Jesus. Verheylezoon 8.50
Who Is Padre Pio? Radio Replies Press 1.00
The Stigmata and Modern Science. Fr. Charles Carty .... .75
The Incorruptibles. Joan Carroll Cruz 8.00
The Life of Christ. 4 Vols. H.B. Anne C. Emmerich 67.00
The Life of Christ. 4 Vols. P.B. Anne C. Emmerich 40.00
St. Dominic. Sr. Mary Jean Dorcy 5.00
Is It a Saint's Name? Fr. William Dunne 1.25
St. Anthony—The Wonder Worker of Padua. Stoddard 2.50
The Precious Blood. Fr. Faber 7.50
The Holy Shroud & Four Visions. Fr. O'Connell 1.50
Clean Love in Courtship. Fr. Lawrence Lovasik 1.50
The Prophecies of St. Malachy. Peter Bander 3.00
St. Martin de Porres. Giuliana Cavallini 7.00
The Secret of the Rosary. St. Louis De Montfort 1.00
The History of Antichrist. Rev. P. Huchede 2.00
The Douay-Rheims New Testament. Paperbound 8.00
St. Catherine of Siena. Alice Curtayne 7.50
Where We Got the Bible. Fr. Henry Graham 3.00
Hidden Treasure—Holy Mass. St. Leonard 2.50
Imitation of the Sacred Heart of Jesus. Fr. Arnoudt 10.00
The Curé D'Ars. Abbé Francis Trochu 15.00
Love, Peace, and Joy. St. Gertrude/Prévot 4.00
The Way of Divine Love. Sister Josefa Menendez 12.00
Mary, The Second Eve. Cardinal Newman 1.50
The Faith of Our Fathers. Cardinal Gibbons 9.00
Manual of Practical Devotion to St. Joseph. Fr. Patrignani 9.00

At your bookdealer or direct from the publisher.

Prices guaranteed through June 30, 1987.

Father Albert J. Hebert, S.M. (Society of Mary—Marists) has been a soldier, religious, and priest. Born in New Orleans in 1913, as a layman he was a member of various Catholic lay organizations including the Catholic Evidence Guild of New Orleans founded by the late Very Rev. Joseph Buckley, S.M.; this apostolate included speaking on street corners in New Orleans. After serving as a Staff Sergeant in the 8th and 9th Air Forces in World War II in the European theater of operations, he studied at Marist College and Catholic University in Washington, D.C., being ordained in 1954. Father Hebert has served in city parishes in Wheeling, West Virginia and in New Orleans, and in mission parishes in Georgia and West Virginia; he also taught at Chanel High School in Bedford (Cleveland), Ohio. At present he is in residence at St. Anne parish in Sorrento, Louisiana (Baton Rouge diocese). Father Hebert has authored several books and has contributed articles and poems to Catholic periodicals; he has also contributed poems to several anthologies. He is included in the *International Who's Who in Poetry*.

GUERRILLA MARKETING
The Original Marketing Bible That Started the Revolution — Now Fully Revised

"A veritable plum pudding of marketing techniques and secrets. More than 100 free, cheap but effective marketing ideas for small businesses. Levinson's marketing tips are designed to encourage customer loyalty and promote subsequent sales."

— *Los Angeles Times*

"In the marketing world, no one knows how to use the weapons of the trade better than industry expert Jay Levinson. He is living proof that his unconventional marketing ideas work."

— *Entrepreneur*

"Resourceful, penny-wise marketing techniques."

— *Kirkus*

"A guru for seekers of economic freedom, including a generation of stressed-out executives and wannabe entrepreneurs. His ideas were conceived long before most had ever heard of flextime. *Guerrilla Marketing*, with its unorthodox bargain basement approach . . . is designed to give small business owners with time and energy — but not a lot of cash — an edge on the competition."

— Greg Cahill, *Pacific Sun*

"A source of inspiration for many independent entrepreneurs."

— *Booklist*

"Levinson is as much a missionary as a guerrilla. His books admonish small businesses to devote more resources to marketing, inspire them to be more aggressive and provide them with creative but inexpensive techniques. They also dispense advice and encouragement to those considering becoming their own boss."

— Michael Gallantz, *Entrepreneur*

IT'S A JUNGLE OUT THERE.

GUERRILLA
MARKETING

Secrets for Making Big Profits
from Your Small Business

Jay Conrad Levinson

Houghton Mifflin Company

Boston   New York

For information about permission to reproduce selections
from this book, write to Permissions, Houghton Mifflin Company,
215 Park Avenue South, New York, New York 10003.

Library of Congress Cataloging-in-Publication Data
Levinson, Jay Conrad.
Guerrilla marketing : secrets for making big profits from your small business /
   by Jay Conrad Levinson.
p.   cm.
Includes bibliographical references and index.
ISBN 0-395-64496-8 (pbk.)
1. Marketing.   2. Small business—Management.   3. Advertising.
   I. Title.
HF5415.L4764   1993
658.8—dc20   93-22334
               CIP

Printed in the United States of America

MP   10   9   8   7   6   5   4   3

I dedicate this book to

Mike Lavin
Thane Croston
Alexis Makar
Lynn Peterson
Wally Bregman
Bill Shear
Leo Burnett
Steve Savage
Sidney Mobell
Norm Goldring

—guerrillas all.

Contents

1
The Guerrilla Approach to Marketing — Updated

ALTHOUGH MARKETING CHANGES so fast that there are daily and weekly publications solely devoted to chronicling the changes, the soul of guerrilla marketing remains unchanged. Updated, to be sure, but not changed at its core. Within a brand-new world of marketing, the guerrilla thrives by warmly welcoming, then adapting to the myriad changes going on all over the place.

The world of marketing has evolved to a new age as computer technology asserts itself, as communications from satellites 23,500 miles away enable guerrilla marketers to advertise on television in prime time for under twenty bucks, as an ugly recession has strengthened the bond between people and their money, and as social causes such as domestic violence, saving rain forests, and curing AIDS have become part of the marketing scene. Although you'll be made aware of the most important changes, I hope this enlightenment is enhanced by the security you'll feel in the comforting fact that this updated guerrilla approach to marketing *works and is proven in action.* Ten years of success for thousands of guerrilla small businesses throughout America underscore this truth. Practitioners are now found around the world. The best will want to know how guerrillas use the latest changes to their best advantage. I wrote this edition for them.

Guerrillas from outer space

Who this book is for

If your business is exceptionally well funded and you have stockpiles of money allocated to marketing whatever it is you are selling, you might take the standard approach and handle the marketing function with big bucks and textbook tactics. But if you have very little or a modest amount of money for marketing, I would advise you to take a radically different approach and handle the marketing function with big ideas and guerrilla tactics.

Guerrilla tactics do not put textbook tactics to shame. But they do provide you with an alternative to standard expensive marketing. They enable you to increase your sales with a minimum of expense and a maximum of smarts.

Goals and shortcuts

You'll best understand the guerrilla approach to marketing once you study a standard marketing textbook. In the standard book, you'll learn of marketing goals and methods of attaining them. In this book, you'll learn of similar marketing goals and shortcuts to attaining them. You'll learn how to do what the big spenders do without having to spend big. Since very little comes to us for nothing, you'll have to do some extra work. But instead of relying on moneypower, you can rely on brainpower.

To keep up with the daily changes that occur in marketing is a Herculean task. I write a guerrilla marketing newsletter and a monthly guerrilla marketing column to accomplish all that Hercules would. The bare-bones essence of marketing has changed only in that we've become more enlightened by it. The weapons of marketing have undergone a revolution. This updated edition of *Guerrilla Marketing* is to keep you abreast of the current state of its art and its science. Although the true nature of guerrilla marketing remains the same, the breadth and technology of marketing has changed dramatically.

Saving the planet

One major change is the use of environmental issues in marketing. Letting prospects know about your environmentally sound manufacturing practices gives them an additional reason to buy from you. Another factor small businesses must deal with is the recession, which has become a sort of unofficial perma-recession. And then there are the crucial advantages of cable and satellite television, not to mention fax machines and desktop publishing for the small-business owner. This updated edition shows you how to prosper from all of these changes.

The Intel 486 is the Colt 45

Guerrillas know that the Intel 486 is the Colt 45 of the nineties and that it will be superseded by another name and number as time and human ingenuity advances. Do guerrillas welcome change? They thrive on it — because they know that their competitors have a tough time keeping up with change. This edition informs you about the marketing changes that will give you a leg up on your competition.

Guerrillas already know that in the 1990s:

- 75 million baby boomers will enter middle age.
- The 18-to-34-year-old market will lose $100 billion worth of spending power.
- Dual-income households and aging Americans will put a premium on time-saving products and services.
- Discretionary income will increase because of the trend toward smaller families and the fact that fewer households are being formed.
- The shrinking middle class will force retailers to aim more for the top and bottom. Some guerrilla companies will successfully manage to do both.
- Ulcers will increase for owners of companies that offer anything that has an unhealthy identity.
- Health care for those over eighty-five will expand 64 percent by the year 2000.
- Home remodeling will enjoy boom times because of the high cost of housing. Space-saving furniture sales will soar.
- Cosmetics and skin-care products will help oldsters look like youngsters. Middle-aged models will become commonplace.
- People seventy-five or older will move to Florida, Nevada, Alaska, and Arizona. They'll be a lucrative market.
- Satellite transmission of local TV will grow rapidly, as will the galaxy of choices available, enabling guerrillas to aim directly at their market, geographically and demographically.
- VCRs will become so widespread that video brochures will be recognized as high-powered weapons, proving their effectiveness to all types of businesses.
- Tomorrow's marketplace will be populated by customers **Warmth in a** who are more demanding, less forgiving, in a hurry, and **cold world** appreciative of warmth and attention to detail.
- The ultimate winners in the nineties and beyond will be companies that are right in front of the buyers at the time the buyers want to buy. Not easy, but possible.
- Your product or service will often be considered exactly the same as that of your competitors. This is because an enormous influx of marketing will create mass confusion and the perception that all offerings are created equal.
- Supermarkets will sell shelf space to companies just for the

privilege of being displayed. Those same supermarkets will have computerized data their scanners compile on your purchases. This means you might buy Cheerios and get a coupon offer from Wheaties.

- Ads will invite consumers to phone in or send for a free sample, enabling guerrillas to compile a list of people who have expressed interest in their product.
- New ways to influence consumer purchases, ranging from in-store TV to high-tech coupon machines, will be developed for use at the point-of-sale.
- There will be a growth spurt in frequent-buyer clubs, modeled after frequent-flier programs.

Brand-new markets

Brand-new weapons

This edition of *Guerrilla Marketing* for these times opens your mind to the brand-new markets of these times: working women, older people, ethnic groups (11 million people in the United States use Spanish as their primary language; 3 million Asians speak little or no English). It brings into focus the new marketing weapons of these times: video brochures, newsletters, 900 numbers, infomercials, video monitors on shopping carts, postcard decks — as well as changes in the older ones: direct mail, telemarketing, free publicity, trade shows, and catalogues.

Three is now ten

Because of the inevitability of change in marketing, it will always be necessary to update the methods and tactics of guerrilla marketing while maintaining its soul and essence. Whereas the first edition of this book called to your attention the *three* most important marketing secrets, this updated edition gives you even more of a head start by imparting the *ten* most important marketing secrets.

One of the seven habits practiced by effective people is called "sharpening the saw" — improving the things you do best. This edition sharpens the saw of guerrilla marketing. In doing so, it provides the guerrilla with a keener edge than ever. With over a million new businesses launched in America each year, the guerrilla needs all the ammunition available to achieve victory. This edition was written to restock your guerrilla arsenal with ammunition, the kind that can make the difference between exceeding your projections or falling far short of them.

Even with the changes in marketing and markets, in media and methods, the guerrilla approach remains the sensible one for all marketers. For entrepreneurs, for new businesspeople, for small businesspeople, it seems almost mandatory. Ask the successful small-business owners who have prospered in the ugly face of an ailing economy and they'll tell you it *is* mandatory that you make the attitude and smarts of the guerrilla part of your permanent mind-set.

If I ran a small or even a gigantic business, I'd take comfort in knowing that my marketing would work and had been proven on the front lines. I'd feel confident knowing that my marketing mind-set was state-of-the-moment. I'm delighted to let you in on the common sense that makes marketing work, but I'm even more gratified knowing the high level of success you will certainly attain as a guerrilla. As one guerrilla to another, I wish you well.

1
What Is Guerrilla Marketing?

MARKETING IS EVERYTHING you do to promote your business, from the moment you conceive of it to the point at which customers buy your product or service and begin to patronize your business on a regular basis. The key words to remember are *everything* and *regular* basis.

The meaning is clear: Marketing includes the name of your business, the determination of whether you will be selling a product or service, the method of manufacture or servicing, the colors, size, and shape of your product, the packaging, the location of your business, the advertising, the public relations, the sales training, the sales presentation, the telephone inquiries, the problem solving, the growth plan, and the follow-up. If you gather from this that marketing is a complex process, you're right.

See marketing as a circle that starts with your idea for generating revenue and completes itself when you have the blessed patronage of repeat and referral business. If your marketing is not a circle, it's a straight line that leads right to the bankruptcy courts.

This book can simplify the complexities, remove the mystique, show you exactly how any entrepreneur can use marketing to generate maximum profits from minimum investments. It can prevent you from making the many marketing mistakes businesspeople make every day.

What this book can do for you

Put another way, this book can help make a small business big. It can aid an individual entrepreneur in making a lot of money as painlessly as possible. Very often, the only factor that determines success or failure is the way in which a product or service is marketed. The information in these pages will arm you for success and alert you to the shortcomings that lead to failure.

Every type of entrepreneurial enterprise requires marketing. There are no exceptions. It's not possible to succeed without marketing.

Assume that you have a fine business background and are well versed in the fundamentals of marketing as practiced by the giant corporations. Admirable. Now forget as much as you can. Marketing for you as an entrepreneur is vastly different than it is for an esteemed member of the *Fortune* 500. Oh, some of the principles may be the same, but the details are different. A good analogy is that of Adam and Eve. In principle, they were very much the same, but they varied in crucial details — and thank heaven for that. When they were lost, I'll bet Adam *never* asked for directions.

You're about to become a master of guerrilla marketing, the type of all-out marketing necessary for entrepreneurial success. Guerrilla marketing is virtually unknown to the large corporations. And be grateful that it is. After all, the large corporations have the benefit of big bucks. You don't.

So you've got to rely on something just as effective but less costly. You've got to rely on guerrilla marketing. I'm happy to report that your size is an ally when it comes to marketing. If **Your size** you're a small company, a new venture, or a single individual, **is an ally** you can utilize the tactics of guerrilla marketing to their fullest. You've got the ability to be fast on your feet, to employ a vast array of marketing tools, to gain access to the biggest marketing brains and get them at bargain-basement prices. Now you may not need to use every weapon in your potential marketing arsenal, but you're sure going to need some of them. So you'd best know how to use them all.

It may be that you will require no advertising at all. But you will require marketing. It may be that word of mouth is so favorable and spreads so rapidly that your venture can reap a fortune just because of it. If so, you can be sure that the word of mouth was motivated by effective marketing in the first place.

In fact, a strong word-of-mouth campaign is part of marketing. And so are business cards. And so is stationery. And the hours you're open. And the clothes you wear. And certainly your location is important in marketing.

Every component that helps you sell what you are selling is part of the marketing process. No detail is too insignificant to be included. The more you realize that, the better your marketing will be. And the better your marketing is, the more money you will make. I'm not talking about sales. I'm talking about profits — the dear old bottom line.

That's the good news. Here's the bad: One of these days, you're going to be an entrepreneur no longer. If you successfully put into practice the principles of guerrilla marketing, you will become fat and rich and famous and will no longer have the lean, hungry mentality of the entrepreneur.

Once you've reached that stage, you may resort to the textbook forms of marketing, for you might be too encumbered with employees, traditions, paperwork, management levels, and necessary bureaucracy to be flexible enough for guerrilla marketing. But somehow I have the feeling you won't mind that state of affairs too much. After all, Coca-Cola, Standard Oil, Procter & Gamble, and General Motors were all started by entrepreneurs. You can be darn certain that they practiced guerrilla marketing as much as possible in their day. You can also be sure that they do all their marketing by the numbers these days. And I doubt if they complain about it.

In time, some of those king-sized companies may be surpassed in size by companies that are now being founded and nurtured by entrepreneurs such as you. How will it happen? It will be the result of a combination of factors. And marketing genius will be one of them. Count on it.

At this point, I'm assuming you understand that you have to offer a quality product or service to be successful. Even the best marketing in the world won't motivate a customer to purchase a poor product or service more than once. In fact, guerrilla marketing can speed the demise of an inferior offering, since people will learn of the shoddiness that much quicker. So do everything in your power to ensure the quality of whatever it is you'll be selling. And once you've got that quality, you'll be ready for guerrilla marketing. **You must have quality**

It is also mandatory for success that you have adequate capitalization — that is, money. Notice I didn't say that you need a lot of money. Sufficient capitalization to engage in guerrilla marketing will be enough. That means you'll need enough cash or cash reserves to promote your business aggressively for at least three months, and ideally for a full year. It might take $300; it might take $30,000. That depends on your goals.

There are loads of small businesses throughout the United States. Many of them offer superb products and highly desirable services. But fewer than one-tenth of one percent of those businesses will make it to the point of phenomenal financial success.

The elusive variable The elusive variable that makes the difference between merely being listed in the yellow pages and being listed on the New York Stock Exchange is the *marketing* of the product or service.

You now hold in your hand the key to becoming part of that tiny percentage of entrepreneurs who go all the way. By realizing that many facets of your business can fall into the category of marketing, you have a head start over competitors who do not see that there is a difference between *advertising* and *marketing.*

The more aware of marketing you are, the more attention you will pay to it. And the increased attention will result in better marketing of your offerings. A great deal of marketing isn't merely poorly executed these days; it's not executed at all! I'd **Fewer than** venture a bold guess that fewer than 10 percent of the new-and **10 percent** small-business owners in America have explored most of the marketing methods available to them. These methods include canvassing, personal letters, telephone marketing, circulars and brochures, signs on bulletin boards, classified ads, outdoor signs, advertisements in the yellow pages, newspapers, and magazines, and on radio, television, and billboards, direct mail, advertising specialties such as imprinted ballpoint pens, samples, seminars, and demonstrations, sponsoring of events, exhibiting at trade shows, and using searchlights, T-shirt ads, and public relations. Guerrilla marketing *demands* that you scrutinize every single one of these marketing methods and more, many, many more — then use the combination that seems best for your business.

Once you've launched your guerrilla marketing attack, you must keep track of which weapons are hitting your target and **How to** which are missing. Merely knowing can *double the effectiveness* **double your** *of your marketing budget.* **effectiveness**

There are absolutely no advertising agencies that specialize in guerrilla marketing. When I worked as a senior executive at some of the world's largest (and smallest) advertising agencies, I found that they didn't have a clue as to what it takes to help an entrepreneur succeed. They could help the big guys, all right.

But they were helpless without the brute force of big bucks. So where can you turn to for help? The first place to turn is to this book. The next place is to your own ingenuity and energy. And finally, you will probably have to go to a marketing or advertising professional to get help with details in the areas where guerrilla marketing overlaps standard marketing. But don't expect the pros to be as tough in the trenches as you are. Most likely, they operate better from high in a posh skyscraper.

Where to get help

Guerrilla marketing dictates that you comprehend every facet of marketing, then employ with excellence the necessary marketing tactics. To understand the nature of this idea, it may be useful to examine the real reason Japan was able to knock the United States off its perch as world leader in the TV, stereo, automobile, and electronics industries.

Industry in the United States has been able to turn out excellent products with a low percentage of rejects — 5 percent. That means that of one million manufactured items, only 50,000 were rejects. Industry leaders recognized that the cost to lower that number would be greater than the profit industry would realize by achieving perfection. So it became an economic truism that you could run a successful manufacturing operation if you limited your rejects to 50,000 per million units. And the public became used to the concept: They complained about lemons, but weren't really all that surprised at them.

Japan, after a horrible defeat in World War II, suffered from an identity of poor quality. For years the phrase "Made in Japan" was enough to elicit a grin from a sophisticated purchaser. How did the Japanese overcome this problem? Japan decided to fly in the face of the economic truism that allowed for a 5 percent reject rate. Japan figured that if the public accepts products even though 50,000 per million are inferior, it might happily embrace products of which fewer than 50,000 were unacceptable. But according to the economists, this would cost a ton of money.

The Japanese, having nowhere to go but up, figured it was worth it. They improved the quality of what they made to the point that right now, they have only 200 rejects per million units. Two hundred rejects versus our 50,000 rejects! And Japan is still working on methods for lowering that 200 figure.

How did Japan do it? By reducing mistakes. Every error that could possibly be construed as a mistake was noticed by people actually hired by industry to count mistakes. In the category of mistakes were included shoddy workmanship, tardiness, breaks that lasted too long, minor flaws in detail work, low morale, and anything at all that impeded production. Weekly, departments within Japanese industrial firms would meet with their hired mistake counters. They were told the number of mistakes made that week, and they worked to reduce that number. By working at it assiduously, they dramatically cut the number of mistakes.

Through almost totally eliminating mistakes, Japan took over leadership in the TV, stereo, automobile, and electronics industries. And as the number of mistakes went down, productivity went up. The country benefited in these two ways by this one action. In all businesses, there are numerous opportunities and numerous problems. The Japanese exploited their opportunities and solved their problems. So it is with guerrilla marketing.

Going all out   Guerrilla marketing involves recognizing the myriad opportunities out there and *exploiting every one of them*. Like the Japanese, don't overlook a thing. In the marketing of any product, problems are certain to arise. Solve these problems and continue to look for new problems to solve, problems of prospects and customers. Businesses that solve problems have a far greater chance of success than those that don't. Today and in the twenty-first century, businesses that save time for people will flourish. Why? Because lack of time is a problem and growing numbers of people in industrialized societies see it as such. The time-saving industry will become a major opportunity.

You must spot these large opportunities, but you won't have the luxury of neglecting the smaller opportunities or overlooking minor problems. You've got to go all out.

Going all out is the foundation of successful guerrilla marketing. By going all out, the Japanese completely reversed the reaction to "Made in Japan" to the point where the phrase now means excellent craftsmanship, attention to detail, and nearly zero defects.

Energy alone is not enough, however. Energy has to be directed by intelligence. Intelligent marketing is marketing that is first and foremost focused on a core idea. All your marketing must be an extension of this idea: the advertising, the stationery, the direct mailings, the telephone marketing, the yellow pages advertising, the package, the whole thing. But it is not enough to have a better idea; you must also have a better argument and a focused strategy. Today many large and supposedly sophisticated companies go to one expert for a trademark, another expert for an advertising program, yet another expert for direct-mail planning, and possibly one more professional for location selection. This is not only costly, it is nonsense. Nine times out of ten each of these experts is pulling in a different direction.

What must be done is to have all the marketing pros pull in a common direction — a preagreed, long-term, carefully selected direction. When this is done, a synergistic effect is automatically created and five types of marketing tactics do the work of ten. The preagreed direction will always be clear if you encapsulate your thoughts in a core concept that can be expressed in a *maximum* of first, seven sentences, then seven words. That's right, a *maximum* of seven. Think it can't be done? Try it for your own business.

Pulling in the same direction

Here's an example. An entrepreneur wanted to offer courses in computer education, but knew that most people suffer from "technophobia" — fear of things technical. Advertisements for his proposed courses in word processing, accounting by computer, the electronic spreadsheet, and more produced little response. So he decided to restate the basic premise of his offering. At first, he stated it thus: "I wish to alleviate the fears that people have regarding computers, so that they will recognize the enormous value and competitive advantages of working with computers." Then, in an attempt to reduce this thought to a seven-word core concept, he reiterated his idea: "I will teach people to operate computers." This seven-word statement clarified his task. Clarified it for him, for his sales staff, for his prospective students.

Later he developed a name for his company, a name that reduced his core concept to three words: Computers for Beginners. This bypassed the problem of technophobia, stated his premise, and attracted hordes of beginners. Before he started this business, his concept ran six pages. By reducing and reducing his basic thoughts, he was finally able to achieve the succinctness necessary to assure clarity. And clarity led to success. It usually does.

The core concept

It's a pretty simple idea to center all your marketing on a core concept. But you can be sure that when you begin to market your offering that way, you will be a member of an enlightened minority and well on your way to marketing success — a prerequisite for financial success.

Here is what guerrilla marketing is *not:* expensive, easy, common, wasteful, taught in marketing classes, found in marketing textbooks, practiced by advertising agencies, or known to your competitors. Be grateful that it is not all those things. If it were, all business owners would be guerrillas, and your path to success would be a paved and marked one rather than a secret, unmarked route to the end of a rainbow with a bigger pot of gold than you ever imagined.

2
Entrepreneurial Marketing: The Guerrilla Difference

IN AN ARTICLE IN THE *Harvard Business Review,* John A. Welsh and Jerry F. White remind us that "a small business is not a little big business." An entrepreneur is not a multinational conglomerate but a profit-seeking individual. To survive, he must have a different outlook and must apply different principles to his endeavors than does the president of a large or even medium-sized corporation.

Not only does the scale of small and big businesses differ, but small businesses also suffer from what the *Harvard Business Review* article calls "resource poverty." This is a problem and opportunity that requires an entirely different approach to marketing. Where large ad budgets are not necessary or feasible, where expensive ad production squanders limited capital, where every marketing dollar must do the work of two dollars, if not five dollars or even ten, where a person's company, capital, and material well-being are all on the line — that is where guerrilla marketing can save the day and secure the bottom line.

A large company can invest in a full-scale advertising campaign run by an ad agency, and that company has the resources to switch to a different campaign if the first is not successful. And if the company ad manager is smart, he or she will hire a different agency the second time around. This luxury is not available to entrepreneurs, who must get it right the first time. Entrepreneurs who are guerrillas get it right because they know the secrets — and so will you.

Get it right the first time

This is not to say that I hold the techniques employed by the big corporations in contempt; quite the contrary. While creating advertising for companies such as Alberto-Culver, Quaker Oats, United Airlines, Citicorp, Visa, Sears, and Pillsbury, I frequently employed big-company marketing techniques. I was acting properly. But to suggest that the individual entrepreneurs I advise employ the same techniques would be irresponsible, not to mention financially wasteful. Instead, I resort to the techniques of guerrilla marketing, techniques that might get me laughed out of a Procter & Gamble or Chrysler Corporation conference room.

Many of the approaches and some of the techniques overlap. Entrepreneurs must govern tactical operations by marketing strategy. And all their marketing efforts have to be weighed against that strategy. They also need to examine all of the marketing avenues available to them. The critical difference is the bottom line. They must keep a far keener eye on the bottom line than do the giant firms.

The critical difference

They must spend far less money testing their marketing tactics. And their marketing must produce results at a fraction of the price paid by the biggies. They may not necessarily handle their marketing efforts better than large companies, but they will be more personalized and realistic in their use of marketing.

Large companies think nothing of producing five television commercials for purposes of testing. Small companies dare not even think the same thought. Large companies employ many levels of management to analyze the effectiveness of their advertising. Small companies entrust the judging to one individual. Large companies look first to television — the most far-reaching of all the advertising media. Small companies generally look first to small newspaper ads in local papers. Both are interested in sales that generate profits. But each must achieve its goals in a dramatically different way.

Often, large companies aim for leadership of an industry, or to dominate a market or large market segment, and they use marketing ploys designed to attain those lofty ambitions. But small companies, or individual entrepreneurs, can flourish merely by gaining a tiny slice of an industry, a fraction of a market. Different wars require different tactics.

Flourish by gaining a tiny slice

Whereas large companies must advertise from the outset and continue to advertise with virtually no interruption, smaller enterprises may be able to advertise only in the beginning and then rely solely upon guerrilla weapons and word-of-mouth advertising. Can you imagine what would happen if Budweiser beer depended on word-of-mouth advertising? Miller beer would sell a lot more six-packs.

An individual entrepreneur may be able to get enough business just by dealing with one gigantic company. An acquaintance of mine was able to survive financially (and in gracious style, I might add) merely by conducting small seminars for one large banking firm. No large company could exist off the income he was generating, but my friend was able to zero in on that one firm until he got his first assignment. After that there were others, and still others. This year, he is conducting his seminars for a large chemical company. Working with companies of that size, he needs very few customers. Needless to say, his marketing was tailored to this reality.

A descriptive brochure sent to a single large corporation may result in enough business to keep an energetic telephone marketing trainer in the chips for a long time. Try finding a New York Stock Exchange – listed company that could do the same. Impossible.

Many entrepreneurs get all the business they need by posting signs on bulletin boards. A large company would never consider such a possibility. If it did, it would be known as Shrinking, Inc., in short order. The point is obvious: Sauce for the small goose is not necessarily sauce for the large goose. And vice-versa.

For example, business cards can be plain and straightforward for big-company executives. The executive's name, company name, address, and phone number are enough. Perhaps a title is also necessary. But for a smart practitioner of an individual enterprise, that business card ought to contain a lot more information. For example, I know a typist whose card has all of the above, along with the message "Legal, theses, statistical, manuscript, résumé, and business typing." Her card does double duty. It has to. That is what guerrilla marketing is all about.

A business card can double as a brochure, a circular, a wallet-sized advertisement. It can open up to become a mini-brochure. People appreciate such mini-brochures. These people know that their time and space are at a premium and that your card saves them time while taking up very little valuable space. The cost to produce such a card is not much more than one pays for a standard card. But the need is different. Lacking a large stockpile of dollars, the small businessperson must make use of all the adver-

The guerrilla business card

tising media available. A business card can be more than a mere listing of one's name, address, and phone number; it can be an advertising medium. To see how much of an advertising weapon it can be for you, call InfoCard at 512-327-3385.

A huge corporation can run radio or television commercials and tell the audience, at the end of each message, to obtain the address of the nearest dealer by consulting the yellow pages. Now that's just dandy when you dominate that section of the yellow pages with the largest ad and the most recognizable trademark and line. But the individual entrepreneur dare not direct listeners or viewers to the yellow pages. That would only alert his prospective customers to the competition, or to the dominance of certain competitors. Instead, the astute entrepreneur directs his prospects to the white pages, where there will be no competitive ads, where his organization's small size will not appear as a detriment, and where recognizable promotion themes and symbols will not woo a customer away.

You have more flexibility   Perhaps the biggest difference between an individual businessperson and a large corporation is in the degree of flexibility each possesses. Here the balance tips in favor of the small business. Because it hasn't indoctrinated numerous levels of management and a gigantic sales organization in the tactics and strategies of its marketing plan, it can make changes on the spot. It can be fast on its feet and can react to market changes, competitive ploys, undeveloped service niches, economic realities, new media, newsworthy events, and last-minute offers.

I recall how a major advertiser once was offered an unbelievably good media buy for a fraction of its normal price. Because the offer did not fit into the company's engraved-in-bronze plan, and because the person to whom the offer was made had to check with so many bosses, the company had to turn down the offer. A tiny business then accepted it: a thirty-second commercial just before the Super Bowl, for the incredible price of $500. The cost of this commercial slot (in the San Francisco Bay Area) normally sold for ten times that amount. But because of lack of flexibility, the giant corporation was unable to get in on the bargain. Speed and flexibility are part of the very essence of guerrilla marketing.

A success-bound entrepreneur must learn to think about marketing and advertising on a different wavelength than does a corporate advertising executive. While you must think about the primary marketing tools much as the executive does, you must also develop a sixth sense for the other opportunities available to entrepreneurs. It may be that a personal letter or visit is in order. A corporate manager might never consider such mundane tactics. Perhaps a telephone marketing campaign is in order. Can you picture Coca-Cola getting involved in telephone marketing to consumers?

The *Fortune* 500 may have big bucks in the same way the brontosaurus had a weight problem. But like the furry, quick mammal, you've got the flexibility, the speed, the disregard of image, that enables you to use radio commercials and also hire high school students to hand out printed circulars on street corners. You don't have a body of rules to follow, a committee to answer to, a set structure to follow. You're a guerrilla. You are the organization. You answer to yourself. You make the rules and you break the rules. And that means you get to be amazing, outrageous, surprising, unpredictable, brilliant, and quick.

You also just may be able to enjoy the rare luxury of sitting back and relying upon consistent word-of-mouth advertising. If you're really good at your work, and know how to generate word-of-mouth marketing, it might be enough to keep your coffers brimming. I know of no *Fortune* 500 companies that can enjoy that amenity.

Incidentally, please understand that what appears to be word-of-mouth advertising is often a combination of newspaper, magazine, radio, direct-mail, and word-of-mouth advertising. But it's the mouth that gets the credit and not the media. Don't delude yourself into believing that you can succeed with no media advertising. Winning with that strategy would be like winning the lottery with your first ticket. It happens, but don't bet your boots or your business.

It's not really word of mouth

Still, it is possible to generate word-of-mouth advertising. There are several ways to accomplish this. The first, of course, is to *be so good at what you do*, or to offer products that are so obviously wonderful, that your customers will want to pass on the good word about you. Another way to get the ball rolling is to *give brochures* to your new customers. This reminds them why they patronized you in the first place and spurs word-of-mouth endorsements. A third way to obtain positive recommendations is literally *to ask for them*. Nobody is better equipped to talk up your company than you — or perhaps your best customer. Tell all your customers: "If you're really satisfied with my service or products, I'd sure appreciate it if you'd tell your friends." Finally, *you can bribe your customers*. Tell them, "If I get any customers who mention your name, I'll send you a free gift (or give you a 10 percent discount) next time you're in." Which of these methods should you employ? As a guerrilla, you should use all of them. Testing will tell.

The point to remember is that no large corporation can succeed by means of word-of-mouth advertising alone, and some entrepreneurs can. But do yourself a favor and don't leave everything up to the recommendations of your happy customers. They probably have more important things to talk about. Even for a guerrilla, consistent marketing is crucial to success.

An overall marketing plan for a person engaged in individual enterprise might consist of a listing in the yellow pages, a mailing of circulars and business cards, a posting of signs, and a follow-up telephoning to prospects to whom the promotional material was sent. That four-pronged effort (yellow pages, mailing, sign-posting, and telephoning) might be all it takes to get a business off and running. You can be certain that no big company has a marketing plan so short and simple — and inexpensive.

Imagine a staple gun and a handful of circulars as the only marketing tools necessary to conduct a business. IBM would boot me out of its corporate offices for suggesting such a thing. But many a successful home-typing service uses these devices and none other. A typist I know started out by typing her circulars, thereby lending credibility to her typing ability. Then she posted them with her staple gun on bulletin boards throughout local college campuses. These days, she posts no more circulars, and her staple gun gathers dust. Word of mouth has taken over, and she gets all the business she needs through referrals.

Entrepreneurs can enjoy month after month of profitable business merely by advertising in the classified pages. I'm sure you've seen rafts of ads by independent contractors while perusing the classified ads. You do look through them, don't you? The classified ads are recommended reading for entrepreneurs. They give you ideas. They alert you to the competition. They clue you in as to current prices. You'll read a lot more about them in chapter 13. The point I'm making here is that classified ads are an **An important tool** important tool for independent businesspeople. They are not a tool for large companies. I doubt if the most professional advertising agencies in the world are well versed in proper use of the classified pages. But the classified pages may be invaluable to free-lance earners.

In *How to Start and Run a Successful Home Typing Business* (Aames-Allen Publishing, Huntington Beach, California, 1980), Peggy Glenn, the author, who also writes of word processing at home, lists an eleven-point advertising program:

1. Hang fliers on campuses and near student gathering places.
2. Ask each school department to allow you to post your fliers.
3. Post a flier in the faculty lounge.
4. Post your flier at placement offices and counseling centers.
5. Leave fliers at the graduate study office.
6. Advertise in the campus newspaper.
7. Post a small sign on the community library bulletin board.
8. Post fliers for special groups such as engineers.
9. Visit a few college departments to see if they need your help.
10. Visit the principals of schools in your community with fliers.
11. Visit private and special schools in your area, leaving fliers.

She admits that this is a lot of advertising. To a typist, it is. To a large company, it isn't. That illustrates clearly how marketing is different for entrepreneurs—inexpensive, yet comprehensive.

Still, there are ten highly significant marketing secrets that must be known by all advertisers, large and small, if they are to succeed. Even the tiniest of entrepreneurs must be aware of them. And that awareness will begin the moment you start reading the next chapter.

3
The Ten Most Important Marketing Secrets

IT FLOORS ME that these secrets are secrets at all. Instead, they ought to be truisms, engraved on brass plaques in the offices of all who market or plan marketing. Yet these proven gems of marketing wisdom have somehow escaped the ken of large and small marketers alike. I sincerely believe that it is next to impossible to market a product or service successfully unless these secrets are known and put into practice. I also believe that merely by learning these secrets, then living by them, you're 80 percent of the way toward a successful marketing campaign.

If you have a small business and want it to become a large business, forget it — until you put these secrets into practice. And if you allow these concepts to become part of your mental marketing framework, you've got a giant head start on those who do not.

The big ten   So as not to keep you in suspense any longer, I'll reveal the secrets right here and now. They can be summarized in ten words, each ending in the letters "ent": commitment, investment, consistent, confident, patient, assortment, subsequent, convenient, amazement, and measurement.

1. You must have *commitment* to your marketing program.
2. You must think of that program as an *investment*.
3. You must see to it that your program is *consistent*.
4. You must make your prospects *confident* in your firm.
5. You must be *patient* in order to make a commitment.
6. You must see that marketing is an *assortment* of weapons.

7. You must know that profits come *subsequent* to the sale.
8. You must run your firm to be *convenient* for your customers.
9. You must put an element of *amazement* in your marketing.
10. You must use *measurement* to judge the effectiveness of your weapons.

Let's start with the first. If you're not committed to a marketing or advertising program, it's probably not going to work for you. I tell my clients that the single most important word for them to remember during the time they are engaged in marketing is *commitment*. It means that they are taking the marketing job seriously. They're not playing around, not expecting miracles. They have scant funds to test their marketing — they must act. Without commitment, marketing becomes practically impotent.

You evolve a marketing plan, revise and rerevise it until it is *a powerful plan for your purposes*. You put it to work, and then you stay with it, no matter what (in most cases). You watch it slowly take effect, rise and falter, take a bit more effect, slide back a bit, start taking hold even more, stumble, then finally grab on and soar, taking you with it. Your plan is working. Your cash register is ringing. Your bank balance is swelling. And it all happened because *you were committed to your marketing program*.

Let's examine that last paragraph. What if you weren't patient enough during the time your plan "slowly" took effect? You might have changed the plan. Many entrepreneurs do. What if you dropped the plan the moment it faltered? You would have lost out. Many marketers do. What if you lost your cool when your sales slid backward? You might have scrubbed the plan. Suppose you dropped it when it stumbled, as virtually all marketing plans do, at least temporarily. Disaster would have ensued. But because you stayed with the plan, because you were committed to it, it finally took hold and did what you wanted it to do. Your success was very much due to your understanding of the concept of commitment. If you had not been in touch with the essence of the concept, you probably would have taken one of the many tempting opportunities to kill the plan — and would have killed your chances along with it. But you understood what commitment means, and it paid off for you.

Understanding pays off

A new sleep shop was opening in Boulder, Colorado. The owner of the business had heard about me, so he flew out to northern California to talk. We hit it off. We discussed the idea of commitment to a marketing program. He admitted that he knew zilch about marketing and turned the whole thing over to me. I developed a marketing plan, secured his approval, then reiterated the necessity for him to commit himself to the program. Mind you, I'm talking about a guy with one little store in a relatively small town.

The marketing started and nothing happened. Six weeks later, my new client called me to tell me he was still committed to the program, but that he hadn't seen much proof of it working for him. He also let me know that he was completely relaxed about the whole thing because he felt he understood about commitment. After twelve weeks, he called to tell me he was beginning to see hints that the program was taking effect. After six months, he opened his second store. After nine months, he opened his third, and at the end of the year, he had five stores. He remained committed to the marketing program and within six years had forty-two stores in Colorado, Iowa, Kansas, Wyoming, and Missouri.

I sincerely doubt that he would have progressed to a point where he could even have justified a second store if he had not stayed with the plan, if he had not understood what I meant about commitment. He had many chances to waver, many chances to become a disbeliever. He had a ton of reasons to veer from the plan. Naturally, it was a well-conceived plan, a plan perfect for his purposes. Commitment to an unwise plan is just plain stupid. And you won't have any way of knowing if your plan is good or bad at the outset — except for low-cost testing, your own intuition, and the counsel of others in whom you believe. But once you believe in your plan, you've got to back that belief with *patience*. Patience is another way of saying commitment.

My sleep shop client's plan called for weekly newspaper advertising, daily radio advertising, strong in-store signs, weekly sales training, consistent customer follow-up, and free gifts for customers during promotions. That was in the seventies. In the eighties, it was augmented by daily TV advertising three weeks out of every four. And for the nineties, though the business was sold for an obscene sum, it might be supported even more by a video brochure. But the framework would remain the same — because the mind-set of the owner would remain that of a guerrilla.

How long does it take to work? My advice to you is to create a sensible plan, then stick with it until it proves itself to you. How long might that take? Maybe three months, if you're lucky. Probably six months. And maybe even as long as a year. But you will never, never, never know whether the plan is working within the first sixty days. Commitment is directly related to time. The longer you live by a plan, the deeper your sense of commitment. If your boat sinks in the ocean and you start swimming to shore, you should not give up if you haven't hit the beach within one hour — even five hours. To survive, you've got to be committed to swimming to that beach. Think of that when you consider altering your marketing plans after a short time.

In working with small clients, I consider the greatest stumbling block to be their inability to understand commitment. Lest you misunderstand, think about the following list each time you run an ad and achieve less of a response than you expected:

The greatest stumbling block

1. The first time a man looks at an ad, he doesn't see it.
2. The second time, he doesn't notice it.
3. The third time, he is conscious of its existence.
4. The fourth time, he faintly remembers having seen it.
5. The fifth time, he reads the ad.
6. The sixth time, he turns up his nose at it.
7. The seventh time, he reads it through and says, "Oh brother!"
8. The eighth time, he says, "Here's that confounded thing again!"
9. The ninth time, he wonders if it amounts to anything.
10. The tenth time, he will ask his neighbor if he has tried it.
11. The eleventh time, he wonders how the advertiser makes it pay.
12. The twelfth time, he thinks it must be a good thing.
13. The thirteenth time, he thinks it might be worth something.
14. The fourteenth time, he remembers that he wanted such a thing for a long time.
15. The fifteenth time, he is tantalized because he cannot afford to buy it.
16. The sixteenth time, he thinks he will buy it someday.
17. The seventeenth time, he makes a memorandum of it.
18. The eighteenth time, he swears at his poverty.
19. The nineteenth time, he counts his money carefully.
20. The twentieth time he sees the ad, he buys the article or instructs his wife to do so.

The guerrilla from 1885

The above was written by one Thomas Smith in London back in 1885. So much for commitment. Now let's talk about another "ent" word, the second of the ten most important marketing secrets of all — *investment*.

Marketing and advertising should be considered *conservative investments*. They are not miracle workers. They are not magic formulas. They are not instant gratifiers. If you don't recognize that marketing is a conservative investment, you'll have difficulty committing yourself to a marketing program.

Marketing is not instant gratification

Suppose you buy a blue-chip stock. If it drops after a few weeks, you don't sell it. You hold on to it, hoping it will go up. And in all likelihood it will. Such is the nature of a conservative investment. Think of marketing the same way. If it doesn't produce instant results, that's because most marketing doesn't. If it does produce instant results, good for you — but don't figure it will always be that way.

Also, don't expect marketing to suddenly double your sales. Although that has happened, it is unusual. Marketing will contribute to slow but steady increases for you. At the end of a year, you'll be able to say that you've invested X dollars in marketing and received X plus Y in sales. Just the way conservative investments are supposed to pay off. Recognizing this, you'll feel good about making a conservative investment in marketing the next year, and the year after that. If you expect more from marketing, chances are you'll be disappointed. If you expect only that, chances are you'll be gratified. And successful.

Stupid example time: I worked with a client who had never engaged in newspaper advertising. We developed a marketing plan for his four eyeglass stores, a creative strategy, and a media plan. We discussed commitment. Then we ran the ads. After four weeks, my client called to tell me he was dropping the entire advertising program. When I inquired why, he told me he had expected his sales to at least double by this time. Yes, he admitted, I had explained that advertising does not work this way. But no, he decided, he didn't want to spend money that didn't produce instant sales.

I wish I had informed him up front that his advertising expenditure was a conservative investment. Perhaps he would have better understood its powers. But instead, he dropped the plan and lost his money. Obviously he didn't have an iota of understanding of the investment concept. People don't invest money and then pull out when there is zero chance of recapturing the expense. But he did. And mind you, he was no dummy in real life. Only in marketing. He was expecting miracles, instant results, dramatic changes. Marketing just does not work that way. So don't expect it. Don't plan for it. Don't lose money because of it. In fact, whenever you spend one dime for any type of marketing, you should actually use the term *investing* to describe your expenditure. By *investing* your money in marketing, you'll earn a lot more money than by *spending* your money in marketing. See the difference?

The third major marketing secret is to make your marketing *consistent*. Don't change media. Don't change messages. Don't drop out of the public eye for long periods. When you are ready to market your product or service, be prepared to put the word out consistently. Consistently means regularly — and for a goodly period of time. It means that instead of running a couple of large newspaper ads once every few months, you'll run smaller newspaper ads, and run them frequently. Instead of airing fifty-five radio commercials in one week every few months, you'll run twelve radio commercials per week every week. You can even drop out of sight one week out of four. As long as you are a consistent marketer, you can pull out of the media for brief periods.

Consistency equates with familiarity. Familiarity equates with confidence. And confidence equates with sales. Provided that your products or services are of sufficient quality, confidence in yourself and your offering will attract buyers more than any other attribute.

Familiarity breeds sales

That's why the fourth secret is to make prospects *confident* in your offering. Confidence is ultra-important to you. More than quality. More than selection. More than price. More than service. Confidence will be your ally. And commitment, as proven by consistent marketing, will breed confidence.

I have a retail furniture client now who has been with me for about twenty years. When she first started marketing her product, she spent a fortune advertising on television. Could she afford it? Of course not. But she believed that television was her key to success. With the number of dollars she had to invest, television was her key to doom because she could only afford to run two commercials per week, even though they were on the highest-rated show at the time. But ratings are virtually meaningless with only two spots a week. It doesn't take a guerrilla to know that she'd be ill-advised to expect TV to produce profits with so few commercials. We'll discuss TV in greater detail later, but for now, suffice it to say that unless you can utilize a medium effectively, you should not utilize it at all.

My client was able to salvage her business from her disastrous TV experience, and she came to me. We talked about commitment, investment, and consistency. We talked about the other seven secrets as well. Since that day, she has run a tiny ad every Sunday in the newspaper, and her sales have continued to rise. Without increasing her marketing expenses as a percent of her gross revenue, she has dramatically increased her sales. It happened over a period of several years. Her store has quadrupled in size, and her profits have followed suit. She's even back on television — this time running ten commercials per day, two weeks out of every four. The key to her glittering success was consistent **Guerrillas have** advertising. She calls her tiny Sunday newspaper ad her "meal **meal tickets** ticket." And she's right. She tells me that almost everyone who comes into her store says they've seen the ad. You'd find that hard to believe if you saw the size of the ad. But you'd find that easy to believe if you knew that she's been running that and similar ads in the same newspaper on the same day for years. People are familiar with her operation. They're confident in her offerings. And they buy from her.

Along with her commitment, her treating marketing like an investment, her being consistent and patient, she has since added a multitude of weapons to her marketing arsenal. This *assortment* of weapons is generating all sorts of new, higher-than-projected profits for her. Guerrillas know that the wider the assortment of weapons you use, the wider the grin on your face when you review your financial statements.

Does she do follow-up mailings to all of her customers? Of course she does. She has learned that marketing doesn't end with the sale; instead, it's the marketing you do *subsequent* to the sale that leads to the juicy profits. It costs five times as much to sell to a new customer as it does to sell the same thing to an existing **The inevitable** customer. So my client is always mailing to existing customers — **payoff** and benefiting from the repeat sales that are the inevitable payoff.

Her store is known as a very *convenient* place to buy. It's open seven days a week. Hours are extended for the convenience of her customers — not for her own convenience. She accepts every credit card under the sun. She takes checks, arranges partial payment plans, delivers, installs, is accessible twenty-four hours a day via voice mail and fax, and even the parking is convenient.

Although she takes much of her business for granted, she knows that her marketing must *amaze* people. So her marketing mentions that her custom-designed furniture is available at factory-direct prices because she has her own factory. The prices are amazing and so is the homemade touch. It enables her to custom-design furniture and offer it at an off-the-floor price. This element of *amazement* attracts attention to her ads.

Most amazing of all, she has doubled the effectiveness of all her marketing! How did she do such a wondrous thing? The answer is *measurement*, as if you didn't know. She measured the effectiveness of all her marketing, asking people where they first heard of her.

In this way, she was able to eliminate the weapons and newspapers that weren't pulling their weight while doubling up on those that gave her the biggest bang for her bucks. The result: a doubling of her profits. The reason: measurement, also called "sourcing" by those in the know.

These ten secrets — as embodied by ten words — are the most valuable secrets you'll learn in this book. They are also extremely difficult rules to follow. **Valuable but difficult**

Your friends, employees, coworkers, partners, family, and suppliers may advise you to change your marketing plan when they don't see instant results. These same well-meaning people will question a marketing program that does not produce a dramatic increase in sales over a short period of time. And they'll be the first to tire of your marketing, become bored with your ads or commercials, be ready for a major change in your message or media. But your customers won't feel that way at all. They'll go through the process of developing confidence in your offering, and you should do everything in your power not to undermine that process. Now that you know these secrets, you won't.

The guerrilla moral: When you do develop your marketing plan, don't give it your stamp of approval until you are ready to commit yourself to it. Don't okay it until you are ready to invest in it with a realistic expectation of return. And don't start implementing it until you are prepared to stay with it on a consistent basis. This is not to say that you can't make changes. Of course you can. And maybe you should. But you can make changes while remaining consistent.

In quick review:

- Your task: make prospects *confident* in you.
- Your secret weapon: *commitment* to your plan.
- Your personality: *patience* describes it.
- Your marketing: an *assortment* of at least twenty weapons.
- Your format: the spirit of *consistency*.
- Your finances: some wisely *invested* in marketing.
- Your energy: apparent prior to and *subsequent to* the sale.
- Your operation: the essence of *convenience*.
- Your creative message: it always *amazes* readers.
- Your unglamourous but ultra-profitable chore: *measurement* of who came in to buy and where the heck they heard of you.

There. Now you can never say you weren't made fully aware of the ten most important marketing secrets. Merely by knowing them and making them a cornerstone of your business, you have a head start on your competition. Now, let's increase that head start. Let's examine what it takes to develop a successful plan in the first place.

4
The Blueprint: Developing a Guerrilla Marketing Plan

IN ORDER TO ENGAGE in successful marketing, you absolutely *must* start out with a marketing plan. But how do you develop one? You engage in research, attend to all details, and give the matter quite a bit of deep thought. Rest assured, the difference between many a success and failure is market planning and nothing else.

A word that you should now start to use and understand is *positioning*. Positioning means determining exactly what niche your offering is intended to fill. Once, I read of an airline that commenced operations during a time when most airline business was drastically down. By establishing a solid marketing plan, the new airline took off with astounding speed. It positioned itself as a high-frequency, no-frills airline that specialized in flights of less than two hours and in connecting passengers with long-distance routes of other airlines. That was a unique position. No other airline in the region offered such benefits. Success came rather easily.

Positioning

To attract further attention, the airline held seat-clearance sales, gave away free fifths of Chivas Regal scotch and Jack Daniel's bourbon, and introduced other innovations into a rather staid industry. None of this happened by accident. All of it came as a result of intelligent market planning and brilliant positioning.

One of the best-known names in American advertising circles is David Ogilvy. After placing several billion dollars' worth of advertising, Mr. O. listed thirty-two things his advertising agency had learned. Of the thirty-two, he said that the single most important decision had to do with *positioning the product*. He claimed that marketing results depended less on how advertising was written than on how the product or service was positioned.

The springboard for marketing

The guerrilla marketing plan or strategy should serve as the springboard for marketing that sells. When doing your own market planning, review your offering with regard to your objectives, the strengths and weaknesses of your offering, your perceived competition, your target market, the needs of that market, and the trends apparent in the economy. This should be instrumental in your establishing a proper position. Ask yourself basic questions: What business are you in? What is your goal? What benefits do you offer? What competitive advantages? When you know the true nature of your business, your goal, your strengths and weaknesses, your competitors' strengths and weaknesses, and the needs of your target market, your positioning will be that much easier to determine, your strategy easier to plan.

Who are you marketing to?

You must also ask and answer: Who is my target market? The answers you may have had when you started in business may vary in the nineties. Many enormous new markets are being identified in the United States, and many guerrilla marketers are enjoying record-breaking profits by aiming at those markets. Guerrilla fact: the more markets you have, the more profits you have.

Three markets that have already emerged as viable target audiences and will be bombarded with marketing in the nineties and throughout the coming century are *older people*, *women*, and *ethnic groups*, especially Asian-Americans and Hispanics.

Marketing to older people

The University of Michigan informs us that older people rely on mass-media marketing even more than on friends and family when it comes to consumer information. Surveys from several sources show that older folks rank health first, financial security second, a closer relationship with God third, and a closer relationship with family fourth. Younger people rank their free time above all else.

Guerrillas know that when communicating with older people, you should use the term "older" rather than "elderly" or "senior citizen." No games, please. When using graphics, show older people as *actively old* and living life to its fullest. Avoid anything trendy. Older people respond well to products and services that appeal to their autonomy and independence. Their eyesight is faltering, so use large type in your printed material. Do you know the magazine with the largest circulation in the United States? It used to be *Reader's Digest*; then it was *TV Guide*; now it's *Modern Maturity*.

Women now start over half of the new businesses in the United States and have higher success rates than businesses started by men. The kinder, gentler, entrepreneurial woman of the 1990s is very different from Mom and Grandma. **The woman of the nineties**

- 61 percent of women think that kids are the best part of life.
- 8 percent eat three regular meals a day with no snacks.
- 16 percent think society could thrive without marriage.
- White women outnumber white men by 2.2 percent; black women outnumber black men by 5.2 percent.
- 22 percent of computer scientists are women, up from 14 percent in 1970; but 99 percent of secretaries are women, the same as in 1970. I sure bucked that trend; my first job was as a secretary in a small advertising agency.
- Women spend three and one-third hours per weekday viewing TV. They're less likely than men to change channels during commercials, but more likely to mute the sound.
- 41 percent of the network audience for baseball are women over eighteen. For NBA basketball, the percentage is 37 percent; for NFL football, it's 36 percent. And all the percentages are rising.

The woman of today has more interests and can be reached through more marketing vehicles than ever before. And the power of women is staggering: Although 79 percent of bed purchase decisions are made by women, 77 percent of the time a man writes the check for the bed. Similar percentages can be found in many other fields offering expensive items, beginning with houses and cars, usually the most expensive purchases people will make in their lifetimes.

Guerrillas not only include women as a target audience in their general marketing, they also direct much of their marketing directly to women and only to women. Their purchasing power is growing with their stature in business.

Let's compare the mother of today, age thirty-seven, with her mother:

Task	% of Time Spent by Her Mother	% of Time Spent by Today's Woman
Job	31	31
Kids	24	34
Husband	15	14
Personal	5	9
Chores	8	5
Cooking	16	8
Parents	3	5

Don't overlook ethnic groups

Now also recognized as a potential lode of purchasing power are ethnic groups, especially Asian-Americans who now number 10 million, many of whom are affluent, educated, and, happily for the guerrilla, have no brand loyalties — yet.

The Hispanic and Asian markets have a combined purchasing power of $216 billion, and they don't assimilate as they used to. They know they don't have to if they don't want to. Changes in communication technology allow new arrivals to retain their cultural and linguistic identities and allow guerrillas to target these markets with pinpoint accuracy. A few other facts to ponder:

- Asians and Pacific Islanders are growing at eleven times the average population rate.
- Hispanics are growing at over five times the average population rate.
- Among Hispanic markets, the Mexican and Central and South American segments are the largest and fastest growing.
- The median household income among Asian families in 1990 was $36,800.
- Some of the least targetable ethnic segments are Puerto Ricans, Filipinos, and African-Americans.
- The highest concentrations of Hispanics are located in, in order: Los Angeles–Long Beach, New York City, Miami-Hialeah, Chicago, Houston, Riverside–San Bernardino, San Antonio, Anaheim–Santa Ana, San Diego, El Paso, and Dallas.
- The highest concentrations of Asian-Americans are located

in, in order: Los Angeles–Long Beach, New York, Honolulu, San Francisco, Oakland, San Jose, Anaheim–Santa Ana, Chicago, Washington, D.C.–Virginia, and San Diego.

Although Asian market segments are the smallest of the major ethnic groups, they have extraordinary growth, above average income, and they're highly targetable.

Guerrillas welcome their business, help them feel welcome, and emphasize the values deemed traditionally important to Asians: *independence, leisure, and family unity as a means to achieve financial success and social status.* Their marketing is devoid of showy displays of personal wealth and individuality, respecting the tradition deeply ingrained in many Asians. Guerrillas know they must emphasize their stability over almost any other benefit. They are aware that Asian-Americans are attracted to businesses that have credibility and experience and that these people have the money to afford high-ticket purchases. The new Asian-Americans are Chinese, Koreans, Japanese, Vietnamese, and Laotians.

To reach ethnic communities, consider placing ads in their newspapers, running spots on their cable TV channels, experimenting with direct mail, and sponsoring events aligned with the groups that are your target audiences. Remember that many ethnic groups rely on native language media for their consumer information.

Many marketing honchos are terrified of ethnic markets, foreign cultures, and unfamiliar languages. Guerrillas accept that challenge, working with ethnic ad agencies. At least one firm, Target Marketing (1-800-659-4905), can help you gain access to and communicate with virtually any ethnic market. More firms with this type of specialization are springing up. There are now several advertising agencies that specialize in serving the huge African-American market.

When you are focused clearly upon your market or markets, you can clarify your market position. Once you zero in on that position for your product or service, you should measure it against four criteria: (1) Does it offer a benefit my target audience **Four criteria** really wants? (2) Is it a real honest-to-goodness benefit? (3) Does **to meet** it truly separate me from my competition? (4) Is it unique and/or difficult to copy?

Unless you are completely satisfied with your answers, you should continue searching for a proper position. When you have finally answered the questions to your own satisfaction, you'll end up with a sensible position — and that should lead you to your goal. Accurate positioning doesn't just happen. It takes a lot of clear thinking, quite a bit of effort. But it's the key to marketing that works. And no guerrilla would think of doing one speck of marketing without a proper marketing plan that includes a positioning statement.

Just before starting on your marketing plan, you should practice thinking big. At this point, your imagination is not a limiting factor, so let it expand to open your mind to all the possibilities for your venture.

If you want, you can make your finished plan up to ten pages long. But at first, try stating it in one paragraph.

The guerrilla marketing plan

Guerrillas create strategies that are seven sentences long:

1. The first sentence tells the purpose of the strategy.
2. The second tells how you'll achieve this purpose, focusing upon your benefits.
3. The third tells your target market — or markets.
4. The fourth, the longest sentence, tells the marketing weapons you'll employ.
5. The fifth tells your niche.
6. The sixth tells your identity.
7. The seventh tells your budget, expressed as a percentage of your projected gross revenues.

Suppose you call your business Prosper Press and you intend to sell books about free-lancing. Let your strategy start with the words:

"The purpose of Prosper Press marketing is to sell the maximum number of books at the lowest possible selling cost per book. This will be accomplished by positioning the books as being so valuable to free-lancers that they are guaranteed to be worth more to the reader than their selling price." Let the paragraph continue: "The target market will be people who can or do engage in free-lance earning activities." Next, the paragraph might say, "Marketing tools to be utilized will be a combination of classified advertising in magazines and newspapers, direct mail, sales at seminars, publicity in newspapers and on radio and television, direct sales calls to bookstores, and mail-order display ads in magazines. The niche to be occupied is one that stands for valuable information that helps free-lancers succeed, the ultimate authority for free-lancers. Our identity will be one of expertise, readability, and quick response to customer requests. Thirty percent of sales will be allocated to marketing."

That's a long paragraph. And it's a simplistic paragraph. But it does the job. It's for a product rather than a service, for an earning venture that entails hardly any contact with the public. This mail-order venture requires very little in the way of marketing, considering all the options. It works beautifully in real life; has worked since 1974.

The plan starts with the purpose of the marketing — that is, it starts with the bottom line. From there, it connects with the benefits that will beautify that bottom line and with those who will contribute to that line — the target audience. The marketing tools are then listed. Next comes the positioning statement, which explains why the offering has value and should be purchased, what the product stands for. The identity (not the image, which is phony compared with the honesty of an identity) comes next. And the cost of the marketing wraps it up.

Dissecting the plan

Take a moment to understand clearly the crucial difference between an *image* and an *identity*. *Image* implies something artificial, something that is not genuine. *Identity* defines what your business is really about.

A business owner gets together with his staff and they develop an image, which is defined by many dictionaries as "a façade." Their marketing reflects this image. People come in and see that the business isn't exactly what they expected. They feel ripped off. They feel distrustful of the company.

Another business owner gets together with his staff and they develop an identity, based on truth. Their marketing reflects this identity. People come in and see that the business is exactly what they expected. They feel relaxed. They know they can trust this company. After all, it said nothing about itself that wasn't true.

Which of these two business owners is the guerrilla? What's better for your company, a phony image or an honest identity? We both know the right answers.

Now let's examine a marketing strategy for a computer tutor:

The purpose of Computer Tutor marketing is to book 100 percent of the company's available time for computer education, at the lowest possible cost per hour. This will be accomplished by establishing the credentials of the educators, the location of the operation, and the equipment. The target market will be local small businesspeople who can benefit from learning how to operate a small computer. Marketing tools to be utilized will be a combination of personal letters, circulars, brochures, signs on bulletin boards, classified ads in local newspapers, yellow page advertising, direct mail, advertising specialties, free seminars, sampling, and publicity in local newspapers, on radio, and on television. The company will be positioned as the prime source of one-on-one, guaranteed instruction in the operation of small computers; positioning will be intensified by office decor, employee attire, telephone manners, and location selection. Our company's identity will be a blend of professionalism, personal attention, and warm, human regard for our students. Ten percent of sales will be allocated to marketing.

Most marketing plans, especially if they are reduced to one paragraph, seem deceptively simple. But *unless* they are simple, they are difficult to execute. A complete marketing plan, which can run as little as three paragraphs — the marketing plan, the creative plan, and the media plan — or as long as 10 or even 110 pages (not recommended), should serve as a *guide*. It need not spell out all the details.

The chairman and chief executive officer of the Coca-Cola Company recognized this need for simplicity when he said, "If I had to state our business plan in one sentence, it would be this: 'We are going to build on our marketing strength in order to achieve profitable growth in the decade ahead.'"

Naturally, the marketing plan does identify the market. It lays out the framework for creating the advertising — as will be seen in the next chapter. It specifies the media to be utilized, along with costs, as will be seen in chapter 6. And that's really all it has to do.

A business plan   A business plan may require support documents such as results of research, the overall competitive situation, financial projections, and other details. But to include those details in the marketing plan itself is to muddy the waters. That's one reason guerrilla marketing plans are brief. A good road map lists the name or number of the highway wherever appropriate, not wherever possible. Like maps, marketing plans with too many details are difficult to follow.

The briefer your marketing plan, the easier it will be to follow. Bolster it with as many support documents as you wish. But don't include support information in the plan itself. Leave the details for other times, other places, other documents. The marketing plan should be the essence of simplicity. If it is not, chances are you haven't thought it through enough. And your employees, once they've read it, should immediately grasp your goals and be on your wavelength because your strategy is clear and direct. Most marketing strategies befuddle instead of enlightening employees. Then again, most employees are never made privy to the marketing strategy of the companies for which they work.

Once you have given your plan the proper thought, brevity, and focus, you can expand it in those areas pertinent to your business. While expanding it, never forget that your prime purpose is to obtain maximum profits. Profits are very different from sales. Anyone can achieve sales. It takes a guerrilla to consistently turn honest profits. These profits will be obtained if you clearly list your goals — all of them, including timing, budgets for everything, and projections. Without projections, you won't have a measuring stick. Your expanded plan should look first to the long range, then to the near future. By looking far enough into the future, you will realize what it takes to get you where you want to go in the style you desire. **Your prime purpose**

You might want to consider what market share you are targeting, what key personnel may be necessary to command that share, what inside services you'll need, and what outside services can be utilized to negate the need for inside services. Whether you list all the potential pitfalls in writing or not, you should think about how to deal with them. If you know what to expect in the way of obstacles, you'll better be able to surmount them as they pop up. And pop up they will.

Many expanded marketing plans include a situational analysis. This entails learning about your key customers, your expected competition, the possibilities, the probabilities, and the reality of the marketplace at the moment. While you are analyzing your situation, always remember to keep your eye on your bottom line. Don't let business get in the way of the purpose of business. The means should not interfere with the end. **Expanded marketing plans**

Computers now enable us to project results based upon hypothetical instances. An expanded marketing plan or business plan may examine those "what if" situations. It should have the framework for incorporating alternative courses of action based upon contingencies. If you wish, it can embrace lists of objectives, priorities, monitoring methods, problems, opportunities, and responsibilities. But an expanded marketing plan is more of a luxury than a necessity. And too many entrepreneurs get waterlogged with details to the point that the flame of their initial thrust grows dim and turns to smoke. Huge corporations do the same when they get carried away with technology and distracted from their original dreams.

Yearly, you should reexamine your marketing plan — whether brief or expanded. Your goal should be to maintain it. The conservative philosophy should apply: If it is not necessary to change, it is necessary not to change.

But whatever bells and whistles you have attached to your basic plan, whatever M.B.A. documentation you have affixed to it, you must still know who you are, where you are going, and how you will get there. You must start with a bare-bones marketing plan, short and simple. And you should not confuse a marketing plan with a business plan. A longer plan can go into details of growth, exact expenditures, and details. But the plans I have included a few pages back are enough to enable you to start and succeed. The first example is for a real company. The second is for a fictional company. These plans can be implemented by entrepreneurs who have a bent toward either mail-order book marketing (you can write or buy the books) or computer education (you can do or delegate the teaching). Both follow a simple formula that can serve as the basis for virtually any venture.

Such plans allow for some flexibility, but not a great deal. For example, Computer Tutor may run only one magazine ad one time in one regional edition, and run radio commercials every single day of the year. The marketing plan would still be fulfilled.

A good marketing plan should not allow for too much flexibility. After all, the plan is created to be followed. If you want

When to make changes

changes, make them *before* you write the plan. *And don't forget to commit yourself to it.*

Once you have positioned your business with a marketing

plan, where do you go? You go on to develop a creative plan that tells what your advertising is going to say. And finally, you create a media plan that tells the exact media details: costs, names of newspapers or radio stations, dates and sizes of ads, frequency of advertising, advertising specialties to be employed, tacks for obtaining free publicity, and the identity of your business.

Okay, you've got a marketing plan that tells how you'll promote your earning endeavor. You've got a creative plan that dictates your message and your identity. You've got a media plan that tells exactly where you'll spend your money. Now, if you've got the rest of your earning act together — the financial side, the legal issues, the accounting, the ability to offer a lot of quality in either your products or your services, and the right mental attitude — you can start earning money.

Many people start at this point, get frigid feet when they see the early results, and stop marketing while they think things over. Think but do not stop. Stopping is not a good idea. If after starting a business and embarking upon a marketing program — which is to say, investing serious cash in promoting the business (serious being anywhere from $100 per month to $1,000,000 per month) — you decide to stop marketing for a while, turn immediately to this page and read the following list of reasons why you *should* continue to market:

1. *The market is constantly changing.* New families, new prospects, new lifestyles change the marketplace. Nearly 18 percent of the people in America changed residences in 1992. Nearly 5 million Americans will get married. When you stop advertising, you miss evolving opportunities and stop being part of the process. You are not on the bus. You are not in the game.

   Why you must continue to market

2. *People forget fast.* Remember, they're bombarded with tons of marketing messages (an estimated 2700) daily. An experiment proved the need for constancy in marketing by running advertising once a week for thirteen weeks. After that period, 63 percent of the people surveyed remembered the advertising. One month later, 32 percent recalled it. Two weeks after that, 21 percent remembered it. That means 79 percent forgot it.

3. *Your competition isn't quitting.* People will spend money to

make purchases, and if you don't make them aware that you are selling something, they'll spend their money elsewhere.

4. *Marketing strengthens your identity.* When you quit marketing, you shortchange your reputation, reliability, and the confidence people have in you. When economic conditions turn sour, smart companies continue to advertise. The bond of communication is too precious to break capriciously.

5. *Marketing is essential to survival and growth.* With very few exceptions, people won't know you're there if you don't get the word out. And when you cease marketing, you're on the path to nonexistence. Just as you can't start a business without marketing, you can't maintain one without it.

6. *Marketing enables you to hold on to your old customers.* Many enterprises survive on repeat and referral business. Old customers are the key to both. When old customers don't hear from you or about you, they tend to forget you.

7. *Marketing maintains morale.* Your own morale is improved when you see your marketing at work, and especially when you see that it does, indeed, work. Your employees' morale is similarly uplifted. And cutting out marketing seems a signal of failure to those who actively follow your advertising. That won't be many people, but it will be some.

8. *Marketing gives you an advantage over competitors who have ceased marketing.* A troubled economy can be a superb advantage to a marketing-minded entrepreneur. It forces some competitors to stop marketing — giving you a chance to pull ahead of them and attract some of their customers. In all ugly economic situations, there are winners and losers.

9. *Marketing allows your business to continue operating.* You still have some overhead: telephone bills, yellow page ads, rent and/or equipment cost, possibly a payroll, your time. Marketing creates the air overhead breathes.

10. *You have invested money that you stand to lose.* If you quit marketing, all of the money you spent for ads, commercials, and advertising time and space becomes lost as the consumer awareness it purchased slowly dwindles away. Sure, you can buy it again. But you'll have to start from scratch. Unless you are planning to go out of business, it is rarely a good idea to cease marketing completely.

Just look at it this way: Does stopping marketing save you money? It does in the same way that stopping your wristwatch saves time. In other words, don't kid yourself.

I hope I have talked you into living with your commitment to your marketing program. This in no way means that you are going to market your business successfully. A marketing plan is necessary — in fact, crucial — for a company or an entrepreneur. But a marketing plan is a bit like a fancy, comfortable, powerful, great-looking car without gas. The fuel that powers your vehicle is the marketing itself: what it says, how it looks, what it feels like. That's where the creative process comes into play in marketing. And that's when it's got to be used with style and power. There's a way of making sure those creative juices flow. I'll let you in on some of the secrets in the following pages.

The fuel that powers your business

5
Secrets of Developing a Creative Marketing Program

PROBABLY THE MOST ENJOYABLE part of the marketing process is the creative part. And if you want to succeed in making your small business big, you should realize that the creative part applies to every single aspect of the process. We'll start by going into ways you can make your advertising itself creative. Later, we'll explore how you can be creative in media selection, marketing planning, and public relations.

I'm not sure who first said it, but almost any marketing person worth his or her salt will tell you that *marketing is not creative unless it sells*. You can pretty much ensure that you'll end up **The creative** with creative marketing if you start out by devising a *creative* **strategy** *strategy*. Such a strategy is similar to a marketing plan, but limited to marketing materials only — and directed solely at their content.

If you think there's a simple formula for establishing such a strategy, you're absolutely right. Here, in the simplest terms possible, is a typical three-sentence creative strategy:

> The purpose of Mother Nature breakfast cereal advertising will be to convince our target audience, mothers of children twelve years of age and younger, that Mother Nature breakfast cereal is the most nutritious and healthful boxed cereal on the market. [This is the purpose of the creative message.] This will be accomplished by listing the vitamins and minerals in each serving of the cereal. [This explains how the purpose will be achieved.] The mood and tone of the advertising will be upbeat, natural, honest, and warm. [This tells the mood and tone, the personality of the product.]

In this one paragraph we have listed the purpose of the advertising, the method by which the purpose can be achieved, and the personality the ads or commercials will have.

You've undoubtedly seen Energizer battery advertising, showing the pink bunny going on and on, even into "commercials" for fictitious products. The creative strategy for that type of marketing might have read:

> The purpose of Energizer battery advertising will be to convince our target audience, primarily males eighteen to fifty-four, that Energizer batteries last an inordinately long time. This will be accomplished by creating an Energizer bunny that marches on and on through the years, powered by an Energizer battery. The mood and tone of the advertising will be humorous and single-minded to embed the idea of Energizer's durability, while making the TV commercials fun to watch.

The first step in developing a creative marketing program is writing a simple creative strategy. You can get a great deal of insight into writing one for yourself if you practice first by writing creative strategies for current advertisers. Pick a newspaper advertiser, a television advertiser, and a direct-mail advertiser and compose three-sentence creative strategies that apply to each of them. Do the same for your competitors. That will help you figure your own positioning and prevent you from becoming a me-too company.

After you've got your own strategy — one to which you have devoted much time and thought — you can embark upon a seven-step program to assure yourself of successful marketing. Let's check all seven steps.

Seven steps to creative marketing

1. *Find the inherent drama within your offering.* After all, you plan to make money by selling a product or a service or both. The reasons people will want to buy from you should give you a clue as to the inherent drama in your product or service. Something about your offering must be inherently interesting or you wouldn't be putting it up for sale. In Mother Nature breakfast cereal, it is the high concentration of vitamins and minerals.
2. *Translate that inherent drama into a meaningful benefit.* Always remember that people buy benefits, not features. People do not buy shampoo; people buy great-looking or

clean or manageable hair. People do not buy cars; people
buy speed, status, style, economy, performance, and power.
Mothers of young kids do not buy cereal; they buy nutri-
tion. So find the major benefit of your offering and write it
down. It should come directly from the inherently dramatic
feature. And even though you have four or five benefits,
stick with one or two — three at most.

3. *State your benefits as believably as possible.* There is a
world of difference between honesty and believability. You
can be 100 percent honest (as you should be) and people
still may not believe you. You must go beyond honesty, beyond the barrier that advertising has erected by its tendency
toward exaggeration, and state your benefit in such a way
that it will be accepted beyond doubt. The company producing Mother Nature breakfast cereal might say, "A bowl of
Mother Nature breakfast cereal provides your child with almost as many vitamins as a multivitamin pill." This statement begins with the inherent drama, turns it into a benefit, and is worded believably. The word *almost* lends
believability.

4. *Get people's attention.* People do not pay attention to advertising. They pay attention only to things that interest them.
And sometimes they find those things in advertising. So
you've just got to interest them. And while you're at it, be
sure you interest them in your product or service, not just
your advertising. I'm sure you're familiar with advertising
that you remember for a product you do not remember.
Many advertisers are guilty of creating advertising that's
more interesting than whatever it is they are advertising. But
you can prevent yourself from falling into that trap by mem-
orizing this line: *Forget the ad, is the product or service interesting?* The Mother Nature company might put their
point across by showing a picture of two hands breaking
open a multivitamin capsule from which pour flakes that
fall into an appetizing-looking bowl of cereal.

5. *Motivate your audience to do something.* Tell them to visit
the store, as the Mother Nature company might do. Tell
them to make a phone call, fill in a coupon, write for more
information, ask for your product by name, take a test drive,
or come in for a free demonstration. Don't stop short. To

make guerrilla marketing work, you must tell people exactly what you want them to do.

6. *Be sure you are communicating clearly.* You may know what you're talking about, but do your readers or listeners? Recognize that people aren't really thinking about your business and that they'll only give about half their attention to your ad — even when they are paying attention. Knock yourself out to make sure you are putting your message across. The Mother Nature company might show its ad to ten people and ask them what the main point is. If one person misunderstands, that means 10 percent of the audience will misunderstand. And if the ad goes out to 500,000 people, 50,000 will miss the main point. That's unacceptable. One hundred percent of the audience should get the main point. The company might accomplish this by stating in a headline or subhead, "Giving your kids Mother Nature breakfast cereal is like giving your kids vitamins — only tastier." Zero ambiguity is your goal.

7. *Measure your finished advertisement*, commercial, letter, or brochure against your creative strategy. The strategy is your blueprint. If your ad fails to fulfill the strategy, it's a lousy ad, no matter how much you love it. Scrap it and start again. All along, you should be using your creative strategy to guide you, to give you hints as to the content of your ad. If you don't, you may end up being creative in a vacuum. And that's not being creative at all. If your ad is in line with your strategy, you may then judge its other elements.

The key to creative advertising is starting with a smart creative strategy. The test of creative advertising is sales and profits. If what you want to sell doesn't sell and generate profits for your business, you are not truly being creative. And creativity doesn't end with the creation of your advertising.

Once you have highly creative marketing weapons — in the form of ads, commercials, signs, circulars, store decor, whatever — you must be creative in the way you use them. I know of a deodorant company that did a lot of TV advertising to introduce its product during the winter. Why the winter, when people are not buying as much deodorant? Because this company lacked the funds to go head-to-head with the big guys. So instead of vying

How guerrillas use marketing weapons

for public attention during the summer, when its competition would be shooting the big guns, it attracted attention during the winter, when no other deodorant companies were advertising and it had the stage to itself.

There are other ways to be creative. You can be creative in the use of personal letters by having them hand delivered or by sending them via Express Mail, Federal Express, or some other out-of-the-ordinary delivery service. You can canvass creatively by wearing a unique outfit and handing a small gift to each prospect. You can be creative in your use of signs by putting them in unusual places, such as in the hands of paid picketers (one of the most unique advertising vehicles I know). Show creativity in the yellow pages by the size of your ad, its message, color, and its graphic treatment. Be creative in the use of newspaper advertising by running six small ads in one issue, rather than one large one.

As you can see, there are limitless ways to exercise creativity in all facets of marketing. In one of my earlier books, *Earning Money Without a Job*, I told of a couple who got married in their boutique, after informing the local newspapers and TV station about the wedding. Naturally, they received a lot of free coverage. (I hope they didn't get married simply to get free publicity.)

Your socks in your mouth

A former boss of mine used to remind his staff that you can be creative by coming downstairs with your socks in your mouth — but what's the point? There should be a reason for your creativity. And it should never detract from your message. The Energizer Bunny is both creative and right on the target message. Such well-directed creativity is hard to find, hard to develop, and hard to compete against. That's why guerrillas place such emphasis on *creativity with a point to it*.

When practicing guerrilla marketing, you must be more creative than your competition in every aspect of marketing. Merely doing it by the numbers isn't enough. You've got to do it properly, do it intelligently, do it clearly, do it creatively, and do it consistently to assure yourself of successfully marketing your product or service. You don't have to know how to write or draw to be creative. All you've got to do is supply the creative idea. You can always hire a person to write or draw for you. But it's not easy to hire a person to be creative about your business for you. That task should fall to you. And you should revel in it. Now let's look at a few examples of creativity in action:

Who will be creative for you?

Example A: A CPA wanted to increase his business, so he wrote a tax newsletter and sent it, free of charge, every three months, to a large list of prospects. By doing this, he established himself as an authority and dramatically improved his business. Not an earth-shaking act of creativity, but it worked like crazy for the CPA.

Example B: A waterbed retail store wanted to rid itself of the counter-culture identity associated with waterbeds, so it relocated in an elegant shopping center, required its staff to dress to the teeth, and hired a man with a voice like God to serve as the announcer on its radio commercials. Great results all around.

Example C: A jeweler wanted to attract attention to himself every Christmas, so he invented outlandishly expensive Christmas gift ideas. One was a Frisbee with a diamond in the center. Price: $5000. One was a miniature hourglass with real diamonds instead of sand. Price: $10,000. One was a jewel-encrusted backgammon set with a price tag of $50,000. The jeweler sold hardly any of these items. But he attracted national publicity and his December sales soared.

Notice that in none of these examples did I talk about the creativity one usually associates with ads themselves. That's the obvious place to be creative. But these examples show how you can be creative in your prospecting, store decor, employee attire, methods of gaining free publicity, and many other ways. If whenever you engage in marketing you train yourself to think that the opposite of creativity is mediocrity, you'll start forcing yourself to use marketing tools in the most creative manner possible.

In case you're wondering where creativity starts, I'll tell you. It starts with *knowledge*. You need knowledge of your own product or service, knowledge of your competition, knowledge of your target audience, knowledge of your marketing area, knowledge of the economy, knowledge of current events, and knowledge of the trends of the time. From this knowledge, you'll not only develop a creative marketing program, but you'll also be able to produce creative marketing materials. **Where creativity starts**

I find that I can glean a lot of knowledge by keeping abreast of world events in the usual manner. I read one weekly news-magazine and ten monthly special-interest magazines. I watch the late TV news most nights. And I read one daily newspaper. Some people are far more attuned to world happenings than that. But that's enough for me. It lets me in on the world situation, the local situation, and up-to-the-minute trends. It also allows me to get a look at the marketing of others — especially competitors of my clients.

Keep up or fall behind   If you're not keeping up, you're falling behind. And guerrillas just can't afford to fall behind.

Armed with all of this knowledge, you are able to do what many people define as the essence of creativity: You can combine two or more elements that have never before been combined. For instance, when 7UP wanted to boost its sales up there with Coca-Cola and Pepsi-Cola, it referred to itself as "The Uncola." This put it in the category of the colas, yet proudly proclaimed that it was different. By combining the prefix *un*, which means "not," with the word *cola*, 7UP exercised great creativity. The advertising person who dreamed up the concept used his knowledge of the art scene at the time by employing psychedelic art in advertisements both in print and on television. His knowledge of his product, his competition, his target audience, and the trends of the day resulted in exceptionally creative advertising. And the proof of that creativity was in the increased sales enjoyed by 7UP. Where did it all start? It started with basic knowledge.

The Marlboro cigarette company exercised creativity when it combined the ideas of a cowboy and a cigarette. The AT&T telephone company used creativity when it combined the ideas of an emotionally charged situation and a telephone ("Reach out and touch someone"). Avis Rent-a-Car showed creativity when it capitalized on being the second largest, rather than the largest, car rental company, and flatly stated, "We try harder." In all of these cases, plus thousands more, creativity started with plain and simple knowledge.

As a guerrilla, you are obligated to become knowledgeable about a broad range of topics. Guerrillas are generalists, not specialists. Guerrillas know that to remove the mystique from **Thinking** the creative process, they must think backward. They must start **backward** by picturing the mind of their customer at the moment that customer makes a decision to purchase. What led to that decision? What were the thought processes? What made them take place? What were the customer's buttons and what did you do to push them? Thinking backward takes you to the needs and desires that are crucial to motivation.

Let's take a moment to examine marketing in the light of psychology. "Skinnerian marketing" would dictate that you modify behavior. This means saying, showing, or doing something that causes a customer to change his or her behavior so as to act in the way you want that customer to act. You gently nudge the customer to buy, to call, to visit, to compare, to clip a coupon, to follow your command.

"Freudian marketing" is addressed to the unconscious — the most powerful part of a person's mind. "Skinnerian marketing" is addressed to the conscious — less powerful, but more easily activated.

Guerrilla marketing is addressed to both the unconscious and the conscious. It changes attitudes while modifying behavior. **What guerrilla marketing does** It comes at the customer from all directions. It persuades, coerces, tempts, compels, romances, and orders the customer to do your bidding. It leaves little to chance. It is the essence of precise planning.

In the nineties, guerrilla marketers understand their role in the community. Their marketing might change attitudes while modifying behavior, yet have very little to do with the product or service itself. I quote from a very successful ice cream company's brochure: "At Ben and Jerry's, we're as concerned about our responsibility to the community, both local and global, as we are about making great ice cream." Then they prove their devotion to humanity by sponsoring altruistic causes such as the Children's Defense Fund, voter registration, peace on earth, saving rain forests, less military spending, and more recycling. Ben and Jerry say, "Business has the responsibility to give back to the community." And this is their creative platform. It sells sanity. It sells honesty. It sells nobility. It sells ice cream. Ben and Jerry sponsor concerts to help spread the word, not about their ice cream as much as about their desire to save the planet.

In the 1950s, this would have been considered crazy. In the 1990s, it's considered brilliant marketing as well as humanitarian. Ben and Jerry's is famous for its good deeds. But Sears? Sears is pushing for recycling these days. And so are Safeway, Bank of America, Coca-Cola, American Airlines, 3M, Anheuser-Busch, Du Pont, UPS, and guerrillas throughout the nation whose names are not yet famous. Backing a noble cause is an option when developing a creative strategy.

Apparel-maker Liz Claiborne buys ads aimed at helping victims of domestic violence. Patagonia, the outdoor clothing company, promotes environmental awareness. Esprit, the clothing

Cause-related marketing

maker, urges people to vote. In 1992, $262 million was spent on "cause-related marketing." This includes causes such as AIDS, healthy eating, and helping the homeless.

This corporate philanthropy started well before the nineties. American Express promoted restoration of the Statue of Liberty in the mid-1980s.

Do creative strategies based upon noble causes work? In 1992, 83 percent of shoppers said they had changed brands based solely upon environmental concerns. Eighty percent of shoppers said a company's environmental reputation is important. Consumers even said they'd spend a 5.5 percent premium for "green" products.

Made in the U.S.A.

Along with this new public and corporate conscientiousness, we see a strong move toward "Made in the U.S.A." products to help our ill economy. Does this work? It does with women and with older consumers. It works better on the East Coast and Midwest than elsewhere in the United States. But people aged eighteen to thirty-five are not very influenced by it, having grown up with foreign-made products in their homes.

Still, in 1992 a *Los Angeles Times* poll listed 45 percent of respondents as saying they avoid products made in Japan. In 1985, that figure was 26 percent. Retailers report that "Made in America" promotions of domestically made apparel increase sales from 25 to 50 percent. These are numbers to be taken seriously. And so should cause-related marketing.

But be careful about centering your creative strategy around rapid societal changes that are more anecdotal than factual. The guerrilla is alert for changes, but knows the difference between a real change and a media-perceived change.

Because industrialized nations are experiencing a major decline in 20-to-29-year-olds, the group that starts new households, the slowdown in sales of big-ticket items is predicted to persist throughout the nineties.

Go with the flow

Guerrillas adapt their marketing, their creative message, and their entire philosophy to the realities of the times. Instead of pushing against the river of change, they go with the flow. And their profitability attests to the wisdom of this attitude.

6
Secrets of Selecting Marketing Methods

IF YOU ARE CONSCIENTIOUS, you can create a dynamite marketing plan, a brilliant creative strategy, and promote a noble cause. Still, there are many places you can go wrong. One way is to run the right advertising in the wrong media. But how do you tell the right from the wrong?

Every method of marketing has its own particular strength. Radio is the most *intimate* of the media, allowing you to spend chunks of time in one-on-one situations with your audience. Sometimes the listeners will be in crowded restaurants. But other times they'll be in their cars or in their homes — alone.

The strengths of the media

The newspaper is a prime medium for disseminating the *news*. And that strength can become your strength. Advertising in the newspaper, other than in the classified section, should be newsy, interruptive, and to the point.

Magazines are media with which readers become more *involved*. Whether they buy individual newsstand copies or subscribe, they take a good, long time to read them. So you can attempt to capture the editorial "mood" of the magazine in your ads. You can put forth more information because readers will be willing to take more time reading a magazine ad than a newspaper ad.

Television is the most comprehensive of the media. It enables you to convince your prospects by means of actual *demonstrations*. Such powerful selling devices as demonstrations are not possible by any other means — except seminars, fairs, and live contacts with audiences. Television allows you to combine words with pictures and music, and to get into the minds of your potential customers in more ways than any other medium. Television advertising can also be very costly, so it must be done properly or not at all. This is not a medium with which to dabble.

Still, cable and satellite TV has put the medium within the reach of *all* advertisers, down to the tiniest. To a guerrilla, this **Prime time** is glorious news. A prime-time TV spot for under $20? This just **for guerrillas** wasn't available in the seventies and eighties. But it is now. And many a small business is becoming a big business as a result of it. Don't take this as permission to play around with TV. Instead, think of it as an invitation to give serious consideration to what some describe as "the undisputed heavyweight champion of marketing."

Direct mail allows you to take *the most careful aim* at your target audience. Created skillfully, direct-mail advertising enables you to go through the entire selling process — from securing your prospects' attention to actually obtaining sales by means of coupons the prospects can complete and toll-free phone numbers they can call. Like TV, direct mail can be very costly when misused. And it's quite easy to misuse. This will continue to be true as postage rates continue to rise and the number of mailed pieces increases. To a guerrilla, postage rates don't mean nearly as much as response rates. If it costs twice as much postage to get three times the response, only a nitwit would save on postage rates. Guerrillas aren't fazed by the blizzard of direct mail assaulting their prospects each day. They know how to break through that barrier: with follow-up mailings, with telemarketing, with unique mailing packages.

Outdoor signs and billboards are superb at *reminding* people of your existence and your reason for being. They do not work well all by themselves, except in rare instances. But they work **The power of** well in combination with other marketing methods. Signs inside **inside signs** are a different matter altogether because they generate impulse reactions right where they ought to — at the place of purchase, where about 75 percent of purchase decisions are made, according to a 1991 study. Worded and designed right, they *capitalize upon the momentum generated by your other marketing.* The great Leo Burnett, founder of one of the three best ad agencies in the world, always reminded us to "plan the sale when you plan the ad." He loved the immense power of inside signs. They would be designed to take off from where the ads left off. These days, those signs might be a video message, a hologram, a moving sign. And you don't need your own inside premises to capitalize upon the power of inside signs. The inside of many other premises will work very well, thank you. As long as your prospects are there, you should try to be there. Consider airports, hotel lobbies, club bulletin boards, stores owned by people with whom you have established tie-in arrangements.

Canvassing takes more time than any other method of marketing, but it is highly effective. It has few limitations and gives you *personal contact*. In many cases, it is difficult to handle the canvassing yourself. But you can delegate the job to a professional salesperson or a college, even a high school, student, depending upon the complexity of your sales presentation. Canvassing is greatly strengthened by mass-marketing methods, which help remove you from the category of complete stranger.

Yellow pages marketing and classified advertisements hit the *very hottest of prospects*. These people are taking the time to look up the kind of information you're offering, so you don't have to expend much energy getting their attention or selling the general benefits of your product or service. This advertising also places you in direct confrontation with your competition. Just knowing that should enable you to be more precise with your message.

Brochures offer the greatest opportunity to go into *great detail* about your product or service. People expect a lot of information from a brochure, so you should feel encouraged to give it to them. This is not an invitation to be boring, but it is a hint that you can be very informative.

Telephone marketing allows you to be even more intimate than you can be in radio advertising — as you know, the most intimate type of advertising among the mass media. This type of marketing provides you with *great flexibility*. It can be used as an adjunct to direct mail or any other marketing method. It can stand alone. It can take a person from total apathy about your product or service to complete readiness to purchase. And you can take orders if your prospects have credit cards. As a guerrilla, you take credit cards — all of them. Just in case folks are up to their limit on Visa and MasterCard, take American Express, Discover, Carte Blanche, Diners Club, even Shell Oil and Macy's if you can. This may seem mercenary, but to prospects, it's convenience, and they appreciate you for making it so easy to buy from you.

Tiny signs on bulletin boards serve to make you *part of the community*, increasing the amount of confidence people have in you. They are also extremely inexpensive, and if your product or service can fill unanswered needs, such signs frequently prove to be the most fruitful of marketing methods. Like yellow page and classified ads, signs on bulletin boards tend to attract serious browsers. Such is not the case with, say, television advertising.

Advertising specialties such as T-shirts and calendars work like billboards and signs to *remind people of your existence*, but they can't do the entire selling job. They can, however, pave the way to acceptance of your offering when used in conjunction with other marketing vehicles. The same goes for the sponsorship of teams and events.

A shot in the sales curve   Many businesses get a terrific shot in the sales curve by marketing at trade shows and exhibits. They find the opportunity there to *make contacts with purchase-minded people* who are thinking about the primary topic of the show or exhibit. The ability to reach people who have this type of mind-set is a great advantage. There are fewer barriers preventing completed sales. Some companies and entrepreneurs obtain all the business they need by this one method of marketing. If you fall into that category, your life will be simpler.

Public relations, encompassing community relations, publicity, and even joining clubs and organizations, is another marketing method that should always be considered. It fits in well with virtually all other methods and often is the key to success. Involvement in community relations — meaning service to your community — helps you make powerful contacts, especially if you work your tail off for the community and not merely to serve your business needs.

Publicity adds a great deal to your *credibility,* and at worst puts your name in the public eye, though guerrillas do not buy into that old lie that "even bad publicity is good publicity as long as they spell your name right." Bad publicity is harmful for your company and your goals. Avoid it at all costs.

Joining clubs and organizations seems also to do what community service does — put you in contact with people who can help you. It seems a bit self-serving to join with that purpose in mind, but many do. And it serves their purposes well. I have a subtle point to make here: *Guerrillas are aggressive in their marketing, but they are never crass.*

With all of these marketing methods available, and all are examined later in this book with chapters of their very own, which do you, as a guerrilla, choose? The answer should be obvious: *as many as you can do well.*

Once you have selected the marketing vehicles that can propel you to your goal, be sure you use them in an orderly, logical manner. This can best be accomplished by using a *marketing calendar.*

Choose the weapons you can use well

A marketing calendar will help make all the elements in your program mesh. It enables you to plan your budget and helps you avoid unforeseen expenditures. It prevents you from engaging in hit-or-miss marketing. It protects you from marketing lapses. It precludes surprises. It aids enormously in planning, buying, and staffing. Clients who operate from one say that after three years, a marketing calendar is their most precious business asset. They tell me it's akin to getting into heaven without the inconvenience of dying.

Most marketing calendars address themselves to the weeks of the year, to the marketing vehicles that will be employed during those weeks, to the specific promotions or events in which you will be engaged, to the length of each promotion, and, when applicable, to whether or not co-op funds from manufacturers will be available to help pay the tab. In addition, some calendars include the cost of the marketing for each promotion.

Armed with such a calendar, as all guerrillas should be, you can see far into the future. The marketing process will come into clearer focus for you. And you will find it considerably simpler to be committed to your marketing program, to see it as the investment it is, and to recognize the consistency that is built into it.

A moment ago, I told you that a guerrilla makes use of as many marketing vehicles as he or she can implement effectively. A marketing calendar lets you know whether or not you can use these methods properly, because it forces you to come to terms with the costs and realities of utilizing the media you have selected.

Let's examine the marketing calendar on page 59 to get a better line on what it looks like. Note that the calendar runs a full fifty-two weeks so that the owner of this small retail store can see

Examining a marketing calendar

well ahead what ads to run, what products to have in inventory, what costs to project, what sales to plan.

The calendar utilizes the *Chronicle* newspaper every single week, but staggers the monthly use of the *Sun*, the *News*, the *Independent-Journal*, and the *Gazette*. It also allows for a testing of the *Times* and the *Reporter*. This seems like a lot of newspapers, but it is clear that the *Chronicle* will be the marketing flagship.

Lengths of the marketing activities vary from one to five weeks, with a healthy balance of long, short, and medium-length events. This prevents the marketing from being too predictable. Radio is used, but not every single week. With such a calendar, Video Vanguard is following a well-conceived plan. Promotions and sales are balanced with periods with no special sales.

Just as you shouldn't run just one week's worth of TV commercials or join a club with no intention of coming to meetings, you should not employ a marketing vehicle unless you are going to use it like a pro. And that means putting time, energy, money, and talent into it. It also means selecting marketing tools that are compatible with your business.

All of the compatible marketing methods that you can possibly employ with skill, and on a regular basis, should be put to work for you. In chapter 4, we saw that the entrepreneur billing himself as Computer Tutor became committed to using fourteen methods of marketing. And that didn't even include decor, attire, and location. Computer Tutor has the option of being a single individual or a multi-employee company, yet its marketing plan calls for the utilization of personal letters, circulars, brochures (we'll get into the difference between these in chapter 12), signs on bulletin boards, classified ads in local newspapers, display ads in local newspapers, magazine advertising, radio advertising, direct-mail advertising, advertising specialties, free seminars, sampling, and publicity in newspapers, on radio, and on television. Sounds like this is going to cost Computer Tutor a huge sum of money. But it won't. You don't have to spend a double bundle to market like a guerrilla. In fact, you may be doing it wrong if you do spend too much money. Mind you, you won't get all that marketing for free. You'll have to pay, or, rather, invest. But it is possible to engage in a large number of marketing methods and save money with each.

Naturally, you start the process of selecting marketing meth-

Video Vanguard Marketing Calendar

Weeks of	Marketing Thrust	Length	Co-opable	Radio	Newspapers	Cost Per Promotion
9/13	Giant Screen TV	1 wk	Yes	Yes	Chron/Sun	$615
9/20–10/4	New TV Set	3 wks	Yes	Yes-2	Chron/News	$1750
10/11–10/18	Video Experience	2 wks	No	No	Chron/IJ	$984
10/25–11/15	Names to Drop	4 wks	Yes	Yes-2	Chron/Gaz	$2044
11/22	Thanksgiving Sale	1 wk	Yes	Yes	Chron/Sun	$615
11/29	VCR Promotion	1 wk	Yes	No	Chron/News	$450
12/6–12/20	Xmas Promotion	3 wks	Yes	Yes	Chron/IJ	$2076
12/27	Last Week to Save	1 wk	Yes	Yes	Chron/Gaz	$611
1/3–1/17	TV Rut	3 wks	No	No	Chron/Sun	$1245
1/24–2/7	Trade-in Time	2 wks	No	No	Chron/News	$900
2/14–2/21	Clearance Sale	2 wks	Yes	Yes	Chron/IJ	$1384
2/28–3/28	Solve TV Problems	5 wks	No	Yes-2	Chron/Gaz	$2455
4/4–4/18	Giant Screen TV	3 wks	Yes	Yes-2	Chron/Times	$2044
4/25–5/2	People Who Love TV	2 wks	No	No	Chron/News	$900
5/9–5/16	Component TV	2 wks	Yes	No	Chron/IJ	$984
5/23	Memorial Day Sale	1 wk	Yes	Yes	Chron/Gaz	$611
5/30–6/13	Credit Is Easy	3 wks	No	Yes-1	Chron/Sun	$1445
6/20–6/27	VCR Promotion	2 wks	Yes	No	Chron/Rep	$976
7/4–7/11	Video Experience	2 wks	No	No	Chron/IJ	$984
7/18–7/25	Videotape Rentals	2 wks	No	Yes	Chron/Gaz	$1222
8/1–8/8	Free Home Demo	2 wks	No	No	Chron/Sun	$830
8/15–8/29	Giant Screen TV	3 wks	Yes	Yes-2	Chron/News	$1750
9/5	Satellite TV	1 wk	No	No	Chron/IJ	$492
9/12	Video Experience	1 wk	No	No	Chron/Gaz	$411

ods by first identifying your target audience. The more exactly you know who your prospects are, the easier it will be to attain accuracy with your marketing plans. Kids don't read newspapers. Teen-age girls rarely read business magazines. Adult males hardly ever subscribe to *True Romance*. Those are the realities of the marketplace, and you have to tailor your selection of marketing methods to them.

Who are your prospects?

Select as many methods as you can. Select only the ones you will be able to do right. And select the ones that will be read, seen, or heard by your target audience.

Although marketing budgets are as unique as snowflakes, you

might get a better bead on your target if you study the budgets of three fictitious companies. One is a small contracting company, Let George Do It, one year old, located in a town of 40,000, but within a marketing area of 150,000. The second is a two-person computer education organization, Computer Tutor, three years old, outside a city of 500,000, in a market area composed of 600,000 people. The third is a retail stereo store, Sounds Great, five years in business, smack-dab within a city of one million people.

How George does it

Let's suppose that Let George Do It grosses $4000 monthly in sales. The owner is willing to spend 7.5 percent of his sales dollars for marketing — a total of $300 per month, or $3600 per year. Computer Tutor takes in $20,000 in monthly sales and invests 10 percent of that in marketing: $2000 monthly, or $24,000 per year. Sounds Great grosses an average of $50,000 in monthly sales. An aggressive 12.5 percent is put back into marketing, permitting $6250 for marketing each month, or $75,000 per year.

Because these companies are not brand-new, they do not have to invest extra heavily in advertising to get public attention. They already have a logotype; they have business cards, stationery, and invoice forms. They even invested from $500 (Let George Do It) to $5000 (Sounds Great) for professional marketing consultation before they got started in marketing. So they each have a marketing plan, a creative strategy, and a media strategy. Their investment with the consultants has also netted them advertising themes, clear identities, and a visual format. Incidentally, the only way Let George Do It obtained such a large amount of consultation for such a low price was by building a sun deck for the marketing consultant as part of a barter arrangement. Computer Tutor and Sounds Great worked a similar agreement, if I know my guerrillas. Look at the table on page 61 to see how these guerrillas would apportion their funds.

George has selected many marketing methods, as you can see. His primary marketing medium is newspapers, yet he obtains quite a bit of business through his signs posted on bulletin boards and his free seminars. Neither cost him any extra money, and both are successful, according to George, because of his newspaper advertising. George installed a skylight for a graphic artist, who in return gave him nearly $1000 in artwork: layouts, illustrations, even type and a finished mechanical, all ready for the

Let George Do It ($300 Monthly)

Marketing Method	Monthly Cost	Comments
Canvassing	$0	Main investment is time
Personal Letters	$0	Main investment is time
Circulars	$20	Cost of $240 yearly, amortized
Brochures	$50	Cost of $600 yearly, amortized
Signs on Bulletin Boards	$0	Posts his own circulars
Classified Ads	$40	Runs ads in two newspapers, once weekly
Yellow Pages	$20	Small listing, one directory
Newspaper Display Ads	$100	Runs ads in one newspaper, once weekly
Direct Mail	$10	Postage only, since he mails his circulars
Free Seminars	$0	Distributes his brochures at these
Trade Show Booth	$10	Built booth himself, one-time cost amortized
Public Relations	$20	Cost of materials only, handles his own publicity
Production	$30	Amortized over one year, traded for a painting by George

printer. George set up his trade-show booth at the Home Improvement Show, where he distributed his circulars freely and established a mailing list. George's $300 monthly investment in marketing runs 7.5 percent of his sales this year. He projects that next year that same $300 will represent only 5 percent of his sales. That is how much he expects his sales to increase as a result of his consistent marketing program. (By the way, the prices quoted here were from 1984; they are remarkably similar ten years later. I guess that's the upside of a recession.)

Time to take a look at Computer Tutor's marketing budget:

Computer Tutor ($2000 Monthly)

Marketing Method	Monthly Cost	Comments
Personal Letters	$0	Uses these to gain corporate jobs
Circulars	$30	Cost of $360 yearly, amortized
Brochures	$80	Cost of $960 yearly, amortized
Signs on Bulletin Boards	$30	Monthly fee to have company's flier posted
Classified Ads	$40	Uses one newspaper twice a week
Yellow Pages	$30	Medium listing, one directory
Newspaper Display Ads	$940	One ad weekly, two newspapers
Magazine Ad (One Time)	$100	One full-page ad in *Time*, amortized over one year
Radio Spots	$400	Spends $100 weekly; on one FM station
Direct Mail	$100	Postage only, since company mails circulars
Advertising Specialties	$30	Cost of computer-oriented calendars
Free Seminars	$0	Distributes brochures at these
Sampling	$0	Offered to corporations
Public Relations	$20	Amortized for one publicity push yearly
Production	$200	Amortized over one year — all production of circulars, brochures, ads, commercials

Computer Tutor gets a lot of referral business. The brochures spur word-of-mouth recommendations. The company's newspaper ads sell people completely, cause people to phone Computer Tutor, where they receive even more of a sales pitch, and motivate people to send for a free brochure. The radio spots direct people to make a phone call. Although Computer Tutor spends nil for telephone marketing per se, it engages in quite a bit of it as a result of responses to the newspaper and radio advertising.

Computer Tutor would love to demonstrate its proficiency on TV, but simply cannot afford it. Each year, a publicity stunt such as free computer lessons for city-hall employees results in free TV coverage. The 10 percent of sales invested in marketing will drop to 7.5 percent next year because of an increase in sales. Actual marketing outlays will remain the same.

The marketing expenditures for Sounds Great are even more ambitious:

Sounds Great ($6250 Monthly)

An ambitious guerrilla

Marketing Method	Monthly Cost	Comments
Brochures	$200	General brochures with no prices
Point-of-Purchase Signs	$205	One-time cost, amortized over one year
Yellow Pages	$200	One large listing in two directories
Newspaper Display Ads	$2800	Two large ads weekly, two newspapers
Radio Spots	$1400	Consistently run on three FM stations
Television Spots	$500	Two one-week TV splashes, amortized
Direct Mail	$300	Three yearly mailings, amortized
Free Seminars	$0	Held at store, sales made afterward
Searchlight	$20	For one yearly promotion, amortized
Production	$625	Amortized over one year

It's interesting to note that Sounds Great, which has the largest of the three budgets examined here, utilizes the fewest marketing methods. However, two methods are used very seriously: radio and newspaper advertising. The radio rates are very low, since spots are purchased through the company's internal ad agency (more about that in chapter 7) at a very favorable one-year contractual rate. The newspaper ads are also available at one-year contract rates, at a substantial discount. Television advertising is used with force, but only two times a year. The cost for the TV time is $3000 for each week.

Like other guerrillas, Sounds Great is now spending a large amount — 12.5 percent — on marketing. This tactic has eliminated several competitors who spent less boldly. Although they were larger than Sounds Great, their marketing did not reflect this. Sounds Great, like all smart guerrilla marketers, plans to spend the same amount on marketing next year, but figures this will represent only 10 percent of sales. The year after, that same amount should represent 7.5 percent of sales. The plan is to spend no less than 7.5 percent on marketing, because the stereo business is highly competitive.

Desktop publishing might cut some of these costs, especially if they include newsletters and a lot of direct mail. But marketing is not a do-it-yourself process (see chapter 27), and desktop publishing is best left to people who know how to do it with style. If that includes you, perhaps you can save money on production when it comes to brochures, circulars, signs, and the aforementioned direct mail.

Reach and frequency

When advertisers discuss media, they talk of *reach* and *frequency*. *Reach* refers to the number of people who will be exposed to the message. *Frequency* refers to the number of times each person will be exposed. Although in some endeavors you should strive for reach, in most, frequency will help you even more. Remember, familiarity breeds confidence, and confidence serves as the springboard to sales.

Before you select any method of reaching the people you wish to reach, think these thoughts: It is not necessary to say everything to everybody, nor is it possible. If you try to say everything to everybody, you'll end up saying everything to nobody or

Say something to somebody

nothing to everybody. Instead, you should strive to say something to somebody. Your marketing message is the "something." Your target audience is the "somebody." Just as you take care in selecting what you will say, you should take equal care in selecting to whom it will be said. Saying the right thing to the wrong people is not acceptable guerrilla marketing. I know that advertising on television does wonders for your ego, but if your prospective customers don't watch much television, it is folly.

I suggest that you set out with the idea that you will employ absolutely every marketing method listed in this chapter, maybe even more. Then start cutting down the list on the basis of who your audience is, whether you can utilize the method properly yourself, and whether you can afford it. With the methods that are left on your list, go to glory. Plunge into each as if it is your one and only. When you combine two marketing methods with two other marketing methods, the total is more than two plus two. A synergistic effect is created whereby two plus two starts to equal five and six and seven. And when you combine five marketing methods with five others, your possibilities for success increase manyfold.

The more methods of marketing you employ, and the greater your skill at employing and selecting them, the larger the size of your bank balance. The idea is to combine the right marketing message with the right marketing media. That's the guerrilla truth.

7
Secrets of Saving Marketing Money

SAVING MONEY IS IMPORTANT to everyone. To consumers. To large companies. And to entrepreneurs — *especially* to entrepreneurs. Don't forget, entrepreneurs for the most part are suffering from resource poverty. So not a penny can be wasted. And all money should pull more than its own weight. But is this possible? Bright entrepreneurs make it possible. This chapter suggests several ways to stretch your marketing dollars without decreasing their effectiveness one iota.

Dollar stretching

First of all, *don't feel that you must constantly change your marketing campaigns*. This costs unnecessary production money and dilutes the overall effect of your marketing. Stick with one campaign until it loses its pulling power. That's hard to do for most advertisers. In the beginning, most people will like your ad. Then you'll become bored with it. Next, your friends and family will get tired of it. Soon your fellow workers and associates will feel ho-hum about it. And you'll be tempted to change the ad.

Don't do it! Let your accountant tell you when to change ads. That's right, your accountant — the person who takes long looks at your profit picture. You can be sure your accountant won't get tired of an ad that is still pulling in business. The important thing is the public's reaction to an ad. It takes a long, long time for the public to get tired of advertising run on a scale that can be afforded by most small businesspeople. By remembering this, you will stretch your media money and save production dollars.

Another way to save impressive sums is to *make use of the concept of barter*. Maybe your local radio station or newspaper

Bartering

doesn't want what you are selling. But they do want *something*. In all likelihood, you'll be able to trade with someone who has that something they want. When that happens, you'll get your media ads for a fraction of their usual cost, since you'll be paying with your own services or goods *at their full retail price*. Guerrillas learn of this exciting and enormous world of barter by calling 714-495-6529 and closely examining the most recent copy of *BarterNews*.

Here's an example of bartering: A stereo dealer wanted radio commercials but felt he couldn't afford the cost. He offered to trade recording equipment, but the station just wasn't interested. The station *was* interested, however, in constructing a new lobby. The stereo dealer found a contractor who wanted new stereo equipment. Result: The contractor received $5000 worth of stereo and television equipment; the radio station got its new lobby; the stereo dealer received $5000 worth of radio time. Yet the dealer's cost was only $2500 in equipment. In fact, his cost was even less than that, because he traded discontinued merchandise that would have had to be discounted.

There are many barter houses in the United States that specialize in setting up such trades, sometimes between as many as ten companies. Find barter houses in the yellow pages in large metropolitan areas, listed under "Barter Services" and also "Media-Buying Services." At least 500 magazines will trade ad space for whatever it is they need. But policies vary at these publications, and trades must be individually negotiated. Just remember that everyone needs something. By learning what your selected media need, you might put yourself in a position to set up a money-saving trade.

When I first learned of the world of barter, it was very much like my first time scuba diving. An entire world existed every day within my own world — and I wasn't at all aware of it. To give you an inkling of the magnitude of barter in today's economy, consider that in 1991, 55 percent of media was not purchased, but obtained by barter.

You can also *save money by getting access to cooperative advertising funds*. Many large advertisers pay cash fees to small advertisers who mention the name of the large advertiser or show its logo in their ads. I know a woman who owns a small furniture store. When she mentions the name of a large mattress company in her ads, she receives a small sum of money from that com-

Getting co-op funds

pany. Naturally, most of her ads mention the name of some large manufacturer that offers these co-op ad funds.

This is worth looking into. It not only helps save money for entrepreneurs, but also lends credibility to their offerings by mentioning the name of a nationally known company. Some companies that offer these co-op funds insist they be the only company mentioned. Others don't care, just as long as you spell their name right. Still others demand that you include their theme line or logo in your ad. A smart entrepreneur, interested in saving lots of marketing money, will include the names of several co-op–oriented companies, thereby saving a large percentage of the ad cost — frequently more than 50 percent. This takes research and prearranging, but if you're interested in saving money, it's worth it.

Talk to your suppliers and simply ask them about their co-op program. If they don't have one, ask them to start one. One of my clients consistently has over half of his marketing costs covered by co-op funds. His business is video rentals; the co-op funds come from movie studios. Very few advertising agencies will help you obtain co-op funds, so it's your job as a guerrilla — and worth every minute you or your designated guerrilla devote to doing it because it significantly reduces your investment in marketing. Who says you can't get something for nothing?

P.I. and P.O.   I also suggest you *put forth the effort to set up a P.I. or P.O. arrangement with an advertising medium.* This is a rather common method entrepreneurs employ to save and make money. *P.I.* stands for "per inquiry" and *P.O.* stands for "per order." Here's how it works. You contact, say, a television station to see if it is interested in a P.I. or P.O. arrangement with you. That means that it gives you television time, and in return, you give it a prearranged sum of money per inquiry or per order.

Suppose you want to sell books for $10 apiece by mail. You strike up a deal with a TV station whereby the station gives you commercial time and you give the station, say, $3 per order. At this point, no money has changed hands. Okay. Now, the TV station provides you with the equipment to produce a commercial heralding your book. Normally, it might charge $100 to run a one-minute commercial, but it gives you the time for free. Then the commercial runs and fifty people order the book. That means the TV station receives $150 (at its $3 per order), which is a good deal for the station. You also come out very well, because you receive fifty orders ($500) and risk no marketing costs. Now, if you can make that same arrangement with one hundred other TV stations, you can clearly achieve very attractive profits without risking marketing outlay.

P.I. and P.O. arrangements are available with many magazines, radio stations, and television stations, more every year. I have never heard of this kind of deal being available with newspapers, but I imagine some far-sighted publishers would welcome the idea. All it takes is a letter to the medium of your choice, outlining the arrangement you're proposing. If the medium feels it can make money on your offer, you're in business. In this way, you can engage in quite a bit of high-level marketing with virtually no out-front costs to you, other than minimal production costs. Of course a TV station might put your commercial in a time slot after midnight, a time slot that couldn't be sold to another advertiser. But you can bet that the TV station wants to make money on the arrangement. Therefore, it will go all out. And if it makes money, you make money.

Many an entrepreneur has made many a dollar with this little-known method of saving marketing dollars. A client of mine sold $3000 worth of his newsletters through a P.I. arrangement with a magazine publisher. The publisher gave free ad space (a full-page ad usually sold for $900) in return for a $50 cut of a $100 subscription price. Thirty subscribers signed up. Result: $1500 for the publisher and $1500 for my client — the first year. Renewals will increase his profits.

The magazine wanted to repeat the ad — on the same P.O. basis. Naturally, my client nixed the offer and paid the magazine full price for the full-page ad.

People enjoy being asked about themselves, enjoy talking about themselves. Take advantage of this human characteristic by *asking questions of your customers*. This can provide you with expensive research data for free. Prepare a questionnaire asking **Free research** your customers all sorts of questions. Some will toss your questionnaire right in the wastebasket. Others will complete every question and provide you with a wealth of information. This research, if obtained through standard research-company channels, would cost you a fortune. But when obtained the way I've just described, this same information costs very little. More about this in the next chapter.

If you are a patient sort, you can save money, lots of it, *by taking advantage of "gang runs."* Large printing companies often run huge amounts of full-color printing on large presses all at once. Sometimes they have an opportunity to run a bit more printing than is scheduled. If you are about to have something printed and wish to save money, let a large printer know that you are interested in being included in a gang run and are patient enough to wait until it happens. Then furnish the printer with the press-ready materials and the paper, and sit back and wait. Eventually, the printer will have that gang run and you will be the happy recipient of a mass of your full-color brochures, obtained at a fraction of the normal price. And all you had to do to take advantage of this money-saving opportunity was to be patient. I've seen clients too impatient to wait for gang runs. They paid five times the price they could have enjoyed if only they hadn't been in a hurry. And the sad thing is that often their rush was unnecessary.

Slow down   Being in a rush is a deterrent to good marketing and to inexpensive marketing as well. If you wish to gain the maximum effect from your marketing and to save money at the same time, avoid rushes like the plague. With a solid marketing calendar, a program that is planned ahead for a year, it will be quite easy to avoid them.

The three   A key thought for you to remember if you wish to save money
variables   is that in marketing, there are three variables — quality, economy, and speed. You get to select *any two* of them. Guerrillas opt for the first two.

You can also save considerable sums of money if you realize that the cost of radio and TV time is nothing if not negotiable. Of course, prime time or drive time is hard to buy, therefore hard to negotiate. But understand that if radio or TV time is unsold, it is wasted forever. Therefore, stations will usually accept prices far below their normal rate-card prices. Deals abound.

To entice new advertisers — that is, entrepreneurs — TV stations will ordinarily offer even more attractive prices. Just knowing this will save you money. Large advertisers do know that rate cards are works of fiction. But small advertisers often believe what they read on rate cards. Don't you believe it. Remember

An offer   that you can save media money by *making an offer you can af-*
you can afford   *ford.* You'll be surprised at how many radio and TV stations will accept your offer.

While we're on the subject of radio and television and saving money, let me emphasize that a vast amount of research has proven that you can accomplish almost as much with a thirty-second commercial as you can with a sixty-second commercial. So save money by cutting the verbiage and saying your message in half a minute. Think hard and you can even do it in less time than that. In 1991, over 80 percent of national TV commercials were less than thirty seconds long. Some are so short, they're termed "electronic billboards" instead of TV commercials.

You can save money by applying this same truism of brevity to your print efforts. Unless it is necessary for you to look important by running large, expensive newspaper or magazine ads, you can attract business just as well by running small, inexpensive, **Ad size** but consistently run newspaper or magazine ads. You may not look as important as the purchasers of full-page ads, but you'll end up making more money. Don't forget: As I emphasized in chapter 3, consistency is the one of the most important factors in marketing. And you can gain that consistency with small ads as well as large ones. Largeness does not produce the consumer confidence that comes with consistency — a truth that can save you impressive sums.

It is axiomatic that shoddy production gives you a shoddy image. Therefore, when running print ads, especially newspaper ads, it is usually silly to save money on production by having the **A silly savings** newspaper or other medium design your ads. Instead, you should have a professional do that work.

There are basically two types of professionals: high cost and low cost. To save the most money and gain the best identity, hire a high-cost to lay out your first ad and create a visual format for you. Then hire a low-cost to do all of your follow-up ads, telling him or her to follow the format created in the original ad. This will not infuriate the inexpensive designer, who will probably be thrilled with the business. And it will not anger the expensive designer, who got a fair sum for the talent expended. The result will be that you will always have sharp-looking ads, even though you paid through the nose only one time. You get the best of two worlds: a classy look and format throughout the life of your marketing campaign, and a low price for the production of all the ads except the first. You shouldn't have to spend high production fees more than one time, but believe me, it is well worth it that one time. Ask any entrepreneur who has employed this tactic.

Remnant space   Have you ever heard of remnant space? Probably not, unless you're in the marketing business. Many national magazines publish regional editions. When doing so, they sell advertising space to regional advertisers. Because of the way magazines are put together, publishers think in terms of four-page units, since it takes one large piece of paper folded in half to make four pages that fit comfortably into a magazine format. Often a magazine will have sold three of its four pages when publication date is right around the corner. What does the publisher do with that one extra page — that remnant space? Sells it at an astounding discount to a local advertiser, that's what. If you wish to be that local advertiser, just contact the publication well in advance of the date you wish your ad to appear, or get in touch with Media Networks, Inc., a company devoted to selling remnant space to local advertisers. The company is national, and its toll-free number, from which you should request a free rate book, is 1-800-225-3457. This company will be able to put your ad in most national magazines, in the regional issues, at a far lower cost than you may think.

For example, during the early 1990s a full-page, black and white ad in *Time* magazine ran in the $80,000 range. Media Networks, Inc., could sell you a full-page black and white ad in *Time* magazine in Tucson or El Paso or Wilmington or Savannah or many other places for under $3000 — a $77,000 savings. Some difference!

While we're on the subject of the cost of advertising time and space, we should take a look at one of the most efficient money-saving strategies in all of marketing — establishing a house advertising agency for yourself. Normal advertising agencies earn their money by receiving a 15 percent discount from publications and broadcast stations where they place advertising. If an ad or commercial costs an advertiser $1000, that same ad space or commercial time costs an advertising agency only $850. This is known as an agency discount, and advertising agencies are entitled to every cent of it. The advertiser would have to spend $1000 anyhow. So by utilizing an ad agency, the advertiser receives professional help at no extra cost, since the advertisement will cost $1000 with or without an agency. And the ad agency picks up $150 for its efforts.

But what if you're too small to require an advertising agency? What if you just plain don't want an advertising agency? You should establish your own in-house ad agency. To do this, you usually need do no more than tell the advertising medium that you are an in-house or internal agency for your business. In some cases, the medium may require that you have a checking account in your agency's name (ten dollars in an account will do nicely). And you may need agency stationery. Again, this is no problem. If your business is called Atlantic Manufacturing, just call your agency Atlantic Advertising on inexpensive stationery you have ordered in the minimum amount.

You are the advertising agency

With this checking account and stationery, you are now ready to be your own in-house advertising agency. And you can save 15 percent on almost all the advertising you place for yourself. You can save on virtually everything but newspaper advertising, where you pay only the retail rate, which is low to begin with. It's so easy to set up an internal agency that I'm surprised more entrepreneurs don't do it. But you can. You can save a considerable sum of money after you do. And your $3000 *Time* regional ad will then cost only $2500.

If you ever do use local television, start out with tight, well-planned scripts. Have a rehearsal session or two prior to the shooting date, then try to shoot three or four commercials in one session. Although the average thirty-second TV commercial costs around $175,000 to produce (thanks to the soft drinks, beers, and fast-food chains), you can get that cost down to $1000 if you shoot several spots at once, work with thought-out scripts, and avoid paying high talent fees to actors and actresses. Once again, some difference! The difference is due to a variety of things. For one thing, full-scale TV productions usually involve large crews for lighting, props, make-up, hairstyling, and moving the camera around. That ordinarily involves union and inflated costs. Guerrillas work with skeleton crews and do not work with unions unless absolutely necessary. They're not anti-union; they're pro-efficiency.

TV production on a shoestring

One of the highest costs in TV production, especially with videotape, is editing. With very well planned scripts, you will need very little editing.

Some advertisers feel that they must have a celebrity to hawk their wares. This adds from $5000 to $500,000 to the tab. Two Michaels command even more: Jackson and Jordan. Guerrillas rely on the power of an idea and save the cash.

Expensive production devices such as complex scenery, special effects, and ornate sets make commercials cost more than they should. Because many people are involved in the actual shooting, each scene may be shot four or five different ways, to stroke four or five different egos. Guerrillas shoot each scene one way and get their ego kicks by making sizable bank deposits.

In addition, TV professionals tend to shoot commercials to suit their own tastes and needs. They can spot flaws that most viewers would never see. So they reshoot and reshoot and reshoot. Guerrillas accept minor flaws and get on with the commercial.

All this adds up to a whale of a difference in money — but not in quality. I have a reel of commercials, each costing under $500. TV pros who have seen them have estimated that the cost of each spot was $10,000 or more. In my opinion, unnecessary TV production costs are murdering many large-company production budgets. The amazing thing is that they are easy to avoid. So avoid them.

Two kinds of advertising   In the final analysis, there are two kinds of advertising: expensive and inexpensive. The expensive kind of advertising is the kind that doesn't work. The inexpensive kind of advertising is the kind that does work — regardless of cost. This chapter has suggested additional ways to save money with your marketing. But you'll save the most if you always make sure to run inexpensive advertising — the kind that gives you the results you want. And that has more to do with quality than cost.

8
Secrets of Obtaining Free Research

IT'S NOT DIFFICULT to turn up a marketing pro who will tell you that the three most important things to do to market anything successfully are to test, test, and test. That is pretty good advice. But it is unrealistic for those with resource poverty, who cannot shell out big bucks for sophisticated research.

The big secret is that you need not shell out any money to learn about your market. If you know what to look for and where to find it, you can obtain crucial information for nary a cent. Let's examine some of the things you might want to find out.

1. What should you market — your goods, your services, or both?
2. Should your marketing feature some sort of price advantage?
3. Should you emphasize yourself, your quality offerings, your selection, your service, or merely the existence of your business?
4. Should you take on your competition or ignore all competitors?
5. Exactly who are your competitors?
6. Who are your best prospects?
7. What income groups do they represent?
8. What motivates them to buy?
9. Where do they live?
10. What do they read or watch or listen to in the way of media?

Ten crucial questions

The right answers to these questions can prove invaluable to a marketing effort. The wrong answers, or no answers, can prove disastrous. Do what you must to get the right answers.

In most cases, great advertising is preceded by great research. There are three prime ways for you to engage in research that will provide you with the information that can make the difference between success and failure, yet not cost you much, if anything. **Enlist your library as an ally** The first is to go to your local library. The reference librarian, one of America's greatest untapped resources, will be able to steer you to just the books and other publications that contain a raft of money-making information for you. Some of these publications have market studies of your area, conducted by companies that paid impressive sums for the data. Others contain studies of products or services such as yours, and indicate the level of their acceptance by the public. Still others include census reports, research reports, industry studies, and more. Whenever I write a book, I find myself in libraries ferreting out information. And I am always dazzled by the expertise of the reference librarians, who not only know where to find information but also seem to delight in the finding. And all the information to which they lead you is free for the asking. The more customer information you have, the better equipped you will be to serve those customers. This is where inquisitiveness pays off big.

A second, and commonly overlooked, way to obtain information is to ask your own customers. If you have a new business, **Your customers have the answers** I strongly suggest that you prepare a lengthy questionnaire for them. On it, ask them everything under the sun.

Large corporations that enclose brief questionnaires with their manufactured items such as TV sets, electric razors, or blow dryers report that fewer than half the questionnaires are returned. These questionnaires consist of five or six questions, even fewer. On the other hand, I had a client who gave each of his customers a fifteen-question questionnaire. Seventy-eight percent of the forms distributed were completed and returned. It seems that many people enjoy providing personal information, just as long as they can remain anonymous.

Suppose you wanted to establish a company that provided auto mechanical services at people's homes rather than in a garage. You might prepare and hand out a questionnaire that asks the following of your prospects — namely, motorists:

We are establishing an automotive service that makes "house calls." To help us serve you most effectively, please provide the following information:

What type of car do you drive? _____

What year is it? _____ What model? _____

How long have you owned it? _____

Who usually performs mechanical services for your car? _____
_____

Would you want these services to be performed where you live?
_____

List the three main reasons you would want "house calls" made to service your car: _____
_____
_____
_____

Would you pay more to have "house calls" for your car? _____

What is your sex? _____ Your age? _____

Your household income? _____

What newspapers do you read? _____

What radio stations do you listen to? _____

What TV shows do you watch? _____

Which magazines do you read? _____

What type of work do you do? _____

Would you purchase products as well as service from a traveling automotive service? _____

Who do you consider to be our competition? _____

Where would you expect us to advertise? _____

Do you have any other comments? _____

In this game of twenty questions, you always emerge the winner. By studying the *questions only,* you can easily see how much you can learn. Just think of how informed you'd be by studying the answers! This kind of questionnaire should be distributed for a number of months, and the answers should be studied each month so trends can be spotted after the business has been established. Notice that the questionnaire did not ask the name or address of the customer, so anonymity was preserved, enabling you to ask many personal questions.

Analysis of the completed questionnaires will show you the kind of people your prospects are, how to reach them through the media, how to appeal to them, and what kind of cars they drive.

You can analyze the questionnaires by grouping the responses to each question. Perhaps you'll learn that the majority of people interested in patronizing your business drive foreign cars. That would alert you to the possibility of doing a mailing to foreign-car owners. Their names are available from mailing-list brokers. It might be that your customers are owners of older cars. Again, you can reach these people with a targeted mailing. Also, the questionnaire will help you focus your advertising on the right people.

From the questionnaire, you can learn who your competition is by learning who usually performs mechanical services for your prospects. You can determine what it is you offer that is most enticing to your customers — again helping you choose the proper emphasis for your advertising. You'll discover the sex and age of your customers, and you'll learn exactly how and where to communicate with them once you ascertain the newspapers, radio stations, TV shows, and magazines that interest them. If your customers are primarily white-collar workers, this questionnaire will inform you of that fact, and you'll be able to tailor your media selection to that reality. You can find out which marketing vehicles will work most effectively for you. And you can obtain a report on your own service.

It is very simple to make this analysis, very useful in helping you determine your marketing thrust, yet extremely inexpensive for you. This information can be used to update or revise your marketing plan. And just think, the only cost was for duplicating the questionnaire — well under $100. This is free research at its best, and frankly, you're nuts if you don't take advantage of it . . . then repeat it every few years to keep you abreast of your market.

The third way to take advantage of inexpensive research is to prepare a questionnaire similar to the preceding one, and hand it to people using the kind of services you provide. That way, you'll be researching serious, rather than potential, prospects. You'll receive fewer returns than the 78 percent my client enjoyed, but you'll learn something — which is a lot more valuable than knowing nothing. Naturally, you won't hand your questionnaire to motorists if you are selling computer education. If that's your business, you'll want your questionnaires in the hands of people entering or departing computer stores. If you are a traveling hair-stylist who makes house calls, hand your questionnaires to people leaving beauty salons or barbershops. Whatever your business, you can find prospective customers somewhere: with their kids at the kiddie playground, at the beach, in the park; downtown; coming out of the hardware store; leaving the ballpark. Chances are, you've already got a line on where they are. All you've got to do is go there and hand them your long list of questions.

How do you ensure that the prospective customers will return your questionnaires? Well, you can furnish them with stamped envelopes. You can tempt them with offers of free (but inexpensive) gifts. You can offer discounts to them if they complete and return your questionnaire. And you can use pure honesty by telling them, atop the questionnaire, exactly why you are asking so many questions. Just be sure to include your address, so that the questionnaires will be mailed (or brought) to the right place.

How to get answers to your questions

It helps if you have an introductory paragraph atop your questionnaire. It should say something like, "We're trying to learn as much as possible from motorists in the community, so that we can offer them the best possible service. We apologize for asking you so many questions in this questionnaire, but we're doing it so that you can benefit in the long run. We promise that your answers will remain anonymous (notice we are not asking for your name). And we also promise that we'll use the information to help you enjoy better automotive service." Such an honest introduction serves to disarm people who resent being asked so many questions; and it does explain exactly why you are doing it.

Once again, you end up with valuable information. Once again, it costs you hardly anything. A true guerrilla will try *all three methods* of obtaining such free research. Then he or she will put the information to work to create a first-rate marketing plan, using reliable data that can aid in the selection of marketing methods, the evaluation of the competition, and the framing of the creative message.

These are not the only methods of conducting inexpensive research, simply the most common and effective. Also worth checking for important data are your local chamber of commerce, your state chamber of commerce, any industry organizations to which you belong, and any industry publications of which you are aware. You might also make a field trip or two to poke around and talk to people in your business but not your geographic area. Guerrillas abet their primary research with these additional sources of knowledge. They know, and so do you, that knowledge is the currency of the nineties.

More sources of inexpensive insight

When questioning your target audience, it might help to list some of the basic needs people have, and ask them to make check marks by those that pushed their particular buttons. Most people **The basic needs** will react to one or more of the following basic needs (known as "appeals" in advertising lingo):

Achievement	Style
Pride of ownership	Social approval (status)
Convenience	Health and well-being
Comfort	Profit
Love	Savings or economy
Friendship	Conformity (peer pressure)
Security	Ambition
Self-improvement	Power

If you have had the feeling that people patronize you because you offer convenience and economy, you may be surprised to learn, via your questionnaires, that they really give you their business because your work adds to their sense of security.

You can engage in more free research by conscientiously studying the other advertising that is going on in your community — not only that of your competitors but that of everyone else as well. Have frank conversations with your customers. Talk with your competitors. If they're from a noncompeting area, tell them about a marketing tactic that worked for you, then ask about any that worked for them; most likely, they'll talk their heads off because you're obviously a person who understands them because you're in the same business. Guerrillas call this "sharing." The way it works is, the more you give, the more you get.

Talk with other businesspeople in your community. You'll find that these sources will provide you with useful information and won't charge you one cent for it. Research can help you save a lot of money and earn a lot of money. Free research can help you save and earn even more.

II
Mini-Media
Marketing

I T IS IN MINI-MEDIA MARKETING that practitioners of guerrilla marketing have their chance to shine. For standard marketers rarely, if ever, resort to such teeny-tiny marketing methods as canvassing, writing personal letters, marketing by telephone, distributing circulars, posting signs on bulletin boards, running classified ads, using signs other than billboards, and putting the yellow pages to work. Fortunately, because the titans do not practice mini-media marketing, you'll come across very little competition in these arenas — except from fellow guerrillas. Be warned, there are more and more of them *daily*, and your close attention to the media will alert you to their presence — as well as educate you by their examples. Be prepared to respond. Giant companies aren't as quick on their feet as you, so you can respond faster.

Your mini-media marketing must still adhere to your marketing plan. It must still be accomplished with talent and style. It must still follow many of the fundamentals. But it gets to break many of the rules, too. For instance, you can make letters highly personalized. You can post one-of-a-kind signs. You can take advantage of the smallness of your business when making telephone calls. Make them personal, friendly, informal, yet professional.

I urge you to utilize as many media as you can possibly use correctly. And I especially urge you to use the mini-media to the max. Big companies don't. This will rarely put a strain on your budget. Production costs will be small. You'll have an opportunity to star in the mini-media more than in the maxi-media, where you can be outspent even if you're not being outthought.

In the mini-media, your size will be an advantage, not a disadvantage. So I hope you'll put most or even all of the following marketing methods to work while you're still small. If you do, you'll know which to utilize when you're large.

Your small size enables you to offer advantages in the area of customer service. Your geographic proximity — including the fact that you're a true-blue local — if your market is your own locality, is a big weapon, possessed by few of the behemoths. You know folks on a first-name basis. You see them regularly. Chalk up one major advantage for your side.

You can provide extremely individualized service, tailored to the realities of your customers' budgets. Few big companies can match you in that area. By necessity, they're forced to run customer service by company policy, and that deprives them of flexibility.

As a guerrilla, you're reeking with flexibility — and it can be translated into service that customers crave. Another point for your team. The mini-media includes maxi-service. Used properly, they can make you a juggernaut. The nineties have brought a multitude of changes in the mini-media, all of which work to the advantage of the entrepreneur.

- Faxes allow you to render speedier service (but don't use faxes for marketing; people resent "junk faxes").
- Computer bulletin boards enable you to zero in on specific target audiences, then communicate by modem.
- Toll-free 800 numbers are less expensive than ever, so you can increase your response rates.
- Catalogues, newsletters, and brochures are simpler than ever to produce, thanks to desktop publishing.
- 900 numbers can be used both as a marketing weapon and as a new profit-center.
- More magazines offer inexpensive regional editions than ever, giving you first-rate credibility at cut-rate prices.
- More newspapers than ever now offer low-cost zone editions that reach prospects in targeted neighborhoods.
- Computer technology allows entrepreneurs to tap into computer networks, communicate with many people at once, and keep more accurate databases.
- TV time, thanks to the growth of cable companies, has

dropped in price to a point that almost any small business can (and should) consider it.

- Satellite TV transmission allows advertisers to home in on very, very specialized markets.
- Home shopping networks enable viewers to buy instantly, providing advertisers with instant gratification.
- Car phones and airphones offer more sophisticated communication options, saving time and opening the door to more personalized service.
- VCR penetration is nearing 80 percent, adding to the attractiveness of a video brochure.
- New breakthroughs in psychology are giving us a clearer view of human behavior, so that we can create more effective marketing.
- New media are springing up all over the place: in a sky full of advertising blimps, on airport luggage carousels, on jet-plane movie screens, at grocery check-out counters, in post-card decks, integrated within major movies and TV shows.
- People are being marketed to while on telephone hold, and they actually appreciate the data while they wait.
- Special-effects TV technology allows small advertisers to get a big-advertiser look without spending big bucks.

I'm just scratching the surface of the new changes in mini-media that have taken place since the original edition of this book. Many of the maxi-media, once the domain of the big spenders, are now your domain, too. As a guerrilla, your eyes must be open to the marketing options of the nineties, and far more of them than ever before. New ones enter the marketing arena on a daily basis. These lovely marketing weapons and technologies are by-products of the age of the entrepreneur. Each one represents an opportunity for you.

Whether or not you capitalize on the opportunity is up to you; whether or not you learn of the opportunities is up to me. And learn you will as soon as you turn the page.

9
Canvassing: Marketing on an Eye-to-Eye Basis

CANVASSING CAN BE the most inexpensive marketing method of all. In fact, it can be free, except for the time you devote to it. And if you're just starting out, time is something you have a great deal of in your inventory. After all, canvassing is merely asking prospective customers for business. During a canvass, which the dictionary defines as "a soliciting of sales," you should engage in three separate steps.

The first step, called the *contact*, is when you first meet your prospect. That first impression counts like crazy. So make your contact friendly, upbeat, customer-oriented, honest, and warm. *Try to establish a relationship.* Smile, look directly into the person's eye, and if at all possible, *use the person's name.* You need not talk about business if you don't want to. And you really shouldn't. Some *Fortune* 500 companies require that their salespeople ask at least three nonbusiness questions before actually getting down to business. You can talk about personal matters, about the weather, about a current event, about sports, or — hopefully, about your prospective customer. That's probably his or her favorite subject.

First impressions count

The second step of a canvass is called the *presentation*. It usually takes longer than the other steps, yet it need take no longer than one minute. During the presentation, you outline the features of your offering and the benefits to be gained from buying from you. Some pro canvassers say, "The more you tell, the more you sell." I'm not sure about that. Depends upon what you are selling. If it is a home security system, your presentation might take fifteen minutes. If it is an offer to wash your prospect's car, the presentation might take one minute or less. Presentations to sell waterbeds take about forty-five minutes; presentations to sell home satellite systems take a day and a half; presentations to sell million-dollar computer switchers take up to a year and a half. The price of your product or service will dictate the time you have to spend on presenting it.

The most important step

The third step of a canvass is the most important part. It's called the *close*, and it is that magical moment when you complete the sale. That happens when your prospect says "Yes" or signs on the dotted line or reaches for his or her wallet or merely nods affirmatively. If you are a poor closer, it doesn't really matter how good you are at the contact and the presentation. You've got to be a good closer to make canvassing work at all.

Before there were any other methods of marketing, canvassing existed. In fact, the very first sale in history probably occurred when one caveman asked another, "Want to trade me an animal skin for this fruit I picked?" No advertising was necessary. No marketing plan, either. Life has become far better since then. But far more complicated, too.

If you think that canvassing is like door-to-door selling, you're right only if you want to do it that way. You can canvass by going from door to door. You can do it in residential neighborhoods, you can do it in commercial neighborhoods, and you can do it at trade shows. Or, you can presell your canvass by first calling or writing the people you intend to canvass. You have a choice of telling them you'll be coming around so that they'll expect you sometime, or actually setting up an appointment. When that happens, it's more like making a sales presentation than canvassing. For most guerrillas, canvassing is something done with little or no advance warning. Sure, it helps if you advertise so that the prospective customers have heard of you when you come calling. But you don't have to advertise. If you make a good contact, a crisp presentation, and a dynamite close, and if you are offering a good value, canvassing may be the only marketing tool you ever need.

Canvassing with intelligence

I mentioned that canvassing can be free, and I wasn't kidding. But canvassing improves when you do invest a bit of money in it. For one thing, you want to look good so as to inspire confidence. That means you should look the part. If you are canvassing store owners with the idea of getting them to sign up for your window-washing business, you need not wear a coat and tie. But it helps if you're wearing spotless work clothes, and even if you have a clean rag dangling from your rear pocket.

The investment increases a bit more if you offer a business card to the person you are canvassing. The card establishes that you are for real and enables a person to give you business later, if not now. It also helps your referral business — if you do a good job. Your investment will be even greater if you decide to canvass using a brochure or circular. If you do produce such materials, either use them as sales aids while you are making your presentation or give them away after you have closed the sale. Don't expect a person to read your sales literature and listen to your sales talk at the same time. Generally I frown on giving out a circular during this contact, since it gives your prospect an opportunity to avoid buying by telling you he or she will "study" your circular, then get back to you. If they don't buy now, figure that they won't buy later. Most of the time, they won't. Another way to see it is that *someone will buy.* Either you'll buy their story about why they can't buy now, or they'll buy what you're selling. Some entrepreneurs give free demonstrations or samples while they canvass. Although this adds to your investment, it is often a smart addition.

Someone will buy

Once you learn the best way to accomplish your canvassing, you will be confronted with several choices. First, will you want to continue using this method of marketing? Second, are you doing it as well as it can be done? Third, should you be delegating the canvassing job to someone else or to several other people? To an organization of sales reps, called distributors? The advantages of canvassing are readily apparent. It doesn't cost much, if anything. It is a great way to get a brand-new business going. It strengthens your contacts, because looking a person directly in the eye is more personal by a long shot than writing a letter, making a phone call, or attracting attention with an ad. Canvassing is also a good way to learn the objections, if any, to your offering. It provides instant results and can be commenced instantly as well. And it lets you be sure that your message is being heard. Like television advertising, it enables you to demonstrate. Like radio advertising, it enables you to be intimate. Like newspaper advertising, it allows you to be newsy. Like magazine advertising, it allows you to involve your prospect. And like direct-response marketing, it is geared to get you a direct response of the positive kind.

The success of canvassing depends upon you and you alone. You can't blame the media if you mess up. And if you succeed, you deserve to get all of the credit. Furthermore, canvassing is very accountable, meaning that you know darned well whether it's working or not. Results aren't always so accountable once you get into the more sophisticated media.

Let's say you have a brand-spanking-new home security com-**A canvassing** pany. You sell and install burglar and smoke alarms. You've **campaign** named your company Always Alert, and you've printed up business cards, nothing else. Your marketing plan calls for you to spend the first two months canvassing for business. The first month, you'll canvass commercial establishments. The second month, you'll canvass homes. Then you'll decide whether to concentrate on businesses or homes, and you'll decide whether or not to continue canvassing for new business. Let's assume you're so short of cash that you cannot afford to run even one ad. I hope that is never the case, but right now, let's stack the deck against you.

Okay, you're ready to make your detailed canvassing plans. What to wear? As a general rule, dress exactly as your prospects dress, whether it be Levi's or a three-piece suit. If you're calling upon businesses, I'd suggest a dark business suit, whether you are male or female. The dark colors — navy blue, black, deep gray, or charcoal — lend authority to what you say. The suit itself implies professionalism. I'd stay away from any accessories that detract from the professional look you wish to convey. I'd also be sure that my hair was neat and my hands were clean, and that I had a handsome case to carry either samples or sales literature provided by the manufacturer. I'd feel so good that a smile would come easily.

Once you're properly attired, the next step is to decide what you'll say during the contact, that first precious moment. It is probably best to make a comment first about the store you are visiting: "I like your window display. It seems just right for this location. My name is Tim Winston. My company is Always Alert. We offer security systems to businesses such as yours. What type of security system do you have now?"

During this contact, you have complimented the prospect on

his or her window display, thereby showing that you noticed it in the first place. I hope you were smiling and making eye contact as you announced your name and the name of your company. Finally, you qualified your prospect with one single question. By "qualified," I mean you determined your prospect's need for your product. If the prospect has a security system and tells you that it consists of both a burglar alarm and a smoke alarm, you can save time by making no presentation whatsoever, and go ahead on your way after first thanking the person for the information imparted. You might inquire if the person is happy with the current security system, and be sure to leave your card behind just in case he or she wishes to make a change later. But you'd be best off keeping the time spent with nonprospects down to a minimum. Once your prospect indicates that he or she already has what you're selling, you should save time for both of you.

At the next store, following a similar contact, the prospect may tell you that they have no security system. That's your cue to make your presentation. While giving it, remember that *whenever you mention a feature, follow it with a benefit*. For instance, "Always Alert features security systems that run on solar power. So they never need batteries. They use up no expensive electrical power. And they are maintenance free." The feature is the solar power. The benefits are freedom from purchasing batteries, from spending money for electrical power, and from taking up time maintaining the devices.

Features and benefits

Continue your presentation, making it as long as it must be, yet as short as it can be. After all, both you and your prospect have other things to do. While presenting, be constantly on the lookout for closing signs. It may be that you have already made the sale and that the prospect wants to buy. But if you don't look for signs that you've said enough, you might end up losing the sale. As the topnotch salespeople say, A-B-C — *Always be closing*.

After you have made your presentation, try to close with a question that requires more than a yes or no answer. Such a question might be, "Well, that about does it. Will it be better for me to install your alarm system Wednesday or Thursday?" Another closing question might be, "Do you intend to pay for your alarm system at the time of installation, or should I bill you?"

Ask and ye shall close

Many excellent books on salesmanship carefully dissect the sale, examining the contact, the presentation, and the close. For reasons of enlarging your bank account rather than catering to my ego, I recommend *Guerrilla Selling* by Bill Gallagher, Orvel Ray Wilson, and myself (Houghton Mifflin Company, 1992). If you're going to be a guerrilla, go all out; don't merely play at part of it.

Canvassing requires salesmanship. It requires a contact, a presentation, and a close. Furthermore, it requires just as much quality in that salesmanship as is needed for the sale of an expensive car or an item of furniture. And it requires far greater salesmanship in terms of quantity. A great car salesman may make ten contacts, presentations, and closes in one good day. You may make ten in one good hour. To succeed at canvassing, you must have enthusiasm about your product, an honest enjoyment of people, and a load of determination.

But if you're to succeed as an entrepreneur, if you're to build your small business into a large one, you'll have to move beyond canvassing, even though it may continue to be part of your marketing mix. The disadvantages of canvassing are that it takes too much of your time, that you can't reach enough prospects even in one high-energy day, and that it is limited in scope geographically. Some of those disadvantages disappear when you start delegating the canvassing to others. But if you succeed at canvassing, you'll soon become itchy to reach more people.

Before we go into ways you can do that, let's try to make you the best canvasser possible. To do that, let's examine the contact, the presentation, and the close in a bit more detail.

First, realize that *somebody* is going to close a sale with your customer. It might be a competitor of yours. It might be a friend of the customer. But it *will be somebody.* That somebody can be **When you have** someone else or you. While your customer is with you, you have **a lot of control** a lot of control over who will close — the most control you will ever have. After you've left your customer, you have very little control, if any. *So while your customer is with you is the best time to close.* And remember: Closing is really the name of the canvassing game. So even though you will need to make a contact and a presentation, you should be thinking "close close close" all along. By doing that, you'll be gradually closing all the time you're with your customer. And that's good. Still, in spite of the importance of closing, it is crucial that while you are making your contact, you think of *that* as the most important part. If you mess up on it, you may not have a chance to move on to the close. Do the contact well, and you may breeze right through to the actual close. That's how important the initial contact is.

If your contact comes from a "cold" call, and your prospect is a complete stranger, take steps to make that prospect a new acquaintance. If your contact comes from a lead — a recommendation from a friend, an answer to an ad you ran, or some other reason to make you believe the prospect can be converted into a customer — refer to that relationship, that bond between you. It will help break the barriers that much faster. You are no longer a complete stranger. Now you are at the very least, an acquaintance of an acquaintance. Here are a few tactics canvassing pros use:

- Greet your prospect warmly and sincerely, using eye contact.

  Guerrilla tips about the contact

- Allow your prospect some time to get acclimated to being with you, some time to talk. Don't come on too strong. But don't waste your prospect's time, either.
- Engage in casual conversation at first — especially about anything pertinent to your prospect. Make it friendly and not one-sided. Be a good listener. But let the prospect know that your time is precious. You are there to sell, not to talk.
- Ask relevant questions. Listen carefully to the answers.
- Qualify the prospect. Determine whether or not this is the specific person to whom you should be talking, the person with the authority to give you the go-ahead, to buy. Try to learn, during the contact, what to emphasize in your presentation.
- Try to learn of your prospect's attitude toward your type of offering. Tune in on his or her fears, expectations, feelings — so that you can tailor your presentation to them.
- Learn something about the person to whom your contact is directed, so that he or she will feel like a person rather than a prospect. Make your prospect like you, for people enjoy doing business with people they like. But don't be phony. Don't be syrupy. The best possible thing you can do is to make your prospect *feel unique* — proving that you recognized his or her individuality and needs.
- Be brief, friendly, outgoing, and truly inquisitive. But be yourself.
- If you're in a retail environment, one of the best questions to initiate healthy contact is "Mind if I ask what brings you into our store today?"

- Even though you are selling, don't think of yourself as a sales-person but as a partner to your prospect. This healthy mind-set improves both your perspective and your chances of closing.

Important elements of your contact are your smile, your attire, your posture, and your willingness to listen and look directly into the prospect's eyes. Your nonverbal communication is as important as your verbal communication. The impression you make will come as much from what you don't say as from what you do say.

It is often during the contact that the sale is cinched. This happens if your contact has truly opened up communications and you have convinced your prospect that you are honestly interested in helping him or her. During a successful contact, each party will have made a friend — and thereby paved the way to a sale, even continuing sales. The contact may be the shortest of the three phases of a canvass. But it does establish the basis for the presentation and the close.

When making your presentation, keep in mind that you are not talking by accident. You are there because of intent on your part. If your prospect is still with you and has not ended the canvass, there is intent on his or her part, too. And the intent is to buy. Either you will buy a story about why a sale cannot be made, or your prospect will buy what you're selling. It truly is up to you. And don't forget: People do enjoy being sold to. They do not like being pressured. They do like being persuaded by honest enthusiasm to buy. Here are some tips to make your presentations flow smoothly:

Guerrilla tips about the presentation

- List all the benefits of doing business with you, one by one. The more benefits a prospect knows about, the more likely a prospect will buy. When compiling your list of benefits, invite your employees and at least one customer. Customers are tuned in to benefits you offer that you may take for granted.
- Emphasize the *unique* advantages of buying from you. You should be able to rattle these off with the same aplomb you can state your own name and address. It is upon these competitive advantages that you should be basing your marketing.

- If your prospect has no experience with what you are selling, stress the advantages of your *type* of offering, then of your specific offering. If you're selling security devices, talk of the value of owning them, then of the value of owning *yours*.
- Tailor your presentation to information learned during your contact — and before. I hope you learned a lot before making any contact. Homework pays off bigtime to guerrillas.
- People do not like to be pioneers, so mention the acceptance of your products or services by others — especially people in their community. If you can mention names and be specific, by all means do so. The more specific you are, the more closes you'll make. But don't be tedious. You can't bore a prospect into buying.
- When you know enough about your prospect, you can present your product or service from his or her point of view. This ability will increase your number of closes dramatically. Emphasize what all of your product or service benefits can do for your prospect, not what they can do for the general population.
- Keep an eagle eye on your prospect's eyes, teeth, and hands. If the prospect is looking around, rather than at you, you've got to say something to regain attention. If your prospect is not smiling, you are being too serious. Say something to earn a smile. Best of all, smile yourself. That will get your prospect to smile. If your prospect is wringing his or her hands, your prospect is bored. Say something to ease the boredom and spark more interest.
- A sales point made to the eye is 68 percent more effective than one made to the ear. So show as much as you can: photos, drawings, a circular, a product, *anything*. Just be sure it relates to your presentation.
- Sell the benefit along with the feature. If the feature is solar power, for instance, the benefit is economy. If the feature is new computer software, the benefit is probably profitability.
- Mention your past successes so the prospect will feel that the key to success is in your hands and there is little chance of a rip-off.
- Be proud of your prices, proud of your benefits, proud of your offering. Convey your pride with facial expression, tone of voice, selection of words. Feel the pride and let it

come shining through. There are 250,000 commonly used words in the English language; there are 600,000 nonverbal methods of communications: stance, facial expression, hand gestures, eyebrow position, and 599,996 others. Learn them and utilize them. They're completely free, another example of pure guerrilla marketing. No cost. High payoff.

- Throughout your presentation, remain convinced that your prospect *will* buy from you. This optimism will be sensed by the prospect and can positively affect the close.

Despite the importance I have attached to the contact and the presentation, I still reiterate that all the marbles are in the close. Effective salespeople and canvassers are effective closers. Aim to be a dynamite closer and your income will reflect this. To close effectively, try to close immediately, rather than in a week or so. Also, remember these thoughts:

Guerrilla tips about the close

- Always assume that your prospective customer is going to do what you want, so you can close with a leading question such as, "Will it be better for you to take delivery this week or next week?" "Do you want it in gray or brown?"
- Summarize your main points and confidently end with a closing line such as, "Everything seems to be in order. Why don't I just write up your order now?"
- Ask the customer to make some kind of decision, then close on it. Typical points that must be agreed upon are delivery date, size of order, method of payment. A good closing would be: "I can perform this service for you tomorrow, the eighth, or the fifteenth. The eighth would be best for me. Which would be best for you?"
- Begin to attempt the close as soon as possible by easing your prospect into it. If that doesn't work, try again, then again. Continue trying. If you don't, your prospect will spend his or her hard-earned money elsewhere — and with someone else. Count on that. Remember: People *like* to be sold to and *need* to have the deal closed. They won't make the close themselves. So you are performing a service when you sell and close.
- Always be on the alert for signs that the time is right to close. The prospect will hardly ever tell you when the time

has come. You must look for hints in the prospect's words *and* actions. A mere shifting of weight from one foot to another may be a signal to close.

- Try to give your prospect a good reason to close *immediately*. It may be that you won't be back in the neighborhood for a long time, or that the prospect will wish to use your product or service as soon as possible, or that prices are expected to rise, or that you have the time and the inventory now but might not have them later.
- Let your prospect know of the success of your product or service with people *like* the prospect, with people *recently*, with people in the community — with people *with whom the prospect can easily relate*.
- Be specific with names, dates, costs, times, and benefits. Evasiveness in any area works against you.
- If the prospect likes what you say, but won't close now, ask, "Why wait?" The prospect may then voice an objection. And you may close by saying, "That's great, and I understand." Then you can solve the objection and close on it. In fact, one of the easiest ways to close is to search for an objection, then solve the problem and close on it.
- If you have not yet completed your presentation but feel the time may be right to close, attempt to close on the most important sales point you have yet to state.
- Always remember that a person knows what you want him or her to do, that there is a reason for your meeting, that your offering does have merit, and that at that moment, your prospect has your offering on his or her mind. Just knowing all these things will make it easier for you to close.
- When a prospect says "Let me think it over," that means "no."
- If you do not close just after your presentation, chances are you have lost the sale. Few prospects have the guts to tell you they will definitely not buy from you. They search for excuses. So do everything you can to move them into a position where they will buy from you. If you don't, a better salesperson will.
- Tie the close in with the contact. Try to close on a personal note. Something like, "I think you'll feel more secure now with this new security system, and that's important. Shall I have your smoke alarm installed tomorrow or the next day?"

Some canvassers are lucky. They get to talk only to people who are honest-to-goodness leads, who have demonstrated an interest in the product or service already. But most canvassers have to make cold calls. Brrr! A pundit once observed, "Throughout history, the most common debilitating human ailment has been cold feet."

But guerrillas are not troubled by this ailment. They thrive on cold calls. They need no introduction, referral, or appointment. They know the key to success is *making the most of the short time they have to attract their prospect's attention.* They also know six hot tips on cold calling:

Hot tips on cold calling

1. *Do your homework.* Learn as much as possible about the company you'll be calling upon. The more you know, the better you can tailor your presentation to the prospect.
2. *Start at the top.* Ask for and speak with the person in charge, the one who can say "yes." Do what you must to find out this person's name and title before you even begin. Anything extra you learn will prove extra helpful to you.
3. *Be brief.* Don't waste anyone's time. Keep your message concise. Brevity in cold calling primes you for success.
4. *Get to the point.* Tell if your offering does the job faster, easier, lasts longer, saves time, saves energy, or whatever. Zero in quickly on the prime benefits of your product or service.
5. *Give references.* Give names of satisfied customers, names that your prospect will recognize and respect. If he doesn't know the name, maybe he'll know the company.
6. *Close the sale.* Make an appointment. Schedule a full presentation or a demonstration. Know before you start exactly what you wish to achieve, and close on that objective. Whatever you do, ask for the order.

If you don't feel comfortable with A-B-C, "always be closing," at least learn to feel comfortable with A-T-C, which means "always *think* closing." If you think closing, your thoughts will carry over to your prospect. And you'll close more as a result. But eventually, you just may want to exercise your powers of selling on larger groups of people. One of the ways to do that is by writing personal letters. So we'll examine the art of creating them in the next chapter.

10
Personal Letters:
Inexpensive and Effective

THE WRITING OF PERSONAL LETTERS — not direct mailings of large quantities of letters and brochures, but simple, personal letters — is one of the most effective, easy, inexpensive, and overlooked methods of marketing. Certainly the large corporations don't consider using this type of communication, because it doesn't reach enough people to enrich their coffers. But it's just the ticket for many an individual businessperson. If you can write clear English, spell properly, and keep your message short enough, you ought to be able to develop enough business through this mode of marketing so that you need not employ many other methods. Even if you're a dismal grammarian, professional typists can usually help put your ideas into acceptable form on the printed page.

The primary value of a personal letter is that it enables you to convey a truly personal feeling and reach a special place in the mind of the reader. You can say specific things in personal letters that are just not practical in any other medium except for certain kinds of telephone marketing. **The personal touch**

For example, you can say in your letter, "Mrs. Forman, your gardenias and carnations look wonderful this year. But your roses look as though they can use a bit of help. I can provide that help and bring your roses back to glowing health." That sure has more going for it than, "Dear Home Gardener, perhaps your garden isn't as beautiful this year as usual. We offer a full range of garden supplies and expertise to aid you."

The point is that in a personal letter you can, should, and must include as much personal data as possible. Mention the person's name, of course. But also mention things about the person's life, business, car, home, or — if you're in the gardening business — the person's garden. By doing so, you will be whispering into someone's ear rather than shouting through a distant megaphone. Naturally, you can't mention personal things unless you know them. So do your homework and learn about your prospective customers: their working and living habits, their hopes and goals, their problems, especially their problems.

Solving problems will be a growth industry in the next century, indeed, forever. Businesses devoted to success are devoted to obtaining information about their prospects. You can get much of this information with the aid of a simple questionnaire, or by personal observation. Include your findings in your personal letter, and you'll be dazzled by the effect.

Doubling the effectiveness

No matter how motivating your personal letter may be, you can double its effectiveness if you do one of two things — or preferably both: (1) Write another personal letter within two weeks; (2) Call the prospect on the telephone.

When you do the repeat mailing, your letter can be brief and for the most part a reminder of your original letter. However, it should also have new information in it, more reasons to do business with you.

When you make the follow-up telephone call, refer to your letters. Ask if the person read them. Talk about the high points. Take advantage of the fact that your letter has broken the "stranger barrier" and you are now on speaking terms with your prospect. Use the phone to develop a relationship. The stronger that relationship, the likelier the person is to do business with you. That relationship will intensify if your letter includes a number of personal references. That will prove beyond doubt that you have sent a personal letter and not a clever mass-mailed flier.

Multiple mailings

These days, with more and more advertising pieces being mailed, people are literally bombarded with letters. One way to make your letter stand out is by making it part of a two- three- or four-letter campaign. Such multiple mailing campaigns are more expensive than single letters, but incredibly effective. Study after study confirms that people patronize businesses with which they are familiar. In the mid-1980s, a study was conducted to ascertain what factors influenced a buyer's purchase decision. Five thousand respondents indicated that confidence ranked first, quality second, selection third, service fourth, and price ninth.

But times have changed, and new research, conducted on the retail level, shows that price is now the biggest purchase motivation, quality the second, and environmental safety third. In another study of retail customers, price was first, selection second, quality third, location fourth, and service fifth. In a recession, when these 1990s studies were conducted, buying attitudes change. Confidence is not included on surveys. But be assured that people still won't buy the lowest-priced item if they don't trust what it buys.

The hot buttons of the nineties

The truth is that reasons for buying vary from industry to industry, from age group to age group, from target market to target market, from circumstance to circumstance. The leading appeal to a mother buying baby food would be different from the appeal to that same mother buying a sports car.

Forget personal letters altogether if you don't have a clear idea of the leading appeal to the people receiving them. Knowing it, along with as much personal data as possible, will enable you to gain the greatest benefit from your personal letter. And what might that be? It could be an order, a request for more data, a meeting with you. You've got to know what you want your personal letter to accomplish before you write it.

By sending out multiple mailings of personal letters, you build customer confidence through familiarity, paving your way to a relationship and a sale. Only an entrepreneur with a carefully targeted market can afford this luxury. A large company has too many prospects to engage in personal letter campaigns.

Understand that there is a difference between a personal letter and a personalized letter. The latter type is really a rather impersonal letter with a person's name in the salutation and within the body of the letter, along with some personal references. The personalization is accomplished by means of a word processor. A personal letter, on the other hand, is extremely personal. It is directed to one person and contains so many specific personal references and so much personal information that it cannot possibly be meant to be read by anyone but the person to whom it is addressed. It is signed in ink — smearable, fountain-pen ink. It has a P.S., possibly even handwritten. Naturally, it has a greater effect on a reader than a mere personalized letter.

One good way to do a personal mailing is to *make it unnecessary for your prospect to respond.* Oh, your letter might have an address or phone number, but in this case it should not ask for a

No response necessary

written reply or a phone call. It should not include a means for responding. It should whet the reader's appetite. However, it should also tell the reader that you will be telephoning within a week to set up an appointment or firm up a sale.

This accomplishes several things. It forces the reader to think about your offer — because it tells the reader that you'll be talking with him or her about it soon. It separates you from the many letter writers who leave everything to the discretion of the reader and require the reader to take action. You leave the reader waiting for *you* to take action, to provide the missing information. *And your letter prepares the reader for your phone call.* When you do call, you will not be a stranger but an expected caller.

This luxury of not including a response mechanism in your letters cannot be practiced by big firms, because it is too inefficient on a large scale. But it is the essence of guerrilla marketing, for it gives you an edge over mass marketers. And it goes to a unique extreme to gain attention.

Appeal to the reader's self-image

The tone of your letter should incorporate business matters and personal feelings and should appeal to the reader's self-image. If written to the president of a company, for example, your letter should mention the responsibilities of a president, the importance of the job, and the problems encountered, and it should be well written, employing a relatively sophisticated vocabulary.

How long should a typical personal letter be? One page. But don't worry about going longer than that if necessary. Be sure to convey all the information you feel you must convey, but do it as briefly as possible. A good rule is to make your personal letter short unless it must be long. And when I say short, I mean one full page of warm, personal, motivating, enticing copy. Because it is a personal letter, it need not have a brochure or circular enclosed — although it may.

Your letter should give the reader relevant information, data that he or she might otherwise not have known. Occasionally, I will remind a prospective advertising client of an upcoming event or a promotion that worked well for another client. A gardener might alert a prospect to a coming season that is right for the planting of certain species. A tutor might talk of advances in education. What it comes down to is *giving something to the reader rather than merely asking for something or selling something.* The information you impart freely might impress a reader with your intelligence, insight, or personality. The prospect might also utilize it with no recognition to you. But the rewards are usually worth the risks.

It is crucial to remember that the letter should not be about you, but about the reader. It should be in the reader's terms, about the reader's life or business. The letter should be loaded with potential benefits for the reader. The greater the number of benefits, the better. The classic advice about such letters is to remember the opera *Aida*. That's a memory crutch to remind you to get *a*ttention first, then *i*nterest the reader, then create a *d*esire, and finally make a call to *a*ction. But perhaps it's simpler just to remember to secure the reader's attention first, then state the benefits of doing business with you, and finally tell exactly what action the reader must take — make a phone call, write a letter, read page 15 of the Sunday paper, expect a phone call, anything, just as long as you say exactly what you want the reader to do.

The letter is not about you

From a purely technical standpoint, I offer these gems of personal-letter wisdom:

- Keep your letter to one page.
- Make your paragraphs short, five or six lines each.
- Indent your paragraphs.
- Don't overdo underlining, capital letters, or writing in margins.
- Do everything you can to keep the letter from looking like a printed piece.
- Sign your letter in a different-colored ink than it is typed in.
- Include a P.S. — and have it contain your most important point and a sense of urgency.

Personal-letter wisdom

Studies show that when people receive personal, and even printed, letters, they read the salutation first and the P.S. next. So your P.S. should contain your most attractive benefit, or your invitation to action, or anything that inspires a feeling of urgency. There is an art to writing a P.S., and you should not sell such a brief comment short. Some personal letters contain handwritten P.S. messages. I recommend this. A handwritten P.S. proves beyond doubt that you have created a one-of-a-kind letter, that it is not a mailing piece that went out to thousands of people.

The potent P.S.

As with a great advertisement, a great personal letter should tell the reader what you are about to say, then tell what you want to say, and finally tell what you just said. This may seem repetitious, but believe me, it's practical in these days of mailboxes filled with direct mail.

I have written myriad personal letters. Probably five in ten get ignored completely. Probably one in ten results in business. But the business from that one is usually so profitable that I can easily overlook the nine rejections. Ten percent is a great response rate compared with the 2 percent aimed for by many mass mailings. To give you some insight into how I create a personal letter, consider this one, to which I clipped a crisp one-dollar bill. I mailed it twelve times with zero business to me, then a thirteenth time that resulted in enough business to keep me grinning for months. It's over a decade old, yet versions of it continue to gain an impressive response. With the tactic of a million-dollar check by me (unsigned) instead of a buck, the letter pulled equally well. The gimmick is strong because it ties in with the letter's promise:

November 6, 1981

H. H. Thomas
Pacific Telephone & Telegraph
1313 53rd Street
Berkeley, CA 94705

Dear Mr. Thomas:

The dollar bill attached here symbolizes the thousands of dollars Pacific Telephone & Telegraph may be wasting by not utilizing the services of a prime quality free-lance writer.

During this year alone, I have accomplished writing projects for Visa, Crocker Bank, Pacific Plan, Gallo, Bank of America, the University of California, and the Public Broadcasting System. Although these companies do not ordinarily work with free-lancers, they did work with me.

In each case, the projects were completed successfully. In each case, I was given more assignments. There must be a reason why.

If you want to provide Pacific Telephone & Telegraph with the best free-lance writing available for any type of project — or if you have a seemingly impossible deadline — I hope you will give me a call.

I have enclosed a description of my background — just to inform you that I have won major writing awards in all the media and that I have served as a Vice-President and Creative Director at J. Walter Thompson, America's largest advertising agency. I guarantee you, however, that I am far more interested in winning sales than winning awards.

By your company settling for mere competent writing, or by having your writing assignments handled by traditional sources, you just might be wasting Pacific Telephone & Telegraph's money. A good number of the *Fortune* 500 companies have already figured that out.

Now, I look forward to hearing from you.

Very truly yours,
Jay Levinson

P.S. If you are not the person who assigns work to free-lancers, I would appreciate it if you would pass this letter (and this dollar) on to the person who does. Thank you very much.

It usually helps if you include a unique or informal enclosure with your letter. A newspaper article, a trade magazine article (especially in your prospect's trade), or a copy of your prospect's ad or a competitive ad helps a great deal, because the reader probably wants to read such material and will appreciate your sending it. In my case, the one-dollar enclosure served to separate my letter from the many others sent to the addressee. I'll bet many of them spent more than a dollar on a brochure. And I figure I'm the only one whose mailing piece was printed by the U.S. Treasury.

Would this letter be effective in the nineties? Judging by the way it has worked so far, it will be effective well into the 2000s. But I would make one change. After the fourth paragraph, I would write a separate paragraph, motivated by the recession, saying: "My fees are not low. But in a recession, you can't afford to take chances with less than the highest possible quality."

Timing

Timing is very important. Be careful you don't mail when everyone else is mailing. Try to time your mailing to coincide with a particular season or the advent of a new competitor, or when you hear word that your prospect may be in trouble and in the market for whatever it is you're offering. Marketing during a recession is very different from marketing during boom times.

During the bleak days of a recession:

Marketing in a recession

1. Market more to your customers and less to your prospects and the universe in general. Rely on, love, and make enticing offers to the people who have already learned to trust you — your customers.
2. Use the telephone as a follow-up weapon. We're talking relationships here, and if you've got one on paper, widen it

to include the telephone, a potent weapon in tough times. When the going gets tough, the tough make phone calls.

3. Eliminate any perceived risk of buying from you. Do it with a guarantee, a warranty, a deep commitment to service. Let the customer know that *the sale is not over until the customer is completely satisfied.* Now that is a risk remover, one guerrillas use to assuage skittish prospects.

4. Keep an eagle eye out for new profit-centers, fusion marketing opportunities, cooperative ventures. Because others are also suffering through the recession, there's a good chance they'll be willing to go along with your idea for a collaborative effort.

5. Instead of shrinking your offerings, go against the grain and expand them. Do what you can to increase the size of your purchases, your selection of profit-producing items, the services you offer.

6. Let your customers know that you are fully aware of the recession and are basing your prices and offerings upon it, making your business a more sensible place to patronize than ever before.

It is important to mail your letter to the person who ought to be reading it. Find out who that is by studying the appropriate directories at your library or, better still, by phoning all the companies to which you hope to mail. When in doubt, mail your letter to the company president, who will either *be* the person you want to reach or will see to it that the right person does read your letter. It's worth a call to the company's phone operator to find out the president's name and its correct spelling. You can be sure that if the president asks a subordinate to read something, it will get read.

With a word processor and laser printer you can send out several thousand letters or more, all of which will appear to be personal letters, for all can be personalized with appropriate comments. But keep in mind that these are *not* personal letters. Only a letter that is chock-full of personal references is really a personal letter.

These you can send out in smaller numbers. And they will give you, the entrepreneur, a big advantage over the huge corporation. So take advantage of this valuable tool if you can. If you do so, you will be practicing guerrilla marketing with maximum skill.

11
Telephone Marketing:
Dialing for Dollars

AMONG THE MANY FORMS of marketing is telephone marketing. In 1982, telephone marketing surpassed direct mail in revenues spent, and the gap has been widening ever since. In 1990, half of all goods and services sold were sold by phone. Telephone marketing is used both by the big guys and by budding entrepreneurs. *Forbes* magazine predicted that telephone marketing would be a prime marketing force in the latter years of this century, and they seem to be on the money.

Currently, there are three ways you can engage in telephone marketing. The first way is individual phone calls made by you or a member of your company. The second way is mass telemarketing, which is carried out by firms specializing in it or by dedicated telemarketing departments and is directed at thousands of potential customers at a time. The third way is by computer. Computerized calling machines actually call prospects, deliver tape-recorded sales pitches, and even pause during their messages so that prospects can answer questions and place orders. This method may be a bit impersonal, and many consider it an invasion of privacy, but it is commonly practiced. And for many a company, it works. Machines aren't hurt by rejection.

A telephone call takes less time than a canvass, is more personal than a letter, costs less than both (unless it's long-distance), and provides you with fairly close personal contact with your prospect. It is hardest to say no to a person's face. It is less hard to say no to a person's voice. And it is least hard to say no to a person's letter.

Guerrillas use telemarketing to make their ads and other marketing efforts work harder. They know that 7 percent of people hang up on all telemarketers, that 42 percent hang up on some telemarketers, and that 51 percent listen to all telemarketers. Bless that teensy majority.

What happens to telemarketers

What kind of companies use telemarketing? Mainly they are businesses that sell to other businesses, but often it is a business out to sell directly to a consumer. The ones that succeed plan the entire phone call: the objective, the words spoken, the mood and tone, and the follow-up.

As with advertising, telephone marketing should be part of an overall marketing program. And it should be a continuing effort. One phone call isn't enough. If a member of your company makes the phone calls, certain incentive policies should be instituted. For instance, you should always pay your designated callers both by the completed call and by the completed sale. Even if you use a salaried employee, add incentive bonuses to the salary.

How guerrillas talk

No matter who does the calling, proper voice training is a good idea. Talk clearly. Use short sentences. Talk loud enough, but not directly into the mouthpiece; talking across the mouthpiece gives the most effective voice transmission. Your voice should project authority and warmth while instilling trust. Your message should be stated as concisely as possible. Whatever you do, don't read from a script. However, research shows that it's always a good idea to memorize a script, changing any words that feel "uncomfortable." The script must be so well memorized that the words sound as though you know them by heart, as natural as the Pledge of Allegiance. Don't use words that feel strange to say. Find words and phrases that come naturally to you. Guerrillas are in full control of their telemarketing and do not recite awkward speeches to their prospects. Doing so is bad business — more personal than a computer pitch — but still not worth doing if not done right.

Memorized words are best

Studies in varied industries consistently show that a memorized telemarketing presentation always produces better results than the same presentation from an outline. It may be more humanistic to let the caller use his or her own words, but few callers have the ability to summon the right ones. Gone are the days when it was recommended that callers use an outline, or "thought flow." Still, the more naturally conversant you sound, the more sales you'll make. And that takes practice.

If you are more comfortable using an outline to structure your phone presentations, be sure to heed the following guidelines. If the outline is longer than one page, there is probably too much in it and you should try to streamline it. An outline not only creates a structure for your thoughts and ideas, but also helps keep the call on track when the person at the other end redirects it. Even if you do work from an outline — against my recommendation — it's still a good idea to write a script of a phone call. Once you have written the script, you should do three things with it: (1) Record it. See what it sounds like. After all, you'll be using "ear" words that are heard, rather than "eye" words that are seen. There's a big, big difference. (2) Make sure the recorded script sounds like a conversation and not like an ad. Leave room for the person being called to respond. (3) Make it a point not to restate the script but to rephrase it. State the same selling points. Present them in the same order. But use words with which you are comfortable. Your telephone outline should be able to accommodate several situations. After all, if your prospect decides to buy just after you've started, you should be prepared to close the sale and end the conversation.

Notice how your friends, and probably even you yourself, assume different voice personalities when speaking on the phone. This is subtle, but it's there. Try to eliminate that telephone personality and bring out your most conversational qualities by actually practicing on the phone — talking to a tape recorder or to a friend. If you're going to do a good amount of telephone marketing, engage in role-playing, with you as the customer and a friend or associate as you. Then switch roles. Role-playing gives you a lot of insight into your offering and your message. Keep doing this until you are completely satisfied with your presentation.

Your telephone personality

Many telephone solicitations crumble when objections are made. These objections are really opportunities in disguise. Many successful telephone salespeople (and nontelephone salespeople) are able to close sales when handling objections. In fact, "close on the objection" is a sales credo for many pro sellers. One way to handle an objection is to rephrase it. Merely by doing that, you can sometimes dissipate it. "We're already buying from

The value of objections

someone else," says the person at the other end. "Oh, you're completely satisfied with the price, quality, and service you're currently receiving and feel there's no room for improvement?" By rephrasing the objection, you not only defuse it but create an opportunity for yourself.

When calling a potential customer, try to establish a real relationship with that person. You may not ever speak to him or her again, but you should try to create a bond between the two of you. Do it with a couple of personal questions or observations. Ask the person about some non – job-related subject. Relate as human beings before you relate as salesperson and prospect. You **Find the** probably have some interests in common. Meet on that common **common ground** ground if possible. Even though the two of you should relate as people, make no mistake: Your purpose in making the phone call is to make a sale. So go for it. As with the standard canvass or sales presentation, think in terms of contact, presentation, and close.

Remember, your contact should be brief and warm. Your presentation should be concise, yet loaded with references to benefits. And your close should be clear and definite. Don't pussyfoot. There is nothing wrong in most instances with asking for the sale. Just don't do it in such a way that a yes or no answer can be given. Close by saying something like, "What will be the most convenient way for you to pay for this, check or credit card?"

A script that The following script is from a telephone marketing program **worked** that was used in conjunction with a direct-mail program. This makes for a potent combination. These days, with direct-mail advertising growing so rapidly, it makes a lot of sense to follow up a mailing with a phone call. For guerrillas, it's almost mandatory with big-ticket sales. In this instance, the mailing was followed two weeks later by a phone call. A week later, another call was made. The program worked. Direct mail alone would not have worked.

The one-two Hello, Mr. _____ ? This is _____ . I'm calling for the Wilford **punch** Hotel in Los Angeles. Have you ever been to the Wilford? _____ When was the last time you were in Los Angeles? _____ Recently, we sent you an invitation. Did you receive it? _____ Are you the person who makes out-of-town meeting arrangements for your firm, or is it someone else? _____ Do you plan to take us up on our special offer now, or do you plan to request more information? _____

As you may recall, we are offering special prices and complimentary services to companies that hold meetings at the Wilford between April first and June thirtieth. Will your company be holding a meeting in Los Angeles during that time? _____ Did you like the special offer we made to you? _____ Do you have any questions about it? _____ Do you usually have meetings in hotels such as the Wilford? _____ What size meetings? _____ Where do you ordinarily meet? _____ I think you might be interested in holding a meeting at the Wilford. Don't forget, during the period from April first to June thirtieth, we're offering:

- Special room rates
- Complimentary meeting room
- Complimentary wine with dinner
- One free room for every fifteen booked
- A complimentary coffee break daily
- Discounts on audiovisual equipment
- Preregistration for your people
- A suite for the meeting planner

Doesn't all that sound good? _____ You get all these benefits with a minimum of only fifteen guest rooms.

Is there anything else we might offer you? _____ When do you plan to hold your next meeting? _____ When would be the best time to arrange a reservation for your group at the Wilford? _____ Would you like to make the arrangements right now or later? _____ When? _____ Is there any other person at your company that you suggest I contact? _____ Thanks very much for taking this time to speak with me. _____ Good-bye.

As you can see, a good phone script calls for lots of questions, so that the person called will feel he or she is part of the process and will not feel "talked at." Whatever you say on the phone should be part of your overall marketing and creative plans, so measure your scripts against your marketing strategies.

The downside to telemarketing is that most calls are poorly scripted. It takes talent to create a good call. That means more than a way with words. A guerrilla telemarketing script helps telemarketers overcome employee turnover, despondent moods, lack of enthusiasm, and rejection daze. It keeps callers on track and ensures that prospects receive accurate data — all the while allowing for natural telephone conversation. It even raises and answers objections.

Most scripts fail because they don't give enough credence to

**The downside
of scripts**

the very important human element, and because telemarketing is now regarded as suspicious by an increasingly sophisticated public. Be sure your scripts are tight, yet loaded with warmth. Hard to do? You bet it is.

The guerrilla script

Be sure your script has tons of humanity built into it, with room for give-and-take. Let the telemarketer add his or her own words and phrases to the script. The more comfortable the telemarketer, the more relaxed the prospect. Relaxed prospects are good to have.

Keep your script to a maximum of one page, single-spaced. Paragraph one introduces the caller and the company. Paragraph two gives the reason for the call or makes the offer. Paragraph three highlights the benefits of the offer. Paragraphs four and five close the sale or set the stage for the next step, possibly a personal appointment.

Your script should contain a good reason for your call and a way to get through the secretary barrier. You have fifteen to twenty seconds to gain or lose your prospect's attention, so don't waste one second or one word. Guerrilla scripts contain about four interest-creating comments and flow directly to the benefits. They build rapport right off with questions.

Good scripts have systems to handle objections to the sale and to close the sale. You'll need a system to test and improve your script. More about this later.

Get set to be rejected

You've got to be prepared for massive amounts of rejection when you embark upon a telephone marketing program. For this reason, employee turnover in telephone marketing firms is tremendous. On the other hand, telephone marketing is so instantly effective for some companies that they set up what are known as boiler-room operations. In these operations, several people gather in one large room, which is often partitioned. Each has a phone. And each can see the others. Each person makes call after call, trying to make as many sales in as short a time as possible. When a sale is made, a signal is given, such as an upraised fist. Seeing this signal, the other phoners give a reciprocal signal to show that they recognize the success. This seems to give a lift to the group morale and helps the telephone salespeople deal with the horribly high number of rejections. It also seems to nourish enthusiasm.

The boiler room

You can set up your own boiler-room operation. Or you can hire one. Many telephone marketing firms exist — more now than ever, because just two decades ago none existed. These firms are permanent boiler-room operations. They operate from their own facilities, using their own scripts, tailored for your needs, and their own telephone sales pros. They charge by the hour and by the call. And many companies find them well worth the expense. If you ever consider establishing your own boiler-room setup, first look into the economics of hiring an outside firm with a going operation. These firms can put their facilities to work for you or they can set up an operation for you, training your people to be masters at telephone selling.

One of the great advantages of telephone marketing is that you can obtain an instant response to your offer. You can deal with objections and overcome them. You can, by using a boiler-room operation, talk to literally thousands of people per day. In doing so, you can categorize the people you have called as customers, near customers, and noncustomers. In rare instances, you can accomplish all of your marketing by phone. Some companies do.

Such marketing works far better for businesses selling to other businesses than it does for companies selling directly to consumers. This is because consumers at home have little time for business, but businesspeople in their place of business do have a bit of time for business matters, even those that come by phone. High-ticket sales are one of the reasons for telemarketing success in business-to-business transactions. Whereas with individual consumers, profits tend to be far lower, making telemarketing to them less cost-efficient.

Be sure you don't expect telemarketing to do more than it can do. A financial organization mailed a letter to its prospects, offering a free gift to those who requested a brochure. Telemarketing to the brochure requesters netted many personal appointments. It was during these appointments that sales were closed. Although sales may be closed on the phone, often telemarketing is merely a crucial cog in a big machine.

To succeed with telemarketing, know which benefits turn on your prospective customers. Give prime emphasis to the benefits you feel have the most impact. Be sure you are speaking with the right person. Make a specific offer — preferably a special offer that is not available to all people at all times.

The more people you call, the more sales you'll close. Of every 20 people you *call*, you'll probably make contact with only

Succeeding on the phone

about five on your first try. The others will be busy, sick, away, on the phone, or otherwise indisposed. Of every 20 people you *reach*, you may close a sale with only one right there on the phone. So you can see that you'll have to make about 100 calls to close one sale. That might sound like a lot, but to a true-blue telephone marketing pro it means that a mere 1000 phone calls will result in ten sales. Figuring an average of three minutes per call (some will take up to ten minutes, but most will take less than one minute), this means that 50 hours of calling will result in ten sales.

This also means that you'll either spend one hard workweek on the phone, or you'll hire someone to be on that phone for you. If your profit per sale is great enough, you should give serious consideration to marketing this way. If ten sales aren't nearly enough, perhaps you should think about using other marketing methods. For some entrepreneurs, ten sales in one week means joy, wealth, and fulfillment. If that's you, and you feel telephone marketing makes sense for your offering, utilize it before your competitors discover its powerful capabilities.

If you have an in-house calling department, don't let them call for more than four hours a day. The rejection rate is so high that it may cause death — for all I know. I do know that so much rejection dampens enthusiasm, sometimes permanently.

Three things to do

To help you get your act together, find out what's new in telemarketing by contacting AT&T and your own local telephone company, both of which conduct regular telemarketing seminars (a guerrilla activity by King Kong – sized guerrillas). Three things that both groups will tell you is to test, to test, and to test. What they are referring to are your scripts, your callers, and your target markets.

Recognize that although you are pleased with the results of your telemarketing — and you will be if you combine it with other guerrilla marketing methods — it can always be improved. That's why guerrillas never stop testing their scripts. They will constantly experiment with new words, phrases, and ideas. As a result, their response rates continue to rise.

This chapter has discussed only part of telemarketing, the part known as outbound telemarketing, where *you* make the phone call. An entire other part, inbound telemarketing — how you handle calls to you — involves proper telephone demeanor and is more in the domain of large businesses than guerrilla small businesses.

Still, you should know that a toll-free number can increase your response rate by 30 to 700 percent. If you deal with local prospects and customers only, you should avoid having a toll-free number since people like dealing with local companies — it's that confidence factor again. Should you feel you must have a toll-free number, be warned that if it spells out a word, people probably won't write it down because they figure they'll remember it. But the truth is they won't. That's why the toll-free phone number for the free catalogue offered by Guerrilla Marketing International is 1-800-748-6444. I give that number when I give talks on guerrilla marketing, and people write it down. If I said a word instead of all those digits, they'd probably trust their memories and we'd get fewer calls.

Toll-free numbers

Telemarketing is a superb mini-marketing weapon, already doubling as a maxi-marketing weapon, and I encourage you to give it a try, especially if you're selling to businesses. In 1990, the average telephone transaction — contact to closed sale — worked out at higher than $300 per call when one business telemarketed to another. Maybe you can improve on that figure. This guerrilla sure hopes so.

12
Circulars and Brochures:
How, Where, and When

LET'S GET THIS STRAIGHT right at the outset: There is not much difference between a circular and a flier, but a brochure is a different kind of animal. To me, circulars and fliers are short and single-minded; a brochure is longer and more detailed than either. My dictionaries don't shed much more light on the subject, so we'll have to live with my distinctions.

Distribution   There are several ways to distribute circulars and brochures. They may be mailed alone or as part of a mailing package; placed in mailboxes; slipped under doors or windshield wipers; handed out at street corners, at trade shows, or wherever lots of prospects congregate; given to prospects and/or customers; placed in racks that say "Take One" or on counters for general distribution; or even dropped from airplanes. I don't recommend the latter.

If you're going to distribute many pieces, make them circulars, because circulars are less expensive per piece. If you are distributing relatively few pieces, you might opt for the more expensive brochures.

Form and content   The simplest form of circular is a single sheet of paper, printed on one side. Printing on both sides makes matters and format a tad more complex. Printing on both sides of two pieces of paper — each folded in half — makes a booklet, which I call a brochure if it is loaded with information, printed or visual. If it isn't, it's not really a brochure, but a folded circular. Some brochures run as long as twenty-four pages. When planning to produce such materials, remember that when you fold a sheet of paper in two, you have a total of four pages (two on each side).

So generally you must think in terms of four-page units. Brochures are ordinarily four or eight or twelve pages. Some brochures have panels that fold rather than pages that turn. Usually, these are six-panel brochures — three panels on each side. If you start with a standard 8½ x 11 piece of paper, folding it twice makes it ready to become a six-panel brochure and the ideal size for a standard #10 envelope.

The format isn't nearly as important as the content. And the content must be factual information, enlivened with a touch of style and romance. Unlike ads, which must flag a person's attention, a brochure or circular already has that attention. So its primary job is to inform with the intention of selling. Most brochures, and some circulars, use artwork. Sometimes this is intended to keep the piece visually interesting. But most of the time, its purpose is to explain, inform, and sell.

What's the big idea?

When writing a circular, think first of the basic idea you wish to express. Then try to marry a picture (art or photograph) to a set of words. After you've stated your idea as briefly as possible, try to explain more fully what you are offering. Always be sure to include information about how to get in touch with you: address, phone number, place to find you.

George's circular

I know an entrepreneurial-minded contractor named George. He markets his services well, and decided he'd improve business even more by distributing a circular or a brochure. Here's the way he proceeded. Being no dummy, George started out with a circular to see how this marketing vehicle would work for him. If it worked well, he might upgrade it to a brochure. On the circular, he had a drawing done of a man (George) doing five tasks at the same time in front of a house. Above the drawing, he listed his company name, which, incidentally, made a dandy headline for his circular: Let George Do It. Beneath that headline and picture, he briefly stated his offering:

George builds sun decks and patios.
George installs skylights and hot tubs.
George paints and puts up wallpaper.
George does masonry and electrical work.
George also designs and makes building plans.

LET GEORGE DO IT!

Call George at 555-5656 any time any day.
All work guaranteed. Contractor's License #54-45673.

Not very fancy, but quite explicit. The cost for George to write this circular was nil. An art student did the illustration for $50. And the cost to produce about 5000 of the circulars, including paper, was another $100. So George ended up spending about $150, which comes to three cents per circular. Even if printing costs had been higher — and they are — George would have spent less than a nickel per circular. And without paying for color, George was able to get a colorful circular by the ingenious use of colored ink on a colored paper stock — dark blue ink on light tan stock.

George then distributed his circulars by several methods: He mailed 1000; he placed 1000 on auto windshields (he had a high school student do some of this for him); he distributed 1000 more at a home show in his area; he handed out 1000 more at a local flea market; and he held on to 1000 to give to satisfied customers to pass on to their friends and neighbors. Being bright as a penny when it comes to saving money, the enterprising George also asked each of his customers where they had heard of him. When they said, "I saw your flier," George asked where they got it. This way, he learned which of the five methods of circular distribution was most effective.

Now that's guerrilla marketing. Not expensive whatsoever. But very effective. One job could recoup for George his entire marketing budget for circulars. And since 5000 circulars were distributed, you have to believe that George got more than one job.

George's brochure
Perhaps George will decide to put out a brochure someday. As a first step in planning a good one, he'd think in terms of photography, so that he could show actual pictures of work he has accomplished. And because he has such a comprehensive offering, he'd figure that an eight-page brochure was needed to do the trick. He'd use a simple 8½ x 5½ size, which is half the size of a standard 8½ x 11 sheet of paper. Unless the brochure was full-color — a good idea because color increases retention rate by 57 percent and proclivity to buy by 41 percent — all type and photos would be in black ink. The paper stock, either glossy or not, would be white or some other light color.

He'd plan to use the same drawing on the cover that he used on his circular. After all, if it worked once, it ought to work again. And it makes good economic sense. So his cover would show his drawing, list his company name (which fortunately doubles as a headline and a brochure title), and maybe, but not definitely, list the other copy points from his circular. Let's say he does list them, since he wants to impart as much information as possible. *Repetition in marketing is far more of a good thing than a bad thing.*

Following his cover page, page one, his second page might list a bit about George. It would indicate his experience, his training, and jobs he has accomplished, and would list his skills and offerings. It might even include a photo of him. It would lead up to the other things he is about to say.

Page three would show photos of a sun deck and a patio, and would give a description, about five sentences long, of George's capabilities in this area. Page four would show photos of a skylight and a hot tub that George installed. Again, five or six sentences would indicate his expertise. Page five would show photos of a room that George painted and another room that George papered. It would also include a bit of copy attesting to George's talent at painting and papering. Page six would feature photos of houses with masonry and electrical work by George. One would be an exterior shot and the other an interior shot. Again, copy would describe the work accomplished. Each of these pages, by the way, would repeat the short copy lines from the cover. For example, the seventh page, showing a gorgeous room addition designed and built by George, would have as its headline, "George also makes building plans and building designs." A few sentences of copy would follow the photo. The copy would not have to be brief. Don't forget, the purpose of the brochure is to inform.

Finally, George's eighth page, the back cover, would give the name of his company, his phone number, his contractor's license number, and probably a repeat of the best photo from the interior of the brochure. Such a brochure might cost George as much as one dollar per unit. But it would be worth it, when you consider George's profit per sale.

A solar-heating company for which I created a brochure had a special problem. They realized that a brochure would help their business, but the technology in their industry was changing so rapidly that they were reluctant to commit themselves to producing one. Solution: I created an eight-page brochure with a pocket inside the back cover. Within the eight pages, the brochure dealt with all of the aspects of solar technology that were not changing: its economy, its cleanliness, its responsibility to the environment, its acceptance and success in all parts of the world. Within the pocket were inserted separate sheets dealing with specific equipment as technology marched forward, as it has. These could be replaced at will. Price lists, also replaceable at a whim, could be put there as well. This enabled the company to have a brochure and flexibility at the same time.

Let's look at another example. A jewelry-making firm in San Francisco manufactured beautiful but very expensive jewelry. To add an element of value, it produced a lavish brochure — full-color, glossy, and photographed in the most glamorous parts of San Francisco. Each two-page spread contained one gorgeous photo of the San Francisco area and one photo of an item of jewelry. This lent an air of value to each piece of jewelry that could not have been created with a single photo. It connected the jewelry store with San Francisco, where tourism is the largest industry. A brochure was just the ticket.

One of my clients sent a photographer on a dream assignment: to visit Mexico and shoot photos of a wide variety of villas and condominiums that my client was renting to people for vacation use. These photos were later made the basis for a colorful brochure. Without the photos, the brochure could only have dealt with villa and condo vacations in a theoretical sense. The photos brought the theory to vibrant life. The brochure helped the company quadruple its sales. Without a vehicle to show the many villas and condos, complete with beaches, pools, balconies, lush living rooms, and spacious bedrooms, the company could not have made its point. Less than a brochure could not have done the job.

A brochure success story

Still another company was able to grow from tiny to tremendous merely by the proper use of a brochure. The company owned the patent on a new product that replaced the old-fashioned blowtorch. But it couldn't communicate all of the advantages of its product with ads or letters or phone calls. Personal demonstrations were impractical because of logistics problems. A brochure was the answer. It was incredibly detailed, listing all of the advantages of the product and all of the famous-name companies using it, and showing several exciting shots of the product in use. The brochure included a pageful of testimonials from satisfied users, and it described the technical data in such detail that even the most nitpicking engineer would be impressed. In addition, it was very handsome. This inspired confidence in the company, and it grew like Topsy. To this day, the company's primary marketing tool is that brochure.

And so it is with a number of other companies. They have a story that does not translate well in advertising but becomes brilliantly clear when the details, both verbal and graphic, are communicated in a brochure. If yours is one of those companies, you can afford to spend a great deal of your marketing budget producing a knockout brochure. The cost, including everything, runs anywhere from $500 to $50,000. But don't let the $50,000 figure dazzle you. That's only $4166.67 per month, a lot less than many companies spend on media advertising alone. Perhaps you won't even need the mass media. Perhaps a brochure will do the trick for you.

Although some businesses benefit almost every time they give away their brochure, there are times not to give one away. If you have a store and distribute brochures to your potential customers, that gives them an excuse not to buy. They can tell you that they want to look over your brochure before buying. I advise my clients, except those selling very expensive items, *not* to give their brochures to shoppers — only to people who have purchased or to people who are on their way out anyhow.

I also advise people who run newspaper or magazine ads that contain a lot of information to consider using those ads as brochures. Merely reprint them and add front and rear covers by printing on the back of the folded-in-half advertisement. Often the magazine will do this for you for peanuts.

Brochures for peanuts

If you don't have the budget for large ads, you might consider running small ads offering your free brochure. I know a man who earns his entire income (a six-figure income, I might add) by running tiny ads in myriad publications, offering his free brochure in each ad. The people who request the brochure are serious prospects. They took the time to write for the brochure. They are interested in what he's offering. My friend's brochure does his entire selling job for him. It describes his offer, gives the details, and asks for the order. His ads and his brochures are his only marketing tools, and he is very successful as a one-man show. This demonstrates how important a brochure can be.

A mighty important point: When printing your business cards, think of them as mini-brochures. On them print your name, address, phone number, logo, and theme line, of course, but also include brief body copy — as much as you can fit. Some clever entrepreneurs hand out double-size business cards, folded in half. The outside of the cards has the standard business-card information. The inside has a headline, beneath which are listed several features and benefits, products and services. These cards look like business cards but work like brochures. And brochures work well.

To see what a twenty-first-century business card will look like, make a simple phone call to InfoCard at 512-327-3385 and request a sample. It will be sure to plant healthy ideas in your mind.

Electronic brochures

If anything does a brochure's job better than a brochure, it is an *electronic brochure* — a five- to nine-minute version of a printed brochure. The cost of duplicating videos is under $2 and falling. The cost of producing videos is $100 to $10,000 per minute. The lower cost is if you do it yourself — not recommended. The higher number is for letting a first-rate video production company handle it. Guerrillas find a happy medium somewhere between the two.

The video brochure

A *video brochure* — and about 80 percent of Americans have access to a VCR — will give more of an impression of worth and value than a printed version. Prospects will view it, then probably view it again with one or more people. They may give it to a friend or associate, not likely with a printed brochure. The purpose of such a brochure is just the same as a printed one — using words, pictures, music, emotions, intellect, demonstration, and believability to create a desire to buy your product or service. Don't let the medium create the delusion that you're now in show business. Guerrillas don't fall into that enticing trap.

Guerrillas do not send video brochures to people on a mailing list, such as huge corporations can and a few automobile manufacturers have done. One car maker sent a video introducing the local dealer's name at the beginning, starring the car with glitzy cinematography in the middle, then ending with *the recipient's name superimposed across the video image* — it was the first of many personalized video brochures. Guerrillas like the idea of personalization and are wowed by the potency of video information. Still, they send their video brochures *only to people*

By request only *who request them.*

People learn of videos through magazines, direct mailings, trade shows, and other modes of communication. When they request one, it should be sent free, with no obligation. Whatever you do, send a personal letter along with it, just as you would with a printed brochure. Follow within ten days with a phone call or letter. A request for a video should be construed as the first step in buying. Be sure to follow up — don't lose the momentum you've created.

Maybe you don't require visual input to tell your business story. Perhaps you can do it with words. Put your words onto tape and offer an *audio brochure*. About 95 percent of Americans have access to an audiocassette player. A growing number of Americans have commutes of over half an hour. Instead of listening to the radio, they'll probably listen to your five- to fifteen-minute tape. They know it's a way to learn while saving time.

The audio brochure

Create a video brochure according to a strategy, just as you'd create a printed brochure. Only, say as much as you can *visually*. Realize that your visuals will communicate more powerfully than your verbiage, so keep the visual excitement to a maximum. Be sure the visuals pertain to your company and aren't merely special visual effects substituting for a solid idea.

A video brochure is jazzy and more dynamic than a printed piece, but its purpose is still to make a sale, either all by itself, in concert with a sales rep who is present while the tape is being shown, or in tandem with a direct-mail letter, card, or a phone call. In numbers there is strength. In visuals there is strength. As great as your video brochure may be, it is only as powerful as your idea.

Electronic and printed brochures can be expensive mistakes, so don't say anything you'll want to change within a year. Do it once and do it right. Then do your darnedest to follow up on everyone who requests any kind of brochure.

13
Classified Advertising Hints: Making Small Beautiful

WHEN YOU THINK OF CLASSIFIED advertising, you probably think in terms of finding a job, looking for a car, selling a sofa, buying a boat, or locating a house or apartment. Think again. Classified advertising can also be used to support a business. And many a flourishing enterprise exists primarily on the pulling power of classified ads.

On a random weekday, my local newspaper featured classified ads for a ticket-selling firm, a number of attorneys, an advertising medium, a pregnancy consultation center, a credit association, a fortune teller, a job-finding service, several books, a game arcade, a psychic adviser, a rent-a-mailbox firm, a ghostwriter, several introduction services, a group of escort services, two full columns of massage businesses, one and a half columns of firms offering loans, unique telegram companies, hairstylists, barbers, moving companies, auto transport firms, travel agencies, calligraphers, gobs of home-service entrepreneurs, tropical fish stores, pawnbrokers, coin and stamp dealers, antique dealers, auctioneers, TV dealers, computer equipment stores, musical-instrument stores, a horse ranch, boat dealers, a flying school, two résumé-writing services, loads of schools, tutors, employment agencies, auto and truck dealers, motorcycle dealers, hotels, rooming houses, bed and breakfast places, rest homes, guest houses, realtors, business brokers, motels, and mobile-home dealers. And this was a weekday, not even a Sunday. I wouldn't even attempt to list the entrepreneurial enterprises using the Sunday classified section. Do your own homework and see for yourself — in your own community.

If all of these entrepreneurs and/or businesses use the classified section, it makes sense for you to consider it, too. I notice that many of these advertisers have had ads in the classified section for more than ten years. And I know that they wouldn't spend their money there if they weren't getting handsome returns.

In my files, I have magazines with far more classified ads than are in the newspaper just mentioned. And I'm sure you know of newspapers — many of them, and the number keeps rising — that consist of nothing but classified ads. Obviously, classified ads work as a marketing medium. And if you can see any advantage for your company in using this medium, a bit of investigation and investment on your part is worthwhile.

Generally, there are three places you can run classified ads: in magazines, in daily newspapers, and in classified-ad newspapers. If your offering requires proximity to your customers, forget the magazines. And if your offering is national in character, forget the newspapers. There is little likelihood that you'll want to run classified ads in both local newspapers and national magazines — unless the papers you select are in localities spread throughout the country, and you want to combine that advertising with national magazine advertising.

Where to run your ads

You are probably noticing that more and more magazines are offering classified advertising. They know that the many new small businesses just plain can't afford a display ad, and they have this deep longing for revenue. So they offer classified advertising sections for entrepreneurs. Look long and deeply into this because the cost is relatively low to get into a major magazine and because the classified section is generally at the back of the magazine.

Guerrilla hint: Because 61 percent of Americans read magazines from the back to the front, your economical classified ad will have a decent shot at being read.

As you may have heard, it doesn't cost an arm and leg to run a classified ad. And you'll usually be offered a frequency discount. This means that if your five-line classified ad costs you $20 to run one time, it will cost only, say, $18 per insertion if you run it three times, and only $15 per insertion if you run it five times. The more frequently you run it, the lower your cost

How much it costs

per insertion. This is called a frequency discount. Classified ad charges are based upon the number of words, the number of lines, or the number of inches. It depends upon the publication. The cost of the ad is also based upon the circulation of the publication — both in quantity and quality.

Many people read the classified ads each day. Some read them to find specific bargains. Others read them merely to browse via the newspaper. And still others find them the most fascinating part of the newspaper. Check them yourself. See which ads draw your attention. Also notice which classified-ad categories catch your attention. By reading through the ads, you'll get a sense of whether or not your business can profit from this method of marketing. You'll also begin to learn, by osmosis, what to say in a classified ad and what not to say. Although classified ads are short, fraught with abbreviations, and devoid of illustrations, they are not as simple as they may seem. If you decide to give the classified-ad section a go, there are a few concepts that you should keep in mind.

Writing strong ads For one thing, keep your headline short — and be sure you do have a headline, printed in all capital letters. Don't use abbreviations unless you are sure that people will understand them. While living in England, my wife and I searched for an apartment by scanning the classified ads. Many said that the rental included CCF&F. At first, we were completely thrown by that. Do you know what it means? Later, we learned that it stands for "carpets, curtains, fixtures, and fittings." We also learned that most Britishers already know that.

Don't use esoteric terms in your ads unless you're sure that most of your readers (99 percent) know the meaning. Write in short sentences. Try to sound more like a human being than a want ad. And be sure you include a way to contact you. More than once I've seen an ad with no phone number or address.

In most instances, publications have people who can help you word your want ads. I suggest that you use these people as guides but do not slavishly follow their advice. If they were brilliant writers, they'd probably be paid for their writing and not for taking want ads. If you are a good writer, write your own classified-ad copy. If not, go to a pro. Don't rely on the person who takes the ads to write your copy, but do rely on that person's experience.

Word your ad in such a way that it contrasts with other ads

in the same section. And choose that section very, very carefully. Some newspapers have categories that do not appear in other papers. Such categories include: attorneys, announcements, Christmas items, computers, and so forth. Be sure that you advertise in the right category. Make that plural. You may want to place your ad in more than one category.

Strange as it may seem, classified ads often outdraw display ads. So don't think that just because an ad has no picture and doesn't cost much it's not going to be effective. Many companies run display ads and classified ads in the same newspapers on the same day. They claim that the ads reach different classes of consumers.

I earned about $500 per month for at least a dozen years working about half an hour per month. I did it with a classified ad. I ran the same ad, with minor changes in wording, all twelve years. After I had been working for a few years as a free-lance writer, I'd learned quite a few important things about free-lancing, things nobody had ever told me, things that weren't written in books. So I wrote a book and published it myself. I called the book *Secrets of Successful Free-Lancing*. And although it had but forty-three pages, I priced it at $10. The reason I charged $10 was because I sincerely felt the book was worth it. The book cost me about $1 to print, including type and binding. Advertising ran about $3.33 per book. So I figured that I made $5.67 per book. Here's a sample of the classified ad I ran:

> I EARN MORE AS A FREE-LANCER THAN I DID AS VP/CREATIVE DIRECTOR AT J. WALTER THOMPSON. I loved my JWT days. But I love now more. I live where I want. I work only 3 days a week. I work from my home and take lots of vacations. To do the same, read my incisive book, *Secrets of Successful Free-lancing*. Send $10 to Prosper Press, 123 Alto Street, San Rafael, CA 94902. $11 refund if you're not completely satisfied.

A money-making ad

Notice how my ad used standard language rather than want-ad language. When I've run other classified ads using "people talk," I've also had good results. A regularly worded ad appearing in a sea of want-ad-worded ads tends to stand out.

The cost of the ad was $36 for one inch in the publication in which it originally appeared. And the entire ad fit in one inch in the classified section. For every dollar I invested in the ad, I averaged $3 in sales, $2.50 in profits. It cost fifty cents to mail it, envelope included.

For me, the biggest challenge (and biggest problem) was to find enough places to run the ad. After all, everybody isn't a prospect for a book on free-lancing. I ran the ad in three advertising trade magazines, two art-director publications, two writers' magazines, the *Wall Street Journal*, and four opportunity magazines. Some of these publications drew a great response every time I ran the ad — and I ran it every three months. Others didn't pull well for me, so I discarded them from my schedule. But by sticking with the four publications that worked, I was able to bring in around $500 per month in profits — after paying for the ads, the books, and the mailing. I had all the orders mailed directly to a mail-order-fulfillment house that mailed out the books on the day orders were received, put the names of the people who ordered into a computer, and sent me the checks weekly — coded so that I knew which publications were working best.

People in the mail-order book business report that a 5 percent request rate for refunds is about par for the course. My requests for refunds were 1.2 percent. And don't forget, I offered an $11 refund for a forty-three-page $10 book.

The half-hour per month I spent on this business was used to keep tallies on the pulling power of the various magazines and to fill out deposit slips for my bank. There was not a lot of money from this endeavor, to be sure. But $500 per half-hour isn't anything to complain about. And just think — my only method of marketing was classified advertising.

That book is no longer available by that title because I enlarged it to help more than just free-lancers. It is now available in two versions: *Earning Money Without a Job* and *555 Ways to Earn Extra Money* — both published by Henry Holt and Company, in updated editions in 1991. In fact, it was the response to those books that prompted me to write *Guerrilla Marketing* in the first place. Enough about me. Back to your marketing.

Many marketers use the classified ads only to check out the pulling power of products, claims, prices, copy, headlines, and appeals. It's an inexpensive way to gain valuable information. Once you have a proven winner, you can then put forth your message in display ads if you wish. But remember, classified ads sometimes pull better than display ads.

A friend who advertised his books in *Psychology Today* found that classified ads, at 25 percent of the price of display ads, pulled considerably better than display ads. The kind of classified ad he ran is called a *classified display* ad, available in most publications. This is an ad that appears in the classified section but has a box around it and features dark, large display type. It costs more than regular classifieds, less than regular display ads, and depending upon the offering, pulls better than both in many instances. They're worth checking into.

Classified display ads

It is a false economy to keep your classified ad as short as possible. Don't use too many adjectives, but do use a lot of facts. Aim to be as clear in your message as you can. Remember that your classified ad is really your sales presentation. So don't hold back on features if your offering has features to boast about. You may end up spending several dollars more because your ad is longer, but if it pulls in sales, this will easily outweigh the extra cost. *The cost of all advertising is measured not in dollars, but in response.*

When thinking about classified advertising, think first in terms of clarity, then in terms of reader interest. You've got to capture your readers' attention. Do it with a catchy word such as GHOSTWRITING! or with a cogent headline such as NEED EXTRA MONEY? Keep in mind that you have but a fleeting instant to gain attention. The way to get it is with your short headline. The rest of your copy should follow directly from the headline. The GHOSTWRITING! headline might be followed with this sentence: "A professional writer will write, rewrite, or edit your letter, essay, manuscript, or advertisement so that it sings." The NEED EXTRA MONEY? headline might be followed by copy that begins with: "Obtaining the extra cash you need is not as hard as you think." If I needed money, I'd read on. Wouldn't you?

The idea in your classified ad is to maintain the momentum created by the headline. Write copy as though you are talking to one human being and not to a mass audience. Although you should mention as many features and benefits in your ad as you can afford, you should also practice the selective withholding of information. Merely by omitting certain facts, you may generate phone calls, visits, or whatever type of response you desire. The information you withhold may be the price, the location, or some other data the reader needs to complete the picture. Just be

Talk to one person at a time

careful not to withhold enough information so that you attract a horde of unqualified prospects.

A good exercise for classified-ad writing is to write your ad as though it were to be a display ad in a newspaper. Then start cutting copy to make the ad shorter and shorter. Finally, you will be left with the pure facts. But remember, shortness does not equate with quality. Pepper your facts with a few adjectives, with word pictures. "I can paint your house so that it gleams like the day it was built" sounds a whole lot more appealing than "House painting at reasonable prices."

Though classified ads need not be as short as possible, they must nonetheless motivate your prospective customers. They must create a desire to buy. One advertising genius who specializes in classified ads claims that the key to success in the classifieds is simplicity and tight copy. If you think that is easy to achieve, you are wrong. It's tough to be simple, tough to be brief. The writing of classified ads is a very special art. The ads must be well written or else they will not inspire confidence. Just because they're short does not mean they can be shabby.

Study the winners

To gain the greatest possible insight into writing successful classified ads, I suggest that you spend some library time. Look through current newspapers and magazines, studying the classifieds. Then look at one-year-old issues of the same newspapers and magazines. Check to see which ads are in both the new and the year-old publications. Those must be winners, or the people running them would not be repeating them. By studying them, you can learn what it is that makes them so successful. Is it the headline? The offer? The price? The copy? Apply whatever you learn to your own business.

Many large businesses that run high-powered advertising and marketing programs, making use of TV, radio, magazines, and other publicity, still use the classified section. They recognize that there are some people who read classified ads when looking for, say, antiques or certain automobiles. So don't think classified ads are small potatoes. There are even advertising consultants who specialize in classified ads. You give them your ad copy and they give it back to you, improved, and with a list of publications in which it is likely to elicit a response. If you will be marketing a product or service nationally, consider not only national magazines but also newspapers in multiple markets.

If our friend George were to run a classified ad in a local

newspaper, he'd probably run it in the "Home Services" section, and it would say something like:

> WANT A SUN DECK? PATIO? SKYLIGHT? HOT TUB? Let George do it! George can give you those things plus masonry work, electrical work, and building plans. Free estimates. Call 555-5656. All work is fully guaranteed.

Fact is, a person with an offering similar to George's did run such an ad. After it appeared only six times, he had to withdraw it because he couldn't handle all the work. I wish you the same success.

Remember that classified ads in newspapers allow you to home in on a local audience. Classified ads in magazines allow you to home in on a more widespread audience. And all classified ads allow you to test your strategy, your message and the advertising media you are trying out. They're glorious places to say that magic sentence: "Call or write for our FREE brochure."

Testing the waters

If you feel that classified advertising might be your marketing mainstay, I heartily recommend that you get in tough with Agnes Franz at 602-778-6788. Take out a subscription to her newsletter, *Classified Communication*, which is devoted 100 percent to classified advertising and how to make it work. She'll show you in short order that classified advertising can be big-time advertising even though it comes in short paragraphs consisting of short sentences. She'll even direct you to the directories that list all the magazines that accept classified advertising, and if she can, she'll recommend a few that have proven themselves in action.

Remember: Just because classified ads are small and inexpensive doesn't mean they're ineffective. A true guerrilla marketer tries to find ways to put the power of classified ads to work. Hardly any other medium enables you to talk to honest-to-goodness prospects and not just browsers. There's a huge difference between the two.

14
Signs: Big and Little

THINK OF SIGNS IN TWO WAYS: those that appeal to people *outside* your place of business and those that appeal to people *within* your place of business. The first category consists of billboards, which we'll discuss in another chapter, small signs on bulletin boards, which are discussed in this chapter, window signs, store signs, banners, signs on trees, and poster-type signs. Category two is made up of interior signs, commonly called point-of-purchase (P-O-P) or point-of-sale signs.

Whichever you use, or if you use both, be certain that your signs tie in as directly as possible with your advertising. The dictum, as stated by the late, great advertising pro Leo Burnett: "Plan the sale when you plan the ad." The dictum, as stated by the current, above-average advertising pro Jay Conrad Levinson: "Signs trigger impulse purchases; guerrillas are trigger-happy."

Signs trigger impulse purchases

Your ads will have made an unconscious impression on your potential customers, and your signs will awaken the memory of that advertising and result in a sale. Many people will patronize your business because of your ads. Your signs must be consistent with your advertising message and identity or those people will be confused. If the signs are in keeping with your overall creative strategy, consumers' momentum to buy will be increased. The Point-of-Purchase Advertising Institute tells us that in 1991, 74 percent of all purchase decisions were made right at the place of purchase. People entered a store with a vague notion of buying. They didn't solidify their decision until they were *in the store.* And what do you suppose influenced their decision? In many cases, a package. In many other cases, a sign.

Signs have exceptional power in the realm of malls, hypermarkets (a galaxy of malls), shopping centers, warehouses, supermarkets — large spaces where many businesses are competing for the eye and business of passers-by. Many smart retailers have used their signs and their decor to tie in with the times. The idea is to match confidence in the offering — accomplished with mass marketing — with a reason to make an impulsive purchase. This is, in part, accomplished by the use of a sign. Make that match and — bingo! — you've made a sale.

Most exterior signs are there to remind, to create a tiny impulse, to implant inclinations a wee bit deeper, to sharpen an identity, to state a very brief message. As a rule, exterior signs should be no more than six words long. Some successful signs have more than six words, but not many. Probably the most successful of all have just one to three words. **How many words on a sign?**

Right now, since we're talking about the power of words — few words — let's examine some of the strongest words in the English language. Many are used in headlines. Many are used in signs. Almost all are used in advertising.

Psychologists at Yale University tell us that the most persuasive words in the English language are: **Sign language**

you	results	love
money	health	discovery
save	easy	proven
new	safety	guarantee

To that list, I would hasten to add:

free	why	announcing
sale	yes	how
now	benefits	fast
secrets		

Now that you know these words, I'll bet you can come up with some dandy signs.

Frequently, motorists make abrupt decisions (and right turns) when they pass windows with huge banners proclaiming SALE! or FREE GIFTS! or SAVE 50%! As you probably know, it doesn't take many words to convince some people that they ought to buy from you — right now.

And many famous businesses were built with signs and signs alone. I instantly call to mind Burma-Shave (for which I had the privilege of writing two signs that were actually "published," or shall I say "roadsided"), Harold's Club in Reno, and Wall Drug Store of South Dakota. These are nationally famous businesses. Many locally famous concerns marketed their wares the same way. You can be sure that the Burma-Shave people, Harold, and Mr. Wall were all pioneer guerrillas, for they blazed trails that led directly to the bank. They also incensed coming generations of environmentalists, who claimed the signs were encroaching upon the beauty of America. Lady Bird Johnson spearheaded this movement and it's never going to die. So be aware of it, and don't put up exterior signs that will be picketed by planet-savers. As a guerrilla marketer, you must stay in touch with trends, and I, for one, am heartened by the nation's growing concern with the environment as indicated by new marketing strategies, use of recyclable materials, and production measures to guide our species toward cosmic sanity.

Mike Lavin, a true "green guerrilla," wanted one more unique way to promote his Berkeley business. A healthy mixture of environmentalist and capitalist, Mike was able to have his cake and eat it, too, by erecting, in a field, a large sign frame with no sign inside the frame. Beneath his see-through creation was a smaller sign that said "Scenery Courtesy of BERKELEY DESIGN SHOP."

Other exterior signs that usually work well are those that say such things as VOTE FOR LEVINSON, GARAGE SALE, FLEA MARKET, PARK HERE, and GAS FOR LESS. Perhaps the most profitable investment a retail business owner can make is in a red neon sign that says OPEN. Not a lot of creativity in the copy for those signs, to be sure. Nonetheless, they work. Failure to make a sign investment early on may mean making a sign investment later on, investing in a GOING OUT OF BUSINESS sign.

Effective sign graphics   Almost (but not quite) as important as the wording of the sign is the overall look of the sign. By this I mean the picture or pictures, the lettering style, the colors, and the design of the sign. A powerful graphic lends more power to the words. A sign that says FRESH DONUTS can be made doubly effective if it shows donuts growing in a meadow like flowers. If the sign says DELICIOUS

DONUTS, it can be more motivating if it shows a picture of a grinning little girl holding a donut with a giant bite taken from it or a close-up of a donut in the process of being dunked.

Usually, it makes sense to use very light lettering against very dark background colors or very dark lettering against very light colors. Using one type of lettering makes for easier reading than using more than one type. The words on the sign should be as large as possible while leaving room for the picture.

Keep in mind that although your sign should be expected only to remind, and not to make an actual sale, it will be better if you do go for the jugular and try like crazy to make the sale from the sign. Large advertisers with humongous marketing budgets can use signs for reminding only. But guerrillas have to get more mileage from their money. So although they know deep down that signs remind, they also realize that it is impossible to sell *some* people with a sign, and they go for the sale with the sign.

Consider also the "clutter factor." Are there many other signs nearby? If so, your sign should stand out. If not, you can approach the creation of your sign with a different mind-set. In England, when designing an outdoor sign campaign for a product that promised economy, we took the clutter factor into account and introduced black and white signs that contrasted with the surrounding sea of color signs. Our black and white beauties not only won awards but, more important, won customers. Had we used color with the same words and pictures, we would not have enjoyed such a high level of success. Our uniqueness, which tied in directly with our promise of economy, helped us stand out and make our point.

The clutter factor

A powerful visual image should be created if you are going to use many signs. The Marlboro cowboy comes to mind immediately. Because you want your sign to be instantly identifiable with you, a graphic identity is highly recommended. The look should be unusual, connected with your company's identity, and suitable for being maintained over a long period of time. Consistency. Remember?

The only punctuation mark with which you need be concerned is the exclamation mark. It lends a tone of excitement. Questions marks, while of use in print advertising, take too much reflection time to be utilized on signs. Stay away from them unless you have a good reason to break that rule. Commas and periods usually are not necessary with six-word messages. And long words are to be avoided whenever possible.

Making a sale with a visual image plus five or six words calls for a lot of thought, a lot of creativity. As with all other marketing devices, a great sign starts with a great idea. If you lack the idea, your words and pictures will probably end up plain vanilla. But with the right words and the right pictures, along with the right idea and the right location, a sale can be made.

Little signs do a lot

Guerrillas must fight their battles with every single available weapon. And small signs on bulletin boards have proven to be extremely effective weapons for many an entrepreneur. I'm talking about signs on cars as small as 3 inches by 5 inches. Even business cards. A sign need not be big to attract customers. Little signs do the job, too.

What kind of businesses and individuals might avail themselves of this minor a medium? Tutors. Gardeners. Plumbers. Typists. Writers. Baby-sitters. House sitters. Movers. Accountants. Room renters. Music teachers. Nurses. Answering services. Pet groomers. Cleaning people. Painters. Astrologers. Mechanics. Printers. Seamstresses. Decorators. Tree pruners. Entertainers. And a whole lot more.

If your business has any prospects who have occasion to see bulletin boards, perhaps you should use small signs on bulletin boards to promote your business. You'll find such bulletin boards, as do countless eager board readers, on campuses and in libraries, cafeterias, dormitories, company rest rooms, offices, supermarkets, Laundromats, locker rooms, bookstores, pet stores, sporting goods stores, barbershops, hairstyling salons, toy stores, and sundry other locations. Most major cities have hundreds of such locations; many small towns have as many as five or ten.

You can either post the signs yourself or you can hire companies that specialize in posting the signs for you. In the San Francisco Bay Area, where I live, a local company called The Thumb Tack Bugle provides this service. In 1981, it serviced 80 locations; now it services almost every location in the Bay Area, a number that tops 600. Their chief rival is The Daily Staple, a company that was spawned by the obvious success of sign-posting. The point is — this is a growing medium, and guerrillas must be aware of it because of its efficiency and low cost.

In most instances, your sign must be replaced on a regular basis (monthly or weekly). But sometimes it can stay in place for years. In a few cases, you'll have to pay a tiny fee to post your sign, but often this method of marketing is free (if you do your own posting). The companies that post for you promise to place your sign on a guaranteed number of boards — a large number, I might add — and they'll also replace it on a regular basis. Unless you've got the time to check your signs, look into these posting services. You can find them listed in your yellow pages under "Signs" or "Bulletin Boards." If signs do work for you, consider allowing one of these companies to handle all of that work for you, so you can concentrate on your primary way of earning money.

A crucial point to remember is to keep the lettering on your sign very clear. Fancy lettering is a definite no-no. Typewriter type is fine. But clear, handsome hand lettering is probably best. If you haven't the proper calligraphic skills, ask a pro or a friend with immense talent to letter your sign for you. Remember to keep your copy short and to the point. Incidentally, it is okay to make copies of your signs. One original plus a slew of copies and enough thumbtacks, and you've got the marketing tools to make yourself a success.

No fancy lettering, please

If George of Let George Do It posted bulletin-board signs throughout his area, they'd be very similar in wording to his circular. In fact, a sign for George might say:

LET GEORGE DO IT!

George builds sun decks and patios,
installs skylights and hot tubs,
does masonry and electrical work,
and designs building plans.

Call George at 555-5656 any time any day.
All work guaranteed. Contractor's License #54-45673.

George probably wouldn't even need a 3 x 5 sign. Instead, he could post his circular. Circulars have a charming way of doubling as small signs.

Amazingly, there are some businesses that need only promote via this wonderfully inexpensive method of marketing. Perhaps you can be one of them. Although guerrilla marketers should utilize as many marketing methods as they can effectively, they should also save marketing money whenever they can do so intelligently. Promoting your business with 3 x 5 cards is a true saving of marketing money. In fact, if you do the lettering and the writing and the posting, it's free.

At this point, if you own and operate a computer, you're **Desktop** wondering if you can use desktop publishing to help you produce **publishing** and design signs. The answer is that you certainly can — and **your signs** should — if you've got the right software, skills, and taste.

Armed with those weapons, you can use your desktop publishing prowess to produce newsletters, direct mail, brochures, and a host of other marketing tools. The technology is getting easier than ever. People are used to a higher quality of production in the marketing materials they are exposed to. The opportunities for a business with desktop publishing capabilities are endless. Just be sure you devote your time to the areas where it can most help your business. If that includes desktop publishing, great. If you love it, but should be doing something else, delegate it to someone else. A hallmark of the guerrilla is in the intelligent apportionment of time.

Ornate graphics are generally not necessary when marketing with small signs, though borders, typography, and little illustrations enliven most signs. If you post on a regular basis, it's a good idea to change the wording — but not the basic message — of your sign periodically. It's also a good idea to use different-colored paper so that your sign stands out from the rest. But be careful that your paper color does not impair the clarity of your ink color. Green ink on green paper makes for a very green but very unreadable sign. If you use green paper, make it light green — and make your ink a very dark color. Don't forget: Your major purpose is to motivate prospective customers, and if they can't read your message, they can't be motivated.

Take a field trip I suggest that you visit a few places where signs are posted in your region and notice the clever ways people are utilizing this unique marketing method. When I look at the galaxy of signs on bulletin boards, I get the feeling that many entrepreneurs are true guerrillas. Of course, that is not necessarily true. Merely using such a method does not make one a guerrilla marketer. But a guerrilla marketer does seriously consider such a method when developing an overall marketing plan. And a true guerrilla doesn't think it is at all silly to combine radio advertising, newspaper advertising, and bulletin-board advertising in his or her marketing strategy. Would General Motors consider such a tactic? Is the Pope Buddhist?

Be sure to make your headlines large. Make plenty of signs. In fact, it's a good idea to make about ten at a time and staple them together. Tack the whole packet to a bulletin board and carefully letter the words "Take One" atop your signs. This way, people can not only read your sign but the serious prospects can take one home with them for future reference — and to pass it along to someone who is looking for a product or service exactly like yours.

If you place signs on ten different bulletin boards, be sure you engage in the same kind of research you would employ if you were testing any other type of marketing. Ask your customers, "Where did you learn of my business?" When they tell you that they saw your sign, ask, "Where did you see it?" This way, you'll be able to pinpoint your best sign-posting locations. The more you can home in on your most productive marketing methods — including such subtleties as wording, sign color, sign location, and lettering style — the more successful you'll be.

It won't hurt for you to call some of the people who have posted signs in your area and ask about their effectiveness. Ask how long they've been posting signs, where they post them, whether the one you saw was typical, which locations seem best, and what success stories they may have heard. People are surprisingly open with information like this, and many enjoy being singled out as experts.

Interior signs require far more creativity than exterior signs, and you are allowed to use far more words. In fact, you are encouraged to.

Point-of-purchase signs are considered by those who use **P-O-P** them to be extremely effective because they create impulse sales. They also put forth extra selling energy and cross-merchandising opportunities. A person comes in to buy a pen, sees a sign that says briefcases are marked down, and buys a briefcase, too. That's cross-merchandising.

P-O-P signs make it easier for customers to locate and select products. They serve as silent salespeople, as aids to the actual salespeople. They demonstrate product features. P-O-P signs give customers product information, reinforce the ad campaign at the retail level, offer premiums and discounts, and actually generate sales all by themselves.

Many manufacturers offer free point-of-purchase materials to their customers. If you purchase from a manufacturer, you should ask if P-O-P materials are provided. If not, request some. Most manufacturers are happy to comply. They'll set you up with signs, brochures, display racks, window banners, display modules, counter cards, window cards, Plexiglas merchandisers, posters, display cases, stand-up signs, and more. Just ask.

The growth of in-store signs is causing the giant advertising agencies to change their attitudes toward this nonglamourous medium. They can't help but notice that during the 1980s, in-store media expenditures doubled, outgrowing more traditional vehicles such as television and print. The in-store sign industry is

Couponing growing. And growing along with it is couponing, part of the in-store experience with Americans. Approximately 45 percent of all cereal is now bought with a coupon, compared with less than 20 percent back in 1987. But most ad agencies don't take in-store signs and couponing as seriously as they should. You, as a guerrilla, will not make the same mistake.

New video technologies are creating opportunities for in-store marketers. TV monitors are cropping up over product displays and store shelves, at checkout counters, and even on shopping carts. This very definitely is a happening medium. As a guerrilla, you can get in on the new technologies while the big guys are waiting around to see how well they work. Many new marketing weapons are ideal for guerrillas because of their low cost, nontraditional nature, and ability to let guerrillas market like the big dudes (and dudettes) before the biggies even get started.

In the 1980s, telephone marketing was an emerging marketing force, according to *Forbes* magazine, and it was right on the button. In the 1990s, *Adweek* claims that P-O-P is the emerging force. The reason for P-O-P advertising's popularity is its ability to connect mass media marketing with the consumer at the time of purchase. This makes it cost-effective. To give you an idea of the growing size of this market, the Point-of-Purchase Advertising Institute estimates that in 1991, $7.5 billion were spent making P-O-P materials, compared with $5.5 billion spent in 1981. Some surveys indicate that in the near future P-O-P materials will make up 80 percent of many advertisers' budgets.

Plan the sale As I mentioned earlier, the basic rule in creating any adver-
when you tising is to plan the sale when you plan the ad. That means that
plan the ad you shouldn't think in terms of a person reading your ad or hear-

ing your commercial. Instead, think of the person at the moment of purchase. Is your message designed to motivate the potential customer at that crucial moment? By nature, almost all P-O-P marketing materials are. P-O-P signs get to people when the getting is good. They are there. They are in a buying mood. They are thinking in terms of the type of merchandise or service you offer. P-O-P advertising gives them many reasons to buy, or at least it should.

Many a smart guerrilla has run an ad, then blown it up into a five-foot-high poster, mounted it, and used it as a sign — inside the place of business, outside the place of business, and in the window. This is a way to market intelligently while saving lots of money, and it ensures that the interior signs will tie in with the ads.

Interior signs can be used to encourage customers to touch your offering, taste it, try it out, and compare it with the competition, and also to explain complex points by means of clear graphics. Remember: 74 percent of all buying decisions are made right in the place of business, but even half that number would be impressive. It should cause any guerrilla to take the use of signs very, very seriously.

What signs can do

The Institute points out that today decisions to buy are less casual than they once were, and that people need to be convinced right there, at the point of sale. If your business is in a location where your customers will come to browse or buy, the Institute says you should consider your aisles to be your "trenches" — where the true battle for customer dollars takes place. Since many battles are won or lost in the trenches, your point-of-purchase materials should be as potent as possible.

While the other marketing methods and materials create in the customer a desire to buy, as well they should, point-of-purchase signs promise instant rewards. Americans love instant gratification, if not faster. True guerrillas recognize that people patronize their businesses on purpose, not by accident. And they capitalize on the presence of prospects by using motivating, informative signs. Some have lengthy copy. Some have brief copy. Some go into detail about product features and benefits. Some contain lists of satisfied-customer testimonials. Some display ornate graphics. Some point out advantages of related merchandise. But each is there to move as much merchandise or sell as many services as possible.

You might want to walk the aisles of successful businesses in your area to find out how they use point-of-purchase signs. To learn even more about point-of-purchase signs, drop a line, requesting free information, to POPAI, 60 East Forty-second Street, New York, New York 10165.

Whenever possible, signs should be employed to pull the trigger on the gun already cocked by aggressive guerrilla marketing.

15
The Yellow Pages:
Making Them Turn to Gold

IF YOUR BUSINESS IS ALREADY off and running, you probably know quite a bit about the yellow pages, having learned it from the yellow pages sales representative, not to mention real-life experience. But if your business has not yet started, it's a great idea to name it something that will appear as the first listing in its category in the yellow pages. For example, a new storage company called itself Abaco Storage. It didn't advertise, except in the yellow pages. Success came to the company that first year, and phone inquiries resulting from the first listing in the yellow pages were clearly responsible.

The first thing to decide is whether or not your business is the type that can benefit from yellow page marketing. Do most people look there, as they do for storage companies, to find a product or service such as yours? If you are a retailer, chances are that people will consult the yellow page phone directory and find out about you. But if you're an artist or a consultant, people will probably find out about you through other sources. Once you've decided you should be in the directory, determine which directory or directories. Will one be enough? Or, as is the case in large metropolitan areas, will you have to be in five or ten? The answer may be clearer after you've considered these findings by the Small Business Administration:

Must you be in the yellow pages?

- The average independent store draws the majority of its customers from not more than a quarter of a mile away.

- The average chain store draws most of its customers from not more than three-quarters of a mile away.
- The average shopping center draws customers from as far away as four miles.

Some businesses draw customers from as far away as 100 miles — especially in wide-open areas such as North Dakota and Iowa. Furniture stores attract business from an average distance of ten miles away. One of my enterprises, Guerrilla Marketing International, draws business from throughout the nation. How about your enterprise? If you think you should run yellow pages ads in a number of directories, decide whether the ads in other areas should be as large as or smaller than your primary area ad. Decide whether you should have an advertisement or a listing. Decide whether the listing should be in dark, bold type or in regular type. My publishing business is listed in but one directory, in normal type. It is not the type of business that attracts yellow pages searchers. But some of my clients have large yellow page ads in three directories, small yellow page ads in five more directories, and bold-type listings in six other directories.

The cost for a large number of listings is assessed monthly, and it's steep. Find out the names of other companies in your business category and try to learn what percentage of their business each month comes from people who have located them through the yellow pages. I have some clients who obtain 6 percent of their business from people who first learned of them by consulting the yellow pages. Others obtain 50 percent of their business that way.

Where do you list yourself? You must do the groundwork to see how, where, and whether you should make use of a strong yellow pages program. Now you know some questions to ask and answer. Here's another: In which categories in your yellow pages directory will you list yourself? For example, if you run a sleep shop in which you sell beds and bedroom furniture, should you list your shop under "Furniture," "Mattresses," or "Beds"? Can you do with one listing, or do you need to pay for several? Answer: You'll probably have to list where people look. And they look in all three categories. One of life's necessary bummers.

A prime advantage A prime advantage of listing in the yellow pages is that you can appear as big as your biggest competitor, as large as the largest business of your type in town, and as well established as the oldest business of your type in town. Although directories differ from yellow pages publisher to yellow pages publisher (and there are several), usually the largest space unit you can purchase is a full page in some cities, a quarter of a page in others. Since these are also the largest ad spaces available to your competition, you can appear equal in size. And you can take advantage of this by running a more powerful ad than your competition.

Some bright entrepreneurs, who realize that a great deal of their business comes from people who consult the yellow pages, spend the majority of their marketing budgets on this medium. But here's a crucial truth: Unless you totally dominate your section of the yellow pages — I mean run the only large ad and the only good ad — you should never, in your advertising on radio and/or television, when directing people to your store or phone number, say *"You'll find us in the yellow pages."* If you do that, you will be spending your media dollars turning people on to your direct competitors.

Never direct them to the yellow pages

Believe me, many people innocently do that. They run a fine radio commercial, tell listeners to find them in the yellow pages, then sit back while nothing happens. Why? Because in the yellow pages, the listeners learn of several other places they can buy the product or service being advertised. Nope. If you don't appear as the clear choice within your category of the yellow pages, steer people away from the yellow pages. Tell people, "You'll find us in the white pages of your phone directory." There, in the peace and quiet of the noncompetitive white pages, listeners and viewers can learn your phone number, your address, and even how you spell your name. And they'll not be aimed in the direction of any of your competitors.

Now that that's understood, let's talk about how you must think of the yellow pages as a marketing vehicle, an advertising medium, an opportunity to sell. Many people think the yellow pages are merely a place to put their phone numbers in large type. Silly thinking. The yellow pages are an arena for attracting the business of active prospects. They are a place to confront prospects on a one-to-one basis. You are selling. Others are selling what you sell. The prospect is in a buying mood. Understand that opportunity, and you'll be able to create yellow pages ads that translate into sales.

Readers are in a buying mood

More and more yellow pages directories are now giving you the chance to use color in your ad. If you're springing for a large ad, or even a small ad, do it. Clients from around the country tell me it's worth the investment. Many directories also give you a chance to participate in coupon promotions by placing coupons for discounts on your offering in the back of the directory. Not enough results are in yet to evaluate that type of yellow pages marketing. I'd suggest calling a few coupon advertisers in your area and asking if the coupons work. Maybe it's a hidden gold mine. Maybe it's a disaster area. A guerrilla would check into it.

The electronic yellow pages   A guerrilla would also inquire about the electronic yellow pages. The way this works is that each ad contains a toll-free number that prospects can call for further information. You can update the information on a monthly basis. This is already in progress, and as with coupons, the jury is still out on it. Contact your local yellow pages rep to see if the service is available to you and what kind of results it has been getting for others.

If you decide to run one large ad in the yellow pages directory for your locality, you may decide to run smaller ads in outlying directories. So you may need a large ad and a small ad. Maybe even more. At any rate, it's too expensive to run yellow pages ads that are poorly written. And most of them are. By putting a bit of thinking into the content of your ad, you can greatly increase your yellow pages response rate.

I'm familiar with a local business that was attracting 2 percent of its sales with yellow pages ads. Two percent isn't all that good, but it does represent a fair sum of money at the end of the month. So the business couldn't eliminate that particular marketing tool. Instead, it changed its ad copy. That's all. The result was a 600 percent increase in business from yellow pages ads. The store now drew 12 percent of its sales from people who first learned of it through those pages of yellow.

What accounted for this dramatic increase? The owner of this store, which carried a goodly selection of beds — by no means the largest in the area but big enough to enable her to promote her products seriously — understood the mind-set of yellow pages readers. She realized that people who consult the yellow pages are actively looking to find specific information. But she also realized that you can usually motivate people more effectively if you get them to agree with what you are saying — to the point where they say yes to questions you are asking.

The bed store owner asked a question to which the person looking in the bed section of the yellow pages directory would always answer yes. The question was, "Looking for a bed?" Naturally, the answer was yes, and the reader read on. Whatever buttons the reader had regarding beds were intentionally pressed by the ad. The advertiser did not feel self-conscious about putting forth a lot of information. She also recognized the nature of the medium and actively sought the business of her prospective customers.

The answer must be yes

See the two-column by five-inch ad on page 145 as it appeared in the San Francisco yellow pages. That other advertisers in the same directory used the same space to list their names, phone numbers, and little else is a good indication that if your offering is suitable for yellow pages advertising, you have a splendid opportunity.

The do's and don'ts

If you use the yellow pages, here are the do's and don'ts:

- Do list a whole lot of facts about yourself.
- Do make your ad look and "feel" classier.
- Do treat it like a personal communication, not a cold listing.
- Do let folks know if you accept credit cards or can finance.
- Do gain the reader's attention with a strong headline.
- Do let people know all the reasons they should buy from you.
- Don't let the yellow pages people write your ad.
- Don't run small ads if your competitors run big ads.
- Don't make your ad look or sound boring.
- Don't forget to use graphics to communicate handsomely.
- Don't list your business in too many directories.
- Don't treat your ad less lightly than a full-page magazine ad.
- Don't hold back on the data; people are looking in the yellow pages for information. Give it to them, lots of it.

Lucky for you, the yellow pages are a misunderstood advertising medium. Now for the first time, specialized yellow pages advertising companies are being formed to help businesspeople take advantage of the opportunities offered. The yellow pages deserve your careful attention. But there is absolutely no reason why you *must* advertise there. If in doubt, read the yellow pages where you live and see what your competitors think about the whole idea.

III
Maxi-Media
Marketing

M AXI-MEDIA MARKETING refers to the mass-market media, such as newspapers, magazines, radio, TV, billboards, and direct mail. Mistakes cost dearly in this area. The competition may be able to outspend you dramatically. For instance, the average cost to produce a television commercial in 1991 was in the neighborhood of $180,000. Some neighborhood. And that's for a thirty-second live-action commercial. You've got to add to that the cost of running the commercial, and running it often enough.

Don't be put off by that high number. It's high because of the fast-food chains, beer and soft-drink companies that spend lavishly to create a desire for what they make. Still, you should not think of maxi-media marketing as expensive. That is not the case. Expensive marketing is marketing that does not work. If you run one radio commercial on one local radio station and it costs you only $10, but nobody hears it or acts on it, you have engaged in expensive marketing. But if you've shelled out $10,000 to run one week's worth of advertising on a large metropolitan area radio station and you realize a profit that week of $20,000, you have engaged in inexpensive marketing. Cost has nothing to do with it. Effectiveness does.

When a guerrilla marketer uses the mass media, he or she does what is necessary to make them effective, therefore inexpensive. A guerrilla is not intimidated by the mass media but is fascinated by them, finds ways to use them with precision, carefully measures the results, makes them part of an overall marketing plan, and realizes that using them calls for a combination of science, art, intuition, and business acumen. A guerrilla knows what maxi-media marketing is all about: selling and creating a powerful desire to buy.

Since I first wrote this book, a marvelous revolution has taken place in maxi-marketing: It is now more affordable and more sensible for teeny-tiny companies than ever before. Responding to the growing number of small businesses — which comprise 98 percent of all businesses — the advertising media have bent over backward to attract business.

They have done this by offering far lower prices than ever before. TV costs have plummeted to where even George of Let George Do It can afford to go on the tube. Magazines and newspapers are now available on regional and zone editions. Radio stations offer extremely attractive package rates. Postcard decks have made direct mail extremely affordable and attractive to right-thinking guerrillas. The maxi-media are not only within your reach, but right up your alley because you can do what the big guys do without spending big to do it.

In truth, these are the golden years for entrepreneurs. They get to compete in arenas where their presence used to be unknown. They get to take on the big players when it comes to attracting the attention — and the disposable income — of the American public.

Technology has changed so that breakthroughs such as desktop publishing, laser printing, satellite TV, cellular telephones, fax machines, voice-mail, and electronic mail are now beyond the stage of guerrilla engineers and into the arsenals of guerrilla marketers. Be aware of these technologies. Embrace them before the big corporations do. You're a guerrilla, lithe and agile. Your big competitors may be bright and wealthy, but they're moving through the molasses of their big-company bureaucracies — meetings, committees, reams of memos, and layers of decision making make them clumsy.

Be known for your quality, innovation, flexibility, and responsiveness to customer needs. Be known for epic service. Enter with confidence the world of the maxi-media. There has never been a better time to be a guerrilla. So go get 'em while the getting's good.

16
Newspapers:
How to Use Them
with Genius

WHETHER YOU'RE USING the mini-media, the maxi-media, or no media, as a guerrilla you should be aware of the changes always taking place in the U.S. marketplace. Because of the baby boom from 1946 to 1964, the median age in the United States is moving steadily upward. Soon it will exceed thirty-six. People are living longer as well. In fact, *Newsweek* accurately predicted that in the 1990s, the second biggest job opportunity will be in the field of geriatric social work (the biggest will be in industrial robot production).

In the market of today — and tomorrow — the old will be older than they used to be. Back in 1900, only 4 percent of elderly Americans were older than eighty-five. Today it's more than 10 percent — about 3 million people in all. Those eighty-five and older are the fastest-growing age group in the American population, according to the U.S. census.

We're older than we were

The population shift to the Sunbelt — Texas, Florida, Arizona, and California — will continue. Immigrants will account for 25 to 33 percent of our population, with Hispanics superseding blacks as the largest minority group. Ten percent of the population will be Hispanic. More and more minorities will move to the suburbs. The number of Asian-Americans will skyrocket.

Marketers must be aware of these trends as they begin to consider newspaper advertising. In most areas, a large number of newspapers are available. They all reach specific audiences. Which newspapers, which audiences, are best for you? Since there are metropolitan newspapers, national newspapers, local

Which newspapers are for you?

newspapers, shopper-oriented newspapers, classified-ad newspapers, campus newspapers, business newspapers, ethnic newspapers, and daily, weekly, and monthly newspapers to choose from, you can see that your work is cut out for you. You must make your selection skillfully.

By far the major marketing method used by small business is newspaper advertising. Of course your type of business may not benefit from business advertising. But if you think it may, pay close attention.

Newspapers offer a high degree of flexibility in that you can decide to run an ad or make changes in it up to a couple of days before the ad is to run. Radio gives you even more flexibility in that regard, allowing you to make changes up to the day your spot is to run. Magazines and television marketing allow you the least leeway.

A newspaper test

If you don't have a clear-cut favorite newspaper — favorite being defined as most local and most appropriate for your ads — there is a test you should use. Remember that there are most likely far more newspapers in your region than you ever imagined. Run an ad in as many of the newspapers in your area as you can — there may be as many as thirty. Use coupons in your ads. Have each coupon make a different offer, such as $5 off or a free book or a 15 percent discount or a free plant. In the ad, request that the customer bring the coupon when coming to your place of business, or mention the coupon when calling you.

By measuring the responses, you'll soon see which newspapers work, which don't work, and which work best of all. You don't have to run ads in all thirty newspapers to learn which is the best paper. Maybe you'll only have to test in three or five or ten papers. But you are nuts unless you test. And be sure to determine what generated the customer's response — the offer or the newspaper. You can do this by means of a second test. Make a different offer in the most effective paper. If it still pulls well, you've got a horse to ride.

Don't forget, we're talking about advertising in terms of a conservative investment. So don't waste your money advertising in a paper that you happen to read or that your friends happen to recommend or that has a supersalesperson selling ad space. The paper you eventually select will be the one in which you advertise consistently. That paper is the one to which you will commit your marketing program, your regularly placed ad, your money, your hopes. So select with the highest care possible. The paper must have proven itself in your coupon test. It should be the one read by prospective customers in your marketing area. A monthly paper is not preferable. Use it, if you wish, but make sure your major newspaper is at least a weekly, if not a daily paper.

Marketing is part science and part art — and the art part is very subjective. The artistic end of marketing is not limited to words and pictures but also involves timing and media selection and ad size.

The importance of your ad's appearance is not to be underestimated. Far more people will see your ad than will see you or your place of business, so their opinion of your business will be shaped by your ad. Don't let the newspaper people design your ad, and don't let them write the copy. If they do, it will end up looking and sounding like all of the other ads in the paper. Your competition is not just the other people in your business, but **Your real** everybody who advertises. **competitors**

You're out there vying for the reader's attention with banks, airlines, car companies, cigarette companies, soft-drink companies, and who knows what else. So give your ad a distinct style. Hire a top-rate art director to establish the look for your ad. Later you can ask the paper to follow the design guidelines set down by that art director. But at first, either you or a talented friend or a gifted art director should make your advertising identity follow your marketing plan — and do so in a unique manner. You won't win customers by boring them into buying. You've got to create **Create a desire** a desire. And a good-looking ad helps immeasurably, even measurably if you do your tracking.

I must caution you that perhaps one in twenty-five newspapers has a first-class art department that can design ads with the best of the expensive graphics companies. Put another way, twenty-four out of twenty-five newspapers have art departments that can help you waste your marketing money by designing ordinary-looking ads. The same goes for copy. Newspapers will help write your copy — because they want you to advertise. Give your marketing money to charity instead. Or spend it on a great ad writer who can make your ad sing, motivate, cause people to sit up and say, "I want that." If you have a winning ad, your marketing money can be safely invested in newspapers with the expectation of a high return.

Select the type used in your ad for readability and clarity.

Don't use any type size that is smaller than the type used by the paper. In fact, even type that size is too small. Make it easy for the reader to read your ad. If you decide to make your ad look different by having it appear in black with the type appearing in white (a process called reversing the type), be sure that the black ink doesn't spill over into the white letters, obliterating them. It happens every day. Don't let it happen to you. Newspapers are notorious for making good-looking ads come out faint and un-readable as a result of their particular printing process. Be sure that you or your art director check out your ad with people from the newspaper's production department to see if the ad will print well.

The right size ad   Then there's the matter of size. Of course, a full-page ad is probably best. But you won't want to pay for a weekly full-page ad, so you must make do with something smaller. What size can you comfortably afford?

Newspapers charge you by the line or by the inch. There are fourteen lines to the inch. If the newspaper charges, say, $1 per line, you are paying $14 per inch. If you want your ad to be fifteen inches high and three columns wide, you multiply $14 by fifteen, coming out with $210, then multiply that by three, for a total ad cost of $630. If you run an ad that size weekly, it will cost $2709 per month. (I multiplied the $630 by 4.3, because that's the approximate number of weeks per month.) If that charge is too high, you can run a smaller ad, one you can afford. Some people can run a weekly ten-inch ad (two columns by five inches) all year every year and enjoy a 25 percent sales increase each year. Other people want more of an increase, so they run a larger ad and run it two times a week. A lot depends upon the cost of advertising in the particular paper.

Dominating the page   Most full-sized newspapers are twenty-two inches high. If you can afford it, run an ad that is twelve inches high or higher. That way, you'll be sure your ad is above the fold. Most full-sized newspapers are six columns wide. So you can be certain of domi-nating the page with a four-column by twelve-inch ad.

That's a great tack, and if you use it you won't be wasting your money. But you can save a bit of money if you run a smaller ad with a powerful and unique border. An ad does not have to dominate a page to be seen. It merely has to interest the reader, then create a desire, then motivate the reader to do something you want him or her to do.

If you run your ad in a tabloid-sized newspaper rather than a full-sized newspaper, you can save money by running a smaller ad. A ten-inch ad seems a bit buried in a large newspaper, but it stands out in a tabloid. Many Sunday newspapers have tabloid-sized sections, and you can save money by using them. But don't use them just for that reason. Be sure that your prospects read that paper and that section.

Run it on the right days

What are the best days to run your ads? It differs with different towns and different businesses. Ask your local newspaper's space salesperson for a recommendation. Generally, Sunday is the day that the most people read the paper and spend the most time with it. But can your business succeed by running ads on days your doors are closed? Some businesses can. If yours can, give a nod to Sunday.

Monday is a pretty good day if your offering is directed to males, since many males read the Monday papers carefully because of all the sports events that went on the preceding weekend. Saturday is also a fairly good day, since many advertisers shy away from it and you'll have less competition. Some papers make Wednesday or Thursday their food day, so the papers are loaded with food and grocery ads.

You'll have to observe the papers yourself, then ask the person who will be selling the ad space to you. That ad space comes a lot cheaper if you sign a contract for a given number of lines or inches per year. Ask about the discounts you can receive for volume usage. They are quite substantial — a fringe benefit of consistent advertising in the same paper.

The best placement

In most cases, the best place to have your ad appear is as far to the front as possible, on a right-hand page, above the fold of the paper. But few, if any, papers will guarantee placement unless you sign a King Kong – sized contract. The main news section is also considered to be an optimum place for an ad, because of high readership by a large cross-section of the paper's circulation.

Because of the nature of your product, you may want to run your ad in the business section, the sports section, or the entertainment section. Run your ad where competitors run theirs. If you have no competition, run your ad where services or merchandise similar to yours are being offered. Why? Because that's where readers are conditioned to look for offerings such as yours.

Incidentally, readers most likely will read your ad, because study after study shows that newspaper readers read the ads almost as intensively as they read the stories. Because of the power of graphics, some ads attract more attention than the actual news stories. Use graphics in your ad, but go easy. Generally, more than three or four pictures — whether art or photography — is too many. But that's a rule that is both useful to know and useful to break. I've broken it successfully more than once. I've also run very successful ads that have only one illustration or photo.

When selecting your newspaper, you of course want to know its circulation. And you also want to know if the paper's circulation is in your marketing area. Otherwise you'll be paying for wasted circulation. A good thing to keep in mind is that when you hear a circulation figure, you can multiply it by three and learn how many people are actually reading the paper. When a family has a subscription to the paper and two adults and three kids read each issue, that only gets counted as one subscriber. When a woman buys a copy of the paper to read on the bus on her way home and her husband reads it when she arrives home, that, too, gets counted as one reader, according to circulation statistics. So newspaper circulation figures are one of the few marketing statistics that are understated.

Reprint your ad   If you have a truly good ad — one that tells all the features and benefits of your offering — consider making multiple reprints of it and using them as circulars, customer handouts, mailing pieces, or interior signs. They cost very little, and most of their cost was spent when you had the ad produced. And remember, you can blow up the ad and make it into a poster.

Don't forget that many people newspaper shop before they buy. That is, they scan the papers before going out to purchase a product. Keep that in mind when running your ads. If your product is aimed at a particular group of people, such as businesspeople, consider running your ad in a business paper rather than a metropolitan paper. If your offering is geared to discount hunters, run your ad in shopper-oriented papers. If it will appeal to college kids, advertise it in the campus paper. A finished newspaper marketing plan usually calls for ads in a number of papers, some primary, others secondary. The combination you choose can be the key to your fortune. You want to obtain exceptional results from both primary and secondary newspapers. Exceptional results mean many sales. And many sales come from many inquiries, be they in the form of phone calls, visits to your place of business, or even letters.

To increase the number of inquiries you receive through newspaper advertising, first and always remember to put your name and primary message continually in front of readers. In addition, put the following tips into action:

1. Mention your offer in your headline.
2. Emphasize the word *free* and repeat it when possible.
3. Restate your offer in a subhead.
4. Show a picture of your product or service in action.
5. Include testimonials when applicable.
6. Do something to differentiate yourself from others who advertise in the newspaper. That means all others — not just your direct competitors.
7. Say something to add urgency to your offer. It can be a limited-time offer. It can be a limited-quantities offer. Get those sales now.
8. Put a border around your ad, if it is a small ad. Make it a unique border.
9. Be sure your ad contains a word or phrase set in huge type. Even a small ad can "act" big if you do so.
10. Always include your address, specific location, and phone number. Make it easy for readers to find you or talk with you.
11. Create a visual look that you can maintain every time you advertise. This clarifies your identity and increases consumer familiarity.
12. Experiment with different ad sizes, shapes, days run, and newspaper sections.
13. Consider free-standing inserts in your newspaper. These are increasingly popular and may be less expensive than you imagine.
14. Try adding a color to your ad. Red, blue, and brown work well. You can't do this with tiny ads, but it may be worth trying with a large ad.
15. Test several types of ads and offers in different publications until you have the optimum ad, offer, and ad size. Then run the ad with confidence.
16. Be careful with new newspapers. Wait until they prove themselves.
17. Do everything in your power to get your ad placed in the front section of the paper on a right-hand page above the

fold. Merely asking isn't enough. You may have to pay personal visits. Be a squeaky wheel.

18. Don't be afraid of using lengthy copy. Although lengthy copy is best suited for magazines, many successful newspaper advertisers employ it.

19. Run your ad in the financial pages if you have a business offer, in the sports pages if you have a male-oriented offer, in the women's pages for household services and products, in the food pages for food products. The astrology page usually gets the best readership. But in general, the main news section is still the best location for ads.

20. Study the ads run by your competitors, especially their offers. Make yours more cogent, more concise, sweeter, different, better.

21. Keep close records of the results of your ads. Experimenting doesn't mean a thing if you don't keep track of the experiments.

22. Be sure your ad is in character with your intended market.

23. Be sure your ad is in character with your product or service.

24. Be sure your ad is in character with the newspaper in which you advertise.

25. Try to use short words, short sentences, short paragraphs.

26. Don't put your address on a coupon only. If you use a coupon, have your address appear on it and outside of it, so that if the coupon gets clipped, your address will appear anyhow.

27. Use photos or illustrations that reproduce faithfully in newspapers.

28. Always put the name of your company somewhere at the bottom of your ad. Don't expect people to get the name from the copy, the headline, the picture of the product, or the picture of the storefront. Still, putting your name into your headline is generally a good idea. At least put it in the subhead.

29. Say something timely in your ad. Remember, people read papers for news. So your message should tie in with the news when it can.

30. Ask all of your customers where they heard about you. If they do not mention the newspaper, ask them directly: "Did you see our newspaper ad?" Customer feedback will be invaluable for you.

31. Aim your ad, in most cases, to people who are in the market for your offering *right now.*
32. If you're not going to use newspapers solely as a support medium, that is, to support your other marketing efforts, be sure you use them weekly or stay away from them altogether. Occasional use doesn't cut it.

These tips, your common sense, the quality of newspapers in your community, the newspaper production department, the newspaper representative calling upon your business, and the presence or absence of your competitors in the newspaper should be prime considerations in your decision to include or exclude newspapers from your guerrilla marketing mix.

17
Magazine Advertising:
Its Value to Entrepreneurs

WHOEVER HEARD OF A small-time entrepreneur advertising in well-known and respected national magazines? You have now. Magazine advertising has been the linchpin for many a successful small business. Remember, the single most important reason people patronize one business over another is confidence. And magazine advertisements breed confidence by instilling familiarity and giving credibility. *A properly produced magazine ad,* **The credibility** *preferably of the full-page variety, gives a small business more* **factor** *credibility than any other mass marketing medium.*

Consumer confidence will not necessarily be gained from one exposure to your magazine ad. But if you run the ad one time, you can use the reprints of that ad forever. One highly successful company ran a single regional ad in only a single issue of *Time* magazine, then used reprints of the ad (reprints are available at a fraction of a cent each) in its window and on its counter for more than fifteen years after the ad had run. Reprints were also sent in direct mailings. Even mailings in 1993 can contain an ad reprint saying "As seen in *Time* magazine" — heavy-duty name-dropping from an ad run one time back in 1973. Now that's getting mileage out of magazine advertising. Several bright entrepreneurs have run an ad one time in a regional edition of a national magazine, then mailed out reprints in all future direct mailings — each time gaining for their products the confidence that prospects ordinarily placed in the magazine itself.

You see, that's the whole point of magazine advertising for small businesses. It gives them a great deal of credibility. And credibility creates confidence, which translates to sales. And profits. If people feel that *Time* magazine is reliable, credible, trustworthy, and solid, they will feel those same things about the companies that advertise in *Time*. So if you wish to gain instant credibility, advertise in magazines that can give it to you.

Don't forget, I'm not talking about running your ad in the entire edition of the magazine, just in your regional edition, and just one time. Not all magazines have regional editions, and unless you are running a classified ad, you may as well forget those that don't, unless you have a large budget or a product or service with national appeal. But many magazines do have regional editions that can save you a fortune.

Regional means affordable

The number of publications offering these affordable methods of reaching the target audiences of a small business is growing fast. It takes a media-buying service to keep up with the maximedia's efforts to woo budgets from small business. That's one reason guerrillas use them.

Remember that most people do not realize there are regional editions at all. When they see your full-page (or smaller if you engage in fusion marketing and split the cost of the page with one, two, or three others) ad in *Time* magazine, they'll be quite impressed that you are advertising in a respected national magazine. And they'll turn that state of being impressed into a state of confidence in your offering. Check your library for the latest issue of *Consumer Magazine and Agri-Media Rates and Data* (published monthly by Standard Rate and Data Service, Inc. — known as SRDS), and you'll learn which magazines have regional editions, and how much they charge for advertising in them.

If you run a small display ad for a mail-order venture in a national publication, you should do as much testing as possible. An inexpensive method of testing is to avail yourself of the split runs offered by many magazines. By taking advantage of them, you can test two headlines. Send your two ads to the publication, being certain to code each ad for response so that you'll be able to tell which of the two headlines pulls better, and ask the publication to split-run the ads. One headline will run in half the magazines printed; the other headline will run in the other half.

Test as you go with split runs

For example, a manufacturer of exercise equipment once ran a split-run ad with a coupon. One headline said STRENGTH-EN YOUR WRISTS FOR BETTER GOLF! and the other said STRENGTHEN YOUR WRISTS IN ONLY 2 MINUTES A DAY! The coupon in the first ad was addressed to Lion's Head, 7230 Paxton, Dept. G6A, Chicago, Illinois 60649, and the coupon in the second ad was addressed to Lion's Head, 7230 Paxton, Dept. G6B, Chicago, Illinois 60649. Even though the coupons looked alike, it was easy for the advertiser to tell that the appeal of two minutes a day was far stronger than the appeal of better golf, even though the advertiser had guessed ahead of time that the golf headline would attract the better response. How could the advertiser tell that his guess was wrong? Because the responses to Dept. G6B ran four times higher than those to Dept. G6A. Incidentally, the advertiser could also tell by referring to those responses that they came from *Golf* magazine (G) and that they were in answer to an ad run in June (6). So the code allowed the advertiser to tell three things: the publication, the month run, and which of the two ads drew the best response.

Measuring by coding   Coding can be even more complex so as to tell you the year, the ad size, and other information. Some publications allow you to do a triple-split run and not just a double, enabling you to test three headlines rather than two. If you can test three headlines, do it. Let your audience make your judgments for you whenever possible. After you count up the coded responses, you will know which headline is best. And the cost of the test itself will have been minimal. The magazine's split-run capability will have saved money for you while giving you valuable information. Now you can run the successful ad with boldness and confidence.

Don't count yourself out of advertising in national publications because of the cost. You can cut down on that cost by establishing an in-house advertising agency, by purchasing remnant space or space in regional editions, and by purchasing a tiny space unit — say, one column by two inches. Or you can advertise in the classified section that is available in many national magazines. Also, many magazines offer enticing discounts to mail-order advertisers. And virtually all magazines offer impressive merchandising materials: easel-back cards, reprints, decals with the name of the magazine (for example, "as seen in *Time*"), and mailing folders. The magazine's advertising sales representative will be happy to tell you about all of the merchandising aids offered. Be sure you take advantage of them. They will be useful at your place of business, in your window (if you have one), and in other advertising you do.

Merchandising aids

Your business will be helped if you simply mention "You've

probably seen our ad in *Woman's Day* magazine." And these materials can be used as enclosures in direct mailings, as enclosures with personal letters, as signs on bulletin boards, as counter cards, as display pieces at trade shows, exhibits, or fairs, and as part of a brochure or circular. The cost of these powerful guerrilla marketing aids is ridiculously low, sometimes even free, so use them to the fullest extent. Magazines can help you market your offering immediately and well into the years ahead. It's the years-ahead part that's going to result in profitable business for you.

When the waterbed industry was in its infancy, growth was dramatically spurred when Chemelex, a manufacturer of waterbed heaters, ran full-page ads in *Time, Newsweek,* and *Sports Illustrated*. Chemelex then distributed reprints of the ads to retailers throughout the country. The retailers prominently displayed the ads throughout their showrooms, and the industry grew to the point where it turned from a hippie-image industry into a steady $2 billion per year furniture-image industry. One reason: the instant credibility gained by advertising in highly credible publications.

Magazine advertising offers other attractive advantages. You can target your market much better with magazines than with newspapers. Instead of reaching a general circulation, you can reach people who have demonstrated an interest in skiing, gardening, do-it-yourselfing, snowmobiling, or you name it. This results in very little waste circulation. Everyone who sees your ad is a prospect. And one of the basic tenets of guerrilla marketing is to talk primarily to prospects and not to browsers.

Target your market

A good guerrilla marketer also considers advertising in magazines other than consumer magazines. There is a whole world of trade magazines out there. Almost every trade and profession has its own publication or, more likely, group of publications. Because you want to home in on prospects, you should consider advertising in some of these trade publications, because they are subscribed to and read cover to cover by large numbers of prospective customers. This is especially true if your product is at all business oriented.

Don't forget trade magazines

So go to your library, locate a copy of *Business Publication Rates and Data,* another directory published by SRDS, and look through it. Try to find publications in which you might advertise your products or services. You'll find many, many magazines you've never heard of, and quite a few may be read by prospective buyers of what you sell. I've always been amazed at the amount of information in SRDS — as it's called in the ad biz. If you find a couple of magazines (newspapers are also listed) that might be right, send away for sample copies. I predict that you'll be pleasantly surprised at the large number of marketing opportunities available to you in trade publications. You may find entrepreneurs with whom you can team up for greater sales. You may realize that you ought to be advertising in some of these publications. And you will learn a lot of inside information about your type of business. Most likely, you'll want to subscribe to at least one trade magazine just to keep abreast of new developments in your field.

Standard Rate and Data publishes a host of directories that may be of use in your business. If I ran a business school, I'd make it mandatory to spend a day looking through SRDS publications. Success-bound students would petition for more days. If you want to subscribe, write to Standard Rate and Data Service, 5201 Old Orchard Road, Skokie, Illinois 60077, or call them at 708-256-6067.

The colorful guerrilla Another important advantage of advertising in magazines is you can use color much more effectively than you can in newspapers. If your offering is oriented to color — if you are marketing fabrics, for instance — consider advertising in magazines just to show off the hues and tones. Magazines are better suited to lengthy copy than any other medium. The reason is that people buy magazines with the idea of spending time with them, unlike newspapers, which are read quickly for news. Magazines involve their readers, and your ads may do the same.

It is primarily because of guerrilla marketers that magazines now publish so many regional editions. Now that you know this, look through your local issue of *Time*, or *TV Guide*, or *Better Homes and Gardens*, and notice how many regional advertisers are using those media, how many of them utilize color to show off their product, and how many of them run long-copy ads. Notice the ones that share the cost of a full-page even though they run different half-page ads. Most important, remember that in all likelihood these advertisers could never afford a national ad in the same magazine. But the growth of the entrepreneurial spirit in America has necessitated an increase in regional editions. Advertisers in these regional editions know that by advertising in a major magazine, they are putting themselves in the big leagues. Their ad might run on the page next to an ad for General Motors or Rolls-Royce or IBM. Not bad company for a guerrilla, no? But after all, guerrilla marketing lets you play in the big leagues without first struggling through the minor leagues. **You're in good company**

It has been over twenty years that many major magazines have been available to minor advertisers, but most small business owners are oblivious to the fact. Guerrillas avail themselves of these major magazine opportunities and all of their merchandising aids as a key to successful marketing. For at the same time that it gives you credibility within your community, it gives you respect in the minds of your sales staff, your suppliers, and even your competitors.

If you're a thinking entrepreneur, you'll utilize magazines in several ways. You will advertise regularly in a magazine that hits your target audience right on the nose. You will advertise only one time in a prestige magazine, so as to use its merchandising aids. You will use the classified sections of national magazines if you are in the mail-order business. And you will use the display sections of national magazines if what you have to sell is too big for the classified sections or if your chosen magazine runs no classified ads. **Using magazines properly**

It may be that you want to advertise in a national magazine because of the status, the huge circulation, and the easily identifiable audience, but do not have the money for a large-enough ad. No problem. In that case, use a two-step process. You might also consider *marketing with your own magazine*. In a fusion marketing effort with three or four other companies with the same types of prospects, you can produce your own beautiful, glossy magazine, replete with elegant photos, stylish writing, and fancy paper stock. **Your own magazine**

To make this magazine work for you and your marketing collaborators — who each have several full-page ads in the magazine and are the only advertisers — you must mail it to a carefully selected audience, consisting mostly of your customers and those of your fusion partners. Your identity will be impressively conveyed through the editorial material, the style, and the ads. The readers will develop a tighter bond with you, much tighter than if you had invested this money in mere advertising. The cost of this endeavor is high — nearly a dollar per reader. This figure is based upon 100,000 copies of the magazine, about $25,000 each for you and your three other fusion partners. The same reader that costs you one dollar by this advertising method costs you only half a cent for a full-color, full-page ad in a standard magazine. But that's like comparing apples with emeralds.

With your own magazine, you have total control of the editorial environment, can run as many ads as you want, and can eliminate ads by competitors. Phooey on them. This idea is already being used by MCI, Federal Express, Philip Morris, Benetton, and others. Is it cheap? No way. Is it guerrilla-like? If you do it with fusion partners, it is. You don't have to be a big guy to market with big ideas.

If you are practicing guerrilla marketing to the hilt, you will mention your national magazine advertisements in the other media you use: on the radio, in your direct-mail advertisements, on your signs, in your yellow pages ads, in your personal letters, in your telemarketing — wherever you can. "As seen in *Fortune*" carries a lot of prestige.

Do the two-step   Guerrillas excel at *doing the two-step*. Step one is to have a magazine (or any publication) run a small display (or classified) ad that hits the high points of your offering, then tells readers to call or write for *free* information. When they respond, send them your brochure and a motivating sales letter (step two). Follow up with still another letter if they do not order. Consider selling or renting their names to mailing-list brokers. These people buy and sell or rent names and addresses of many different types of consumers. Find them in your yellow pages under "Mailing Lists." The two-step process lets you tell your entire story but does not entail the high costs of large-space advertising. It also gives you a large number of salable names, and you can be sure these are valuable names for your own mailing list.

This two-step process worked for an entrepreneur friend of mine after the running of a large ad failed. In the classified section of *Psychology Today*, he ran a classified display ad telling readers that they could earn a legitimate college degree — B.A., M.A., or Ph.D. — right from their homes. Then he told them that they could secure free details about the offer by writing him. My friend later told me that he made a great deal of money with this two-step process, but that it was twice as much work as the one-step process that I was employing at the time to advertise the free-lancing book I had written and published myself. Soon he was able to employ someone to handle the detail work for him, and his two-step ads continue to run in *Psychology Today* as well as in more than thirty other publications. It has been over eighteen years since the first ad ran.

I tell you this story to emphasize that if you come up with a winning magazine ad, you may be able to run it in a multitude of magazines. The result of this can be a multitude of profits. You can run your proven money-maker for years and years in a wide selection of publications. To a guerrilla, few marketing situations are as delightful.

But the prime reason for using magazines is the lasting value of the ad. I recall placing a full-page ad in *Newsweek* for a client. After the ad was run, the client asked each customer where he or she had heard of his company. At the end of one week, only five people claimed to have seen his ad in *Newsweek*, where it had run only one time. At the end of one month, that number climbed to eighteen people. And after a full year, a total of sixty-three customers said they had first heard of the company through its ad in *Newsweek*. And that's not even the impressive part! The really significant aspect of this story is that the entrepreneur blew up a reprint of the ad to the size of an enormous poster — five feet high — then mounted it and placed it outside his place of business. Thousands of customers patronized his business because of that huge poster.

The prime reason to use magazines

Newsweek turned out to be his most effective advertising medium that year — and yet he placed but one ad there. To make matters even more wonderful, the *Newsweek* page was purchased at less than half the going rate, because it was remnant space. The magazine had sold three full-page ads to regional advertisers and had one page left over — a remnant. So my client was able to buy the space for a fraction of its original price.

If you are interested in advertising in any particular magazine, call the local representative of the magazine and say that you are definitely a candidate for any remnant space and that you should be phoned when it is available. You may wait a bit, but it will be well worth the wait. Do Coca-Cola and AT&T practice this tactic? No. But do successful guerrilla marketing people practice it? You bet their bank balance they do!

Most small-business owners never even consider advertising in magazines. That's because they don't know about regional editions, remnant space, in-house agency discounts, the two-step process, and valuable merchandising aids. Now that you do know about these lovely aspects of magazine advertising, give serious consideration to the medium.

18
Radio: It Costs
a Lot Less Than You Think

UNLESS YOU HAVE A GOOD friend who owns a radio station, most of your radio marketing will be of the paid, rather than free, variety, though remember, in 1991, 55 percent of all media was obtained via barter, according to the head of one of the nation's largest media-buying services. It is possible to have stories or interviews about your product or service on the radio, and it may be that those will cost you nary a cent. In chapter 26, we'll go into ways of obtaining free publicity on the radio and in other maxi-media. But as far as this chapter is concerned, you'll have to pay or trade for your radio marketing. For purposes of simplicity, let's talk paying.

Although newspapers are the primary marketing media for most small businesses, and direct mail has taken over second place, radio does come in a strong third. Radio advertising can be used effectively by a company with a limited budget. And radio can help improve your aim when you're trying to reach your target consumers. Radio helps you establish a very close **Radio is intimate** relationship with your prospects. Because of its intimate nature, it brings you even closer to them than newspapers do. The sound of an announcer's voice, the type of musical background, the sound effects you use to punctuate and enhance your message — all of these are ammunition in your radio marketing arsenal. All can help win customers and sales for you.

Although it is true that you can, if you try, pay $450 for a single thirty-second radio commercial on a large commercial radio station, you can also, if you try, pay $5 for a single radio commercial on a smaller, less popular station. You'll certainly talk to far more people with the $450 spot. But you'll be talking to more than a few people with your $5 commercial.

Now don't think that you can spend $5 and feel that you are involved in radio marketing. But if you spend $5 times five spots per day ($25), and you run your spots four days a week ($100), three weeks out of four, you may be able to say that for $300 a month you are adequately covering the listener profile in the community that particular radio station covers.

Because radio listeners are notorious button pushers and change stations a lot, you're probably going to have to run radio spots on more than one station. This is a rule to know and to break. But make sure you know it. One station does not a radio campaign make.

How many stations do you need? Well, you may really need only one. But you'll probably need three or four or five. It may also be that you have the type of offering that lends itself so well to radio that you'll need no other ad media and can dive headlong into advertising on ten stations. Some of my clients have. One of the advantages to being on so many stations is that by carefully tracking your audience response — that is, learning which stations are bringing in the business — you can eliminate the losers and narrow your radio marketing down to proven winners. You can also use the coupon-type testing we explored in the chapter on newspapers. That means you pick, say, five stations and run commercials on all five. In each commercial, make a different offer — money off, free gift, 50 percent reduction — and ask listeners to mention the offer when they contact you. By keeping assiduous track of the offers mentioned by your customers, you'll know which stations to drop (maybe all of them) and which to continue with (maybe all of them).

How many stations?

Unless you really keep track of all of your media responses, you are not a guerrilla. If you run your ads and keep selecting media on blind faith, you are closer to a lemming. You've got to make your marketing as scientific as possible. This is one of those rare instances where you can measure the effectiveness of your media scientifically. Avail yourself of it.

If you have salespeople, ask them to track responses. If you're the person taking orders from customers, then you must track responses. Ask the customers, "Where did you hear of us first?" If they say radio, ask, "Which station?" If they name a station that you don't use, ask, "Which stations do you ordinarily listen to?" If that doesn't net a solid response, prompt the customer, naming a few stations, one of which you use. It's a drag to do this, but it's a bigger drag to waste marketing money and bankrupt a business. Do everything you can to learn which stations are pulling in customers and which are not. After you've been marketing seriously for a year or three, you can cut down on your media tracking, though I do not suggest that you do. If you start learning for sure which stations pull best, you may feel that you need no longer ask. But until you are certain, you must ask. Because stations and people change, it is a good idea to keep track constantly.

What kind of stations?   There are many types of radio stations: rock and roll, rap, middle of the road, country, public, all news, talk show, drama, Spanish language, religious, black, top forty, bubble-gum rock, jazz, oldies, intellectual, avant-garde, local interest, farm-oriented, progressive rock, reggae. Which are most likely to be listened to by your audience? Although it is possible to divide radio stations into twenty-one categories, as I have just done, it is first advisable to divide them into two categories — background stations and foreground stations.

Background vs. foreground radio   Some radio stations play *background* programming. That means they play music that is generally a background sound. People talk, converse, work, play, iron, cook, and do myriad other things with background radio sounds. The music does not get in the way, does not command attention, does not distract. Unfortunately, because people are not actively listening, the commercials are also in the background. Oh, sure, when a person is driving home with the radio on, all alone, the commercials — and the music — move up from the background. But in general, all music stations are background radio stations. And many music lovers have cassette tape decks in their cars, not to mention their homes.

All radio stations that are sports, religion, all news, or all talk are *foreground* radio stations. They are in the foreground of people's consciousness. They command attention. They do distract. They are poor stations to have on during a conversation, during work, during situations that require your concentration. As a result, the commercials that are broadcast on them are likely to attract more active listeners. These people pay closer attention to commercials because they are actively listening to the radio. They don't have it on some back burner of their mind, as is the case with background radio. This is not to say that foreground radio is better than background radio for advertising. But I do want you to be aware of the difference between the two.

Active listeners are best

There are other differences as well. Talk radio is hosted by "personalities" more than music radio is. All music radio requires is a person to say what music just played and what music is about to play, though sometimes this is on tape. Talk radio requires more listener rapport, more informal chatter, more personal asides.

Here's a guerrilla tactic that works gloriously well on foreground stations when it is appropriate. Suppose you have a new company that sells, say, computer instruction. Invite a talk radio personality to take a few lessons. Then buy time on that personality's station. Rather than give him a sixty- or thirty-second script for your commercial, which you might ordinarily do, give him an outline — and invite him to ad-lib as much as he wants. The result is usually a sincere commercial, far longer than the commercial for which you have contracted, that has loads of credibility. If your product or service is worth raving about, you can count on most personalities to give it their all. You only have to pay for a sixty-second spot, but you may end up with a three-minute spot at no extra cost.

A guerrilla radio tactic

That is about the only instance in which I'd advise you to put your message into the hands of the radio station. In virtually all other instances, I suggest that you have the radio station play recorded commercials, which you can tape either at an independent facility or at the station itself. Don't make the mistake of furnishing scripts to the station. Although some of their announcers may do a great job of reading them, other announcers may make mincemeat out of them, reading them with no conviction, no enthusiasm, but with oodles of errors. Murphy's law has a way of asserting itself at radio stations: If the commercial can be messed up, it will be. Protect yourself by furnishing finished tapes only — unless you can get a personality to breathe true life into your script.

Just as it is bad business to let a newspaper write your newspaper ad copy, it is also a grave error to let a radio station write your radio ad copy. Most stations will be all too willing to vol-

Who writes your commercial?

unteer. Don't let them. They will have the script written by someone not quite good enough to be paid as a writer, who will, by
force of habit, make your commercial sound just like everyone
else's commercials. One of the most asinine methods of saving
money is to let the station write your advertising. They'll do a
C+ job for you, and as a guerrilla, you need an A+ if you're
going to commit to a medium.

If the station offers to produce your spot, that's a different
story. Check out their equipment. Probably it is all right. Listen
to their announcers. If you trust their equipment — as measured
by the sound of finished commercials produced on it — and you
like one or more of their announcers, let the station voice and
produce the commercial on tape for you. Generally there is either no charge or just a tiny charge for this service. And in most
cases, but not all cases, it is worth the price.

Thirties and sixties   Should you run thirty-second spots or sixty-second spots? A
thirty-second spot is usually far more than 50 percent of the cost
of a sixty-second spot. But in most instances, what you can say in
sixty seconds can also be expressed in thirty seconds. So go with
the shorter spots even though they are not great values. In the
long run, they'll give you more bang for your budget. If, however,
you have a complex product or service, you'll just have to run a
full sixty-second spot. Some advertisers achieve superb results
with two-minute commercials. So take as long as you must to
state your message; but make it thirty seconds if possible.

Music hath charms   A long-time radio pro once told me that if he had to cut
33 percent of his radio advertising budget, but could spend that
33 percent on a music track for his commercials, he'd gladly do
it. He believes that the presence of music lends a powerful emotional overtone to the commercial. And I agree. Music can convey what words frequently cannot. And music can be obtained
very inexpensively. You can rent it from the station's rights-free
music library. You can have a music track made by hungry musicians who will record a track for very little money, appreciating
the exposure they will receive. Or you can purchase an expensive music track — made expressly for you or taken from a hot
record — and use it so much that the amortized cost is mere
peanuts.

I know an entrepreneur who made a deal with a composer
who had recently released a record album. The entrepreneur,
upon learning that the cost of the particular music he liked was

$3000, said that he'd pay the composer $100 per month for a full year. If, at the end of that time, he was still in business and wanted the music, he would then pay $3000 in addition to the rental fees he had paid. If he had not made it in business, he would merely be out the rental fees and the composer would still have the music. It sounded like a fair deal for both parties, so the composer agreed. At the end of one year, the composer did receive his $3000, in addition to the $1200 he had earned for renting out his music. His total gain was $4200. The entrepreneur, who at the time could barely afford the $100 rental, later could easily afford the $3000. Result: Everyone came out a winner.

If you have to use announcers and musicians who are members of the various unions (Screen Actors' Guild and/or American Federation of Television and Radio Actors), be wary. Union costs and paperwork are overwhelming, and you might be better off doing all in your power to avoid unions. I only work with unions when I absolutely must. And when I do, I have all the paperwork handled by an independent party. Unions and guerrillas mix like gasoline and fire.

As music adds new dimensions to your selling message, so too do sound effects. Use them when you can, and remember that radio stations (and most production facilities) have libraries of them and rent them at nominal costs. Just be careful you don't get carried away with their use.

When writing your commercials, keep in mind that you have but three seconds to catch and hold the attention of the listener. **Three crucial** So be interesting during those first three seconds and say what **seconds** you have to say, lest the listener's attention stray elsewhere. Be sure you use "ear" words rather than "eye" words, and whatever you do, repeat your main selling point. Also, repeat your company name as many times as you comfortably can.

A successful way of putting together radio commercials is to put the president of the company into a recording booth and interview him or her. Let the interview go on for twenty or thirty minutes, or even longer. Then use small sections of the interview as ingredients — sound bites — in future commercials. Sound bites are ideas expressed, simply and briefly, in a short time. The concept was spawned for the political process by public relations pros, who themselves are named "spin doctors" by the media. This is based upon their ability to give the proper "spin," or public perception, to the activities of the firms they represent. Spin doctors can create the perception that an oil company is a group of ardent environmentalists. As a guerrilla, you can be your own spin doctor, selecting your own sound bites from the interview for your marketing. It's important to remember that trust is the key — you never want to be *perceived* as a spin doctor; you only want to put the right "spin" on your marketing. Your use of selected interview sound bites must come across as different, believable, and best of all, allow the president of the company (you?) to go out on a limb publicly — a good idea.

A rich, meaty spot that worked   The following script is reprinted not because it won Radio Commercial of the Year honors in Chicago, but because it successfully sold dog food at a not very generous savings. It is a sixty-second spot and cost very little to produce.

ANNOUNCER:	Ladies and gentlemen! The makers of Perk dog food — the rich, meaty, energy-giving, delicious dog food — now bring you one minute of rich, energy-giving, delicious . . . *silence*.
SOUND:	*(Five seconds of silence)*
MAN:	*(Whisper)* Aren't you going to say anything about the big Perk sale?
ANNOUNCER:	*(Whisper)* Shhh! This is supposed to be silence!
SOUND:	*(Four seconds of silence)*
MAN:	*(Whisper)* Won't you even remind people that if they buy three cans of Perk dog food during the sale, they get five cents off?
ANNOUNCER:	*(Whisper)* Quiet!
SOUND:	*(Four seconds of silence)*
MAN:	*(Whisper)* But this is important! Aren't you —
ANNOUNCER:	*(Whisper)* Will you be quiet!!
MAN:	*(Whisper)* Yes, but —
ANNOUNCER:	*(Whisper)* I mean now!
MAN:	*(Whisper)* Yes, but the big Perk sale! You've got to say something about how now is the time to stock up on Perk because people can get five cents off when they buy three cans!
ANNOUNCER:	*(Whisper)* I'm not going to say a word! Now quiet!
MAN:	*(Whisper)* Then I'm going to say something —
ANNOUNCER:	*(Loud whisper)* Keep away from that microphone!
MAN:	*(Loud whisper)* Listen, everyone . . . *(Louder)* Perk is having a big sale, and —
SOUND:	*(Scuffling and fighting sounds. Man yells "Oof!")*

That was a humorous commercial and the humor worked to gain attention. In a more serious vein (and even more economical because it uses one announcer instead of two), here's a straight-forward spot as it might be broadcast, in thirty seconds, for a service-oriented entrepreneur:

> MALE VOICE: (*Over music*) If you dislike the inconvenience of driving your car to a mechanic, you'll like the convenience of having the Mobile Mechanic drive to your car and fix it while you're relaxing at home. If you're not happy with the price of having your car tuned up at a garage, you'll be very happy with the bargain price of having your car tuned up at home by the Mobile Mechanic. Keep your car in top shape, conveniently and economically. Call the Mobile Mechanic. Find him in the white pages of your local phone directory. The Mobile Mechanic. Call him.

Although most announcers can easily fit seventy words into a thirty-second spot, studies indicate that people listen more atten-tively if the announcer talks faster and crams more words into a short space. Thank Columbia University for making that study and giving speed talk a shot in the arm, and remember it when **Speed talk** making your commercials. A few radio hints for guerrillas:

- Save money by running ads three weeks out of every four, **Radio hints** not all four. **for guerrillas**
- Concentrate your spots during a few days of the week, such as Wednesday through Sunday.
- The best time to run radio advertising is during afternoon drive time, when people are heading home. They're in more of a buying mood than during morning drive time, when work is on their minds.
- When listening to the radio commercials you have just produced, be sure you listen to them on a car-radio-type speaker, not on a fancy high-fidelity speaker like those pro-duction studios use. Many an advertiser, dazzled after hear-ing his commercial on an expensive speaker system, has be-come depressed when hearing what the commercials really sound like on the type of sound system most people have in their cars.

- Consider radio rate cards to be pure fiction. They are highly negotiable.
- Study the audiences of all the radio stations in your marketing area. Then match your typical prospect with the appropriate stations. It's not difficult.

How much can radio do?

Unless you simply cannot see your way to using radio, do give it a try. You'll appreciate its flexibility, its ability to allow you to make last-minute changes, and the way you can home in on your prospects on the basis of station format, time of day, and day of the week. I have a client, very successful, who owns a furniture store. Although he uses many marketing media — newspapers, yellow pages, billboards, point-of-purchase signs, and direct mail — he spends 90 percent of his marketing money on radio advertising. With such a high concentration of dollars in just one medium, does he qualify as a true guerrilla? He sure does!

He has learned through the years that radio reaches his exact audience and motivates them to come into his store. He runs his commercials on anywhere from six to ten stations, and he often runs the same commercial fifteen times in one day. What's more, he's never off the radio, using it fifty-two weeks per year. Because he has learned how to use this medium to the benefit of his bottom line, he is a true guerrilla marketer. After experimenting with all kinds of marketing mixes, he finally decided that radio was the medium for him. He uses it a lot. He uses it with music. He uses it consistently. And he makes so much money that he is now able to live a luxurious life in Hawaii while his business, located in the Midwest, continues to flourish. Although many factors are responsible for his success, he gives most of the credit to radio advertising. He is living proof that you can prosper in style even as a one-medium guerrilla. But things rarely work out that way.

19
Television:
How to Use It,
How Not to Abuse It

ALTHOUGH TELEVISION IS THE MOST EFFECTIVE of all marketing vehicles, the undisputed heavyweight champion, it is also the most elusive and easiest to misuse. It is elusive because it is not as simple as it seems, because it requires many talents, because it is not normally associated with small businesspeople, and because it is dominated by giants who give entrepreneurs a mistaken impression of how it should be used. Just remember: You cannot use TV as Coca-Cola and McDonald's use it unless you have their money. But you can use it. It is easy to misuse because it does seem straightforward, because almost anyone can afford to run one or two television commercials, because it is readily available, because it is the medium that strokes the entrepreneur's ego the most tantalizingly, and because it requires a whole new discipline. Television is not, as some believe, radio with pictures.

But television has changed in many ways, all of them favoring guerrillas. The cost has plummeted to where a thirty-second commercial in prime time runs around $20 even in major markets. The targeting ability has improved to where you can run commercials in specific city neighborhoods, in selected suburbs, right in your community. The options have broadened to where satellite and cable TV let you pick TV channels that hit your audience smack-dab in their viewing patterns. Using a big dish called an uplink, satellite TV is broadcast upward to one of twenty-three communication satellites. The satellite then sends

The plummeting cost of TV

the TV signals down to earth where it is picked up by nearly 3 million Americans on their home satellite dishes and by cable stations. To give you an idea of how many choices today's TV viewer equipped with a satellite dish has, consider the selections available on the twenty-three communication satellites now in orbit. Each satellite can broadcast on twenty-four transponders, or channels, but few use all twenty-four. Still, our choices are

The bountiful options of TV

bountiful:

ABC
Able Telecommunication
  Service
Action Pay Per View
Acts — Family
  Programming
Agnet — America Agricul-
  ture Network
Agrivision
Alaska Satellite TV
All News Channel
American Entertainment
  Network
American Movie Classics
American Transportation
  TV Network
America's Disability
  Channel
Arab Network of America
Arts and Entertainment
Asia Network
Black Entertainment TV
Bravo — Cultural Pro-
  grams and Movies
Cable Video Store
The California Channel
Canadian Broadcast
  Corporation
Caribbean Super Station
The Cartoon Network
CBS

CCSN — Community
  College Satellite Net-
  work TV
CFTM — Montreal (in
  French)
Channel America
Cinemax East — Movies
Cinemax West — Movies
CNN — Cable Network
  News
Consumer News and
  Business
Comedy Central
Cornerstone
  TV — Religious
Country Music TV
Courtroom TV Network
C-Span I — Live and
  taped coverage of the
  U.S. House of Rep-
  resentatives plus
  committees
C-Span II — Live and
  taped coverage of the
  U.S. Senate plus
  committees
CTN — Christian TV
  Network
CTNA — Catholic Tele-
  communications
  Network

The Discovery Channel — Nature programming
Disney Channel East — Family entertainment
Disney Channel West — Family entertainment
E! — Entertainment
EENET — Emergency Education Network
Empire Sports Network
Encore — Movies
ESPN — Sports
Eternal Word TV Net — Catholic programming
The Family Channel East
The Family Channel West
Family Net — Religious
Flix — Movies
Fox
Galavision — Spanish
Greensheet — Shopping
Headline News
Home Box Office East — Movies, entertainment, sports
Home Box Office West
Home Box Office 2 East
Home Box Office 2 West
Home Box Office 3
Home Shopping Club
Home Shopping Club II
Home Shopping Net — Infomercials
Home Shopping Spree
Home Sports Entertainment

Home Team Sports
House of Commons
The International Channel
Jade Channel — Chinese news
JSO — TV feed to Japan
KBL — Pittsburgh sports network
KCNC — NBC in Denver
Keystone Inspirational
KMGH — CBS in Denver
KRMA — PBS in Denver
KTLA — Los Angeles sports, movies
KTVT — Dallas, Texas, Rangers baseball
KUSA — ABC in Denver
KWGN — Independent in Denver
Las Vegas TV Network
The Learning Channel
Lifetime — Health, medical, cooking, women's programming
Madison Square Garden — Sports
Main Street TV
Midwest Sportschannel
Mind Extension University — Accredited college classes (*For more data, call 1-800-777-6463*)
MOR Music TV
The Movie Channel East
The Movie Channel West
Movie Greats Network
MuchMusic — Music videos
Music Television East

Music Television West
NACTAV Network —
North American Chinese network
NASA Select TV
The Nashville Network
National Christian Network
NBC
Nebraska ETV Network
New England Cable News
New England Sports
Network
New Inspirational Network
NHK — TV feed to Japan
Nickelodeon — Children's
programs and old TV
shows
The Nostalgia Channel
Open Public Events
Net — North Carolina
Pass — Detroit sports
PBS
Playboy at Night
Prime Network
Prime Sports
PrimeStar
Prime Ticket Network
ProStar — Sports and
events for commercial
establishments
QVC Shopping Network
RAI — Italian, variety
Satellite Market USA
Sci-Fi Channel
SCOLA — International
news, in the language of
origin
Shop at Home
Shop at Home II
Showtime East

Showtime West
The Silent Network —
Programming for the
hearing impaired
SkyVision — TV reception
only
Spice — Adult programming, pay per view
SportsChannel — Ten
transponders on one
satellite
Sports News Satellite
SportSouth
Step — Educational
Programming
StoryVision — Computer
data storybook for
children
Sunshine
Network — Sports
Superior Livestock
Tavern TV
TBS — Atlanta sports
Telemundo — Spanish
Three Angels — Seventh
Day Adventist
TNT — Movies, sports
The Travel Channel
Trinity Broadcasting
Turner Premiere
TV 5 Quebec
TVN Pay-Per-View — Ten
transponders on one
satellite
TVNC Iqualuit — Far
North American
Univision — Spanish
USA Network — Variety,
sports, movies
The Vacation Network

ValueVision — Shopping
channel
Video Hits-1
Viewer's Choice 1 — Pay
per view
Viewer's Choice 2 — Pay
per view
VISN Interfaith Network
WABC — ABC in New
York
The Weather Channel
The Weather
Network — Canadian
WGN — Independent TV
from Chicago, featuring
sports

World Harvest TV
WPIX — Independent TV
from New York, featur-
ing the Yankees
WRAL — CBS in Ra-
leigh, North Carolina
WSBK — Independent TV
from Boston, featuring
sports
WWOR — Independent
TV from New York, fea-
turing sports
WXIA — NBC in Atlanta

Whether your interest is education, international news, movies, adult programming, network TV, kids, business, information, shopping, religion, sports, travel, weather, or a skyful of
other topics, chances are that it's on satellite.

Cable stations select their programming from both local
sources and all these satellite options. Some cable systems have
only five choices; others have over fifty. The number is growing. And notice that there are eleven different home shopping
channels.

As TV technology, cable systems, satellites in orbit, and
videocassette ownership — now approaching 80 percent — have
changed, so have viewing patterns. Guerrillas know that the ten **What folks watch**
prime uses of TV sets are, in order:

1. Network television
2. Local television stations
3. Public Broadcasting System
4. Playing rented tapes
5. Recording on-air programs for later viewing
6. Cable movie channels
7. Other cable channels
8. 24-hour music videos
9. Video games
10. Monitor for a home computer

Guerrillas also know that some uses of TV have died down while others have become growth areas. Right now, the eleven *fastest growth areas* for TV set use are, in order:

1. Playing rented tapes
2. Public Broadcasting System
3. Cable movie channels
4. Other cable channels
5. Recording on-air programs for later viewing
6. Local television stations
7. Viewing home movies
8. Playing video games
9. 24-hour music videos
10. Monitor for home computer
11. Network television

When you were a kid, network TV ruled the roost. Today it is hanging in there, but not enjoying a growth spurt.

The sophisticated viewer   TV viewers are now more sophisticated than ever. They've been around the block when it comes to TV advertising spots, and they have opinions about the spots that you should know: 31 percent find TV advertising spots to be misleading; 24.3 percent find them offensive; 17 percent think they are informative; 15.9 percent think they are entertaining.

If you are planning to test TV for advertising to your market, you should give cable serious consideration. The markets with the highest cable penetration are Palm Springs, California (88 percent), Santa Barbara–Santa Maria–San Luis Obispo, California (85 percent), Laredo, Texas (85 percent), Parkersburg, West Virginia (82 percent), Elmira, New York (79 percent), Bluefield–Beckley–Oak Hill, Virginia and West Virginia (79 percent), Odessa–Midland, Texas (78 percent), Lafayette, Indiana (78 percent), Johnstown–Altoona, Pennsylvania (78 percent), and Hartford–New Haven, Connecticut (78 percent). Cable TV, as you can plainly see, is growing, and it's becoming more and more affordable.

Voila! Now small-business owners can advertise on TV, on any satellite-delivered cable show, for somewhere in the $20 range — or less! You can advertise on prime time, cherry-pick the subscriber neighborhoods and suburbs in which your spots appear, pick stations such as MTV, the Nashville Network, Arts and Entertainment, the Discovery Channel, and loads more — *for not much more than the cost of a radio commercial.* Never before has TV been more available and desirable to owners of small businesses. Guerrillas in droves are, at this very moment, discovering the awesome power of TV, and I suggest that you do the very same.

Awesome power, teensy prices

You might want to look into interconnects, companies that serve as middlemen between the cable companies and small-business owners who want to go on TV but can't afford standard spot advertising or network TV. Ask your media-buying service how to get in touch with your local interconnect company. They're all over the place, concentrating on big cities.

But television can be effective only if you use it enough. And enough is a lot. Enough is expensive. How much is enough? Many experts say you can measure how much enough is by understanding rating points. A GRP, or Gross Rating Point, is calculated on the basis of one percent of the TV sets in the TV marketing area. If one million TV sets are in the area, one rating point equals 10,000 sets. The cost of TV advertising is determined by the size of each GRP in the marketing area, and advertisers pay for a given number of GRPs when they buy advertising time. The experts advise, and I agree, that you should not consider TV advertising unless you can afford to pay for 150 GRPs per month. Those can come in the form of 75 GRPs per week every other week, or 50 GRPs for three weeks out of four, or even 150 GRPs for one week per month. How much a single rating point costs in your area depends upon the size of the area, the competitive situation, and the time of year. Points tend to cost more around Christmas shopping time — October through late December. They tend to cost less during the summer when reruns are being shown. GRPs in small towns cost far less than GRPs in big cities.

How much is enough?

The price ranges from about $5 per GRP in a small town to about $500 per GRP in a big city. Although TV costs have dropped, these numbers have remained constant. The lower costs are the result of pinpointing smaller audiences and more limited geographic areas.

Can you start small in TV and then build up? Only if you start out by buying 150 GRPs for one month and have the funds and emotional endurance to hang in there for a minimum of three months. If you can't do that, don't fool around with TV.

But if you can afford to pay for the proper number of rating points — and you can if you live in a low-cost TV marketing area such as those found in many rural sections of the United States, or if you are well funded — you'll find that TV can do many **What TV can do** things the other media cannot. It allows you to demonstrate, to act, to dance, to sing, to put on playlets, to show cause and effect, to create a lively identity, to be dramatic, to reach large numbers of people, to home in on your specific audience, to prove your points visually and verbally — all at the same time. No other medium provides so many advantages to the advertiser at one time.

Of the various times you can advertise on the tube, unless you're going to economize by running on cable channels, steer clear of prime time — the 8:00 P.M. to 11:00 P.M. period when so many people are watching. You can realize better values — more viewers per dollar — by using fringe time, the time before and after prime time, especially on local affiliates of the big networks. You might also look into daytime TV, which attracts many women viewers. The audience size is smaller and so is the cost. The time period past midnight, when few people are watching, is very inexpensive and can prove a springboard to success. Some postmidnight shows have ratings so low they are unmeasurable. That also means, happily, that they are inexpensive.

If you truly want to advertise on television, find out what shows your prospects watch, then run commercials on those shows. Many of the shows are available on cable. For example, when the solar energy industry was in its infancy, aggressive marketing people soon learned that the same people who watch *Star Trek* tend to buy solar energy units. They also learned that men who watch science-fiction movies, not sports, have a proclivity toward solar power. Some solar energy companies went to the bank as a result of that fascinating information. Even though *Star Trek* was in its tenth series of reruns, it still proved to be a marvelous and inexpensive vehicle for solar heating marketers. Talk shows, which frequently attract an older audience, were determined to be poison for solar energy sellers. Their product simply did not appeal to seniors — at least at first it didn't. Today it does, as solar energy becomes more and more acceptable as an alternative source of power, and as media coverage of solar applications becomes generous, appealing to our increasing number of environmentally aware citizens.

To get the most out of TV, keep in mind that TV rate cards, like radio rate cards, are established as the basis for negotiation and are not to be taken as gospel. In fact, if you're going to go on to television, you should retain a media-buying service to make your plans and buys for you. They'll charge about 7.5 percent of the total for their services, but they'll save you more than that. Many small businesspeople make their own buys, thinking they are getting good deals. But the media-buying services, which purchase millions of dollars' worth of TV time monthly, obtain bargains that would shock the small businessperson.

Media-buying services

Another warning about buying your TV advertising directly: TV salespeople have a powerful way of putting the egos of their commercial clients to work for them. Some convince an advertiser that he or she would be a terrific spokesperson. The advertiser, enjoying the strokes to his or her ego, then goes on TV and presents the commercial in person. Sometimes, but rarely, this is effective. Generally, the advertiser loses as many sales as he or she gains. Frequently the advertiser becomes a laughingstock but continues to present the ads because his or her TV salespeople wouldn't dream of risking their sales by telling the truth. Don't let your ego get in the way of your TV marketing when it comes to buying the time or presenting the information. If you've watched enough TV, I'm sure you get the gist of what I'm saying.

I strongly suggest that you look into cable TV. It just may be that you can afford to market your offerings on television because of the new cable availabilities. Instead of going on TV and reaching the 90 percent of the audience who are out of your marketing area, you can telecast *only* to people within your marketing area. As cable (and satellite TV) is making TV more and more affordable to more and more small businesses, the networks are losing their shirts. In 1991, they lost $625 billion to cable. And TV is still in a state of flux — all favoring the guerrilla. So be one! And get yourself onto the tube.

Cable is able

Also, videocassette recorder sales are skyrocketing — nearly 80 percent of Americans have access to one at this writing, compared with 45 percent in 1984 — letting audiences view postmidnight programming anytime the next day. Stay tuned. These are very interesting times from the standpoint of television.

If you do decide to invest in television marketing, there are many methods by which you can cut down drastically on the cost of producing TV commercials, which currently runs an estimated $179,000 for a thirty-second spot. Truth is, you can turn out a very good thirty-second spot for about $1000. And even that figure can be reduced as you increase your TV savvy.

How to produce a TV spot

First of all, let your TV station provide all the *production* assistance. Not the writing. Let *them* put up the equipment and furnish the camerapeople, the lighting experts, the director, the all-important editor. Don't let them write the spot. If you do, it will look like all their other homegrown TV commercials. Instead, either you or a talented individual you coerce, barter with, or hire should write a tight script. The left side of the sheet of paper upon which the script is written is reserved for video instructions. On that side, describe every single action the viewers will see, numbering each one. The right side of the script paper is for the audio portion. These are the sounds the viewers will hear. Again, number each audio section, matching it up with the appropriate video section so that the audio and video make a team.

If necessary, and it usually is not necessary, make a storyboard. A storyboard is a pictorial representation of your script. It consists of perhaps ten "frames," or pictures. Each frame contains a picture of what the viewers will see, a description of what will be happening, and the message that will be heard while the action is taking place. Storyboards tend to be taken too literally, however, and do not allow you the leeway to make changes during production. Those little changes are often the difference between an ordinary and an extraordinary commercial. Most (but not all) people have the imagination to understand a commercial from a script alone. If the people you are working with don't, you just may have to resort to a storyboard. Artists charge from $10 to $505 per frame, so you can see how utilizing storyboards will make costs rise.

While working in major ad agencies, I had to prepare a storyboard for every commercial I wrote. And I know that I wrote over a thousand. Many art directors enjoyed gainful employment because of my active typewriter and the traditions of advertising agencies, which called for storyboards. Since I've been working on my own, I have written well over a thousand commercials, and only five or six required storyboards. Yet the commercials were no less successful than those I made using storyboards that swelled the budget.

Intense pre-production

You can also save money by having intense preproduction meetings with all who will be involved in the production of your commercial. Meet with the actors, actresses, director, lighting person, prop person, everyone. Make sure everyone knows what is expected and understands the script. Make sure the timing is on the button and not one detail is unexplored. Then hold at least one tightly timed rehearsal. Have the people involved go through the motions before the cameras are running. By doing so, you'll be able to produce two commercials in the time usually necessary to produce one. You'll even be able to fit three commercials into the same production time, if you're good enough. When you are paying $1000 per day for equipment and crew, that comes to $333.33 per commercial when you do three commercials at once. A far cry from the average cost of $179,000. That $333.33 figure was true in the 1980s and remains true in the 1990s. All it takes is shopping around plus the attitude of a guerrilla.

To keep the cost down, which is one characteristic of a guerrilla, you will have to avoid expensive union talent and crew whenever possible (in some union cities such as Los Angeles and San Francisco, this is not easily done), get everything right the first time as a result of well-planned rehearsals and preproduction meetings, and plan the editing when you plan the spot. Editing videotape can be very expensive — $250 per hour and up. So plan your shooting so that little editing will be necessary. And know that most experts tell you that it's in the editing room that the commercial is really made. So make it a point to be there watching — and opining — when the editing takes place. It's an important process of guerrilla learning.

Film or tape

Whether you shoot with film or tape usually won't make much difference in your final cost. Film allows you to use more special effects, has more of a magical quality because it has less "presence" than tape, and allows for less expensive editing. But with film you have no instant feedback. If someone goofed, you won't know it till the film is processed. With tape, you can replay what you have shot immediately, and if anything is wrong, you can redo it. No processing is necessary. As to which is better, there is no correct answer. Both can be ideal, depending upon the circumstances. But if you are planning to have the station help with production, better plan on videotape. Stations don't usually film for you. That's okay; guerrillas seem to opt for tape.

What makes a great TV commercial? Well, Procter & Gamble, one of the most sophisticated advertisers in the United

States, frequently uses "slice of life" commercials, which are little playlets, the type that seem boring and commonplace. But with the big bucks P&G puts behind them, they work extremely well. And many companies have made a bundle copying this format. So don't knock them if you are considering TV as a marketing vehicle. You can learn plenty from P&G. I certainly did.

There are a few guidelines that will help you regardless of the type of commercials you wish to produce:

Remember always that television is a *visual medium with audio enhancement*. Many ill-informed advertisers look upon it as the opposite. A guerrilla marketer knows that a great TV commercial *starts with a great idea*. Try to express that idea visually, then add the words, music, and sound effects to make it clearer and stronger. Try viewing your commercial with no sound. If it is a winner, it will make its point with pictures only.

Where a great TV spot starts

Again, go with thirty-second spots rather than sixties, and if you are using TV for direct response, such as for ordering by toll-free number, try two-minute spots. They're very effective. Say that phone number at least three times.

Keep in mind that, as with radio, you have three seconds to attract the viewers' attention. If you haven't hooked them right up front, you've probably lost them. So say what you have to say in a captivating manner at the outset. Say it again, in different words, in the middle of your spot. Say it a final time, again in different words (or maybe even in the same words), at the end. Don't fall into the trap of making your commercial more interesting than your product. Don't allow anyone to remember your commercial without remembering your name. There are bushels of sob stories about commercials that won all sorts of awards while the products they were promoting died horrible deaths. You want sales, not awards, praise, or laughs.

Communicate to their eyes

When you can, *show your product or service in action*. People's memories improve 68 percent when they have a visual element to recall. So say what you have to say verbally and visually, especially visually.

The following thirty-second commercial not only won first prize at the Venice TV Film Festival but caused the advertiser to withdraw it from the air because he was unable to keep up with the demand for his product. The basic idea to be conveyed in the commercial is that this particular cookie, known as "Sports" and manufactured by a company called Carr's, has more chocolate on it than any similar cookie. Simple enough? Here's the script:

VIDEO	AUDIO
1. OPEN WITH TWO SLAPSTICK CHARACTERS FACING THE CAMERA. ONE IS TALL AND ONE IS SHORT. TALL ONE SPEAKS.	1. (*Tall man*) Good evening. Sidney and I would like to prove that Carr's Sports have the most chocolate — by showing you two ways to make chocolate cookies.
2. SHORT MAN SMILES WHEN HIS NAME IS MENTIONED, BUT LOSES THE SMILE WHEN HE HEARS THAT HE IS A COOKIE.	2. Imagine Sidney here is a cookie.
3. TALL MAN LIFTS HUGE CONTAINER MARKED "CHOCOLATE" AND POURS REAL CHOCOLATE FLUID ONTO SHORT MAN.	3. Now take your cookie. Cover it with chocolate.
4. CAMERA TILTS DOWN TO SHOW POOL OF CHOCOLATE AT SHORT MAN'S FEET.	4. Effective, but not much stays on. Carr's makes Sports a better way.
5. CUT TO THE TWO MEN. TALL MAN NOW CARRIES SHORT MAN, HOLDS HIM ABOVE A TUB MARKED "CHOCOLATE." TALL MAN THEN DROPS SIDNEY INTO THE TUB.	5. Pop the cookie in chocolate.
6. CUT TO SHORT MAN'S HEAD SURFACING FROM THE CHOCOLATE. AS IT SURFACES, MORE CHOCOLATE IS POURED ON IT.	6. Top it up, and when it is set . . .
7. DISSOLVE TO SHORT MAN NOW ENCASED IN CHOCOLATE AS HE IS LYING DOWN. TALL MAN STANDS PROUDLY ABOVE HIM.	7. . . . you have your cookie with all your chocolate on it.

8. TALL MAN HOLDS OUT A CARR'S SPORTS PACKAGE AS CAMERA ZOOMS TO CLOSE-UP OF IT.	8. That's how Carr's makes Sports.
9. HAND SETS PACKAGE DOWN NEXT TO SHORT MAN, STILL ENCASED IN CHOCOLATE. MAN LOOKS AT PACKAGE.	9. Carr's Sports — the bar of chocolate with the cookie in the middle. Right, Sidney?

The commercial, which cost about $1500 to produce, including everything, states the premise right up front. In the beginning the two characters are whimsical, so the viewer's attention is caught. The commercial is very funny. But the product is always the star. All the talk is about the product. The theme is chocolate. And the viewer makes a clear connection between Carr's Sports and chocolate, which was the basic idea all along. Viewers are told in frame one that the product has the most chocolate. In frame seven, the point is made again. In frame nine, it is made one more time. Even if there were no words, viewers could tell what the commercial is all about and could understand the connection made between Sports and chocolate.

The commercial uses no music, has ninety-three words instead of the pedestrian sixty-five, and employs humor to make its point. Humor, often referred to as the most dangerous weapon in advertising because it is so frequently misused, works well here, selling a product that retails for about seventy-five cents. And the spot makes full use of television's ability to demonstrate product advantages. Best of all, the commercial is so much fun to watch that viewers could watch it several times without becoming bored with it. They must also have remembered the name of the product, in view of the sales that resulted.

This just goes to show that you don't need a huge budget and a fancy jingle to make a successful commercial. As a marketing man, I am far more proud of the sales than of the awards won by this commercial.

Because so many people, estimated now at 70 percent, have remote controls with both their TV sets and their VCRs, there's a big chance, estimated at 67 percent, that your commercial will get "zapped" — either shown at fast forward, or muted, with the sound off. Does this steer guerrillas away from television? No, it does not.

Instead, guerrillas take heed of this ugly reality by working with it, not against it. They make their TV commercials remote-proof by telling their stories visually, using words and music, but not really requiring them because their pictures make their point. They show their names — often throughout the commercials — by superimposing them in the lower corner of the screen, à la CNN. **Overcoming zapping**

And they show their commercials enough times to their target audiences that they begin to see the results of this ultra-powerful guerrilla marketing after a few months. A few months? Why not instantly? Because TV, as high potency as it is, does not bring about instant results unless you are having a limited-time sale, making a limited-time offer, or using TV as a direct-response medium, providing viewers with a toll-free number and enough information to make the decision to buy from you.

You're going to be a happy guerrilla if you *lower your expectations for TV in the short run*. Over time, TV will work its miracles for you. Only they won't be miracles. They'll be the result of your patience combined with your knowledge that no medium does as much to sell your offering as television. **TV miracles**

Yet, even with your newborn confidence with this medium, keep in mind that you've got to have a great product or service for TV to do its job for you. You've got to be aware that the 1990s are shaping up into a decade that responds most to the basics. The hot buttons of this decade are the functionally elegant, the plain and simple, what is healthy and sensible, what is politically correct, what is environmentally responsible, what is good for America, and what is solidly positioned as mid-price.

Once you've got offerings that live up to those consumer demands, that's when TV can be most effective for you, the guerrilla. That's when to use and not to abuse TV.

20
Outdoor Advertising:
What It Can and Cannot Do

OUTDOOR ADVERTISING CONSISTS of billboards, bus ads, taxi signs, painted walls, and outdoor signs. Let's deal with billboards first. Rare is the entrepreneur who can survive on billboard advertising alone — although it can be done. We have already chronicled the successes of Harold's Club, Wall Drugs, and Burma-Shave, but these enterprises really used outdoor signs, not billboards. Billboard advertising — and to use the term advertising is somewhat of an overstatement — is really reminder advertising, for the most part. It works best when combined with advertising through other media.

Each year, an Iowa entrepreneur I know runs a month-long one-cent-sale promotion on the radio and in newspapers. He supports the radio and newspaper advertising for a month each year with billboards, too. His sales rise an average of 18 percent. With billboards alone, this would never happen. But the billboards add an important ingredient to his marketing mix. He uses them only once a year to promote his furniture business. And they work wonderfully.

Two magic words   But billboard advertising doesn't have to be strictly reminder advertising. In some instances it can lead directly to sales. In regard to this, let me stop right here and tell you the two most important words you can use on a billboard. They are not at all like the high motivation words we discussed several pages back — not at all that obvious. The two magic words that can spell instant success for you if used on a billboard are *next exit*. If you can use them on your billboard, it may do a full-blown job of marketing for you. For example, a new store in the San Francisco Bay Area that did not have enough money for most marketing could afford one billboard. And that billboard, fortunately, was able to display the words *next exit*. Success came rapidly and overwhelmingly. Of course, the store had to do everything else right to succeed, and it did. But the billboard must get the prime credit. If you can't use those two words, these three also work well: *two miles ahead*.

Most of the time, you cannot buy just one billboard. Usually you've got to rent ten or twenty billboards at once. Some are in all winning locations. Some are sure-fire losers. You must take the bad with the good. But sometimes, through cogent arguing or through some loophole in the billboard firm's policies, you can lease just one beautifully located billboard. If ever you can, do it. Otherwise, be careful. Consider using billboards if you have a restaurant, tourist attraction, garage, gas station, motel, or hotel. But look with disdain upon billboard advertising if you've got a business that will not have instant appeal to motorists. If you have a car wash that really is at the next exit, a billboard might just be the ticket. If you have a computer-education firm, forget it. A billboard can, however, help you maintain your identity — if your identity is already established.

When to use billboards

The Marlboro cigarette company is able to maintain its cowboy identity with billboards. It wouldn't even have to use any words, though it does. But if you are thinking about using billboards simply as reminders and haven't invested a lot in your identity, as Marlboro has, scratch that idea from your marketing plan.

To ascertain whether or not you want even one billboard, find out how many cars pass the billboard site each day. This is known in the business as the traffic count. Billboard firms have that data at their fingertips. Find out also the type of traffic passing by. Trucks won't be able to patronize your car wash. On the other hand, homeward bound affluent suburbanites may be interested in your take-home restaurant.

When planning a billboard, keep the rules for outdoor signs in mind. Rarely use more than six words. Remember that people are probably driving around fifty-five miles per hour when they glance, if they glance at all, at your billboard. Keep it simple for them. Give them one large graphic upon which they can concentrate. Be sure the type is clear. Be sure the words are large. If

Six words only

the traffic count remains more or less the same at night, be sure your board is illuminated. That costs more than a nonilluminated board but may be worth the extra bucks.

Billboard companies are open to price negotiation, although they may not appreciate my putting that down in print. They are also amenable to location negotiation. Once I wanted a specific location and was told that in order to get it, I'd have to rent nine other billboards — all in dismal locations. I said I was not interested. A couple of weeks later, I was offered the billboard along with only four other locations, also dismal. Again, I said no. Finally, I received a call from the sales rep saying I could have the one location I wanted, but the price would be significantly higher than originally quoted. It would have been a good deal, and I wished I could have said yes. But by this time, my client's monies had been committed. So we all lost out. Too bad the rep hadn't made me the same offer in the beginning. I could have used "next exit" on the billboard and had one more success story to report here.

In addition to attracting direct sales on occasion, billboards help guerrillas in three other instances:

1. When you are new to an area and want to make your presence known
2. When you want to tie in with a unique advertising campaign or promotion
3. When you have an idea that translates ideally onto a billboard, and you can rent just one board

An example of the third instance is a roadside cider stand that sells cherry cider grown from trees visible from the highway. A gutsy entrepreneur might display a billboard with the entire center section cut out so that motorists can see right through the billboard to the cherry trees. A simple line of copy at the top (or bottom) might say: CHERRY CIDER FROM THESE TREES — NEXT EXIT. I know it is seven words long, but it's okay to break the rules occasionally, just as long as you know them and have a good reason for breaking them when you do.

Producing your billboard One of the more attractive aspects of billboard advertising is that if you supply the design, the billboard company will produce the billboard for you. That means the company will handle blowing the artwork up to a size that will fit on the billboard. Billboard sizes are measured in sheets, with one sheet approximating the size of a large poster. The usual size is a 24-sheet. Whatever you do, make sure your billboard fits in with the rest of your advertising campaign. The Iowa man was able to present his message in six words on his immensely successful billboard only because the message had been explained more fully elsewhere. A guerrilla uses billboards like darts. A guerrilla either says "next exit," "two miles," or "five minutes ahead," ties his or her billboard in directly with a strong campaign, or uses a single billboard with surgical precision. No guerrilla uses a "next exit" billboard for the usual one month or three months. After testing the merits of a billboard, a guerrilla signs a one-year, three-year, or five-year contract for such a board. A guerrilla contracts with a billboard company to erect a billboard in a place where "next exit" can be used, if one does not yet exist there. And a guerrilla still realizes that a great billboard isn't much more than a great reminder.

I would suggest that you avoid the use of billboards unless there is a compelling reason to use them. Drive around your community and carefully note the local companies that use billboards. Then talk to the owners of those companies and find out if the billboards work. Unless you are in a business that competes with theirs, you'll probably get a straight answer.

Sometimes a guerrilla can get several fellow guerrillas to collaborate on a billboard. This brings the cost of the board down considerably and puts it within range of many an entrepreneur. If two or three companies share a board, the cost may be low enough to enable each of them to use the board on a full-time basis, as part of their overall marketing plan.

Call the billboard representatives in your area and listen to their sales pitches. Perhaps they can enlighten you as to special opportunities, new boards to be erected, chances to go in on billboards with other companies. Chances are, you won't be persuaded to put even the tiniest billboard into your marketing plan. But you've nothing to lose by talking with them. So do it. Better yet, listen to them. If you have a well-known theme, billboards might be for you. As with many other marketing media, it may be worth your while to test their efficacy. Different towns respond in different ways to billboards. Maybe you live in a town that gets motivated by billboards. Los Angeles seems to be the billboard capital of the universe, with a multitude of ornate moving billboards in high-traffic locations — all heralding movies, stars, shows — but never Preparation H. Maybe you are located near a street that is ideal for a billboard. If that's the case, I recommend testing. If you test a billboard for a month or two and nothing happens, you're not out all that much money. But if you never give it a try, and then your biggest competitor tries billboards and goes to glory with them, you'll kick yourself from now till Sunday.

Share-of-mind advertising

Billboard marketing is, almost without exception, *share-of-mind* advertising. Share-of-mind advertising is advertising that attempts to win sales down the road by implanting a thought or establishing an identity. It tries to win for you a constantly increasing share of the minds of the people in your marketing area. It does not normally prove effective in a hurry, cannot be translated into results, and is only profitable in the long run, if ever. *Share-of-market* advertising, on the other hand, is advertising that attempts to win instant sales. It tries to win for you a constantly increasing share of whatever market your offering belongs to. Share-of-market advertising is the kind of advertising that is the most effective, the most instantly translated into results, and the most profitable in the short run. Most entrepreneurs are a bit too concerned with cash to worry about shares of minds. They want increased shares of markets, and they want them right now. So consider using billboards, but don't expect to attract highly motivated prospects through them.

Buses and taxis

You can expect about the same, perhaps a little more, from bus signs, both interior and exterior, and interior or exterior taxi signs. These may be employed as part of a marketing plan that calls for the use of signs in targeted urban areas. These moving signs are seen by many people, a lot of whom may be serious prospects. Taxi signs are seen by people throughout the metropolitan area. Bus signs are usually seen by the same people — bus riders and people who live along the route. Of course buses don't always travel the same routes taxis do. But this should be kept in mind if you're thinking about using both bus signs and taxi signs.

A client of mine enjoyed a great deal of success attracting temporary office workers with signs placed inside buses. The client was an agency that provided these workers to large employers, and the signs were designed to appeal to both the workers and the employers. If your product or service is located near a bus line, you should consider placing signs on that particular bus line —

on the exterior of the buses. Such signs will not serve as a complete marketing plan, but they can be an effective part of one.

Learning where your prospects go will help you determine the best location for outdoor advertising, whether it be placed on a billboard, a bus, a painted wall, or a sign on a barn. For example, if you sell a new type of tanning oil and a paintable wall is available near a sunbathers' beach, grab it. If you market agricultural products or services and a paintable roof is available on a well-traveled country road, rent the space and paint it with your message. Give serious thought to placing a sign outside your own place of business. A good sign often results in good business. A poor sign invites disaster.

What makes a bad outdoor sign? Lack of clarity. Lack of **A bad sign** uniqueness. Fancy lettering. Bland colors. Tiny words. Improper placement. What makes a good outdoor sign? Readability. Warmth. Good location. Uniqueness. An identity that matches that of your business. Clarity from afar, from moving vehicles, on dark nights. Good colors. Make certain that your sign communicates what your business is all about. For instance, "Moore's" tells us a lot less than "Moore's Stationery." To gain community acceptance, try to have your sign designed in such a manner that it fits in with the character of the community. Garish signs may be dandy in some locations and horrid in others. Conservative signs may be just the ticket on some streets, and a ticket to doom on others. Be sensitive to the tastes of your community.

Always be on the lookout for potential sign locations. I know a guerrilla marketer who could not secure a billboard near his place of business. But he was able to persuade the owner of a drive-in located within one mile of his business to sell him space on the back of the drive-in screen. It's no accident that the back of the drive-in screen faced a heavily traveled freeway.

Successful guerrilla marketers tell me that one of the most important signs they have is the neon one that says OPEN. Some **A neon money-** remind me that the high cost of neon signs prevents a few busi- **maker** ness owners from using them, necessitating instead the eventual expense of a GOING OUT OF BUSINESS sign.

Don't allow yourself to be hemmed in by a small imagination. But remember that advertising seen by speeding motorists has less impact than advertising seen by relaxed prospects — the type that might take the time to read a direct mailing from you.

21
Direct-Mail Marketing:
Pinpointing Your Prospects

ATTENTION ALL GUERRILLAS! Direct marketing is where it's at. Direct marketing is the name of your game. Direct marketing has a built-in mirror that reflects the true effectiveness of your advertising message. All other forms of marketing have much to be said for them, but direct marketing has more. All other forms of marketing can help you immensely, but direct marketing can help you more.

Direct marketing refers to direct-mail, mail-order, or coupon advertising, to telephone marketing, direct-response TV, postcard decks, door-to-door salespeople, home shopping TV shows, or any method of marketing that attempts to make a sale right then and there. It does not require a middleman. It does not require a store. It requires only a seller and a buyer. And because of that, much unnecessary game playing is removed from the marketing process, leaving only accountable results. Let me repeat that

Accountability is all word: *accountable*. When you run a radio commercial or a newspaper ad, you do all in your power to make sure that it works, but you don't really know if it does. But when you engage in direct-mail advertising, the form of direct marketing upon which we will concentrate in this chapter, you'll know clearly whether or not your mailing worked. Either it did or it didn't. If it worked, you'll know how well it worked. And if it failed, you'll know how dismally it failed.

Direct-mail advantages Along with its all-important accountability, consider some of the other advantages of direct mail over other advertising media:

1. You can achieve more accurately measured results.
2. You can be as expansive or concise as you wish.
3. You can zero in on almost any target audience.
4. You can personalize your marketing like crazy.
5. You can expect the highest of all response rates.
6. You can use unlimited opportunities for testing.
7. You can enjoy repeat sales to proven customers.
8. You can compete with, even beat, the giants.

Along with those eight advantages come eight rules of thumb:

1. The most important element is the right list.
2. Make it easy for the recipient to take action.
3. Letters almost always outpull mailing packages with no letters.
4. The best buyers are those who have bought by mail before, a rapidly growing number.
5. Do anything to get your envelope opened. (A list of hints is coming up later in this chapter.)
6. Keeping good records is paramount.
7. Testimonials improve response rates.
8. Remember that *nothing is as simple as it seems.*

In true guerrilla fashion, I also offer you eight tips for gaining the response rate you want with direct mail:

How guerrillas gain responses

1. Ask for the order in the headline of your brochure.
2. Always tell the person what to do next.
3. Blue is a dandy second color, but red with black is generally the best-pulling direct-mail combination.
4. Don't overuse red; use it primarily for highlights.
5. Experts say the four most important elements in direct mail are the list, the offer, the copy, and the graphics. Guerrillas pay close attention to each.
6. The fastest-growing segment of the direct-mail industry is nontraditional mailers — those who haven't used direct mail in the past.
7. Direct-mail success comes with the cumulative effect of repeat mailings. Make them repetitive, yet different from one another.

8. Direct-mail spending by consumers tripled between 1980 and 1990; expect more growth in the current decade.

The normal response rate

Guerrillas realize that when it comes to determining the normal percentage of return on direct mail, *there is none.* You'll have to determine your own, then go about improving it — the name of the game in direct mail.

Right now, about 40 percent of direct mail is from national advertisers, 25 percent from local advertisers, 20 percent from mail-order firms. The average U.S. household receives an average of 104 pieces of direct mail each week. To a guerrilla, this means a slimmer chance than ever for a great response rate and a more acute need than ever for true creativity in your mailings. Keep in mind that more money is spent on direct mail than on magazines, radio, or TV. Remember also that over 95 million Americans responded to direct-mail pitches in 1991, that one in six Americans purchased six or more items via this maxi-medium, that older people want less mail while younger folks want more, and that nonprofit groups use direct mail to raise up to 90 percent of their funds. Finally, keep in mind that with postal rates rising, amateurs are being forced away from direct mail, leaving a lush new universe for guerrillas.

The least expensive method

Those same guerrillas are grateful that direct mail is the least expensive method of marketing — on a per-sale basis. The overall cost may be high, but if it works for you, it is inexpensive marketing. There are many books, many articles, many chapters devoted to enlightening marketers on the intricacies of direct-mail marketing. Read them. Keep reading. For a guerrilla, marketing is part art and part science. Direct mail is more science than art. This is not to downplay the art of creating a successful direct-mail package. But for now, let's focus on the science, the things we already know.

Test, test, then test

For instance, we know that the three most important things to do if you are to succeed at direct marketing are to test, test, and test. If you know that and do that, you are on the right road. If you play it by ear, you will probably fall on your ear. Direct marketing is growing faster than any other type of marketing. More and more people trust it. More and more people enjoy the convenience of being able to shop and buy by mail. More and more people want to be spared the lack of parking places, high fuel costs, irritable sales clerks, and crowded stores. They turn, therefore, to companies that make their products or services available through direct mail. In 1991, 94 percent of Americans purchased something by mail. They obviously appreciate the convenience and the saving of time. With a mailing, *you have a good chance of getting through to people.* Studies show that 60 percent of people say of direct mail, "I usually read or scan it"; 31 percent say, "I read some of it, don't read some of it"; 9 percent say, "I don't read any of it." The bottom line: You have a shot at reaching 91 percent of your audience. That's a healthy number.

More on the science of direct mail is embodied in the *60-30-10 Rule.* Sixty percent of your direct-mail program depends upon your using the right list of people; 30 percent depends upon your making the right offer; 10 percent depends upon your creative package. You can make it extra creative if you take to heart these three tips: **The 60-30-10 rule**

- Brightly colored envelopes grab attention. Although red and blue are time-honored direct-mail colors, the nineties are proving that yellow, orange, and pink merit consideration, too. But white is always a safe, good bet.
- Oversized addressing stimulates the unconscious pleasure people gain from seeing their name in print. The larger, the better.
- A white #10 (business-sized) envelope with a first-class stamp and no return address is especially intriguing and gets rave notices when it comes to response rates. Look into it (that's a guerrilla hint to test it).

The complete honesty that results from direct-mail marketing is invaluable. Because it is so *accountable,* it lets you know if you have done a good job making your offer, pricing your merchandise, constructing your mailing package, writing your copy, timing your mailing, selecting your mailing list. Soon after you have accomplished your mailing, you learn whether it worked or failed. That's what I mean by accountability. During the past few years, more of my work than ever before has been in the area of direct response. That is because companies are moving rapidly into direct-response marketing. They are learning that the feedback is instant and accurate when they employ this marketing vehicle.

But before studying the secrets imparted in these pages, you must honestly ask yourself whether or not your product or service lends itself to direct marketing. If you have a product or service, or are trying to select a product or service, to market through direct-mail or mail-order marketing, you should first consider several factors. You automatically consider them when asking and answering these questions:

Checklist for direct marketers

- Is there a perceived need for the product or service?
- Is it practical?
- Is it unique?
- Is the price right for your customers or prospects?
- Is it a good value?
- Is the markup sufficient to assure a profit?
- Is the market large enough?
- Does the product or service have broad appeal?
- Are there specific smaller segments of your list that have a strong desire for your product or service?
- Is it new? Will your customers perceive it as being new?
- Can it be photographed or illustrated interestingly?
- Are there sufficient unusual selling features to make your copy sizzle?
- Is it economical to ship? Is it fragile? Odd-shaped? Heavy? Bulky?
- Can it be personalized?
- Are there any legal problems to overcome?
- Is it safe to use?
- Is the supplier reputable?
- Will backup merchandise be available for fast shipment on reorders?
- Might returns be too huge?
- Will refurbishing or returned merchandise be practical?
- Is it, or can it be, packaged attractively?
- Are usage instructions clear?
- How does it compare with competitive products or services?
- Will it have exclusivity?
- Will it lend itself to repeat business?
- Is it consumable, so that there will be repeat orders?
- Is it faddish? Too short-lived?
- Is it too seasonal for direct-mail selling?
- Can an add-on to the product make it more distinctive and salable?

- Will the number of stock-keeping units — various sizes and colors — create problems?
- Does it lend itself to multiple pricing?
- Is it too readily available in stores?
- Is it like an old, hot item, so that its success is guaranteed?
- Is it doomed because similar items have failed?
- Does your mother, wife, brother, husband, girlfriend, boyfriend, sister, or kid like it?
- Is direct mail the way to go with it?
- Does it fill an unfilled niche in the marketplace?

These questions were posed by Len Carlson, who for thirty years has sold about 10,000 different items from a direct-marketing company called Sunset House. They were listed in *Advertising Age*, in an article written by Bob Stone, president of Stone and Adler, a direct-response firm in Chicago.

You've got to ask yourself these hard questions and come up with answers that please you — and if you can't, either you've got to discard the idea of direct mail for your particular product or service, or you've got to make some major changes in your offering. If as few as five of your answers to these thirty-seven questions are not the right answers, you may be going in the wrong direction. This checklist can serve as a handy guide to direct-marketing success. Luckily, you have these questions to save you from spending money unwisely.

Only after you are satisfied that you ought to proceed into the world of direct marketing should you take the next step — which is to understand the relationship of direct-response advertising to non-direct-response advertising. Rather than giving you my words about that relationship, I would like to quote from a speech made to the Direct Mail/Marketing Association's 65th Annual Convention by David Ogilvy — the head of a major advertising agency that has offices worldwide. Keep in mind that David Ogilvy's agency is a standard agency, not a direct-response agency, although it now has a branch called Ogilvy and Mather Direct. Here is a portion of Mr. Ogilvy's talk:

Direct is different from indirect

> In the advertising community there are two worlds. Your world of direct-response advertising and that other world — the world of general advertising. These two worlds are on a collision course.
>
> You direct-response people know what kind of advertising works and what doesn't work. You know to a dollar.

You know that two-minute commercials are more cost-effective than thirty-second commercials.

You know that fringe time on television sells more than prime time.

In print advertising, you know that long copy sells more than short copy.

You know that headlines and copy about the product and its benefits sell more than cute headlines and poetic copy. You know to a dollar.

The general advertisers and their agencies know almost nothing for sure, because they cannot measure the results of their advertising. They worship at the altar of creativity. Which means originality — the most dangerous word in the lexicon of advertising.

They opine that thirty-second commercials are more cost-effective than two-minute commercials. You know they're wrong.

In print advertising, they opine that short copy sells more than long copy. You know they are wrong.

They indulge in entertainment. You know they are wrong. You know to a dollar. They don't.

Nobody should be allowed to create advertising until he has served his apprenticeship in direct response. That experience will keep his feet on the ground for the rest of his life. The trouble with many copywriters in ordinary agencies is that they don't think in terms of selling. They have never written direct response. They have never tasted blood.

Until recently, direct response was the Cinderella of the advertising world. Then came the computer and the credit card. Direct marketing exploded. You guys are coming into your own. Your opportunities are colossal. . . .

Ladies and gentlemen, how I envy you. Your timing is perfect. You have come into the direct-response business at the right time. You are onto a good thing. For forty years I have been a voice crying in the wilderness, trying to get my fellow advertising practitioners to take direct response seriously. Today my first love is coming into its own. You face a golden future.

David Ogilvy's speech was considered so important that he was the keynote speaker, and yet his entire speech was delivered on videotape. Goes to show that it's the content that counts. And the words just revealed to you are loaded with meaning. I hope you heed them. I hope you realize the enormity of Mr. Ogilvy's truth: If you don't know about direct-response marketing, you don't know about marketing.

According to technical experts in the field, direct marketing is not a fancy term for mail order. It is an interactive system of marketing that uses one or more advertising media to effect a measurable response and/or transaction at any location. We have the magazine *Direct Marketing* to thank for this definition.

That same publication reminds us that marketing is all the activities involved in moving goods and services from seller to buyer. Then *Direct Marketing* makes a crucial distinction. It says that direct marketing has the same broad function as standard marketing but also requires the maintenance of a database. This **The database** database records the names of customers, prospects, and former customers. It serves as a vehicle for storing, then measuring, the results of direct-response advertising. It also provides a way to store, then measure, purchasing performance. And finally, it is a way to continue direct communication by mail and/or telephone.

Risk-wary advertisers are shying away from the mass market media, choosing instead to target their prospects directly. These advertisers might have invested 50 cents a person to reach a general audience in the past, but in the 1990s, they're putting up $1 for someone whose demographic and economic profile indicates they're predisposed to making a purchase. From Waldenbooks' Preferred Reader Program to Liz Claiborne's store-based computers to Hyatt Hotels' Gold Passport program to Prodigy's on-line buying to the myriad of frequent-flier programs, retailers and advertisers are hoarding information on exactly who their customers are, what they bought, and what they are likely to buy in the future.

Scads of information pulled from scanners, coupons, and even a check-cashing card pinpoint exactly where a person lives, how many people they live with, how much they earn, what they drive, read, and eat, even what kind of toilet paper they use. Every right-thinking guerrilla is building a database because so few markets are growing. Companies are desperate to hold on to their current customers.

Looking into the future, *Direct Marketing* reminds us to consider interactive TV as an up-and-coming selling device. This **Interactive TV** device, already in use in test markets and in the many home shopping shows now on TV, lets shoppers see items on TV, then order them immediately. Eventually, interactive TV will probably be the major vehicle employed by large users of direct marketing.

The value to you is potentially enormous. You get to home

in on your prospects with amazing accuracy. You can be selective in regard to age, race, sex, occupation, buying habits, money spent on past direct-mail purchases, education, special interests, family composition, religion, marital status, and geographic location ranging from state to county to town to Zip Code to block. Expensive? Yes. But it's the real cost to build lifetime customer loyalty.

Prodigy Services, a computerized on-line information and interactive shopping service, listed 1.7 million subscribers in 1992, proving that people will happily shop from their easy chairs. According to a survey by Simmons Market Research Bureau, 65 percent of Prodigy's subscribers graduated from college, and nearly half live in households earning $75,000 or more. Nearly 200 advertisers currently allow people to buy from them through Prodigy. Because the company has sunk at least $1 billion into its business, it has no serious competitors in the on-line consumer market. But this is still the wave of the future and not the present.

Home shopping networks Video shopping networks are already with us, as you gleaned from the chapter on television. In 1992, video home shopping sales topped $2 billion. A whopping 70 million people watch Home Shopping Network; 28 million watch Cable Value Network; 18 million watch QVC Network. And those numbers are growing, along with the mailing lists compiled by the home shopping networks.

Your customer mailing list If you have the soul of a guerrilla, you will have been compiling your own mailing list from the day your business began. The list should naturally start with your own customers. From there, you can expand it to include people who have recently moved into your area, and people who have recently been married or divorced, or become parents. You can eliminate people who have moved away — a full 18 percent of Americans, nearly one in five, moved in 1992.

You might engage in a simple direct mailing of postcards to customers, informing them of a sale you will have the next week. They will appreciate the early notification and might show their gratitude by purchasing from you. You might also engage in a full-scale direct mailing, using what is now known as the "classic package," which consists of an outer envelope, a direct-mail letter, a brochure, an order form, a return envelope (maybe post-paid, maybe not), and often even more.

Whatever you do, the process begins when you decide exactly what it is you wish to offer. How will you structure that offer? Then you must select your mailing list. If you haven't got the names already, you can purchase them from a list broker (look under "Mailing Lists" in your yellow pages). Take care. Be sure you buy a clean, fresh list. The broker (and the price) can give you clues on this. You must be certain that you know all the costs involved: postage, printing, writing the mailing, artwork, paper, personalization (individualizing each letter by name and address, rather than saying "Dear friend" or the like), and repeat mailing costs. Your gross sales, minus these costs and your production, handling, and shipping costs, will constitute your profits. Be sure you make financial projections and know your break-even point.

According to Lynn Peterson, a former direct-mail executive in the direct-response arm of a major advertising agency who helped mastermind mailings for some of the nation's largest direct marketers, the three biggest secrets that can be disclosed to a direct marketer are:

Secrets and errors

1. Pick your list with the utmost care.
2. Structure your offer in such a way that it is extremely difficult to refuse.
3. Plan your projections so that you earn a profit.

Ms. Peterson was also asked to describe the three biggest errors made by direct marketers. Never one to be inconsistent, she said they were:

1. Failure to pick the right list or lists.
2. Failure to structure an offer properly.
3. Failure to plan projections with enough foresight.

Along with her insights into making direct mail a money-maker for your company, I offer these gems:

Guerrilla direct-mail gems

- Printing your most important sentences in a second color will increase sales enough to warrant the extra money. Be sure you choose a bright, pleasing color.
- If you've got a two-page letter to send, use two pages. Printing on both sides of one page is a false economy and gets you right where it hurts — in your response rate.
- Restate your main offer on your response form. The repeti-

tion will be good for you as well as motivating for the reader.

- Illustrations or photos incorporated in your letter will also improve your response rate. Just be sure that the graphic element adds to the offer or the promise.
- The worst months for direct mail are June, March, and May. The best are January, February, and October.
- Guerrillas juice up their offers — and response rates — with free gifts for ordering, a photo of the free gift on the envelope, or a free trial of their product or service. As you are learning, something free always aids in marketing.

These are not the old days

In the old days, a direct-mail campaign meant a letter. Today it means a letter, two or three or five follow-up letters, perhaps a follow-up phone call or two, and finally, one more direct-mail letter. Many entrepreneurs engage in weekly or monthly direct mailings.

There are a multitude of decisions for you to make when you embark upon a mailing, so it is crucial that you know the right questions to ask. In addition to deciding about your mailing list, your offer, and your financial projections, you'll have to decide whether to mail first class or third class. Will you personalize your mailing? Will you have a toll-free number available for ordering? Which credit cards will you accept? Will you need to alter your pricing because you'll be selling direct? This seemingly simple subject becomes more complex as you learn more about it.

Getting them to open the envelope

The envelope for a direct mailing merits a chapter of its own. Executives should not be sent envelopes with address labels. For maximum response, their names must be typed on the envelope. And for selling stationery, feminine products, or political candidates or causes, a handwritten envelope provides a wonderfully personal tone. Envelopes can be standard size (#10) or oversize (6 inches by 9 inches), manila, covered with gorgeous art, foil-lined, or window-type. They can have a return address, or, to pique curiosity, omit the return address.

One of the best devices you can use on an envelope is a "teaser" — a copyline that compels the recipient to open the envelope. Examples of successful teasers are: "FREE! A microcalculator for you!"; "Want to get your hands on $10,000 extra cash?"; and "The most astonishing offer of the year. Details inside."

As you can see, there are myriad ways to get a person to open an envelope. And that is the purpose of the envelope — to interest the recipient so that he or she will open it and read the contents.

Guerrillas know that people read the addressee name first, then they look at the teaser copy, and finally they read to see who sent it. Was it the Office of the President? The Awards Committee? The IRS? If it has the name of the person's bank, it always gets opened. No teaser is needed. I doubt if the IRS needs one either.

When planning your own envelope, determine the needs and wants of your target audience. Remember that you can always use the back of the envelope and that 75 percent of the people holding it will read it. Figure that you've got three seconds to get them to open it. So say something enticing to motivate that action. Examples:

- Free gift enclosed
- Money-saving offer inside
- Wealth-building secrets for the nineties
- Private information for your eyes only
- Did you know you can double your profits?
- What every business like yours needs to know . . .
- How to add new profits for only six cents a day
- See inside for exciting details on (virtually anything)
- Read what's in store for you — this week only!

The idea of teaser copy is not to be cute, clever, or fancy. The job is to be *provocative*, to entice the recipient into opening the envelope. Sure, it's only an envelope, but guerrillas know that it's often the key to a successful or a failed mailing.

You should almost always include a P.S. in your letter. They get read with regularity, far more than body copy. Many direct mailings now include what are known as lift letters — little notes that say things such as "Read this only if you have decided not to respond to this offer." Inside is one more attempt to make the sale, probably a handwritten message called a "buck slip," signed by the company president.

Always end with a P.S.

Be sure you guarantee what you are selling, because you are not as "in touch" with customers as you would be with a store-sold product or service, and they will want the reassurance of a guarantee.

The most effective direct-mail efforts allow people to buy with credit cards. "Bill me" also works well as a rule. An element of urgency, such as "offer expires in one week," increases the response even more. Guerrillas always put a time limit on their direct-mail offers.

Whatever you do, make your offer clear, repeat it several times, keep your message as short as possible, and ask for the order. Don't pussyfoot around. Ask people to do exactly what you wish them to do. Then ask them again.

Let them order by phone   I also recommend toll-free phone numbers, which can triple the response rate. Every day, three-quarters of a million Americans order $225 million worth of merchandise by phone.

When you create a direct-mail ad with a coupon, make the coupon a miniature version of your ad, complete with headline, benefit, and offer. In short, make it a brief summary of the advertisement. Some direct-mail pros write their coupons or response devices before they write their ads. This is called "working backward" and guerrillas see the wisdom in it. Working backward helps you immensely when you write the letter or brochure — because it helps you remember what you want the recipient to do.

Where should your mail-order ad appear in a publication? The best place, although relatively expensive, is the back page of a newspaper or magazine — where response can be as much as 150 percent greater than from the same ad inside the publication.

And while considering direct marketing, always consider including an insert with your bill. People certainly open bills, so that means they'll probably see your insert. And you'll get a free ride because the bill is paying the postage for the insert. Another type of insert is the free-standing type that often appears in newspapers or magazines. These are known to be very effective. So check with your newspaper or magazine rep to find out about their services with regard to inserts.

Freeman Gosden, Jr., president of Smith-Hennings-Gosden in Los Angeles, has come up with a direct-mail marketer's checklist. He offers these points for consideration:

- Look at the mail as your reader will.
- Keep your primary objective foremost in your mind.
- Does the number-one benefit hit you between the eyes?
- Does the number-two benefit follow close behind?
- Does the message of the mailing package flow?
- Does the outside envelope encourage you to open it — now?
- Is the letter the first thing you see upon opening?
- Does the letter discuss the reader's needs, product benefits, features, endorsements, and ways to respond?
- Do graphics support the copy?
- Does the reply card tell the whole offer?
- Is there a reason to act now?
- Is it easy to reply?
- Would you respond?

The almighty catalogue

Catalogues are a whole different ballgame, part of direct mail, to be sure, but a very different part. As your business grows, you will probably require a catalogue to spur your direct marketing. When you do decide to market with a catalogue, be absolutely certain that your catalogue has the right positioning, the right merchandise selection, the right kind of merchandise, the right graphics, the right use of color, the right size (thirty-two pages is considered optimum), the right headlines, the right subheads, the right copy, the right sales stimulators, and the right order forms. Also be sure that you have formulated your projections correctly. Other than that, direct marketing with catalogues is a piece of cake.

If you run a mail-order business, your catalogue will be the heart of your business. It will be a mighty contributor to your bottom line. The success of your mail-order catalogue will be contingent upon your having customers who have already had one or more satisfactory transactions with you. That means that when they receive your catalogue they will trust you and will have confidence in your offerings. It also means catalogues are not for people just starting a business.

Be prepared to invest in your catalogue. A friend of mine who ran a successful mail-order company ($2 million in sales, with $500,000 in marketing expenses) spent 50 percent of his marketing money on direct mail, 30 percent on catalogues, and

20 percent on mail-order ads. Does it sound as if he believed in catalogues? Well, he didn't believe enough. Later he changed his marketing budget so as to spend 15 percent of his marketing money on mail-order ads, 20 percent on direct mail, and 65 percent on catalogues. He had learned that his catalogues were the most important selling tools he had. In fact, he used to say he was in the catalogue business rather than the mail-order business. My friend became a millionaire in the business, so take heed of his words.

Think of your catalogue as a specialized form of direct mail. It is like a store on paper — a complete presentation of your merchandise. The items within your catalogue should reflect the interests of your audience and should be similar in nature. If you sell outdoor equipment, your customers won't want to buy gourmet foods from you. They look upon you as a specialist, and your catalogue must nourish that belief.

To print a catalogue you should have about 25,000 customers. That's a lot. But if you want to earn a whale of a lot of money, you'll have to start developing a customer list that long. The big money — the truly large sums — will come to you when you send those customers your catalogue. What if you don't have 25,000 customers? Create an inexpensive catalogue, perhaps a mini-catalogue of eight pages, with just black and white photos.

Preparing a catalogue is quite a serious project. Once designed, it can be printed for 5000 customers or 5,000,000 customers. But the amount of work required to get the catalogue ready for the printer makes it cost-ineffective unless you print up 25,000 copies. That's just a rule of thumb, but it's a good one.

Catalogue costs   If your catalogue contains only 100 items, the cost of your art direction, copywriting, and photography, plus the charges for your type, photostats, and paste-up, will run about $8000. Your printer will charge about $2000 as a make-ready (getting ready to print) fee. The cost of the printing (in black and white plus one color) for an 8½ x 11 format on regular paper, sixteen pages, will run about twenty cents per catalogue. Postage will run another twenty cents. So the 25,000 catalogues will cost about $20,000 by the time they're in the mail — about 80 cents each. Assuming you have a gross profit margin of 55 percent, you will have to sell at least $1.25 of merchandise per catalogue mailed. You must sell $31,250 worth of goods just to break even. That's not easy. But if it's your first catalogue, breaking even isn't too bad. It builds business. And the next year, when you have 50,000 customers, most of your catalogue work will already have been accomplished. You can pick up most artwork and copy from the first catalogue, and your in-the-mail costs will be substantially reduced. Therefore you ought to make a very impressive profit on your catalogue the second year, even more the third year, and still more each succeeding year. But as with all other forms of guerrilla marketing, you must be patient, must not expect miracles, must consider your expenditures as an investment, and must remain committed to your catalogue marketing program.

Up till now, we've been talking about mailing your catalogue to your own list of customers. If you purchase outside lists, even exceptional ones, you should not figure on a return that is more than 85 percent of that realized by mailing to your own list. So test other lists very carefully before plunging in and mailing a million catalogues. Whatever you do, you must mail your catalogue for Christmas. People want to buy at that time, and you've blown an important opportunity if you do not mail to them then.

A few more pointers about catalogues: Work with your printer to determine the optimum number of pages, the paper **Catalogue pointers** stock, the format, and the print run. Naturally, your printer must be experienced in catalogue production to do this. Find one that is. Also, don't produce full-color catalogues until you can mail 200,000 or more of them. Use the front and back covers of your catalogues, along with your order form, to sell merchandise. They are very effective. Stay away from group-item shots. Display your merchandise item by item and don't try to be artistic. Instead, be clear. Steer clear of models, because they can increase your costs more than is necessary. If you sell clothing, it's almost impossible to avoid using models, but do so if you can. Also, it is not a good idea to mix photos with illustrations. Choose between the two and stay with your choice.

Your copy should be simple, straightforward, and concise. Forget cleverness and give the facts, along with the benefits. Better to give the features and the answers to any questions that may come up than to be too brief. If you can possibly write the copy yourself, do it. You have a feel for the merchandise, or at least you should.

By all means, bind an order form into your catalogue. And **Bind in an order form** offer some merchandise on that order form. Bribe people to order more than they ordinarily would. For instance, tell them that if they order $25 or more in merchandise, they will receive a free gift, and if they order $50 or more, they will receive a better free gift. And promise them a doozie of a gift if they order $100 or more. Try it. People just love free gifts. Don't you? Also include on your order blank a brief letter from you to your customers. Make it warm, personal, and not too long.

Richard Thalheimer of The Sharper Image does a wonderful job, not only with his warm, personal letter, but also with the copy and graphics in his catalogue. Fortune's Almanac is beautifully written, as are many more — L. L. Bean, the J. Peterman Company, Hammacher Schlemmer, and Seventh Generation come to mind. But writing and graphics are only part of the job, as you now know.

Guerrillas do the whole job, which starts with *giving people what they want*. What else do people like about catalogues?

What people like about catalogues

1. 36 percent say *convenience* is what they like most.
2. 19 percent give the nod to *more variety*.
3. 17 percent like *low prices* (hard to find in my Tiffany catalogue, and it's quite a successful one; has been for a long time).
4. 6 percent say they go for the high quality offered.
5. 22 percent list the inevitable "other" or list nothing.

After the 78 percent who have good things to say about catalogues finish reading or ordering from them, what do they do with them? Forty-two percent save them; 41 percent toss them; 10 percent pass them on; 7 percent say "it depends."

Guerrilla guidelines

If you're thinking of mailing a catalogue, follow these guerrilla guidelines:

- Set specific objectives on what the catalogue should do for your business.
- Define your audience so that you know who will receive your catalogue; that helps in creating and producing it.
- Pre-plan all the elements of your catalogue before going into production: products, prices, fulfillment, and more.
- Make all the hard decisions up front: which products to include, which to exclude, how production will be handled.

- If possible, group your offerings into clearly defined groups so that the catalogue is not a hodgepodge.
- Make a rough outline of the contents of your catalogue, including everything you wish to have in it — everything.
- Determine the exact format you want: size, typeface, color or not, paper stock, binding.
- Make a layout that is organized, logical, and pleasing to the eye of your target audience. Think of their eyes only.
- Plan, write, and perfect the copy. Then set up a timetable and stick with it.

As you can tell, the business of producing and mailing catalogues is complex. But after the first year, it is exceptionally profitable — if you do it right. If you think you might ever offer a catalogue, start putting your name on as many catalogue mailing lists as possible. Then you can expect your mailbox to be filled with informative examples every day but Sunday. Mine is.

Keep in mind that the number of Americans ordering at least one thing from a catalogue is fast approaching 95 percent, and the percentage continues to grow. There must be a reason.

Even if it isn't practical for you to use catalogues, I hope you will try direct mail if it is at all feasible for your business. If you do, you will get a head start by using the major marketing method of the future.

Try a small number of mailings first. Test always. Learn from each test. In truth, if you break even while testing, you are doing fine. The goal is to come up with a formula that can be repeated and expanded. If you ever obtain a publicity story about your business, consider enclosing reprints of it in a mailing.

Breaking even is fine

In my own experience as an entrepreneur and as a direct-response specialist, I have found that envelopes with teaser lines get a better response than those without. I have found that short letters work better than long letters, that long brochures work better than short brochures, that postcards often make superb mailers all by themselves. I have learned that it is worth the time to check out many lists before selecting one, and that one's own customer list is a gold mine when it comes to direct mail. I know that a single mailing isn't nearly as effective as a mailing with one, two, or more follow-ups, and that a mailing with a phone follow-up is frequently best of all.

A guerrilla will either realize that direct marketing is not the way for his or her business to proceed, or will utilize direct marketing with intelligence, reading books about it, talking with direct-marketing pros, and making it his or her most cost-effective marketing method. Strange as it may seem, the majority of people like to receive mailings from businesses; so don't feel self-conscious, and put the U.S. Postal Service to work for you.

IV
Non-Media
Marketing

NOW THAT YOU KNOW YOU can market your products and
services through mini-media and maxi-media, you should
also know that you can succeed without using media at all. You
can invite groups to your place of business to hear speakers.
You can put on programs for these groups if they won't come to
you. You can stage exhibits at fairs. You can display your offerings
in model homes or auto showrooms or restaurants or other non-
media places where groups of people will see them. You can participate in your local Welcome Wagon, which helps newcomers
to the community and enlightens them as to products and services available. You can talk with fellow merchants and entrepreneurs and arrange to exchange information, assistance, and ideas
with them when possible. You can hold sales training sessions for
your own people. You can ask the manufacturers that supply you
for their aid in marketing. You can develop incentive plans to
spur your people to greater heights. You can hold open houses
and parties. You can create dazzling window displays.

Coming up are even more ways that successful entrepreneurs
can promote their businesses without using the media — at least
not directly. Some of these methods ought to become part of your
marketing plan if you are serious about success. They are hard to
develop. They require painstaking detail work. They are far more
complex than they appear. But they are worth your time and
effort, and for many a guerrilla they pay off handsomely.

Is it possible to succeed using only non-media marketing?
Yes. But it is easier to succeed with a combination of mini-media,

maxi-media, and non-media marketing. There are far more non-media marketing opportunities available to you than there are media opportunities. *Use as many as you can.*

The way you answer the phone has a powerful influence over how people will feel about your company. Either an untrained, unfriendly voice will turn off a potential or, worse yet, a current customer — or a warm, welcoming voice will make the caller want to do business with a company such as yours. Is this media? No. Is this marketing? It is. So are the neatness of your premises, the smiles prospects receive upon entering, the respect for their time displayed when they place an order or make a request. If you know the name of your customer and use it, that's personalized marketing on a face-to-face basis. Guerrillas know the importance of eye contact in non-media marketing such as trade shows and of greeting people who visit their business.

Let me give you a prime example of non-media marketing that is so unusual it doesn't fit into any chapter. Although it's unique, it is the spirit of common sense. This guerrilla marketing technique helps you obtain the names of prime prospects, a noble endeavor. To do it, guerrillas invest in high school students on bicycles. The roofing guerrilla pays a student $1 for the address of each home in the community that needs a new roof. The gardening guerrilla pays $1 for the address of each home that could do with some quality gardening. The paving guerrilla pays for the address of each home that needs work on its driveway.

These guerrillas know that they will get only about thirty to fifty new addresses a month, not a lot. But at each address is at least one human being who needs a new roof or a manicured garden or a smooth driveway. And that person is probably soothed by the fact that you're a local business. Guerrillas get the names of these people from the reverse phone directory, then write to them in a highly personalized way, pointing out the problem and offering a solution. The tactic of securing these names of honest-to-goodness prospects involves no media. Then guerrillas use the mini-medium of a personal letter to make everything happen (as is so often the case). I predict that you will get a lot of mileage from the non-media weapons you employ — in the form of PR, reprints of PR, and a warm, cozy relationship with your entire community, if not the entire planet.

Non-media marketing also includes your own attitudes. Your willingness to abide by guerrilla marketing principles indicates the right spirit of *competitiveness*. Your belief in the benefits of your product or service is manifested in the *enthusiasm* that spreads from you to your employees to your customers. These attitudes are non-media marketing in that they influence people, but don't cost you a cent for media. Combine them with media — and get ready to soar.

22
Advertising Specialties and Samples: If You've Got It, Flaunt It

ADVERTISING SPECIALTIES ARE ITEMS on which the imprinted name (and sometimes the address, phone number, and theme line) of the advertiser appears. Examples of advertising specialties are ball-point pens, scratch pads, briefcases, calendars, key chains, paper-clip holders, caps, T-shirts, pins, playing cards, shopping bags, belt buckles, decals, banners, lighters, license-plate frames, fanny packs, and more, lots more.

Consider these specialties to be the equivalent of billboards. That means they are great for reminder advertising. They are usually terrible as your only marketing medium. They do, however, put your name in front of your prospective customers. And your prospects don't even have to leave home or office to see them. As part of a marketing mix, that's a very good thing. As you well know by now, familiarity is one of the keys to success. And there is no question that ad specialties breed increased awareness.

Yet that's just the tip of the advertising specialty iceberg. Those free gifts — and that's the whole idea — to give them away gratis — can be used to leverage many a sale, and our nation abounds with billionaires who realized the power of something free. As a Fuller Brush man while in college, I was amazed at how free samples worked like magic as door openers. Procter & Gamble is famed for its generosity with free samples.

Everyone loves free gifts

Advertising specialties make your prospects and customers feel good about you, especially if the specialty items are valuable. I remember that a businessman buddy of mine was ecstatic upon receiving a digital clock-pen. He spoke with reverence of the supplier who gave it to him, and he continues to show his loyalty to the firm. A specialty item with a high perceived value does breed a sense of unconscious obligation, to be sure. And if you can purchase a breakthrough type of inexpensive product for your deserving prospects *and customers,* by all means give it serious consideration. There are no particular industries or businesses that benefit more than others by this marketing medium. But if, for example, you come across a unique and advanced measuring device, and your prime prospects are contractors and carpenters, you'd be well advised to give it a shot. Be proud to put your name on such a gift. Guerrillas never put their names on anything shoddy, anything that will break at a dirty look, anything that doesn't make them proud to give it away.

Give away a sample

Be proud to use sampling, too, if you sincerely believe that by providing exposure to your product or service you will win loyal customers. Choose sampling over advertising specialties every time, if it comes to making a choice. Both involve giving something away. Both win friends and create favorable associations. But sampling accomplishes these things by means of freebies that are more pertinent than advertising-specialty items, valuable as they may be.

I strongly suggest that you examine the use of ad specialties if they seem to lend themselves to your type of business. If, for example, you are a mobile auto mechanic, it's a dandy idea to give your customers and prospects key chains (for their car keys) with your name and number on them. On the other hand, if you are a computer consultant, handing out key chains makes no sense whatsoever. But handing out small guides to software makes a lot of sense.

Selecting the best ad specialties

I have gained a wealth of information from the following tactic. I would consider my line of merchandise or services very carefully, then look in the yellow pages under "Advertising Specialties" and pick out the best ad — judging it by the amount of information it gives and its credibility. I'd call the rep listed in that ad and ask him or her to pay me a visit. While still on the phone, I'd tell the rep who my target audience was and ask the rep to recommend specialties that have worked for others in my line. I'd also ask about new ad specialty items that haven't yet been tried. Each year, a plethora of new items come onto the market, and a good rep regularly alerts his clients to the new ones. When the rep paid me a visit, I'd take the time to look through his or her pleasantly cumbersome catalogue of available specialties, and perhaps I'd get ten ideas that hadn't occurred to the rep.

I'd also ask the rep to tell me about upcoming specialties, gift ideas, and specialties that I might recommend to my own clients. I might decide that none of the specialties are for me. But at least I'd know a lot more about what is available, what certain specialties cost, and what use other companies have made of this method of non-media marketing. Perhaps I wouldn't want to use a specialty item now but would want to use one later.

I must admit to a prejudice toward calendars as an advertising specialty. I'm not talking about ordinary calendars. I'm referring to gorgeous calendars that most people will happily hang in their homes or offices, then look at almost every day. I have such calendars in my own home, and I have patronized the companies that gave them away. (I'm not really sure whether my business was instigated by the calendars; probably not, but one can't be too sure of one's unconscious thought processes.) And I have recommended the use of handsome calendars to my clients. They have used them and continued to use them. One of the reasons I like calendars as ad specialties is that people tend to look at them a lot. One of the reasons I do not like, say, playing cards, is that people tend not to look at them a lot, and when they do, they look at the side without your name and logo.

Marketing daily with calendars

If you do decide you want to distribute calendars, you've got to make that decision in the summer, at the very latest, so that the right calendars with the right inscriptions can be in your hands at the right time — probably in early November.

You might also consider scratch pads. Imprinted scratch pads have become very effective lead-generating gimmicks for salespeople, I'm told. What you do is pay a printer to stick a photo, your name, address, phone number, and theme line on a sheet of paper, then print up a bunch of sheets that are made into scratch pads — or Post-its — each sheet of the pad an ad for you. Next, distribute those pads — free, naturally — to your prospects. Either hand them out or mail them. People tend to keep such pads by their phones or on their desks. They use them to write notes to themselves. Every time they look at one of the scraps of paper, they see the name of your offering. Of course even the hottest offer will not motivate them to pick up the phone and order whatever you are selling unless they need it. But when

Put your name on their scratch pad

they do need what you have to offer, chances are your name will come to mind first. And that's a big help to any guerrilla.

As with other types of marketing, the key here is repetition. Because it takes time to become known in a community, it's important to keep circulating new scratch pads.

I know of a real estate salesman in Southern California who estimates that he earns between $15,000 and $20,000 in commissions per year from listings generated by his scratch pads. He sounds like a real guerrilla in that he obviously tracks his sales leads like crazy, and then even translates them into dollar figures.

There are no hard and fast rules as to who should use ad specialties, when they should be used, or how they can be used best. But your ad specialty rep probably has many tips for you. If George, of Let George Do It, were to consider advertising specialties, he might like the idea of calendars and rulers, maybe ball-point pens, and possibly even scratch pads. Or George might let his altruism come shining through by giving away auto litter bags with his name on them. But George would probably not get involved in giving away freebies until his business was well established.

The cost of an individual advertising specialty is tiny. But the volume in which you must order each specialty is not tiny. I once gave away felt-tip pens for a business I was running. The cost of each pen was less than a dollar. But I had to order 300 pens before the manufacturers would put my name on them. At the time $300 sounded like a lot.

A client of mine who is very successful at fund raising for public schools gives away pens with his name, company name, and phone number on them. His costs are even lower than mine were, because he orders so many pens. His pens, by the way, are neither felt-tip nor ball-point. Because he's a real guerrilla, he gives away a new type of pen. People perceive it to be a breakthrough product, and they associate him with innovation.

His company achieved tremendous profitability by using advertising specialties as a key ingredient in its marketing mix. Prospects were sent a letter or postcard with a color picture of a free gift such as a microcalculator or a quartz desk clock — both available for under $2. The teaser said "A free gift for you!" and the recipient, being of the human race, would open the envelope and learn that merely by requesting more information, the gift would be given without obligation. From this point on, the company

Free gifts as door openers

gave the gift, paid a personal call, telemarketed, sent another letter, made a phone call or two or three, and prospered to a point where it was one of the 100 fastest-growing companies in America. All because of advertising specialties? Of course not. But they did a bang-up job of getting that door open, never an easy task.

In regard to the copy on your ad specialty, don't make the mistake of leaving it off entirely. I suggest that you include your name, address, phone number, theme line, and as much copy as will tastefully fit on the item. Not much will fit on a key chain or a pen. A bit more will fit on a calendar. But use restraint and remember that people won't hang a calendar if it looks like an ad. Nonetheless, it is possible to convey more information than the usual name and address. A guerrilla markets at every opportunity. Still, I caution you to use good taste more than hard sell.

A final hint: Talk to people who give away ad specialties themselves. Ask if they consider them effective. Ask them to recommend a good rep. Ask about cost-effectiveness and how long they've been using ad specialties.

I'm knocked out at each year's crop of new advertising specialties. Several are exciting and economical inventions. Clock-pens, solar calculators, Lucite-framed quartz desk clocks for a buck — don't let any winners pass you by. If there is any potential reason for you to invest in this low-cost marketing method, see to it that you find out about the new specialties each year. They can't help you all by themselves — but they won't hurt you either, unless they break on day one. **New ones every year**

If you're considering using advertising specialties as a guerrilla marketing tool, you should have an idea of what your target market might want in the way of a free gift. The October 1992 issue of *Business and Incentive Strategies* magazine reported on a survey conducted to see what sorts of incentive items people most like to receive from their employers for special performance. Say what you will about stereotypes, but when merchandise incentives were offered, men preferred electrical gadgets while women chose clothing. For merchandise incentives worth over $1000, men went for big-screen TVs while women selected a new wardrobe. In travel incentives, women's top choices for vacation activities were relaxation, sightseeing, and culture. Men opted for relaxation, sports/outdoor activity, and sightseeing. For an overseas travel destination, both men and women picked Australia **Insights into sales incentives** and New Zealand as their top choice. For domestic trips, women wanted to visit the Pacific Northwest while men were attracted to the links and beaches of the Southwest. The favorite incentive for both men and women (as if you didn't know) was money — preferred by 51 percent of the men and 56 percent of the women. One thing about crisp, green American cash: You don't have to question its quality.

If you're giving out free samples, the quality of your offering is as or more important than with a free gift. Sampling can help you all by itself if the quality's there. And it can kill you if your product or service is at all shoddy. Guerrilla marketing can hasten the failure of your business by letting more people know faster about the faults of your offering.

I consider sampling to be the most effective marketing method. Of course I am assuming that you have an excellent product or service. If your product is wonderful, sampling will help it take off in a hurry. You've got to have the ability to service the people you sell, and you've got to offer true quality. But if you do, sampling works wonders.

One of my marketing idols, Procter & Gamble, spends a fortune on sampling. So do other large, successful, sophisticated marketing concerns. But that does not rule out guerrillas. In fact, before this chapter ends, you'll know of six instances where sampling helped small-businesspeople realize healthy profits.

You'll have to examine your offering to see if it lends itself to sampling. Most offerings can be sampled. The first one that comes to mind is a car. You certainly won't want to give away a sample car. But almost all auto dealers offer free test rides. That's a sample. And it succeeds. Usually, and especially when you are offering a service, your sampling must be offered to one person at a time. But if you are offering a product, perhaps you can give away several of your items as free samples.

At my current address, I've received in my mailbox free samples of toothpaste, detergent, shampoo, cigarettes, and chewing gum. I continue to use the toothpaste. And we buy the new detergent. I doubt if any other marketing method would have persuaded me to switch brands so quickly. In time, more sampling will probably woo me from the brands I currently use. Like most Americans, I'm a fickle consumer, though I've driven my Buick GS-400 convertible 325,000 miles with the same engine and transmission. (When it had 300,000 miles on it, I took a photo of it, with its fancy new gold paint job, and sent it to Buick, along with a letter thanking them for making such a grand car; a month later I received a two-line form letter signed by a machine. I'm ashamed of such an unguerrilla-like response from the city of my birth.)

Naturally, it costs a bundle to give away free samples. But if you can look upon the cost as a conservative investment, you might be tempted to engage in sampling rather than radio advertising. It's worth thinking about. I cannot think of a more guerrilla-spirited marketing method. It is the essence of honesty, since it forces you to offer quality, and people will appreciate you for it. What's more, your competition probably doesn't do it. Not for the lazy or unimaginative, it is an optimum marketing vehicle for guerrillas. **That's the spirit!**

Now here are the six examples I promised you on how sampling works: **Examples of samples**

In the early days of waterbeds, people considered the beds to be a fad, a mere offshoot of the counterculture. To overcome sales resistance to the new product, a retailer offered a free thirty-night sleeping trial: He would deliver and install the beds, then make a phone call thirty days later to see if his prospects wanted him to pick up the beds or were willing to pay for them. Ninety-three percent of the people were willing to pay for the beds. Sampling paid off.

Another entrepreneur was launching a newsletter. He advertised in magazines. He engaged in direct mail. Both got mediocre results. Then he mailed free sample copies to prospects. Instant success. Sampling came through. Incidentally, it cost him a total of $500 to try the sampling; he realized $7000 in profits from the attempt.

A third guerrilla was marketing a large-screen television set of his own design. Very few people took the time to visit the showroom in which it was displayed. So he took out ads offering free home trials. Soon he had to discontinue the ads because the response was so great. And even better than the response to his trial offer was the fact that 90 percent of the respondents purchased from him after sampling. That is the main idea, you know.

A fourth guerrilla, an office manager who baked chocolate chip cookies and sold them at flea markets on weekends (earning more doing that than through her office-manager salary), engaged in sampling. She baked two sizes of cookies. The tiny ones were free samples. The large ones were $1 each. She gave away the tiny ones — one per customer. More than half the customers were then tempted by the enchanting flavor and crispy goodness of the sample to purchase one or more of the $1 variety. One more case of sampling that worked.

Thus far, I've told you about two samples of merchandise that were loaned rather than given away (waterbeds and large-screen TVs) and two samples that were given away permanently (newsletters and cookies). What you can learn from this is that it does not take a giant company to engage in sampling, and sampling can be employed even if your product is too large or too expensive to give away. Free sampling can provide instant results that are not achievable through any other marketing method.

If it is at all possible to allow your prospects to sample your offering, let them. Are you a consultant? Offer a free one-hour consultation. If George, of Let George Do It, wanted to show people how good he is at home repair, he would have no trouble giving away free samples. A project, accomplished in one hour, would do the trick. And George would, in all likelihood, benefit greatly from his sampling, not to mention his new, budding relationship with a grateful prospect. The large-screen-TV entrepreneur had to make his sampling come alive through advertising. His ads called attention to his sampling. So you can see that some sampling depends upon other methods of marketing. But some sampling can work on its own.

My fifth guerrilla sampler, a person who washed windows for commercial establishments, frequently washed the windows of his prospects for free. This demonstrated his proficiency, his speed, his method of working. It also netted him several large customers. And it didn't require any advertising to get started.

Sometimes I see ads in marketing publications for writers who offer to write for free — just to prove how good they are. If they are indeed good, this advertising-then-sampling combination nets them quite a lot of business. Hardly anyone turns down something that is offered free. It seems that I'm seeing more and more ads of that type these days. It may be that the economy is tough as nails, but it also may be that people are catching on to the effectiveness of this method of marketing.

Example six also involves a person who offered a service. He offered to come to my residence weekly and wash my car, and promised to wash my car that night for free, to show how good he was. I could see the results of his work the next day, realize how convenient his service was, and then when he came back, sign up for it. Was I ever tempted to say no to his offer? Of course not. In fact, he made it nearly impossible to say no. The next morning, my car was gleaming. The next evening, he knocked on my door and asked if I wanted the same service every week. That man had earned himself a steady customer with one free sample. It probably took him fifteen minutes to wash my car. But it demonstrated to me how good he was, how convenient he was, and what a nice fellow he was. That his price was definitely not competitive didn't even enter my mind.

By giving me a sample of his great service, the car washer caused me to think positive thoughts about his offering. So I was won over quite easily. I wonder if he could have ever obtained my business through other methods. Let's see. He could have talked me into buying from him by canvassing. And in a way, his initial contact with me was a canvass. He might also have signed me up through telephone marketing, but I'm not so sure I would have signed. It certainly wouldn't have been as easy a sale as the sampling was, since he couldn't have proven his worth over the phone. A personal letter might have impressed me, but it wouldn't have given the opportunity for give and take that the personal contact did. It also wouldn't have let him prove his point. I would have read his circular or brochure with interest. But since I had never had a car washer who paid house calls, I might not have given the matter serious thought. And a sign, a classified ad, or a listing in the yellow pages would certainly not have won my business.

None of the maxi-media marketing methods would have worked as well. Newspapers, magazines, radio, TV, billboards, direct mail — I doubt if any of them would have made me an instant customer. Certainly if he had put his name on an advertising specialty, I would not have signed up so quickly. But sampling did the trick for him. And it might do the trick for you — in a hurry.

Instant customers

Such sampling of services is very expensive if you place a price tag on your time, and believe that terrible lie about time being money (time is far more valuable than money; stop kidding yourself), but very inexpensive if you think of out-of-pocket expenses only. Sampling is quite different from other methods of

Time is not money

marketing because it does not depend upon repetition. One great sample will do it all. Before you purchased this book, perhaps you looked through a few pages. Maybe you looked at the table of contents. If so, that was sampling on the part of the bookstore. And it worked. I bet sampling will work for you, too. Use it if you possibly can.

23
Free Seminars and
Demonstrations: Show and Sell

I HAVE A CLIENT WHOSE business is computer education. His classes are unique, effective, and impressive. But standard marketing methods didn't attract many customers. So he decided to hold a free seminar on computers for people who knew nothing about them. He placed an ad and over 500 people showed up for the seminar.

Had he teamed up with a great salesperson, he might have sold his program to as many as 50 percent of the people attending. But he'd never dreamed so many people would show up, so the number of people he sold on his series of lessons was closer to 5 percent. Next time he holds a free seminar, he'll be a lot better prepared to close his sales. In fact, he might even hire a professional salesperson.

Many people who give paid seminars or courses for a living advertise free seminars with ads in the business sections of newspapers. One speed-reading school advertised its free seminars with television commercials. An income tax expert markets his free seminars by means of publicity stories coupled with radio commercials on talk-oriented stations. Many entrepreneurs earn a great deal of money with paid seminars and courses. But they cannot attract large numbers of people to paid seminars and courses merely through newspaper ads, so they attract them to free seminars, then convert them to paying customers.

As one guerrilla to another, I sincerely recommend the same tactic to you. I recommend, if it is at all feasible for your type of product or service, that you advertise in the newspaper that you are holding a free seminar on the topic most closely connected with your product or service. Then obtain as many customers for your free seminar as you can. They may purchase your products or they may sign up for your service. If you hold a decent seminar, they will.

Give valuable information

When I say seminar, I really mean lecture. Give your audience valuable information and demonstrate your expertise or your product's efficacy for, say, the first forty-five minutes. Then spend the next fifteen minutes selling whatever it is you wish to sell. What I am talking about is a fifteen-minute, straight-from-the-heart commercial — delivered by you or by someone you hire. The entire process takes one hour. After that, you sign up the prospects. Unlike professional seminar leaders, you probably won't be signing them up for a paid seminar (unless selling information is your business). But you will be allowing them to buy your offering. And they'll want it because your message, your demonstration, your enthusiasm, and your proven expertise will have created within them a desire to purchase from you.

There is no question that an in-person commercial is better than a radio or TV commercial. Certainly a fifteen-minute selling opportunity will pan out better than a thirty-second selling opportunity. For this reason, seminars and demonstrations are being utilized more and more to market products and services.

A seminar is a sample

In a sense, a lecture or demonstration is very much like a sample. Your prospects get to see for themselves what you have to offer. They probably get to touch it, if it's a product, and they get to ask questions, whether it's a product or a service. They get to learn more about your offering this way than they do by standard marketing methods. And just as sampling convinces many people that they should buy a good product, so can your seminar.

Two key factors

Before I write one more word, I should emphasize that a free seminar/demonstration amounts to marketing in a vacuum unless two other factors are present. First, your free imparting of information must be advertised, so that you'll have a large group of prospects. Advertise in the newspaper, on the radio, or on TV. Go for the free publicity that is readily available when you're offering a free seminar. Tell the truth in your ads as to the contents of the seminar, and try to attract honest prospects, not just warm bodies. Second, be sure that either you or an associate can sell your offering to those prospects after the seminar is over. My client was a brilliant lecturer. People listened intently to his every word. They enjoyed looking at him and listening to him. As a lecturer, he was first rate. But as a salesman, he was eighth rate. He had no inkling of how to close. He had no instinct for blood. He didn't have the kind of personality that could take advantage of the momentum his lecture had built. So he signed up only 5 percent of the audience, rather than the 50 percent that was possible.

If you can, demonstrate your product or service at your seminar. Keep in mind that although what you are offering is free, people are giving up their time. They are traveling to the place where you are holding your seminar. And they have expectations, based upon your ad. You must give them value in exchange. You must live up to their expectations and move beyond them. You must treat them as if they have paid to hear you. You should make sure that even if they do not buy from you, they still feel that their time was well spent. Perhaps they'll buy from you later.

Where should you conduct your seminar? At your place of business, if possible. Just rent the chairs you'll need. Perhaps you'll conduct it outdoors, if you are demonstrating gardening skills or the like. Perhaps you'll conduct it in a gym, if you want to show and sell exercise equipment. Eventually, you'll be able to hold it on the premises of a "partner" with whom you have a *fusion marketing arrangement* — a collaboration of marketing talent, money, and ideas. (Read more about the fascinating topic of strategic alliances in *Guerrilla Marketing Excellence*, Houghton Mifflin, 1993.) Most seminars are held in motels or hotels where seminar facilities are readily available. Such facilities include a lectern, a microphone, a blackboard, chairs, and easily available coffee, water, and rest rooms. It is also advisable to offer free parking. If you have a store, a free seminar held there will work best. It will show your prospects where you are and what you sell. For instance, a seminar on decorating held in your furniture showroom is a natural.

Where to conduct seminars

People appreciate useful information. They appreciate it all the more when it is free. When you conduct a seminar or workshop, when you give a lecture, when you demonstrate a product or service, you prove your expertise. You establish yourself as an authority. You gain credibility. Even if people do not buy from you right then and there, they very well may buy from you later. There is a tactic, however, that some very successful (and very high-pressure) businesses employ to get the maximum number of

You're the authority

people to buy right then and there. They establish three "sales points" on the way to the exit. Upon conclusion of the free seminar, the speaker tells the customers that they can either sign up for the paid seminar at a particular table or with specific representatives located throughout the room. Probably four reps are present to sign people up. Prospects who do not buy must then pass the three sales points before leaving the room. At each, they are given a different sales pitch, stronger each time. Some people sign up in the main room, others at the first sales point, and still others at the second sales point. Another group signs up at the third sales point. Only a tiny group — who have world-class sales resistance — leave the building without putting their hands to their wallets. Sounds a bit pressured for this guerrilla.

This practice is common among some consciousness-raising groups. It is the hardest of all possible sells, and it is not easy to resist. As you can see, it takes several people to accomplish. But it does work. And if you care about profits more than you care about social propriety, you might employ it.

Free seminars, even without triple-teamed closes, can be a bonanza for you, and you should try to market with them if you possibly can. It may be that your business just doesn't lend itself to seminars. If you operate a window-washing business, a car-washing business, or a mail-order publishing business, perhaps seminars are not for you. But if you run an income-tax preparation, instructional, or retail furniture business, perhaps they are.

Think about the field in which you operate. Can you give a lecture for forty-five minutes on any aspect of it? Which aspect? How will this tie in with your offering? Do you have the showmanship to lecture for forty-five minutes and hold the attention of your audience, or should you delegate that task to someone else? Do you have the salesmanship to close sales right then and there, or should that, too, be the job of an associate? What will you be selling at the seminar? Will it be products? Services? Books? Lessons? A paid seminar? Products or services of a fusion marketing partner?

As with sampling, if it is at all feasible, simply try to offer one free seminar to market your business. It can be a lot of fun. And it can be extremely profitable, with a lower cost per sale than advertising in any newspaper or on any radio station. It will give you both immediate and long-term benefits. You'll get to mention in future marketing that you have lectured in your field, led seminars in your area of expertise. Giving free seminars is a very innovative way to market.

Giving a seminar that's not at your own place of business will run you about $50 to $200 for the room, plus whatever it costs to buy coffee or juice for your guests. If you will keep them for only an hour, you need not provide refreshments, but if you plan to go longer than that, it's a good idea to have them. Some morning seminars also offer free donuts. Even donuts are weapons in the arsenal of a practitioner of guerrilla marketing. Guerrillas know the dynamic power of small details.

Seminar costs

To the cost of the room and refreshments, add the price of the ads you'll be running and any seminar materials you'll be handing out. After your seminar and sales pitch are completed, you can add up your receipts, then divide them by the total cost of the room, the ads, the refreshments, and the materials. That will give you your cost per sale. If it is low enough, continue to market this way. In fact, it doesn't have to be low. Even if you sell ten people a $1000 product that costs you $100 and it runs $1000 for your room and ads and handouts, you will have earned $10,000 while spending $2000 — a cost per sale of $80. This is a high cost, but it's minuscule when compared to your $900 profit on a $1000 product. That is why so many free seminars are being offered these days. That, plus the opportunity to talk to honest-to-goodness prospects, people who have already shown that they will expend time and effort to learn more about your field.

Demonstrations can be given not only at seminars, but also in homes, at parties (be sure you consider party-plan marketing for your business), in stores, at fairs and shows, in parks, at beaches, almost anywhere. People are attracted to small crowds, and a free demonstration will almost certainly attract a small crowd. At a free demonstration, which is much shorter than a seminar — no more than five minutes — be prepared to sell and take orders immediately afterward. Folks who give seminars and demonstrations often have cohorts all set to accept customers' credit cards, checks, and cash. The person giving the demo or seminar is usually too busy answering questions to take orders. So be sure you have that base covered.

Demonstrate

A free demonstration need not be marketed in the same way as a seminar. Just showing up at a high-traffic location, or placing some well-conceived signs may do the trick. Of course, it is okay to advertise and distribute circulars. But those things may not be necessary. It will be necessary, though, to provide the showmanship and salesmanship.

Can you demonstrate your product or service effectively? Be sure you ask yourself and answer honestly. If you can say yes, by all means give it your best shot. Rarely will you be afforded so golden an opportunity.

Throw a party

A few moments ago, I mentioned the idea of giving your free seminar or demo in a party situation. More and more items every year are being marketed through party-plan marketing. Here's how it works: A person becomes a party-plan representative for a company. Let's say it's an art gallery, since so many of them engage in this kind of marketing. No, wait — let's say it's *your* business. You throw a party for all of your friends and close acquaintances, just as Tupperware party-planners have been doing for decades, and very successfully as I'm sure you've heard.

At the party, you serve coffee and pastries, maybe even little sandwiches. You also give a well-planned sales spiel about whatever you are selling. You show examples, conduct a brief seminar, distribute samples, or give a demonstration to the assembled throng. The lighting is optimum. Music especially selected for the occasion may be playing in the background. Your enthusiasm is bubbly and contagious. You're obviously proud of your offerings. It shows. Your friends start to like them, too. And the prices! They sound so low. A buying frenzy starts. Fifteen of your offerings are sold. They sell for an average of $100 apiece. But you purchased them for $25 each, including everything, from your supplier.

Each $100 sale results in $75 for you. You have a right to feel proud of yourself. You earned $1125 for the night and spent only $50 for refreshments — a $1075 profit. And that's just the start. Now you tell your friends that they can do the same. And some do. The word spreads. The parties spread. Soon they're being held in several towns. Naturally, you get the lion's share of sales from the parties thrown by the people you've signed up. You're raking in the bucks. Your buddies, along with strangers who are enthused about what you sell, are raking in the bucks. Your suppliers are doing very well, thank you. You are very, very, happy that you engaged in party-plan marketing.

Can you? Here are the types of companies that do already: exercise-machine companies, art galleries, kitchen-equipment companies (such as Tupperware), women's clothing manufactur-

ers, vitamin manufacturers, X-rated product companies (the bur-
geoning "pleasure" industry), cosmetics manufacturers, computer companies, and lingerie manufacturers. The list is not
shrinking.

Such parties are ideal places for demonstrations. And the
people attending *are already conditioned to buy.* You can't beat
that kind of situation if you're a practicing guerrilla. Of all the
places at which free seminars or demonstrations can be held, parties certainly rank up there near the top.

About the only disadvantage of free seminars and demonstra- **Have seminar,**
tions (except for parties) is that you must do quite a bit of travel- **will travel**
ing. Either you or a person you delegate. You can't keep holding
free demos and seminars in the same area over and over again.
You've got to go on the road and talk to fresh prospects. But you
can make these free sessions part of your marketing plan and give
one or two per year. A guerrilla would find some way to utilize
them. Will you?

24
Trade Shows, Exhibits, Fairs: Making a Public Spectacle

SOME WILDLY SUCCESSFUL ENTREPRENEURS employ only one major method of marketing: They display and sell their wares at trade shows, exhibits, and fairs. They realize that many serious prospects will attend these gatherings, so they put all their efforts into exhibiting and selling their merchandise (they usually sell products rather than services). This is not to say that their show booths are their only marketing vehicles. But they are their primary ones. And in a few instances, this is the only way a person needs to market. I don't like telling this to you for fear it might encourage a lax attitude, but it is the truth.

The marketing plan of many a guerrilla consists of appearances at four major shows or fairs, plus circulars or brochures to be distributed at the shows. Nothing else. And to be sure, nothing else is needed.

I once attended a large national furniture show with a client who owned a chain of furniture stores. He very much wanted to be one of the first people through the doors at the three-day event. When I asked him why, he told me that he would first breeze through the show, making notes and looking at all the exhibits. Then he would quickly return to the displays that had caught his attention and order a full year's worth of items, making certain to get agreements that he would be the exclusive outlet for each item.

Sure enough, it took him, with me hot on his heels, a mere thirty minutes to walk the miles of aisles. Then he spent the next two hours dickering with the manufacturers or distributors that tickled his fancy. At the end of two and one-half hours, he was delighted, having signed up for a year's worth of purchases, all with exclusive arrangements. And just as happy as he, maybe even happier, were the handful of entrepreneurs who had attracted his attention with their merchandise, displays, salesmanship, and readiness to grant concessions. I well recall the look on one man's face when he realized that in only ten minutes he had sold half a million dollars' worth of goods. Fifty thou per minute is a pretty luscious sales rate.

The $50,000 minute

I suggest that you browse through a copy of *Tradeshow and Convention Guide* at your library, or order a copy from Budd Publications, P.O. Box 7, New York, New York 10004, to learn of a multitude of shows at which you can display your offerings. You'll find more than you think, and believe me, the shows will be worth checking into.

There are a couple of ways to display what you sell at such shows. One way, the standard way, is to rent a booth for several hundred dollars, set up a display, and give it your best. Another way, guerrilla-like in character, and a fine method of testing the efficacy of trade shows as a non-media marketing medium for you, is to visit a show, find a display booth that offers merchandise compatible with yours, and strike up a deal with the exhibitor whereby you share a portion of the next booth the exhibitor rents. That means you pay part of the rental fee, assume part of the sales responsibility, and allow your items to be displayed and sold along with those of your new compatriot.

Two ways to display

Visiting such shows is a revelation to the astute guerrilla. When you visit one or two, you will learn of products that compete with or complement yours. You will also discover products that knock your socks off — products with which you would love to become associated, and possibly could, as a fusion marketing partner. You'll learn the right way to display goods, and the wrong way. You'll pick up some dandy ideas for brochures, signs, and demonstrations. You'll learn a heck of a lot from the mistakes of others — people who have great merchandise but don't know how to market it. And you'll meet people who may be able to help you distribute what you sell.

Be a visitor

Let's look at a case in point. A man-and-wife team who marketed greeting cards all by themselves by calling on stationery stores were soon alerted to the existence of stationery shows at which greeting cards are displayed. There, they were told, they could display their own cards and make sales, they could team up with other card manufacturers, and better yet they could meet distributors who could distribute their cards throughout the country. The two budding entrepreneurs went to the show, checked out the cards and displays of others, and met several representatives who offered to distribute their cards. Because they were greenhorns at the business, they were delighted, and they signed on with several of the reps.

Business picked up for them that next year. But in talking with a few fellow card sellers, they learned that there are basically two kinds of reps one meets at shows. Some are ordinary reps who conduct an ordinary amount of sales activity, and achieve ordinary distribution in ordinary stores. Those, alas, were the kind of reps the man-and-wife team had signed up. The other kind of reps are known as Rolls-Royce reps. They have the ability to move prodigious numbers of greeting cards by distributing only in high-volume stores and expending a great deal of selling energy.

The next year, the man and wife went to the stationery shows and signed up with only Rolls-Royce reps. By signing with them, the couple increased their sales fivefold over the year before, propelling themselves into a deliriously wonderful tax bracket. So if you are looking for national distribution of your goods, look for Rolls-Royce reps at major trade shows.

While displaying your products in your own booth — something you will most likely want to do after you are ready to take on large orders — you will have a great opportunity to engage in four other types of marketing at the same time:

Market with more than your display

1. You'll be able to hand out circulars. I suggest that you hire someone, preferably a gorgeous woman (or a gorgeous man, if women are your prime prospects), to distribute your circulars while walking through the show. The cost to hire the person will be about $75, and for that, she or he will pass out as many as 5000 circulars — all inviting people to visit your booth. If you do that, you will instantly rise above most of the other exhibitors, since they will not be practicing such a guerrilla-like tactic. You'll also attract more prospects.

2. You'll be able to give away brochures. Because brochures are more costly than circulars, you won't want to give as many away. But by disseminating them at your booth only, you'll be able to narrow the distribution down to serious

prospects only. And your brochures will do heavy-duty work for you. Many people attend shows and exhibits merely to collect brochures. Then they study the brochures and place their orders on the basis of the information they've gleaned. So this is a chance to make your brochure a powerful sales tool. Be sure to get the names and addresses of the people to whom you give brochures. Just ask for their card.

3. You'll have a great chance to demonstrate your goods to real prospects who are in a buying mood. You can demonstrate your offerings to large groups of people. And since your competitors will probably be at the show too, you'll have a good opportunity to prove the advantages of your product.

4. You'll have ample opportunity to give away free samples. Rarely will you be afforded the chance to give samples to so many potential customers. So if it's possible to let people sample your merchandise, a show or exhibit is the place to do it.

Perhaps now you can see how entrepreneurs avail themselves of the opportunities at shows with 100 percent effort, and why they concentrate their marketing energies and dollars on shows.

Pay close attention to this next guerrilla secret. It frequently spells the difference between astonishing success and depressing failure. It is quite obvious, or so I thought until I saw exhibitors who didn't understand the concept at all. So let me make it even more obvious right here and now. Your main purpose in having **The main thrust** a booth at a trade show, fair, or exhibit is *to sell your product.* If it's not that, then it's to *get quality names for your mailing list.* Sure, you want to display, to demonstrate, to educate. But you really want to sell. So you've got to have the means to take orders right there at your booth. You've got to have a person there who is dedicated to selling. You should aim for a large volume of sales at the show itself, in spite of the fancy brochures you will be passing out. Don't forget the furniture store entrepreneur I wrote about at the start of this chapter. He visited the shows to look and then to buy. He didn't care about brochures. He wanted to place his orders at the show.

If you do not sell a lot of what you want to sell at a show, you may have failed in this marketing effort. Don't feel great because you have given away cartons of brochures, made gobs of friends, obtained loads of contacts. That's fine, but if you have not sold a large volume of what you are selling, you have not taken advantage of the glorious opportunity afforded you by such shows. I recall two competitors at a national show. Both had attractive displays. Both gave imaginative demonstrations. Both handed out compelling brochures. But the first company figured that the show was a place to display — so it made zero sales. The second company, a new, small, young partnership, figured that the show was a place to sell — so it made $4.5 million in sales during a three-day period. I believe I've made my point.

Before wandering off to the fair, there are two guerrilla tactics for you to know about trade shows. The first involves the recognition that there are prospects and there are large, hot prospects. If you've done your crucial pre–trade show homework, closely perusing the trade magazines and talking with industry insiders, you'll know exactly who the big fish are. These large, hot prospects deserve to be invited to your hospitality suite at a hotel near the trade show. In it, intensify your personal bond with these people. Don't sell. Make your friendship closer.

All prospects aren't created equal

The second tactic is mandatory for companies that didn't sell a lot at the show. It is to *follow up within ten days on the prospects you met*. Write them, call them, and keep the memory of your offerings fresh in their minds. Without follow-up, you're probably just wasting your time at a trade show. And you know how important your time is — far more important than money. If you run out of money, any guerrilla can find ways to generate more. But if you run out of time, no guerrilla tactic can alter that reality.

Follow up within ten days

Many craftspeople sell all the crafts they make at one or two yearly shows. They spend most of the year making their items, then spend a few weeks — at two three-week shows — selling them. Often, no other marketing is necessary for them. But generally, to succeed at marketing in a show, exhibit, or fair, you need a combination of marketing tools: a professional-looking and beckoning display; a supply of informative brochures; a larger supply of enticing circulars to be passed out at the show; a method of demonstrating, sampling, or showing off your goods; and at least two high-energy salespeople. If you have all of those, you are a guerrilla and you have primed yourself to succeed.

Your exhibit at the trade show should be as professional as you can afford. New technology in audio-visual presentations makes it possible for you to stage a continuous multimedia extravaganza — including slides, film, videotape, and music. Lighting can be combined with this multimedia display to literally spotlight your products as they are being featured in your multimedia show. As the visual images dance before the eyes of your prospects, and as music soothes their conscious minds and gains access to their unconscious, the tape-recorded voice of a master motivator tells your audience that they should buy from you, that they should trust you, that they should give their money to you. And there you can be, order pad at the ready, all set to sign, seal, and deliver.

Dancing visual images

That's the best possible scenario for a trade-show exhibit. If you can't afford it, work down, step by step, including as much as you can.

In most big-city yellow page directories are several columns of "Display Designers and Producers." These businesses offer such lovelies as modular exhibit systems. They will construct or they will rent, and they will even store your exhibit while you're not using it. They'll make a miniature model of your exhibit before you give them an okay to build the real thing — or ten real things. They craft handsome exhibit displays of wood, plastic, cardboard, or metal. They make displays of any size, wired and ready to go.

I'm always impressed and educated when I walk through a display warehouse. I discover great ideas for future displays. I get a good fix on current prices, both for renting and for purchasing. Because the technology is moving so rapidly, it's a good idea to make a yearly visit to one of your area's largest display companies. Ask to see the best they have. And remember — you may be able to afford it if you go in with a few other compatible companies. Case in point: At a recent waterbed trade show, the best exhibit was a multimedia display using holograms and laser technology. It was paid for by a mattress maker, a heater manufacturer, and a bed-frame company. Each of these three compatible companies got a first-class reputation for 33 percent of the first-class price.

The display warehouse

Of course, you can always build your own display. If you have the time, talent, and equipment, give it consideration. But do me a favor. Before you do it yourself, look at what is available to you now. That's what your competitors will probably use. Can you do better? Can you keep abreast of new developments?

Just as important as an award-winning display are the people who man — or woman — your booth at the trade show. They should be talented in several areas. Here are a few tips:

1. Staff your booth with *enough* people. Not doing so can be fatal. I recall a show booth that was manned by two marvelous company reps. They were backed by a beautiful display. At one point, one of the reps was having lunch and the other was visiting another booth. The only person left was a lackadaisical fellow who didn't really understand the company's business and was really hired to be a gofer. Naturally, that was when two of the biggest customers in the industry visited the booth. They couldn't get answers to their questions, couldn't get an explanation of a new product being introduced, so they moved on and gave their business to someone else. Don't blow your opportunities. Be sure that a top-rate person is always at the booth. To do that may require at least two, and if you can arrange it, even three, top-rate people to attend the show and attend to the exhibit. One of those people must always be on hand to answer questions and take orders.

2. Be sure the people staffing your booth are *personable, extroverted*, and *friendly*. You don't want an introverted genius up there on your stage. Some people serve best from within the inner sanctum of the company. Others are made for the road.

3. Do what is necessary to staff your booth with *knowledgeable salespeople*. Knowledgeable alone isn't enough. Sales-minded alone isn't enough. At a trade-show exhibit, your staff must be both.

4. Ascertain that the people staffing your booth have a *high energy level* and won't burn out too soon. Trade shows are exhausting. It's hard to stand up and be bright and charming all day, three days in a row.

5. Carefully select people with the *proper social graces* to represent you at trade shows. Trade shows invariably mean parties. I've seen enough people get embarrassingly drunk at such parties to realize that their energies on the exhibit floor were wiped out by their antics on the sixteenth floor.

At trade shows, glorious things can happen for your company. It is possible — and I know of at least three instances in which this happened — to make one contact who will place an order so large **Gigantic orders** that it will put you on easy street for at least a year. A woman who invented a paper-towel dispenser printed her circulars on paper towels, then gave them away at her booth — dispensed from the dispenser she had invented. One buyer placed an order with her for 250,000 units. Was this due to her unique way of supplying information? Maybe yes, maybe no. But she sure wouldn't have made a sale that size had she not been at the show. And she may not have attracted attention had she not developed such a unique way of sampling, demonstrating, and providing information.

There are more trade shows today than ever before. That means you've got to know which to attend, which to exhibit at. Except for the big national trade shows, most people attending a trade show come from a 100-mile radius. They come to buy, to see what's new, to investigate the competition, to spot trends, and to find new tools and services that can help their companies profit. If you're attending a trade show, these are the things you **How to attend** must know: **a trade show**

- Know just what you want to accomplish.
- See the entire show; profits hide in esoteric places; small companies with exciting products are often in inexpensive locations on the fringes of a show.
- Prioritize by visiting the important exhibits first.
- Bring a sturdy, lightweight case to hold show materials.
- Wear comfortable shoes and take breaks to lighten your load. A trade show is not as exhausting as a full-court basketball game, but many attendees will tell you that it comes very close.

If you're an exhibitor, recognize that the show begins long before the show. Pre-show promotion sets your show marketing in motion. Remember that your job is to get your prospect's attention and time, then show how you can help the prospect profit. This will occur if you realize certain truisms about shows:

- Select the right shows, guiding your selection with past experience, quality of the sponsor's past shows, who the audience is, and who the other exhibitors are.
- Guerrilla rule of thumb on show selection: The more valuable the show is to your prospects, the more valuable it will be to you.

- Important criteria to consider include location, timing, convention center, on-site services, and your display.
- Guerrillas are definitely party animals and know they will ring up the most sales with a party for sizzling prospects in their hotel hospitality suite.
- Know for certain whether you want to penetrate your existing market or expand into a new market, know if you're going for sales or leads.
- Don't send any trade-show reps who will long for home so they can get down to real work. The real work is at the show.
- Be absolutely certain that your booth blends with your marketing identity and your current marketing theme.
- Because people don't like to walk into a booth where they might feel trapped, be sure your booth has an open feel.
- If you can, include a hands-on demonstration or something that people can handle. Studies show that folks love to touch things.
- Research reveals that location has very little to do with the amount of traffic at your booth; believe it.
- Keep things very easy to understand; a few large pictures are better than many small ones. Be sure your company name is highly visible. This is all-too-often overlooked.
- Know all your costs. These include rent, displays, electricity, carpeting, furniture, transportation, lodging, food, entertaining — hey, that's a lot! Keep track or you may end up kidding yourself.
- Experts say the profitability of a show is determined primarily by the quality of your people and how they work a booth. Be sure they take breaks every four hours and see the entire show as early as possible to gain a feel for the competition.
- Quickly separate the serious prospects from the browsers. Don't spend too much time even with the serious prospects; there are many others to meet.
- Have no chairs in the booth unless you *plan to close sales there — and I hope you do.* Visitors won't disturb seated staffers. If you must have a chair and table setup, put it in a quiet corner.
- Don't give away too much literature. People get overloaded. Save your best for *major prospects during follow-up.* With

qualified leads and notes made at the show, follow-up will
be effective. *Start with a thank-you note within one week,
or otherwise you'll probably be completely forgotten.* What a
waste of time, energy, and money! Don't let it happen.

A few guerrilla tactics that have worked for others before the show   **Guerrilla tactics**
will also work for you:

- Send prospects a small packet of Epsom salts and an offer of
  free footpads at your booth.
- Send an invitation to pick up a free product from your
  booth.
- Send a photo or drawing of your booth so that your visitors
  can easily spot you.
- Send a map of the exhibit hall marked to show your booth,
  the rest rooms, the food stands, pay phones, and all the
  exits.
- Send an entry form for a contest to be entered at your
  booth.
- Send a show schedule with a time to visit your display.

Perhaps your business simply cannot make sales at such public
gatherings. But if there is any way you can utilize this marketing
tool, do it. At such events, making a public spectacle of yourself
is more of a virtue than a vice.

25
Miscellaneous Marketing Tools: Services, Searchlights, Contests, T-Shirts, Newsletters, and Guerrilla Media

EVERY FEW MONTHS, NEW MARKETING weapons are developed. Some are ingenious. Some are ridiculous. All are worth examining. Just because a marketing device is new doesn't mean it is bad. Probably the most amazing moment I spent during my career in big-time advertising agencies occurred while I was working in England. We had persuaded a large manufacturer of anti-acne products, the largest in the country, to experiment with television advertising. This was in 1968, hardly the Dark Ages.

After a three-month test, during which sales went right through the roof, we prepared a plan calling for the year-round use of television. When we presented it to the client, he told us he did not plan to include television in his marketing program. We wanted to know why, since our test had been enormously successful. "Because frankly, gentlemen," the client countered,

Beware of fads "I am not convinced that television is here to stay."

I suppose you can take the same attitude when examining new methods of marketing. But even if a method is hot for only one year, a guerrilla should avail himself or herself of it during that year. It doesn't have to be "here to stay" in order to help your business. Any help you can get should be gratefully accepted.

Moped marketing Perhaps you've heard of moped advertising. That's a type of marketing in which you pay a company and provide them with a sign advertising your product or service. Then they have one of their employees, usually clad in a bikini, drive a moped into high-traffic areas where your sign can be seen by large numbers of people. If you are marketing sunglasses, tanning oil, or soft drinks, it makes a lot of sense to employ this medium at beaches. Mopeds can go where buses and cars cannot. They can go to parks and ballgames and parades — wherever lots of people congregate. This is a new marketing medium. It may or may not be here to stay, but it can be of help to you. It's certainly here to stay if "here" is Southern California beaches.

There are other, less obvious marketing tools that you probably have heard of. Matchbooks, for one. Package inserts, too, though they are really part of direct marketing. Searchlights are successfully used by many a retailer. But if you live in a community that frowns upon their use, better steer clear of them. Bench advertising is another medium that is available in certain towns, but not many. Might it be right for you? What about T-shirt advertising? If your business might benefit from this method of marketing, give it consideration: Some businesses (and many are small businesses) get impressive results from commercials run in movie theaters and drive-ins. The cost is very low. Can this medium influence your prospects? If they are movie-goers, maybe so.

In addition to these marketing tools, you can use bumper stickers to broadcast your message. Baseball hats with the name of an advertiser are ubiquitous in the United States, not to mention across the waters as well. Maybe you'll market with buttons like many political candidates do (though half of them lose). And then there are decals. And imprinted sun visors. There's skywriting. And you can use banners that are towed by airplanes. Let's not forget blimps, once a mainstay for Goodyear, now flying high for many other marketers. Less popular these days is the device of A-frames, known as sandwich boards. These are worn by people parading in front of large groups of other people, and they tell of the benefits of buying from you or announce special offers. As a guerrilla, you have an obligation to give serious consideration to many of these off-the-wall marketing devices.

Bumper stickers, blimps, and buttons

I recall being approached by people from a company called Johnny-Ads. They told me that they placed signs on the inside of doors in rest-room toilet cubicles, renting the space from building managers. That explained their name. It also seemed to me to be an invasion of privacy. I mean, if you can't be free from advertising while on the john, where can you be? Although I did not sign up for a three-month trial of ads in latrines, I did hear some glowing stories of success achieved by others using the medium. Since that time, however, I have heard nothing about the company.

Rent a picketer

There are now several companies that offer to market your services with picket advertising. One of these is called Rent-a-Picket. Another is called Positive Picketing. You pay them a set amount and they have their employees parade in front of your place of business carrying picket-type signs that say wonderful things about you. It's unique, all right, and it may even be here to stay. It is certainly marketing. And for you, it might be worthwhile. As a practicing guerrilla, you can stage this marketing event by yourself, working only with your own employees. If you use any picket marketing, be sure to contact the media. Because the medium is such a hoot, I'll bet you can get free media coverage — in the newspapers and possibly on television.

Such advertising methods — searchlights, skywriting, pickets, rest-room ads, computer diskettes, and the rest — should be perceived the same way you perceive billboards. They are reminder advertising. They help keep your name in the public eye, and they call attention to your prime attributes. But they probably can't do the job all by themselves. Still, one or more of them might be made part of a smart marketing plan. And computer

Floppy disks as media

diskettes can do a whale of a selling job for you, as they have for others.

Computers themselves have come onto the marketing scene and made themselves a boon to guerrillas in six areas:

Ways computers help guerrillas

1. More fresh and up-to-the-moment customer mailing lists
2. Burgeoning-with-important-information databases
3. Motivation to publish a newsletter or catalogue
4. Ease, accuracy, and automation in direct mailings
5. Computer graphics — for print and video
6. Ability to tap into on-line information services

You can expect the computer to influence guerrilla marketing even more as we move into a new high-tech century. You'll see how by the end of this chapter.

If you have a place of business where you occasionally run promotions, a searchlight to call attention to a late-night sale may work as an attention-getter for you. I know of a waterbed retailer who once filled a waterbed mattress with helium and tied it to a rope. Then he let it float over his store, where it could be seen for miles. The cars that drove by didn't all stop, but many slowed down and noticed the store. The owner of the store says that the stunt enabled him to sell his average monthly volume in one day and to double it within one week. Crazy, but it worked.

And so it is with many unusual marketing methods. As a small entrepreneur, you can take chances that many well-established large companies wouldn't try. Take advantage of your smallness. Experiment. Try making up your own advertising implements. If you make up ten signs, you can hire ten high school students to affix the signs to their bikes, then ride the bikes wherever your prospects might be. Would this work for you? Or perhaps you could arrange to have a truck with bells drive through neighborhoods alerting the community to your offerings. Ice cream companies do. Political candidates do. It's worth looking into if you think it might work and won't offend the neighbors.

Just because certain marketing methods are rarely used, or because you've never heard of them, doesn't mean they won't be effective for you. During the next year and every year thereafter, two or three fascinating ad vehicles will be invented. TV cable interconnects for low-cost prime time come to mind. Shopping cart video monitors, too. And classified advertising TV channels, not to mention the ubiquitous home shopping networks. Marketing while people are on telephone hold was new at one time, but it's now standard for many a guerrilla company. Keep your eyes peeled for more. If you honestly feel that they can help you — not just as gimmicks, but as sales tools — give them a try. For example, if you are marketing a rock concert and you know of a beach where lots of potential concert-goers hang out, it might make a lot of sense to market your concert on a banner pulled by an airplane. And it shouldn't be too tough to find a plane owner who offers such a service.

Keep your eyes peeled for new media

Publish an annual report, especially if you're not a public company. It's a unique and rather wonderful way of communicating with your customers and prospects. It will get inordinately high readership because no small companies publish annual reports — everybody knows that. Or at least they didn't until guerrilla marketing became so necessary.

Annual reports aren't only for biggies

Market by providing extra services such as child care and baby-sitting services. Several exercise centers, for example, have increased their clientele by offering such services free of charge — and well supervised.

Remember that a videotape brochure cuts way, way down on the cost of a sales call. The 7 percent response rate to video marketing is quite attractive compared with the 2.5 percent expected of most direct mailings.

You might plan to regularly publish a newsletter, as many companies do — but some do poorly. To do yours right, you've got to know the do's and don'ts:

Newsletter do's and don'ts

- Do remember that newsletters should motivate prospects to buy while helping them in general.
- Do provide valuable, timely, brief information.
- Do make your newsletter easy to read and easy to look at.
- Do give a host of fabulous ideas; be known as an important source.
- Do let a professional designer create a great-looking format for your newsletter.
- Don't let your designer create a costly, elaborate format.
- Don't publish on a random basis; become habit-forming.
- Don't send to people who never respond to any of your offers.
- Don't give outdated, untimely, hard-to-use information.
- Don't make your newsletter too long; they're popular because they are not time-consuming to read.
- Don't forget what people buy: solutions to their problems. Newsletters, thanks to desktop publishing and a realization of the importance of time, are now easier and more sensible to add to your arsenal than ever before.

Marketing with a 900 number

Should you market with a 900 number? First off, realize that most people now associate 900 phone numbers with scams and porn. They also know they'll be hit with a dialing fee and they don't really want to pay it. That's why some companies look askance at 900 numbers. But Procter & Gamble ran a sweepstakes with a 900 number, costing 75 cents a call. Of the quarter of a million people who entered, only 24,000 used the 900 number, and P&G has no immediate plans to use a 900 number for its next promotion. Still, if you want to market this way, know these nine facts:

1. Callers with a 900 number will be fewer than with a free 800 number, but will be more qualified.

2. 900 numbers are terrible for obtaining leads, but marvelous for generating hot prospects.
3. A 900 line can help build a qualified base of prospects if you offer something other than your main offering. Example by a large guerrilla: Kimberly-Clark offered parents a 900 number that played a personalized lullaby. Now they gain revenues from the more than 100,000 calls they received.
4. Your 900-number callers can be categorized by forty different demographic and psychographic clusters. The 900 service offering this information is called Prizm 900. Ask your local phone company about it.
5. When supplying prospects with data, offer to fax it to callers who use your 900 number. Many, needing your data and needing it this instant, will gladly pay the $5 toll for the call.
6. A 900 number can generate revenues without sales when used to give people an edge in sweepstakes and an extra incentive, such as a special discount, for purchasing. Notice that I did say *revenue without sales.*
7. Samples can be distributed to very qualified people if they can request the samples only by calling your 900 number.
8. Memberships and subscriptions can easily be sold through a 900 number, which offers prospects more convenience and instant gratification.
9. Using a 900 number is a proven way for fund-raisers to obtain money from small contributors.

You win with contests

Also consider contests and sweepstakes. These definitely do attract people, even though they may not be attracted to your primary offering. Those who enter do become involved with you, and involvement can lead to sales. Just remember that the purposes of contests and sweepstakes are (1) to get names for your mailing list, (2) to separate you from the ranks of strangers, and (3) to entice people to enter your store in order to enter the contest. Be sure you place the entry boxes in the rear of the store so that entrants can scope out your other offerings while they try to win that free trip to Hawaii.

Certainly you have seen ads or received mail that screams "You have been selected," or "Fabulous Sweepstakes," or "You may have already won $1,000,000," or "Be a winner." Some sweepstakes experts believe that although people may not have money for food, they do have money for sweepstakes. In fact, the experts say, "When times get bad, sweepstakes get good."

In 1990, sponsors spent an estimated $250 million on prizes, plus far more than that advertising the sweepstakes. Between 1989 and 1992, according to the Promotion Marketing Association of America, the number of contests and sweepstakes grew by more than 34 percent. Contests and sweepstakes used to be shunned as legally and morally dubious. But they have now become a mainstay of American marketing. For that reason, they are worth considering. If you do get involved, be sure you do everything on the up-and-up. Check with your lawyer to be sure you are not conducting an illegal lottery when you are asking folks to guess the number of coins in a bottle.

If you want to attract a lot of foot traffic to a particular location, give thought to running a contest that requires people to come to your place of business to enter, and to return to see if they have won. These days, smart marketers are learning that everyone should win something. Whatever that is, it should be enough so that they do not resent you and associate your offering with their loss. The best prize of all, better than cruises and convertibles and round-the-world trips, is cash. No surprise there.

The gambling instinct   People seem to want to gamble; even charities are jumping onto the contest bandwagon. So let your imagination run rampant. I know a retailer who filled a gigantic container with goldfish. Then he advertised his contest: "Guess the number of goldfish in the container and win $1000!" His traffic count (and his sales) rose so dramatically that the $1000 prize didn't even put a minor dent in his budget. Because he was a guerrilla, he gave 25-cent plants to everyone who entered — after the prize winner was announced. Again, people came in to collect their prizes, and while they were there, well, they purchased something else. Are you surprised?

Different communities have different laws regarding contests. I'm sure you've seen the disclaimer "Void where prohibited by law" appended to many a sweepstakes entry form. So don't leap into this type of marketing without first consulting the local authorities.

Contests always attract attention. What you want to do is attract the attention of *prospects*, and not just people. Because people want not only to make money but also to save money, try marketing with price-off coupons. If you're a retailer, use creative tags on your merchandise. Perhaps each tag can offer a different percentage discount. Then you can advertise a "Mystery Tag Sale." It's not a completely new idea, merely a variation on an old one. But it can, and does, work.

Giving "spiffs," or special commissions, to salespeople who surpass a certain goal or sell a specific item is also an effective method of marketing. Can you put it to work to increase your own sales?

Exciting, ever-changing window displays can also be effective. You're in luck if you can use them. And even if you don't have your own display window, you may be able to strike up a deal with someone who does, another person for your growing list of fusion marketing partners. Just imagine the difference between a store that has a window display and one that doesn't. Enormous!

How much is that doggie in the window?

I know of a fancy hairstyling salon that kept a poster in its window advertising a nearby clothing boutique. The boutique displayed a poster for the salon. Both gained extra sales as a result. The cost? Nil. The only price was the few seconds it took for someone to come up with the idea. As you know, guerrillas are all too happy to invest time instead of money when it comes to marketing.

Maybe you can market and *save* time. Who does that? Users of cellular telephones, that's who. Does that mean all guerrillas need one? Here's a test to answer that for you:

Cellular phones save time, make money

- Including commuting, do you spend two or more hours per day in your car for work?
- Do you conduct at least 20 percent of your business by phone?
- Do you often have unproductive time on the road?
- Are you often in locations where you are unable to be reached on the phone by others?
- Do you make frequent stops at pay phones to make calls during the day — and sometimes have to search for a pay phone?
- Have you ever lost business because you failed to get phone messages in time or didn't return a call promptly enough?

- Does your business require that customers be able to get information to you whenever necessary?
- Do you frequently need to reschedule appointments or inform people if you're running late?
- Are you often driving alone, and could it benefit your firm if you had an in-car meeting with someone?
- Do you ever get ideas while driving that you would like to put into effect right away?

If you answered yes to only two of those questions, you should look into a car phone. If you answered yes to four or more of the questions, experts say your car phone might pay for itself. I resisted having a car phone for years. Now I wonder what the dickens I ever did without it.

All of the miscellaneous marketing methods are valuable to one entrepreneur or another. They very often make the difference between a profit and a loss. But they rarely can serve as the foundation for a marketing program. They should be used as adjuncts to a solid mass-media program. You've got to prevent your public from becoming callous to your marketing, and these miscellaneous marketing tools do the trick.

Although many miscellaneous marketing tools remain forever miscellaneous — that is, never enter the marketing mainstream — they are not to be ignored. Guerrillas look under every rock, peer around every corner, examine every opportunity. You never can tell when you might make a flurry of sales from a moped sign displayed before thousands of prospects in a park on a sunny day.

Postcard decks   A decade ago, nobody heard of postcard decks — those decks of twenty or thirty postcards encased in clear plastic, addressing the same topic — business, psychology, kids, whatever — and mailed to a specific target audience. I receive postcard decks centered on business offerings. My wife receives them focused upon psychology products — books, tapes, seminars, and directories. Each postcard has a different advertiser's name on one side and room for a stamp (no need to make these postpaid). The other side has a time-limited offer: discount, freebie, two-for-one deal, something tempting. Today postcard decks are the fastest growing area of marketing. The cost is very low and the response rate is in the 20 percent range. Proof of their effectiveness is that in 1990, a full 89 percent of advertisers using postcard decks repeated the tactic. You can be sure they wouldn't have tried it a second time if it hadn't worked the first. These postcard decks are glorious ways to start the selling momentum. To learn more about them, call 800-323-2751.

So keep your eyes — and your mind — open to new media by studying the marketing publications. *Adweek* is my favorite; I recommend subscribing. Call 800-722-6658.

Keep your eyes open to the hot new products of the times. Perhaps you can turn them into a marketing tool or offer them as an incentive or gift. For the nineties, the hot items and markets will be:

Hot items for the nineties

Rain-forest goods	Rollerblades
Portable phones	Airbags in cars
Doggie day-care	Slow food
Beach umbrellas	Liquid diets
Sports drinks	Living wills
Goddess worshippers	Birkenstocks
Vegetarians	Nannies
Depressed people	Men's hats
Environmentally friendly	Army families
items	Oversized TVs
Early retirees	Mountain bikes
White appliances	Balding people
Beach volleyball	Latchkey kids
Supersized bookstores	Step-families
Condoms	Micro-TVs
Catalogue buyers	Sports utility vehicles
Mini-vans	

Other new products may be called to your attention on a regular basis with a subscription to *Product Alert,* a twice-monthly briefing on new packaged goods, or its companion publications, *International Product Alert, Lookout Nonfoods,* and *Category Report* — covering five product categories. Get more details by contacting Marketing Intelligence Service Ltd., at its toll-free number, 800-836-5710. Be warned, some of the subscription rates run $1000.

As these publications alert you to new products, *Adweek, Advertising Age, Inc., Entrepreneur, The Wall Street Journal,* and perhaps even your local newspaper regularly inform you of new media — from ads in elevators to electronic bulletin boards accessed by your computer.

And keep in mind that once upon a time, newspapers, magazines, radio, and direct mail were miscellaneous media.

Guerrilla media

For guerrillas with deep computer expertise but not deep pockets, digital media technology offers cost-effective options. These exciting new marketing tools let you support your basic message wherever you want, focus more sharply on your niche markets, open doors to new markets, and reach higher percentages of your existing customer base. With these media, you can create world-class marketing materials with the finest production values.

Lou CasaBianca, president of New Media (415-456-1914) and a leader in the field of new guerrilla media, encourages entrepreneurs to use their computers to design and print business cards, stationery, packages, brochures, circulars, direct mailings, newsletters, and media ads. Off-the-shelf software can put all these tools at your disposal. And database software can help you monitor and respond to trends and to changes in your customer base.

Computer-driven voice-mail devices can help you get the most out of telemarketing media such as 800 and 900 phone services. They can also prove ultra-valuable to you combined with product demos, seminars, trade-show exhibits, and the more advanced media of videodiscs, cable TV, desktop publishing, multimedia presentations, and infomercials. The proliferation of audiocassette players and VCRs makes the new media available to virtually every potential customer, and the growing use of computers widens your audience even more.

When to get your feet wet

I encourage guerrillas to get their feet wet in the area of computer-based production, although I warn them to tread carefully in this area. Guerrilla media production can be complex and technically demanding. So you've got to choose between doing it in-house, hiring a consultant, or retaining a company to handle the task for you. Just beware of companies that are using outmoded equipment and technology. The real truth, though, is that with the right equipment and expertise you can produce nearly every form of guerrilla marketing material in-house more cost-efficiently than by paying an outside vendor.

How do you start with these new technologies? By talking with a good consultant who will demystify the new media options for you and advise you on the *appropriate* combination of guerrilla media for your company. Note that underlined word. *Overkill is not necessary.* You don't need complicated or overly high-tech media components, merely the ones that can do the right job for you for the least money with the fastest turnaround.

Even the newest and smallest companies can exploit guerrilla media techniques to the maximum. Just keep in mind that these tools are the means to an end — not an end in themselves. Your goal is more profitable marketing communications.

The means to an end

Guerrillas will take advantage of the technological options that are either already at our disposal or fast approaching. These include personal computers, modems, fax machines, electronic bulletin boards, and interactive compact discs. Entrepreneurs who have technophobia will be left in the dust of the computer-literate guerrillas. Yesterday people *asked* if you have a fax machine. Today they *assume* you do. The costs of these guerrilla media devices are tiny compared to the potential return. In very little time, you will realize they have added to your personal productivity, not to mention your company's profitability.

To gain further insight into guerrilla media, I suggest that you consider a subscription to *Marketing with Technology News* (phone: 212-222-1765; fax: 212-678-6357). This newsletter is published once a month by fax. It covers fax broadcasting, fax-on-demand, videotext, FM subcarriers, cellular communications, audiotext, and the latest breakthroughs in marketing technology, including a marketer's resource catalogue.

The reasoning behind fax marketing is based upon the ideas that "less is more." People are inundated with information and have time only to glance at most of it — and the sooner it arrives the better. Speed is omnipotent. Fax marketing also helps guerrillas combat rising postal rates by aligning marketers with declining phone rates. I don't, however, recommend unsolicited faxes, or "junk faxes," as a nonadoring public has christened them.

Now that you have opened your mind to marketing with fax machines, open it more to consider voice-mail as a weapon of guerrilla marketing. To gain specific information about voice-mail in your part of the world, contact your telephone company.

Mine, here in California, offers a voice-mail package that includes call forwarding, a message waiting indicator, and a special dial tone that tells you when you have a message, along with the expected message receiving capability twenty-four hours a day, seven days a week. Callers are transferred automatically to voice-mail whenever your phone is busy or unanswered, and they receive a personal greeting with your own voice (or anyone's voice, for that matter). They can leave a detailed message for you to review any time and retrieve from virtually any touchtone phone. You can use the system to send a message to one person or a whole group with a single phone call. You can even add paging notification and call transferring to an attendant.

The phone company will manage your voice-mail system and take care of all additions, deletions, and mailbox options: length of message, number of messages, messages to save, length of greeting, and paging notification. You can have a single mailbox — personal message center — or many mailboxes, one for each person in your employ if you want.

Costs for this guerrilla medium are lower than you might imagine, and the phone company owns the equipment. You don't have to purchase anything; simply pay a monthly fee.

Your prospects and customers are getting used to voice-mail and appreciating its ability to get through to you even when you're not around. As with many new technologies, people seemed to resent voice-mail when it was first introduced, but they don't mind it nearly as much these days. And owners of small businesses wonder how the heck they got around without it.

At the heart   The good Mr. CasaBianca tells us that the personal computer is at the heart of the new guerrilla media. The Apple Macintosh and DOS or Windows – based IBM-compatible PCs are examples of the types of systems that can deliver the power you want. Guerrillas of the nineties are converting their computers from passive tools into pro-active assistants. The selections of your computer, software, and media peripherals will be among the most important decisions you'll make in building your guerrilla media capability. The technology of all these components will improve with time. But if you don't act now, you'll lose out on the income they can provide for you starting right now. *Waiting is not a good idea.* I purchased my own computer gadgetry ten years ago. Had I waited until prices dropped and technology improved, I would have made my purchase yesterday, losing out on the bundle of money my computer enabled me to make during that decade. Buy now and upgrade later; that's what the pros tell you to do.

The emerging guerrilla media mentioned here can give you the clout of a *Fortune* 500 company, can target your message in a broad spectrum of media, and can reach a diversity of markets. Right at this moment, these are referred to as new media. But I remember when stereo music, microwave ovens, cordless phones, and quartz watches were considered new. Guerrillas have a knack for spotting the necessities from among the passing novelties. They know that their company's future depends upon their overcoming any insidious signs of technophobia.

Overcome that technophobia!

26
Public Relations: Instant Credibility

PUBLIC RELATIONS MEANS exactly what it says. But it is also accurate to say that it means publicity — free stories and news about you and/or your company in newspapers, magazines, newsletters, and house organs, on radio and TV, and in any other type of media.

What's good about PR   Here's what is good about publicity: It is free. It is very believable. It gives you and your company a lot of credibility and stature. It helps establish the identity of your business. It gives you authority. It is read by a large number of people. It is remembered.

Many entrepreneurs feel that there is no such thing as bad publicity; that as long as you get your name out there before the public, that's a fine thing. But guerrillas know that bad publicity leads to bad word-of-mouth marketing, known to spread faster than wildfire. Bad publicity is bad. Good publicity is great.

What's bad about PR   There are even some bad things about good publicity, though I only mean bad in a relative sense. You have no control over publicity. You have no say-so as to when it runs. You have no control over how it is presented. It is rarely repeated. You cannot buy it. You cannot ensure its accuracy.

On balance, however, publicity is an excellent weapon in any well-stocked marketing arsenal. And any marketing plan that fails to include some effort at public relations is a marketing plan that isn't going all out.

Public relations offers, as an unstated but ultra-valuable benefit, decades of staying power. Reprints of positive publicity can be framed, made parts of brochures, included in ads, put onto flip-charts, and leaned upon for precious credibility. The day the story appears is a heartwarming one, but the years afterward are when the marketing power abounds. When you can do it, use reprints of the story to empower your marketing. But you can't always do it.

When I was advertising my self-published book *Earning Money Without a Job* (since revised for the nineties and published in 1991 by Henry Holt and Company, New York) in various magazines and national newspapers, I was spending about $1000 per ad. Each ad was bringing in about $3000 in sales. The book was not available in bookstores and could be purchased only through my mail-order ad. Then a reporter from the *San Francisco Chronicle* purchased a copy of my book. Because I lived in the vicinity, and because he took a liking to the book, he called to see if he could come to my home and interview me, and asked if he could bring along a photographer. It didn't take me long to extend a warm welcome to him and his camera-bearing associate.

PR power

The interview lasted about an hour and included a brief photo session. A few days later, an article about me and my book appeared in the main news section of the newspaper. Accompanying it was a photo of me. Well into the article was the address to which the $10 purchase price (now it's less) could be sent. Within a week, I received over $10,000 worth of orders! The article had not solicited orders, did not really try to sell the book, and mentioned the address and selling price in a place where only serious readers of the article would find them. More than $10,000 in sales, and the marketing didn't cost me one penny.

As wonderful as I felt about the results, I felt just as frustrated at not being able to repeat the process. I sent the article to other newspapers, letting them know I was available for interviews. I continued to advertise the book, still achieving a fair degree of success. But never again have I been able to earn so much money with so little effort. Because my mama didn't raise a moron, I have made reprints of the article and used them as parts of mailings and press kits. So I have received a bit more mileage from the publicity. Although I know of similar stories, and indeed have arranged and taken part in them, never has the value of PR hit home as sweetly as in that instance.

The reporter felt that my book was newsy, since it promised honest information on how people could earn a good living without having to hold down a job. And that is probably the single most important factor in obtaining free publicity: providing news worth publicizing.

A fascinating P.S. to that PR tale is what happened to the reporter, Mel Ziegler, who interviewed me. He took the concepts of my book to heart, quit his job at the *Chronicle*, and opened a **Banana Republic** store, the first of an empire, called Banana Republic. That chain **is born** hit it monstrously big with its line of safari clothes, then a harbinger, it seemed, of fashion to come. It hired professional writers to describe its offerings in its catalogue, which was beautifully written and designed. But alas, what appeared to be a trend turned out to be a fad, and Banana Republic began discontinuing its safari-oriented travel merchandise, added more mainstream clothing lines, and was since purchased by the mainstream clothing giant, The Gap. The Gap is very tuned in to the times with regard to styles, prices, marketing, and selection. Because of its demonstrated genius at merchandising exactly what its target audience wants, I predict bigger and better, although less exotic, things for Banana Republic. I don't think Mel Ziegler minds one bit.

Let me clarify here that if you want to, you can pay for public relations. You can hire a PR person, pay him or her a monthly or project fee — anywhere from $500 to $25,000 per month — and let that person do what is necessary to secure free publicity. PR people are experts at it. They have the contacts, the experience, the insights. They have made all the errors, they have learned from them, and they are usually well worth their fees. But because you are a guerrilla, I want to let you know in this chapter of ways you can do what PR people do. That way, you'll be able to get the publicity and you won't have to pay anyone a dime.

Moment of truth time: The way to succeed at public relations **Where it's at:** is to have *publicity contacts* — people at the media who you **publicity contacts** know on a first-name basis. It's one thing to mail a proper press kit to the proper managing editor at a publication. It's another thing to call Nancy at the paper and say, "Nancy, let's have lunch tomorrow. I have some information that will definitely interest your readers and I want you to have it first. I'll pop for the lunch."

Nancy, because she enjoys free lunches, but primarily because she knows and trusts you, has lunch with you. Never forget that *the news media need you more than you need them.* If you have news, they'll listen. So Nancy listens and the next day, there's a story about your product or service or company in her newspaper. When you pay a PR pro a steep fee, you're paying for a gob of Nancys, and those publicity contacts are usually well worth the price.

Make no mistake: A public relations pro works very hard and intelligently. So you'll have to put in the same kind of effort and intelligence. To succeed at gaining free publicity, you must have three things: the imagination to generate real news that is worth publicizing; the influential contacts to whom you can offer your news for publication or broadcast; and the persistence to follow through and see that you get the coverage you want.

Believe me, I was very lucky when I received the free publicity for my book. I had done nary a thing to get it. Didn't use much imagination. Had no contacts. Wasn't persistent. But I reaped rich rewards. Unfortunately, life does not usually work that way. You've got to knock yourself out to get the "free" publicity that helps so many companies. Instead of paying for the publicity with money, you pay with work: phone calls, writing, time, and determination. But all that effort will be worth your time. People who expend it say that PR really stands for *profit*.

If you do something good, you should get credit for it publicly. If you contribute money to charity, that's good — and it is a basis for PR. If you donate merchandise, that too can result in a publicity story. Just be sure you let the local media know of your altruism. And find newsy ways of being altruistic.

One of the most important public relations tools is the annual report. As a rule, entrepreneurs don't publish one. But why not? It need not conform to the usual annual report sent to shareholders. It need not talk money. It can be a report that contains information valuable to your customers. When you do publish such an annual report, send some copies to the media. Let them enjoy your creativity. Nudge them to give that creativity some "ink." And by all means, send your annual report to your prospects.

The guerrilla annual report

When you give a speech on a topic related to your business — and I recommend that you give them when you can — see to it that there is press coverage. After all, you are speaking because you are an authority on your topic. If the public learns that, they'll possibly reward your expertise with their patronage.

Recently, I went to a restaurant that was jammed. I hadn't

seen any advertising for the restaurant, so I asked some friends there how they had heard of it. They told me they had been invited to an opening-week party — all the food they could eat. The restaurateur must have lost his shirt that week. But he gained it back — with a matching wardrobe and more — in the following weeks. Most likely, he wrote all that free food off as a marketing expense. That's what it was.

Members of the press are frequently invited to "press parties." At these parties, cocktails or beverages and a meal or hors d'oeuvres are served, and frequently a presentation is made. It's a short one, but attractive and hard-selling. The purpose is to woo the press with wining and dining, then win their hearts with a dramatic presentation of the facts. Naturally, the facts are about a new business or a new direction for an old business. It's no surprise that the press coverage following these parties is tremendous. Guerrillas hold their press parties at unique places such as ferryboats, railroad cars traveling to interesting destinations, penthouses, haunted houses, parks, baseball diamonds, and art galleries.

Have a press conference If you have a relatively momentous announcement to make, consider holding a press conference. Attract the press by letting them know you will tell them something newsworthy. Be sure, however, that you live up to that promise. And be sure you can answer hard questions.

When a crisis develops in your community, do what you can to alleviate the problem and gain free publicity at the same time. When a flood hit the area in which I live, an enterprising businessman furnished free hamburgers to the volunteer relief workers. He must have given away 600 burgers. But his business was written up in five newspapers, mentioned on three radio stations, and shown on television. Well worth the 600 burgers. This is not taking advantage of an unpleasant situation as much as it is being "publicity aware." A guerrilla smells opportunities like that every time. An accident in a snowstorm closed Vail Pass in Colorado. Traffic was backed up for many blizzardy miles. Snowbound motorists were astounded when a person from the local Domino's delivered hot pizzas to their cars. Did that result in new customers and free publicity? You guess.

A major-league PR pro once told me that nearly 80 percent of the news is "planted" — sent to the media by publicity firms and lobbying groups. Sometimes planted news deals with politi-

cal topics; sometimes it deals with industrial topics; and sometimes it deals with products or people. That PR pro repeated what
insiders know — newspapers are hungry for real news. If you can
furnish it, they'll gladly publish it. But telling a newspaper that
you are having a sale is not news. Informing a radio station that
you have started a business is not news. News needs a slant to it,
a hook that will interest people. If I wrote a publicity release saying that I had written a new book called *Earning Money Without
a Job,* that would not really be news. But if my release stated that
now there is a new way to combat unemployment, it would be
news. And that might be a reason for a newspaper to write about   **The hook**
my book.

You communicate your news by writing a publicity release.
Address your release to as specific a department as you can —
Sports, Entertainment, Business, Food, whatever — and use the
name of the editor of that department. Get it by phoning the newspaper and asking. If your news is really hot, send it to the news
or city editor. If your news item is homier than hard news, send
it to the feature editor. Tailor your publicity release to the personality of the medium for which it's intended. A release for a newspaper might be longer and more detailed than a release for a radio
or TV station. The latter media probably require more brevity
and spice.

When writing a publicity release for any medium, you   **Writing a**
should use the format that is generally followed and that is ap-   **publicity release**
preciated by most media. Put the date in the upper right-hand
corner. Type in the name of the person to contact for more
information, probably yourself. Be sure you include your phone
number. Write the release date next. The item may be for immediate release, in which case you say that — using those exact
words: *For Immediate Release.* Or it may be for release after September 19th, 1994, in which case you say that. Next, you have
the option of providing a headline. I always do, and I recommend
that you do the same. But if you don't want to, the newspaper
will do it for you. And even if you supply a headline, the newspaper will probably change it.

Then type your release. Double-space it. Use 8½ x 11 paper
and leave wide margins. Begin one-third of the page from the
top. When you move on to a second page, identify your story at
the top of that page, in the left-hand corner. Write in short, clear
sentences. Do not use long words or adjectives. Do not give opin-

ions. State facts. To indicate the end of your release, type either a ##, a ***, or a -30-, centered, below the last line.

What do you say in your release? Say who it is about, what it is, where it is, when it is, why it is, and how it came about. Say all that in your first paragraph if you possibly can. Read your local newspaper and notice how deftly most reporters can work that who, what, where, when, why, how data into the very beginning of most articles.

It also helps immensely if your release is accompanied by a very short note. It's okay if that note is handwritten. On the note, explain in as few words as possible why you are sending the release. When you can, and when it is appropriate, enclose an 8 x 10 black and white glossy photo. Make it an interesting photo because newspapers want to be as interesting as they can.

Even if you are armed with a perfect release and send it to the right person, there's a good chance it will be ignored. If you hand it to the right person, there is less chance of it being ignored. If you give it to the right person over lunch, that's even better. And if you give it to the right person over lunch and that person is an old friend of yours, that's best of all, though no guarantee of publication.

That's why I say that publicity contacts are so very important. If you lack those contacts and the time to have lunch with all the editors and news selectors at the various media, you'll have to keep phoning the person to whom you mailed your release until it gets published. That's where persistence comes in. Don't forget, there are many people trying to get their stories in. Squeaky wheels receive the grease . . . or ink.

Send out your release about ten days in advance of the date you wish it to appear. This gives you time to phone the editor and suggest that the newspaper or other medium cover your story, and allows you to make suggestions for other picture possibilities. It gives the paper — or the station — time to fit the story in, thereby increasing its chances of being used. And it lets you be absolutely certain that the release gets delivered in time.

How George got free PR   Suppose you are George of Let George Do It. You want free publicity. You decide it would be newsworthy to build a unique barbecue pit in the local park. You secure permission, then write your release. Accompanying it is an 8 x 10 black and white glossy photo of you working on a project of which you are very proud. You include a cutline or caption pasted (not clipped) to the bottom of the photo and folded back. It says, "Award-winning patio being built by patio designer George Richards, owner of Let George Do It, Hessel Avenue." The accompanying release says:

February 1, 1994

Contact: George Richards (707) 555-3463
LET GEORGE DO IT, sponsor
115 Hessel Avenue
Sebastapol, CA 91554

FOR IMMEDIATE RELEASE

DESIGNER TO BUILD BBQ PIT AS GIFT TO CITY

George Richards, of Let George Do It, a local contracting firm, will construct a barbecue pit of his own design in Marvin Park on Friday, April 28, as a gift to the city.

Richards, whose patios, sun decks, and barbecue pits have won awards for design excellence, said, "I've drawn up a design that will fit right in with the city's personality. I don't think there's a barbecue pit in America quite like it."

The gift to the city, to be constructed on the third anniversary of Let George Do It, has been approved by the town planning commission. "The people in this town have been very receptive to my designs," said Richards. "I feel it is high time I express my gratitude."

Richards will cook and serve hamburgers on the newly designed barbecue pit when it is completed Friday evening. The public is invited to view the new addition to Marvin Park and to enjoy the hamburgers — while they last.

*　　*　　*

The best thing that could possibly happen would be for the newspapers to publish the release as sent, then do a follow-up story on the celebration following the completion of the barbecue pit, complete with a photo of George and his creation. Perhaps you can't build a barbecue pit for your city, but you can still gain free publicity if you do things such as teach classes in your area of expertise, publish a newsletter on it (a nifty marketing tool in itself), pen a column, or write articles. All of these things help establish you as an authority. Because of the free media coverage you'll get for your work, word of your expertise will get around, and it will sink into the minds of your prospects.

The best marketing plans usually call for a combination of advertising and public relations. The two go hand in hand. One is highly credible but gives you no control. The other has less credibility but gives you complete control. Together, they supply most of the pieces of the marketing puzzle.

Be newsy   Even if you have the best of contacts and the most dogged of attitudes, the bottom line is still that you have to provide news to get a free publicity story or interview. If a Martian lands on the roof of your store, you'll have made that news without even trying. But usually you've got to generate the news, as George did when he built a barbecue pit for the city.

There are ten ways guerrillas can create news all by themselves. Most likely, you can garner free publicity by employing at least one of them.

Ten ways to create news

1. You can tie in with the news of the day. If you're a computer tutor, a person who teaches people how to operate computers, you can issue statements that pertain to the news stories about computers, positioning yourself as the expert.
2. You can stage an event — a computer fair or a free computer seminar — during which you show the public how computers work.
3. You can release useful information. In your copious reading, maybe you'll come across an item in which your community will be interested. Include it in your press release. You can obtain such useful business data from directories such as those published by American Business Directories. Call them at 402-593-4600 and ask for their free brochure.
4. You can form a committee to study how computers can help the community — by lowering taxes, for instance. It need not be that, but find some slant.
5. You can give an award or a scholarship each year. People love awards, and perhaps you can invent one that ties in with computer education.
6. You can make a prediction using your computer. If it is startling enough, and pretty likely to be true, it will be news and will enhance your reputation as an expert.
7. You can celebrate your own business anniversary by providing free computer lessons for a week. This is the same principle as George's donation of a barbecue pit.

8. You can do something incredible. Maybe you could keep a talking parrot at the place where you give computer lessons. The parrot, naturally, would talk computerese ("Polly wants a printout"). Maybe you could get married in your computer classroom. Maybe you could paint a mural of a computer on the outside of your building. Keep it in good taste, but make it amazing.

9. You can surprise your prospects — and media — by giving something away for free such as a computer course scholarship, an award for kids using computers, an appearance by a local celebrity, a public demonstration of computer technology.

10. You can locate a memorable spokesperson who will serve as a living, breathing marketing weapon. It might be a local entrepreneurial success, a local sports star who uses a computer, an inexpensive, recognizable person who will appear at your demos and trade shows, maybe even in your other marketing weapons.

So as not to leave you only halfway home in your quest to be your own PR pro, and to give you a shortcut to succeeding at do-it-yourself public relations, here are ten guidelines that will help you get the coverage you want:

Guidelines to obtaining PR coverage

1. Determine exactly what sets your product or service apart from your competitors'. The media is not looking for humdrum news.

2. Practice communicating your message. Actually rehearse what you'll say to the media. Put it in writing. Say it aloud. Keep it clear, crisp, and concise.

3. Become a familiar name at local clubs, organizations, and associations likely to support your effort. Good research will pay off here.

4. Introduce yourself to newspaper, magazine, TV, and radio pros. You know all about the importance of contacts.

5. Find media biggies at social meetings, local conventions, and events likely to attract them, such as fund-raisers. Join their clubs and hangouts. This includes their bars and restaurants.

6. Study all your options — magazines, newspapers, radio, TV, supermarket circulars, trade journals, free event list-

ings, new publications, public service announcements on local radio stations, even public radio and television.

7. Watch and listen to talk shows. If you have a talk show topic, call the host. If you don't have one, develop a hot topic. Good guests are hard to find.

8. Call radio stations and request a free media kit. This will show you what they want while giving you a handle on how to prepare your own kit.

9. Realize that the media always need *hard news* of interest to their readers. If you have any, tell them of it.

10. Consider staging your own special events to attract prospects, sell to customers, and to generate media attention. This is often an easily obtainable ticket to PR.

Join in Another part of public relations is to join civic clubs and community organizations. That may be your most important marketing tool. Although you will be doing your duty as a member of the community, you will also make lots of contacts with people who can give you business and with people who will refer business to you. I hope you don't join just to obtain business. In fact, if you do, your true motivation may be discovered, causing you to lose business. But if you join to aid your fellow man, you'll most likely end up with important contacts. If you work hard and diligently for the community, folks will assume that you run your business the same way, and they'll want to do business with you.

Despite all the other marketing you do, possibly the most effective will be joining organizations. The only marketing many successful entrepreneurs do is to join as many clubs as possible. I'm sure you've heard that a lot of business is conducted on golf courses. Just as much is conducted in meetings, at lunches, in steam rooms, at dinners, and over cocktails with fellow members of a club.

A true guerrilla puts as much effort into public relations as possible. To a guerrilla, everything that one does publicly is really **Sponsor** public relations. That includes the sponsoring of events, teams, **something** floats, tournaments, and more. You'll obtain sales much more slowly from sponsoring a Little League team, bowling team, or homecoming float than you will from some other marketing methods. But some entrepreneurs report that although the sponsorship of events does not result in quick sales, it does help their other methods of marketing take effect more quickly. There's no question that you will make sales. You will gain credibility, too, and you will become known as part of the community. You'll cause folks to feel good about you. Don't underestimate the power of favorable association. Some major advertisers who spend millions on TV commercials test those commercials to find out only if they have resulted in the company's product having a more favorable association in the minds of viewers. So it is true that sponsoring events will cause more favorable public association in a hurry. But sales in a hurry? No way.

Still, if you want to establish yourself as part of the community, consider sponsorship. Sponsor a turkey race at Thanksgiving, a toys-for-the-homeless collection at Christmas, Little League teams during the summer, and bowling teams during the winter. This will do everything good for you — except win instant sales. Because you are a guerrilla, however, you will be gaining those sales from other marketing methods. And since that's the case, perhaps you should spring for a sponsorship. It doesn't cost all that much — just a few hundred bucks, in most cases. And what it does not buy in quick profits it does buy in good will.

Among those who should consider sponsorship are new businesses that need to establish their identity, companies that sell items intended for the audiences of the events sponsored — for example, sporting goods stores sponsoring any type of athletic team — and companies that feel they must become more involved with the community. Sometimes community involvement is beneficial for political reasons.

Who should consider sponsorship?

Consider your own business. If there is not a good reason for you to sponsor teams or events, you probably should not do it. Don't do it just for your ego, and don't do it merely because your kid asked you to. But do it if you can, for a true guerrilla utilizes as many marketing tools as can be properly employed. And it doesn't take much cash to employ this particular tool properly. But it means you should show up for games — even if your team has one win and ten losses. Such dedication to a community team will translate, and rightly so, as dedicated treatment of your customers.

Actually, doing it for your kid isn't always bad marketing. If your company has been earning money for many years within the community, there is absolutely nothing wrong with giving some of those profits back. By putting a Little League team on the field, outfitted in snazzy uniforms heralding your company name, you will be making a charitable contribution and marketing at the same time. Nothing wrong with that.

Frankly, many teams and events are sponsored for the benefit of the sponsor's ego. If you want to massage yourself the same way, just be sure you know why you are doing it.

It may be that you can take advantage of the timing of certain events. For instance, if a homecoming parade, featuring floats and queens and brass bands, ties in with a specific promotion you are having, join right in. Sometimes you can collaborate with a fellow entrepreneur and co-sponsor a float.

Many astute people believe that you should not become involved in community relations for the profit motive alone. They believe that if you sponsor teams or events for the sake of the community you will prosper, but that if the sole purpose of your sponsorship is to earn extra dollars you will fail to prosper. Give that some thought. I believe it to be true. Deep down, I feel that you do owe something to your community if you are succeeding.

Lubricating the wheels   What sponsorship really does is lubricate the marketing wheels that are already turning for you. People aren't going to buy from you because they saw your name on a uniform. But they may buy from you if they saw your ad in the newspaper *and* your name on a uniform.

There is still another reason why some companies sponsor events: They may be resented if they do not. If you are operating in a small town where most of the businesses sponsor teams, you'll just have to pay those civic dues — or run the risk of offending the members of the community.

It is also true that the success of your business may depend upon the health and stability of your community. And your sponsoring of an event or a team will contribute to that health. That helps you in two ways. It helps your region and it helps your business. Without doubt, sponsoring events or teams or causes or floats gets you recognized as a solid citizen, as a kind, generous, helpful, friendly human being — a pillar of the community. And that helps your business, regardless of your intent. Guerrillas can be philanthropists, too. No law against it.

The cost of sponsorship is going to be time as well as money. Not too much of each, but some of both. You can't sponsor a team and fail to show up for its games. You can't back an event and then divorce yourself from it entirely. Word will get out that you are in it for the money alone, and that will cause you to lose more sales than you'll gain.

In some cities there are no events or teams to sponsor. Although you may want to, you may be unable to add this weapon to your marketing arsenal. If that's the case, perhaps you can create an event. Think about doing that if you have the opportunity. If yours is a growing community, your initiative, which costs very little now, will be worth a lot later. You will have positioned yourself in the right way, in the right place, at the right time. Perhaps you'll never again have that chance. Perhaps one of your competitors will start a cause, a league, or an event and assume a leadership position. Don't let that happen. As a guerrilla, *you* should take the leadership position.

A client of mine sponsored a 10-kilometer run with the proceeds going to the town's favorite charity. Each of the entrants received a free T-shirt with the name of the event on one side, the name of the sponsor on the other. The race is held once a year. The T-shirts are worn throughout the year.

The payoff from sponsorships will differ from that connected **The payoff** with other marketing tools. Don't shortchange that payoff, however. It might be a feeling of warmth toward your business by the community at large. It might also be a new contact, a new customer, a new source of profits for your business. Perhaps at a league meeting you'll meet someone who can direct fifty new customers your way. Maybe you'll be awarded a gigantic sale seven years after you've sponsored the event. This is not at all uncommon.

By sponsoring events, you create the opportunity to meet new people, make new friends. And because your business, rather than you, is doing the sponsoring, it will probably be the benefactor of the gratitude. Little political favors may fall your way, such as better positioning in the local newspaper for your ads, better timing on the local radio station for your commercials, new contracts coming your way. None of this will be measurable, in the classic sense, but little of it will be accidental. Your sponsorship will be the cause. Increased profits will be the effect. Will it always work that way? Not always, but sometimes. Now that you know the value of sponsorship, look into it.

27
Producing
Professional Marketing

IT IS POSSIBLE TO HAVE a first-rate product or service, a well-conceived marketing plan, brilliant positioning, a dynamite creative strategy, a topflight business location, a gorgeous package, an ideal name, and a memorable theme line, and still have your business fall flat on its face. It is not only possible but commonplace.

The reason? Your marketing materials look just awful. Your words sound horrible. Your advertising is a real turn-off. You have sunk all your money into media, and you have skimped on production. That is a mistake no guerrilla would ever make. A diehard practitioner of guerrilla marketing knows that marketing has an intangible quality that defies number, defies logic. It is the way marketing "feels." And that "feel" is determined by the look and sound of the marketing. If it is bad, you can't hide it. You can't hide it if it is good, either, but you won't want to.

Beyond CPM   Non-guerrillas measure advertising strictly by CPM. That stands for "cost per thousand," and it refers to the cost in media dollars to reach one thousand people. If a radio commercial costs $100 and it reaches ten thousand people, your cost per thousand — your CPM — is $10. That is considered a relatively high CPM. Some CPMs get down to $3, as is the case with widely viewed TV shows. And $3 is not a high price to pay to reach one thousand people.

But true guerrillas look far past the CPM. First, guerrillas **Your** realize that the *cost per prospect* is more important than the cost **metamessage** per thousand. Second, guerrillas are highly sensitive to the *meta-*

message of their marketing. The metamessage is the unspoken part of the marketing process. It is the true emotional impact of the advertising, which really cannot be measured at all. As you might sense, it is the "feel" of your marketing.

The metamessage of your marketing reaches not merely the conscious mind of your prospects but also the unconscious. That is why it is so difficult to measure. I suppose it can be gauged only by sales results over a long period of time. One thing is certain: *You have complete control over it.* That's the good part. Here's the not-so-good part: It costs to send out a positive metamessage. Producing professional marketing materials costs quite a bit of money. On the other hand, it costs very little to produce unprofessional marketing materials. In fact, it costs so little that many would-be guerrillas are wooed away from success by the temptation to save a buck on production.

Reflecting on my own experience with clients over the years, I realize that 40 percent of them, usually the big ones, spent too much on production. This did wonders for their egos, but not their sales. They confused their prospective customers with too much style and not enough substance. Their electronic marketing — radio and TV — reeked with so much fluff and unnecessary window dressing that the message became cloudy. Another 40 percent of my clients, usually the smaller ones, spent too little on production. They invested in media advertising but not in artwork. They bought a lot of time and space but not a lot of talent. They decided that they could write the copy themselves, that their friends could do the artwork. They allowed radio stations to write their radio spots. They allowed newspapers to lay out their newspaper ads. The result was usually schlocky-looking marketing that had an amateurish feel. They produced marketing like cheapskates, and it showed. That means that *only 20 percent of my clients spent the right amount on production.*

Keep in mind that it is very easy to overspend, and even easier to underspend. You will be advised to spend far more than you ought to, possibly by a friend or associate, frequently by a production facility, maybe by an advertising agency. You will also be advised to spend more than you ought to, probably by a media rep who wants those extra dollars for a commission and for more ads or commercials for you. Bad advice, all of it. Don't let it ruin an otherwise good marketing effort. Advice on spending less money may also come from your accountant and a few fellow employees. You might want to listen to them, but I'd suggest taking that advice with a grain of salt.

Ten percent should do it   Here's some *good* advice: Reserve *about 10 percent of your marketing budget for the production of marketing materials.* That means you should set aside quite a few dollars for creating professional ads and commercials, handsome signs and brochures, and motivating messages. Most likely, you'll spend a lot of that production budget up front. That's how it usually works out. You can amortize those funds over a long period of time. Let's say you plan to spend $36,000 over one year to market your product. That comes to $3000 per month. This means that you should spend $3600 producing ads and marketing materials.

If you are a new company, or if you are an old company just coming to your senses, you may want to invest in a logotype, or logo. That is your symbol — a visual representation of your company such as McDonald's golden arches or Shell's shell. It should include your name, though Shell's doesn't and really doesn't have to after nearly a century of exposure. Your logo will appear on your signs, in your ads, on your business cards, stationery, and brochures, in every single place you can think of to put it. It will become associated with you. To produce a logo, a good art director will charge anywhere from $250 to $50,000. You'd be overspending if you went the $50,000 route — though large corporations have spent more than double that — and you'd be underspending if you paid an art student $50 — unless he or she was a highly talented student destined for marketing greatness. They do exist, and art schools are where you find them.

A professional logo   Because you'll be using it for so long and in so many different applications, invest in a first-class logo. If this means you write a check for $500 to $1500 up front, you can amortize that expenditure over the length of time you are in business. In the long run, it may come to only a few dollars per month. Truth is, you should not even consider the money you spend for a logo as part of your production budget. It's above and beyond that budget.

Say you are quoted a price of $500 to produce an ad. Sounds like a lot. But if you run that ad over the course of four months, it comes to only $125 per month — a small sum for production. And $500 should buy you a darned good-looking ad. Naturally, you won't want to spend a lot of money on an ad you will run but once. But remember, guerrillas run their ads more than once, more than twice. They run them until the ads stop pulling in business. If you let your newspaper lay out your ad, and if you write the copy, it may only cost you $50 to produce an ad, but the ad may never pull in any business. So it's really not much of a savings for you. It amazes me when a person signs up for a $10,000 TV schedule, then wants to run a $150 commercial. Seems to me that's a savings in the $150 department and a waste of money in the $10,000 department. Don't let it happen to you.

There are three ways that you as a guerrilla marketer can produce advertisements or commercials. One way is to *do it all yourself.* You handle the graphics, the writing, and the ad production. If you are a creative genius and have experience producing ads, that will save you a lot of money. It may eat into the time you spend running your business, but if you're the best person to write your copy and create your layout, a rare bird in my experience, go to it.

Three ways to produce

A second way to have your advertising production done is to *turn the work over to an advertising agency.* For many entrepreneurs, that's a good idea. Advertising agencies earn 15 percent of your media dollars. In effect, though, you get their services free. If you buy $10,000 worth of radio spots, it will cost you $10,000. If you use an ad agency, it will still cost you $10,000, but it will cost the ad agency only $8500, since as an accredited advertising agency it gets a 15 percent discount from the media. So you get the ad agency's expertise, its planning ability, the time it invests placing the advertising for you, and even its writing talents — and you don't pay anything for services rendered. You pay only for type, illustrations, and a camera-ready mechanical.

As a guerrilla, you may want to set up your own house ad agency so that *you* can earn the 15 percent discount, but perform your own services. In this case, most standard advertising agencies charge on a fee basis these days, the fee depending upon the amount of work and time required to service your account.

If you have a too-tiny budget, most ad agencies will turn up their noses at you. But if your budget is hefty, advertising agencies can save you a lot of time and trouble. And they provide a great deal of much-needed expertise. Word-of-warning: If your budget is small, your advertising account, while pitched by senior management, will probably be assigned to green-behind-the-ears employees. That's not always bad, but it's a gentle hint that if you're going to use an ad agency, use a small one that will treat your small company like an important client.

Most entrepreneurs, however, produce their marketing materials a third way. They *use independent contractors to fill in the gaps* in their marketing ability. A success-oriented entrepreneur will hire a smart marketing consultant to help draft a marketing plan and a creative strategy. The consultant is paid a fee — one time — and that's it. The fee covers either several projects or anywhere from one to three months. If he or she is needed down the road, then another fee is charged. Maybe you'll want to keep a consultant by paying a monthly retainer fee for continuing counsel.

A smart entrepreneur might also have an ongoing relationship with an art director. That person designs the logo, the ads, the brochures, the circulars, the yellow pages ads, the mailing pieces, the signs — everything that needs designing. The art director is paid by the hour, by the ad, or by the project. Usually, it is by the hour.

You might also hire a copywriter who charges by the hour or by the ad. And you might employ a media-buying service to place all your ads for you, at a charge of from 3 percent to 10 percent of the cost of running the ads. Since a media-buying service can save you 15 percent, the 10 percent it may charge actually amounts to a savings of 5 percent for you. At times, you might also wish to hire a professional research firm that charges by the project. And you might need the services of a photographer or an illustrator. Be sure they all follow your marketing plan and pull in the same direction.

Use properly or not at all

As I have counseled a number of times, and will continue to harp on because it is so important, you should utilize as many methods of marketing as you can *properly* utilize. The same holds true for marketing production. Do as much of it yourself as you can do properly. Farm out the rest to talented professionals. In all likelihood, you are a pro at your business. And you should use people who are pros at the business of advertising production. That combination of pro and pro is a tough combination to beat.

Seven areas of expertise

An effective printed piece, be it ad, brochure, circular, or point-of-purchase sign, requires expertise in seven different areas. The first area is the idea. *Don't forget that all great marketing starts with a great idea.* It is not important that you be the person who gets the idea. It is very important that you be able to judge the idea. If you can't distinguish a good idea from a bad idea, find someone who can. That's the most important part of marketing.

The second area is *copywriting*. To begin with, somebody has to come up with a winning headline. To be successful, the headline should either state the idea succinctly or interest people so much that they'll want to read the copy. The copywriter must have the ability to write flowing, motivating copy. No particular style is right or wrong. But in general, copywriting should be clear, easy to follow, crisp, and believable. Many people believe that because they can write, they can write copy. If that were the case, there wouldn't be such a large number of copywriters earning in excess of $150,000 per year for their golden prose. There is a huge difference between writing in the English language and writing advertising copy designed to create a desire to buy.

The third area is *graphics*. The most important aspect of graphics is the design and layout. An art director must take the words and pictures and arrange them in such a way that the reader's eye will flow from one element to the next, free and easy. There must be no hint of confusion. The ad should look appealing, should invite readership by its look. It is not easy to create such ads. That's why some art directors are paid fancy salaries, also in excess of $150,000 yearly, to lay out advertisements. They possess a graphic sense that combines aesthetics with motivation, art with psychology. You need an ad maker to design ads, not merely a designer. An ad that merely looks good is a bad ad. The ad must look good and also communicate exactly what you wish to communicate.

The fourth area is *pictures*. The pictures may be illustrations or photos, black and white or color, small or large, one or many. The art director makes that decision. The illustrator or photographer then takes over and draws or shoots the picture that helps bring the marketing plan to life. I have had clients pay $12,500 for a single photo session and feel that the shots were worth every cent. I've had clients spend $150 for a photo session, too. They weren't as captivated as the big spenders, but the $150 did the job of helping them grow to become a company that could afford the higher figure. If you are superb with a camera or if you can illustrate with pizzazz, perhaps you can handle the picture portion of your advertising. But chances are, you'll be better off hiring a pro. Fortunately, most people recognize their lack of talent at art. Unfortunately, most people fail to recognize their lack of talent at writing.

The fifth area is *typography*. There are books and books of typefaces you can select. With such a wide selection, which is the right kind of type for your advertising? Should it be a serif typeface — one with letters that have little tails and curlicues? Or should it be a sans serif typeface — one with clean, stream-lined letters? Should you use italics? Boldface type? All capitals? What is the right size of type for the headline? The subhead? The body copy? The theme line? A type expert or art director must be able to answer all of those questions and answer them correctly. Otherwise, a lot of money may go down the drain. I've seen many ads that had everything right except that the type was unread-able — either unclear or too small. Any ad with unreadable type is a sad waste of money, space, time, and energy. Daily, you see typefaces that can and do give people headaches.

The sixth area is *paste-up*. That means pasting on a board or sheet of paper the type that has been set, the headline, the illustration or photograph, the logo, the border, and any other element that goes into the ad. The paste-up person, when prepar-ing the mechanical — a term used to describe the pasted-up ad — must place and paste with precision. He or she follows the design formulated by the art director and pastes all the pieces together to make a camera-ready ad.

The seventh area is *photostating*. Once an ad has been thought up, written, laid out, illustrated, set in type, and pasted up, it must be photographed and a photostat of the ad must be made. That's what you send to the newspaper. That ensures that the ad will appear as you want it to appear. The art director should already have contacted the publication to find out its printing idiosyncrasies, so that the ad will print well. Once that is done, your ad quality is assured if you send a perfect stat to the paper.

It is the rare guerrilla who possesses expertise in all seven areas. Even the most proficient ad makers are expert in but a few. Generally, one person thinks up and writes the ad, a second per-son serves as art director, paste-up person, typographer, and stat maker, and a third person handles the photos or illustrations. That, as I said, is generally the case — meaning more than 50 per-cent of the time. In many cases, however, the art director thinks up the ad. In some cases, one person does the writing, a second person handles all graphics and production responsibilities, and either of the two people gets the idea for the ad. It doesn't matter where a good idea comes from.

Your job, as a guerrilla, is to exercise the right judgment in **Judgment is all** all of these areas. You need not be able to do any one of these tasks, but you must be able to distinguish good from bad in all seven areas.

One of the most successful entrepreneurs I have ever known, Mike Lavin — a true guerrilla in every sense of the word, inventor of the BioFirm Mattress, the best-selling mattress in Berkeley, California, and proprietor of the Berkeley Design Shop, which became a local landmark because of his marketing — had zero talent in all seven areas but had exceptional judgment and resourcefulness. His judgment helped him recognize his own limitations, helped him distinguish a good ad from a bad ad, a good commercial from a bad one, good copy from bad copy. His resourcefulness led him to the people who could supply the talent he needed to run prime-quality ads. Although he didn't contribute one word to his copy, he never ran a bad ad. His success, both financial and personal, was astonishing. He built a company that used all of the media — and I mean all. First, he sold waterbeds, then added other beds, then futons, then invented a breakthrough mattress design, then added space-saving furniture, then added children's furniture — changing with the times and the needs of his market. There was not a single major marketing tool that he failed to use. And yet he had no innate marketing talent, merely brilliant marketing judgment and instincts. That's all you need to be a guerrilla. That plus patience and aggressiveness.

Needless to say, it will cost you money to secure talent in the seven areas required. And remember, I'm just talking about printed marketing materials. You'll require even more talents for television marketing. And radio advertising calls for professionalism in six areas: the idea, the writing, the voicing, the music, the sound effects, and the mixing. As with print advertising, you yourself don't have to have talent in these areas, merely good judgment. And you must know how to locate expert production studios.

As with cognac, when it comes to marketing production, you usually, but not always, get what you pay for. Learn what you'll be paying for by checking the portfolios of the pros you plan to select. Be wary of those who talk of awards. Be attracted to those **Results over** who speak of results. **awards**

In most parts of the country, seminars are often presented for entrepreneurs. Some seminars are geared to teaching you how to produce your own marketing materials. If such seminars come to your area (check with a local community college, a chamber of commerce, or the extension division of a local university), sign up for one. Sign up for more than one if production turns you on. If it does, ask yourself, "Is this the best use of my time for the business?"

Now that you are taking the marketing process seriously, start developing a radar for good marketing and bad marketing. Both kinds are all around you. The more you observe, the more you learn, and the more you learn, the better you'll be able to market.

Guerrillas use pros With all of my recommendations that you handle much of the marketing yourself, I encourage you to hire a pro to create your marketing materials. Unless it is something at which you really excel, you are usually far better off giving it to a pro — or to several pros. To find them, merely set aside a few days to visit graphic-art firms and view the work they have done for others. Visit writers and art directors and look at ads they have created. Listen to radio spots they have written and produced. View TV commercials for which they have been responsible. Only if you do it that way will you get a feel for the marketplace. When looking at the work of these people, ask two questions: (1) How much did it cost to produce? (2) What were the sales results? Concern yourself more with the answer to question two than question one. You'll find the publication *Adweek* to be a rich source of local marketing talent.

Co-op advertising You can save sacks of money and get to use beautifully produced ads, commercials, brochures, and signs if you make use of co-op advertising. If you are a manufacturer, you can gain a lot in local sales by joining a good co-op program. If you are a retailer or distributor, you can gain welcome funds for your marketing budget by obtaining co-op money. Co-op funds and materials are made available to entrepreneurs by large companies. If you deal with one, ask about their co-op advertising program. If they don't have one, ask them to create one for you. Never hurts to ask. To obtain first-class marketing help in the way of money, ads, and more, co-op advertising is an area worth exploring.

Only after you have assembled the proper marketing aids will you be able to combine the best stated message with the best metamessage. It is the combination of the two that will result in success. One without the other just won't do it.

When thinking about marketing — an activity in which you should engage more and more — try to think long-term while you are thinking short-term. Don't just look at the week ahead. Look also at the months and years. Your marketing efforts will add up. Your identity will not come easily or quickly but will be built over time. And everything you do in the way of marketing will contribute to that identity. If you see that you may have to spend $1000 to produce an advertising piece, think of other ways the piece can be used. Maybe you can turn it into a sign. Perhaps it can also serve as a customer handout. Possibly it can be the basis for a brochure. Maybe it can be used with interchangeable headlines and become two ads. Perhaps it can be the major part of a mailing. And you may be able to use it for five years or longer. By getting the most mileage out of your marketing materials, you will save a lot of money. Suddenly, that $1000 figure looks a lot more reasonable. Why, with enough deep thought on your part, it might even seem inexpensive.

In addition to getting as much mileage as possible from your marketing, do everything you can to create brand names for your products. People trust brand names. They have confidence that a brand-name item will perform better than a non-brand-name item. Don't make the mistake of thinking that brand names belong only in the province of the big guys. Brand names can be used by anyone who wants to create them. Smart marketing people, big and small, want to create them.

Become a brand name

Mike Lavin, of Berkeley Design Shop fame, has only one retail store but he created a brand name for the mattress he invented. He calls it the BioFirm Mattress. He has marketed and advertised and promoted it so long and so enthusiastically that local people now ask all over town for the BioFirm Mattress. The mattress is available only at his store, of course. He has created a brand name that, in his community of 125,000 people, outsells Serta, Sealy, Simmons, Sears — all the big guys. And he's just a little guy with limited resources and a single showroom, but a stunning profit and loss statement, along with a permanent grin. Ask him about the Herculean power of brand names.

According to the *Harvard Business Review*, entrepreneurs are going to have to start developing their own brand names. There is a new selling environment. People want uniqueness, want names they can trust. Creating a brand name gives the people what they want and gives you what you want: consumer confidence. A good approach to take is to give your customers *more than their money's worth*. If you sincerely try to do that, to go the extra distance, provide the extra service, give the extra quality, you'll be able to convey that attitude in your marketing. You'll be a better marketer if you think that way. And word will spread, too.

The department store, Nordstrom, is famed for its customer service. Its name is synonymous with superlative service. One day, the store received a call. Something a customer purchased had broken and the customer wanted it fixed — pronto. That day, Nordstrom had a salesperson stop by the person's house to make the repair. The broken item hadn't come from Nordstrom, after all, but from Sears. The Nordstrom person fixed it anyhow, charged nothing, and contributed yet another tale to the treasure trove of service stories that has made Nordstrom a name that people know they can trust. Do that for your company, too.

There is no mystique to marketing, as you have seen. It is nuts and bolts and is fairly easy to dissect. But marketing is difficult to do properly. Never forget that no matter what your business really is, *people will think of it as your marketing portrays it*. If you run cheap-looking ads, that's what people will think of your product or service. Don't believe those people who tell you that you'll never go broke underestimating the intelligence of the American public. Instead, figure that the American public is about as intelligent as your mother. And you know that she is no dodo. In reality, she is a good representative of the public. She won't be won over by gimmicks and special effects.

Involve your employees

If you have employees, make sure they are completely aware of your marketing program. They must reflect all that is conveyed in your marketing. After all, people will come to you because of that marketing, and they will expect certain things from you. Your salespeople or representatives must have attitudes that are consistent with the messages you have been putting forth. Guerrillas not only have all employees and associates read their marketing plans but also insist that all employees read every ad and hear every commercial. If they do, they'll be able to relate that much better to customers and will know what the customers are looking for. They will know what is being communicated in advertising and will be able to help the business live up to its marketing.

One of the most important attributes a guerrilla can have is patience. Wait for that marketing plan to take hold. Stick with it. If you have thought it through, it will pay rich dividends. If you expect instant results, your plan will never have a chance to shine, to motivate, to sell. Lean on your marketing materials as much as you can. Post your ads on your door, in your window, on your walls. Be proud of them. Create each ad with the care you would use if it were your only ad.

You are probably reading this book because you own your own business or because you are considering owning your own business. I doubt that many people would invest money and time in a marketing book unless they were involved in the marketing process. It may be that you are in the marketing department of a company. But it is more likely that you have your own company. Merely by purchasing or taking the time to read this book, you have proven that you already know the crucial importance of marketing. In our competitive society it is more important now than ever. Because you purchased a book dealing with guerrilla marketing, you are a person who wants to market more effectively than your competitors. You are now equipped to put better marketing to work for you.

Entrepreneur magazine, a worthy publication for any person who considers himself or herself an entrepreneur, publishes an entrepreneur's credo in each issue. Because I suspect that you are a small businessperson who wishes to become a big businessperson, and because I believe you are an entrepreneur, I will repeat the credo by which you may already live:

Words to live by

I do not choose to be a common man. It is my right to be uncommon — if I can. I seek opportunity — not security. I do not wish to be a kept citizen, humbled and dulled by having the state look after me.

I want to take the calculated risk, to dream and to build, to fail and to succeed.

I refuse to barter incentive for a dole; I prefer the challenges of life to the guaranteed existence; the thrill of fulfillment to the stale calm of Utopia.

I will not trade freedom for beneficence nor my dignity for a handout. I will never cower before any master nor bend to any threat.

It is my heritage to stand erect, proud and unafraid, to think and act for myself, to enjoy the benefit of my creations and to face the world boldly and say: This . . . I have done. All this is what it means to be an entrepreneur.

Now you have risen above the level of entrepreneur. Just as the entrepreneur has advanced beyond the wage slave, being freer, more responsible, and a greater taker of risks, the guerrilla has advanced beyond the entrepreneur, being a mite harder working, a bit sharper, slightly more of an explorer, often more successful. As the age of the entrepreneur and individual enterprise comes more and more into the forefront in America, the need to be a guerrilla is more and more acute. And to be a guerrilla requires an attack.

V
Launching Your
Guerrilla Marketing Attack

A WELL-EQUIPPED ARMY led by a top-rate general in possession of a well-conceived battle plan will win no battles — unless those battles are launched. In real life, that army can assure a blessed peace merely by its presence. But marketing isn't as simple as real life.

You are constantly under attack by your competitors — all vying for that limited disposable income to be spent by your prospects. Your presence, plan, and general don't amount to a hill of Rice Krispies if they just sit there, snapping, crackling, and popping. You're going to have to launch your own attack. To some people, this is a sorry situation. They don't have the smarts, the stomach, or the imagination to launch, much less succeed at, an attack.

But you do. You've got it all — the data, the motivation, the insights, and the arsenal of weapons to stake out a territory and get your fair share, even more. You'll be able to achieve your goals because you know what those goals are. They are clearly spelled out in your marketing plan.

You also must now realize that if you don't attack, you'll lose the battle. Others are coming down the pike by the hundreds of thousands, and they're all bent on victory. You are dead meat unless you act. So you've got to do something. You've got to do it with the acumen of a guerrilla, and although you must act with patience, you must also act now — right after you complete this book. No shilly-shallying around.

One of the hallmarks of the guerrilla is a penchant for ac-

tion. When they hear there's a battle coming up, they plan, anticipate, visualize, and understand victory. They take the actions that victors take, and they keep up the attack permanently, always aware of what the heck is going on — information most small-business owners lack.

These people have learned that marketing is not an event, but a process. It begins in a room where they map their battle plan. Then they take it to the streets in the form of mini-media, maxi-media, and non-media — utilizing the weapons that they can use with skill. Understanding how and why marketing works, they are armed with their ten-word guerrilla credo: commitment, investment, consistent, confident, patient, assortment, subsequent convenient, amazement, and measurement. They are now ready to take the actual steps to launch an attack.

Do they launch all of their weapons at once? Of course not. That would be time-consuming, confusing, intimidating, and expensive. Guerrilla marketing attacks are precise, easy to control, inexpensive, and intimidating only to the competition. Success requires knowledge of specific aspects of the science of psychology, plus an unstoppable inner will to win. The knowledge and the will aren't usually to be found between the covers of a book. But they're in this manual for guerrillas, and they're coming in just a moment.

But first, step back and take a look at marketing in the context of business, in the context of *you.* Use this perspective for honest self-evaluation. I'm asking you to do this because in a study to determine why so many products fail, the answer turned out to be painfully obvious: *the boss.*

A 1992 Innovation Survey from Group EFO Limited, the eighth annual survey of its kind, showed the number-one reason for product failure isn't the competition, the trade, the recession, a failure of creativity, or a shortage of ideas. It's the chief, the honcho, the top banana. A startling 63 percent of new-product managers say *top management at their companies do not have a clear strategic vision of the role of new products.* "Lack of strategic direction" is the leading factor in new-product failure. Absence of management commitment tied for second with such factors as price-value relationship, product delivery, and point of difference. Guerrilla marketing can't save companies that have low marks in those areas.

Fully 83 percent of new products brought to market in 1993

failed to reach their business objectives, according to the respondents' projections. Fingers were also pointed at guilty parties for failure to market aggressively: only 47 percent said their companies put their best marketing people on new products. To illustrate the pitiful lack of creativity in creating products, 87 percent of the products respondents' companies brought to market in 1992 were line extensions — new versions of old products — while only 4 percent created a new product category. These figures pertain to new products and to large companies, but all entrepreneurs can learn important lessons from them.

Management for the twenty-first century must improve on them. Guerrillas will require new skills and will have to fill new management roles in addition to running the marketing show:

- You'll have to scale economies.
- You'll have to offer speed and flexibility.
- You'll have to understand data processing.
- You'll need the knowledge to create intelligently.
- You'll have to know the exact way to position.
- You'll have to know how to maximize profits.
- You'll have to know how to create value.
- You'll have to constantly refine your operation.
- You'll have to consistently reexamine your strategy.

How will you possibly do all these things? By being a true entrepreneur and not an implementer, by developing coaching and not just controlling skills, by identifying and nurturing employees with the right attitudes, and most of all, by understanding your customers inside and out, backward and forward, upside and down.

The more you know what makes your customers tick, the better able you will be to push their hot buttons, gain repeat business from them, enjoy referrals from them — and create the kinds of products and services they want. All this takes is a knowledge of human behavior, and you'll start gaining that knowledge when you turn the page.

28
How Guerrillas
Use Psychology

THE FIELD OF PSYCHOLOGY has undergone a major transformation since I was majoring in the subject at the University of Colorado. I remember how upset I felt upon hearing, as we approached graduation, that there were no fixed laws in psychology, only theories.

Here, I had spent nearly four years of my life learning theories (and skiing) instead of hard, tangible facts. No wonder so many people majored in engineering, where the numbers add up in no uncertain way, or English Literature, where the words are unarguably printed right there on the page. But psychology and theories? Didn't sound very solid, though it certainly was fascinating.

Since my college days, psychology has changed even more than I have. Many of the theories have been discarded after proving worthless or false. Other theories have emerged, and marketing guerrillas have learned how some of these aspects of human behavior can be applied in marketing.

The best example of this — and the one you've just got to remember as long as you market — is that *purchase decisions are made in the unconscious mind.* You do not, as you may have thought, consciously select a brand to purchase. Instead, your unconscious mind, that inner, deeper portion that comprises about 90 percent of your brainpower, figures out what brand you should purchase, then sends its message to your conscious mind. There, where the words are spoken, you order or pick up a specific brand. You thought you were making a conscious decision,

Where purchase decisions are made

but your conscious mind was merely a tool of your unconscious one.

All alone, that's a fairly shocking piece of information — different as it is from the conventional wisdom. But marketing geniuses do not look at that law all alone. They also are entranced at the law that tells us *how to access the unconscious mind*. We didn't know how to do that while I was studying about minds in college. We figured that hypnosis was one way, but we weren't sure. *Today we are sure that you can access the unconscious mind through repetition.* Advertising leaders from Rosser Reeves to Leo Burnett have frequently made the same point.

How to access the unconscious

So you put two and two together and you see that by repetition of your message, you can gain admission to that holy place where purchase decisions are made. Empowered by that simple fact, you begin to understand why marketing works the way it does. And you make a mental note to apply this new awareness in all of your future marketing. It will manifest itself in repetition. That will be one of the "secrets" to your profitability.

When I was in school, none of the professors talked about left-brained people and right-brained people. Today, still, not many advertisers, even the biggies, act upon the enormous economy this discovery represents to enlightened entrepreneurs.

Left-brained and right-brained

Studies show that 45 percent of Americans are left-brained and react to logical appeals while ignoring emotional appeals. Another 45 percent are right-brained and are stimulated by emotional appeals, disdaining logic for the most part. The final 10 percent of us are balanced-brained. Because most marketing is created without regard to this psychological reality, nearly half of mass marketing is wasted. Better still, *I know which half:* In some marketing, it's the kind aimed at the nearly half of Americans who are left-brained; in other marketing, it's the type created for the nearly half who are right-brained. Most marketing aims in the opposite direction of about half of its potential audience. As a guerrilla, you can hit 100 percent of the people to whom you market if you *aim your marketing at both left- and right-brained people.*

Left-brained people love logical, sequential reasoning. You offer them a brochure with ten reasons to buy from you and they'll read every word. Is that good? Not necessarily. Since half the population is left-brained and half is right-brained, you're missing half of your market. Those right-brained people, who are influenced by emotional, aesthetic appeals, have zero interest in your ten reasons to buy. So you create a brochure with gorgeous graphics and words that tug at their heartstrings. Is that good? Not necessarily, because such a brochure would miss out on all those left-brained people who don't care a whit for pretty pictures and mushy words.

Guerrillas, therefore, are very careful to aim their marketing materials at both left-brained and right-brained people. They know that their target audience is probably 45 percent left-brained and 45 percent right-brained. So they put forth logical appeals to buy — blended with emotional reasons. Nobody is overlooked. Their brochures have both the ten reasons to buy *plus* the appeals directly to the heart. This is not a big deal, but the losses suffered by ignorance of this aspect of human behavior are a humongous deal. **Aim at two targets**

There are exceptions to the left-brained, right-brained aim I advise you to take. If your audience is computer scientists, they're probably left-brained to begin with, so your marketing can be the very model of logic.

However, if your audience is artists, most likely they are right-brained and will buy because of emotion. And you should know that except for the most analytical of souls, almost everyone is influenced by appeals to the basic emotions. To add force to your marketing by giving your prospects motivation to buy, you can rely on one of the following emotional appeals: **The basic appeals**

- Achievement
- Pride of ownership
- Security
- Self-improvement
- Status
- Style
- Conformity and peer pressure
- Ambition
- Power
- Love

Your job is to find out which of these emotions will most set your customers and prospects into motion — or to find another that will do the job better.

As you can benefit by appealing to emotions, maybe you're

in a business where you can also appeal to the *senses*. Do it whenever you can and consider yourself lucky to have the opportunity. Guerrillas do all they can, by conversation and observation, to learn which senses most motivate their prospects. These examples show how they put their findings into action by enlisting the senses as allies:

> *Sight:* "That looks great on you."
> *Sound:* "Hear the massive power in that engine?"
> *Touch:* "Feel the richness of those fabrics."
> *Smell:* "The clean, fresh aroma is pure delight."
> *Taste:* "These are remarkably delicious tomatoes."

As you can surmise, guerrillas are both emotional and sensible. This sensibility manifests itself in their understanding of the need to create powerful bonds.

A great deal of repeat business never occurs because the business owner makes a strong business bond with his customer, then leaves it at that. The guerrilla is all for business bonds, but knows **The human bond** that the strongest are braided with the strength of a human bond. So the guerrilla first makes the human bond, then the business bond. As the years pass, both bonds are intensified, strengthened, made permanent. This does not mean that the guerrilla spends a lot of time socializing with his or her customers. Instead, it means that in all interactions, the person is treated first like a human being — with a family, a business, hobbies, interests, opinions — and then like a customer. When the human bond is powerful, the business bond is lasting. When the business bond exists without the human bond, its existence is fragile.

Psychologists have asserted that one of a human's most powerful needs is for an identity. A way to cater to this need is to form a club and make the customer a "member" of your "customer club." Membership privileges might include a membership card, framable certificate, newsletter, special discounts, advance notice of special events or sales, free gifts, car window decal, refrigerator magnet, a greeting card or gift at holiday time, maybe even a birthday card. Sometimes it includes a gift that is personalized with the names of both the guerrilla marketer and the customer. This further strengthens the individual's sense of identity with your business.

Stay in touch with your members, offering them new prod-

ucts, new services, and offerings of your fusion marketing partners. Naturally, these offerings will be in the best interests of your
customers, so life is working out well as your customer benefits
first and you benefit as a direct result.

To add more power to your human bond while increasing
your members' sense of identification with your company, edu-   **Educate your**
cate them on how they can succeed better at their businesses.   **customers**
Sometimes that will mean purchasing from you; sometimes it
will mean purchasing from others — or not purchasing at all.
Educational marketing is effective, potent, rare, and just the
ticket for a guerrilla. By helping your customer — even if there
is no immediate gain for you — the eventual gain will make the
wait worthwhile.

The whole concept of "eventually" takes on special meaning
to guerrillas who know that most, but not all, people respond to
determination — another law of human behavior.

Dennis Holt, a friend who happens to also own what may be
the world's largest media-buying service, tells this story about
himself: While he was about halfway through a sales presentation
for his company to an advertising executive, the exec, his face
only inches from Holt's, snarled, "I don't like you. I don't like
what you do. I don't ever want to see you again. I'm insulted that
you came into my agency to pitch me. Get out." Holt got up,
pulled out a pencil and paper, and said, "I'm putting you down
as a firm maybe."

Holt never let up. He called the executive weekly. The first
four years the agency chief refused to take his calls. The fifth
year, he finally picked up the phone only to beg Holt to stop
calling. Thirteen years after their first encounter, that same
executive hired Holt's company, and more specifically, Dennis
Holt, to handle his media buying. Holt's determination, along
with the fact that *he is always a pleasure to be with* — a crucial
guerrilla tactic — is why his little media-buying service purchased over $1 billion in media in 1991. Determination alone
wouldn't do the job. Charm was part of the recipe.

Don't think you're limited in your canvassing and sales presentations to only the approximately 250,000 words commonly
used in the English language. Guerrillas aren't limited by such
paltry numbers. They've boned up on the latest findings from the
psychology world, and they know there are 600,000 non-verbal   **Non-verbal**
gestures they can use. Even better, they've learned that *people*   **marketing**

respond more to non-verbal cues than to verbal ones. So they learn the proper stance, the right facial expressions, when to smile, when to lift an eyebrow, what crossed arms mean, what a furrowed brow means. Non-verbal communication, i.e., body language, is part of communication and, therefore, part of marketing.

Sophisticated sales training techniques include videotaping the top salespeople, then showing the other sales staff members the video — pointing out the non-verbal gestures that lead to sales. Dissected, a fifteen-minute sales pitch may have 500 non-verbal gestures, most subtle, many highly effective. When you learn that in most organizations, 20 percent of the people accomplish 80 percent of the sales, you've got to figure that the 20 percent do a lot of non-verbal communication — unless they're in telemarketing. In that case, their voice inflections, volume, and pitch do as much selling as the words they use. Do they understand the science of speaking effectively? They do. They do. Success hardly ever happens by accident.

Guerrillas pay close attention to another critical maxim of marketing that focuses on the psychology of human beings: *Make every customer and prospect feel unique.*

Make each feel unique

This guerrilla tactic leads right to the vault, yet is the most unusual to see in practice. It describes the best possible way for your customer or prospect *to feel* after an encounter with you — either by phone or in person. It's almost like asking you to be a psychologist.

I admit it is difficult to get people to feel this way without appearing phony. It is also difficult because it requires hard work and cannot simply be finessed with a warm smile or a firm handshake.

Still, you've got to make each customer and prospect feel unique and important, not like a consumer, not like a member of a demographic group, not even like a well-treated customer. Instead, each should be made to feel like the special individual that he or she is — with feelings, beliefs, values, problems, and personality traits unlike those of any other human being on earth. If you convey knowledge of the person by your remarks, actions, and service, you will go a long way toward making that person feel unique. This is not easy to do. But if you do it, you will have a customer for life — *because hardly any other companies do it.* Even if they know the importance of making a person feel unique, they haven't got the knack, the data, or the information to accomplish it. As a guerrilla, you've got the small size to do it with every one of your customers.

Just ask yourself: When was the last time a business owner made you feel unique — like an extraordinary, one-of-a-kind person? Maybe once or twice, but probably never. That's because it's too hard to collect the information and remember it when dealing with the person. But that's a piece of cake to a guerrilla because the guerrilla has made customer reverence part of his very essence. That's your job.

It is now possible to add still another reason for people to buy from you — to aid a social cause. If they patronize your business, they'll gain all the benefits you offer — *plus* they can help save the environment, or stop AIDS in its tracks, or cure multiple sclerosis, or save whales. Maybe they will buy from you simply because you're an American and they're worried about the state of the economy in the United States, so they patronize businesses that are true-blue American.

Remember that aligning yourself with a noble endeavor gives you an opportunity to engage in *cause-related marketing*, a method of overcoming the "purchase guilt" that many consumers feel, and another method of using psychology along with your normal competitive advantages. If you can let them feel that they've helped the world while buying your product, you're doing a favor for them, for you, and for the world. Cause-related marketing is an act of philanthropy on your part, and the world needs and appreciates it. There are many sick, homeless, displaced, and disabled people who need all the help they can get. If your business can devote even a small percentage of its profits — or better still, its sales — to a good cause, there's a good chance that many winners will emerge.

Cause-related marketing

The eighties were a "greed" decade. The nineties are a "green" decade with more awareness of environmentally safe or damaging products than at any other time in history. In 1991, a Roper Poll revealed that consumers said they'd be willing to pay a 5.5 percent premium for green products. Since 1989, recycling has been up 15 percent for glass and cans, up 21 percent for newspapers. Seventy percent of consumers are against postponing tougher emission standards for the automotive industry. The world, and so the marketing directed at it, is always changing, as if you didn't know.

Greed then, green now

As you pursue the psychological edge that can make or break

a sale, these days, a call to patriotism in purchasing is often heard and heeded. The appeal to buy American is strong, as shown by the numbers: In 1992, a *Los Angeles Times* poll listed 45 percent of respondents avoiding products made in Japan. In 1985, that number was 26 percent. The percentage of people who believe that when they buy imports they're responsible for putting Americans out of work has risen to 57 percent. Retailers report that "made in America" promotions of domestically made apparel increase their sales from 25 to 50 percent. Wal-Mart, America's biggest retailer at this writing, has gone on record as being deeply committed to American sources. The company says it has repatriated 130,000 jobs based on that decision.

The downside of this patriotic marketing is that it might appear to cater to the hate and fear instincts in people. Be sure if you embrace cause-related marketing, especially the red, white, and blue variety, that it is not at the expense of other peoples or ethnicities. Guerrillas never alienate potential prospects.

To gain the closest psychological bonding with your prospects and customers, be certain that you know the most possible about them, then marry that information to the understanding you have of your own product or service. Just what is its identity? What does it symbolize to your market? What are its inherent emotional appeals? Logical appeals? Cultural appeals? As true product differentiation is harder to come by and even tougher to sustain, perceptual associations will play a greater role in setting products and services apart from one another.

See yourself as others see you   That's why it's so crucial for you to understand precisely what your business really stands for in the eyes of your target audience. Research can tell you. Ideally, it's what you want it to stand for. If not, changes are in order. Understanding what your offering means to your market is something you should always strive for. You must be aware that the public perception of your product or service will probably change over time, necessitating continuing research via questionnaires.

In 1992, a national poll by New York advertising agency Warwick Baker & Fiore revealed that people who shop at stores have changed their shopping habits. Nine out of ten shoppers who go to the store for frequently purchased items go armed and ready with a specific shopping strategy in mind for saving money. These shoppers have been categorized into five basic groups:

- *The Practical Loyalists,* 29 percent of shoppers, look for ways to save on the brands they will buy anyway. The confidence they have in these brands cannot be shaken by low price alone. **The psychology of shoppers**
- *The Bottom-Line Price Shoppers,* 26 percent of all shoppers, buy the lowest-priced item with little or no regard for brand. This number is up from 14 percent in the mid-1980s.
- *The Opportunistic Switchers,* 24 percent of shoppers, use coupons or sales to decide among brands and products that fall within a mentally preselected group.
- *The Deal Hunters,* 13 percent of shoppers, flat out look for the best "bargain" and are not brand-loyal. Understand that "bargain" refers more to value than to price.
- *The Non-Strategists,* only 8 percent of shoppers in the nineties, do not spend the time and effort to strategize their shopping.

As you might expect, the recession is largely responsible for this fundamental change in consumer behavior, yet the behavior is expected to continue even after economic recovery is in full swing again. Although confidence will reign supreme as the unconscious motivator for selecting one brand or business over another, recessions cause consumers to clip coupons, cut corners, shop in bulk, and patronize warehouses and price clubs.

Nineties consumers are savvy shoppers, buying on pure benefit and price relationships. And although the largest group of them are loyal to their brands, increasing numbers are loyal to their dire financial straits and are forced to forsake longtime loyalties. Guerrillas do all they can to maintain their current customers while winning over the new breed of sophisticated, yet savings-minded consumers.

If you use psychology in your marketing, you'll do every single thing in your power to cater directly to your audience and capitalize not only on its universal buying habits, as I've just described, but also on its special idiosyncrasies, regardless of how wild this may make your marketing appear to the outside world.

Mad magazine, known for its irreverent humor and wacky views of American life — also for its consistent profitability — gave a free pin to all new subscribers. In keeping with its identity, it didn't treat the pin as it deserved to be treated, as an insignifi- **A Mad example** cant object, but instead wrote of it in terms that only its subscribers could love:

> Each and every *Mad* Pin is precision crafted by machines that are turned On and Off by hand. These *Mad* Pins will not be sold in any store — we know, we tried getting any store we could find to sell them and nobody would touch them. Due to the special nature of this offer, the number of Official *Mad* Pins commissioned shall never exceed the demand. Each Official *Mad* Pin is so valuable it will be personally delivered to your home by an official United States Government employee, dressed like a mailman.

You can be sure that each person who received a pin felt unique and identified just a wee bit closer with *Mad*.

Do I recommend this tactic to all guerrillas? I definitely recommend the tactic of being sensitive to your own market. The accuracy of your marketing attack will depend upon that sensitivity.

29
How Guerrillas Win Battles

THERE IS ABSOLUTELY NO MYSTERY to why guerrillas prevail when others fall by the wayside. They know how to launch a marketing attack and when to do it. They know which battles to fight and which to ignore. They know where to turn for support. They have learned how to win, beginning with one battle, and continuing as the battles get larger and more numerous. They have also learned how to avoid the greed and blind instinct to grow beyond their capabilities and into a heap of trouble.

Working backward, assuming you're going to do what it takes to be a guerrilla, be sure you know how to deal with success. Most people lack the skill. It is an infrequently encountered talent, and yet without it, you're going to find yourself in deep waters. A good rule of thumb is to *engage in no expansion until* **Don't expand yet** *you have eliminated all of the mistakes in your current operation.* Otherwise, your mistakes will be magnified and multiplied. When you begin to hit new profit highs month after month, you'll be tempted to go for the gold and grow. If that's what you really want, go for it — but not until you've fine-tuned your mistake-radar to the realities of your company. Any mistakes you find are red flags warning you against growth. Don't ignore those flags.

To get to the point where you even seriously *consider* expansion, you're going to have to engage in the four steps necessary to **The four steps** launch your marketing attack, then launch it at the right time.

The four steps seem to get harder as you take them, not a bad arrangement since it always helps to have the easiest part in the beginning to build your confidence.

Step one is to plan your marketing. This entails a few crucial tasks, all of which can easily be accomplished by a good, hard-working guerrilla in one tough week, not counting the research time that must precede this endeavor:

- Select the marketing weapons you'll use.
- Create a guerrilla marketing plan.
- Create a guerrilla creative plan.
- Create a guerrilla media plan.
- Develop a guerrilla marketing calendar.
- Decide the priority order of launching your weapons.
- Decide who will be responsible for launching each.
- Decide who will be responsible for tracking each.
- Decide exactly when each weapon will be launched.

It starts out easy

There. That's all there is to the first step of launching your devastating attack. I told you it would be relatively simple. I also told you that the second step would be a bit harder.

Step two is to launch your weapons. Non-guerrillas, if confronted with a list of, say, fifty-five weapons to launch, would be so overwhelmed they'd run for cover, or more likely, never launch an attack at all. But the guerrilla knows that there is no reason to launch all the weapons at the same time. A sane way to look at it is to figure on about eighteen months, maybe a year, to launch all the weapons you said you'd launch. There never has to be or should be a rush. And every weapon must be used properly. The people responsible for launching your weapons know who they are; those same people know when to launch them, so there are no surprises — except to your competition.

Hang in there

Step three is to maintain the attack. Sorry, this is no arena for devotees of instant gratification. Little that you do will give you instant results. Feedback will be sparse or nonexistent. You won't be able to stop yourself from questioning your marketing plan. But don't ask too much of it. Remember the Marlboro man and take a horseback ride into the sunset. Bide your time.

Unless you maintain your attack, there is no way it will succeed for you. The money — and the time, energy, and imagination — you have invested in marketing will be lost forever. It would be like shredding a stock certificate because the stock dropped a couple of points. Keep embedded in your mind that this is the way it's supposed to be. It is tough to continue investing

your money while seeing little or no return. Some business own-
ers might construe this state of affairs as a failure on their part.
But guerrillas know that people don't fail; they only quit trying.
They cease maintaining.

This is the time to hang in there and win that all-important
confidence that guerrillas are supposed to win. But, sadly, this is
where most business owners get cold feet and sweaty palms. They
panic, abandon their marketing plan, change their media, fire
their advertising agency, and decide that newspapers, direct mail,
telemarketing, television, or any combination of these doesn't
work for them. Of course it doesn't! It has to be maintained over
a period of time — three months to a year — to work.

Just last week, a client excitedly called to tell me that he was
overloaded with business. I wasn't surprised. He was shocked! He
had been actively marketing for six months, and during the first
five, not much happened. During the sixth month, *everything*
happened. And it all was good. Those prospects he had spoken
to five months earlier decided that now was a good time to take
him up on his offer. Those *other* potential customers he contacted, also five months ago, figured that this was a good time to
buy from him. His telephone was ringing incessantly and the
callers were all ready to undergo that magnificent transition from
prospect to customer. The seeds had been planted; they had been
lovingly nurtured. Now the harvest was taking place and the
farmer was shocked! If you maintain, you'll harvest. If you don't,
you won't. Maintenance is not glamorous work. But it does work. **Don't be shocked**
And don't be shocked when it does. **when it works**

Step four is to measure your attack. This is where you will
work the hardest because it is one royal pain to measure the effectiveness of marketing, but it's your job — and if you do it, you
can double the effectiveness of your marketing budget. Stated
another way, if you don't do it, you can halve the effectiveness of
your marketing budget.

Only by measuring can you improve your marketing calendar. Only by finding out which weapons worked and which were
duds can you maximize the good ones and eliminate the bad
ones. You learn about the effectiveness of your marketing by asking people where they heard of you.

Ask them in person, when completing a sales receipt, at the
outset, in a questionnaire, at any opportunity — because it is so
important for you not to waste one cent of your marketing

money. If you don't find out where people first learned of your company, you are wasting your marketing money. That's just no way for a guerrilla to conduct business, and so the guerrilla devises methods and policies that capture this information from every customer, and in many cases, from every prospect.

Measuring becomes a mite easier when you've formalized the procedure for any employees who are in a position to track responses, such as including a blank space on your order form with room for the original source of this customer, "forcing" the employee to ask and learn it. Some businesses that do this or have their phone operators ask prospects "Where did you first hear of us?" say that they've got their measuring chore "on automatic" — that is, have devised a system where everybody is asked for this data.

But measuring is never a cup of tea. Keep it forever in mind, however, that measuring actually will double your efficacy and translate to dramatic increases in your profits — the whole purpose of guerrilla marketing in the first place.

The ideal small business of the 1990s and the decades beyond will realize that *the past is not the key to the future.* Although the sun continues to rise in the east and Uncle Sam requires you to pay your just share of taxes by the ides of April, marketing has changed and will continue to change. Guerrillas are positioned for these changes. To adapt, they know that survival and prosperity are not so much a matter of money as a matter of time, energy, and determination.

An arsenal of profit-producers

To market with acumen and success today, you've just got to launch a guerrilla marketing attack. Stock your arsenal with these profit-producing tips for the nineties:

- Forget the past when planning the future. Changes that represent opportunity will take place in service, technology, prospect sophistication, quality expectations, available options, and competitive marketing savvy. Be ready or be lunch.
- Refocus on your marketing strategy. Anticipate response. Be sure your plan is clear and brief enough for all major employees to read it. Don't change your marketing merely for the sake of change, or a bad case of nerves.
- Expand your niche. Expand it by offering what your com-

petitors don't do well. Expand it by targeting markets too small for big competitors. Expand it by discovering the new markets that change creates. Strategies to consider for expanding your niche are: *speed, service,* and *specialization.*

- Assess your passion. Assessing is done with your mind, a left-brained activity, as you now know. Passion you feel with your heart — a right-brained characteristic. Combine your mind and heart to see if you truly still feel passion for what you do. If the fire's gone out, move on to your next bliss. No guerrilla attack can succeed without a burning desire to win.
- Trust your marketing. In a world with much change, marketing can stand out by changing the least. Maintain your thrust and identity, but broaden your media, add more target markets, and reexamine your pricing.
- Become your customers. The moment you are in their shoes, you'll see changes from their perspective, see your company from their viewpoint, see any changes that are needed.
- Make each customer feel unique. I repeat this because most of your competitors will be unable to do it, and you'll gain an enormous advantage if you can. Learn so much about your customers' lives and businesses that when they see or hear from you, they'll instantly remember that you recognize what makes them special.
- Hang in there. When times change, the normal tendency is to make changes in wholesale lots. This is not necessary. What is necessary is that you make some changes, even make them on a constant basis. Hang in there with your mission, but in service and quality, be a rolling stone.
- Hone your awareness of needs and problems. Guerrillas know that the path to profits is smooth when it is directed to filling needs and solving problems. Needs and problems change, but guerrillas have methods for spotting them.
- Do more fusion marketing. Many businesses, large and small, are aware of changes, yet unaware of how to act. One way to act is to team up with new collaborative marketing partners who can help you spread the marketing word and cut marketing costs — benefiting both fusion marketing partners.

- Know what your prospects and customers expect. Be assured that they expect more and better. You've got to be ready to exceed those expectations, even new ones.
- Create a new competitive advantage. Change opens many doors, and guerrillas rush through to offer exactly what new consumers want. They want speed. They want service. They want value. They want technology that works.
- Do more follow-up with existing customers — and prospects — than ever. Do more than any competitor.
- Engage in constructive discontent. Stop talking up your business with your associates, and start questioning it. Informed criticism helps you keep abreast of changes.
- Don't lower your prices just because others are doing it. Instead, consider maintaining or even raising your price, then justifying it with more service or increased convenience.
- Develop a reverence for measurement. Become an accountability freak, measuring marketing weapons, employees, staff and company performance. Every component is accountable, so change won't leave you behind.
- Recognize that your best marketing investment is yourself. Invest time and energy learning to negotiate the subtle intricacies of change in your marketing and your managing. The times, your competition, your marketing, the marketing process itself, and you — they all are a-changing.

When to launch your attack

Be sure that you realize these changes are all working for you when you launch your guerrilla marketing attack. The two best times to launch it are exactly the same as the two best times to plant a tree: twenty years ago — and today.

Regardless of your lofty achievements, regardless of your successes, regardless of the size to which you grow, it will always be possible to bring to marketing the imagination, the ingenuity, and the comprehensiveness of thought of a guerrilla. If you approach your task with the soul and the spirit of a guerrilla primed for the times, in spite of the hordes of competitors, my bet's on you. I'll see you in the trenches. And at the bank.

Acknowledgments

THE ACKNOWLEDGMENTS SECTION may be the least enjoyable part of a book for the reader, yet writing it is one of the most enjoyable parts for the author. It is only in the Acknowledgments that the people responsible for the spirit of the book receive the recognition they deserve.

First on the list is Michael Larsen, my agent. Upon hearing me speak on marketing at a luncheon meeting, he dashed up to me and told me that I ought to write a book based upon my speech. From that moment on, *Guerrilla Marketing* started taking shape. Gerard Van Der Leun, my original editor at Houghton Mifflin, earned my gratitude for believing in the book and adding crucial touches of spark and soul. My current editor, Betsy Lerner, gets heaps of Brownie points for much of the scope and style of this updated edition. Steve Lewers, marketing guru at Houghton Mifflin, is the driving force that spawned the edition in the first place.

The people to whom this book is dedicated should also be singled out for the public appreciation they merit. Mike Lavin has always been a full-scale, high-energy practitioner of guerrilla marketing. Thane Croston trusted guerrilla marketing with enough faith to build an empire. Alexis Makar believed in guerrilla marketing and succeeded big-time as a result. Lynn Peterson learned, lived, mastered, and inspired with it. Wally Bregman showed me the value of fighting for guerrilla marketing with guerrilla-like tenacity. Bill Shear masterminded the spread of the word about guerrilla marketing, a constant guerrilla role model. Leo Burnett taught me more about marketing, guerrilla marketing, advertising, and life in general than any other mentor I've had, and I consider myself lucky to be able to make that statement. Steve Savage is the gutsiest guerrilla experimenter I know and is willing to take the risks that must be faced high on the ladder to the top, where he is perched. Sidney Mobell was a guerrilla long before I knew him, yet he allowed me to merge my own guerrilla tactics with his. And Norm Goldring has practiced guerrilla marketing to the point that his company is now one of the three largest businesses of its kind in the world.

I also want to thank the late Howard Gossage, who was the first to hire me as a professional guerrilla and teach me how much fun there is in the process of marketing.

During the writing of this book, I was constantly impressed by my daughter, Amy, who juggles childraising, full-time work as a mental health counselor, and graduate school with aplomb. And finally, I offer a deep bow and a warm kiss to my wife, Pat, who has always believed in me, encouraged me, understood me, put up with me, shared precious time with me, inspired me by her every action, and loved me.

I am fortunate, indeed, to owe acknowledgment to so many superb people.

Information Arsenal for Guerrillas

Albrecht, Karl, and Lawrence Bradford. *The Service Advantage: How to Identify and Fulfill Customer Needs.* New York: Dow Jones–Irwin, 1989.   **Books**

Antin, H. Brad, and Alan H. *Secrets from The Lost Art of Common Sense Marketing.* Clearwater, Fla.: The Antin Marketing Group, 1992.

Applegath, John. *Working Free: Practical Alternatives to the 9-to-5 Job.* New York: AMACOM, 1981.

Baty, Gordon. *Entrepreneurship: Playing to Win.* Reston, Va.: Reston Publishing, 1974.

Bayan, Richard. *Words That Sell: A Thesaurus to Help Promote Your Products and Ideas.* Chicago: Contemporary Books, 1987.

———. *The Marketing Revolution.* Philadelphia: Swansea Press, 1985.

Bencin, Richard L. *Strategic Telemarketing.* Philadelphia: Swansea Press, 1987.

Benn, Alec. *The 27 Most Common Mistakes in Advertising.* New York: AMACOM, 1978.

Benson, Richard V. *Secrets of Successful Direct Mail.* Savannah, Ga.: Benson Organization, 1987.

Berkman, Robert I. *Find It Fast: How to Uncover Expert Information on Any Subject.* New York: Harper & Row, 1987.

Bly, Robert W. *The Copywriter's Handbook.* New York: Dodd, Mead, 1985.

Bobrow, Edwin E., and Dennis W. Shafer. *Pioneering New Products: A Market Survival.* Homewood, Ill.: Dow Jones–Irwin, 1986.

Bonoma, Thomas V. *The Marketing Edge: Making Strategies Work.* New York: Free Press, 1985.

Bove, Tony, Cheryl Rhodes, and Wes Thomas. *The Art of Desktop Pub-*

312 INFORMATION ARSENAL FOR GUERRILLAS

lishing: *Using Personal Computers to Publish It Yourself.* New York: Bantam, 1986.

Breen, George, and A. B. Blankenship. *Do-It-Yourself Marketing Research,* Second Edition. New York: McGraw-Hill, 1982.

Brodsky, Bart, and Janet Geis. *Finding Your Niche . . . Marketing Your Professional Service.* Berkeley, Cal.: Community Resource Institute Press, 1992.

Buell, Victor P. *Handbook of Modern Marketing,* Second Edition. New York: McGraw-Hill, 1986.

Daniells, Lorna M. *Business Information Sources.* Berkeley: University of California Press, 1976.

Day, William H. *Maximizing Small Business Profits.* Englewood Cliffs, N.J.: Prentice-Hall, 1978.

Dean, Sandra Linville. *How to Advertise: A Handbook for Small Businesses.* Wilmington, Del.: Enterprise Publishing, 1980.

Dible, Donald M. *Up Your Own Organization.* Santa Clara, Cal.: Entrepreneur Press, 1974.

Dirks, Laura M., and Sally H. Daniel. *Marketing Without Mystery.* New York: AMACOM, 1991.

Drucker, Peter F. *Innovation and Entrepreneurship.* New York: Harper & Row, 1985.

Ehrenkranz, Lois Beekman, and Gilbert R. Kahn. *Public Relations/ Publicity: A Key Link in Communications.* New York: Fairchild Books, 1983.

Eichenbaum, Ken. *How to Create Small-Space Newspaper Advertising That Works.* Milwaukee: Unicom Publishing Group, 1987.

Eicoff, Al. *Eicoff on Broadcast Direct Marketing.* Lincolnwood, Ill.: National Textbook Company, 1987.

Feinman, J. P., R. D. Blashek, and R. J. McCabe. *Sweepstakes, Prize Promotions, Games and Contests.* Homewood, Ill.: Dow Jones–Irwin, 1986.

Fisher, Peg. *Successful Telemarketing: A Step-by-Step Guide for Increased Sales at Lower Cost.* Chicago: Dartnell, 1985.

Foote, Cameron S. *The Fourth Medium: How to Use Promotional Literature to Increase Sales and Profits.* Homewood, Ill.: Dow Jones–Irwin, 1986.

Gallagher, Bill, Orvel Ray Wilson, and Jay Conrad Levinson. *Guerrilla Selling.* Boston: Houghton Mifflin, 1992.

Gosden, Freeman R., Jr. *Direct Marketing Success: What Works and Why.* New York: Wiley, 1985.

Gray, Ernest. *Profitable Methods for Small Business Advertising.* New York: Wiley, 1984.

Hawken, Paul. *Growing a Business.* New York: Simon & Schuster, 1987.

Hecker, Sidney, and David W. Stewart. *Nonverbal Communication in Advertising.* Lexington, Mass.: Lexington Books, 1987.

Hisrich, Robert D. *Marketing a New Product.* Menlo Park, Cal.: Benjamin/Cummings, 1979.

Hodgson, Richard S. *The Greatest Direct Mail Sales Letters of All Time.* Chicago: Dartnell, 1986.

Joffe, Gerardo. *How to Build a Great Fortune in Mail Order* (7 volumes). San Francisco: Advance Books, 1980.

Jones, John Philip. *What's in a Name?: Advertising and the Concept of Brands.* Lexington, Mass.: Lexington Books, 1986.

Kamaroff, Bernard. *Small-Time Operator.* Laytonville, Cal.: Bell Springs, 1981.

King, Norman. *Big Sales from Small Spaces: Tips and Techniques for Effective Small-Space Advertising.* New York: Facts on File, 1986.

Kuswa, Webster. *Big Paybacks from Small-Budget Advertising.* Chicago: Dartnell, 1982.

Laing, John. *Do-It-Yourself Graphic Design.* New York: Facts on File, 1984.

Lant, Jeffrey L., Dr. *The Unabashed Self-Promoter's Guide.* Cambridge, Mass.: Jeffrey Lant Association, 1983.

Lavin, Henry. *How to Get — and Keep — Good Industrial Customers Through Effective Direct Mail.* Pompano Beach, Fla.: Exposition Press of Florida, 1980.

Lazer, William. *Handbook of Demographics for Marketing and Advertising.* Lexington, Mass.: Lexington Books, 1987.

Lesly, Philip. *Lesly's Public Relations Handbook,* Third Edition. Englewood Cliffs, N.J.: Prentice-Hall, 1983.

Levinson, Jay Conrad. *Guerrilla Marketing Excellence.* Boston: Houghton Mifflin, 1993.

———. *Guerrilla Marketing Weapons.* New York: Plume, 1990.

Lewis, Herschell G. *Direct Mail Copy That Sells!* Englewood Cliffs, N.J.: Prentice-Hall, 1984.

———. *How to Make Your Advertising Twice As Effective at Half the Cost.* Chicago: Bonus Books, 1990.

Lodish, Leonard M. *The Advertising and Promotion Challenge.* New York: Oxford, 1986.

Louis, H. Gordon. *How to Handle Your Own Public Relations.* Chicago: Nelson Hall, 1976.

Lyons, John. *Guts: Advertising from the Inside Out.* New York: AMACOM, 1987.

Maas, Jane. *Better Brochures, Catalogs and Mailing Pieces.* New York: St. Martin's, 1984.

Mackay, Harvey. *Swim with the Sharks Without Being Eaten Alive.* New York: William Morrow, 1988.

Malickson, David L., and John W. Nason. *Advertising — How to Write the Kind That Works*. New York: Scribner's, 1977.

McCafferty, Thomas. *In-House Telemarketing: A Master Plan for Starting and Managing a Profitable Telemarketing Program*. Chicago: Probus, 1986.

Miles, John. *Design for Desktop Publishing*. San Francisco: Chronicle Books, 1987.

Nierenberg, Gerard I. *The Art of Creative Thinking*. New York: Cornerstone Library, 1982.

Ogilvy, David. *Confessions of an Advertising Man*. New York: Atheneum, 1980.

———. *Ogilvy on Advertising*. New York: Crown, 1983.

———. Edited by Joel Raphaelson. *The Unpublished David Ogilvy: His Secrets of Management, Creativity, and Success — from Private Papers to Public Fulminations*. New York: Crown, 1987.

Ortland, Gerald T. *Telemarketing: High Profit Telephone Selling Techniques*. New York: Wiley, 1982.

O'Shaughnessy, John. *Why People Buy*. New York: Oxford, 1987.

Phillips, Michael. *Honest Business*. New York: Random House, 1981.

Phillips, Michael, and Salli Rasberry. *Marketing Without Advertising*. Berkeley: Nolo Press, 1986.

Pope, Jeffrey. *Business to Business Telemarketing*. New York: AMACOM, 1983.

Rapp, Stan, and Thomas L. Collins. *Maximarketing: The New Direction in Promotion, Advertising and Marketing Strategy*. New York: McGraw-Hill, 1987.

Reynolds, Dr., Don, *Crackerjack Positioning: Niche Marketing Strategy for the Entrepreneur*. Tulsa: Atwood Publishing, 1993.

Ries, Al, and Jack Trout. *Marketing Warfare*. New York: McGraw-Hill, 1983.

———. *Positioning: The Battle for Your Mind*. New York: McGraw-Hill, 1980.

Ross, Tom, and Marilyn Ross. *Big Marketing Ideas for Small Service Businesses*. Buena Vista, Col.: Accelerated Business Images, 1991.

Sandstrom. *The Ultimate Memory Pack Remember Anything Quickly and Easily*. Granada Hills, Cal.: Steppingstone Books, 1990.

Schollhammer, H., and Arthur Kuriloff. *Entrepreneurship and Small Business Management*. New York: Wiley, 1979.

Seglin, Jeffrey L. *The McGraw-Hill 36-Hour Marketing Course*. New York: McGraw-Hill, 1990.

Settle, Robert B., and Pamela L. Alreck. *Why They Buy: American Consumers Inside and Out*. New York: Wiley, 1986.

Siegel, Connie McClung. *How to Advertise and Promote Your Small Business*. New York: Wiley, 1978.

Slutsky, Jeff. *Streetfighting: Low Cost Advertising Promotion Strategies for Your Small Business*. Englewood Cliffs, N.J.: Prentice-Hall, 1984.

Smith, Cynthia S. *How to Get Big Results from a Small Advertising Budget*. New York: Hawthorn, 1973.

Soderberg, Norman R. *Public Relationships for the Entrepreneur and the Growing Business*. Chicago: Probus, 1986.

Stansfield, Richard H. *Advertising Manager's Handbook*, Third Edition. Chicago: Dartnell, 1982.

Swann, Alan. *How to Understand and Use Design and Layout*. Cincinnati: Writer's Digest Books, 1987.

Throckmorton, Joan. *Winning Direct Response Advertising: How to Recognize It, Evaluate It, Inspire It, Create It*. Englewood Cliffs, N.J.: Prentice-Hall, 1986.

Todd, Alden. *Finding Facts Fast: How to Find Out What You Want to Know Immediately*. Berkeley: Ten Speed Press, 1979.

White, Matthew. *Turn Your Good Idea into a Profitable Home Video*. New York: St. Martin's, 1987.

Witcher, William K. *How to Solve Your Small Business Advertising Problems*. Scotts Valley, Cal.: Mark Publishing, 1987.

Periodicals

Advertising Age, 740 N. Rush St., Chicago, Ill. 60611.

Adweek, 5757 Wilshire Blvd., Los Angeles, Cal. 90036 (1-800-722-6658).

Direct Marketing, Hoke Publications, 224 7th St., Garden City, N.Y. 11535.

Entrepreneur, Chase Revel, 631 Wilshire Blvd., Santa Monica, Cal. 90401.

Harvard Business Review, Soldiers Field Rd., Boston, Mass. 02163.

In Business, The JG Press, Box 323, 18 S. Seventh St., Emmaus, Pa. 18049.

Inc., United Marine Publishing, 38 Commercial Wharf, Boston, Mass. 02110.

Journal of Marketing, American Marketing Association, 222 S. Riverside Plaza, Chicago, Ill. 60606.

Standard Rate & Data Service (11 directories), Macmillan, Inc., Skokie, Ill. 60077.

Venture: The Magazine for Entrepreneurs, 35 W. 45th St., New York, N.Y. 10036.

Audio

Cluff, Douglas D., and Lesa M. N. Bell. *Power Marketing: 5 Easy Steps to Turn Small Advertising Budgets into Big Profits*. New York: Adweek Books (1-800-722-6658).

Dunn, Dick. *How to Write Great Copy.* New York: Adweek Books.
Lazarus, George. *The Marketing Edge: Six Pros Tell You How to Get It* (six interviews). New York: Adweek Books.
Levinson, Jay Conrad. *Guerrilla Marketing.* Mill Valley, Cal.: Guerrilla Marketing International (1-800-748-6444).
———. *Guerrilla Marketing Attack.* Mill Valley, Cal.: Guerrilla Marketing International (1-800-748-6444).
———. *Guerrilla Marketing Weapons.* Mill Valley, Cal.: Guerrilla Marketing International (1-800-748-6444).

Index

You can continue to be a guerrilla with
The Guerrilla Marketing Newsletter!

The Guerrilla Marketing Newsletter provides you with state-of-the-moment insights to maximize the profits you will obtain through marketing. The newsletter has been created to furnish you with the cream of the new guerrilla marketing information from around the world. It is filled with practical advice, the latest research, upcoming trends, and brand-new marketing techniques — all designed to pay off on your bottom line.

A yearly subscription costs $49 for six issues.

All subscribers to *The Guerrilla Marketing Newsletter* are given this unique and powerful guarantee: If you aren't convinced after examining your first issue for 30 days that the newsletter will raise your profits, your subscription fee will be refunded — along with $2 just for trying.

To subscribe, merely call or write:

Guerrilla Marketing International
260 Cascade Drive, P.O. Box 1336
Mill Valley, CA 94942, U.S.A.
1-800-748-6444
In California, 415-381-8361